Shamans, Sorcerers, and Saints

A PREHISTORY OF RELIGION

SHAMANS SORCERERS AND SAINTS

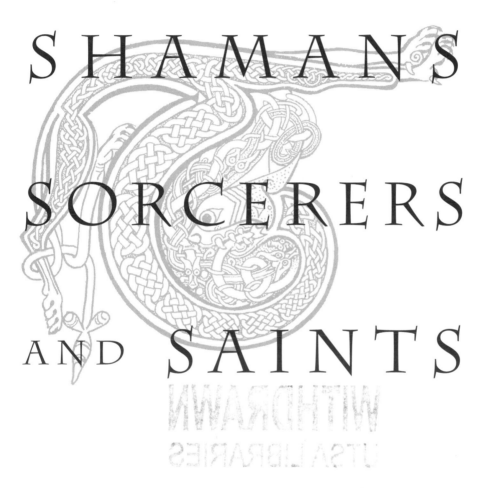

BRIAN HAYDEN

Smithsonian Books
Washington

© 2003 by the Smithsonian Institution

All rights reserved

Copy editor: Jean Eckenfels

Production editors: E. Anne Bolen and Joanne Reams

Designer: Brian Barth

Library of Congress Cataloging-in-Publication Data

Hayden, Brian

    Shamans, sorcerers, and saints : a prehistory of religion / Brian Hayden.

      p.   cm.

    Includes bibliographical references (p.) and index.

    ISBN 1-58834-168-2 (alk. paper)

      1. Religion—History. I. Title.

    BL48.H368   2003

    200′.9′01—dc21   2003045695

British Library Cataloguing-in-Publication Data are available

Manufactured in the United States of America

10 09 08 07 06 05 04 03   5 4 3 2 1

∞ The paper used in this publication meets the minimum requirements of the American National Standard for Information Sciences—Permanence of Paper for Printed Library Materials ANSI Z39.48-1984.

   For permission to reproduce illustrations appearing in this book, please correspond directly with the owners of the works as listed in the individual captions. Smithsonian Books does not retain reproduction rights for these illustrations individually or maintain a file of addresses for photo sources.

To René, Erik, and Séline

Contents

Preface

I have long thought that a comprehensive book by an archaeologist on the prehistory of religion was overdue. In the course that I taught on this topic, no one text was broad enough or theoretically suited. As my own ideas on the topic developed and evolved over the last 15 years, more and more pieces began to fit together into a relatively coherent picture that I finally considered to be worth publishing. The marriage of ecology and religion is a little-explored domain, but one that I think has a great many potential insights to offer about ourselves and our religious feelings. If some of the arguments presented do not seem entirely iron-clad, I would remind the reader that archaeology is still a fairly young discipline and that our data base is often slim. Given these circumstances, we must always approach interpretations by judiciously weighing relative probabilities. This is, in fact, true of all sciences, even those that seem to deal in "hard facts." Archaeology is simply less developed than the older sciences in this respect. I have tried to adhere to the classic tenets of the original Greek Academy of Athens, where Plato taught. These academicians maintained a healthy skepticism toward all explanations. However, they thought that since decisions had to be made, the best way to proceed was to lay out all the competing theories together with all of the known relevant data. Each theory was then harshly criticized, and the one that stood up the best was deemed the most useful basis for making decisions. In this classic sense, this is an "academic" work. However, I have tried to present the observations and arguments about the past in a way that is easy to read and grasp for a wide range of students and interested nonstudents.

In writing this book, I have tried to remain cognizant of the fascination that prehistoric religion holds for many people from diverse backgrounds, both academic and nonacademic. In order to make this book useful to as many people as possible, I have limited the use of technical terms and the discussions of issues only of interest to specialists. Thus, I have not gone into the details of the different Upper Paleolithic cultures, or indeed, even mentioned them by name or discussed all their variability. Nor have I delved into the traditional subdivisions of the earlier Paleolithic or the many local Neo-lithic cultures, or the detailed arguments about domestication. These issues are discussed in standard textbooks on archaeology. On the other hand, I have tried to provide key references to many of the concepts that may not be readily obtainable by students or other academics, so that these and other areas can be explored more fully if readers wish to pursue certain topics. Moreover, in a book of this size, it is impossible to cover all religions of the world throughout all time periods. Thus, I have selected examples of what I perceive to be the most representative or the most important developments in religious life over the past two million years. As a prehistorian, I have understandably emphasized the prehistoric periods of religious development rather than the major religions of the historic period. Thus, some major religions such as Islam, Buddhism, and Medieval Christianity are not really dealt with at all in this book. There are many other comprehensive volumes dealing with these aspects of religious life whereas there are few that deal with prehistoric religions, and most of these are only for very selected periods. I hope that the resulting balance is both readable and enjoyable while at the same time providing critical documentation for key aspects of past ritual life. Perhaps it would be best to view the chapters in this book as useful introductions or starting points for examining specific issues and topics rather than any definitive summary of established interpretations about prehistoric religions. The interpretations and suggestions presented in this volume are my personal assessments of what appear to be the most sensible interpretations of the information now at hand, leavened with suitable cultural ecological assumptions. Over the last 15 years, it has been fascinating to see this project come together, and it has been one of the most interesting projects of my career. I have been unusually lucky in being able to visit some of the most important sites by dint of being at the right place at the right time. My visits to the caves of Enlène, Lascaux, Bernifal, Arcy, and Bruniquel are some of the most fascinating archaeological and personal experiences that I have ever had, and I am very grateful to those who made these visits possible. There are many individuals to whom I owe great debts for sharing their time, knowledge, hospitality, and insights with me. Foremost is Huguette Hayden, who encouraged me to undertake this project, provided key insights into ecstatic states from a psychiatric viewpoint, and introduced me to mainstream researchers in transcultural psychiatry. Also of great help in the research for this volume have been Jean Clottes, David Lewis-Williams, Polly Wiessner, Wolfgang Jilek and Louise Jilek-Aall, Sophie de Beaune, François Rouzeau, Tran Quoc Vuong, Ralana Maneeprasert, Larry Keeley, Stanislaus Sandarupa, Paul Dutton, Trevor Watkins, Richard Sobel, Denise Schmandt-Besserat, Marek Zvelebil, Mark Blackham, Dan Monah, and Fritz Muntean. I am especially grateful to the Centre for Distance Education at Simon Fraser University for enabling me to develop this text and permitting me to use it, including many illustrations, in this published version. I am extremely appreciative of the cooperation of its directors, Colin Yerbury and Joan Collinge as well as the work done on this manuscript by members of the Centre, including Yvonne Tabin (associate director), John Whatley (program director), Jane Cowan (senior editor), Wendy Plain (co-ordinator of Course Production), Barb Lange (for page layout), and Production team members: Sigie Diebold, Greg Holoboff (Art), Barb Lange, Melanie Monk, Doris Oh, Lesley Rougeau. Many thanks go to Scott Mahler of Smithsonian Books for undertaking this project, Emily Sollie and

Joanne Reams for troubleshooting all the queries and conundrums involved in getting this book to print, and Jean Eckenfels for her copy-editing skills. Jennifer Provençal (who also contributed portions of Chapters 2 and 3) and Suzanne Villeneuve ably piloted the manuscript through its many revisions for which I thank them from the bottom of my heart. I am also very grateful to all those authors and publishers who have generously given their permission to use their photos and illustrations in this volume. Many others helped in a wide variety of ways including the Count Begouën, Lindi Brown, Séline Hayden, Mike Clarke, Elizabeth Carefoot (art), Greg Ehlers (photography), many musicians, students, pagans, witches, elves, and ancestors. I am extremely grateful to you all!

CHAPTER 1

Delving into the Past

At some time during the mist-shrouded past, human beings acquired an inherent tendency to believe in the supernatural. Today, that predisposition is found in a large portion of people in virtually every human society. Religious belief can be considered a fundamental characteristic of human nature that has proven impossible to eradicate by totalitarian political movements, the logic of hard science, or the commercialization of life. Worship of the supernatural has played a critical role in the emergence of the first complex societies, and religion has been the focus of incalculable amounts of time and energy throughout the cultures of the world (Figs. 1.1, 1.2). Despite this central role in human development, prehistorians have tended to shy away from serious attempts to deal with the topic except on an ad hoc basis. There is no general overview of religion in the archaeological literature. There are no posited principles dealing with the broad evolution of religious behavior. There are no syntheses from an archaeological point of view of this universal and highly important aspect of human societies.

Religion embodies ideas and values that many prehistorians think are inaccessible from the material remains of the past. Thus, theories on prehistoric religion have remained speculative for far too long without any clear resolution of issues or basic theoretical foundations. Although there are many books on specific aspects of prehistoric religion, none have addressed its general development and evolution. This book takes an initial step toward establishing a synthesis and formulation of some basic principles. My goal is to understand why religion is so important in cultures as well as to individuals, why religion takes different forms, and what it ultimately may mean. The emphasis of this book is on *traditional* religions in traditional societies (both prehistoric and contemporary), *not* on the major world religions that currently cover the globe.

As you will see, this book is quite different from most other books on archaeology or anthropology. Rather than dealing with dusty artifacts, abstract kinship systems, or bizarre customs, this book is about fundamental issues of what it means to be human. What are the abilities that make us unique in the animal kingdom? What fundamental

Fig. 1.1. Each year, innumerable pilgrims are drawn by their religious beliefs to Mecca to worship at the Kaaba, the most sacred place in the Islamic world. What powerful emotions inspire people to travel thousands of kilometers to share this experience? From A. Wavell, *A Modern Pilgrim in Mecca.* London: Constable & Co., 1912.

Fig. 1.2. Prehistoric communities undertook gargantuan building projects in the name of their deities such as this monumental Temple of the Sun at Teotihuacan, near Mexico City. Why did so many people contribute so much time and energy to make these religious structures, sometimes spending hundreds of years in the tasks? Photo by B. Hayden

values, feelings, and expectations lie at the core of our being? What is our emotional and spiritual heritage? How is it expressed today? How did our ancestors express it? (Fig. 1.3). To the extent that these feelings have been submerged in a sea of technology and civilizing influences, dredging up powerful intuitive experiences from our distant past not only has the potential for changing the way we look at the world around us but for changing our values, our priorities, and thus our very lives. We will be dealing directly with meaning in a world that has become largely divested of meaning: the meaning of our rituals and the meaning of our place in the world. In

Fig. 1.3. Our ancestors were hunters and gatherers who probably had beliefs and religious practices similar to modern hunter-gatherers such as this Aranda Australian Aborigine decorated for a ritual performance. From B. Spencer and F. Gillen, *The Arunta,* Fig. 89. London: Macmillan, 1927.

short, we will be dealing with religion, the religion of our ancestors. Our trip into the past will be long and sometimes involved, but it can be exhilarating, too, if we follow our instincts.

The general premise of this book is that basic religious behaviors of the past, and present, have been shaped by two factors: ecology and an innate emotional foundation in humans that distinguishes us from other animals. This emotional foundation specifically consists of the ability to enter into ecstatic states via a number of techniques and to create strong, emotionally binding relationships with other people (or institutions or ideals) associated with those states. These factors become crucial in understanding the origins of the human penchant for religious experiences (Chap. 2), archetypes, and shamanism (Chap. 3).

Ecological factors come into play when they modify the context of this innate emotional foundation either in terms of economic conditions (in their widest sense, including subsistence) or small group political relationships. Economic and political factors become especially significant with the development of socioeconomic hierarchies and the first complex societies (Chaps. 5–8). The first temples (Chap. 6), megalithic monuments like Stonehenge (Chap. 7), and the pyramids of Egypt (Chap. 11) can all be viewed as adaptations to specific economic and political conditions. This first chapter introduces the major issues and concepts that will guide our journey into the supernatural realms of the distant past. Our first task is to develop a clear understanding of what distinguishes traditional religion from more modern "book" religions.

Traditional Religion Is Not Like Formal Religion

Most people profess to know what religion is, having been to either churches or temples at some point in their lives. However, experiences with modern temples and modern religions do not equip us with an understanding of what traditional religions are like. In fact, some authorities on traditional religions, for example, Joseph Campbell (1985:52), have even argued that modern religions are like a vaccination against the real (traditional) thing. What would bring scholars to say this? We will find out shortly. But before we begin, I would like to emphasize the enormous gulf that exists between the general modern experience with religion and what our ancestors experienced.

One of the challenges of writing this book is to try to convey a real sense of what traditional religions are like. This is extremely difficult to do in a book because traditional religion is experiential, not intellectual. It is like jazz. No amount of written description can convey what it feels like to listen to jazz. In order to understand what jazz is, it is necessary to have heard jazz. Similarly, in order to know what traditional religion is, we have to undergo some of the subjective experiences that make up traditional religions. Even if we only get a superficial taste of these experiences, the exercise will have been worthwhile.

Understanding *contemporary* traditional religions in this fashion is essential if we really want to understand *prehistoric* religions. Fortunately, there are a number of important stepping stones that can help us reach this goal. First, there are many ethnographic accounts of traditional religions that describe what those rituals were like. Second, there are a number of important ethnographic films of traditional rituals in which it is possible to see what traditional rituals were like. Third, there are modern practitioners of traditional religions as well as many alternative religious groups that use the same techniques and open up many of the same spiritual doors as traditional religions. Fourth, there are many scientists and psychiatrists who study specific aspects of traditional religious experiences such as altered states. Finally, I like to encourage those interested in traditional religions, and archaeology in general, to adopt an informed "experiential" approach to understanding the phenomena we study. This entails trying to see and experience the world from the perspective of our ancestors or others that we are interested in.

In archaeology, the experiential approach means not just digging up artifacts and studying them in the laboratory but trying to make and use them. It means camping in the areas that would have been used by past peoples and developing a personal understanding of the resources, amenities, and problems associated with survival in that location. It may even mean trying to live off the land or building shelters or clearing land to grow crops using ancient technologies. In the study of religions, it may mean visiting sacred locations after fasting, taking sweat baths, or experiencing sensory deprivation for a few hours in a flotation tank or a cave.

There are, however, dangerous conceptual traps in dealing with ancient and traditional religions. These impede our understanding and can distort reality. Some of the most important traps include romanticizing and utopianizing the past (Chap. 7) and ethnocentrism. Ethnocentrism involves judging other cultures and beliefs by one's own very narrow beliefs and values. It is common for some people to laugh at the beliefs of others but find their own beliefs perfectly valid. In religion, ethnocentrism is expressed by the view that "our" sacred books are true, but that others' are only imaginative stories.

For instance, an ethnocentric person would laugh at Egyptian or Greek myths of death and resurrection (Osiris and Dionysus) as mythical stories, yet maintain adamantly their own belief that the death and resurrection of Jesus Christ actually happened, as did his virgin birth and other miraculous events in his life. Stories of virgin births are common in other cultures, too (see Chaps. 11 and 12; also Campbell 1968:311), but are rarely taken seriously by Westerners.

Archaeologists and anthropologists usually try to avoid such traps through special training. They strive to understand all human behavior in all cultures in terms of the inherent logic of the culture or in terms of adaptive responses to specific conditions in their environment, whether physical, social, or political. Some of the prehistoric and modern cultures that we will consider are identified in Figure 1.4. Adaptation at the cultural level is the improvement of an individual's or group's survival prospects, or standard of living, through decision making on the part of individuals in the community. Archaeologists and anthropologists attempt to discover the inherent logic and reason for all types of human behavior whether religious or profane. They strive to avoid making judgments about other cultures or their practices and beliefs unless crimes against humanity are involved. If you are to benefit from this book, you, too, must try to divest yourself of ethnocentrism.

TRADITIONAL VERSUS BOOK RELIGIONS

Beginning with William Howells (1948:2–5) scholars have distinguished two major religious traditions in the world: "book" religions and "traditional" religions. While the world is clearly more complex, this basic distinction is useful for emphasizing the difference between most people's urban Industrial religious experiences and the kinds of religious experiences that tend to typify traditional, non-Industrial communities. The distinction is therefore helpful in opening up new perspectives about prehistoric religions.

Book religions are simply defined as major world religions that have a scripture of some sort describing supernatural beings and providing a moral code. The most familiar book religion scriptures include the Christian Bible, the Islamic Koran, and the Judaic Torah. Traditional religions do not have such written scriptures but are passed on from generation to generation as oral and experiential traditions. On the surface, this is a simple enough distinction; however, there are other, much more profound differences beneath this surface. These are discussed under the following eight headings.

1. *World View:* In most book religions, that which is considered sacred or divine is generally to be found somewhere distant, separate from material existence. Typically, god, or the gods, are located in the heavens, above the world. In contrast, for traditional religious practitioners, the sacred is everywhere. It is potentially immanent in everything: animals, plants, people, rocks, the ocean, mountains, the sky, and celestial bodies. The traditional sacred essence can erupt from its dormant state from any thing at any time. Moreover, and this is especially important, under the right conditions using appropriate procedures involving traditional rituals, paraphernalia, and special places, people can reestablish contact with the sacred. Of all the differences between Judaism and the earlier pagan Hebrew practices, the idea that the sacred was in everything was the one that made the prophets of Yaweh the most wrathful

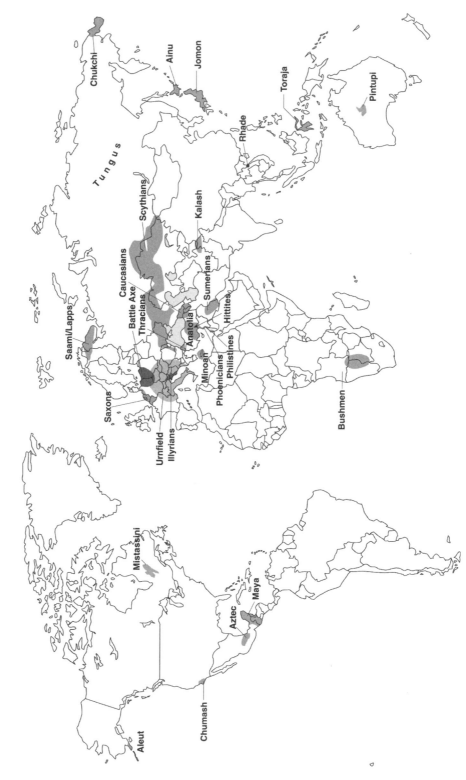

Fig. 1.4. A map of the world showing the locations of the most important prehistoric and ethnographic cultural groups discussed in this book. Drawn by Greg Holoboff.

(Eliade 1978:354). It is a critical difference. The use of the term *sacred* in traditional contexts is also quite different from the usage that most people were taught by church, mosque, or temple members. The essential traditional meaning refers to the presence of vital forces of creation and life in an object, experience, or place, in contrast to profane items and experiences that seem dull and lifeless. But this will become more apparent as we progress.

2. *The Sacredness of Food and Dance:* Food, drink, music, and dance were all part of ritual feasts and were all thought to be especially favorable for contacting sacred forces, currying their favor, and even forming a lasting bond with them. The sacrifice of animals and the eating of meat was a powerful and sacred event that only took place as part of ritual feasts (Fig. 1.5). Feasts, food, and dance formed the warp and the weft of traditional religious fabric in many cultures.

   These are also things that the early fundamentalist missionaries fumed about when trying to convert the pagan European tribes (Miles 1912:170). In most book religions, food and drink are entirely secular or nonreligious objects. In the Industrial societies that we live in today, the consumption of meat is taken for granted in our daily meals. We have become completely divorced from any sacred aspects of killing animals or eating meat. In our culture these activities are profane in nature. In many book religions, music and dance were also considered profane or even dangerous unless closely supervised and controlled by religious authorities. Even today, there is a widespread tradition in many Appalachian communities that the devil resides inside fiddles and can stir up powerful emotions when the fiddle is played. This is why religious fiddlers put rattlesnake tails in their fiddles—to keep the devil at bay (Melvin Wine, personal communication). Similarly, stories about priests in the Canadian Maritime provinces holding community meetings where people had to burn their fiddles or suffer condemnation are recollections among the older generations.

3. *Ecstatic Experiences:* In the vast majority, if not all, traditional religions, entering into ecstatic states is *the* religious experience. It is a direct connection with the sacred forces of the universe and is therefore promoted as desirable. This is vividly demonstrated by the use of masks in traditional rituals. Traditional masks are sacred creations and transform the wearers into the beings that the masks portray (Fig. 1.6)—a far cry from the profane way masks are generally used today.

   In book religions, individual ecstatic experiences are frowned upon, discouraged, or cloistered away. No masks are used in rituals because wearers might become influenced by the spirits embodied by the masks. There seems to be an underlying fear that private contacts with the sacred (even by the standard clergy) might lead to rival cults, political instability, or uncontrollable behavior. In book religions, authorities try to limit direct experiences of the sacred to the most important religious authorities. It is above all this aspect of traditional versus book religions that has led scholars like Joseph Campbell to say that book religions are inoculations against the real thing.

4. *Participation:* While not everyone may enter ecstatic states in traditional religions, many community members sometimes do. Rituals are participatory for a broad segment of the community. People either experience ecstatic states themselves, enter into other types of altered states, play music, sing, dance, eat sacred foods, keep rhythm, or make costumes and other paraphernalia (Fig. 1.7). Rituals are certainly

Fig. 1.5. In Southeast Asia, as in much of the non-Industrial world, elaborate ceremonies featuring animal sacrifices are common occurrences. In the Torajan highlands of Sulawesi, Indonesia, a water buffalo has its throat cut (below), while many people walk in a funeral procession across the sacrificial ground (above). Photos by B. Hayden.

structured so that they are welcoming and open for everyone's active participation.

Participation in book religions tends to be much more of a spectator event with one or few clergy manipulating sacred objects and conducting rituals in front of the massed congregation. Special efforts are often made to awe worshipers spectators with wondrous architecture or the riches of clothes or ornaments. Even the officiating clergy rarely if ever enter into ecstatic states. Rituals are routine and run by the book. As long as the correct words are said and the correct things are done, the ritual is viewed as successful. There is no necessary emotional involvement or transformation of consciousness, whereas in traditional religions, these aspects are essential. It is appropriate, here, to mention that not all people in traditional communities were religious or interested in achieving the ecstatic states to be described in Chapter 3. Those individuals who were concerned about religious matters and who could easily enter into altered states of consciousness are the people that are usually referred to when discussing traditional religions. They constitute the traditional "religious person."

Fig. 1.6. In traditional religions, masks are commonly used and are meant to be worn by participants in rituals so that the participants may be transformed and become the mythical being that the masks embody. Photo by Greg Ehlers.

5. *Life Attitude:* In book religions, there is a tendency to view this world as a somber and solemn place, or one that should be. The major philosophical themes are that if we endure the sufferings inflicted on us by fortune and society here, we will be rewarded in the afterlife. This world is a painful place and therefore we should try to arrange our spiritual development so that we can get out of this existence. Material things are bad; the flesh is sinful; mortify the flesh and emphasize the afterlife, and so on (see Chaps. 11 and 12).

Although it may be stretching the point somewhat, I think that a reasonable case can be made that traditional religions try to connect people to the sacred forces of the universe in a more celebratory fashion, epitomized by rituals with food, drink, music, and dance (Fig. 1.8). Despite frequent adversity, traditional religious people experienced a strong connection to the land, the plants, and the animals. These experiences were celebrated and viewed positively in many ways. People interacted with nature on an individual basis and talked with nature, enhancing subjective feelings of being alive. There are many times when plants, animals, and nature appear to be playing practical jokes on people living and working in fields and forests, and these are undoubtedly the source of inspiration for the many trickster spirits like coyote and raven that appear in Native American mythologies.

Fig. 1.7. Participation in rituals is much more pervasive in traditional religions than "book" religions. Here, tribal Akha girls in the hills of Thailand perform a traditional dance with sticks while other members of the community beat out rhythms, play music, sing, and call out to the girls. Photos by Michael Clarke.

6. *Goals and Morality:* Roy Rappaport (1999:325) has argued that there is a major difference between book religions and tribal religions in terms of morality and ethics. For the followers of book religions, the primary goal of life should be to live in a state of purity, without sin, so that they may be united with the sacred forces *after* death. Religion is a codified coherent ethical system for achieving this goal. Book religions are above all else *moral systems.*

   In contrast, tribal religions are not moral systems. The main goal of the traditional religious person is to be in contact with sacred forces all the time during this life and to celebrate this connection with ritual. Techniques for achieving this goal are the most important elements of traditional religions, and groups are often open to trying out new techniques. In addition, the other goals of traditional religious practitioners are usually very practical rather than moral. They seek to influence divine forces for the benefit of themselves or their communities—for healing, fertility, protection, or similar cares. Rituals sometimes even take on the flavor of business contracts. Higher level ethics, morality, and philosophy are of secondary interest or are even inconsequential.

7. *Central Mysteries:* For book religions, the central mysteries revolve around actions of the deities or moral aspects of the universe (especially why evil or pain exists). In contrast, Mircea Eliade (1959:147) has argued that for the traditional religious person, the central mystery is *life*—where it comes from, where it goes, what affects it, and how it transforms and is continuous from year to year and from generation to generation.

8. *Exclusivity:* Because book religions are ethical systems, usually based on the teachings of key historical figures such as Mohammed, Christ, or Buddha, book religions tend to consider other belief systems as not fully ethical or valid. Generally they are intolerant of other belief systems, even when they do not actively campaign to eliminate

Fig. 1.8. Feasting is a central part of traditional rituals and ceremonies. Here, leading Akha women share a meal for a lineage ritual feast, and display their jewelry. Photo by Michael Clarke.

them. Therefore, book religions transcend ethnic groups and tend to become imperialistic (Howells 1948:5). In contrast, traditional religions easily accept other religions as being equally valid and are tolerant of beliefs in other deities.

It is undoubtedly possible to add to this list, but these are the major distinctions discussed by scholars like William Howells, Joseph Campbell, and Mircea Eliade, with a few of my own elaborations. While some people like to point out the fundamental similarity of all belief systems in the world, it seems to me that there are many fundamental differences, as just indicated. We will see a number of others in later chapters involving relationships with gods, basic values, behavior versus belief, explanations of evil, tolerance of others' beliefs, control over people, and so on. These distinctions will be elaborated and refined as we progress through the last two million years of prehistory, especially in Chapter 3, which deals with shamanism. Before proceeding to discuss the earliest origins of human religious behavior, it is necessary to discuss explanatory frameworks in a bit more detail so that we will have a clear understanding about the direction of our journey into the past and what kinds of phenomena and factors we are going to pause over and ponder.

CULTURAL ECOLOGY DEALS WITH BEHAVIOR

In this book I will primarily use an ecological approach (encompassing both cultural ecology and political ecology) since it is most suited for answering *basic* questions about why religion developed and why its fundamental characteristics changed over time. Other approaches, discussed shortly, will be useful for understanding different aspects of religions.

Cultural ecology is the study of how ecological factors (environment, reproduction, survival, and the use of energy sources) affect human behavior and cultural institutions (Steward 1955). It studies the relationships between people and the natural world, especially how people adapt to the world around them including other people. Cultural ecologists, like most archaeologists, use scientific procedures in order to evaluate competing ideas about the past. They make the details of their theoretical models explicit so that they can be more easily evaluated, and they develop hypotheses in order to test their models by obtaining new observations about the past. A healthy "academic" skepticism toward *all* explanations characterizes the scientific approach (see Preface). Because there are so many conflicting theories about prehistoric religions and because there has been so little archaeological testing of these ideas until now, most of the ideas in this book should be considered as hypotheses or models that still need to be verified by future research.

In contrast to scientific frameworks, other approaches may emphasize the importance of subjective feelings as in mysticism, phenomenology, art appreciation, hermeneutics, or romanticism. These other approaches do not emphasize skeptical analysis or the testing of ideas about the past. One of the premises of cultural ecologists maintains that (a) when people spend large amounts of time, effort, and resources on a specific type of behavior, (b) when that behavior persists over long periods of time, and (c) when the behavior is widespread, then there is likely to be some adaptive benefits to such behaviors. All of these factors describe traditional religions (Rappaport 1971:23, 28). Complex religious behavior and beliefs are certainly widespread, being present in the simplest technological societies in the world such as the hunting and gathering tribes of Australia (Eliade 1973), the Kalahari Desert (Lewis-Williams 1994, 1995b; Lewis-Williams and Dowson 1989), and Tierra del Fuego (Chapman 1982). Simple agricultural tribes such as the hill tribes of Southeast Asia or in tribal Africa also have complex religions (Kammerer 1986; Alting von Geusau 1983). In more technologically complex societies, powerful chiefs created major temples to their ancestors and deities in Polynesia and Africa, while rulers of early states erected even larger statues and temples (Kirch 1984; Lloyd 1978).

In fact, religion, together with language, kinship systems, technology, and political organization are cultural universals of the human race. Religion has persisted from a very early time in our development and consumes enormous amounts of time and energy. Even among materially simple and small-scale societies such as hunters and gatherers, rituals have been observed that have consumed 400 man-weeks of work, enough time to have built a small hill fort or to have written several Ph.D. dissertations (Jones 1977:201). Given such time and energy investments, we may well wonder: how can traditional religion be viewed as adaptive in terms of cultural ecology? We shall begin to answer this question in Chapter 2.

Archaeologists generally use some form of cultural ecology when attempting to reconstruct the social and economic organization of bygone cultures. This is basically the approach advocated by Julian Steward (1955) and William Sears (1961). Ake Hultkrantz (1966) provided an important pioneering lead in studying religions from a cultural ecology perspective, and I will use many of his principles in identifying different "types of religion" as resulting from adaptations to different environmental and economic conditions, for example, religions of simple hunter-gatherers (Chap. 4), religions of trans-egalitarian groups (Chap. 5), religions of pastoral nomads (Chap. 8), religions of chiefly elites (Chap. 7), and others.

In my approach to cultural ecology, I assume that most people in traditional societies such as the Kuma (Reay 1959:191–92), especially more aggressive individuals, seek to promote their own self-interest or at least make decisions based upon the options they think will benefit themselves most. The study of the complex economic and social strategies employed by individuals or groups to promote their own self-interests is what I refer to as "political ecology"—an approach that we shall encounter in Chapters 5–12. However, for most people, I assume that the most important issues are survival (food, shelter, and defense), reproduction, and achieving a comfortable cushion in terms of a standard of living. These are the main ecological imperatives. It is certainly true that not all individuals adhere to these basic imperatives all the time (Hayden and Cannon 1984), although most of the time, most people do. Therefore it is necessary to take these imperatives into account and see how far they can take us in terms of explaining cultural and religious developments.

Ecological principles also emphasize the necessity of generating and maintaining a wide range of physical characteristics, behaviors, and beliefs because these are the building blocks of adaptation and evolutionary change. In cultural terms, it is often people or groups on the fringe of mainstream society who conceive of and try out new ideologies, social relationships, economic strategies, marital relationships, or configurations of power. Historically, most of the main religious and social or political movements of the world (including Christianity, Islam, Buddhism, and political democracy) began as just such fringe groups. Many of the alternative lifestyles and ideologies promoted by contemporary fringe groups could become adaptive given appropriate economic or other changes in today's societies. The long-term evolutionary viability of most cultures is safeguarded by permitting or even encouraging creative fringe groups. Therefore, we always expect to find some eccentric or nonconformist people and values in all societies.

Cognitive Frameworks Deal with Symbols

In contrast to cultural ecology, which emphasizes the practical benefits of behavior and beliefs to the individual, many cognitive anthropologists and structuralist or "postmodern" archaeologists argue that culture is an independent system of ideas. In this view, the structured relations of cultural ideas and values shape human behavior. Moreover, these ideas and values are passed on to succeeding generations so that they "reproduce" themselves and perpetuate the system. According to the more extreme proponents of this approach, cultural traditions and values exert such a strong influence that people become blinded to their own self-interests and are driven to adopt beliefs and behaviors simply because they are part of the tradition they grew up with (Sahlins 1981; Renfrew and Bahn 1996:464; Harris 1979:278–82). Such views are especially common in attempts to explain elaborate gift giving and feasting such as the potlatch (Rosman and Rubel 1971:90, 205–6), the Mesoamerican cargo system (Carrasco 1961; Cancian 1965), or the lavish tribal funerals in Southeast Asia (Kammerer 1986). All these events may leave hosts temporarily or even permanently destitute.

There are major problems with these extreme views, and such explanations are incompatible with a cultural ecology approach *when dealing with costly, persistent, and pervasive behaviors.* As we shall see in later chapters (Chaps. 5–8), traditional people are no economic lemmings being driven to self-destruction by unquestioned cultural norms (see also Hayden 1995). Most people are generally sufficiently intelligent to see where their own best interests lie (Rappaport 1971:32, 1999:120–30), particularly if major expenditures of time, effort, and resources are involved. It now seems clear that when people spend lavishly on gifts and feasts, they are competitively investing surpluses in bids to maintain or improve their self-interests and ultimately their adaptive position.

There is certainly a useful role for the cognitive approach when dealing with symbolic interpretations (see Chaps. 6–10), and there is a good deal of truth to the view that cultural values influence our behavior since we must all adopt conventions of behavior that will enable us to interact successfully with the people around us. We cannot demand that people adopt a language that we have invented, or insist on driving on the opposite side of the road from the norm, or go to work naked. But my experience in traditional societies, as well as from reading descriptions in the literature, have made it clear to me that few people ever blindly accept costly cultural values to the detriment of their fundamental self-interests. Certainly, there may always be a few, and there may be exceptional circumstances such as the defense of one's family, community, or ethnic group. However, most people appear to be forced to accept cultural practices that are contrary to their self-interests because of severe consequences and/or the lack of better alternatives. In other cases, cultural values are used as tools to get what one wants. As Marvin Harris (1979:271–78) has observed, people selectively use cultural rules to justify their behavior and manipulate situations to their own advantage. In this respect traditional societies are much like the great moral books of the world, such as the Bible. One of the great values of these books is the large number of contradictory rules they contain that allow individuals to select a rule to suit their immediate needs. This is one reason why such works have endured over centuries and millennia: something can be found in them to deal with almost any situation according to one's desires. The Bible, for instance, exhorts us to turn the other cheek when we are wronged (Luke 6:27–35; Matthew 5:39) but it also says, "an eye for an eye, a tooth for a tooth" (Exodus 21:24). Religion has probably always been used to explain why things happen, such as earthquakes, or why things such as sacrifices must be performed. Although practices like human sacrifice may have been carried out within a religious framework, many religious beliefs really only rationalize events and justify actions for economic, social, or political goals.

In the traditional societies with which I am familiar, cultural rules and norms certainly exist and are held to be immutable or absolute. Yet, even in the most tradition-bound cultures studied by anthropologists such as the Maya of Guatemala (Hayden and Gargett 1990), the Australian Aborigines (Morphy 1991; Mulvaney and Kamminga 1999:418–19; Guenther 1999:428), and the hill tribes of Southeast Asia (Kammerer 1986), there have been startling changes to traditional economies, social relationships, and beliefs in the last century. How did these changes come about if these groups were so tradition-bound that they overlooked their own self-interest?

When I carried out ethnographic work in these three cultures, I was constantly surprised by the readiness of some portions of each community to experiment with new technologies, new relationships, new ideas, and new ideologies. I saw Australian Aborigines building African-style shelters after having seen photographs from Africa. Their religions are reported to be the most conservative in the world, yet following the earliest contacts with Europeans, new totemic spirits such as liquor bottles and bulldozers were incorporated into their "dreamtime" sacred songs and myths (Mulvaney and Kamminga 1999:418; Guenther 1999:428). I also found that in the most religious communities of the Highland Maya there were a surprising number of self-professed agnostics or atheists. About 10 percent of the people simply did not care about rituals or supernatural beliefs, while another 10–20 percent had abandoned their traditional beliefs in favor of new belief systems being promoted by missionaries from outside. In Southeast Asia, Karl Izikowitz (1951:321) found the same proportion of atheists and agnostics among the very remote and tradition-bound Lamet, and he also recorded many instances of people rejecting the values or rules that they were brought up to believe in, such as the economic and political deference that is supposed to be shown to elder brothers as lineage heads. In the same vein, Marie Reay (1959:131) observed that most people in the Kuma culture of New Guinea did not have a working knowledge of their own religious doctrines or myths, even though these were accessible. Presumably they simply did not care about these matters. The Kuma did participate in all the traditional rituals, but only accepted the religious concepts to varying degrees. These observations provide strong reasons for rejecting the extreme cognitivist contention that people in traditional cultures are and were prisoners of the belief systems that they grew up with.

Furthermore, in Southeast Asia, I found that almost all cultural rules and even basic values were subject to qualifications or were modified when changes were perceived as advantageous (Leach 1954:8, 10, 221, 262–63). Similar observations come from ethnographers working elsewhere in the world (Cashdan 1980; Shnirelman 1990; Chagnon 2000). Moreover, people who broke community rules could almost always negotiate to avoid heavy penalties if they had enough support. Edmund Leach (1954:129, 145–48, 160, 167, 179–86, 245), Georges Condominas (1977:38, 86, 108, 111, 123, 139, 151, 156, 166, 208, 330, 336, 338), and Polly Wiessner and Akii Tumu (1998) vividly report the constant stream of pressures and litigations in traditional societies in Southeast Asia in which cultural rules were bent, warped, invented, changed, or ignored in order to accommodate the interests of the most powerful individuals in the communities. As Paul Radin (1920) pointed out long ago, there is an enormous gulf between the cultural and religious rules that people give lip service to and actual individual behavior or even acceptance of those rules (see Rappaport 1999:118ff.). This is one reason why cultural ecologists emphasize actual behavior rather than belief as the essential core of cultures. Roy Rappaport (1999:140ff.) in particular has argued that verbal claims to abstract qualities are easy to make and often are empty proclamations. If such claims are to be believed, they must be backed up by physical proof such as acts, performance of rituals, and/or the creation of valued or monumental objects.

The ecological view of traditional societies is very different from that generally found in cognitively oriented anthropological or archaeological studies. In the ecological view that I am advocating, traditional political power (the ability to influence decisions in a community) plays a critical role in understanding behavior, beliefs, and changes in cultures. In turn, the command and use of resources and manpower is critical for understanding the development of political power. That is why I sometimes refer to this approach as a political ecological one (*political ecology* can be defined as the study of how the available resources, demography, and technology influence the decision making, or power structure of communities).

While the strength of ecologically based explanations is in dealing with costly behaviors, ecology is usually not very successful in dealing with questions of the meaning of symbols or rituals for users, makers, or observers. Ecology may help us understand why symbolic systems like writing, numbers, or signs are used, but there is rarely any basis for determining why a culture chose a specific number such as 2 or 3 or 4 as sacred or what such a number might symbolize (the dual aspects of the yin/yang, the three classes of society, the four directions of the universe). Nor is ecology very well equipped to deal with historical choices, which may persist over long periods, such as the Babylonian decision to divide the sky into 12 astrological signs, a system still reflected in the 12 hours of our clocks and watches, or the Saxon decision to name their days of the week after gods (i.e., Thursday after Thor), a practice we still continue.

Historical and cognitive cultural explanations do clarify these kinds of phenomena quite well and these approaches will help us understand some interesting aspects of traditional and contemporary religions. Thus, it is important to distinguish between trying to explain the occurrence of a general type of behavior such as raising stone monuments or building temples (an ecological problem) and explaining the symbolic meaning that makers, users, and observers attribute to those behaviors, such as to worship ancestors, the sun, or other concepts (a cognitive problem). The distinction should become apparent as we chronicle religious changes over the last two million years. Both approaches are useful and can help us understand past religions, and I will use both approaches in this book. However, in many archaeological cases, there are few or no clues as to what religious symbols meant, and in those cases we are restricted to dealing with the more basic ecological questions of why people began to use ochre, bury the dead, use deep caves for rituals, raise large stones, or build towering temples.

Accounting for Religious Change

One of the most important features of human cultures that archaeology deals with is change, especially change over time. Understanding why changes take place in culture is ultimately the essence of understanding culture itself. It is one of the great intellectual adventures of our time and there is no consensus on this issue. It encompasses religious change, and religious change is a central concern of this book. There are many different philosophical windows from which students of culture look at traditional societies, but not all of them can account very well for changes in cultures. Some people, following Stephen J. Gould (1989), see no rhyme or reason in the biological or cultural changes of the past two million years. For them everything is viewed as due to chance or random events (Flannery 1968, 1986). If humans were eliminated from earth, they argue, the chances that other intelligent life would evolve are infinitesimally small.

Others, like cognitivists and structuralists, tend to ignore the dimension of time and change, or perhaps see change as due to random cognitive events, inspirations, or great ideas that are generated by a nebulous internal dynamic and spread by contagion or by elevating people's "awareness."

Similar views are that cultures change because of nebulous winds of change in the world (cultural "spirits of the times" or "zeitgeists"), as argued by James Deetz in *In Small Things Forgotten*. This view is compatible with art historians and many humanists who coined these terms to explain changes in art styles and fashions. They, however, give few answers to questions about why zeitgeists change.

There is also a strong recent tendency to view the nature of others, other cultures, and past changes, as ineffable, unknowable, and totally subjective. For such people (hermeneuticists, postmodern deconstructionists, extreme postprocessualists), there is no reality except the subjective reality (Shanks and Tilley 1987; Hodder 1986), and one may even wonder if that can stand on its own in such a navel-centered conceptual world. Ken Wilber (1996:26) and others (Harris 1992, 1993; Mukerjee 1998; Yengoyan 1985) have described such approaches as nihilism being promoted by those who want to manipulate public or other opinions for their own purposes and conceal the true nature of reality.

Mystics, feminists, and political reformers often insist that we can change the world by raising people's consciousness, and they presumably believe this is why changes took place in the past. Nor should we forget fundamentalist explanations of change, whether the specific versions are Christian, Islamic, Judaic, Hindu, First Nations, or other varieties. According to many of the fundamentalist views, the fall from grace or separation from a sacred past created the present world, and divine influences or battles between good and evil still determine the outcome of many events. We could continue to explore these different approaches for many pages, together with the different approaches dealing with how we can know what the world is really like, and how it operates.

I will focus, however, on using cultural ecology to understand basic forms of religious change since I think it has greater explanatory potential than the other approaches. In contrast to a single set of cultural norms or values or rules that govern behavior and thought in communities, I adopt the view that there is *always* a broad range of other behaviors and beliefs that vary from individual to individual. The entire range of these behaviors and beliefs is available to all members of a community to adopt or ignore or even

Fig. 1.9. Popular, and even professional scientific, writers sometimes suggest that the great religious monuments of the world, such as Stonehenge (shown here), were built because of religious fervor and charismatic leaders. Cultural ecologists suspect that there were much more practical reasons. Photo B. Hayden.

to invent new forms. Of critical importance is the notion that *what determines which beliefs and behaviors will be adopted by most individuals is the perceived benefit that will be derived from adopting specific beliefs or behaviors.* The individual is the decision-making unit in cultural change and so we must account for cultural changes on the basis of individual decision-making criteria rather than cultural spirits or diffusing norms.

While there is certainly variability in decision-making criteria from individual to individual, the vast majority of people seem to place most emphasis on the benefit to themselves, whether directly or indirectly. The cultural beliefs and behaviors available to them are like cultural tools. In any given situation, individuals first establish a clear idea of the outcome they desire, and then they choose the "tools" (technological, social, ideological, or other) most appropriate for achieving those ends. From a cultural ecological point of view, economic conditions, in particular, constrain outcomes and choices so that in many traditional societies, where economic and environmental conditions do not change, there is little if any change in beliefs or behaviors. People simply find that the traditional solutions work best, although periodic experiments and deviations certainly must occur.

Many popular writers (Barry 1805:102; Wernick 1973) and even some professional archaeologists (Weaver 1972:75) propose that religious monuments requiring huge amounts of human labor, such as Stonehenge or the Pyramid of the Sun in Mexico (Figs. 1.2, 1.9), were built because of religious fervor. From a cultural ecological perspective, this suggestion is ridiculous. Why would such large numbers of people suddenly develop such religious zeal? Why did such fervor only occur in very restricted areas of the world and only for a few thousand years out of the millions of years of human existence? Who could have persuaded so many people to undertake such huge projects involving so much time and effort for so long a time? To students who believe in such powers of persuasion, I have offered $1,000 if they can persuade enough people to quarry and carry a 10-ton megalith to Simon Fraser University and erect it using *only* their powers of persuasion concerning supernatural concepts (i.e., no rewards or monetary benefits can be offered to people to induce them to undertake this task). I have never had anyone take me up on such an offer and I do not expect to be paying anyone in the future.

Within the cultural ecological perspective, it is above all when the environment changes (whether subsistence, economic, social, or political aspects of the environment)—when new alternatives with clear practical benefits become available—that major cultural and religious changes tend to occur. It is then that individuals can propose new ways of doing things. It is under these conditions that they may receive receptive responses from others in their community. Thus, Elizabeth Cashdan (1980) found that when the fiercely egalitarian Bushmen of Botswana settled down near cattle ranches and began receiving salaries that provided security from famine, they quickly abandoned their staunch sharing values and became much more individualistic. Similarly, I found that when evangelical missionaries entered the Guatemalan Highlands in a quest to convert the pagan Maya, they had enormous success in the communities where they provided agricultural assistance, low-interest loans, medical facilities, and employment. In other communities they had little success. In much earlier contexts, Polly Wiessner has documented the remarkable impact on cults, rituals, and culture that the introduction of the sweet potato had in New Guinea, where it greatly increased the food surpluses that people could produce (Wiessner and Tumu 1998). Such examples could be multiplied many times over. They all demonstrate the fundamental role that practical benefits play in changing traditional belief systems. These are some of the considerations that we, too, will be examining in our journey through the past.

SUMMARY

A basic distinction in the panoply of religions throughout the world is between "book" religions and "traditional" religions. In their extreme expressions, these polar opposites differ in terms of worldviews; attitudes toward life, ecstatic experiences, food, sex, music, and dance; ideas about sacred realms and basic mysteries; exclusivity; religious goals; and participatory roles. Trying to convey a tangible sense of what traditional religions are like is the biggest challenge of this book. Traditional religious experiences are so alien to most Industrial denizens that we must cross a fairly forbidding experiential and intellectual abyss to achieve even a modicum of understanding. But understanding traditional religions is the most important thing that I would like people to carry away with them when they have finished reading this book.

Another challenge is to provide readers with a firm sense of the role that ecological factors played in the major developments of prehistoric religions. In my experience, people in traditional societies rarely uncritically accept ideas or values that they are taught. People constantly evaluate ideas and practices that require major expenditures of time, effort, and resources. When religious changes occur on a broad scale, cultural ecology leads us to ask what practical benefits might be associated with the newer forms. Can religions really be viewed as adaptive? Is there really a relationship between environment (in its widest sense) and resources, on the one hand, and major religious phenomena on the other? These are the issues that we will begin to explore in the next chapter.

CHAPTER 2

The Making of Humanity
and the Origin of Religion

Archaeology confronts some of the most fundamental questions that we can ask about ourselves and our place in the universe: questions about what it means to be human, how humans evolved, what culture is, why religion exists, and how any of these things can be considered adaptive. We have seen that religion is a universal cultural phenomenon and that many people have an innate penchant for religious experiences, especially ecstatic experiences. The question that this chapter addresses is how such tendencies have become an integral part of the human psyche. Answering this question will also take us into more profound problems such as the origin of many of the other human emotional characteristics, some consideration of the structure of the brain, archetypes, and a definition of religion. These are all weighty topics to delve into, but each is fascinating in its own right.

To begin with, it is useful to realize that there are many different opinions about why religion exists and is so widespread (Waal Malefijt 1968:42ff.). These include suggestions that religion is the result of:

- intellectual attempts to explain dreams, death, nonlogical thoughts (Tylor 1958; Jaynes 1976), or mistakes in reasoning (Frazer 1959)
- the need to sanctify social conventions (Durkheim 1961; Young 1965; Rappaport 1999:4–5, 7, 286, 304, 322–24)
- means for establishing political power or high status (Dietler 2001)
- the psychological need to reduce childhood or adult anxieties or conflicts (Roheim 1972; Parsons 1952; Freud 1913, 1939; Tuzin 1984; Malinowski 1954; Oubré 1997:16–17)
- incidental by-products of other adaptive changes to the brain, for example, increased size, complexity, and linguistic functions (Boyer 1994, 2001; Webber, Stephens, and Laughlin, 1983)
- recognition of real paranormal or supernatural phenomena (Winkelman 1982)

- ways of adapting to harsh environments for survival (Hayden 1987) or for decision-making needs (Rappaport 1971)
- very early healing techniques (Winkelman 2000:251)

While it is fashionable to use psychological or social (Durkheimian) models to explain the origin of religion, these approaches are unsatisfactory for a number of reasons from an archaeological and ecological point of view. First, the amount of time and effort invested in many religious activities such as the building of Stonehenge are far beyond what one would expect of any simple anxiety-reducing behavior, unless entire populations were extremely phobic. Moreover, high levels of anxiety do not accord with any ethnographers' observations that I am aware of. In fact, ethnographers sometimes remark on the surprising *lack* of concern that hunter-gatherers and horticulturalists display about the future. High levels of anxiety would hardly have been adaptive for early hunters and gatherers, and they do not seem to characterize any other intelligent mammals. Moreover, spending large amounts of time and energy in any activity that had no real adaptive value would have placed early humans at a distinct disadvantage in the harsh and fiercely competitive environment in which they evolved.

Second, developing an inherent tendency to enter into ecstatic or altered states of consciousness must have involved major transformations of the physical structure of the human brain. In ecological theory, such changes are incomprehensible unless they also confer advantageous survival benefits; that is, unless these changes are in some ways *adaptive.*

Third, it might be argued that the expansion of the brain's neocortex and especially the dominance of the left hemisphere (see Music Is in the Hemispheres, below) were adaptive because they made culture possible at the cost of suppressing functions of earlier parts of the brain. In this view, the function of religion is to reduce the stresses between these different parts of the brain (Webber, Stephens, and Laughlin, 1983). This explanation has a relatively narrow scope, however, accounting only for ritual behavior. In contrast, ecological explanations such as those to be discussed cover a much wider range of behavior, including sharing, alliances, and kinship. In addition, ecological explanations encompass unique types of human behavior that are difficult to understand under other paradigms. Such behaviors include the human reaction to rhythms and their link to rituals, the acceptance of new values presented while in ecstatic states, and the notion of higher principles or beings. None of these features might be expected to occur if the main function of religion was simply to reduce internal mental stresses. Raw expressions of emotions would presumably be more effective for that purpose.

Thus, there are a number of reasons for thinking that the ecological approach is more useful than others for understanding the origins of religion. Given the universality of religion, the magnitude of effort, time, and resources consumed in religious behavior, and the persistence of religion over tens or hundreds of thousands of years, cultural ecologists argue that there must have been important adaptive advantages to religion during our evolution. What those advantages were is not very apparent, but I will provide one scenario that I think is a good explanatory candidate. I will not evaluate the numerous other attempts at explaining the existence of religion here since that would take up many pages, but some of the problems with the other approaches may become evident as we delve into the topic.

Our Ancestors Evolved under Pressure

It is important to begin by recognizing the magnitude of the changes that were involved. Over the course of some three to four million years, our ancestors underwent profound evolutionary changes in their bodies and brains. They changed from 50-pound weaklings who could scarcely walk upright, had no ability for human speech, and had brains a quarter the size of ours, to upright walking, running, talking, highly intelligent humans with robust bodies and large brains. There were many other subsidiary changes as well, but the main point is that these magnitudes of change do not come about as the result of random genetic influences or drift tendencies. These changes took place in an extremely short time period (for biological evolution), which required extremely *strong selective pressures*. In blunt terms, this meant that during this formative period, a very high percentage of our ancestors were dying before they could reproduce and only those with better abilities to walk and talk, think, and experience religious states had good chances of surviving. Nonecological explanatory models for the existence of religion generally do not appeal to any force powerful enough to remodel, restructure, and recast the human brain into its present form in terms of strong innate penchants for religious experiences and other related emotions.

Thus, psychologists, ethnologists (scholars who study traditional societies), and others have neglected dealing with the origins of the neurophysiological foundations of religion. However, those who study the evolution of humans (physical anthropologists) have avoided dealing with this issue as well. They have concentrated almost completely on gross physical changes (in locomotion, body size, dentition, brain size, posture), using these to frame their concepts of human evolution. Physical anthropologists have almost completely neglected human emotional characteristics in their considerations of evolution and the emergence of distinctive adaptations of human beings. In this chapter, I propose a bridge between these two extremes. If the reason for human religious tendencies is to be found anywhere, it will be found in the evolution of an entire array of very distinctive human emotional characteristics that form an important part of our genetic heritage. This distinctive emotional array is just as important as our distinctive posture, our ability to walk and talk and make tools, and our ability to analyze or remember things.

Hunters and Gatherers Hold the Key to the Origins of Religion

We may begin by asking what traditional religion does. In order to answer this, we cannot use experiences from modern Industrial societies. We must delve into the nature of religions among hunting and gathering peoples—nomadic people in small bands without agriculture or domesticated animals, people living much closer to the lifestyle of our ancient ancestors. Hunter-gatherers and their religions may hold the keys to many questions about religion and human evolution because our ancestors followed an entirely hunting and gathering way of life from the first appearance of humans (Fig. 2.1), over two million years ago, up until the advent of agriculture, a scant 5,000 to 10,000 years ago in most areas of the world (see Chap. 4). This means that for more than 99.5 percent of human existence, we have lived as hunter-gatherers. If the length of a football field represented the length of human existence, agriculture would come in only 12 inches from the goal line and civilizations would only appear in the last 6 inches. Thus,

A
B
1
m.
0
Stone tool
Bone
A
B

Fig. 2.1. The nomadic hunting and gathering way of life (as represented above by a Western Australian shade and sleeping shelter) seems to have been established over 1.75 million years ago on the basis of shelter, food, and tool remains left at Olduvai Gorge (below). Note the brush windbreak surrounding the back of the shelter and the refuse pattern surrounding the living area similar to the prehistoric example. Photo by B. Hayden. Olduvai plan from M. Leakey, *Olduvai Gorge,* Vol. 3, Fig. 7. Cambridge: Cambridge University Press, 1971. Reprinted with the permission of Cambridge University Press.

all of our distinctive emotional reactions, including religion, evolved under hunting and gathering lifestyle conditions.

All human beings carry around a lot of genetic baggage picked up in the course of our evolution as hunter-gatherers (Eibl-Eibesfeldt 1989). It influences our emotional reactions to provocations, stress, the opposite sex, our parents, religious experiences, and many other facets of our environment in its widest sense. Unfortunately, we cannot simply put this baggage down and walk away from it when we might like to. It has become part of our bodies. Fully modern physical human forms, indistinguishable from people today, appeared between 50,000 and 100,000 years ago and seem to be fully modern in behavioral terms as well.

Thus, if we are to ask why our penchant for religion evolved, we *must* seek the answers among prehistoric hunters and gatherers. One of the great advantages of archaeology combined with cultural ecology is that it is possible to investigate peoples and cultures from this very remote time period. So, allow yourself to be transported temporarily to our ultimate ancestral home, Africa. The time is some three million years before the present, when our ancestors were those 50-pound weaklings who still spent a great deal of time in trees eating fruits, ants, greens, and occasional small animals.

EARLY HUMANS HAD TO TRANSCEND ADVERSITY OR DIE

What were the strong selective pressures that transformed our early ancestors from a rather unpromising weakling (compared with other primates) into a primate that came to dominate the globe? Such questions preoccupy the minds of many physical anthropologists and there are diverse opinions. However, in all major opinions the changes in the hominid skeleton, brain, and technological abilities are veiwed as developing as the result of pressures from the environment. Opinions only differ as to the nature of the stresses responsible for the changes. The leading scenario at this time focuses on some major climatic changes that had important impacts on the vegetation of Africa (Foley 1994; McKee 1994). These changes began about five million years ago when our early ancestors and other, larger primates, were living in African jungles and forests. As time passed, many of these lush forested areas began to dry up, including much of the area now occupied by the Sahara Desert, the eastern African savannas, and southern Africa (Fig. 2.2). The fruits and vegetables that formed the staples in the diets of the early primates became harder and harder to find in these more arid areas, and competition must have become fierce as periodic droughts occurred, similar to the severe droughts that struck the Sahel areas bordering the southern Sahara in the 1980s (the same recent droughts that brought people together for aid concerts such as the Live Aid concert for drought relief in this area). The droughts of recent decades have been largely caused by people who overgrazed cattle and removed subsurface water. The droughts of several million years ago were caused by natural climatic changes, but the results were very similar: misery, widespread starvation, death, and large-scale population movements. These are conditions that can certainly account for major changes to a population's behavior and gene pool.

In the competition for the remaining resources and forested areas, our early ancestors were apparently on the losing end. Larger primates seem to have monopolized the remaining forested areas, leaving the early protohumans out in the dry, relatively treeless savanna. For an animal adapted to eating fruit and vegetables, the savanna is not a place

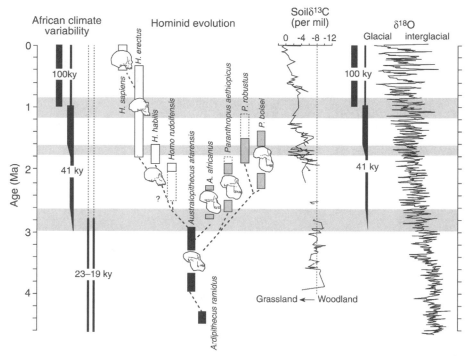

Fig. 2.2. Over the last 4 million years, the climate in many parts of Africa became progressively drier resulting in an increasing replacement of woodland by grassland. It was against this environmental backdrop that the first humans evolved. Reprinted with permission from P. de-Menocal, "Plio-Pleistocene African Climate," *Science* 270:58. Copyright © 1995, American Association for the Advancement of Science.

where it is easy to survive, especially in the dry season. There is certainly food, but most of it is underground or in the form of animal meat on the hoof. Neither of these sources of food would have been easily acquired by early protopeople who lacked claws for digging, the ability to run quickly, or the teeth necessary to kill animals or cut through hides to remove flesh. The initial environment must have been extremely inhospitable and enormous numbers of those early protohumans must have died on the savannas during the drying up of African forests. Great numbers must have also been killed by the predators like lions, cheetahs, and hyenas that roam the savannas. In the forest, trees always provided escape routes from predators. On the savanna, the lack of trees meant that primates unable to escape or defend themselves would likely become predator dinners (Fig. 2.3).

Before looking at how this situation could have resulted in changes that made us human, two important points need to be mentioned. First, rapid evolutionary changes generally do not result from single, unexpected, entirely new, "miracle" mutations. Rather, natural selection seems to work most effectively where there is already some incipient expression of a trait that can become adaptive under changed conditions, for example, an ability to make alarm sounds as a precursor to the development of language. We will see other examples shortly. The second point is an irony of nature in which severe adversity seems to lead either to death and extinction or to a transcendence of the situation through transformation. This is as true in psychological, social, political, and shamanic terms as it is in genetic terms. If adversity does not crush us, we may become stronger and better individuals by making extraordinary efforts and sacrifices to overcome our problems.

Fig. 2.3. One of the survival pressures created by the spread of grasslands was undoubtedly the increased difficulty of escaping from predators such as this lion, which has treed a family of baboons on the African savanna. In woodland habitats primates could have simply traveled in the trees. From S. Washburn and I. DeVore, "The Social Life of Baboons," *Scientific American* 204(6):65.

In fact, this is one of the major lessons of shamanic tales and fairy tales the world over, as we shall see in Chapter 10. Individuals or groups that never face any adversity do not tend to grow or advance. The bigger primates that retained control of the luxuriant fruit-rich forests are still there—little changed from five million years ago. They did not have to change. In the case of our early ancestors, the entire prehuman species came perilously close to being eliminated from the face of the earth by the adverse conditions on the savanna. The entire protohuman population may have been reduced to a few tens of thousands, or even several thousand individuals at some points (Ambrose 1998). The transcendence of this nadir in prehistory is one of the most remarkable stories of biological evolution. What were the key elements of this transformation? Three kinds of changes were particularly important: skeletal changes related to posture and locomotion, technological changes, and emotional changes.

The Evolution of Human Hands and Feet
Bullied out of the forest, the protopeople must have been concerned first with how to avoid becoming a lion's meal. Few primates can stand up or walk on two feet for more than a few minutes. Nor can they move particularly fast on the ground. However, the *incipient* ability to stand and walk does exist among most apes and probably existed among ancestral protohuman populations as well. Contrary to many expectations centering around the human brain as our adaptive reason for biological success, the first skeletal changes taking us on the road to humanity were *not* in the head but in the hands and feet. Changes in posture and locomotion were the first notable adaptations of these populations, occurring some three to four million years ago (T. White 1980). Clearly,

individuals forced to live on the savannas who had incipient bone shapes that helped them stand and walk,
rather than excel at climbing trees, survived more often
than those who were less able to do these things. These
survivors passed on their genes to their children, who
also tended to survive more successfully. Individuals
lacking these abilities, or even those who were less
adept, undoubtedly trailed behind when groups fled
from predators and thus were more likely to be over-
taken and killed.

Standing and running may have been very adaptive
for escaping lions and other predators; however, using
one's hands was also undoubtedly effective. While we
lack claws or other defensive body parts such as the large
canines of male baboons, we can use our hands to throw
objects, just as chimpanzees sometimes wave branches
or throw things to try to frighten other animals away
(McGrew 1992; Goodall 1971:114, 116, 210, 247,

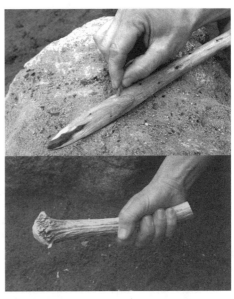

277). Any protoperson who could throw a stick or stone hard enough and accurately
enough to make a predator think twice about attacking would be far more likely to survive than others who could not manage to throw objects effectively. Again, the incipient
ability was probably present in our ancestral primate predecessors (as it is in chimpanzees), and there must have been substantial variability within populations between
those that had hand shapes favoring accurate throwing or "precision grips" (like holding
a pencil, picking up a coin, or throwing a spear) and others who, like most primates,
only had "power grips" (like clenching fists or holding clubs; Fig. 2.4), which were not
very good for throwing. These are factors governed by the bone structure of the hand
and by the ability to coordinate the proper movements neurologically. The ability to
throw forcefully and accurately is also dependent upon an upright posture similar to that
used by baseball pitchers or javelin throwers (Fifer 1987). Thus, the major early changes
to the skeleton that make humans different from other primates can be fairly easily accounted for by changing environments and natural selection leading to new adaptations.

Fig. 2.4. One of
the evolutionary
changes to the
human skeleton
that undoubtedly
helped protohu-
mans survive on
the savanna was
the change in
hand structure
that enabled indi-
viduals to grasp
and throw objects
in a precise fash-
ion. This "preci-
sion grip" is de-
picted above;
other primates
only have "power
grips" as depicted
below. Photo by
Greg Ehlers.

TECHNOLOGY MADE US DIFFERENT

With the double spectres of starvation and large predators confronting the physically ill-
equipped protohumans, rapid change was critical to avoid extinction. Once again, an incipient behavior probably provided a valuable springboard for evolutionary change. This
was the use of tools. Chimpanzees today use a relatively wide assortment of very simple
tools, such as sticks stripped for extracting termites from their holes, stones used to crack
open nuts, or branches or stones used to frighten away other animals (Goodall 1971;
McGrew 1992). The protohuman populations probably acted in a similar fashion when
they found themselves on the inhospitable savanna. It was essential to find ways of getting at the major sources of food there. While they did not have claws for digging up
roots, they appear to have found ways of using sharpened digging sticks (Fig. 2.5). These
were undoubtedly one of the simplest and earliest innovations of our ancestors (Hatley

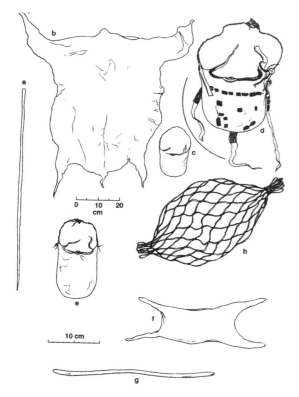

Fig. 2.5. The digging stick (a simple stick sharpened at one end for digging) is one of the most universal tools used by hunter/gatherer women. It can be used to dig up roots and small animals or for defense. It was probably one of the first tools to be made with stone implements by our ancestors. Together with simple carrying devices such as skins the digging stick (item a) comprises the only tool carried by women in many foraging bands as can be seen in this inventory of women's tools. From R. Lee, *The !Kung San*, p. 125. Cambridge: Cambridge University Press, 1979. Reprinted with the permission of Cambridge University Press.

and Kappelman 1980), and digging sticks continued to be used by all hunter-gatherers right up to the present.

Similarly, what they lacked in sharpness of tooth or swiftness of foot, protopeople made up for through stealth and stalking and the throwing of sharpened sticks—the first spears and throwing sticks. These developments also must have made defense against predators far more effective. It undoubtedly took a long time to develop the physical changes necessary to make these strategies fully effective. Hunting large animals probably began as scavenging carcasses that other predators had left behind and breaking open the remaining bones for marrow. Perhaps this stage was followed by the use of sticks and stones to frighten away predators from more recent kills. Protohumans would have had to perfect the precision grip and to refine certain neurological features in order to effectively make and use tools for hunting or chasing away predators from their kills. It would be necessary to develop motor coordination as well as the mental ability to predict game locations and to coordinate groups of hunters, possibly using some form of language. The first good evidence that we have for such changes appears about two and a half million years ago when stone tools essential for shaping and sharpening sticks and cutting up carcasses first appear in the archaeological record (Fig. 2.6). Home bases also appear shortly afterward, indicating that individuals were probably sharing food, living in families, and perhaps using some form of language (Isaac 1978). If these early humanoids were using language, some form of religion may have already been present. There are those who would argue that language implies the existence of sacred concepts in order to distinguish truth from lies (Rappaport 1971:30; 1999:4–5, 7, 286, 304, 322–24).

Once again, individuals with hand shapes allowing better precision grips, postures that enabled them to throw hard and accurately, and mental abilities that enabled them to predict game movements and coordinate hunting strategies must have had better chances of survival on the savanna. Individuals who had genes putting them at disadvantages in these areas would have died more frequently and their genes would have eventually been eliminated. As tools and hunting became mainstays of human survival, the brain also began to increase in size. Scholars have typically assumed that this growth enabled individuals to make better tools and to better coordinate their hunting or other subsistence activities. However, there is another possibility—one related to the distinctive emotional characteristics of humans that also emerged during this period.

EMOTIONS ENHANCED OUR CHANCES OF SURVIVAL

In addition to the physical and technological changes that marked our ancestors' transformation into humanity, I suggest that they also forged emotional bonds that helped them survive in the inhospitable environments in which they were forced to live (Hayden 1987, 1993a). In order to understand how this bonding took place, it is necessary to examine hunter-gatherer lifestyles a little more closely. One of the basic ecological characteristics of most hunter-gatherer societies is that their resources are scarce and fluctuate from season to season and year to year, especially in savanna environments, where rain showers may render one area relatively lush while the neighboring area may stay dry. Under such conditions, survival often resembles a lottery. One group may have enough food to live comfortably one year while their neighbors may be close to starvation, whereas the situation may be reversed in another year. The principal technique that hunter-gatherers throughout the world developed in order to cope with such recurring crises was to establish alliances with other bands, both near and, especially, far. When disaster and famine struck, they would have the option of moving out of afflicted areas and going to other areas where the situation was not as severe. The strategy of long-distance mobility is extremely adaptive and is used by all migratory large mammals and birds. It is difficult to imagine that protopeople on the savanna would not have also tried to use this strategy. However, this is not as simple a prospect as it might seem. Primates tend to live in groups that defend their territories, and virtually the entire landscape would have been occupied by other bands of hunter-gatherers with little incentive to share their territories with outsiders.

Under these conditions, there are only two ways of moving into lands occupied by other groups. One is to go to war and try to kill or displace the original inhabitants; the other is to make friends with them so that they will be willing to act as hosts in time of need. In fact, all simple hunter-gatherers seem to have used both strategies. They maintained enmities with some groups that they might want to go to war with, but they also maintained strong alliances with other groups. Both strategies were costly but essential

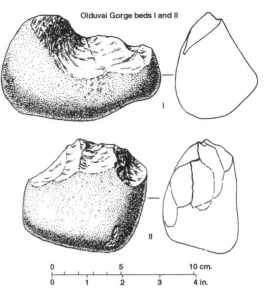

Fig. 2.6. Simple stone chopping tools constitute some of the first material remains of the earliest humans. They were probably used to manufacture digging sticks and spears that made human existence on the savanna a viable option 2.5 million years ago. From M. Leakey, *Olduvai Gorge,* Vol. 3, Figs. 8 and 9. Cambridge: Cambridge University Press, 1971. Reprinted with the permission of Cambridge University Press.

for survival. Warfare was costly in terms of deaths, injuries, and risks of failure. Alliances were costly in terms of the time and gifts and other investments necessary to ensure that the pledges of help from allies would be honored when needed. It is above all the alliances that concern us, for it is here that emotional bonds become important. The formation of socially definable alliances for survival is a unique characteristic of humans. It is important to realize that such alliances were not based on intellectual, rational thought, but on emotional bonds. As Gregory Bateson has pointed out (see Rappaport 1999:401), reason and rational thought cannot provide a secure or sound basis for social life. By themselves they only serve self-interests; they become pathogenic and destructive of life. Social systems require transcending the rational. Thus, it is doubtful whether we should seek the basis of human evolution in terms of the development of a "rational," intelligent brain. Rather, it was the development of unique emotional characteristics that was critical to human evolution.

In order to be able to call upon far-off acquaintances for help, especially if they are experiencing some stress from food shortages themselves, it is necessary to establish very strong emotional bonds—bonds of friendship, kinship, mutual obligations, and even supernatural bonds. These all seem to have evolved in tandem. In order to maintain these bonds in a strong, responsive state, it is necessary to revalidate them constantly by periodic visits, gifts, and participation in mutual emotionally bonding experiences. Family members or friends who have not been seen for years and only come around when they are in dire need are bitterly resented by most people. Foul-weather friends run the risk of not being recognized by those from whom they ask help. Minimally, they might receive a cold shoulder. Those that stay away generally rue their dire days. This is why emotions become so important for survival and adapting to hostile environments. I suggest that early hunter-gatherers developed a unique repertory of human emotions to create lasting bonds between individuals and groups—emotions that would weather times of stress and need and serve each family by helping it obtain assistance from other allied groups.

Among the most widespread of these bonds were those between parents and children, as well as between children and grandparents or the siblings of parents (see especially Bloch and Sperber 2002). This was the foundation for socially defined kinship and families, which have become universal and unique characteristics of all human societies compared with other animals. Where strong emotional bonds between parents, children, or siblings living in different communities existed, it would have been difficult to refuse help when it was requested. The rudiments of such emotions can be found in other primates like chimpanzees, especially between mothers and their children (Goodall 1971:174–80, 109, 124, 242; Eibl-Eibesfeldt 1989:169). Some chimpanzees maintain close affective relationships with their mothers far into their adult lives. However, early hunter-gatherers strengthened and elaborated these emotions to the point that they became effective aspects of social technology (the use of social relationships to secure food or other resources). Bonds between male and female partners and long-term relationships would also have been adaptive in maintaining strong emotional bonds between *both* parents and their children. Close emotional ties between parents were undoubtedly strengthened by adaptive physical changes such as the loss of estrus (the swelling and reddening around the female genitals that occurs in other primates at the time of ovulation) and the development of secondary sexual characteristics such as female breasts and male beards, making sexual bonding a stronger and more regular feature of family life rather than a once-a-month affair at the time of estrus (Lovejoy 1981; Strassman 1981; Symons 1979; Turke 1984, 1988).

Thus, while rudimentary emotional ties to parents undoubtedly existed among protohumans, it was the harsh savanna conditions and natural selection that transformed those incipient emotions into the strong kinship bonds that most people instinctively feel toward their immediate family and others that are closely related. People with these emotional tendencies would have had a better chance of finding safe havens in times of distress than people who did not have such emotional bonds. People with stable families and strong emotional ties to immediate family members living in other areas would be more likely to survive times of stress and thus would have passed on to their children genes favoring strong emotional bonds based on family interactions. Those without such strong ties would be more likely to perish when droughts or disasters struck. Natural selection under these harsh conditions could mold the human emotional psyche into a distinctive constellation unique in the animal world and set the stage for socially defined kinship systems to emerge among human populations.

What if one's children also lived in heavily stricken areas, or what if one's parents had died and there were no children old enough to marry into bands in other territories? Other means of emotionally bonding people together would have also been useful, if not essential. It has been suggested that laughter evolved as a universal way to form mutual bonds and alliances (Small 2000). Some techniques were culture specific. Thus, the Bushmen of South Africa developed *hxaro,* a special gift-giving relationship. They also had special relationships between people with the same name. The Cree of Canada developed strong mutual bonds via hunting-partner relationships. Of most interest for the theme of this book is the fact that virtually all hunter-gatherers have strong ritual relationships. I have argued previously (Hayden 1987) that it is precisely the earthshaking emotional experiences created in ecstatic religious rituals that were adaptive in this respect for early hunter-gatherers. Rappaport (1999:3, 48) has also noted that emotions are the source of ritual and that religion stems from ritual. Thus, it is to emotions that we must turn to understand religion.

There are few circumstances that can shake commitments made when one enters into ecstatic states and when one experiences the strong emotions that arise from connections with forces that seem to be beyond the self and beyond this world. These forces are even stronger than ties to parents or brothers and sisters, as families of people who have been "converted" by various contemporary cults have found out to their dismay. Religious forces are much stronger than the massed might of totalitarian regimes bent on the destruction of religion, as has been demonstrated in a number of communist countries over the last century. Religious forces and experiences can be far stronger than logic, reason, or science. When dealing with ecstatic religious states, and even the milder forms of religious experience, we are dealing with powerful emotions that commit people to ideals that no earthly external conditions appear capable of altering. Winkelman (1992:120) cites research showing that brain opioids such as those released in ecstatic states promote social bonding. Unbreakable social bonds are precisely the kinds of emotional bonds that early hunter-gatherers required in order to establish alliances between groups that would help them survive periodic disasters. And, in fact, rituals among groups like the Australian Aborigines always involved participants from more than one group. Given the sparse population densities of most hunter-gatherers, with only a handful of people in every 100 square kilometers, an alliance between even a few bands would represent territories of many thousands of square kilometres and many different types of environments or microenvironments.

PEOPLE THAT PRAY TOGETHER, STAY TOGETHER

This bonding is, in essence, what I suggest the original function of religion was among hunter-gatherers. Like kinship emotions, religious emotions created bonds and moral imperatives of cooperation, mutual help, and sharing between bands that would not be broken no matter how dire the circumstances. Groups that had the potential for such religious emotions and used them by holding rituals in which participants entered into ecstatic states, communicating with common deities or totemic ancestors, would be more likely to survive because of mutual help in times of need. Groups that did not follow such sacred imperatives might be found after severe crises as dessicated corpses in the sands—reviled by survivors as object lessons of what happens to those who do not follow the ways of the gods or ancestors. In this way, natural selection could have progressively strengthened and intensified the human penchant for religious experiences and the ability to enter into ecstatic or altered euphoric states.

Along these same lines, Polly Wiessner (1998) has suggested that the proclivity for people to accept indoctrination (in religious or other terms) was originally adaptive because it counteracted the natural in-group loyalties of small, closely related family-based groups, thus increasing their chances of survival. By "indoctrination" Wiessner means the ability of some people to make others accept beliefs, values, or concepts and adopt them as their own above their short-term self-interests. Observations of the use of ritual alliances for the purpose of gaining access to food in times of need come from Australia (Yengoyan 1976; Strehlow 1965), the American Southwest (Ford 1977), the Bushmen of South Africa (Wiessner 1977, 1981, 1982, 1986) and hunter-gatherers in general (Harris 1971:296–302). Rappaport (1971; 1999:322–23) has also argued that sanctification of some values is necessary for acceptance of critical social values.

Using religious ecstatic states in severe environments in order to sanctify imperatives of helping spiritually related people probably comes as close as possible to achieving the unquestioning acceptance of cultural values as can be achieved—the cognitivist's ideal. However, even in this case, only a portion of the population must have entered into ecstatic states (depending on the severity of conditions) and only a portion of the people probably even fully accepted these belief systems. Some variability in the indoctrinability of people would have been essential to maintain the potential for future change. Even in families, not all members always help parents or siblings in need. However, under rough conditions, no matter what one's personal beliefs or convictions, social pressures from family members or others probably provided enough pressure to ensure widespread conformity in people's behavior as long as periodic harsh conditions reinforced the adaptiveness of the family and ritual ecstatic bonding complex.

There is undoubtedly a rudimentary neurological basis for experiencing ecstatic states in many mammals. This seems to consist of the tendency to enter altered states under conditions of starvation, stress, and intoxication. Such states may be adaptive during periods of starvation because they reduce unnecessary motor activity and concentrate all the body's energy reserves in the internal organs and the brain, placing most bodily and mental functions in a state of suspended activity that can be reversed if conditions improve, thus prolonging an individual's ability to live. The release of neurochemicals associated with ecstatic states under stress conditions may have also helped animals ignore pain and fatigue in critical struggles for survival (Prince 1982:413). I argue that it is no coincidence that the techniques most widely used for inducing altered and ecstatic states of consciousness in humans generally feature extremes of stress, including induced starvation, thirst, physical exhaustion, sleep deprivation, shock, and others (discussed in the next chapter). These stress conditions are the doorways to the deepest religious experiences. They may also explain why there is a close relationship between people under the most stress (such as the poor) and high frequencies of supernatural experiences, ecstatic religious movements, and sorcery accusations (Lewis 1989).

As we shall see, drugs have also been used to gain access to religious experiences and open up doors to other realities. The effect of drugs is not specific to human beings either. Many other animals have dreams or hallucinatory experiences, are susceptible to altered states resembling hypnosis, seek out intoxicating altered states, and exhibit signs of consciousness or even intuitive knowledge of conditions not immediately apparent (Capitanio 1986; Rosenblum and Paully 1984; Serban and Kling 1976; Siegel and Jarvik 1975; Rodriguez and Wrangham 1993; Parker, Mitchell, and Boccia 1994; Oubré 1997:152, 155; Bardens 1987). Thus, in developing the unique ritual and religious complexes to which humans are so attached, there was certainly a substantial preexisting genetic foundation with which Mother Nature could work.

Rhythm and Dance Enhance Rituals

Why are music and dance among the most valued experiences of people in virtually all cultures, from the nasal droning ritual chants of Australian Aborigines, to the sacred beat of North American Indian drums, to the complex polyrhythms that infuse all aspects of traditional African life? Singing and rhythmic beats are integral parts of the great feasts in New Guinea, Australia, and Africa. In today's Industrial cultures, concerts have been among the largest gatherings ever organized and many billions of dollars are spent every year for these seemingly nonproductive activities. Why are they so alluring and entertaining? Why do they captivate and enthrall so many people?

If we look at some of the other basic emotional responses that distinguish humans from other animals, we find a number of faculties that are both innate and closely associated with traditional religions. These uniquely human emotions include bonding or closeness stemming from the giving or receiving of gifts or the sharing of food (Eibl-Eibesfeldt 1989:340–58; this is also present in rudimentary forms among many primates); emotional responses to rhythms and songs; responses to costumes, masks, body painting, and drama; entering into altered states through dancing; laughter; and establishing close emotional ties through the sharing of feelings, events, and ideas via sophisticated communication (i.e., language). To the extent that all of these aspects made ritual a more effective way to bind individuals together emotionally, they would have *all* been adaptive and thus positively selected for through natural selection. For instance, Roy Rappaport (1999:222, 228) has emphasized the numinous bonding effects that group rhythms and dancing has on participants as the result of involving their entire bodies and psyches in a unified group movement, creating a unified body of people. The dances and rhythms induce altered states, are pleasurable, and require self-surrender to the group. They meld everyone together. This enjoyable feeling of being part of the larger whole, or transcendence of the self, may well be the main reason why so many people today participate in a wide range of group activities from sports to concerts to volunteer work.

Language is another unique human characteristic. People seem innately predisposed to communicate and structure their communication in certain basic ways (Chomsky 1972, 1986). There have been many suggestions as to why language became so adaptive for our early ancestors, often centering on the usefulness of communication for hunting or as a by-product of other factors such as larger brains, problem-solving needs, or tool making (Calvin and Bickerton 2000; Diamond 1959:262). However, it is also useful to look at language from the perspective of fostering survival alliances between groups. Rather than facilitating hunting, I would suggest that language became the universal social glue that enhanced the effectiveness of all the other social technology strategies: kinship, ritual, gift giving, visiting, and food sharing. Above all, these are the behaviors that make humans truly distinct from other animals. Communication and sociability are critical elements in expressing and conveying emotions and in creating social bonds. Most hunter-gatherers that I am familiar with spend far more of their time socializing and talking than they do hunting or gathering. Getting food usually only takes two to five hours a day (Hayden 1981), whereas talking and laughing occurs all day long in the Aboriginal camps of Australia where I stayed.

Perhaps human rationality and intelligence are only epiphenomena that facilitate the *elaboration* of social ties, technology, and culture. In fact, the size of the neocortex in primates appears to be largely determined by the group sizes that characterize individual species, that is, by the amount of social activity occurring in groups (Dunbar 1992). Far more important than intelligence for understanding our large brains, I would argue, are the emotions that drive human behavior in distinctive ways and structure human interactions. It is the innate response to music and rhythm and ecstatic experiences as well as our sophisticated sociability that make us different from the rest of the animal world in behavioral terms. This is a major part of our ancestral biological heritage. These emotions define what it means to be human and constitute the most important experiences that we can have. These are the experiences that humans should revel in rather than try to exorcize from our bodies and minds. To repudiate our distinctive emotional heritage is akin to cutting off the distinctive features of our hands and feet. It is basically the emotional human heritage that accounts for the massive amounts of money spent on concerts, plays, gifts, churches, dances, and films the world over. These are the modern expressions of our universal emotional foundations established hundreds of thousands or millions of years ago. The foundations are still there although they may have acquired new facades.

SCIENCE EXPLORES THE MIND

Over the last few decades, remarkable progress has been made in exploring some of the physical foundations of our minds and emotions. It is worth mentioning three of these advances that are relevant to the present discussion: differences between the right and left hemispheres of the brain, the triune structure of the brain, and the entoptic structuring within the brain.

MUSIC IS IN THE HEMISPHERES

Some of the latest research (Gazzaniga 1998) has confirmed that the right and left hemispheres of the brain each tend to specialize in different types of thinking and motor activities (Fig. 2.7). The right side of the brain specializes in creative aspects of life, including visual and spatial perceptions, dancing, music, imagination, poetry, holistic or synthetic views, and perhaps magical impressions. The left side of the brain specializes in the analytical and intellectual activities, such as mathematics, language abilities, bookkeeping, figuring out how things work and why, schoolwork, report writing, and military planning. It would be interesting to determine whether the tendency for humans to be right-handed emerged with this hemispheric differentiation, since the right hand is usually the one associated with the left brain, that is, with the hemisphere that would be best for taking care of technological tasks and writing. There is some evidence to show that early hominids developed much more pronounced hemispheric asymmetries than are found in other primates (Bradshaw and Rogers 1993:223) and that early hominids were, in fact, right handed, while other primates display little if any handedness (Falk 1980; Toth 1985).

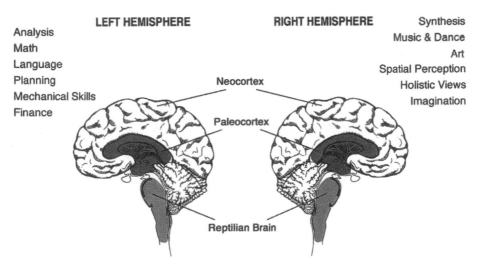

Fig. 2.7. The human brain underwent significant evolutionary changes during human evolution. These included a dramatic expansion of the neocortex and the penchant for each hemisphere of the neocortex to specialize in different types of mental processes (analytical ones on the left, and synthetic-artistic ones on the right). The brain also exhibits an underlying "triune" structure featuring a reptilian part of the brain for basic metabolism, a paleocortex (old mammalian) part of the brain governing basic instincts and emotions, and a neocortex (new mammalian) part of the brain dealing with learning and higher synthetic abilities. Drafted by Greg Holoboff and B. Hayden.

Fig. 2.8. Masks are commonly used in traditional religions. They help transform individual states of consciousness, and, like many ritual devices, may facilitate the integration of mental activity in different parts of the brain. Photos by Greg Holoboff and Greg Ehlers.

The Triune Brain

There is another fundamental division within the brain that parallels major evolutionary developments. In this division, according to Paul MacLean (1973) and Carl Aurell (1989, 1994), there are three major components (Fig. 2.7): *the reptilian brain* (the upper brain stem and midbrain), *the old mammalian brain* (the limbic system or paleocortex), and *the new mammalian brain* (the neocortex). The reptilian brain evolved during the age of dinosaurs. It controls very archaic bodily functions such as metabolism, digestion, respiration, and basic motor reactions but also releases neurochemicals involved in the production of altered states of consciousness (Oubré 1997:133–34; Winkelman 2000). The old mammalian brain was added onto the reptilian brain when mammals began to emerge around 100 million years ago. This part of the brain plays an important role in many of the emotions and drives that govern animal (and our) behavior. Such emotions involve hormonal regulation of fear, joy, self-defense, sex, eating, searching, play, drinking, terror, fighting, sadness, empathy, love, and foreboding.

The neocortex, or new mammal brain, is an additional layer of the brain with many wrinkles and fissures on its surface (what we usually see in movies or pictures of human brains). This part of the brain became greatly elaborated during primate evolution, although more rudimentary forms exist in other mammals. It is responsible for the analytical and creative thinking of the hemispheres mentioned above. The neocortex is probably also responsible for making sure that some of the more primitive emotions do not get out of hand in social contexts, as suggested by Webber, Stephens, and Laughlin (1983). Archaic reptilian and mammalian emotions are still powerful forces, and they can easily become socially disruptive or destructive. Although under special conditions there is considerable flexibility between these three sections of the human brain in terms of their specific functions, under normal conditions there are strong tendencies for the brain to function as a set of separate subsystems similar to those described. Exactly where the neural centers for distinctive human emotions of kinship, rhythm, dance, and ritual might be located is less clear, but the old mammalian brain (limbic system) or the right neocortex would certainly be logical places to explore.

In an innovative article, Webber, Stephens, and Laughlin (1983) suggested that one cause of some mental disorders like obsessive-compulsive neuroses was an excessive domination of the logic-oriented neocortex over the older emotional parts of the brain so that the older parts could not function properly. These researchers proposed that entering into ecstatic states, specifically through the wearing of masks (Figs. 1.6, 2.8), was an important means of temporarily releasing the stranglehold of the neocortex over the older brain and letting the older brain act out emotions and other behaviors that would have otherwise been blocked, thus restoring a healthy balance and functioning to the brain. Oubré (1997:10) notes that the subjective experience of enlightenment is associated with electrical storms in the temporal lobes and the limbic (old mammalian) parts of the brain, which seems to provide some support for the ideas of Webber, Stephens, and Laughlin (see also Winkelman 1986; 1990:321; 2000:128, 131–45, 167–68, 196). Their arguments could clearly be extended to other forms of ecstatic experiences, especially possession dances and rituals of renewal. It seems possible that other creative behaviors, such as playing music, painting, acting, performing magic, and even dreaming, could also serve the same functions. In fact, it is worth suggesting that the essence of creativity may lie in holding the neocortex at bay just long enough to let the emotions of the older brain express themselves but not to the extent that they become destructive or chaotic. This scenario seems to me to be the most plausible of the explanations of ritual and religion as "by-products" of brain evolution, whereas the evolutionary reason for the development of the neocortex in this specific configuration may have been to create or consolidate social bonding through intense, nonnormal emotional states.

ENTOPTICS

At a much more specific level, there are visual patterns that the neural structure of our brain throws up into our fields of vision when we have gone for too long without any visual stimulation, especially under conditions of stress. These are points of light, or squiggly lines, or even more complex shapes that can combine with realistic images under the right conditions. These phenomena are called "entoptic" images and are generally considered to result from the "hard-wired" structure of our brains. They will play an important role in understanding the cave art discussed in Chapters 4 and 5 (also see "Entoptics: The Brain Creates Its Own Images" in Chap. 5).

ARCHETYPES

While the concepts discussed thus far are relatively grounded in ecological theory and brain physiology, there are other concepts that are more debatably linked to the physical foundations of our psyches. These include notions of archetypes (pronounced *ar'-ke-types*). Carl Jung (1969a; see also Boff 1987:222–41), the noted Swiss colleague of Sigmund Freud, argued that certain images kept recurring with constant emotional associations among his patients. He viewed these as symbolic complexes that were innate in the minds of many if not all peoples, or at least among certain populations. He referred to these archetypes as forming the "collective unconscious" of humanity— a fundamental structure of symbols and meanings produced over millions of years of evolution. Most of the symbols are of very basic images (Fig. 2.9), such as water, fire, serpents, lovers, masculinity, femininity, father-figures, mother-figures, wise elderly people, heroes, journeys, antlers or horns, soul flight, world centers (axis mundi), portals

Fig. 2.9. Archetypes are symbols that seem to have natural significance and often emerge in many different cultures independently. One example is the symbolism of power, virility, strength, vitality, and supernatural embodiment associated with antlered or horned men such as this example from Mongolia. Other well-known examples come from many Indian groups in the United States and from Celtic Europe. See also Figs. 3.3 and 5.12. From J. Halifax, *Shaman: The Wounded Healer,* pp. 82–83. London: Thames & Hudson, 1982. Originally from An Imperial Progress through Central Asia by Tsar Nicholas II.

or doorways, dark forests, the color red, the moon, the sky, the sun, drums, or circles. Some authors argue that several of these images have universal or near-universal symbolic or emotional values, especially water, earth, the sky, the hearth, and world centers (Eliade 1959). Other scholars argue that there are innate reactions to such phenomena as deep drum sounds or specific drumming rhythms (Tuzin 1984; Needham 1967; Neher 1962; Jilek 1982:25ff.; Boyer 2001). Pascal Boyer argues that, confronted with a potentially infinite variety of symbolic representations, the neurological characteristics of the human mind consistently focus on a fairly narrow set of attributes to represent the supernatural. In particular, spirits and gods almost universally defy natural and social laws in their appearance, powers, and behavior. He maintains that this is to create strong, unforgettable impressions on our minds. Similarly, he suggests that the early adaptive importance of recognizing potential social relationships has resulted in the tendency to look for human or social characteristics in natural and supernatural environments—generally referred to as "anthropomorphism." Hence, the human aspects often attributed to supernatural beings and our fascination with natural objects that resemble faces (such as the "face" visible on the Martian landscape from satellites) appear to result from human tendencies that began and were positively reinforced at least three million years ago (see Fig. 4.6). Some archaeologists have also argued that humans are innately attracted to, and impressed by, objects that sparkle, shine, or transmit light (Taçon 1991; Clark 1986:5–6; Hamel 1983). These types of items often occur among ritual paraphernalia or costumes of people in the most diverse locations of the globe. Objects that sparkle or shine usually have understandable symbolic associations with water, light, or celestial objects.

Even among other primates some images carry innate emotional reactions such as the panic attacks produced by displaying images of snakes, death masks (a lifelike mask of a person's or animal's face with the eyes closed and a comatose expression) or fantasy masks (Kohler 1927:322; Masataka 1993)—perhaps an incipient basis for the emotional effect some people experience in putting masks on or painting their faces or bodies. The extent to which these or other symbols are innate in the human mind, or natural reactions to aspects of our environment, is still largely open to debate. Nevertheless, some symbols such as horns or antlers are so widespread among the cultures of the world that I will sometimes refer to them as archetypes, irrespective of whether their ubiquity is due to the spread of a popular idea that easily impresses people, or to more fundamental symbolic associations in their psyches.

ASKING ULTIMATE QUESTIONS

We can describe many of the developments that have led to the human brain and to our distinctive religious experiences. However, description does not adequately deal with the ultimate question that interests most people. Namely, is there anything real behind religious beliefs and experiences or is it all smoke and mirrors—only a sanctification of a society, as Durkheim or Rappaport would have it, or an opiate for the masses, as Karl Marx put it? Does the supernatural really exist, and if it does, what is it like? Is there any existence after death?

In the entire realm of human inquiry, these are the most difficult questions to answer. There are many extreme positions, and I am no Solomon. What I think can be said, however, is that *if* there is another dimension of a spiritual nature, it is most likely that we can make contact with it at the moment of death. At that moment, any consciousness we have that is capable of perceiving other dimensions is leaving the physical body and the physical world behind and is focused on other possible realms and states of being. If we have the ability to apprehend or enter other dimensions of reality, death should open those doors for us. Therefore, near-death experiences provide one of the few lanterns that might guide us through the thick fog that surrounds such questions. Lee Bailey and Jenny Yates (1996) set out the most comprehensive overview of this topic. Because inducing ecstatic experiences often involves states that potentially lead up to death (such as starvation, dehydration, physical exhaustion, and extreme pain), they may also be similar to near-death experiences in providing some insight into other dimensions. However, it is clear that the specific content of ecstatic experiences can easily be colored by cultural and personal values, so that if any useful information is to be obtained from ecstatic experiences, it must be on the most general level, similar to the seeing of white light and the feelings of blissful greetings reported by patients experiencing near-death events. Specific content such as the appearance of one's ancestors or visions of saints should never be taken as proof of their real spiritual existence. This will be discussed more fully in the last chapter.

It also seems clear that the interaction between any other dimension that might exist and the world that we know on a daily basis is rare, unpredictable, and almost random. However, when such events occur (often only once or twice in a lifetime), the outcomes are so remarkable that they seem to defy any kind of scientifically established causality. Hard-core scientists scoff at paranormal claims because the events can be imitated by trickery or fabrication, or because they do not stand up to statistical testing. But a random selection of even a few people from any community is almost certain to come up with some surprising personal anecdotes of events that defy rational explanation and seem to defy all the laws of probability. Carl Jung (1969b) called such events "expressions of 'synchronicity'"—the unlikely coincidence of events that seems to be governed by symbolical or personal connections, sometimes centering on apparently trivial or otherwise meaningless details, such as the repeated encounter of a specific number like "1812" many times in a day.

Over the years, I have discussed these issues with students in my classes, and I have al-

Accounts of Synchronistic Experiences

Waking up in the middle of the night from a nightmare in which I saw our house engulfed in flame and my Dad's friend Marvin and his daughter Trena in the flames. The next morning, we (my family) got a phone call that the two had passed away the night before in a fire in their garage. Trena was asleep in his office and when the fire broke out he went to save his daughter, and the two died of smoke inhalation in the process.—T.M.

I had a dream once of a friend who was living in Costa Rica. I dreamt that he had come home and that he and I were able to hang out again. The day of the dream, I went out and ran into him near a friend's skateboard store; he had come back without notice (for a personal reason) and was trying to find my new phone number from the owners of the skateboard shop.—J.S.

The most intriguing synchronistic event that I have ever experienced revolved around three windows located in the lower wall of a huge building that was a long-term care facility. I used to observe these windows from a distance of about one block from the transit buses that I rode each morning on my way to lectures at the University of Calgary. There was nothing spectacular about the windows, no unique framing, no delicate lace curtains, no special lighting, just square black holes in a tan brick wall. For some reason I always positioned myself on the bus so that I could observe those three windows as I rode past. At the same time, I was never motivated enough to investigate the building or check out what was behind those three windows. I rode the bus on that same route for two years, always observing those windows. Then I moved to another part of Calgary and forgot all about them.

Some four years later, having finished both my first university degree and my international chef's curriculum requirements, I returned to Calgary from a sojourn of traveling, broke as usual. Desperate for a job, and planning to return to university, I noticed an ad for a permanent part-time cook at an institution named the Bethany Care Centre. The address of the institution was actually on another street that the building faced onto, it consisting of seven floors (with two full kitchens) as it did. I was very surprised when I realized it was the same building that held the mystery of the three windows. I was even more surprised to discover that the kitchen I would be working in was the room behind those three windows.

I worked at the Bethany for almost four years on a part-time basis while pursuing a degree in forest ecology. Most of that time was spent in the kitchen with the mysterious three windows. There was a very beautiful shy girl who always worked there. She had a degree in economics and was working on a second degree in nursing. Toward the end of my tenure at Bethany, just before I started working for the Alberta Forest Service, that shy girl and I went out four times in one month and then went out and got married.

Today, some twenty-one years later, we live in Hope, B.C., and have four happy yappy healthy children.—T.V.

When I was twelve years old, my father died on March 27th. On that day, and for several days after, I spent a lot of time in my backyard (my dad's favorite place). I noticed with curiosity that on those days, whenever I went outside there were two mallard ducks swimming around our pool. This was odd, because although we often saw ducks in the air, and occasionally on the lawn, they had previously avoided the pool (I thought due to the chlorine). I was pleased to see them on those days and found my gaze following them for hours. The funeral came and went and so did the ducks. Nothing too odd, until the following year. We lived in another house, in another part of the city. On March 27th I walked outside to see two mallard ducks swimming around my pool. I was pleased to see them, and remembered the last time I had seen a couple of mallards (both male) was one year prior. Again, not too odd.

The following year, my uncle on my father's side died on March 25th. We went to Quebec for the funeral to be held on the 28th. We stayed in a small hotel/motel which had a pool which was partially drained and badly in need of cleaning. In what was becoming clockwork, on March 27th, on our way to the car, we noticed two mallards swimming in the shallow, dirty water. Now this was becoming quite odd, as it was the third year in a row and mallards in March in Ontario and Quebec are uncommon.

Year 4, I was living on my own in a small apartment in a concrete jungle of a neighborhood. On this year I had awoken unaware of the date. However, when I walked outside to see two male mallards sitting on my small front lawn by the sidewalk, I was dumbfounded: March 27th. When water was involved it was almost understandable, but this was getting rather bizarre.

Year 5, yet another part of the city, downtown Toronto, March 27th, two mallard ducks in a concrete water fountain.

Year 6, on March 27th, in yet another location, two mallards sitting on the picnic table in my backyard, extraordinarily brave in view of my stalking cat less than two meters away.

Year 7, my first year in Vancouver, at my sister's house off Commercial Drive. March 27th and two male mallards on her front lawn.

Year 8, March 27th, two male mallards in the outdoor pool of my building. I'll admit I went looking for them—it was too cold to swim.

Year 9, the last year of the ducks, March 27th, and two male mallards in the Vancouver Airport parking lot.—J.P.

ways been surprised by some of the extraordinary accounts that they related. Up to 60 percent of the students in some classes reported having at least one experience of precognition in their lives. I include some of the more interesting ones here as examples that indicate the existence of synchronicity or precognition or other kinds of phenomena not currently explicable by the widely accepted models of science.

Similar events have been described by trustworthy scholars (Mishlove 1975:176) and in historical biographical accounts of natives such as Black Elk, who tells how one of his premonitions saved his entire band from being killed (Neihardt 1961:147–49). But he also tells of visions that never came to pass. It seems that even for the most psychically gifted people it is often difficult to tell when one is in touch with a real supernatural insight versus a delusion. In addition to self-deception, there is a substantial history of outright charlatanism when dealing with the supernatural. Yet, even taking into account the fraudulent cases, notable scholars such as the psychologist William James (1961) have investigated these phenomena and gone "on record for the presence, in the midst of all the humbug, *of really supernormal knowledge.*" Moreover, police sometimes use information from psychics with remarkable success in finding bodies or solving crimes, as was the case with Mindy Tran in Kelowna, British Columbia (Fitzgerald 1999).

Scientists have attempted to determine whether such faculties really exist in people and what the magnitude of such effects might be. Because of the sporadic and unpredictable nature of these kinds of events, these researchers have generally adopted a statistical approach in investigating what they refer to as "psi" phenomena (parapsychological psychic events or powers). They conduct hundreds or thousands of experiments involving the prediction of random number sequences, telepathic communication of cards or symbols, remote viewing, and similar information. In the most comprehensive overview of all the experiments conducted in the past half century in this field, Jessica Utts (1995) concluded that even the most rigorously controlled scientific tests displayed results that were significantly beyond what one would expect from chance alone, although sometimes the effects were small. These tests included a remarkable series commissioned by the United States Central Intelligence Agency and carried out by the Stanford Research Institute and Science Applications International Corporation.

These statistical tests, like Black Elk's anecdotal accounts, seem to indicate that whatever effects may be present, they sometimes are dramatically accurate but are also often inaccurate. As yet, no one has been able to develop a technique to distinguish accurate from inaccurate psi impressions. As the physicist Sir Arthur Eddington (in Wilber 1984:206) phrased it, we need to create criteria for distinguishing mystic illusion from mystic reality. That is a daunting task.

To me, these accounts seem to indicate that there is another dimension of some sort, but it is difficult to determine its exact nature. There is no lack of conflicting claims as to what it is like from the many religions of the world as well as from mystics and new age practitioners. However, they are not the only ones to take such questions seriously. There has always been a minor contingent of scientists (including many of the most brilliant ones) who have argued that the physical laws are not enough to explain the patterning and evolution that occurs in the universe. For religious fundamentalists such features are proof that god exists. Scientists with broader views of the universe have argued for the existence of special forces in the universe. Biologists used to refer to this as the "vital force" in evolution ("vitalism") as opposed to purely reductionist views (Williams 1997). More modern versions refer to such a force as "anticipation" (Burgers 1975; Davies 1980) or "self-organization" (Waldrop 1992; Bak 1996; Bak and Chen 1991), meaning that there are certain patterns that almost seem to preexist and slightly favor certain mutations, organizations, or kinds of events. Chaos theory also emphasizes the fact that patterned structures appear to be inherent in many situations that initially appear to be nothing but random chaos (Waldrop 1992). As Ken Wilber (1996:26) puts it: "Something other than chance is pushing the universe." Some physicists note that extreme reductionist approaches may describe basic particles, but they poorly account for complex structures, just as descriptions of words, grammar, and letter combinations can never convey the messages of Shakespearian plays, much less their distinctiveness or brilliance (Mermin 1990).

In physics, many leading scientists have held almost mystical views about reality, the universe, and our ability to understand what it really is. I especially recommend the selections in Ken Wilber's *Quantum Questions.* Among these are writings from notable physicists such as Werner Heisenberg, Louis de Broglie, and Erwin Schroedinger (founders of quantum mechanics), Sir James Jeans and Sir Arthur Eddington (prominent theoretical physicists and astronomers). These physicists argue that although the physical world exists, it is not the essence of reality, only one possible state. Reality is spiritual; science probes reality through a veil of symbols (e.g., mathematical equations), but direct experience of our conscious minds can lift the veil in places and reveal the real spiritual nature of things. Physical objects are illusions.

For these leading physicists, scientific and mystic appreciation of our world are on an equal level of direct experience, and both approaches have concluded that strict causality does not exist. The supernatural is outside space-time dimensions but can be experienced like other physical senses rooted in space-time reality. Beauty and harmony are real factors affecting the structure of the universe, just as time is directional. The mind and consciousness play key roles in our universe.

Lest we become complacent in our four-dimensional perspective of reality, many physicists are convinced that our universe is really structured by many more dimensions—as many as 13–18 with our familiar perceptible universe "confined to a three-dimensional 'membrane' that lies within a higher dimensional realm" (Arkani-Hamed, Dimopoulos, and Dvali 2000; see also Freedman and van Nieuwenhuizen 1985). Quantum mechanics in particular has produced visions of the universe that seem to defy reality as we know it and imply instantaneous transmission of information (Watson 1997). Some versions of quantum mechanics, such as that proposed by John Wheeler, even propose that the state of the universe depends on humans and the questions they ask about it (Barrow and Tipler 1986; Horgan 1992).

One of the themes of several sciences is the unacknowledged role that information must play in the structure of the universe—a theory perhaps compatible with Jung's concept of synchronicity. This has perhaps been articulated best by Ed Fratkin, a millionaire maverick physicist who became a full professor at the Massachusetts Institute of Technology at the age of 34. According to him, information is as important to the structure of the universe as matter and energy (Wright 1988). This is a view probably shared by Sir James Jeans (in Wilber 1984), who argued that the universe was pure thought at both of its extreme size ranges: the subatomic level and macrocosmic level of creation. Anthropologists, too, like Roy Rappaport (1999:109–17), have argued that information is the third underlying component of the universe (together with matter and energy). However, the way in which information functions in the universe has been largely unexplored by mainstream scientists. If it, in fact, does largely operate in a different dimension, it might well account for many of the "supernatural" events that constitute the most common types of synchronistic anecdotes, such as knowing who is calling on the phone before you pick up the receiver (without the benefit of call display!).

What Religion Is

Like culture, there are dozens and perhaps hundreds of different definitions of religion depending upon one's theoretical orientation and the specific problems that one is trying to address. Arguments have flared about the distinctions between religion and magic, myths and rituals, and other related concepts. I do not propose to enter into this fray. Few of the distinctions that anthropologists argue about, such as the distinctions between religion and magic, have any relevance for archaeological inquiries. For convenience, I provide a glossary of terms with my preferred definitions at the end of this book. There are many other books that offer alternatives and discuss these issues in considerable depth. For my purpose as an archaeologist, I am relatively comfortable with Clifford Geertz's (1975:9) definition: *"A religion is a system of symbols which acts to establish powerful, pervasive, and long-lasting moods and motivations in men by formulating conceptions of a general order of existence and clothing these conceptions with such an aura of factuality that the moods and motivations seem uniquely realistic."*

Probably one of the most powerful, widespread, and ancient expressions of religion in these terms is shamanism. And it is to shamanism that we turn in the next chapter.

Summary

One of the major challenges to cultural ecology is to explain how and why religious behaviors became universal aspects of humanity. The fact that religious behavior involves great amounts of time and effort indicates that it should have had some important adaptive role that helped early humans survive. Physical anthropologists usually focus on skeletal changes, intellectual changes, and technological changes that helped people survive drastic climatic deteriorations in Africa millions of years ago. Ritual behavior and other unique human emotions are generally overlooked. Yet these features can be viewed as important means for creating and maintaining strong emotional bonds between people in alliances that constituted mutual help relationships between distant bands. The ability to use these relationships in order to move to other band territories and be accepted by the resident populations was critical for survival in times of crisis. This is likely the real adaptive value of kinship, language, gift giving, food sharing, and shared ecstatic ritual experiences. All these human characteristics probably evolved together as adaptive ways of dealing with life-threatening crises. The first material indication of these mutual-help alliances may be reflected in the movement of small amounts of stones used as tools over long distances beginning about 50,000 years ago (Mcbrearty and Brooks 2000:513–16); however, such alliances do not necessarily have to leave physical traces, and they would have been so adaptive that they may well have existed much further in the past. Additional unique human emotional features such as innate responses to drumming, music, dance, and drama undoubtedly enhanced the effectiveness of rituals in creating strong emotional bonds; and it is no coincidence that traditional rituals generally feature all of these other "arts." These arts, and especially ecstatic experiences, are the essence of our human heritage. To be truly human means to experience that heritage, to sing and dance and experience ecstasy—as James Campbell put it, to "follow one's bliss." This was the essence of religion for our ancestors, and it constitutes quite a different perspective from the book religions of today.

The physical and emotional changes that took place during human evolution were also accompanied by some major changes in the structure of the brain, including its division into two hemispheres with different functions and into three separate levels dealing with physical functions, emotional functions, and intellectual functions (the triune brain). Some researchers suggest that people have specific emotional reactions to or symbolic associations with images such as water, fire, or horns. These are called archetypes, but the degree to which they are an innate part of the human psyche remains to be investigated.

Whether the gods or any supernatural dimensions really exist is an open question. However, on the basis of personal experiences, many people are convinced that something odd certainly is part of the universe, whether we choose to call it magic, information, self-organization, the supernatural, or quantum spookiness. There is no lack of anecdotes of strange events that cannot be accounted for in terms of current mainstream science.

CHAPTER 3

Shamanism

An Ancient System

There has probably been more written about shamanism than any other aspect of traditional or prehistoric religions, for both popular and scientific audiences. Numerous authors suggest that shamanism has extremely ancient roots, almost as old as human consciousness, and that it may be one of the oldest types of religions in our history (Halifax 1982:5; Winkelman 1990:319–21; von Gernet 1993:74). Many authors also suggest that shamanism is a cultural ecological "type of religion" specifically adapted to nomadic or hunting-gathering conditions (Hultkrantz 1973; Winkelman 1990; 2000:6, 58). Because the topic is so large, we will pause briefly before plunging into the Paleolithic past in order to develop a clear idea of what shamanism is and isn't, depending on one's definition. Where shamanism fits in the overall picture of prehistoric religion will be dealt with in the following chapters.

WHAT IS SHAMANISM?

There are many differing opinions on just how shamanism should be defined. As a result, there are differing ideas about whether shamanism is a near-universal phenomenon or whether it is only to be found in Central Asia and Siberia, where the term was originally identified and defined (Fig. 3.1). The word "shaman" comes from the Tungus term, *šaman* (pronounced *sha-man* with both of the *a*'s being short as you would pronounce *map*). Campbell (1983:157) notes that shaman may be derived from the word *ša*, "to know." Most writers agree that the essence of shamanism entails going into a trance (although intensities may vary) in order to travel to spirit realms where the shaman generally attempts to perform some useful task such as healing a person by recovering their soul, fighting off destructive spirits, obtaining information about the location of game, or guiding the dead to the land of spirits (Figs. 3.2, 3.3). Hultkrantz (1973:34) probably provides the best discussion and definition of a shaman. His definition is: "a social functionary who, with the help of guardian spirits, attains ecstasy in order to create a rapport with the supernatural world on behalf of his group members."

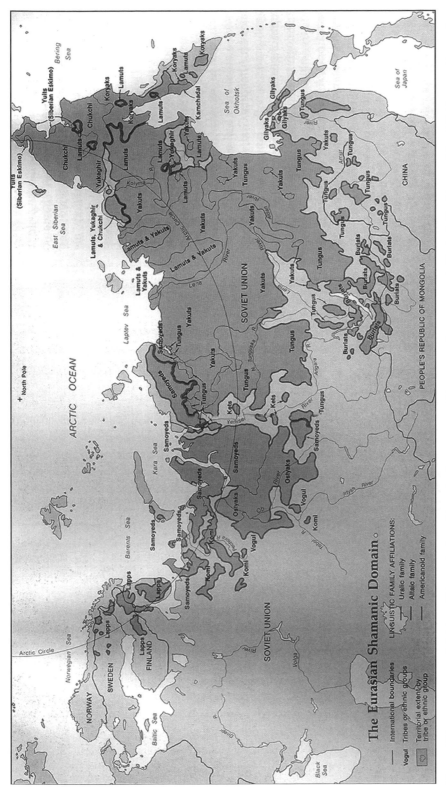

Fig. 3.1. Using a very narrow definition of "shamanism" would restrict the occurrence of shamans to the areas more darkly shaded in this map. Most definitions would extend the distribution of shamanism considerably farther in the Old and New Worlds. Created (after the work of Leo Frobenius) for Joseph Campbell's *Historical Atlas of World Mythology* (New York: Van der Marck Editions, 1983), copyright © Joseph Campbell Foundation (www.jcf.org), used with permission.

Fig. 3.2. This is one of the earliest photographs of a traditional shaman in Mongolia. From a photo by Sakari Pälsi, in the National Museum of Finland, Helsinki.

There are many other common characteristics, but this definition clearly separates the shaman from priests (who rarely if ever go into ecstatic states to help others), mystics (who may go into ecstatic states like shamans but tend to be asocial and do not fulfill roles as healers or helpers), cult leaders, curers, or magicians (who do not go into trances), counsellors, and social workers. Given this basic definition, many scholars agree that shamanism also exists in most of the traditional societies of the Americas, Australia, in Southeast Asia, possibly in pre-Christian Europe, and among hunter-gatherers of Africa (Winkelman 1990).

It is important to realize that shamanism is not a religion per se but rather a religious technique that can be used within many different religious frameworks. Although there are some broad constraints involving trance and the spirit world, there is no set pantheon, no dogma, and no set ritual. Shamans function equally well among hunting and gathering tribes as among agriculturalists, and they continue to exist in many Latin American nation-states, comfortably calling upon saints as allies. Shamanism is a component of religious activity; it does not necessarily constitute the totality of a group's religious beliefs or activities. In addition, the shaman tends to be a specialist to varying degrees. Anyone in a community with the ability to enter into trances, or perhaps even into moderate altered states of consciousness, can be a shaman. Sometimes, as among the Bushmen of South Africa, many people take on this role. More commonly, there are only a few people in a community who are considered especially gifted in being able to enter into trance states and effectively cure others or perform other socially important tasks. Many times, these tasks are outside of the main religious ceremonies of a group. One goes to the shaman when one is sick or in need of help. In contrast, one goes to the owner or spiritual leader of a sacred site (who is not necessarily a shaman) when it is time to perform ceremonies to promote abundance of certain plants or animals. Nevertheless, in small communities such as those of the Arctic, the shaman often does organize social and spiritual events for fun and amusement as well as other ritual purposes.

The Good, the Bad, and the Ugly

The shaman is one of the most intriguing and most complex figures to be found in traditional societies. On the one hand, shamans have been reviled by missionaries, psychologists, doctors, and others as psychopaths or mentally unstable charlatans (see Jilek 1971 for a discussion of this issue). On the other hand, shamans have been eulogized by anthropologists, explorers, and new-age spiritualists as cultural repositories of art, history, medicine, and welfare. What is the truth? As usual, the truth is composed of parts of both of these views. It is true that immediately prior to becoming shamans, many people experience severe stress or illness, either physical or mental. However, if they do not conquer or control these illnesses, those afflicted either die or remain infirm or mentally ill. It is precisely the shaman's ability to overcome and control these severe conditions by entering into an altered state of consciousness that places him or her in a special position.

Once a person has entered into an altered mental state and loses contact with the reality of the everyday world, this experience may facilitate their entrance into similar altered states in later situations (Fig. 3.4). Master-

Fig. 3.3. The Tungus of Siberia were noted for their shamans. The one depicted here in an eighteenth-century woodcut is a Lapp. Note the drum, antlers, and animal feet. From J. Campbell, *Historical Atlas of World Mythology: The Way of the Animal Powers,* Fig. 273. New York: A. van der Marck Editions, 1983. Original Johannes Schefferus, 1674, Lapponia, Frankfurt.

Fig. 3.4. Typically, shamans enter into trance states during their journeys to the spirit worlds. In some cases, such as depicted in this seventeenth-century engraving of a Lappish (Saami) ceremony, the shaman may lose normal consciousness. From J. Campbell, *Historical Atlas of World Mythology: The Way of the Animal Powers,* Fig. 302. New York: A. van der Marck Editions, 1983. Original Johannes Schefferus, 1674, Lapponia, Frankfurt.

ing these altered states also involves methods of reestablishing contact with normal reality. There is generally a range of traditional techniques that other shamans or assistants can use to help a shaman both enter and return from their altered trance states. It is, above all, this control over the ability to enter and return from ecstatic trance states that identifies potential shamans. This is why Eliade (1964:4) and others (Halifax 1979:20) call shamanism a "technique of ecstasy" and the shaman the "technician of ecstasy."

Despite their temporary losses of contact with ordinary reality, which have long been misunderstood as mental illness or instability, many researchers have argued that shamans are among the most intelligent, wise, motivated, artistically gifted, and healthy people in a community (Eliade 1964:30; Elkin 1977:12.13). It is often the shamans who remember and tell (and create) the myths that form the core of cultural mythologies. There are many suggestions that the first images of gods like Odin, Osiris, and Orpheus are based on shamans or supershamans. Often the shamans organize evening social events to communicate with the spirit world, to tell stories or myths, beat drums, sing songs, dance, and perform spectacular feats of magic (Fig. 3.5). The shaman is *supposed* to embody the forces of good for the community and combat evil forces (Eliade 1964:509; Halifax 1979:21). It is the shaman who provides the underlying philosophy of life and explains why someone is sick or the deer have not appeared. Shamans provide answers to many questions about which modern science is silent. According to some scholars (Lommel 1967; Lewis-Williams and Dowson 1989), shamans are the originators of our artistic tradition. As a result of all their roles, shamans have become mystics, artists, entertainers, magicians, scientists, philosophers, psychotherapists, politicians, poets, specialists of the soul, and masters of ceremonies.

However, it is perhaps too easy for us, who are so far removed from traditional life, to overromanticize the shaman. While all of the above is certainly true, it is also true, as Eliade (1964:12) puts it, that "no other religious experience is more subject to distortion and aberration" than ecstasy. If power corrupts, supernatural power can corrupt in spades. This is the essential message of some of the most popular books and movies of the twentieth century. In J. R. R. Tolkien's *The Lord of the Rings,* it is Sauron who has become corrupted by his supernatural power and it is Gandalf who refuses to touch the ring of power because he knows that he, too, would become corrupted. In George Lucas's *Star Wars,* it is Darth Vader who has been corrupted by supernatural power. In traditional societies, shamanic power that could be used to cure could also be used to kill. Typically the shaman's power to kill was supposed to be directed at people outside the community; however, even within communities there must always have been some hesitation in crossing a shaman, for one could never know what a shaman might do when he was alone and out of sight or hearing. As Winkelman (1990:318) notes, all shamans seem to engage in some malevolent magic.

There is no shortage of accounts of benevolent shamans. But there are certainly numerous accounts of shamans who no longer functioned for the good of the community. Joseph Campbell (1983:20, 164–70) relates a number of instances of shamans trying to kill each other with their spiritual powers. He concludes that one of the characteristics of shamans is their involvement in intense and vicious psychic battles; he even goes so far as to label some contemporary shamanism as a devolved form of sadomasochism. If psychic power did not work, many shamans did not hesitate to use physical means.

Fig. 3.5. During shamanic "seances," shamans are reputed to work many supernatural feats such as flying through the air (above) and making drums beat by themselves while the shamans are bound (below). These exploits were graphically portrayed by Rasmussen in his accounts of Eskimo folk tales. From K. Rasmussen, *Across Arctic America.* New York: G. P. Putnam's Sons, 1927.

Campbell tells of one shaman in an Inuit community who had killed eight people, fortified his house against the entire community, and was still feared. Another shaman killed a family of seven so that he could marry their daughter. These may have been extreme incidents but clearly show that shamans were often no saints.

Not all individuals chosen for shamanic roles might be considered ideal caregivers by contemporary standards. Mental instability was also often used as a sign that an individual was suitable for shamanic work, although they might not have been suited for social roles (Eliade 1964:498).

If it could be dangerous to live among shamans, it could be even more dangerous to be a shaman. Not only was it necessary to ward off the real or imagined psychic attacks of other shamans, but when disasters struck, community suspicions invariably turned toward the less popular or more antisocial shamans in the community. William Walker (1998:272) provides a number of accounts of shamans and other ritual leaders who were accused of bringing plagues, droughts, disease, and death to their communities. The community response was generally to kill those thought to have the power and motives for doing evil. When I lived among the Highland Maya of Guatemala, I heard many similar stories of bad shamans who had suddenly disappeared while walking along isolated trails, their remains sometimes found hacked up in the jungles or stuffed down karstic crevices in the limestone mountains. I also recorded a number of stories of mass expulsions of those thought to be working evil against the community. Similar events are described by Condominas (1977:208, 327) for hill tribe communities in Vietnam.

Not all shamans are noted for their joviality, either. In fact, the ones that I have met among the Maya Indians of Guatemala and the Hmong hill tribes of Thailand were all relatively taciturn, a trait also noted by Campbell (1983:170). Those shown in early films or photographs of shamans also seem relatively somber (Fig. 3.2).

The Shamanic Universe Is Sacred

Shamanic ceremonies are long, relatively monotonous events. However, there is a good reason for this, just as there is a good reason for the elaborate costumes and objects that many shamans use in their ceremonies. In order to understand the use of these material items (some of which show up in the archaeological record), we must understand more about the concepts and philosophy of shamanism.

To begin with, the shamanic view of the world and the sacred forces in it is the same as the traditional religious view of the world as described in Chapter 1. Because this view is such a fundamental aspect of shamanism (and so alien to most people's Industrial upbringing), it is worth exploring a bit more at this point.

For the shaman, as for all traditional religious people, there is a vital force that imbues everything in creation. It is this vital force that is responsible for creation, existence, and life. It is the powerhouse of the universe and it permeates people, societies, buildings, plants, rocks, animals, the clouds, the soil—everything. All things partake of some aspect of this spiritual essence and, through it, all things are interconnected. This force is said to be immanent in the world. Life, in particular, is the manifestation of this force. It is this vital force that people refer to when they talk about "the sacred," not the book-religion concept of being pure (free of sin), good (living by a set of commandments or church rules), or holy. In order to understand what the sacred represents for shamans, think of "vital forces." Perhaps "The Force" as portrayed in *Star Wars* is not so far from the traditional view of sacred forces. In fact, Joseph Campbell's research on traditional religion was the major inspiration in developing the concepts and script used in the *Star Wars* film series (Stocker 1997). For traditional religions, *the sacred vital force* is what is most important in the world and what traditional artists try to portray in their art (Fig. 3.6; Rappaport 1999:385). For them, manifestations of sacred forces are the most important reality. The actual physical forms that we see with our eyes are simply illusory shells shielding sacred realities from our eyes—an attitude not too different from that of the leading physicists described in Chapter 2. The essential role of the shaman is to make contact with that force and to affect it in ways that lead to desired outcomes, whether for healing, favorable weather, or seeing the present or future states of the world.

All the world is alive and interconnected by this sacred force. Other things, animals, or plants in the world have their own force that can affect the vital forces in individuals. This, too, is why eating plants or killing animals and eating meat is a sacred activity for traditional religious people. For traditional people, we are what we eat, not only physically but also in terms of vital forces. Life and creation is and probably always will be the great mystery. Traditional views maintain that the vital force is somehow implicated and responsible. In the traditional view, sickness occurs when our personal vital force departs from our body or is lost. It is the shaman's role to attempt to bring that force back and restore it to our bodies. He does this by traveling to the supernatural world and making contact with supernatural forces there, often engaging in battles with the forces of destruction. He uses "medicines" to help cure the sick, but these medicines are not the type that pharmacists sell in bottles. They are certain minerals or plants or other natural objects that have special intensities or other qualities of sacred forces that can help heal the sick or transform normal consciousness. Thus, native medicines and "medicine men" have special meanings. They pertain to supernatural rather than chemical remedies.

Fig. 3.6. Shamanistic art often attempts to portray the inner reality or vital forces of objects. Sometimes this takes the form of showing bones, organs, or muscles within people or animals and is known as the X-ray style of painting. This Australian Aboriginal painting of a kangaroo is one example. Photo by Greg Ehlers.

According to traditional philosophy, it is possible to connect with this vital force and experience it using certain techniques. However, this contact can also occur spontaneously and unexpectedly. It may simply erupt from something in our everyday experiences, whether from a bull, a person, or the sky. Many of the classical Greek and other traditional myths that describe gods as suddenly appearing probably represent just such eruptions or manifestations. It is above all the connection with vital forces—the direct experience of them unimpeded by our physical or rational mind—that gives the ineffable feeling of being alive even if this may sometimes be terrifying. For traditional religious people, and for modern ones, the euphoric feeling that accompanies the best musical or dance experiences provides some inkling of what it means to be connected to the sacred. The same euphoria is typical of almost any creative activity when we feel that we have made a special connection and that some kind of special vital force is flowing through us. To make music or poetry or to dance in this fashion is to transform our inner world. It is intensely blissful and enjoyable. To connect to sacred currents is to feel as though one has melded with eternal forces, as though one can live forever as part of them, whether ancestral beings, musical ecstasy, or artistic revelations. As others have argued (Lommel 1967; Lewis-Williams and Dowson 1988; Rappaport 1999:385), it seems probable that ritual and art do originate from such experiences with traditional sacred forces.

Obviously, just the act of playing music or dancing does not automatically mean that a person will have a euphoric experience connecting them with sacred forces. The mere act of doing something, in any domain, is never enough. Other factors are involved that we will discuss shortly. *Any* act can be performed in either a profane (nonsacred) or a sacred fashion. If it is done in a sacred fashion, the connection is made and the world lights up. We feel euphoric. If it is done in a profane fashion, there is only the taste of staleness in our mouths and the world seems gray. Robert Graves (1948:11–12, citing Housman) argued that the test of "real" (sacred) poetry was whether it sent shivers down a listener's or reader's spine, put goosebumps on their skin, made their hairs stand on end, and constricted their throats. By this, he meant, that real poetry stirred the vital forces within readers. Common, or profane, poetry does not have that ability. The same can be said about "real" versus profane music and dance and drama and art. Consider *Starry Night* by Van Gogh, or the visions of the world by Burchfield (Fig. 3.7), and compare them with almost any of the contemporary schooled paintings of the late nineteenth century.

The "real" is enjoyable, euphoric, invigorating, and ecstatic. By comparison, the rest of our lives are profane, as if we were in a dream, or a fog, or a depressed state. This is why religious people in traditional societies yearn to be in a sacred state all of the time or as much of the time as possible. To be in such a state all of the time would be heaven

Fig. 3.7. Many artists are inspired by the vibrant forces that they feel in the skies, mountains, trees, plants, and animals around them. They attempt to express these realities in their art as can be seen in many paintings by Van Gogh and Charles Burchfield. This is one such painting by Charles Burchfield, titled *Autumnal Fantasy.* From N. Maciejunes and M. Hall, *The Paintings of Charles Burchfield,* Fig. 128. Columbus: Columbus Museum of Art, 1977.

and might well feel like an eternal experience. This is part of what is meant by the "sacred." It is not an easy concept to explain in a book. I therefore urge readers to experiment a bit, summon up a bit of courage, forget feelings of ridiculousness, and follow the suggestions in "Talking with Trees."

Illustration by Bill Edmaler

TALKING WITH TREES

In order to better appreciate the traditional view of the world and the activities of shamans, it is extremely helpful to adopt an experiential approach. This means not just reading about abstract concepts or experiences from the comfort of an armchair or couch or bed, but actually going out and trying to see the world from the traditional perspective. This may seem like a daunting undertaking, but the following experiment is relatively simple, and most people find that it is rewarding or at least helpful. It is absolutely harmless, and it only requires about a half an hour of your time. The goal is to experience a tree as a living entity and, if possible, to establish some communication with the tree. Trees are patient, quiet beings. To hear what they have to say, you also must be patient and quiet. Keep in mind that some remarkable insights have come about from sitting under trees. Newton conceived the theory of gravity while sitting under an apple tree. Buddha experienced nirvana and understood the goal of life while sitting under a banyan tree. So be prepared. Anything could happen!

To begin, you will need some water (and you can add a bit of fertilizer or compost or manure). A blanket or pillow often makes things more comfortable. Next, find a tree that you seem to be attracted to, preferably one where you can be alone and undisturbed by other people, noises, or events. Older trees tend to have more character. Go up to the tree and introduce yourself in your normal conversation voice. Take a few minutes to examine the tree in detail. How old do you think it is? Does it look healthy? Are there any signs of trauma, any scars or large broken branches? What does it smell like? Try standing against the tree for a few minutes. Try lying down on your blanket and looking up at the three dimensional fractal mandala created by the interarching branches for a few minutes. What kinds of feelings do these experiences give you? Tell the tree that you have come to talk with it and that you have brought a small gift. Then pour the water (and/or fertilizer) around the tree and sit on your blanket or find a position that will be comfortable for the next 30 minutes or so. Some people like to light incense when they meditate, but this is a bad idea for this exercise. Trees probably do not like smoke of any kind.

Once you are comfortable, standing or sitting, look again at the tree and relax. When you feel comfortable, close your eyes and relax even further. It is important to relax as much as possible. Make sure that there is no tension in your muscles, especially the muscles around your neck, shoulders, jaw, eyes, ears, and your scalp. When you feel relaxed, bring your attention once again back to the tree. Now, try to see what kinds of impressions occur to you. These impressions may be visual images, they may be emotions that you feel, or they may be thoughts. If any extraneous thoughts occur, bring your focus gently but firmly back to the tree. Any experiences concerning the tree may be very subtle at first, but keep waiting and watching until some impression forms and then try to follow it. Above all, stay relaxed. How do you feel? Happy, sad, serene, anxious, safe, aggressive, tired, energetic? What is your overall impression of the tree and of its feelings, of its concerns and experiences as a living thing? How does it relate to you or to other things in its environment or to the seasons?

After you have explored your own feelings and impressions as fully as you can, thank the tree and gradually become aware of the noises that are in the surroundings. Gradually bring your mind back to an awareness of the rest of the world around you. Then return home and write down your experiences. Even if they only obtain some very general impressions, most people find this experiment both rewarding and fun. The particularly striking experience of one student even moved her to describe it in poetry.

Tree of Thanks

My roots run deep
the full length of this yard,
covered by the soft moss and
grasses of spring to come.

Each year I stretch a little
further down to the earth
and up to the sky.
You don't notice for I
have always been
to you the apple tree
outside your window.

Birds, trust and love me
their tiny talons scratch
the surface of my bark
causing a quivering shiver to run
down my spine.

The sun
hot
heals my wounds and
excites me with warmth
so deep
that I spring forth

in joy
ripe, luscious fruit, dripping
with juice.

Caresses of the summer breeze
tickle my extremities
so much I am taken away
with the freeness
I allow my very leaves to
travel with that sacred wind.

You don't notice
for I have always been
to you the apple tree
outside your window.

Thank-you for sitting so close,
skin against my bark
For a moment we are united
and my story is yours.

—Michele Lavery

Shamans Use Archetypes to Transform Themselves

When a person connects to the sacred vital forces of the universe, things start happening and experiences soar. You feel like you are riding a wave and are master of the world. You feel like a king or queen, or at least a prince or princess. This is the fundamental message of fairy tales—an aspect that we will examine in detail in Chapter 10. But there are also some inherent dangers in trying to connect to the sacred forces of the universe (Eliade 1958a:370). As Walt Disney's sorcerer's apprentice found out in the film *Fantasia,* if we are not very careful, these forces can easily get out of hand and destroy us and others. These vital forces are much like electricity (Jilek 1982:73; Clottes and Lewis-Williams 1998:23). They are powerful forces that permeate things but cannot ordinarily be seen. If controlled, they can be used for wonderful and beneficial things, but when they are out of control, they can be as destructive as a lightening bolt. Dabbling with such forces can be like putting your finger into an electrical socket. Shamans generally prepare for such connections, although sometimes they are caught in maelstroms of the universe's forces and come close to death as a result. This can happen during their physically gruel-ing initiations or when they are engaged in powerful mental battles with malevolent su-pernatural forces while in deep trance states. The fact that they survive indicates that they they have mastered control over those forces and know how to deal with them without perishing. This is the essence of the shamanic initiation, whether planned or unplanned. The initiation consists of coming face to face with the most powerful natural or biological or psychological forces that Nature can throw at humans. Not all initiates do survive (Robinson 1963). The shaman must transcend those forces and emerge as a new, more powerful, stronger person—one who has demonstrated his or her ability to control natural forces—very much as protohumans transcended their harsh environ-ments many millions of years ago. As Wade Davis (2001) stated it, shamanism is always about the release of one's wild genius. This is quite different from the priestly attempts to control economics and politics that characterize hierarchical religions.

Fig. 3.8. Remarkable instances of the mind's mastery over the flesh are part of some religious practices in the world. In the Phuket "Vegetarian" festival in Thailand, spirit mediums use these mortifications of the flesh as an indication that they harbor powerful spirits.

Typically, shamans enter into nearly delirious states using a number of techniques that will be discussed shortly. Under such conditions, reality becomes a fuzzy concept, and the stories told of shamanic initiations frequently have fantastic qualities to them. Shamans typically tell of how they starved and froze over the course of many nights and days; how spirits pierced their bodies with deadly spears; how the ravens came and plucked out their eyes or stripped the flesh off their bones; how their bones were scattered by wild animals; and finally, how the shaman's own spirit caused the bones to be gathered together and flesh put back on them once again and life breathed back into his body (Campbell 1983:170, 175; Halifax 1982:7; Elkin 1977:18–21; Eliade 1964:53ff.). Or, if the shaman does not "die," he suffers remarkable tortures (Fig. 3.8; see also Figs. 3.15, 3.16). I have listened to native people who told of their training and how they had to sit in winter ponds or streams until the ice formed around their necks (see also Olson 1936), or how they had skewers put through their chests and were hung like dead carcasses from ropes. Eyewitnesses, scientists, artists, and photographers have often documented extreme instances of the mastery of the flesh through self-inflicted wounds (Fig. 3.8). While some shamans' accounts are clearly fantastic, delusional, or meant to impress listeners, there is always an important core of truth to them. Shamans used these accounts and feats to impress others with their supernatural abilities or connections (e.g., E. Cohen 2001).

The theme of death and resurrection is extremely common in all shamanic initiation stories and is repeated in shamanic tales of curing, such as the Chukotka tales related by Kira Van Deusen (Tkalich, Tkalich, and Van Deusen 1993). Breaking through the barriers of the rational mind into the realm of subconscious vital forces is the "great work" of shamans and mystics. It is the "great abyss" that must be crossed, the cardboard of reality that Captain Ahab had to punch through in order to apprehend the great white whale of supernatural reality as represented by Moby-Dick. Death is perhaps an archetypal metaphor or symbol for this transcendence and transformation (Fig. 3.9); it is a symbol for the end of one part of a person's life and the beginning of a new life. Bones also seem to have a universal archetypal symbolic value as objects that house the vital life force of animals and people. When the flesh is gone, bones still seem to be permeated with a residual glow of the original person or animal. They are often viewed as the "seeds" of a new life. Oral traditions of many people the world over tell stories of bones being brought back to life (Ginzburg 1991:249, 261; Van Deusen 1996:68).

The goal of shamans is to find the correct balance or equilibrium point between tapping into sacred forces and the ability to control them. If the rational neocortex of the brain relinquishes too much control without proper preparation to older reptilian or paleomammalian parts of the brain where raw emotions dwell, the experience could turn ugly and destructive, as exemplified by the ecstatic bloodlust of Norse berserker warriors or the wild frenzies of the followers of Dionysus, who tore apart living animals, or the members of cannibal societies on the Northwest Coast of North America. If too much vital force is encountered, the shaman could become permanently insane or die, rather like those who opened the Ark of the Covenant in *Raiders of the Lost Ark.* How much and what kind of vital force can a shaman contact at one time without being burned? What safeguards can be used? What are the techniques of control?

Fig. 3.9. In the shamanic world, as in many metaphysical traditions, death is often used as a metaphor for profound individual psychological changes. In Western tarot cards, Death is generally interpreted in this fashion. From *The Paris Tarot,* edited by André Dimanche. Société le Jeu de Marseille, 1984.

Ethnographically, we find that virtually all the elements of a shaman's costume either assist in making connections to sacred forces or assist in controlling them and ensuring that they do not harm the shaman (Fig. 3.10). These are almost always items that have strong symbolical associations that influence one's mental states, self-confidence, and energy levels. Some of these items may have symbolic value only for specific cultures or individuals. However, many of them are extremely widespread and may be considered archetypes. These include bones, bright shiny objects, feathers, and objects that make tinkling noises. Antlers or horns are also widely used and are associated with wisdom, strength, regeneration, potency, and wealth (Halifax 1982:35, 82). There are also talismans and other objects in the shaman's pouch (or medicine bag) made of similar materials (Fig. 3.11). Rattles are commonly used. Masks can also be worn to prevent recognition by enemy spirits or enemy shamans. The drum is perhaps the most powerful item in the entire shamanic repertoire, and sometimes the only item, although it is not universally used (Fig. 3.12).

The drum is generally decorated with important protective and powerful symbols, but much of its power comes from the universal effects of its sound. The shaman may

Fig. 3.10. The shaman's costume can be relatively plain as in Figs. 3.2 and 3.25; however, typically there are many symbolical elements attached as talismans, charms, and powerful symbols. This Siberian shaman holds a feather and a drum with tinklers; his costume is embroidered with sacred symbols and is decorated with bones, feathers, tassels, small animals, and pouches containing powerful substances. From J. Campbell, *Historical Atlas of World Mythology: The Way of the Animal Powers,* Fig. 287 (from a nineteenth-century engraving in *Moeurs et Costumes de la Russie*). New York: A. van der Marck Editions, 1983.

have words of power and special magical techniques for protection as well. He also carefully trains himself ritually and mentally for the ordeal, creating certain automatic reflexes, reactions, and associations in order to control actions and internal mental states and to return to a normal condition. This is one of the most important functions of rituals for anyone dealing with altered or ecstatic states. In dangerous situations, shamans can also enlist the help of assistants and other shamans who know how to bring the shaman back to safety if he finds himself in trouble.

Above all, the shaman uses ethereal intermediaries and spirit helpers to protect himself when dealing with sacred forces. These are usually spirits of animals, but sometimes plant spirits or pure spirits unattached to any physical forms are also used. In medieval Europe, witches' animal familiars very probably played a similar role. All such helpers are thought to have potent supernatural powers. Animals in particular seem to be more instinctual and appear to have a more direct connection to sacred vital forces than humans, with their cultural rules, languages, shelters, comforts, and other buffers that separate them from directly experiencing the forces of Nature. Powerful animal spirit allies can often go where shamans cannot go and do what shamans cannot do. Spirit helpers are also more manageable than dealing directly with the raw powers of the cosmos. They are essential elements for effective shamanic work in supernatural realms, as so many shamanic stories illustrate. All of the above elements provide ritual security for shamans during their work. With this security net in place, shamans can brave their way into supernatural realms and do battle with the forces of chaos and destruction. How shamans enter those realms and make connections with sacred forces is one of the most interesting features of humanity.

Altered States of Consciousness and Ecstatic States

In order to connect with the sacred, shamans enter into ecstatic states that are fundamentally the same as ecstatic states used in other traditional rituals and by reclusive Buddhist, Christian, and other mystics. Some African American Christian churches such as the Institutional Church of God in New York also regularly induce ecstatic states in

Fig. 3.11. This box belongs to an Eskimo shaman on Diomede Island. It contains a copper bell, a sea bird mummy (wrapped), a hawk skull (wrapped), tassels of fur from unborn seals with wolf fur, a small ivory spoon, two ermine pelts, an ivory bodkin, a small amulet of leather and fur, a fossil tooth, and stone implements for making labret holes in lips. Courtesy of the Alaska Museum.

people attending their services. There are many ways to produce ecstatic states, but first it is necessary to define *ecstatic state* clearly. To begin with, an *ecstatic state* is a type of altered state of consciousness. The term *altered state of consciousness* is widely employed in psychology, but it is a broad category used for almost any transitory condition that is not normal consciousness. There are *many* different types of nonnormal consciousness (Ludwig 1969:10–13; Tart 1969). These include daydreaming, energetic states of possession, near-death experiences, artistic rapture, endorphin highs from jogging, alcoholic distortions of time and space, and the myriad types of different experiences induced by such drugs as tobacco, amphetamines, opiates, hallucinogens, and toxins, to mention just a few. Of particular interest are the altered states that enable people to handle or walk on fire (Fig. 3.13). Such mastery of fire is often associated with shamanism (Halifax

Fig. 3.12. The shaman's drum is his most powerful tool. Shamans often decorate their drums with powerful symbols of their helping animals, the sun, the four directions, or maps of their spirit worlds. The Siberian drum on the left shows the world divided into an underworld and a heavenly realm where shamans ride flying horses or birds among the sun, moon, and stars. The drum on the right depicts the four world directions with a sun in each quadrant. Left, from a drawing by Ostiak-Samoyed in *Asia* 24(4), 1929. Right, drawn from a photo in A. Lommel, *Shamanism: The Beginning of Art,* Fig. 28. New York: McGraw-Hill, 1969.

Fig. 3.13. One of the recurring feats associated with powerful shamans or other supernatural workers is the ability to handle or walk on fire. Here a Yao tribesman in Thailand has walked into a fire and proceeded to pick up coals with his hands and throw them in all directions. Photo by Mike Clarke.

1982:23). The ability to handle fire without being burned seems to be a worldwide phenomenon made possible only by entering ecstatic states or developing unshakable faith in one's ability to carry out such projects successfully (perhaps together with certain anxiety levels; Kane 1982; Katz 1982a:364). However, devotees who, I presume, become overconfident and are not in the appropriate mental state are sometimes burned very badly (Cohen 2001:98).

For psychologists (e.g., Ludwig 1969:13; in Jilek 1982:22; Jilek 1989), *some* or all of the following characteristics should be present in order to classify someone as being in an altered state of consciousness:

1. cognitive disturbance (e.g., impairment of memory, attention, or judgment)
2. feelings of some loss of self-control
3. a sense that time has slowed down, speeded up, or stopped
4. fluctuating emotions (especially elation to depression)
5. hallucinations or perceptual distortions
6. distorted perceptions of one's body
7. attaching increased meaning or significance to subjective experiences, ideas, or perceptions
8. inability to communicate the nature of one's experience
9. feelings of rejuvenation
10. susceptibility to suggestion

Many people experience several of these kinds of effects in mild forms during the course of a normal day. They can drift into and out of daydreams where time seems to slip away and ideas or experiences become unusually meaningful, or emotions fluctuate in recalling events, or parts of one's body may seem distorted. The same effects sometimes occur when dancing, playing, or listening to music, or when concentrating on work. In addition to the many different types of altered states of consciousness, there are also varying degrees of alteration (Rappaport 1999:229, 377). And the deeper one goes into a specific kind of altered state, the more dramatic the effects can become, as everyone knows who has had a bottle of wine as opposed to a glass. Similarly, when discussing the ecstatic states of shamans, it should be realized that sometimes this is only a relatively mild state, in which the shaman is conscious of most events in his surroundings. But shamans can also enter very profound ecstatic states, in which they are only aware of the events that they perceive on the altered planes of existence.

Irrespective of the varying intensity of these experiences, it seems apparent that the ecstatic states experienced in traditional religions and by shamans are a subset of altered states (Fig. 3.14; Winkelman 2000:115, 147). We might refer to them as "sacred ecstatic experiences" (SEEs). Joan Halifax (1982:9) suggests that ecstasy may be experienced by shamans above

Fig. 3.14. Sacred ecstatic states seem to be particularly strong experiences that can occur when a person enters into an altered state of consciousness with cultural values that predispose the person toward sacred ecstatic experiences and when individuals are motivated to have such experiences and have made appropriate ritual, mental, and physical preparations for them. Drafted by Greg Holoboff and B. Hayden.

all when they first encounter sacred forces and learn to control them, while repeated experiences may lead to more routine forms of altered consciousness. Michael Harner (1980) has called this specific type of experience the "shamanic state of consciousness" (see also Winkelman 2000:114, 125, 147–53). It is essentially the same as what Eliade and others refer to as the "shamanic ecstatic experience" and is probably the same as what psychiatrists refer to as the "mystical experience." While there seems to be no clearly agreed upon definition of ecstatic experience, it undoubtedly encompasses a wide range of mental states, including many nonmystical or nonshamanic forms. Dictionary definitions refer only to ecstatic mental states as characterized by feelings of overwhelming emotion and loss of reason and/or self-control. However, despite the wide array of behaviors that could be encompassed under the heading of "altered states," it is predominantly the shamanic and religious forms that are of interest to us here.

For psychiatrists (Kaplan, Freedman, and Sadock 1980:998; Winkelman 2000:131), these experiences are probably manifestations of the right hemisphere of the brain, although others argue that ecstatic or enlightenment experiences must involve both the right and the left sides of the brain or the subduing of both sides (Saver and Rabin 1997; Turner 1986:165; Oubré 1997; Rappaport 1999:228). As noted in Chapter 2, it seems possible that the limbic system (the old mammalian brain) may also have a role to play or that different parts of the brain may produce differing types of ecstatic experiences such as possession states versus trance states (see Winkelman 2000:131–45). The characteristics of most of these SEEs according to psychiatrists like Kaplan (see also Rappaport 1999:220, 377–79) are:

- ineffability: the experience cannot be described in words but is a unique emotional experience;
- enlightenment: feelings that the mystery of the universe has been plumbed and that an immense illumination or revelation has occurred; many times concepts, rhythms, images, or tonal sequences are altered in novel ways so as to make more sense or feel better, more invigorating, or more inspired;
- fleeting duration: the experience may last only a moment or for several hours;
- passivity: the person is willing to let other powers direct actions and thoughts;
- transcendence: mystic unity with higher forces, which sometimes seem to dissolve opposites; everything is encompassed; time does not exist. These higher forces are not always conceived of as deities or spirits but can also be ideals (such as political parties, aid groups, environmental groups, business associations, or sports groups), charismatic people espousing specific ideals, or even specific types of activities such as music or physical fitness. The feeling of timelessness probably also leads to associations of these experiences with eternal forces of the universe.

One additional characteristic should be mentioned. While many or perhaps all of these states are euphoric, they can also be painful to experience. This may seem like a paradox, but you may understand this phenomenon more clearly if you think of musicians like the Beatles who cry out in pain that they have blisters on their fingers but who cannot stop playing because the energy flowing through them is so intense and mentally euphoric. They simply choose to disregard any physical discomfort while the ecstatic state lasts. These days, many musicians take pain killers so that their physical discomforts do not stop or distract them from having peak experiences while playing. Others may be seen grimacing in pain. Similarly, South African Bushman trance dancers must transcend fear and pain to attain and remain in their states of euphoria (Katz 1982b), and some argue that the presence of pain and fear actually enhances the feeling of euphoria (Prince 1982:415–18). Perhaps because of these characteristics, some authors like Prince (1982:413) suggest that the underlying endorphin system may have evolved to enable animals to continue struggling or fighting in life-threatening situations despite severe pain and fatigue, thereby increasing their chances of survival. The Nordic berserkers and Indian Gurkha fighters who did not stop fighting even though they were critically wounded provide graphic illustrations of how endorphins and ecstatic states could function in this fashion.

Within this realm of ecstatic experience, Gilbert Rouget (1985:6–11) distinguishes two very extreme forms. One is typified by sensory deprivation, stillness, solitude, and visualized images or hallucinations. Entering these states is intentional and voluntary, not a response to a crisis or part of an initiation. This is the *trance* state of meditators and monks (I have transposed Rouget's labels "trance" and "ecstasy" so as to conform more with what I feel the English terms imply). Rouget's other type of ecstasy is typified by sensory overstimulation with many people and much noise. There are no hallucinations, but people generally cannot recall their experiences either. These are typical *possession* states often triggered by personal emotional stresses or crises. As descriptions by Wolfgang Jilek (1982) and others make clear, actual rituals often involve both of these states but in a sequential order, usually with isolation and sensory deprivation preceding overstimulation. Many shamans also use drums and other percussive instruments, but essentially they try to shut out other stimulations and conduct solitary rituals for curing, the events of which they can usually recall after their rituals. Thus, there is some blurring between Rouget's extreme forms, but in their extreme expressions they do appear quite different. Winkelman (2000:114, 125, 197) suggests that shamanic ecstasy may be a third basic type, characterized by the overstimulation and paralysis of the sympathetic nervous system so that the parasympathetic nervous system can dominate the brain's activities at least for a brief time. It is likely that most shamans and other traditional ritualists experience primarily this third type of ecstatic state, in which trance and ecstatic states alternated or at least were ecstatic states in which people could recall events and where there was no emotional stress involved.

Although these sacred ecstatic experiences are "ineffable," and people feel that they cannot really express them, some have tried. Traditional people that Wolfgang Jilek (1982:73) talked with described incredible energy, exhilaration, and feelings of being high: "I was jumping three feet high and I had such a thrill, a terrific feeling as if you were floating, as if you were in the air, you really feel high. I've only had such a feeling once before in my life when I was on heroin mainlining, but then I went through hell afterwards, it was terrible—but with *sye'wen* [spirit power] you get this feeling without the terrible aftermath" (E.M.).

The "Eightfold Path" Leads to Sacred Ecstasy

As with any characteristic in the biological world, there are always variations. Some individuals have much stronger physical or behavioral manifestations of certain characteristics than others. So it is with abilities to enter into altered and ecstatic states. At the far extreme, some individuals spontaneously and frequently enter into sacred ecstasies. These individuals, like Sri Ramakrishna (Barrett 1998), are generally revered as holy men. At the other extreme, some people never seem to be able to enter into ecstatic states, no matter what the condition. Between the two extremes lie the majority of people, who can enter into varying degrees of ecstatic states depending on the conditions and their intensity.

Buddhist teachings describe an eightfold path to proper action, each path representing a different means of opening doors to a spiritual life (Bodhi 1984). Similarly, we might conceive of a multifold path to ecstatic experiences. This is really simply a metaphor for the idea that there are many different ways to achieve ecstasy, depending on personal experiences and predilections or cultural backgrounds. Some cultures heavily emphasize specific techniques or predispose people to using them from constant daily experiences, such as the use of rhythms in Africa. However, there is a certain body of techniques that seem to be especially powerful for most people, and these are almost universally recognized and used by traditional societies for entering into sacred ecstatic or altered states (Winkelman 1982). There is considerable research indicating that the trance-inducing effects of these techniques are securely rooted in the human neurological system (Tuzin 1984; Jilek 1982; Prince 1982; Winkelman 1986, 1990, 1992, 2000; Boyer 2001) and were probably selected for during human evolution as critical elements in ritual-based alliances. Perhaps they can be considered as a very basic form of archetype.

The main goal of *all* these techniques is to release the stranglehold that the conscious rational mind has on our thoughts and experiences (Winkelman 2000:167). The goal is to open up the channels of communication and experience to other parts of our brain such as the right hemisphere and the older emotional parts of the brain. Virtually all traditional cultures in the world believe that to contact the supernatural realms, it is necessary to enter into altered or ecstatic experiences. As Webber (Webber, Stephens, and Laughlin 1983), Jilek (1982:29) and others have noted, this is a health-restoring process that generally imparts a feeling of immense satisfaction if not euphoria to those involved. However, getting the rational conscious mind to relinquish its grip on thought and emotional control is no easy task for most people. It is the abyss that must be crossed, the board that must be pierced, the "death" that must be endured. In traditional societies, it takes a long time to accomplish this goal, many monotonous hours or days of boring the rational active mind into quiescence and submission, rather like trying to calm down a room full of hyperactive children. All the techniques (except the use of drugs) involve long, slow, and boring processes. The rational mind quickly puts up defenses when it gets bored and tries to get out of the situation, throwing up arguments about how absurd or useless the entire undertaking is or making other objections. Getting past these rational-mind defenses is one of the hardest mental tasks that most Industrial people can face. However, this quality of long, monotonous preparation time for traditional rituals is why many scholars have said that if a ritual is done quickly, or if it always has something "of interest" happening, then they know that it is not a genuine traditional ritual.

What, then, are the techniques of our "eightfold path" to ecstasy? For convenience, they are listed here. As you can see, there are many more than eight paths, but we can still refer to it symbolically as the eightfold path. Some of these are relatively self-explanatory; some have already been mentioned in passing; others deserve more comments.

Perhaps perfumes, incense, and certain foods could be added to this list as well as several new technological techniques, such as the use of biofeedback devices to train one's mind to maintain alpha or other brain wave patterns. Still other techniques may be developed in the future. However, our major concern here is with traditional techniques.

Physiological Techniques

Wolfgang Jilek (1982:22–49) provides an excellent overview of the physiological bases for some of these techniques, especially the use of rhythms and repeating light flickers (see also Tuzin 1984; Needham 1967; Prince 1982; Achterberg 1987:346; Brauchli, Mitchell, and Zeier 1994; Winkelman 1986, 1990, 1992). As music therapist Johanne Brodeur stated it, "Music will reach a child at a very primitive level, through the reptilian brain, the innermost part of the brain. The child doesn't have to process it or use any higher cortical function. It just responds spontaneously" (Boxall 1990). Realizing that there is a physiological basis for the effects of rhythm and drumming on our mental states takes us a long way toward understanding why the drum is so prevalent in shamanism and other ritual contexts (Figs. 3.2, 3.3). Such a physiological basis makes it probable that the unique human use of rhythm in rituals goes far back into the prehistory of religion and probably had an important adaptive role to play in early human evolution. In effect, the first musical instruments were probably rhythm instruments:

The "Eightfold" Path: Techniques of Ecstasy

Physical or Psychophysical Techniques

1. Fatigue and sleep deprivation
2. Sensory deprivation (darkness and silence) or sensory overstimulation
3. Fasting (induced starvation) and dehydration (thirst)
4. Pain and stress (physical or emotional)
5. Rhythmic breathing or hyperventilation
6. Extreme temperatures (hypothermia and extreme heat)
7. Shock
8. Deep percussion, driving rhythms, sound patterns, song, and dance
9. Relaxation or overstimulation (hyperactivity)
10. Rhythmic light flashes (photic driving)
11. Sex
12. Drugs
13. Blood loss

Mental Techniques

14. Disorientation and confusion
15. Impossible mental tasks (riddles, mysteries)
16. Altering identity, physical appearances, and behavior (face and body painting, masks, costumes, and drama)
17. Monotonous repetition
18. Meditation and prayer
19. Ritual (church services, totemic reenactments)
20. Involvement with a higher ideal or conceptual framework (service to god, working for humanitarian or political causes)
21. Motivation or cultural values (expectations of trance states, wanting to become a shaman)

clapping sticks, bones, rocks, and drums. No other animal responds to rhythm and music the way human beings do. Some animals have mechanical rhythm built into their running gaits or sexual copulations, but no other animal uses rhythms outside these mechanical contexts. Just try getting your cat or dog to show any interest in, or response to, music or rhythms, even the most captivating ones.

In contrast, humans in any culture instinctively respond to rhythms and music, even at very early ages. Music and rhythms are used in therapies to cure people of emotional and mental illnesses. When everything makes the right connections, rhythm and music can catapult us into ecstatic experiences in which it seems that the vital forces of the universe are coursing through our bodies and minds, guiding us in the dance, taking over the playing, inspiring us to perform in unthought of ways. It seems that we are riding the waves and currents that power the cosmos. I heard that someone once asked Michael

Coleman, the famous Irish fiddler of the 1950s, what he did when he went into his basement to play his violin by himself. He was reported to have replied in all seriousness that he talked with god. The same sentiment is expressed often by those who play drums seriously, like Mickey Hart (1990) and most African drummers (Hodges 1992). They feel that their music takes on a life of its own and that an outside force is being channelled through them and playing *them* like an instrument. Puccini, too, said the music for his opera, *Madame Butterfly,* "was dictated to me by God; I was merely instrumental in putting it on paper and communicating it." Johannes Brahms expressed the same feeling when he said that "Straight away the ideas flow in upon me, directly from God" (Cameron 1992:2). The experience is so intense for some people that they become music addicts, spending their lives oblivious to the rest of the world, always searching for the special door that will open again and allow them to make the connection to those same forces. Some studies indicate that even simple chanting can trigger neurophysiological changes leading to transcendent experiences (Oubré 1997:16).

The age-old genetic adaptation to the musical beats and sounds that enhanced ecstatic ritual bonding and helped create stronger alliances for survival is still with us (see Chap. 2). It still draws people in large crowds to dances and concerts. At many of these events, spheres of mirrors and stroboscopes create lighting effects that mimic flickering firelight at night. These repeated light patterns can have effects similar to repeated sounds. At certain frequencies, they can alter many people's states of consciousness dramatically. The mesmerizing effect of driving in snow storms with large white snowflakes repeatedly hitting the windshield against a dark sky is a common experience in northern latitudes. Similar effects can occur unexpectedly. Just outside Vancouver, the Port Mann Bridge was built across the Fraser River about 30 years ago. From the time that it opened, stories about the bridge being haunted circulated, and I knew several people who refused to cross the bridge, especially at night. Other people claimed to feel funny when they crossed the bridge, or even almost lost consciousness, waking up just in time to avoid accidents after they had driven across it. To me, it was readily apparent what was going on, for the designers of the bridge had placed continuous rows of meter-length fluorescent lights along the sides of the bridge, and each light was separated from the others by a black spacer band. At 80 kilometers per hour or so, the effect at night was a very annoying flickering light pattern that was driving many people into altered states of consciousness and creating a real safety risk. It took city engineers a few years to realize what was happening, but today those lights are never used and another lighting system has been put in place.

Other physical techniques for inducing altered and ecstatic states are extremely common in traditional religions throughout the world, especially for initiation rituals. These include fasting, dehydration, physical exertion, pain, fear or other strong emotions, special breathing patterns, sensory deprivation or overstimulation, partial asphyxiation, shock, temperature extremes, and blood loss. Once again, Jilek (1982), Katz (1982b), Campbell (1983), and others provide excellent examples of these techniques from North American (especially the Northwest Coast) and South African Bushman contexts. On the Northwest Coast, for example, initiates were suddenly "clubbed" (touched with powerful psychic objects), and if they did not faint from the shock, they might be dragged from their houses to ceremonial locations where they were subjected to all the

Fig. 3.15. Exhaustion, ritual preparations, personal commitment, and pain have been used by various groups to create some of the most profound spiritual experiences. One of the most famous examples involves the Sun Dance ceremonies of the Plains Indians, which culminated in young participants being hung up by skewers thrust through their skin and weighed down by bison skulls attached to them. From George Catlin, *O-kee-pa: A Religious Ceremony and Other Customs of the Mandans.* London: Trübner, 1867.

aches and pains of life in "one heap." For four days, with constant drumming and singing, initiates were blindfolded, stripped, forbidden to talk or move, deprived of sleep, dehydrated, placed under heavy covers, starved, teased, grabbed, lifted, bitten, hit, and punched in order to make them "die." Some initiates also had to run barefoot in the snow until exhausted, dive and swim in ice-cold water carrying heavy stones, pierce or cut their own flesh, and dance to unceasing rhythms. The Sun Dance initiations of the Plains Indians in North America were even more extreme. Skewers were inserted into the chests and backs of initiates. Then they were suspended by ropes tied to these skewers (Figs. 3.15, 3.16). Under such extreme conditions, initiates occasionally did, in fact, die (Cohen 2001:62).

Prince (1982:415–19) suggests that any threatening situation, real or perceived, has the potential for releasing endorphins (the natural opiates of the brain) and triggering euphoric ecstatic states. Frequently many techniques are combined, as in the Winter Dance initiations described by Jilek (1989) and in the traditional North American sweat lodge (Fig. 3.17), where fasting, drumming, darkness (sensory deprivation), temperature

Fig. 3.16. Modern mystics such as Fakir Musafar sometimes use physical pain to trigger their body's endorphin system and create ecstatic experiences. Photo by Charles Gatewood with permission of V/Search Publications, San Francisco, from *Modern Primitives: An Investigation of Contemporary Adornment and Ritual,* 1995.

extremes, and lowered oxygen consumption (an effect of steam vapors) all combine to create powerful altered or ecstatic experiences.

Whenever physical fatigue or pain reaches a certain limit, natural endorphins are released in the body to block the pain, and they create euphoric states of varying intensities. It is thought that this endorphin system was adaptive because it allowed people, and animals, to continue to function under situations of extreme pain or exhaustion and therefore overcome life-threatening situations and thus survive. Prince (1982) devoted an entire issue of the anthropological journal *Ethos* to the exploration of the role of endorphins in shamanic and traditional religious experiences. These are the same body chemicals responsible for "joggers' highs," the highs of other athletes, anorexic highs, and the ecstatic experiences some women report during childbirth. Some mystics, both traditional and modern, seem to specialize in the use of pain to transcend their rational being and achieve ecstatic states (Vale and Juno 1989). Their experiences are so extreme (Fig. 3.16) that it seems that they represent the far end of the natural spectrum where endorphins must kick in very easily and in strong doses. I doubt that the average person would be able to voluntarily endure these experiences without a great deal of prior preparation (fasting, exhaustion, sleep deprivation, and so on).

The milder forms of pain-induced euphoria associated with exhausting work also undoubtedly provide the foundation for certain mystical traditions like Gurdjieff's (1963) and Ouspensky's (1979) that emphasize intensive hard physical work as a means to become enlightened. By staying up until late hours, dedicated musicians also use extreme mental and physical fatigue, perhaps unwittingly, to enhance their euphoric musical experiences. Similar states of exhaustion are produced by starvation and emotional stress, probably leading to the claims that only artists who have been poor and who have suffered can create great art, for only they have opened the door to connections with vital forces, inspiration, and ecstasy. Nor can there be much doubt that workaholics who spend long hours on projects at night also lapse into altered or ecstatic states and get "high" on their work. It is in part these altered states that motivate them to keep taking on more and more projects, irrespective of how antisocial it makes them.

Prince (1982:415–19) also suggests that states of terror, such as those experienced when we are faced with the threat of death or threats to our own sense of worth or in-

Fig. 3.17. Sweat lodges such as this one used by the Thompson Indians of British Columbia, were small, dark structures where temperatures from heated rocks and steam reached the limits of tolerance and generally led to altering the consciousness of participants. From J. Teit, *The Thompson Indians, Memoirs of the American Museum of Natural History,* Vol. 2., Fig. 1. New York, 1900.

tegrity, or other panic situations, can all release endorphins into our brain. Given all these paths to ecstatic experiences, perhaps we should not be surprised if people who work hard and long hours in agricultural fields, day after day in the hot, dehydrating rays of the sun, sometimes experience ecstatic states and epiphanies or hierophanies—sudden manifestations of sacred forces in their environments—or even appearances of satyrs, saints, or other spirits. When combined with other powerful stimuli, the ecstatic effects can undoubtedly be truly dramatic. For example, when exhausted Greek shepherds in the mountains saw cosmic lightning cannonballs illuminate the night skies, thundering off ridges, cliffs, and canyon walls, they must have felt overwhelmed (just as we do) as though they were in the midst of the great elemental forces—divinities in action.

Many people also consider sexual orgasm as a physically based ecstatic state that provides a doorway to experiencing the sacred vital forces of the universe (Fig. 3.18). Whether the experience involves endorphins or should be considered as a special case of ecstatic experience is open to debate. However, many traditional religions recognize human intercourse as a sacred act that makes an important connection between the world we live in and sacred forces (Eliade 1978:372). It is especially important to perform sacred sex during the planting, growing, or harvesting seasons for agricultural people. This is the "sacred marriage" of the ancient Middle Eastern kings, the "great rite," the foundation of Tantric Buddhism, and the core of many religious mysteries.

MENTAL TECHNIQUES

All of these physical techniques are fairly effective for putting the rational mind out of commission, sometimes bludgeoning it into retreat, and reducing it to a barely

Fig. 3.18. Ecstatic states experienced during sex are viewed as important sacred experiences in many traditional religions perhaps the most notable of which is Tantrism. Here, two Tantric deities celebrate cosmic union through sexual union.

conscious level to enable the more archaic levels of our brains to reassert control and expression. There are also mental techniques, some of which may come as a surprise, such as riddles. The rational mind thrives on stimulation and the analysis of incoming information or changes in the state of the environment, assessing possible dangers, opportunities, transgressions, and compliances. It is, in effect, a very good computer. Without sufficient incoming information, the rational mind tends to shut down or go dormant and lets other parts of the brain assert themselves, such as when we dream. Monotonous and repetitious stimuli have the same effect. The rational brain perceives no interest in endlessly repeating unchanging phrases (mantras), sounds (chants), rhythms, or images. It lets everything go on automatic pilot and checks out into a more energy-saving dormant stage. In contrast, the older parts of the brain revel in the repeated, the familiar, and the ritual (Winkelman 2000:246–49). These are the reasons why relaxation, monotonous repetition, drumming of a constant beat, sensory deprivation, meditation, prayer, and ritual are effective doors to ecstatic or altered states. This is also why meditation generally involves either repeated phrases, attempts to empty the mind, or attempts to focus on single images or concepts, and why meditation and prayer are generally supposed to be performed in silent, darkened rooms with no interruptions.

Our rational brain can also be overloaded with so much stimulation that it temporarily shuts down, much as home computers do when they receive conflicting data or a data overload. Similar systemic breakdowns seem to occur when the rational brain is given tasks that it simply cannot handle or situations that it cannot interpret. The neocortex, or new brain, in effect, gives up if it cannot process information and lets the old brain take over more control to see if the result will be any better. Thus, high levels of search activity, such as night vigils, or the altering of one's own appearance so that the brain is not sure of its identity (see the discussion of masks in Chap. 2 and Fig. 2.8), or any source of deep-seated confusion and disorientation can lead to partial or even complete breakdown of the rational system of the brain. Mick Jagger's film, *Performance,* provides an excellent portrayal of this process—in this case it is used to usurp a victim's vital forces. It has been suggested that this is precisely why many religions incorporate incomprehensible "mysteries" that seem completely contradictory, or why Zen masters give their disciples unsolvable riddles (koans): "What is the sound of one hand clapping?" "If there is no one in the woods to hear a tree fall, does it make any sound?"

Shamans, too, generally have a fairly good repertory of unfathomable mysteries including the unity of opposites and the melding of the sexes. The widespread use of riddles in the European tradition may have originally had a similar origin. Certainly, many of the Anglo-Saxon riddles were used in ritual contexts (Williamson 1982:37).

Perhaps the most dramatic example of uninterpretable inputs creating a breakdown of the rational brain and entry into an altered state was documented by the Canadian Broadcasting Corporation a few years ago. They reported a surprising upsurge in the cult membership of a particular charismatic preacher who began to operate in the Toronto area. Both the media and the police began to investigate the activities of this leader. They found nothing strictly illegal, but there was a clear manipulation of the public. One investigative reporter went to a public cult meeting and reported that the charismatic leader first made everyone feel welcome and comfortable and then gradually began to use more and more contradictory and abstract statements that made no logical sense but sounded profound. At first the reporter tried her hardest to follow the meaning of what was being said and to make sense of it, but after only five or ten minutes, she simply gave up and found herself becoming more and more mesmerized, as did many other people in the hall. Once in such an altered state, people are extremely prone to accept suggestions that are presented to them, as psychiatrists and historians have noted. It probably comes as no surprise that after 40 or 50 minutes of listening to gobbledegook, spectators were given very clear messages that they totally enjoyed themselves and understood the revealed truths. They were asked to make as large a monetary contribution as they could in order to make it possible for this good work to continue. To get a better idea of these effects, see "Gobbledegook Can Alter Your Mind," page 74.

INTENTION AND VALUES

Are the above techniques sufficient on their own to induce ecstasy and religious experiences, especially if taken to extremes? Some people think that they are. Others, like Henry (1982), Suedfeld (1980), Jilek (1982:24), and Ludwig (1969:13) are convinced that individual intentions and expectations, together with cultural expectations and experiences are critical for determining the specific nature of many altered states of consciousness and for inducing sacred ecstatic experiences. If people grow up seeing shamanic trance healing being performed by large numbers of adults in their community on a regular basis and listening for hours on end to rhythms and chants, as children of the South African Bushmen do, and if people are also expected to engage in this activity, they are far more likely to successfully enter into a sacred ecstatic state than if they grow up in an Industrial middle-class environment. Even entering into altered states such as hypnosis is dependent largely on a person's motivation and desire to be hypnotized and/or to act out socially unusual roles.

Intention and motivation are perhaps some of the major features that differentiate sacred experiences from profane ones. Winkelman (2000:243–45) notes that the meanings associated with certain symbols within cultures can create emotional and physiological reactions when the symbols are evoked. In a similar vein, Alpert (1995:100) argues that the nature of one's experience after taking hallucinogenic mushrooms is largely determined by the specific rituals associated with taking the mushrooms.

Gobbledegook Can Alter Your Mind
(and Your Pocket)

Trying to get the rational mind to process things that are not rational, things that confuse it, or things that it simply cannot make sense of, can be a powerful technique for shutting down the "new brain" or at least the left side of it responsible for logic and keeping us on track for those long-term life goals. Trying to make sense of seemingly profound gobbledegook will give you some inkling of what this is like. The following is an example that I made up. Try getting a friend to read this to you aloud while you listen intently to try to understand it. In fact, try having your friend read it several times. How do you feel after having listened to it? If your friend suggested that you both should go out for lunch and that you should pay for it after the reading, what would you say? Alternately, try reading this passage to a friend, and then ask him or her for a favor.

Listen very carefully to what I say:
The talking is the important thing, nothing but the talking;
for the talking is truth and yet not the truth.
The talking is the word and the word is one. The word is many.
The talking is everywhere, yet it is nowhere.
The talking turns back on itself, but is not talking, and must go forward.
There is talking in the earth and on the earth and through the earth.
But there is only one true talking—
The talking that I am talking,
And I am talking that talk to you, now,
Listening to my talking, going forward, feeling backward.
Can you hear me walking in my talking?
Listening in my talking?
The forces that are balking at my talking,
Moving through and few, flowing and glowing,
Surging and herding, crying to climb the divine.
Can you see my talking, smell the flocking?
Birds are walking, giraffes are gawking.
Break the sound of the talking,
Taste the sap from the earth.
Open the table, walk the window, pop the name, run the letter.
Come. Sit by me. Let blue run through your fingers.
And, the talk will begin.
For, the talking is the important thing, nothing but the talking.
(Repeat again from the beginning.)

In the same way, the person who engages in profane eating, profane music, profane sex, or profane drug use has no interest in, or perhaps no awareness of, sacred ecstatic experiences. Such people are not motivated to experience the sacred nature of themselves or the world. These people often use activities to escape from problems or are simply not religious in the traditional sense. They do not see the world as a magical, wonder-filled, alive environment. Give two people (a shaman and a street person) a drum and ask them to beat it at exactly the same rate for the same length of time and in the same environment. Compare the experiences afterward and they will be totally different. Taking drugs is not necessarily good or bad, but the way they are used and the intention and the preparation of the user for the experience can make a great difference in the subjective effects the user experiences. If drugs were legalized on the condition that all users had to undergo supervision and training by a bona fide shaman, society would undoubtedly be in a much better state than it is now. However, even then, shamans could not necessarily supply the *motivation and control* that many authors insist is essential for most sacred experiences (Ludwig 1969:13; Jilek 1982:24; Katz 1982a:355). Both motivation and control over various kinds of stressful situations depend to a very large degree on the individual and on personal or cultural training, just as students or athletes are trained to deal with problem solving or competitive situations.

Of all these mental techniques, perhaps the most potentially troublesome, but the most adaptive for us in the past, is the association of one's self and one's activities with higher ideals or conceptual frameworks. In the past, these higher entities were ancestors, totemic beings, or other supernatural manifestations that ensured the upholding of traditional values critical for group survival (sharing, kinship bonds, ritual bonding with and marriage between other communities, and other similar values). Linking exhausting, painful, or sexual experiences to higher principles is perhaps a necessary element in creating sacred ecstatic experiences for many people. It results in the mystic union of one's self with more encompassing aspects of the universe. This feeling of understanding the higher principles of the cosmos—how the universe, or parts of it, operate—is also undoubtedly why many people derive great pleasure in conducting scientific research.

Nobel laureates and the best physicists say that there is nothing more thrilling than discovery. For them, ecstasy and spirituality derive from discovering how parts fit into a whole beyond the immediate senses, whether these are scientific principles or moral orders (see Pauli in Wilber 1984; Heisenberg in Wilber 1984:41; de Broglie in Wilber 1984:117). Major breakthroughs in creating theories about our world (whether they are true or not) undoubtedly involve substantial reorganization of the brain so that previously unconnected neural circuits become integrated into a wider network. Long, stressful periods of exhausting attempts to solve difficult problems certainly must enhance the elation of these experiences, and such states probably facilitate the creation of overarching models, as many students know who have struggled with problems until early morning hours only to come up with an inspired solution at the last minute before a project is due. This same feeling is probably present to some degree in any successful problem-solving activity, whether figuring out why the lawn mower does not work or how black holes function. The inherently pleasurable nature of problem solving may well be an adaptive aspect of most mammalian brains, in which exploratory and learning behaviors are critical for survival.

Among humans there need not be any explicitly formulated intention to link a particular experience or altered state to a higher principle, although this undoubtedly facilitates the entry into ecstasy. Sometimes these linkages can derive from the general background of expected behavior, such as at hunter-gatherer curing ceremonies or even vague, barely conscious personal values such as validating one's involvement in a personal relationship or a youth movement value system. There are major advantages for musical groups who link their performances to popular causes such as the "Live Aid," "Band Aid," and "Tears Are not Enough" concerts and recordings (concerts for famine relief in Africa in the 1980s or the 1971 Concert for Bangladesh). These "cause-related" performances provide powerful and effective higher principles that greatly enhance people's tendencies to have ecstatic listening and dancing musical experiences of varying intensities. This, in turn, enhances performers' popularity and recording sales.

Whatever the ultimate reason, humans certainly seem to derive an innate satisfaction from emotional connections involving *meaning,* especially involving elevated principles. Sacred ecstatic experiences generally result from feelings of ecstatic union with such elevated principles. Material symbols are often used to represent these meanings and the symbols therefore become emotionally powerful. Prestige objects in traditional societies generally are imbued with these kinds of meaningful symbols and also entail substantial costs. While low-cost material symbols may have existed for hundreds of thousands of years without leaving much trace besides some ochre crayons, symbols with the form of prestige objects only start to occur when surplus wealth begins to accumulate in transegalitarian societies (as discussed in Chap. 5).

Higher principles can come in many forms. We have already mentioned supernatural forms, political causes, humanitarian aid, involvement in youth movements or new ideologies, and even personal relationships. Clubs, service organizations, sports groups, other activity groups, families, charities, businesses, work, health, and education are all other good candidates. Almost any activity can be viewed by some people in terms of a higher principle for which they are willing to make sacrifices and which might potentially trigger sacred ecstatic experiences under the appropriate circumstances. However, for most people, some principles are much more powerful than others, especially divinities and appeals for humanitarian aid. These are perhaps not very different from the evolutionary context that made emotional reactions and the supernatural unique human features in the first place, many millions of years ago on the African savanna.

Unfortunately, today, many unscrupulous groups use these same age-old techniques in order to build personal empires and to exploit individuals. Because people are highly susceptible to suggestions when they enter altered or ecstatic states, manipulative groups often use people's devotions to ideals such as humanitarian aid to make their recruits work exhausting hours, to sing or dance constantly, or to engage in other trance-inducing activities. Such groups then use these altered states to bind and bend people to the self-centered purposes of the groups' leaders. These techniques are nothing more than the tools of sacred technology being misused. Like fire, electricity, nuclear power, or computers, sacred techniques can be used either for positive personal growth and to benefit the community or they can be used for negative or disempowering purposes. This issue will be addressed again in Chapter 13, but in general, be extremely wary of any organization or group that appeals to your ideals and systematically demands exhausting commitments of your time and efforts.

Probably none of the techniques that have been discussed work equally well for every person. People differ in their proclivities and their abilities to exert mental control over different kinds of stresses. Some people respond much more emotionally to music than others, some people are more easily carried to rapture by participating in sports, others by meditation or fasting. What are your proclivities? What have been your most ecstatic experiences? What would you do if you wanted to have an ecstatic experience?

Shamans Fly Up the World's Axis

So, once a shaman succeeds in entering an ecstatic state, what happens next? In totemic cults where ancestral animals are invoked, participants must perform some ritual action such as dancing or acting out ancestral actions. In possession cults, in which another supernatural "entity" takes control of a person's body and mind, almost anything can happen, although the person usually ends up acting out personal frustrations or desires, for example, by acting aggressively or sexually or making requests of other people. In contrast, in shamanism, there is a mission to be fulfilled. Most often, the shaman must travel to the spirit realm in order to retrieve the vital force, or soul, of someone who is sick or to obtain some other important commodity from the beings that inhabit that realm (fire, the year's grain harvest, information on the hunt), or to keep the forces of destruction at bay for the community.

How does one find the way to those supernatural realms? Shamans almost universally employ a device called the *axis mundi,* the "axis of the world," or the "world tree" (Fig. 3.19). This is a pole, tree, column, shaft, mountain, or other projection that connects the world of the spirits (both above and below) and the world of mortal people on earth. The axis mundi is the point of connection to the supernatural. The shaman arrives in these spirit realms by traveling up or down the axis mundi, often on a magical mount, usually a horse or bird. The shaman rides or flies until he finds the afflicted soul and the enemy spirits that are holding it (Fig. 3.20). Then the battle ensues.

Flying to reach spirit realms is especially common, and therefore many shamans emphasize costume elements that represent feathers or birds or wings. In fact, many shamans have special relations with birds, especially raptors such as eagles or hawks (Halifax 1982:23, 86). As a result, flight, or riding animals, and world trees or poles are intimately associated with most shamans (Vastokas 1977). Similar journeys involving personal transformation and magical helpers are the core themes of many fairy tales (Jack and the Beanstalk, for instance), and suggestions have been advanced that journeys of all kinds are archetypal symbols representing shamanic travels and adventures for most people (Campbell 1949). Some shamans stand on actual physical poles (Fig. 3.21) as dramatizations to their communities of the reality of the world axis (Campbell 1983:152–53). Many Celtic communities still have sacred trees where supernatural encounters might take place.

One of the most important implications of the axis mundi concept is that it divides the universe into separate levels. There are usually three levels: the upper level (reached from the top of the tree), where spirits reside; the middle level, where humans and

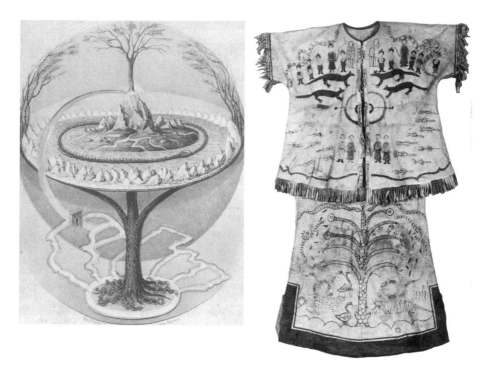

Fig. 3.19. The world tree is a central symbol for many shamanic cultures. The two examples portrayed here are the Norse sacred tree, Yggrasil (left), and the world tree as portrayed on a Tungus shaman's costume (right). Left: from *Northern Antiquities,* 1847. Right: from J. Campbell, *Historical Atlas of World Mythology: The Way of the Animal Powers,* Fig. 300 (original photo from American Museum of Natural History). New York: A. van der Marck Editions,1983.

Fig. 3.20. With the help of spirit animals or birds, shamans frequently fly to the spirit realms where they perform their work, as depicted in this Eskimo drawing by Jessie Oonark. Reprinted with permission of Ernest Mayer, the Winnipeg Art Gallery, and the Public Trustee for Nunavut, estate of Jessie Oonark.

animals reside; and the underworld, where earth spirits, fairies, gnomes, and frequently the dead or unborn reside. This type of division of the world is extremely common in the shamanic world as well as other cultures, including our own with its earth, heaven, and hell. It pervades our mythologies, both past and present (Tolkien's hobbits live in Middle Earth). While such concepts are very common, they may not be absolutely universal.

Another important, probably unexpected characteristic of the axis mundi is that it has many manifestations. It is not like the single physical axis of the earth that passes through the North and South Poles. Rather, there is a spiritual world axis for every culture and every community. And, within each community, there is a spiritual axis for every social group, every kinship group, and every house.

Fig. 3.21. Another means of traveling to the spirit realms is often portrayed as climbing up into the sacred world tree. In some cultures, such as the Mapuche of Chile, shamans may literally climb up a pole or a sacred tree to undertake their work. From J. Halifax, *Shaman: The Wounded Healer,* p. 85 (photo by Louis Faron). London: Thames & Hudson, 1982.

It would be useful to put this book down for a few minutes and go to each room, doorway, window, and outside area of your own home in order to try to determine where you think its axis mundi is located. Many traditional cultures have altars that serve as an axis mundi in each house, but few contemporary houses have such features.

It might be interesting, too, to consider where the traditional axis mundi of early European houses was located. You may be surprised to find that it is still active and still has an enormous influence on the ritual life of nearly every single house in the Occidental world. We still live, in effect, with the shamanic legacy of our ancestors, although you probably don't recognize it as such. See if you can guess what this is with the help of a few clues.

The first clue is that for Indo-European ancestors, the hearth was the most important focus of house activities. People would gather around the hearth for warmth; they would transform raw food into cooked meals at the hearth; they would eat and repair tools or work fibers around the hearth at night. The hearth was the center of social activity, a place to exchange information or to tell tales, and it was vital in fulfilling many bodily needs.

The second clue is that the hearth was also the most sacred part of the house. There were goddesses of the hearth, like Roman Hestia. The broom was a sacred implement of the hearth. And when any communication with ancestors or spirits took place, it was at the hearth, where incense might be burned or food offerings left. Most people are familiar with the trance-inducing effects of an open fire's warmth, flickering light, and crackling noises. On dark, silent winter nights, these hypnotic effects must have been es-

Fig. 3.22. World trees and poles are still part of Western culture. They take the form of Christmas trees and maypoles (seen here). Sacred trees and poles can generally be identified by their elaborate and colorful decorations. Photo by Stevie Doucet.

pecially strong and led to many altered states. In effect, the hearth and the smoke rising up from it to the heavens formed a natural axis mundi of the house. In the pastoral nomadic days of the Proto-Indo-Europeans, the hearth was in the center of a tent or yurt and the smoke rose up through a central smoke hole. In later agricultural homes, the hearth was still in the center of the house and there was still a smoke hole. Shamans or others wishing to contact the ancestors or spirits would mentally rise up on the column of smoke and exit through the smoke hole to fly or ride to the realm of the spirits. Similarly, any spirits that came to visit a household came through the smoke hole and down the column of smoke into the house.

The third clue is that it was not until the later medieval period that chimneys began to be used, and even then, they were used by the elites. Chimneys only became part of ordinary households much later, in the eighteenth and nineteenth centuries.

So, what major spirit visits every household every year and enters through the smoke hole? Have you ever wondered why Santa Claus comes down the chimney? It is certainly a most unusual and difficult way to enter a house and seems entirely mysterious unless we understand something about Indo-European houses and shamanism. In general, important spirits were supposed to visit households at certain times of the year to confer blessings on households, and they often left signs of their visit and their blessings. Odin, a Germanic deity with great supernatural power and insight, came from the north lands in the middle of the winter, riding his eight-legged horse, Sleipnir, and left blessings in all the good pagan households, just as Santa Claus rides through the sky pulled by eight reindeer. Riding flying horses, stags, deer, or reindeer is a typical means of magical or shamanic transport as well as a symbol of abundance (Halifax 1982:82, 86). Among the Celts of Scotland, the great goddess, Brigit, also came to visit each household on her feast day, the second of February—Brigit's Day, subsequently transformed into Candlemas and then into Groundhog Day. Like Santa Claus, Brigit came down the smoke hole or chimney and left a sign in the ashes of her visit and her blessing for the house and took a bit of the food that was left for her by the family. In many houses today, food is also left by the chimney for Santa Claus.

Santa Claus is only one aspect of a much broader pattern that still endures today, albeit at a largely unconscious level. People still carry out the rituals but are only dimly aware of their meaning or the reasons for performing them. For instance, what does the Yule tree represent that families decorate every year? Although claims are sometimes made that the origin of the custom dates back only to the eighteenth and nineteenth centuries, this is the case only in well-off Industrial cities. In traditional rural areas of

Fig. 3.23. Another shamanic element that survives in Western culture is expressed in the traditions of witches flying through the air to perform their work and ascending up the chimneys of houses like shamans of earlier times. Left: a woodcut by Hans Baldung Grien, 1514, appearing in R. Guiley, *The Encyclopedia of Witches and Witchcraft*, p. 254. New York: Facts on File, 1989. Right: an illustration by George Cruikshank (nineteenth century) appearing in D. Valiente, *An ABC of Witchcraft*, p. 109. Surrey, B.C.: Phoenix Publishing, 1973.

Europe there are widespread and age-old traditions of decorating trees around wells for special ritual occasions like May Day and both the summer and winter solstices (Miles 1912:269–71). The Romans, too, decorated their houses with evergreens and lights for the midwinter Kalends festival (Miles 1912:168, 269, 271). Aside from the specific symbolism of these trees and poles (discussed in Chap. 6), it is worth noting that the Yule tree is, in effect, a temporary axis mundi set up in our household. It is meant to make a very important connection between the family and the supernatural realms.

But, there is another lesson to be learned from the Yule tree. How do we know that it is a sacred object? What reveals its sacred nature to us or anyone who sees it? It is precisely the things that distinguish it from ordinary trees that indicate its sacredness. It is the *decorated* nature of the tree, with all its colored balls, lights, stars, and other ornaments, that identifies it as a sacred tree. There are no natural trees that look like Yule trees with all their decorations. The same is true of maypoles. It is their decoration with ribbons and garlands that identifies them as sacred poles, world poles (Fig. 3.22). The same is true of churches and altars. From these examples, an important principle emerges for interpreting prehistoric remains, namely, *sacred objects are usually distinguished from ordinary objects by their decoration* (Rappaport 1999:50).

Yet another contemporary manifestation of the concept that supernatural spirits and shamans fly through the air, entering and leaving homes via smoke holes or chimneys, are the witches portrayed as riding through the air at Halloween (Fig. 3.23; see also Ginzburg 1991:73, 90, 93, 109, 257). Like shamans, they typically had animal spirit allies and entered ecstatic states. In the late medieval and Renaissance periods of Europe, they, too, were generally thought to leave and enter houses by the smoke hole or chimney and frequently rode brooms, one of the sacred implements of the hearth that connects people with other realms. Rural folk would often go to witches for healing or help in spiritual matters, and, like shamans, witches could also curse, or at least they were often blamed for misfortunes.

Does Shamanism Work?

In these days of momentous medical advances and increasing popularity of alternative medical approaches, the most important question that many people want answered is whether shamanism really works. In dealing with the occult or supernatural, as in dealing with scientific claims, we need reality checks to determine whether a concept or approach deserves our attention or whether we are wasting our time on delusions and fabrications. There have been no studies to test the effectiveness of shamanistic healing that I am aware of. However, numerous doctors and researchers have drawn attention to the very important role the mind plays in catalyzing the healing process using the body's own immune system and other internal resources. Herbert Benson (1996; Roush 1997), the founder of Harvard University's Mind/Body Medical Institute, in particular, has explored these relationships. There also exists a considerable body of medical and biological literature that documents these same effects (Sternberg 2000; Dossey 1993; Cousins 1989). The most recent study of antidepressant drugs found that 75 percent of their effectiveness relied on placebo effects, that is, suggestion effects (Enserink 1999).

Probably least controversial of the research are those findings in the burgeoning field of psychoneuroimmunology (PNI). This field explores the relationship between psychology and biology. Researchers like Cohen and Herbert (1996), Bartop (1977), Schleifer (1983), Stone (1994), Futterman and colleagues (1992), and Lefcourt, Davidson-Katz, and Kueneman (1990) have all found significant relationships between emotional state and biological function. Perceptions of control over one's life and situation have also been studied by Reynaert and colleagues (1995), Wiedenfeld (1990), and Greer (1991). In each of these studies, the *perception* of having some measure of influence or control over one's own health state was shown to greatly influence patients' mental and physiological health.

In a particularly important study by Simonton and colleagues (in Hall 1983), 150 terminally ill patients with medically incurable cancer and a prognosis of one year to live were enrolled in a treatment program using relaxation, visualization, and guided imagery, not dissimilar to traditional shamanic techniques. Two years after their diagnoses, which predicted death within one year, 63 of the 150 patients (40 percent) were still alive. Of the 63 patients who were still alive two years after they were considered terminally ill, 27 percent had stabilized and 22 percent showed no evidence of cancer. Other studies have supported these kinds of effects of mind in disease progression (Antoni et al. 1991; Radojevic et al. 1992; Fawzy et al. 1993; Meares 1978, 1979).

Aside from the mental imagery techniques used by many traditional shamans, the use of "hands-on" therapy has proven medically effective as well. Over the last several decades an alternative treatment called "therapeutic touch" or "laying on of hands" has been studied and shown to provide significant effects on disease and health (Meares 1978; Krueger 1975; Quin 1984).

Impressive results have also been documented in the field of hypnosis and suggestion. In a groundbreaking study on the effects of suggestion, Ikemi and Nakagawa (1962) were able to randomly elicit or inhibit allergic skin reactions using only suggestion. These results have been supported by similar studies on hypnosis and suggestion by Black (1963), Wink (1961), Willard (1977), Hall (1983), and Mason and Black (1958). In light of the above medical research it is clear that many traditional shamanic techniques can have predictable, measurable, and beneficial effects on the human biological body. Thus, it is hardly surprising that such techniques have persisted for many millennia.

While there may be grounds for arguing about whether shamans really have any effect in the spirit world, there can be little doubt that by manipulating powerful symbols in which patients believe, by performing emotionally powerful enactments of supernatural battles that their patients believe are literally taking place, and by using realistic sleights of hand to convince patients that maleficent materials have been removed from their bodies, the shaman can galvanize the patient's own biological and mental defenses into action by stimulating old-brain survival mechanisms. These natural defenses can frequently defeat disease and restore the patient back to good health (Winkelman 1991; 1992:117ff.; 2000:77, 107 144, 184–94, 116, 224, 234–35, 253–68).

Do shamans use tricks and sleights-of-hand in their cures? Of course many of them do, but only to increase the effectiveness of the belief in the cure for the patient and participants. This does not mean that shamanism is an invalid or bogus practice or belief system. Such shamanic practices are similar to, but probably much more powerful than, the well-known placebo effects of doctors prescribing sugar pills to some patients. However, the shaman must also be part psychotherapist in order to deal with psychosomatic illnesses and real mental illnesses. The shamanic ceremony and the family or social support that usually accompanies the healing are probably much more effective in dealing with both psychosomatic and mental illnesses than standard Western medicine. More than one anthropologist has also drawn attention to the basic similarities between shamanism and Western psychotherapy in terms of using shared world myths between patient and healer (theories of the subconscious and early experiences in Industrial societies versus traditional religious worldviews of soul loss and recapture). The healer proposes that the patient's problem lies with his or her relation to the mythic world, the healer attaches the patient's emotions to transactional symbols in the mythic world, and the healer manipulates these symbols to help the transaction of emotion (Dow 1986; Lévi-Strauss 1963:Chap. 10; Jilek 1993).

Minimally, at this level, shamanism works. It is probably the best solution to situations in which there is effectively no medical technology except the use of herbs, which shamans also use. However, shamanism is not a miracle cure-all. It was essentially ineffective in stopping the smallpox, influenza, and other deadly epidemics that ravaged native populations in the Americas during the early years of European contact, killing anywhere from 50 to 90 percent of the original inhabitants of the hemisphere. On the other hand, as Jilek (1982:109–28; 1993; 1994; Jilek and Jilek-Aall 1978, 1990) notes, shamanism frequently has success where modern medicine fails, especially in treating addictions, depressions, or perhaps even common colds. He provides clinical documentation from the Northwest Coast of North America on the effectiveness of spirit dancing in treating psychophysiological disorders as well as antisocial, neurotic, and aggressive behavior (Jilek 1982:96–97).

Shamanism Varies throughout the World

Michael Winkelman (1990:319–21) argues that shamanism was once universally practiced throughout the world when only hunter-gatherers roamed the earth. While this may have been true, today there are many variations between cultures in the occurrence

Fig. 3.24. In the Arctic, landscapes tend to be bleak and barren, such as the land surrounding this old Hudson's Bay Company building in Iqaluit. Nights are exceptionally long, snow cover tends to absorb sounds, hunger can be a regular feature of life, and movement is restricted for long periods. These conditions of sensory deprivation predispose many people to spontaneously enter altered states of consciousness. Photo by Barbara Winter.

of shamanism, in shamanic costumes, in the use of drums, in specific techniques of curing, in supernatural concepts, and perhaps even in beliefs about the axis mundi. We have already tarried too long in the shamanic world to be able to explore these variations. For further documentation, you can consult the works of Eliade (1964) and Hoppal (1992). Before leaving this topic, however, it is worth mentioning one clear ecologically related variation of shamanism. This involves the use of drugs to induce ecstatic states.

In the far north, in the circumpolar environments, life is periodically very harsh. Temperatures are extreme, people often go hungry for days, the snow-covered landscapes are monotonous, and the winters are plunged in perpetual darkness and stillness except for the wind (Fig. 3.24). There is little fuel for fires. Sensory deprivations can be almost absolute for long periods of time. If there is a place on earth where people might be expected to break into spontaneous altered or ecstatic states, the far north is it. In fact, breakdowns of people's contact with reality are so common that there is a specific name for them: Arctic hysterias (Foulks 1972). Under these conditions, little additional stimulus is generally needed to put shamans and their audiences into altered or ecstatic states, which probably accounts for many of the extraordinary tales of shamans' seances, such as flying through the air and spirit visitations. In short, no drug-induced states of ecstasy are needed in the far north.

In the much more lush environments of Central and South America, however, life seems to be much easier, more stimulating, and more varied. There is no prolonged sensory deprivation, not as much starvation, not as much pain and suffering—or so some people argue. Under these conditions, it is much more difficult to enter into ecstatic states unless they are artificially induced by prolonged isolation, fasting, and other techniques, or by the use of drugs. Many people contend that because psychotropic plants and animals (such as toads) abound in these warmer areas, shamanism has taken a very different developmental turn in these areas (although central Asian shamans also used *Amanita* mushrooms). Shamans in these tropical areas are considerably different from shamans farther to the north. They do not generally use drums; they do not have elaborate costumes; they rely on drugs to achieve ecstatic states (Furst 1972); and there is more energetic acting out of spirit confrontations (Fig. 3.25), as can be seen in Napoleon Chagnon's documentary video *Magical Death*. The suggestion is also sometimes made that these drug-induced experiences seem less real than experiences stemming from the use of other physiological or mental techniques. Under

Fig. 3.25. In the lush forests of the tropics there is a great deal of sensory stimulation, and food is generally available. Under these conditions, many individuals, for example, the Yanomamo shamans depicted here, resort to psychotropic substances in order to enter into altered states. From N. Chagnon, *Yanomamo: The Fierce People,* Fig. 29. New York: Holt, Rinehart & Winston, 1977.

the influence of drugs, the shaman's images may be less his own and less under his control. The same might be said of the alcohol-induced ecstatic states of shamans that I met in Guatemala. It is not my place to make value judgments in these areas, although I would note that even if drugs can be useful in opening up new perceptions, their systematic use was ultimately abjured even by Carlos Castañeda's Don Juan.

It is also worth mentioning that, in general, both men and women can become shamans, although some cultures emphasize one sex or the other. There are also some cultures that have fairly strong traditions of shamans changing their gender or becoming bigendered, especially in the Plains and western North America, far Northeast Asia, island Southeast Asia, and East Africa (Campbell 1983:174). Shamans generally have quite high social status, sometimes more from the fear that they instill than from their good works; and in more complex cultures, there are actual social ranks or grades of shamans, a topic that will be dealt with again in Chapter 5.

Shamanism Lives in the Industrial World

It is often easy for filmmakers and popular writers to romanticize about the past and the traditional pre-Industrial world. Mystics can be portrayed as living in peaceful surroundings and meditating. It may seem as though pondering koans and achieving ecstatic states was easier under those conditions. Perhaps for some reclusive mystics or shamans, fasting alone for 30 days in the Arctic, this was the case. However, from my experiences, traditional communities are anything but tranquil. There are always crying children, barking dogs, squawking chickens, squealing pigs, noisy insects, all living cheek by jowl and intruding on anyone's ability to concentrate. Life is seldom easy by Industrial standards. It is physically hard and demanding and offers little free time. There are also nuisances like insects and rats scampering overhead, making noise in the thatch, or occasionally dropping onto people below. Perhaps this is why monasteries were built in the past. Today, it is probably far easier to find quiet, isolated rooms for meditation in Industrial communities than it was under traditional conditions.

In today's society, has shamanism disappeared entirely, or are there vestiges that remain besides our seasonal nods to visiting spirits at Christmas, Halloween, and Groundhog Day? Many of the world's myths appear to have been forged from the template of shamanism, especially those featuring death or severe trials, journeys to the underworld, and rebirth.

- Odin, one of the Germanic gods, was hung on the world tree and had one eye plucked out by ravens in order to learn the secret of the runes (Ginzburg 1991:139);
- The bones of the Egyptian god Osiris were gathered together and brought back to life;
- The Sumerian goddess Inanna descended to the land of the dead and returned;
- Persephone, the Greek goddess, was abducted by Hades into the underworld but brought back (together with all plant life) by her mother for six months of the year;
- Orpheus descended to land of the dead to bring back his lover;
- Aphrodite, the goddess of love, also descended to the land of the dead to bring her child Adonis back to this world;
- Odysseus' epic journey took him to fantastic lands and sorcerers' abodes;
- Ishtar, the Babylonian goddess, went to the underworld to bring back her lover;
- Beowulf, the early Germanic warrior, slew a supernatural dragon;
- Jesus Christ was tortured and killed and rose from the dead to help others;
- Indian yogis also suffered physical pains and self-tortures in order to achieve spiritual wisdom and enlightenment (Eliade 1982:57ff).

In many of these stories, it is interesting to note the recurring theme of not eating or drinking while in the underworld—anyone who does must stay in the underworld forever, and for this reason Persephone must return to the underworld. The theme also occurs in North American myths (Jilek 1992:92). In European myths, fairies often take humans to their banquets and give them food from their supernatural realms (Ginzburg 1991:108); the human emerges after the meal to find that an entire century has passed—or never emerges at all. Are these myths the only other shreds to remain of our shamanic heritage?

While it may be difficult to find any individuals who have undergone a traditional shamanic initiation or who go forth into the spirit world to retrieve the lost souls of those who are sick, there are a number of specialized roles in Industrial societies that seem to have taken on some of the specific functions of the shamans of yore. I have already mentioned the psychotherapists who, in effect, journey into the realms of the subconscious spirits in order to battle the demons of the subconscious and heal the sick (but not in ecstatic states). There are other people who have taken over the social role of the shaman and who, like shamans, behave in ways outside social norms. These people induce ecstatic states in other people in social contexts employing drums and singing, powerful symbols and costumes, and drugs or alcohol. Perhaps it can be said that they heal feelings of anomie or soul loss among many adolescents. They provide emotional release and feelings of well-being. These are the music stars of young generations (Hutson

1999, 2000; Wallis 2003). The most recent manifestation of this facet of shamanism is the rave.

> In general practice, a "rave" usually refers to a party, usually all night long . . . where loud "techno" music is mostly played and many people partake in a number of different chemicals, though the latter is far from necessary. . . . At a rave, the DJ is a shaman, a priest, a channeller of energy—they control the psychic voyages of the dancers through . . . manipulating the music, sometimes working with just a set of beats and samples, into a tapestry of mind bending music. A large part of the concept of raves is built upon sensory overload—a barrage of audio and very often visual stimuli are brought together to elevate people into an altered state of physical or psychological existence. http://www.plur.ne.mediaone.net/rave.html

Summary

Shamanism is one of the most fundamental aspects of traditional religions. It provides a good example of an ecologically related type of religion, since it seems to be based on adaptive abilities to enter into altered states together with specific social and economic conditions of nomadic peoples such as hunter-gatherers (Winkelman 1990:320–21). It is not universal, but it is very widespread and of undoubted antiquity, as we will see in the next chapter. Its defining characteristics are the use of ecstatic (or sometimes only altered) states in order to retrieve souls of the sick from malicious spirits or to obtain information or other benefits from supernatural realms for individuals in the community. Unfortunately, shamans are not always as good as romantic Westerners might like them to be. There are both good and bad, as in any profession.

In order to understand shamanism, one must understand the traditional concept of the world as a sacred place imbued with vital forces that can be tapped into for one's benefit or that can erupt unexpectedly. The axis mundi (world tree) and a three-tiered universe also figure prominently in the shamanic world. There are many techniques for entering into altered and ecstatic states, but the intensity of these states can vary considerably from mild to extremely intense levels. When people are in altered or ecstatic states, they become very susceptible to suggestions and values or concepts that may be promoted by others (Jilek 1982:28). Therefore, the specific content of ecstatic visions (such as Christ, Buddha, Kali, the Book of Mormon, Davidian revelations, or Temple of the Sun) should never be taken at face value as representing reality, whether on earth or any other plane of existence. If there is a message about reality in these experiences, it must be sought in the general nature of the experience (such as the simple existence of more powerful forces), not in the specific details, revelations, or associated dogmas.

Shamanism and early ecstatic religious states have conferred upon our bodies and our culture a legacy that we cannot divest ourselves of. It erupts irrepressibly in our music emporiums. It structures many of our institutions and behaviors. It enchants our children and strikes respondent cords in their hearts. Now that we have explored the key concepts of this foreign yet dimly familiar realm, it is time to look in more detail at the first actual archaeological signs of religious behavior in which our ancestors engaged.

CHAPTER 4

The Primal Paleolithic

On 21 June 1970, in the Great Desert of Australia, I witnessed the transformation of a man into his remote ancestor. Other men beat out entrancing rhythms and droned nasal chants for hours. The man entered a sacred space and existed in a sacred time. With a sliver of glass, he opened a vein in his arm, letting his blood pour out, enough to fill a small bowl. Then, with the help of others, he decorated his body with white and red plant fluff, using his blood to make it stick to his body in strange ritual shapes, shapes unknown in the natural world. Gradually, the transformation took place until at last it was complete. The man was no longer merely human but had been totally transformed into his totemic ancestor in every movement, look, and feeling (Fig. 4.1). This scene had probably been repeated over thousands of generations stretching back into the most remote times.

No one knows exactly when such rituals began. They may have begun with the advent of language, or even before. They may have begun with the making of the first tools, or perhaps after. They may have begun with the emergence of the most modern human forms, or before. Rituals like the one I witnessed and like the shamanistic trance rituals of the African Bushmen (Katz 1982b) leave virtually no archaeological traces. The stone tools used to make the beating sticks or the costume paraphernalia are no different from the tools used for everyday activities. The fires and meals are not distinctive or different from everyday fires or everyday meals. There are usually no special structures. Even images painted on rock surfaces do not last long. Ochre washes away, and surfaces of rocks erode after thousands of years unless they are protected by special conditions. Thus, rituals like these could have been performed from the very dawn of humanity. And archaeologists would never be able to tell.

Ethnographic observations among hunter-gatherers and other traditional groups provide archaeologists with some inkling of what ritual life may have been like in the distant past. If the ecological conditions and adaptations of the present and past groups are relatively similar, reasonably persuasive arguments can be made that the ritual life of

Fig. 4.1. In traditional rituals, a person's consciousness is transformed by ritual and costumes so that individual identities merge with those of totemic ancestors, as among these Australian Aborigines, or with other supernatural entities. Participants in these rituals feel that they have become their totemic ancestors. From B. Spencer and F. Gillen, *The Arunta*, Figs. 82 and 84. London: Macmillan, 1927.

the past may have been similar to the present. But in all cases, inference about past behavior based on observations of living groups should be treated as hypotheses about the past that need to be tested with archaeological observations before being accepted. Clearly some such hypotheses seem more likely than others, especially if there are similar material remains. There is one important archaeological clue that enables us to determine that something similar to the Australian ritual I witnessed was probably occurring at least by some 300,000 or more years ago. However, before discussing this clue and subsequent developments, it is necessary to lay out the time frame of the Old Stone Age and some of the terms associated with it.

PALEOLITHIC PEOPLE ESTABLISH THE FIRST RELIGIONS

The *Paleolithic,* or *Old Stone Age,* is an old term, coined by prehistorians in the late nineteenth century. It defines the technological period in which people used chipped stone tools for cutting and scraping objects. This period extends from the first appearance of such tools, some 2.5 million years ago, until the appearance of ground stone tools about 10,000 years "before present" (abbreviated simply as B.P.). This is an enormous stretch of time, during which a number of important biological and cultural changes took place (Fig. 4.2). Therefore, it should not come as a surprise to learn that the Paleolithic has been subdivided. There are three major divisions that most archaeologists use, although these vary somewhat from continent to continent:

1. The Lower Paleolithic: from 2.5 million years ago until 250,000 B.P. At this time the only possible indication of religion is the potential presence of ochres and special treatment of human bones.
2. The Middle Paleolithic: from 250,000 to 35,000 B.P. At this time, other indicators suggestive of ritual and supernatural beliefs appear in the archaeological record.
3. The Upper Paleolithic: the period between 35,000 and 10,000 years ago. This is the time when complex hunters and gatherers emerge, together with evidence for special kinds of rituals.

In Chapter 2, we read about how protopeople were transformed into upright, walking, and probably talking, tool-using early ancestors of humans. The first tool makers were a form of human called *Homo habilis,* or perhaps a more primitive form called *Australopithecus.* With gradual improvements in their mental abilities (reflected by increasing brain size), these hominids evolved into a slightly larger form of humans called *Homo erectus* about one million years ago. These were human forms that roamed the earth in the Lower Paleolithic (Fig. 4.2). Archaic, thick-skulled forms of *Homo sapiens* (the species to which we belong) emerged some 250,000 years ago and are associated with *all basic modern forms of behavior* (Mcbrearty and Brooks 2000). One branch of these archaic-looking people became the European Neanderthals, who appeared more rugged than contemporary people (Figs. 4.2, 4.3). These are the human forms that existed in the Middle Paleolithic. There are differing opinions on when the Middle Paleolithic began. I have used a rather early beginning for this period (250,000–300,000) in order to reflect ritual and other cultural developments (Mcbrearty and Brooks 2000). Fully modern-looking people evolved about 100,000 B.P. in Africa but arrived in Europe only about 35,000 years ago, bringing with them Upper Paleolithic technologies. Some

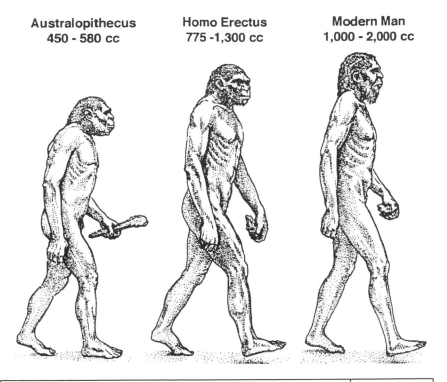

Australopithecus
450 - 580 cc

Homo Erectus
775 -1,300 cc

Modern Man
1,000 - 2,000 cc

Fig. 4.2. This is a time line of the various stages of religious development in the Paleolithic, showing the corresponding climates and human forms associated with each stage. Top: human forms and their brain sizes (cranial capacities in cubic centimeters), adapted from F. Howell, *Early Man,* p. 45. New York: Time-Life Books, 1965. Bottom drafted by Greg Holoboff and B. Hayden.

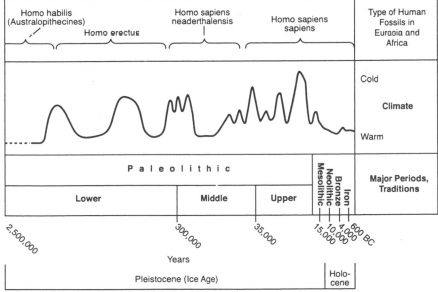

people even argue that Europe was a kind of genetic and cultural backwater far on the outskirts of genetic developments during most of the Paleolithic.

The details of this evolutionary scenario are not critical for our present purposes. Once *Homo erectus* appeared on the scene, and perhaps before, the basic human hunting and gathering adaptation appears to have been set, and subsequent changes over the next

Fig. 4.3. Some of the more plausible versions of what Neanderthals (top right) and Upper Paleolithic people (others) looked like are provided by these striking images by Benoît Clarys and Zdenek Burian. Neanderthal drawing reproduced with permission of the Anthropos Institute, Moravian Museum. Other drawings reprinted with the permission of Benoît Clarys (biface@swing.be).

million years probably represented only refinements. Even the range of *Homo erectus* brain sizes (775–1,300 cc) overlaps considerably with fully modern individuals (1,000–2,000 cc). From a technological and subsistence point of view, the Lower and Middle Paleolithic taken together represent an extremely long evolutionary stretch (2.5 million to 35,000 B.P.) of remarkable stability and very little change. This was the period of generalized, or technologically simple, hunter-gatherers who were the descendants of primates forced out onto the savannas or at least those who managed to survive. That there was so little change over the course of more than two million years is a striking testimony to the relative success of the generalized hunter-gatherer cultural and biological adaptations made by these early ancestors.

The lifestyle of hunter-gatherers is probably the most radically different from Industrial cultures of any existing cultures. All of the archaeological evidence from the earlier Paleolithic periods is consistent with a picture of small nomadic bands (of fewer than 30 people) moving over large areas every few weeks to take advantage of resources in different locations and at different times. As a result, there were no permanent structures. We can also infer that resources must have been scarce, that there was no long-term storage of food, and that population levels were very low. Among contemporary hunter-gatherers

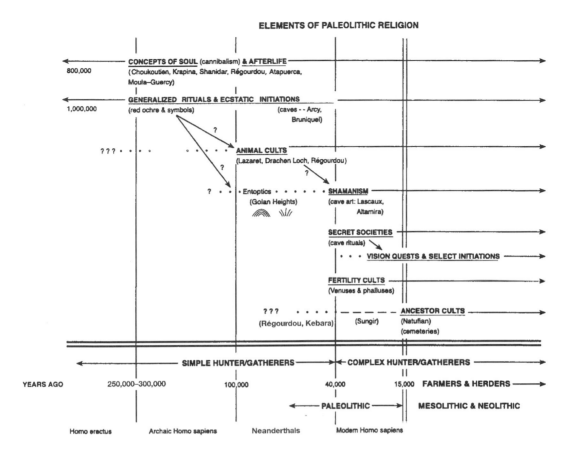

ELEMENTS OF PALEOLITHIC RELIGION

Fig. 4.4. Archaeological evidence attests to a number of different types of ritual behaviors. This graph indicates these various kinds of rituals and when the first evidence for them appears in the archaeological record. Drafted by Greg Holoboff and B. Hayden.

living under such conditions, sharing is imperative for survival, competition using resources is destructive and forbidden, and egotistical behavior is not tolerated. Nor are claims to private property recognized (see Hayden 1993b). As discussed in Chapter 2, it is difficult to imagine this basic hunter-gatherer adaptation working well without some form of cooperative alliances firmly bonded by kinship systems and rituals involving members of different bands. These kinds of alliances were common among remnant hunter-gatherers living in resource-poor environments during the last century.

There are basic similarities between contemporary generalized hunter-gatherers living in areas with limited resources and the characteristics that can be inferred about prehistoric hunter-gatherers during the Lower and Middle Paleolithic. In fact, in terms of what can be inferred from material remains about basic daily behavior, there have been few or no significant changes from the latter part of the Lower Paleolithic until the ethnographic present in places like Central Australia. When I camped with Australian Aborigines sheltered only by traditional windbreaks in their Central Desert, I could see no essential difference between the organization and material remains of those shelters and Acheulian or even Oldowan camping remains left some 100,000 to 2,000,000 years earlier in Africa. Thus, I think that it makes sense to examine closely the basic kinds of rituals and religious organizations of recent simple hunter-gatherers in relation to archaeological evidence. Inferences about early prehistoric religion can be organized under five headings, which I would suggest are typical of "forager" (generalized hunter-

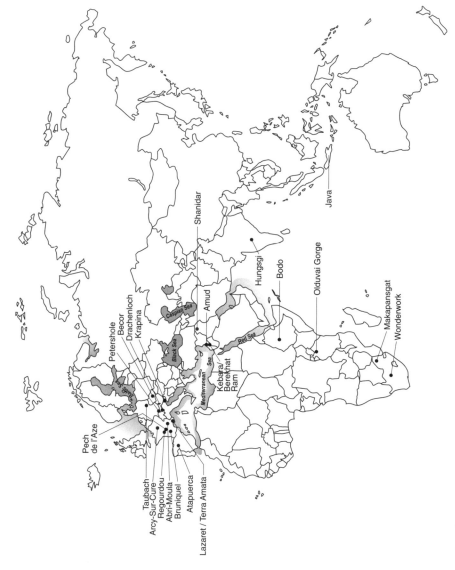

Fig. 4.5. The most important Paleolithic archaeological sites discussed in the text are shown on this map. Drafted by Greg Holoboff.

gatherer) religions: (1) concepts of the soul and an afterlife; (2) generalized rituals and initiations; (3) animal cults; (4) possible ancestor cults; and (5) possible shamanism (Fig. 4.4). These will be discussed in more detail in the following sections.

NOTIONS OF THE AFTERLIFE: GRISLY REMAINS REVEAL RELIGIOUS IDEAS

The first inklings of a notion of soul or afterlife come in the form of a reddish-brown jasper cobble left at Makapansgat, South Africa, about three million years ago (Fig. 4.5). This cobble was water worn and naturally eroded so that it resembles a human face (Fig. 4.6). The closest source for this type of stone occurs 10 km from the site, so evidently the cobble was picked up by protohumans because of its resemblance to a face and was brought to their habitation site (Dart 1974; Oakley 1981). This anthropomorphization of a simple stone represents the first indication of self-awareness and thus perhaps symbolic or even spiritual qualities among our ancestors. Whether such awareness extended to rudimentary concepts of a soul or afterlife is more conjectural.

But there are even more controversial archaeological remains relevant to a discussion of early belief in souls—remains dating back to about a million years ago. These remains reveal the defleshing of skulls and possible evidence for cannibalism. Controversy revolves around whether these remains, in fact, represent cannibalistic or ritual activities, and, if they do, whether such activities really imply notions of souls or afterlives. There are many people in archaeology who are extremely reluctant to embrace the notion that cannibalism was ever a feature of the prehistoric past (Arens 1979; Bahn 1990). Although there is abundant ethnographic documentation that cannibalism was not at all uncommon in the last few centuries (Sanday 1986; Hogg 1966), some authors insist on iron-clad proofs before they are willing to accept this hard-to-swallow notion of our early ancestors.

The early evidence comes from archaeological deposits like those in the 800,000-year-old eating refuse in Atapuerca Cave in Spain, which contain cut-up and smashed bones from six people (Gibbons 1997). In the middle Paleolithic, Defleur and colleagues (1999) have also uncovered incontrovertible evidence of Neanderthal cannibalism (Lorblanchet 1999:69–71 cites additional examples). These finds remind me of the time I was excavating a trash deposit in an abandoned storage pit in Guatemala, some 1,500 years old. Among all the broken pots and discarded avocado seeds, I was surprised to find the bones of a human foot, all still in their articulated position, half shoved in a discarded pot. There was no doubt in my

Fig. 4.6. This remarkable natural stone resembling a human head was picked up by a hominid ancestor three million years ago and left at its camp at Makapansgat in South Africa. It demonstrates a humanlike awareness of self-consciousness and perhaps an artistic sense at a very early time period. Photo courtesy of Geoff Blundell.

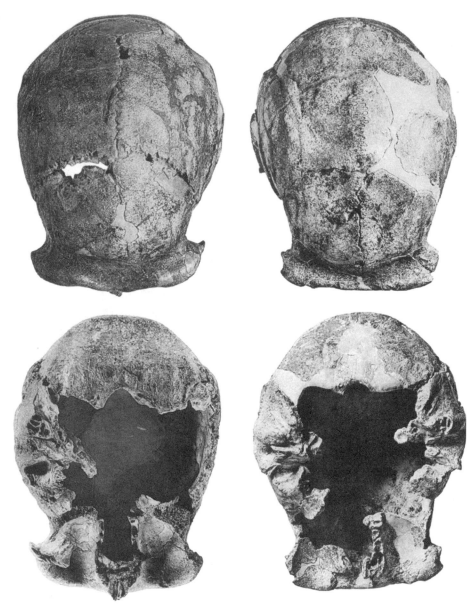

Fig. 4.7. A number of *Homo erectus* skulls, about 400,000–500,000 years old, were recovered from the Choukoutien site near Beijing, China. Almost all of them had their basal portions broken away, as shown here, leading Weidenreich and others to the conclusion that the bottoms had been broken in order to extract the brains for cannibal meals. From F. Weidenreich, *The Skull of Sinanthropus Pekinensis,* pp. 343, 357. Pehpei, Chungking: Geological Survey of China, 1943.

mind that these were the remains of a cannibalistic meal—an impression greatly reinforced when I later read the sixteenth-century accounts of the conquistadors, who described how Indian allies would cut off the hands and feet of slain enemies and eat them because they were the most relished parts (e.g., Lopez 1941:228). Similarly, I have few doubts that cannibalism was being practiced by *Homo erectus* bands in Java and China some 300,000–500,000 years ago (Fig. 4.7). At some of these sites, the skulls were smashed or the bottom of the skulls was broken open, presumably to extract the brain and eat it (Pei 1932; Weidenreich 1943:185–90; Wolpoff 1986). Some skulls had cut marks as well, presumably from defleshing.

Although, a few scholars prefer to search for alternative explanations for these patterns of damage (Jacob 1972, 1981; Bahn 1990; Trinkaus 1985; see also Binford and

Ho 1985), in my view, cannibalism is the most parsimonious interpretation, and strong evidence for it continues throughout the Paleolithic (Villa 1992; Gibbons 1997). Cannibalism is well documented among animals such as rodents, squirrels, lions, jackals, bears, and primates (Goodall 1990:73–80, 162–68; Hiraiwa-Hasegawa 1992:331; McGrew 1992:99, 153) as well as among a wide range of ethnographic human societies. Why should we expect any different behavior on the part of those in the intervening stages of evolution? It is very difficult to interpret the clutch of 12 Neanderthal skulls found at Krapina in northern Croatia with all their bases missing, or the three Neanderthal skulls and other bones with cut marks from Abri Moula in southeast France, in any other way (Defleur et al. 1993, 1999).

However, even if we accept, for the sake of argument, that cannibalism did exist in the early Paleolithic, does this indicate the existence of concepts such as the soul or simply the consumption of deceased community members or even of outside individuals viewed as not quite human? Typically, many hunter-gatherers and simple horticulturalists view any strangers as enemies if they cannot establish kinship or other close connections to someone in the community. Such strangers are often killed. But some people have argued that the intentional breaking open of skulls in order to remove brains has special connotations, for the head is often viewed as the seat of the soul in mankind. Cannibals in recent centuries broke open the base of skulls in precisely the same fashion to extract the brains of their victims in order to acquire their strength and vital forces. Whether the person whose brain was extracted and eaten was an enemy or a relative (in New Guinea, some people ate their dead relatives) makes little difference for the inference that some concept of soul motivated this kind of behavior. The 25 cut marks made with a stone tool on the skull of a 600,000-year-old *Homo erectus* individual from Bodo, Ethiopia, also attest to some special consideration for the dead and a probable mortuary ritual, since the aim seems to have been to remove the skin from the skull (T. White 1986). There seems to be no practical reason for removing skin from skulls since there is almost no meat on the skull. It would seem therefore that some other symbolic goals motivated its removal. The most likely symbolic motives imply some concept of a spirit essence in the skull.

This may be the first clear indication that we have of a concept of soul or afterlife. Most of the sites mentioned above and their remains originate between 400,000 and 1,000,000 years ago. However, even here, the argument that the cannibalistic eating of brains may have been gustatory in nature, without any implications for concepts of souls, may not be easy to dismiss. In fact, chimpanzees have been observed removing the heads of young killed baboons and breaking open the base of the skulls in order to extract the brains, which they apparently relish as a food (Goodall 1971:200). The same may have been true of the early *Homo erectus,* although the cut marks on the Bodo skull are much more difficult to interpret in anything but a symbolic fashion. The evidence for a soul and afterlife concept is considerably stronger after 150,000 years B.P., when intentional burials begin to occur (as discussed below).

Red Paints a Very General Picture: Generalized Rituals, Initiations, and Ritual Ecstasy

The next evidence for some sort of ritual behavior and religious belief comes in the form of the color red, red ochre to be specific. Red ochre is a soft iron oxide that readily imparts its color to anything that it comes in contact with. Ochre occurs naturally in some rocks. Ethnographically, sources of this coloring agent were often highly prized by hunter-gatherers. It was used universally in the hunter-gatherer world as a sacred coloring agent for decorating bodies or tools or ritual paraphernalia, whether in Africa, Europe, the Americas, Asia, or Australia. In fact, long before our ancestors were using ochre for coloring objects or themselves red, there is clear evidence for a fascination with this color. We have already noted the head-shaped red jasper cobble that was transported many kilometers and deposited at Makapansgat Cave by Australopithecines several million years ago. Exotic red nodules were left in late Oldowan deposits one million years ago. And red ochre begins to appear on habitation sites in South Africa about 900,000 years ago (Bednarik 1994:172; Lorblanchet 1999:103–11). These and other early occurrences of ochre represent coloring agents brought into habitation sites but lack clear signs of modification or use. By 250,000 years ago, there is good evidence for the use of red ochre, and sometimes yellow or brown ochres, or black manganese pebbles (Lorblanchet 1999:103–11; Mcbrearty and Brooks 2000).

By the time Neanderthals appeared in Europe some 150,000 years ago, ochre was being brought to some habitation sites on a regular basis and was ground into powder or made into "crayons" (Schmandt-Besserat 1980; Bednarik 1994; Beyries and Walter 1996). Ochres were so important by this time that people were actually mining them in South Africa (Bednarik 1994). When complex hunter-gatherer societies emerged during the Upper Paleolithic (about 35,000 B.P. in Europe), red ochre was widely used, and its use continued thereafter until the advent of synthetic paints in Industrial times.

What can red ochre tell us about prehistoric beliefs and religion? When I initially said that simple hunter-gatherer rituals could be performed for hundreds of thousands of years without leaving any distinctive traces, I mentioned that there was one exception. That exception is red ochre. Red ochre has no utilitarian value. It is strictly decorative and symbolic. We can argue about what the specific symbolic meaning was, but given the special efforts expended to procure and use this material and given the clear ritual associations of subsequent contexts in the Upper Paleolithic and in ethnographic contexts, I think a very good argument can be made for the use of red ochre as having some kind of relationship with ritual behavior.

Some people suggest that coloring materials like ochre could have been used for creating paintings, for body painting, or simply for coloring implements and tools to make them more attractive (Marshack 1981). Certainly, when I lived with the Pintupi tribe in central Australia, I saw many boomerangs and shields and spears covered with red ochre. However, in all these cases, it seemed to me that the use of red ochre was not merely to make items more attractive, but that the use was intimately wed to a very strong ritual symbolism of the group. Red ochre was used to color the traditional string headbands of ritually initiated men in central Australia; it was used to color the white plant fluff during totemic ceremonies; it was above all the sacred color of this group, as it was for countless other hunters and gatherers throughout the world. If it was used on spears and shields, it was to reinforce their connection with the sacred and thus make them more alive, more potent, and more effective.

In a seminal article, Ernst Wreschner (1980; see also Dickson 1990:93–94) argued that all human populations have an inherent, archetypal reaction to the color red. People associate it with blood, life, and death. Its ritual use occurs on all continents. It is, in fact, the most basic linguistic color distinction made by all cultures. Alexander Marshack (1981) extends the associations of red to other domains such as status, age, sex, art, and rituals, but it seems to me that these can be viewed as additional layers of meaning or permutations of the basic underlying symbols. Whether there is such an underlying unity of meaning of red or not, it is inconceivable to me that early hunting and gathering groups would have been painting images or decorating their bodies without some kind of symbolic or religious framework for such activities (Dissanayake 1988). Thus, it seems that no matter how red ochre was actually being used, and no matter what its actual specific symbolism for the earliest prehistoric groups, red ochre symbolized some sort of supernatural connotations at the broadest level of meaning. It is therefore probably one of the earliest indicators in the archaeological record for some sort of ritual, symbolism, and general religious expression. Although rarer, the collection of quartz crystals also began at about the same time (Bednarik 1995:611) and must be seen as a component of symbolic and probably ritual behavior, as probably should the Makapansgat cobble head. At a slightly later time period, Neanderthals were collecting shiny iron pyrites and crystal quartz and carrying them over the landscape, presumably for symbolic enhancement of rituals (Hayden 1993b; Otte 1996:273), just as later groups collected and carried pyrites and quartz crystals, especially coveted by religious personnel (Beaune 1995; Taçon 1991; Condominas 1977:95, 121–23, 143–44, 150, 172; Elkin 1964).

ECSTATIC RITUALS

Thus, during the developmental and intermediate periods of religious development, from 1,000,000 to 35,000 B.P., I think that we can infer, with increasing confidence the existence of what I will refer to as "generalized rituals," and "generalized initiations." Strictly speaking, it is not possible to make more precise inferences about the nature of these rituals on the basis of red ochre or even the few relatively abstract symbols that occur during these first phases of religious development. However, the existence of abstract symbols constitutes one of the few additional lines of evidence for ritual behavior and concepts during the early phases of the Paleolithic. Some of these symbolic representations include: (1) an extremely crude, and perhaps debatable, representation of a person some 233,000 years ago at Berekhat Ram on the Golan Heights (Fig. 4.8; see Marshack 1997a); (2) a series of much clearer concentric arcs engraved on a stone (Fig. 4.9) at Quneitra on the Golan Heights some 54,000 years ago (Marshack 1997b); (3) a shaped and rounded mammoth-tooth plaque (Fig. 4.9) at Tata, Hungary, that had been covered with red ochre about 100,000 years ago, as well as crossed lines finely engraved on a fossil at the same site (Fig. 4.9); (4) a series of paired cup marks carved into a slab of rock overlying a Neanderthal grave at La Ferrassie in France (Binant 1991). There are also

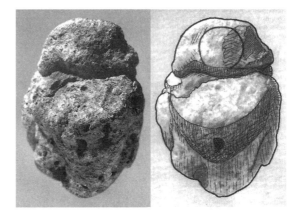

Fig. 4.8. A 233,000-year-old modified stone roughly resembling a human figure was discovered at Berekhat Ram on the Golan Heights. This is the earliest claimed human sculpture in the Paleolithic. From A. Marshack, "The Berekhat Ram Figurine: A Late Acheulian Carving from the Middle East," *Antiquity* 71:329,335 (1997).

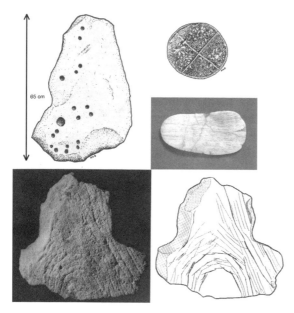

Fig. 4.9. Between 100,000 and 50,000 years ago, simple but clearly intentional abstract art begins to appear on a more consistent basis. Examples include the slab of limestone with paired cup marks that covered an infant burial at La Ferrassie, France (upper left); a fossil engraved with a cross (top right) together with a carefully shaped, smoothed, and ochred piece of a mammoth tooth from Tata, Hungary (middle right); and a series of arcs engraved on a stone from Quneitra on the Golan Heights (bottom). Top left: from R. Bednarik, "Concept-Mediated Marking in the Lower Palaeolithic," *Current Anthropology* 36:610 (1995); published by the University of Chicago Press with copyright by the Wenner-Gren Foundation for Anthropological Research. All rights reserved. Top right: from J. Gowlett, *Ascent to Civilization,* p. 98. New York: McGraw-Hill, 1993. Reprinted with permission of The McGraw-Hill Companies, New York. Bottom: from A. Marshack, "Beyond Art: Pleistocene Image and Symbol," in M. Conkey, O. Soffer, D. Stratmann, and N. Jablonski, eds., *Beyond Art,* p. 55. California Academy of Sciences, Memoir 23, 1997. Used with permission of the California Academy of Sciences.

other sporadic occurrences of zigzags, radiating or parallel lines, or seemingly random marks that cannot confidently be attributed to any symbolic ritual intention (Fig. 4.10).

Robert Bednarik (1995) has suggested that all these simple marks may be the beginnings of attempts to represent concepts graphically. But they also constitute one of the basic patterns that are spontaneously produced with the stimulation of the eye's retina (especially under conditions of altered states of consciousness; see "Entoptics: The Brain Creates Its Own Images" in Chap. 5). Early art motifs may constitute attempts to reproduce such universal visual patterns. Like the use of red ochre, many of the manifestations seem symbolic and some of them (like the mammoth plaque and paired cup marks in Fig. 4.9) seem likely to have been ritual in use or conception, especially when associated with human remains. However, what the exact nature of these rituals was cannot be determined with the evidence now at hand. On the basis of the arguments developed in Chapter 2 involving the survival advantages of participating with other groups in kinship systems and ecstatic rituals connected to higher powers, I strongly suspect that some of these objects and much of the red ochre were being used in ecstatic ritual contexts, probably featuring totemic ancestors.

Much more compelling evidence comes quite a bit later, around 50,000 B.P., when Neanderthals begin entering the totally black, deep recesses of European caves for ritual purposes. Although the popular press often refers to prehistoric Europeans as "cave men," in fact, caves were almost never used for living. Rock shelters (rock overhangs; Fig. 4.11) were far preferred for habitation areas since they were less damp and had much better lighting. They also acted to concentrate the warmth of the winter sun if they were south facing. In the few instances when true caves were used for living at all, camps or structures were always made near the mouth of the cave, where there was both light and shelter. The deep recesses of caves were used only for sporadic ritual purposes.

The earliest documented occurrence of such special use of deep caves is the recently discovered Bruniquel Cave in southwestern France. The entrance to this cave had been

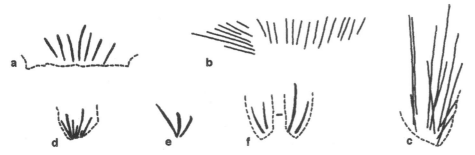

Fig. 4.10. One relatively common engraved motif from the Middle Paleolithic (300,000 to 35,000 years ago) consists of rays of lines such as these. Questions have been raised as to whether these might not simply be incisions left from cutting animal skins, using bones underneath as supports, but in some cases this seems unlikely. From R. Bednarik, "Concept-Mediated Marking in the Lower Palaeolithic," *Current Anthropology* 36:614 (1995). Published by the University of Chicago Press with © copyright by the Wenner-Gren Foundation for Anthropological Research. All rights reserved.

sealed off many thousands of years ago. As a result, no one had disturbed any of the deposits over the many millennia. Only a small air hole betrayed the existence of this underground network of caves. The air hole had been enlarged slightly by its discoverers, but when I entered, it was by far the tightest, most claustrophobic passage that I have ever wormed my way through. Far inside the cave, a quarter of a kilometer from the entrance, as François Rouzaud (Rouzaud, Soulier, and Lignereux 1996) reported, broken stalagmites had been laid down and arranged in two circles, one of which held the charred remains of a fire (Fig. 4.12). There was absolutely no indication that any cave-painting people from the Upper Paleolithic had ever been in the cave, for there were no Upper Paleolithic tools and there were none of the paintings or engravings typical of the Upper Paleolithic on any of the walls of the cave. However, the stalagmite circles were clearly manmade. Rouzaud dated the carbon remains in the ancient hearth and was astonished to find out that it had been lit 50,000 years ago, during the height of the Neanderthal occupation of the area. Neanderthals certainly did not make these stalagmite circles for living in, and there are no tools or food remains evident (although no excavations have been undertaken as yet). Professor Jean Clottes is convinced that

Fig. 4.11. Laugrie Haute in the French Dordogne is one of the best-known "cave" sites in Europe, but it is not a cave at all. It is simply a rock overhang with a big block of stone that has fallen in front of it. These overhangs were so sheltered that modern French inhabitants of the area sometimes built their houses under them, as can be seen here at Laugerie Haute. Photo by B. Hayden.

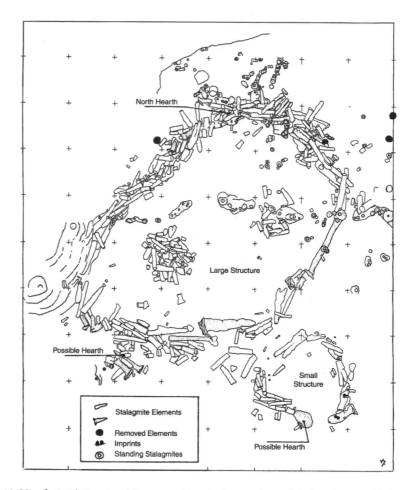

North Hearth

Large Structure

Possible Hearth

Small
Structure

Possible Hearth

Stalagmite Elements

● Removed Elements

Imprints

Standing Stalagmites

Fig. 4.12. Very far inside Bruniquel Cave, several hundred meters beyond the last glimmer of light, Neanderthals apparently built these rings of stalagmites and lit at least one fire some 50,000 years ago. This is one of the first documented cases of the use of deep caves for what must have been ritual purposes with the aim of altering individual consciousnesses for a select group of people. Adapted by Elizabeth Carefoot from F. Rouzaud, M. Soulier, and Y. Lignereux, "La Grotte de Bruniquel," *Spelunca* 60:32 (1996).

these "structures" were being used for ritual purposes. Indeed, there are few other purposes for going so far into black caves other than to experience the darkness and the stillness, to enter into a timeless place where senses and consciousness become altered.

A similar-sized Neanderthal structure also appears to have been built completely in the dark zone about 30 meters inside the Galerie Schoepflin at Arcy-sur-Cure (Fig. 4.13; see also Girard 1976:53; Farizy 1990:307; 1991; Baffier and Girard 1998:18–19), where there were a few tools, broken bones, and a mammoth tusk, which again probably had a symbolic value. The Galerie was certainly not used for normal habitation because, in addition to the darkness, it was very narrow and barely a meter in height. Michel Lorblanchet (1999:76) also notes the early use of these deep caves and cites additional examples such as Cougnac and Grotta della Barura. The simple stone tools found 300 meters inside Drochenhohle Cave may also be from the Middle Paleolithic, although

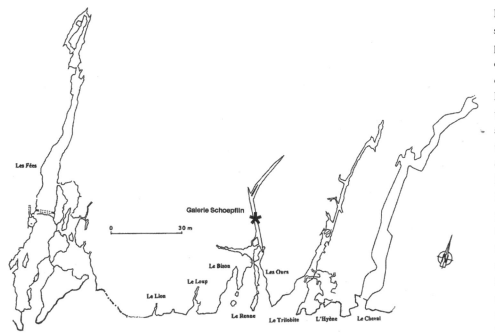

Les Fées

Galerie Schoepflin

0   30 m

Le Bison   Les Ours

Le Loup

Le Lion

Le Renne   Le Trilobite   L'Hyène   Le Cheval

Fig. 4.13. At Arcy-sur-Cure, French prehistorians discovered a long chamber (the Galerie Schoepflin) that had been sealed since the time its Neanderthal occupants had left. Inside the low and narrow passage were the remains of a structure and a mammoth tusk, seeming to represent another ritual use of a deep cave by Neanderthals. From D. Baffier and M. Girard, *Les Cavernes d'Arcy-sur-Cure,* p. 14. Maison des Roches: Paris, 1998. Adapted from originals by P. Guillore, *GSPP—Contribution à l'étude spéléologique des grottes d'Arcy-sur-Cure et de Saint-More,* p. 148 (1964); and R. Humbert, *Fouilles et Monuments Archéologiques en France Metropolitaine. Gallia Préhistoire,* Fig. 1 (1965).

some archaeologists argue for a later date (Tillet 2002). Like the Bruniquel Cave, the entrance to the Galerie Schoepflin had been closed since Neanderthals had last used the cave, preserving everything on the cave floor exactly the way they left it. Thus, I think that the use of these deep caves probably constitutes the first clear material indication in the archaeological record for ecstatic cults, although there is a very good chance that such cults existed hundreds of thousands of years before.

In all rituals and initiations, a sacred area is used or created to serve as the portal to supernatural dimensions. Upon entry, people are considered to leave the ordinary world and ordinary time. They enter another, sacred world and exist in sacred time, which in many respects is timeless, as many stories of people who visit fairy mounds for "a night" indicate, for when they return many years have passed. It is therefore important to establish clear ritual procedures for returning to normal space and normal time. These are essential elements of all ecstatic rituals in traditional religions (Leach 1961:129–36; Eliade 1959), and they were probably also regular components of the earliest rituals and initiations. These experiences were undoubtedly among the most intense and meaningful ones in early hunter-gatherer cultures.

INITIATIONS

Observations of recent hunter-gatherers also suggest that the first human rituals probably involved some kind of healing or initiation ceremonies, and it seems very likely that red ochre could have been used in initiation contexts. In the later prehistoric periods and even up until the nineteenth century, hunter-gatherers occupied a remarkable range of habitats, some with abundant food, others with little food, some with cold or rainy climates, others with hot and arid climates. It is important to keep this variability in mind whenever discussing prehistoric cultures (see Kelly 1995 for an excellent ecological analysis of hunter-gatherer variability). However, in the very early periods at the dawn of humanity, most of our ancestors may have occupied a much more limited range of habitats, especially semiarid savanna parklands, where resources were mobile or spaced far apart and not particularly abundant. Under these conditions, sharing food was imperative for survival, as were alliances of mutual help (see Chap. 2). Egocentric or selfish behavior and any type of exploitation or self-aggrandizement would undoubtedly have been strictly prohibited. This is one reason why hunter-gatherer cultures seem so incomprehensible to Industrial citizens, for promoting one's own self-interests is one of the values that modern society is built on; it constitutes our business ethic.

In his analysis of initiation ceremonies, Frank Young (1965) argues that the elaboration of initiation ceremonies occurs as external threats increase. Certainly, the threat of starvation should be seen as an external threat, but there must also have been threats of attack from predators and enemies or even unknown groups. Thus, adherence by everyone to the sharing, mutual helping, and mutual defense values of these early societies must have been critical for everyone's survival. If someone did not follow these precepts or was thought to be even potentially unreliable, this could threaten the survival of others or of the community. Such people could be forced to leave or even be killed. Thus, severe initiation ordeals probably functioned as tests to determine the strength of new adult members' commitment to the community's well-being. The basic theme of such initiations was: If you are not ready to put up with some pain to join us, we can't be sure that you will help us when times get tough. Youths either went through painful initiations or became outcasts.

In this cultural ecological view of severe initiations, one might expect the most severe forms to occur in the most severe environments, because of the higher frequency and greater intensity of periods of hardship. In Australia, a number of authors have noted that this is precisely what occurs. In the relatively well-watered areas of southeastern and northen Australia, initiations are not notable for their severity. However, as the environment becomes progressively drier, adolescent boys are required to submit to the removal of one of their front teeth at initiation. In still drier environments toward the center of Australia, they also have the foreskin of the penis removed with stone tools at initiation (circumcision). In the most severe desert environments, such as the area that I lived in, boys must also have the underside of the penis cut open with stone knives to expose the inside of the urethra (subincision). These operations are excruciatingly painful. Scarifications and blood letting also form routine parts of initiations and other ceremonies. Among the Pitjantjara of central Australia, Norman Tindale filmed one such initiation ritual in the 1930s involving the circumcision and subincision of a number of adolescent boys. One boy in the film broke down and cried from the pain and his father tried to make light of the boy's reaction. However, Tindale reported to one of my professors that the boy was viewed as effeminate and unreliable as an adult male member of the band. He was later reported to have been killed.

Girls' initiation rites in Australia are not as severe as boys' but can still result in scarification and genital incisions (introcision) in severe environments. In other parts of the world, initiations sometimes took forms such as piercing a part of the body (nose or ear), tattooing, or severing finger joints. It seems clear that *the primary criterion for choosing particular types of initiation ordeals is the pain level that one wishes to achieve in order to test the initiate's reliabiltiy.* The pain is the important feature in these rituals. Pain tolerance is used as proof of commitment. Such ordeals should also leave visibly distinctive marks on the body, so that initiates can be easily recognized, and should not adversely impair normal physical functions. As we shall see in subsequent chapters, painful initiations can also be used for status-related purposes.

The cultural ecological explanations for such seemingly unusual behavior as subincision and tooth removal are far preferable to the cognitive explanations offered by anthrolopogists who see subincision as resulting from the itchy penis of some ancestral being (Berndt and Berndt 1964:145), or from the repeated carelessness of adult men accidentally slipping while using knives and somehow managing to cut their penises (Abbie 1969:149), or as the imitation of birth defects (Abbie 1969:148), or vaginal and menstruation envy (Spiro 1955:163), or the envy of the kangaroo's bifid penis (Cawte 1968). None of these cognitive theories explain why such procedures occur only in the harshest environments or why imitation and envy do not result in subincision rites in other cultures. Nor do these theories account for how some individuals who had such accidents or feelings of envy or ancestral itch managed to convince everyone else in their community to undergo these excruciating ordeals. Finally, these explanations do not account for the rapid abandonment of the subincision and circumcision practices when Aboriginal groups settled down on government reserves or cattle stations, where they were relatively assured that they would not starve even if the environment became harsh. In contrast, this change in behavior is exactly what cultural ecology leads us to expect, and again it demonstrates that people adopt ritual behaviors for good reasons and are not hidebound by tradition when a ritual involves personal discomfort or excessive time or effort, and especially when other options are available.

Given the sparse resources of early hunter-gatherers and the need for sharing, alliances, and mutual support for survival in such environments, it seems highly probable that some sort of initiation ordeal would have been part and parcel of band life even in the earliest times. Such initiations would also be likely to induce ecstatic experiences and would most likely be combined with the forging of ritual alliance bonds. Initiations may have been combined with totemic animal cults or general rituals to create ritually based (or enhanced) alliance bonds. Alternatively, ecstatic alliance rituals, initiation ordeals, and animal cults may have developed as separate strands of religious activity and come together much later in time. I think this is unlikely, but at this point the archaeological evidence does not provide much proof one way or the other. In any event the next indications of religious activity to appear during the flow of the millennia consist of evidence for animal cults and the first human burials.

ANIMALS DOMINATED EARLY PANTHEONS

The cave paintings of the later Paleolithic provide a convenient starting point for the discussion of animal cults. While these will be dealt with in detail in Chapter 5, it is worth noting here that by far the major motifs are animals and that most scholars agree that animal spirits of some sort played a major role in these Paleolithic religions (André Leroi-Gourhan 1965, 1968; Clottes and Lewis-Williams 1998; Bahn and Vertut 1988). This view is consistent with observations from ethnographic hunter-gatherers such as the Australian Aborigines, whose art and mythology is dominated by powerful animal spirits, as well as other groups such as the Inuit, the Northwest Coast Indians, the South

Fig. 4.14. The earliest indication of a belief in animal spirits comes from the mouth of Lazaret Cave in the south of France, where a wolf skull was left in front of the entrance to a hut over 120,000 years ago. H. de Lumley, *Une Cabane Acheuléene dans la Grotte du Lazaret,* p. 220. Paris: Société Préhistorique Française, Mémoire, 1969.

African Bushmen, the Ainu, and many others. As Hultkrantz (1967:59, 143; 1994:359) notes, most if not all hunter-gatherers seem to have a concept of a "master of animals," which is a sort of supernatural animal that rules over animals, prevents unnecessary killing of animals, and ensures their proper burial and their return to the earth in new bodies. The master may withhold animals from people, which explains why animals fail to appear sometimes or go through cycles of plenty and paucity. The master of animals concept is a major form of religious expression among ethnographic hunter-gatherers, and most such spirits have animal forms or at least exhibit some blend of animal and human characteristics, often with transformation capabilities (Campbell 1969:282–98).

Such concepts are very interesting, too, in that they seem to provide animals with souls that reincarnate again and again, no matter how many times their physical bodies are killed and eaten. As a result, hunting is usually a sacred rite linked to the mystery of life, a ritual requiring specific procedures of propitiation in order to maintain the goodwill of animal spirits returning to their supernatural homes and the return flow of animal spirits in new bodies from the master of animals. Thus, animals have souls, and the idea that the physical body can be sacrificed and eaten while the spiritual essence returns to another realm from which it will return in a new body appears to be very widespread and very deeply rooted in our evolutionary past. It is one of the most common concepts in traditional religions of all times and places. Therefore, much religious action is directed toward ensuring a continuing supply of game (Waal Malefijt 1968:301). Moreover, animals are viewed as being stronger, swifter, and more alert than people and in more direct contact with Nature and its sacred forces—and therefore more powerful than people on a supernatural level (Bataille 1980:125–26). Even today, many people feel that certain animals, like cats, have a sixth psychic sense and can sense things or events that humans cannot (Bardens 1987).

Concepts similar to these seem to extend back in unaltered forms to at least 31,000 years ago during the Upper Paleolithic, when the first caves in Europe, such as the

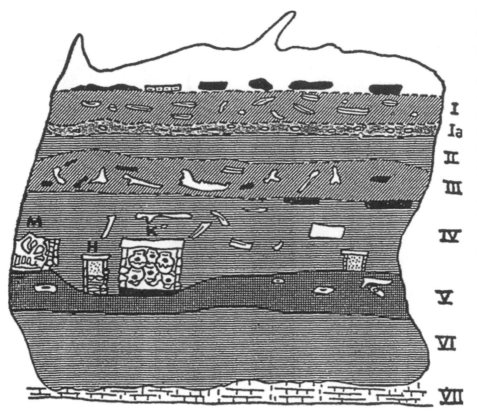

Fig. 4.15. Early excavations at the beginning of the twentieth century reported stone chests, or "cists" filled with bear skulls from Neanderthal times, as illustrated here by Bachler. However, many scholars question the accuracy of these observations given the poor excavation standards of the time, the poor quality of the stratigraphic drawing, and the long delay before these drawings first appeared. From J. Maringer, *The Gods of Prehistoric Man,* Fig. 4. New York: Knopf, 1960.

Grotte Chauvet, were painted (Chauvet, Deschamps, and Hillaire 1995; Clottes 1996). There are earlier indications of animal cults extending back into the Middle Paleolithic, but these are more controversial. The term *cult,* as used here, simply refers to a set of rituals and beliefs centered on a specific theme such as animals, bears, ancestors, emperors, or celestial objects like the sun or moon. The earliest claim for an animal cult has been made by Henri de Lumley (1969:217), who excavated the living floor of an apparent structure inside the Lazaret Cave near Nice in southern France. At the entrance to this structure and an earlier one, de Lumley found the skull of a wolf that he thought had been defleshed and opened to remove the brain. The skull, without the jaw, was then placed at the entrance before the prehistoric inhabitants left, some 120,000 years ago (Fig. 4.14). In a similar fashion, many years later I excavated a dog skull that had been placed in the middle of the floor of a domestic structure of much more recent hunter-gatherers in British Columbia prior to residents departing (Hayden 1997:98). The person I talked to who analyzed the animal bones at Lazaret Cave is less certain that the wolf skull was a ritual offering, since the rest of the wolf skeleton was also there and might simply be the remains of a wolf that had gone into the abandoned cave and died there. This seems possible, but then some structures in British Columbia also had entire dog skeletons left on the floors at the time when the structures were abandoned (Crellin and Heffner 2000:162). It is tempting to adopt de Lumley's interpretation, but without more examples, it may always be open to doubt.

Even considerably later during the Neanderthal occupation of Europe (150,000–35,000 B.P.), there is much debate about the existence of animal cults. In the early twentieth century, excavators at the Swiss cave Drachenloch, found many bear bones and what was reported as a stone slab "chest" filled with bear skulls (Fig. 4.15; see also Bachler 1921). Other caves, such as Petershöhle in Germany, revealed niches stacked with bear skulls (Hormann 1923) or other unusual arrangements (see Kurten 1976:83–107). More modern researchers have argued that caves often have large accumulations of bear bones from bears that die during hibernation and that these bones are moved around substantially by subsequent bears making nests. Some people (Kurten 1976; Pacher 2002) now think that the early reports of bear-skull cults are the products of overactive imaginations, selective observations, and poor excavation techniques. However, the more recent excavations at Régourdou, France, seem to provide better grounds for inferring the existence of animal cults during Neanderthal times.

Régourdou

Régourdou is a collapsed and partially filled-in old cave located only a few hundred meters from the more recently occupied and much more famous painted cave of Lascaux (see Chap. 5). The owner of the site was apparently attempting to locate collapsed entrances to other caves that might contain valuable prehistoric paintings when he dug into a human burial, the grave of a Neanderthal. At that point, archaeologists were called in to recover what they could of the burial and determine its context. The resulting excavations, led by Professor Eugène Bonifay, were carried out in 1957 under very rushed and trying conditions. Subsequent excavations in 1962–65 were conducted under better conditions. Because of the importance of Régourdou and because some doubts had been expressed about the intentional nature of the deposits (Gargett 1989), I went to see Professor Bonifay to ask him about some of the criticisms concerning the interpretation of the remains at Régourdou. He kindly supplied me with a number of unpublished observations and illustrations from Régourdou that I am happy to be able to present here with his permission (see also Bonifay 1964, 1965, 2002; Bonifay and Vandermeersch 1962). He describes the site as the "most extraordinary Neanderthal sanctuary yet discovered."

During the early part of the last glaciation (Wurm I), some 60,000–70,000 or more years ago, sand intermittently was blown and washed into the front of the 25 m diameter cave. It was in this soft sand, particularly near the cave walls, that Neanderthals came to bury someone of importance and to leave a number of ritual offerings in pits and stone coffers and under piles of rocks. At other Middle Paleolithic sites (generally belonging to the Mousterian cultural tradition), there are examples of stone wall constructions, clusters of intentionally arranged stone blocks, and probably symbolic piles of rocks and flint tools (at Pech de l'Azé, Rigabe, Bau de l'Aubésier, El Guettar, Dar-es-Soltane [Gruet 1955; Mcbrearty and Brooks 2000:518], Grotte du Prince [Villeneuve 1906:44], and Baume Bonne [Gagnière 1963; Lumley and Bottet 1962]). Certainly in later times stones or piles of stone or flint were used as offerings or viewed as dwelling places of souls (Kaliff 1997:107ff; Larsson 2000b:184–85). It seems plausible that this tradition began in Neanderthal times. Thus, the occurrence of intentional rock walls and piles at Régourdou should not be viewed as an unexpected development, although some prehistorians have expressed doubts concerning the human origin of the features at Régourdou.

Gargett (1989), for instance, has suggested that pits with bones in them could have been natural dissolution cavities that filled gradually with rock falls and skeletal parts from hyena food refuse or other sources. In the clearest examples from Régourdou, this is manifestly not the case. For example, according to Professor Bonifay's observations (and as corroborated by Professor Norman Clermont, who actually excavated Pit Va [personal communication]), Pit Va cleanly cuts through 70 cm of finely bedded sands terminating abruptly with a flat bottom contour displaying no signs of a dissolution cavity (Fig. 4.16). Most of the lateral walls are nearly vertical and would have collapsed if left exposed for any length of time under natural conditions (contra Gargett's assertion of slow infilling). At the very bottom of this pit, an inverted brown bear skull was found between two cobbles and surmounted by a third cobble. Two bear humeri (upper arm bones) lay to the side. They were crossed, with one end raised by being placed on a rock. Professor Clermont also feels that one end of these humeri had been cut. The form and fill of Pit Va by itself bears very little resemblance to what one would expect from a roof fall or natural type of infill. The occurrence of a flat, teardrop-shaped limestone slab with a hole near its apex about halfway up in the pit fill makes it seem even less likely that the feature was created by natural processes. Slabs with holes in

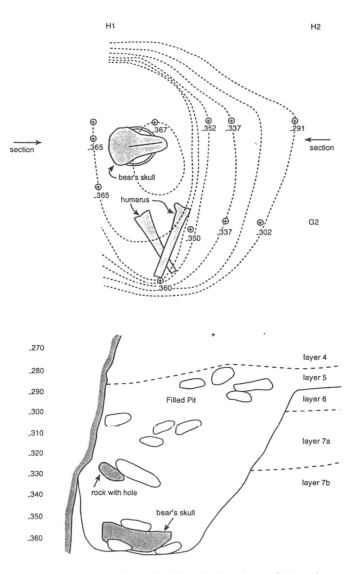

Fig. 4.16. Excavations by Eugène Bonifay at the French site of Régourdou uncovered relatively convincing indications of the special treatment of bear remains by Neanderthals. In Pit Va, shown here, a hole has clearly been dug through the existing layers of soil in the cave and a bear skull with two arm bones have been placed in the bottom between stones. A rock with a hole in it was also placed in the pit and stones scattered over the top after it had been filled in. From E. Bonifay's unpublished drawings and photographs. See E. Bonifay, "L'Hommes de Neandertal et L'Ours (Ursus arctos) dans la grotte du Régourdou (Montignac-sur-Vézère, Dordogne, France)" in T. Tillet and L. Binford, eds., L'Ours et L'Homme. Colloque International d'Auberives-en-Royans (Isère). Liège: Editions ERAUL, 2002.

Fig. 4.17. This is one of the stones with a natural hole in it that was placed with bear remains. This stone is unusual also because its shape appears to have been modified by the removal of several flakes (from the left side) to make it more symmetrical. These stones did not exhibit the same weathering characteristics of the natural stones occurring inside the cave. From E. Bonifay's unpublished drawings and photographs. See E. Bonifay, "L'Hommes de Neandertal et L'Ours (*Ursus arctos*) dans la grotte du Régourdou (Montignac-sur-Vézère, Dordogne, France)" in T. Tillet and L. Binford, eds., *L'Ours et L'Homme.* Colloque International d'Auberives-en-Royans (Isère). Liège: Editions ERAUL, 2002.

them are simply not common occurrences in caves. A similarly shaped slab with a natural hole and modified apex was also found associated with a bear skeleton in the coffer immediately south of the human burial. Although the hole in this slab is natural, the sides of the apex have been shaped by the removal of several flakes, creating slightly concave edges toward the apex (Fig. 4.17). Such features indicate intentional procurement, modification, and deposition. A third, unmodified pierced slab was found in a separate pit. Even today, stones with holes in them are considered lucky or sacred in European folklore and elsewhere (Valiente 1973:175; Schnitger 1989:131, Plate I:2).

In Pit IVb, another cofferlike pit with upright slabs and paving stones at the bottom, bear bones with possible cut marks were deposited. These were covered with more stones on which two bear skulls and a deer skull were placed (Bonifay 1964). However, there are still other indications that the Régourdou deposits are human in origin. All of the stones with a hole, and in fact many boulders and slabs associated with the human burial and ritual offerings, consist of types of weathered limestone that do not occur naturally inside Régourdou Cave or its rockfall deposits. Rather, they occur outside the cave. These stones, as well as occasional quartz cobbles associated with them,

seem to have been intentionally brought into the cave by Neanderthals for premeditated use in rituals (Bonifay 2002). Gargett (1989) suggests that these stones may have fallen into the cave through natural chimneys in the roof, although, according to Professor Bonifay, there is no cone of accumulation under the chimneys, and deposits containing these stones do not occur directly under the chimneys or in cave deposits above the Neanderthal level. Thus, it is difficult to account for their presence by this mechanism. As in other cases of ritual pits in the cave, once the pit had been filled in, a dispersed capping of imported cobbles was left over the pit fill; only a few of these cobbles were transected in vertical section (Fig. 4.16). Gargett's (1989) critique of Bonifay's interpretation of Va is not coherent, and his hypothetical alternative scenario is inconsistent with the facts that have been presented above. There are no rocks in the matrix deposits surrounding this feature that could create his "hourglass" effect.

Pit IIIe provides further corroboration of the human origin of the pits at Régourdou. The digging of this pit seems to have been interrupted and never completed. Perhaps with the unfulfilled intention of returning, the ancient excavator left the modified tool

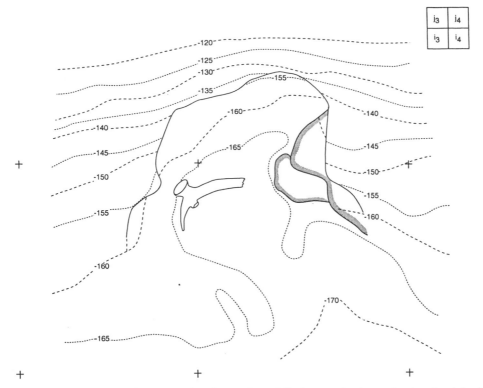

Fig. 4.18. Pit III at Régourdou seems to have been only partially dug out when it was abandoned and the digging tool, a deer antler, was left in the bottom of the pit. Excavators reported being able to detect the digging marks left by the antler on the sides of the pit. Adapted by Greg Holoboff from E. Bonifay's unpublished drawings and photographs. See E. Bonifay, "L'Homme de Neandertal et L'Ours *(Ursus arctos)* dans la grotte du Régourdou (Montignac-sur-Vézère, Dordogne, France)," in T. Tillet and L. Binford, eds., *L'Ours et l'Homme.* Colloque International d'Auberives-en-Royans (Isère). Liège: Editions ERAUL, 2002.

in the pit that had been used to dig it (Fig. 4.18). This tool consisted of the base of a thick, shed antler that had been broken off about 30 centimeters from the base (Fig. 4.19). One of the encumbering basal tines has been broken off, and on the remaining right-angled tine there is use wear resembling that from digging. The result is an antler pick indistinguishable from antler picks found in Neolithic mines and quarries. In addition to this find, excavators who carefully removed fill near the edges of the pit with brushes found clear grooves in the pit walls where fingers or implements had scraped into the sand matrix. As readers might surmise, there is no natural reason for a shed antler to be found in a cave, much less a modified and use-polished one, and less still one in a pit.

There are other similar pits and ritual offerings at Régourdou. However, the most impor-

Fig. 4.19. This is the antler that was found at the bottom of Pit III at Régourdou. The form of its broken main stem is not common under natural conditions, but antler picks with the same shape have been found in Neolithic flint mines. From E. Bonifay's unpublished drawings and photographs. See E. Bonifay, "L'Homme de Neandertal et L'Ours *(Ursus arctos)* dans la grotte du Régourdou (Montignac-sur-Vézère, Dordogne, France)," in T. Tillet and L. Binford, eds., *L'Ours et L'Homme.* Colloque International d'Auberives-en-Royans (Isère). Liège: Editions ERAUL, 2002.

Fig. 4.20. This is a cross-section showing the relative location of the Neanderthal burial at Régourdou, the large cavity containing a bear skeleton, and the wall separating the two. Adapted by Greg Holoboff from E. Bonifay, "Un ensemble rituel moustérien à la grotte de Régourdou," *Proceedings, 6th International Congress of Prehistoric and Protohistoric Sciences, Rome*, Vol. 2 (1965), pp. 136–40.

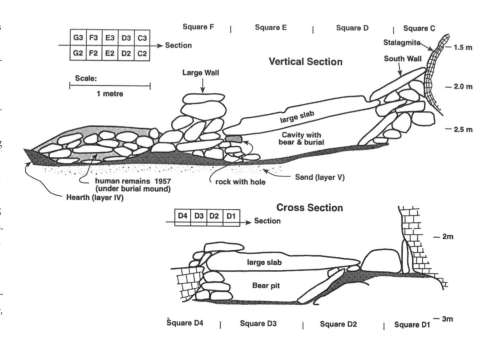

tant is clearly the human burial and the bear coffer associated with it. Near the western wall of the cave, two adjoining shallow prehistoric excavations (about 20 cm deep) removed part of the dark, ashy sands of bed IV (Fig. 4.20). Whether the resulting depression could have been accomplished by natural agencies is not a critical issue. After the creation of these depressions, two substantial dry stone walls (the North Wall and the South Wall) were constructed with a less substantial wall to the east. The North Wall was constructed between the two shallow depressions (Fig. 4.21). Some of the sides of these walls are nearly vertical, a feature that cannot be expected to occur naturally in a cave. As with other features at Régourdou, except for larger rocks, these walls are largely made of imported stones from outside the cave. Moreover, a large, 2-square-meter, 800-kilogram limestone slab rests on the top of these stone walls, creating an ample stone coffer or cist that was *later* filled with sands by natural agencies. To pretend as Gargett (1989) does, that this slab could have come to rest naturally in this position, over an empty void, without breaking and without crumbling the walls that precariously and precisely support it at its edges, strains credulity. Bonifay (2002) also observed that any empty spaces between this slab and the walls were carefully filled in with smaller stones. Large roof fall blocks are uncommon in strata III–VII, and no comparably thin, large slab of roof fall occurred anywhere else in these strata. Below this large slab and partially supporting it was the modified pierced slab already mentioned (Fig. 4.17). The large slab either was intentionally placed in this position by Neanderthals or came to rest in this position due to some extraordinarily remarkable natural agencies. If it was intentionally put in place, it constitutes very strong evidence for ritual behavior, since on the floor of the cavity underneath this slab was something still more difficult to explain in natural terms: the disarticulated remains of a nearly complete brown bear. These bones had been carefully set out and systematically arranged at the bottom of the coffer. In the north, the skull was placed between three stones forming a small protective box near the human burial, while the long bones were set along the sides and the shoulder blades were crossed over each other in the south. Although the bones were weathered over the millennia, excavators reported possible cut marks on the bones in this cist, indicating that the bear had been butchered and then placed in the cist by humans (Bonifay 2002).

Moreover, as Marie-Françoise Bonifay (1989) has noted, brown bears are rare not only in the archaeological deposits of the Perigord for the Paleolithic, but they are rare in natural bone deposits as well. Most of the bears represented at Régourdou were quite young brown bears, as might be expected of bears killed by hunters armed only with spears. The numerous remains of brown bears at Régourdou, as well as the predominance

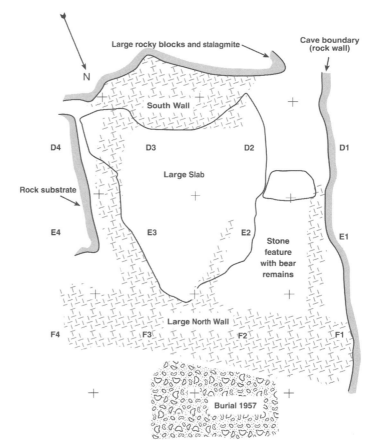

of skulls and foot bones within rock features, should be viewed as indications of special depositional processes that are difficult to explain in natural terms but are common in ethnographic displays of animal skins in which the head and feet are left attached (Maringer 1960:49–54). In some villages of the Saami and Tungus, the skull of the bear was even buried under a pile of stones sometimes in caves (Paproth 1976; Gron and Kuznetsov 2003; Gron, Kuznetsov, and Turov 2001).

Adjoining the north face of the North Wall of the bear cist is the depression and mound containing the crouched skeleton of an adult Neanderthal. The skeleton lay on a pavement of flat stones at the bottom of the depression (Fig. 4.20). Near the foot of the skeleton, two bear lower leg bones (tibias) were found. A large slab of rock covered the rib cage. Lying *directly* on this slab were a flint core, a well-made side scraper, two flakes, and the intentionally *split* half of a bear upper arm bone (humerus), none of which would be expected to occur in such positions by chance. Furthermore, this slab and the rest of the skeleton were covered by a small mound of cobbles and boulders brought from outside the cave as well as an ashy matrix clearly different from the adjacent cultural deposits and the sand that filled the adjoining bear cist and wall interstices. Thus, the natural infilling of the cist was not the same process responsible for the burial of the human remains. Finally on top of the burial mound there was a shed elk (*Cervus elaphus*) antler and above that traces of a small fire consisting of ashes and charcoal.

Fig. 4.21. This is a plan view of the Neanderthal burial and the adjoining bear burial at Régourdou. Adapted by Greg Holoboff from E. Bonifay, "Un ensemble rituel moustérien à la grotte de Régourdou," *Proceedings, 6th International Congress of Prehistoric and Protohistoric Sciences, Rome,* Vol. 2 (1965), pp. 136–40.

Fig. 4.22. Special ritual emphasis on bears as powerful supernatural beings (bear cults) are widespread among cultures living in northern latitudes, as this map illustrates. Created for Joseph Campbell's *Historical Atlas of World Mythology* (New York: Van der Marck Editions, 1983) based on information adapted from R. Gordon Wasson, *Soma: Divine Mushroom of Immortality* (New York: Harcourt Brace Jovanovich, 1972), copyright © Joseph Campbell Foundation (www.jcf.org), used with permission.

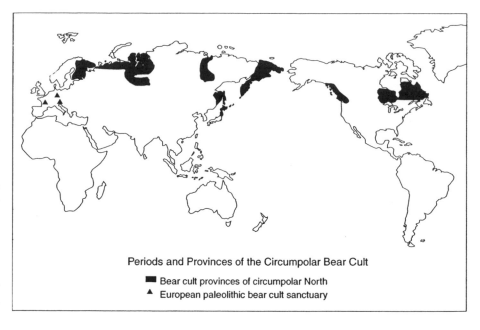

Periods and Provinces of the Circumpolar Bear Cult

◼ Bear cult provinces of circumpolar North
▲ European paleolithic bear cult sanctuary

The position of the skeleton in this depression, the slab flooring and covering associated with carefully positioned artifacts and bones of unusual quality, the use of ashy deposits and introduced boulders to cover the body, plus the fire all indicate that this was an intentional burial. Moreover, given the contiguous location of the depressions containing the bear cist and human burial and the common construction element of the North Wall, it seems probable that all the events represented by the human burial and the bear coffer were contemporaneous and part of a funeral ritual probably involving feasting on bear meat.

Thus, if Professor Bonifay's observations are accurate, Régourdou constitutes a convincing case for some kind of bear-centered animal cult some 60,000–70,000 years ago. The evidence as presented seems impossible to account for by natural processes. Even researchers like the paleontologist Bjorn Kurten (1976:104–5) who are most critical of Drachenloch and other claims for bear shrines in Central European caves readily accept Régourdou as a bona fide bear ritual site. Archaeologists of renown who visited the site during its excavations (Bordes, Movius, Nougier) accepted Professor Bonifay's basic interpretation (N. Clermont, personal communication). Kurten also went on to document the systematic smashing of canine teeth in the bear skulls and jaws at the Neanderthal site of Taubach in Germany. This is another unambiguous example of symbolic behavior indicating the special role of bears in Neanderthal belief systems.

Ethnographically, bear cults are rather common in cold climates (Fig. 4.22; see also Campbell 1983:147–155), and they may provide useful models for further examination of bear-related ritual behavior or even provide some understanding of why bears may have been the focus of earlier ritual behavior in northern regions. Among many northern groups, bears were probably relished for their high fat content (e.g., Le Jeune 1634:25) but respected for their defensive abilities and almost human appearance and behavior. Both Lajoux (2002) and Bonifay (2002) have drawn attention to the frequent importance of the bear as a symbol of death and resurrection (because of its hibernation and reemergence), making it an apt focus for funeral rituals. Moreover, in some myths, the bear, as master over the entire animal kingdom, is sent to earth by his father to understand the problems of humans and to find solutions for them. In a scenario recalling the story of Christ, the bear sacrifices himself for humanity; afterward there is a communion in which the participants eat the body and drink the blood of the bear. This leads to his resurrection (Lajoux 1996, 2002). Thus, the reindeer-herding Lapps of northern Scandinavia had a ceremonial bear hunt and feast after which the bones were buried in approximately the correct anatomical position (Kurten 1976:91). Some of the more remarkable of the bear cemeteries were located in caves (Lajoux 2002). Among the Ainu and east Siberians who still practiced ritual bear sacrifices in the twentieth century, skulls from the sacrificed bears were collected together each year and buried (Maringer 1960:54; Campbell 1983:152; Spevakovsky 1994:106–7); Lajoux 2002). Other hunter-gatherers, like the Ainu, Siberians, Caucasian, and Mistassini Cree, also collect skulls from killed animals and place them in mountain shrines or other special ritual locations (Maringer 1960:49–51; Ianzelo and Richardson 1974) similar to what some excavators refer to as trophylike accumulations of bones at Mousterian sites (see Hayden 1993a). Finally, it might be noted that the identification of the North Star and Big Dipper with bears is extremely widespread in northern hunting cultures. These may even be traditions that have descended to us across some 60,000 or more years. In France, Chantal Jèques-Wolkiewiez argues that animals in Upper Paleolithic myths were portrayed in star constellations. Why should the same not have been true of earlier periods?

ANCESTOR CULTS

The first evidence for intentional human burials occurs during Neanderthal times in Europe and the Near East. As other authors have argued, there are really no practical reasons for burying the dead, especially among nomadic foragers (Belfer-Cohen and Hovers 1992:469). It is far easier to leave bodies exposed to the elements on the ground or in trees. While Paleolithic burials are clear indications of concepts of the afterlife, they also raise the possibility of the existence of very early forms of ancestral cults. Up until about 150,000 years ago, there does not seem to have been any form of burial. When individuals died, they must have been simply left on the ground to decay or to be stripped of their flesh, just as Tibetans leave bodies in the open to be consumed by animals (David-Neel 1932; Hedges 1984:141). It is also possible that early humans could have placed bodies on raised platforms or in trees so that birds and insects rather than carnivores would consume the bodies. This is a practice widely used by Indians on the Great Plains of North America as well as by early European farming communities (Chap. 7). What is most significant when burials begin to appear in the archaeological record is that there is *not* a wholesale change in this traditional practice. It is *not* as though a new belief and ritual system replaced the old practices, and it is certainly not the case that people had suddenly become more conscious of hygiene (Belfer-Cohen and Hovers 1992:469), nor that they had suddenly developed awareness of death. Rather, burial is clearly symbolic. It requires special efforts and is often accompanied by fires or symbolic offerings or selections of special stones.

New beliefs and practices are certainly introduced, but they only seem to involve the burial rites of a few, very select individuals. Rick Schulting (1998b:219–21) argues that new mortuary practices are generally introduced by the most powerful members of communities, and there is considerable support for this in the Paleolithic. Most of the people who died continued to be treated in the same way that people had always been treated; they were simply left to decay. Out of the millions of Neanderthals who lived between 150,000 and 35,000 years ago, less than a dozen intentional burials have thus far been discovered (Binant 1991). Robert Gargett (1999) argues that some of these burials seem to have been partially exposed after death. Excavators of such burials have postulated that bodies could have been placed in cave hollows and protected by branches or wood placed over the bodies, or that they were buried after they had partially decayed elsewhere. These are all reasonable suggestions for some Neanderthal burials, but others, such as those at Régourdou, La Ferrassie, and Shanidar, are much more elaborate. The extreme interpretation that all Neanderthal burials are accidental or natural is difficult to sustain (Riel-Salvatore and Clark 2001). It is difficult to conceive of ten-month-old infants who probably could not even walk, such as those found in Amud Cave in Israel, finding their way into a cave niche on their own and placing the upper jaw of a deer on their own pelvis in order to die. It is equally difficult to believe that their bodies would afterwards be naturally protected from scavengers (Rak, Kimbel, and Hovers 1994; Hovers et al. 1995). The pattern of rare and infrequent burials does not change very dramatically during the Upper Paleolithic after modern humans arrive in Europe. Thus, it appears that the mere act of intentionally burying a body during this time period seems to indicate a special status for such individuals—minimally, an attempt to shield the body from the normal forces of disturbance, out of respect for the person and often probably in an attempt to create a more permanent location of burial that could be easily relocated and revisited.

Why would people want to honor or remember individuals in such a manner? Ethnographically, particularly powerful individuals were most commonly given special burial treatments. For instance, the Aleut complex hunter-gatherers of Alaska placed powerful shamans in cave recesses and retrieved their bodies from time to time to talk with them and to gain some of their power (Laughlin 1980:102). The most successful big men in New Guinea were treated in a similar fashion and were also considered to have special supernatural powers (Solheim 1985; Hampton 1997:99–104, 396; 1999:19, 41). Bones were sometimes removed as talismans carrying the powers of the ancestors to the living bearers of the bones. In both of these cases, there is a strong tendency to pass on material success and supernatural power to succeeding generations, and it is probably the sons and grandsons and great-grandsons who have the most to gain from revisiting the graves of particularly successful and powerful ancestors. This is a pattern that becomes very common with the advent of agriculture and will be discussed in detail in Chapters 6 and 7. At this point, it seems that we may possibly discern the roots of ancestor worship extending far back into the Paleolithic. The ethnographic models certainly provide provocative hypotheses to explore and test further. If kinship and ritual did emerge in tandem as suggested in the last chapter, the concept of ancestors must certainly have been part of the hominid cultural repertory by the Middle Paleolithic.

Is there any other indication that some sort of ancestor worship may have been occurring at this time? Yes. In the first place, the unusual effort and contexts of some of the Neanderthal burials indicate that those interred were of unusual status. At Régourdou, the construction of dry rock walls, a large slab-covered cist with the remains of a bear inside, and the human burial in a mound of rock and soil constitute remarkable indications of special status. In addition, Professor Bonifay (2002) noted that a small fire had been lit on top of this burial mound (Figs. 4.20, 4.21). At La Ferrassie Cave in southwestern France, earth mounds covered Neanderthal bodies just inside a large cave entrance, a context similar to Régourdou. Covering one of the burials was a large triangular slab of limestone with eight pairs of cup marks carved into one surface (Fig. 4.9; Binant 1991; Bednarik 1995). Most remarkably, at Shanidar Cave in Iraq, one of the Neanderthal burials was accompanied by flowers from a number of different plant habitats. Archaeologists recovered and analyzed the pollen and stamen remains that had been preserved in the soil around the body. While skeptics have tried to argue that these remains were contaminants more recently introduced into the soils, their suggestions do not account for the diversity, cave location, depth, and aged condition of these flower remains, which came from a very unusual organic-looking lens of soil directly underneath one of the Shanidar skeletons (see Leroi-Gourhan 1975, 1999, 2000; Hayden 1993b:120). I have discussed the issue with Michel Girard, who helped analyze the original samples, and there simply seems to be no natural agency that could be responsible for these pollen. Arlette Leroi-Gourhan (2000:293) states it succinctly: "Their use in funerary practices is indisputable here."

In addition to these clear cases, some Neanderthal burials seem to be associated with jaws or other parts of game animals, as at Amud Cave in the Levant (Hovers et al. 1995:56; Rak, Kimbel, and Hovers 1994:314), or with unusually fine stone tools as at Le Moustier. However, since most of these burials also occur in deposits that contain bones and stone tools from normal living deposits, some people argue that the items associated with Neanderthal skeletons cannot be convincingly shown to have been intentionally deposited as part of the burial ritual. They might simply be accidentally associated as part of the refuse already in the soil. For other prehistorians, such bones associated with the burials, as well as hearths and entire animals, such as the bear and hearth at Régourdou, constitute good evidence for funeral rituals and feasting among Neanderthals (Trinkaus and Shipman 1992:334–41; Shackley 1980:98).

It is curious that those people who strive the hardest to find natural explanations for the treatment of bear skulls, human skeletons, simple art motifs, grave offerings, and the movement of large rock slabs have little or no hesitation in attributing intentional, artistic, or creative actions to almost identical manifestations when they occur in association with fully modern human physical types. Perhaps not all archaeologists have learned to avoid ethnocentrism. However, the Middle Paleolithic evidence that has been brought to light certainly constitutes solid support for the notion that souls, afterlives, and supernatural power were recognized by Neanderthals. The more elaborate archaeological expressions also provide support for the recognition of a continuing influence or power of the dead in the lives of the living—at least a rudimentary form of ancestral veneration. Offerings and sacrifices to the dead are generally used as a means of contacting ancestors and stimulating them to send fertilizing energy, supernatural powers, or other benefits to the living (Berglund 1976:110ff).

However, there is another reason for thinking that ancestor cults were emerging among some Neanderthals. In two cases, Kebara Cave in the Levant and Régourdou Cave in France, adult males were buried without their skulls (Bar-Yosef et al. 1986). The heads had been deliberately removed before careful and elaborate burial. This may seem like a very strange practice to people in Industrial societies, but among ancestor-worshiping agricultural societies, it is relatively common (Chap. 6). The head is considered the seat of the soul by many groups. Therefore, the head is often retained in a special place either around altars or in special caches. These skulls embody the supernatural essence of powerful ancestors and are used to convey that power to living descendants. Thus, the removal of some Neanderthal skulls before burial is an important indicator of possible ancestor worship by Neanderthals. Similar patterns of elaborate burials for a few people and bone removal continue throughout the Upper Paleolithic in Europe and on into subsequent periods (Cauwe 1996, 1997, 2001; Berg and Cauwe 1996).

SHAMANISM BEGINS EARLY

As we saw in the last chapter, there are arguments that shamanism has very ancient origins. How ancient is a critical question. We have just reviewed some of the earliest evidence for religious behavior from the Paleolithic. Is there any hint of shamanism in the archaeological evidence from the Lower or Middle Paleolithic? Hints there are, but no clear demonstrations. It seems certain that concepts of an "other world" were firmly in place by the time burials first occur, some 150,000 years ago if not before, as indicated by the use of red ochre in general rituals and the defleshed skull from Bodo, Ethiopia, some 600,000 years ago.

It also seems clear that Neanderthals were exploring deep caves, presumably for the purpose of inducing ecstatic or altered states, by at least 50,000 years ago if not many thousands of years earlier given the general arguments presented in Chapter 2 concerning the adaptiveness of ecstatic rituals in creating survival alliances. Altered states and concepts of other worlds are both critical elements in shamanism, but it is difficult to determine if spirit helpers were involved or if they were being used to travel to spirit realms in order to heal the sick or retrieve other useful kinds of information. It has been suggested that shamanism is primarily an adaptation to the early hunting-gathering way of life, with its trying conditions, limited medical technology, and the use of ecstatic rituals, and that it was a universal feature of hunting and gathering societies (Winkelman 1990, 2000:193–94; von Gernet 1993:73). Given the available evidence, it seems entirely possible that the shamanism complex did originate at least by Neanderthal times if not before; however, this cannot be conclusively demonstrated. Stronger evidence can be found in the subsequent Upper Paleolithic period.

POLITICS PLAY WITH PANTHEONS

At the turn of the last century, there was great interest among religious historians in the pantheons of hunting and gathering peoples. Writers such as Fathers Wilhelm Schmidt (1912–55) and Martin Gusinde (1931:2; 1932) were keen to find relict mythological evidence of early concepts of a supreme creator such as might be dimly remembered after the fall from grace and the expulsion from the Garden of Eden described in the Hebrew Bible. About the same time, Friedrich Engels and Johann Bachofen argued that the earliest deity concepts should be those of a mother goddess because women were central to the mystery of birth and life. What evidence from the early phases of the Paleolithic can be brought to bear on these issues? The 230,000-year-old Berekhat Ram artifact from the Golan Heights is the only modified object with any resemblance to a human form, and the resemblance is vague (Fig. 4.8). Aside from that, the best indicators that exist for identifying spirits or gods in the early Paleolithic pantheons are the wolf remains at Lazaret and the bear remains at Régourdou, or possibly the bear skulls in the Alpine caves such as Drachenloch. These certainly suggest that animals or masters of animals or animal totems were key features in early pantheons.

In order to shed further light on this topic, some of my students and I undertook an examination of the beliefs of a broad range of recent hunter-gatherers (Hayden 1987). In the pantheons of simple ethnographic hunter-gatherers who were not in contact with agricultural or more complex cultures, we generally found a wide range of variation. Most of these pantheons, such as the ones in Australia or the subarctic regions of the world, featured different kinds of animal spirits or masters of animals, like the raven, coyote, Sedna the mistress of the sea, bears, wolves, kangaroos, emus, snakes, and many more. Most of these spirits were viewed as "creator" spirits, and myths tell about incidents from their lives that account for the formation of particular rock formations or water holes or the creation of physical marks on animals seen today. Such animals were viewed as having great supernatural or magical powers, and they sometimes played the roles of trickster or culture hero, possibly reflecting powers similar to those attributed to shamans. Most often the role of such tricksters was to show how egocentric, selfish behavior resulted in humiliation and bad outcomes, or how the spirit world could play unpredictable tricks on people and thus prevent them from becoming too self-confident or haughty. They provided an indirect means of critically commenting on individuals' objectionable behavior. Trickster figures in mythology thus bolstered the fundamental egalitarian values of hunter-gatherers and could be expected to be common types of spirits in the Paleolithic pantheon as well.

While the time when they transformed the landscape may have ended in the dimly remembered past, these spirit deities continued to exert powerful influences up to the present, and even today people can sometimes draw upon their influence through appropriate ritual and imitation (Berndt and Berndt 1964:188). Often these animals were considered totemic ancestral beings from whom living families and lineages were derived. Perhaps not surprisingly, our research showed that where animals were more important for subsistence, animal deities tended to be more numerous. In most of these hunting and gathering cultures, there was no supreme being and no mother goddess. Where they occur, concepts of supreme beings seem strongly related to contacts with more complex societies. Even the mother goddess cults, which were found only in northern Australia, appear to have been recent introductions from contacts with agricultural groups in island Southeast Asia (Elkin 1964:226, 229, 237). Nevertheless, in some hunter-gatherer cultures less influenced by complex societies, there was an acknowledgment of a higher role played by the sun and sometimes the moon, and sometimes by a vaguely defined "old man" or old creator who did not have much of a role to play in everyday affairs. These concepts seemed to be strongest in areas where resource stresses were the most severe. In fact, sometimes the sun was associated with particular animals such as eagles, lions, bulls, or bears (Campbell 1969; Rice 1998; Eliade 1958b:23). Even so, most of these celestial deities are not supreme high gods.

If we were to adopt a universal scheme such as proposed for the early belief in a supreme being or a mother goddess, we would have a very difficult time trying to explain why so many ethnographic hunter-gatherer cultures exhibit no traces of such beliefs. Even the very popularized notion of "Mother Earth" does not appear to have been a native concept in the Americas, but a very recent idea generated by romantic Europeans (Gill 1987). What factors could have caused some hunter-gatherers to abandon beliefs in supreme gods or goddesses if such beliefs were as natural or enlightened as their proponents would have us believe? There are no compelling answers. It seems far better to recognize that a wide range of deity concepts has always been available to hunter-gatherers, both today and in the early periods of the Paleolithic and also among horticultural societies (Meggitt 1965:10). People tend to adopt beliefs in those concepts that best fit their concerns and their experiences in subsistence and relations with other groups. The focus on creator animal spirits, masters of animals, and totemic animal ancestors is by far the most common expression in pantheons among simple ethnographic hunter-gatherers. In fact, all three aspects are often intertwined. Because of this widespread occurrence and given our assessment of the nature of the hunting and gathering lifestyle during the early phases of the Paleolithic, it seems reasonable to postulate that similar concepts may have existed in the dim eras that we have been exploring. However, we need to continue to search for ways to test these ideas.

It is interesting to observe that hunter-gatherer concepts of deities and spirits are quite different from modern concepts of gods and therefore it seems likely that earlier beliefs were different as well. Today, gods are considered to have eternal existences. Among hunter-gatherers, as among many other traditional people such as the Maori (Radin 1937:14), these supernatural beings exist only as long as people obey instructions of the spirits and honor them (Berndt and Berndt 1964:188). In a way, totemic ancestors are like real ancestors. As long as the biological descendants continue to procreate, the ancestral DNA is passed on, but if the descendants should fail to have offspring, that expression of a lifeline, too, would die out. Similarly, as long as descendants keep the totemic rituals alive and make ecstatic contacts with the ancestral forces, that totemic spirit will stay alive. When the totemic rituals cease to be performed, that line of sacred forces, too, will die out.

Among hunter-gatherers, the original ancestors of people living today were bears (or bear-people) or kangaroos or other species. According to evolutionary ecology, the original ancestors of people were primates similar to chimpanzees. It is ironic that science has tended to distance itself from such traditional beliefs (and vice versa), since both traditional beliefs of hunter-gatherers and the conclusions of modern archaeology concur in viewing human beings as originating from animals.

SUMMARY
In order to understand the earliest phases of Paleolithic religion, it is essential to have a clear idea about what basic hunter-gatherer life was like, especially the need for alliances in times of stress, the emphasis on sharing and egalitarianism, the prohibitions on egocentric behavior or resource ownership, and the important role of animals. The first material indications of ritual or symbolic activity that come from the archaeological record date from about one million years ago until 250,000 years ago. These indications take the form of cannibalism or defleshing and the use of ochres and shiny minerals. Minimally, these probably indicate the presence of general and probably ecstatic rituals or ini-

tiations and the concept of a soul or afterlife. In the second phase of religious development, from about 250,000 to 35,000 years ago, there is clearer evidence for concepts of the soul and ecstatic rituals in the form of intentional burials and the use of deep caves. There are also major components (but not all the components) of shamanism, so it seems possible that shamanism may have already begun by this phase of development. Ground ochres and elementary graphic symbols appear more consistently, and the first good evidence for animal cults occurs. Some burials may also indicate the beginnings of ancestor cults. If so, kinship systems were certainly established well before this period.

These are all separate elements that can be inferred from different types of material evidence. In reality, many of these different aspects may have been combined into a single religious complex, as was often the case ethnographically. Thus, initiations, animal totemic cults, ecstatic rites, concepts of the soul, and "generalized rituals" may all have been combined into single religious systems. Alternately, they may have been expressed in different kinds of rituals that were more specialized, such as initiations into adulthood that were separate from ecstatic animal cults or separate from various kinds of generalized, nonecstatic rituals. I suspect that many of these aspects were combined very early on in religious development, although this cannot be demonstrated at present. From a cultural ecological perspective, we can refer to the above complex of religious traits as the generalized "forager" type of religion.

In many ethnographic accounts, there are often references to the disparities between the heavy involvement of men in rituals versus the less intensive involvement of women, often with severe penalties for transgressions into the initiated men's ritual spheres (Berndt and Berndt 1964:200, 214). This common feature may be explained by the different roles of men and women in creating alliances between bands. It is men who typically roam the farthest during hunting and gathering, and thus it is the men who take on the responsibility of defense and make first contact with other groups. It would therefore not be surprising if the adult men were more heavily involved in managing the political relationships between bands by creating the most important ritual bonding that maintained alliances.

Beginning with the Upper Paleolithic, some major and dramatic changes took place in religious activity, especially in Europe, where deep caves were painted with spectacular scenes of animals that are among the most inspired works of art ever created. It is to those developments that we now turn.

CHAPTER 5

Complexity in the
Hunter-Gatherer World

Wﬁith the advent of the European Upper Paleolithic, we begin to deal with some of
the most spectacular artistic, religious, social, and economic developments in the history
of mankind. This is the period of beautiful multihued animals painted in the far recesses
of dark caves. This is the period of magnificent ivory carvings and masterpieces in flint
working (Fig. 5.1). This is the period of unprecedented wealthy burials. All of these developments are phenomenal achievements for people living off wild resources. It is also
the first time that we have undisputed dramatic evidence for elaborate rituals and religious concepts. Some of these developments reflect the elaboration of basic aspects of
religion developed during the preceding Paleolithic periods discussed in the last chapter.
These include concepts of the afterlife, ecstatic and animal cults, initiations, and indications of shamanism and ancestor cults. However, other aspects appear in the Upper
Paleolithic and the following Mesolithic period that seem to be new. These include feasting, secret societies, new types of initiation, a greatly expanded use of special sanctuaries,
and fertility cults. I will refer to this constellation of religious elements as the "complex
hunter-gatherer type of religion." In order to understand what happened during the
Upper Paleolithic and the Mesolithic periods, it is necessary to return again to the cultural ecological framework and examine the basic changes taking place in the subsistence
economy to see how these changes affected the social, political, and religious aspects of
these cultures.

Complex Hunter-gatherers Arrive in the World

This last phase of religious development in the Paleolithic coincides with the technological period that archaeologists call the Upper Paleolithic. It lasted from about 35,000 to
10,000 B.P. It is characterized by the appearance of fully modern human forms, which
absorbed or replaced the resident Neanderthal populations of Europe. The production
of flint blades, bone tools, art, and personal decorations such as beads all become much
more common during this period, at least in some areas of Europe. But it is important

to stress the great variability that existed among the Upper Paleolithic and previous cultures.

If Europe seems to have been a genetic and cultural backwater during much of the preceding phases of the Paleolithic, it certainly advanced to the forefront of world cultural developments during the Upper Paleolithic. Some of the cultural developments that we will be discussing simply do not seem to have occurred as early anywhere else in the world. During the very short succeeding period, known as the Mesolithic (about 14,000–8000 B.P.), many of these developments spread throughout other areas of the world. However, even during the Upper Paleolithic, some areas such as the southwest of France were extremely rich in the creation of works of art and ritual elaborations. Other areas such as England, Scandinavia, northern Germany, Greece, and Poland had very sparse populations, limited food resources, and few art objects. One of the goals of cultural ecology is to explain not only the major changes that occur through time but also the geographic variations that occur between cultures.

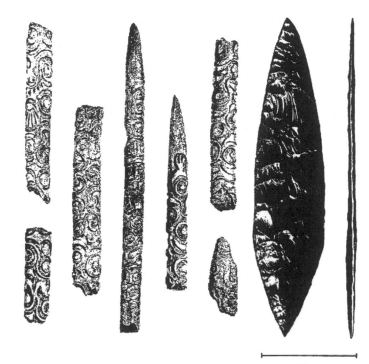

10cm

Fig. 5.1. The European Upper Paleolithic produced the first examples of highly crafted prestige items such as these intricately carved ivory wands and this incredibly thin and large flint biface. None of these items could have served a practical purpose. Items at left: from C. Zervos, *L'Art de l'Epoque du Renne*, Plate 277. Paris: Cahier d'Art, 1959. Right: photo by Greg Ehlers and Fred Kyba.

The Upper Paleolithic in Europe coincided with the last major period of glaciation, interrupted by several relatively short warmer periods (Fig. 5.2). The European landscape was much different from the one we see today. Most of it was dominated by cold grassy steppes, similar to the African savanna grasslands. However, these European steppes should not be thought of as simple equivalents of today's Arctic steppes or African savannas. Because southwest Europe lies at relatively low latitudes, the European steppes were unique in that they supported lush grasslands without the excessively long winters of the Arctic and probably without the excessively dry conditions of the African savannas. The growing season was longer than the Arctic's, the winters shorter, and the summers warmer. Game animals were extraordinarily plentiful during this period, forming a unique environment unparalleled in the world in terms of its rich animal biomass (Dickson 1990:177–78). The animals included such exotic forms as woolly mammoths, mastodons, woolly rhinoceroses, saber-toothed tigers, giant cave bears, horses, reindeer (caribou), bison, and several types of deer and antelope. Many of these animals are now extinct. Many of the herd animals such as reindeer must have undertaken seasonal mass migrations from lush summer meadows high in the mountains of the Pyrenees and the Massif Central of France to the coastal plains during the winter, where the weather would be milder than in the higher mountains (Dickson 1990:153). These migrations

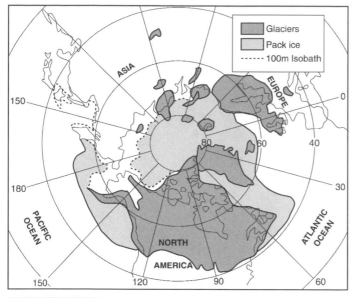

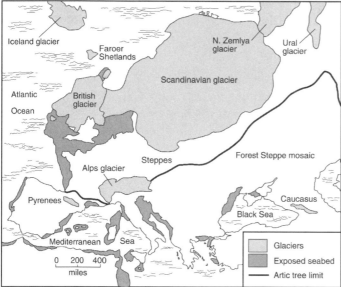

Fig. 5.2. During much of the Upper Paleolithic, ice covered major portions of Europe and altered the rest of the European landscape accordingly. Dense herds of large mammals roamed across the European steppes, providing unparalleled hunting for inhabitants of the time. Adapted from K. Butzer, *Environment and Archaeology,* Figs. 9, 51. Chicago: Aldine, 1971.

seem to have played a critical role in the changes that were to come.

The key concept in understanding the astonishing array of developments in the European Upper Paleolithic is the distinction between generalized, or simple, hunter-gatherers and complex hunter-gatherers (see "Characteristics of Generalized and Complex Hunter-Gatherers"). Generalized hunter-gatherers, on the one hand, are similar to those that have been discussed up to this point. Their resources were scarce and fluctuating, resulting in strong sharing ethics, egalitarianism, high mobility, no large-scale or long-term food storage, small groups, prohibitions on private ownership of most economically important resources, as well as prohibitions on the use of subsistence resources for competitive purposes, while they used ecstatic states and other emotion-based techniques to create alliances for the benefit of the entire community.

Complex hunter-gatherers, on the other hand, have characteristics much more similar to recent and Industrial types of societies. In a very condensed summary of the differences, we can say that the amount of resources extracted from the land is much higher, resulting in higher population densities and reduced mobility (seasonal sedentism or full sedentism). Communities can be relatively large at least on a seasonal basis (up to several hundred or a thousand people). Private ownership of land and resources by families or lineages or corporate groups is common, while surplus food is converted into wealth objects or debts via feasting and gift giving. As a result, competition emerges over the control and use of resources; significant inequalities emerge in terms of economic,

Characteristics of Generalized and Complex Hunter-Gatherers

Resources	Population Density (people per sq. km)	Mobility	Social and Ideological Adaptation	Archaeological Indicators
Generalized hunter-gatherers limited fluctuating vulnerable no storage no small or "occulted" resources	0.01–0.1	nomadic foraging	no individual ownership sharing no economic competition alliances egalitarian society sporadic revenge raiding	no primitive valuables no rich burials no permanent architecture generalized technology few or no storage features small, thin, open-air sites little or no technology for small "occulted" resources and no remains from these resources
Complex hunter-gatherers abundant more stable invulnerable storage small or "occulted" resources are important	0.1–10.0	semi- or full sedentism	private ownership economic competition hierarchical society poor vs. wealthy economic trade increased warfare slavery	primitive valuables (status items, jewelry, etc.) regional trade networks rich vs. poor burials cemeteries with high levels of violent deaths permanent architecture large sites with thick, dense artifact deposits specialized technology for small, "occulted" resources remains of small, "occulted" resources significant storage features

social-political, and religious control; some groups establish hereditary elites or have slaves; and the exchange of exotic prestige goods increases dramatically. In fact, in the Lower and Middle Paleolithic and in later prehistoric cultures where we can be sure people formed generalized forager communities, there are *no* occurrences of prestige objects other than very rare probable ritual items. In contrast, sophisticated art and ritual objects are typically produced as part of the wealth, competition, and political power in complex hunter-gatherer societies. *In fact, the vast majority of technological and social*

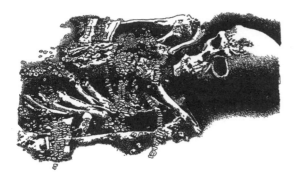

Fig. 5.3. In the richest hunting areas, some Upper Paleolithic individuals, like this man buried at Sungir in the Ukraine, adorned themselves with innumerable ivory, bone, or shell beads, creating lavish garments and bone jewelry. Drawing by Elizabeth Carefoot from a photograph published in 1964. Reprinted with permission of the *Illustrated London News* 245:731.

Fig. 5.4. Early Jomon hunter-gatherers in the Japanese archipelago created the world's first pottery vessels. Subsequently, they produced elaborate vessels like this one that most likely had ritual functions. Photo by B. Hayden.

developments that are usually associated with agricultural communities were actually developed first by early complex hunter-gatherers. These include ground-stone tools, sculptures, jewelry (Fig. 5.3), pottery (Fig. 5.4), record keeping (Fig. 5.15), pet breeding, domesticated animals and plants, the use of metal, complex watercraft, massive architecture or megaliths (Fig. 5.5), large sedentary or semisedentary villages, elaborate burials (Fig. 5.3), slavery, and chiefdom organizations (Hayden 1998). Such features are hallmarks of the difference between generalized and complex hunter-gatherers.

Archaeologists usually consider generalized hunter-gatherers as "egalitarian" societies, or foragers, whereas complex hunter-gatherers represent a new kind of social organization termed "transegalitarian" societies. Transegalitarian societies are intermediate between egalitarian social organizations and strictly class-structured societies such as chiefdoms and early states. Transegalitarian societies are characterized by private ownership of some resources and produce as well as significant social and economic inequalities, but they also have unstable and weakly developed political centralization of authority. For instance, the Lapp reindeer hunters and herders of northern Scandinavia (often compared with Upper Paleolithic reindeer hunters) had a council of male family heads, with a headman and policing officers. Resources were owned by families (Dickson 1990:187).

Transegalitarian social organization begins with complex hunter-gatherers but continues on into the food-producing societies (both horticultural and pastoral nomadic) of the Neolithic and later times as well. If the ethnographic descriptions of the Aborigines of central Australia and the Bushmen of South Africa provide reasonable models of *generalized* hunter-gatherer adaptations, the Northwest Coast Indians of North America and the Ainu of Japan provide reasonable ethnographic models for *complex* hunter-gatherers. The question

Fig. 5.5. Complex hunter-gatherers built monumental structures, such as the longhouses of the North American Northwest Coast, and constructed monumental memorials, such as totem poles and this impressive burial mound at the Scowlitz site in British Columbia. Photo by B. Hayden.

of why the change from generalized to complex hunter-gatherers took place and what the ramifications of these changes are would lead us off on a lengthy, albeit interesting, tangent if we pursued them here. They are dealt with in greater detail in other publications (Hayden 1993a, 1993b, 1995, 1998).

While some people feel that the dramatic changes that were part of the Upper Paleolithic in Europe were due to the evolution of a superior kind of human being (fully modern people as opposed to archaic *Homo sapiens* or Neanderthals), my evaluation of the evidence indicates that biology had no more to do with these developments than it had to do with the European colonial expansion throughout the globe from the sixteenth to nineteenth centuries or the many similar expansions of ethnic or racial groups that have occurred repeatedly over the last 10,000 years (see also Mcbrearty and Brooks 2000). In my estimation, it was a new technology—and above all the successful ability to harvest seasonally massive amounts of food and store such food for long periods of time—that resulted in the dramatic cultural advances in some areas during the European Upper Paleolithic. In essence, I am convinced that the seasonal migrations of large herds of animals from their summer mountain meadows to the winter coastal plains provided Upper Paleolithic groups with the opportunity to harvest massive amounts of meat at certain bottleneck locations created by the deeply incised sections of rivers between the mountains and the coast (Fig. 5.6). While such animal migrations almost certainly occurred during earlier glacial periods, the technological knowledge of how to capture, process, and store large amounts of meat does not seem to have been present.

I like to compare this situation with that of the Northwest Coast, where some of the most complex hunter-gatherers in the world developed because of their ability to harvest and store very large quantities of another seasonally migrating species: salmon. Like reindeer and other herd animals, during most of the year salmon feed over distant, very wide ranges, thereby capturing resources from vast areas. During their migrations, the

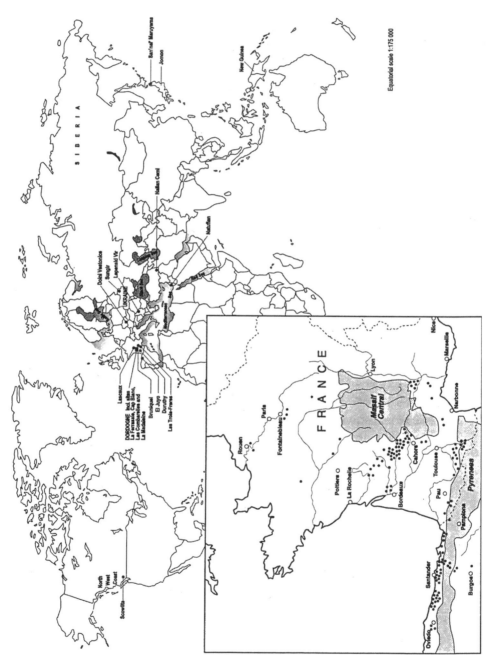

Fig. 5.6. The location of some of the most important Upper Paleolithic sites are shown on this map. Drafted by Greg Holoboff with an inset adapted from P. Bahn and J. Vertut, *Images of the Ice Age*, pp. 38–39. New York: Windward, 1988.

biomass (meat) produced from feeding in these extensive feeding grounds is all concentrated in a very narrow funnel: the continental rivers that millions of salmon swim up in order to lay their eggs. The Northwest Coast Indians intercept the salmon at these bottlenecks and harvest large amounts of fish meat. However, in order to use large amounts of captured fish, it is necessary to carefully slice, smoke, dry, and store what cannot be eaten within the day. This requires a great deal of very intensive labor, and it is also capable of producing a surplus in good years that can be traded to other groups or used to pay for services or for commissioning prestige objects. The key to wealth and power in such a situation is the individual or family control of the most productive resource areas (fishing sites) and control over enough labor to be able to exploit those resources to their full extent. Thus, among the rich, there is often considerable competition for good labor in the form of marriage partners, co-owners, and workers.

It seems likely that something similar was occurring in the most favorable parts of Europe, with migrating herd animals playing the same role in Upper Paleolithic economies that salmon play in Northwest Coast economies. Randall White (1985) has observed that the deeply incised rivers of the Dordogne in France provide ideal funnels for channeling migrating animals. I have canoed down the Vézère River in this region and was impressed by the high sheer limestone cliffs that alternated from one side of the river to the other because of cutbank action on the outside edges of these incised river meanders. These features would have rendered alternating sides of the river impassable to any animals migrating up the river valleys, repeatedly forcing them to swim across the river to traverse the lower banks. After traveling down the Vézère River, I became convinced that White was onto a key element in understanding Upper Paleolithic complexity. Moreover, White observed that the richest Upper Paleolithic sites in southwest France coincide with the natural river fords where most migrating animals would be expected to cross rivers. They are therefore the best bottlenecks from which to capture such animals, and Upper Paleolithic camps were set up near these locations year after year.

These highly productive meat procurement locations concentrated biomass produced over vast areas into very small areas where it could be effectively harvested en masse. Such large-scale seasonal harvests could support many people over the year and produce surpluses in normal years. This scenario provides a rough but very useful model for explaining why art, wealth, complexity, and ritual were so developed in the southwest of France, the north of Italy, northern Spain, and the Ukraine but much less developed elsewhere. Other areas apparently either had lower animal densities or animals that did not migrate to the same extent, or their migrations were not as confined and were more dispersed, making it more difficult to capture large quantities of them. Few other models (such as the population replacement model, the population pressure model, or cognitive models) ever attempt to explain this regional variability in art and rich burials.

Interestingly, the most notable indications of complexity in Neanderthal ritual and social life also come from these same regions of Europe. Both La Ferrassie and Régourdou are in southwestern France in or near important migration river valleys, and Régourdou is only 500 meters from Lascaux, the most famous of all the upper Paleolithic caves. In the Levant, the most notable Neanderthal and Upper Paleolithic burials occur in the same regions, virtually next to each other. Such a coincidence seems far from fortuitous and provides strong support for the notion that regional resource characteristics played critical roles in shaping the more complex aspects of prehistoric culture and religion.

What indications do we have that the richest Upper Paleolithic groups were, in fact, complex hunter-gatherers? First, there is evidence of harvesting, and probably owning, large amounts of meat and creating surpluses or stored reserves based on seasonally abundant resources. Olga Soffer (1989) notes that the first evidence of storage appears in the Upper Paleolithic of Europe, and Alain Testart (1982) has demonstrated the fundamental impact of large-scale, long-term food storage on other aspects of cultures, especially those that characterize complex hunter-gatherers.

Second, faunal evidence indicates that people in the Upper Paleolithic were specialized in the harvesting of large numbers of migratory horses, reindeer, mammoths, and other animals, and that they were filleting the meat in thin pieces, presumably for drying and storing (Dickson 1990:177, 184; Beaune 1995:53, 81, 84; Hayden 1993b).

Third, sites were larger and population densities were much greater than in the preceding Neanderthal times. Some sites were seasonally occupied for thousands of years. Semipermanent pithouses and structures of mammoth bones also appear in the richest areas (Dickson 1990:180–86; Beaune 1995:148, 154–59).

Fourth, clear examples of prestige objects begin to occur on a regular basis in the Upper Paleolithic. These consist of ivory, bone, antler, and amber carvings (Fig. 5.1); beads; ivory implements; shell, amber, and bone jewelry (Fig. 5.3); exotic materials imported from as far as 600 to 1,000 kilometers away; masterworks in flint (Fig. 5.1); and dress costumes of fine buckskin clothing (Beaune 1995:117, 125, 175–79, 185, 247–48; Roebroeks et al. 2000).

Fifth, there are strong indications of private property and substantial wealth differences, not only from the mere existence of prestige items but also from the lavish burials of some individuals with rich grave goods (Beaune 1995:175–79; White 1993; Binant 1991; Roebroeks et al. 2000). Only 40 of about 60 Upper Paleolithic graves are known to have contained jewelry. Probably the most lavish examples of differential wealth yet found consist of an adult and two adolescents buried at Sungir in the Ukraine with over 10,000 ivory beads, plus ivory spears, ivory bracelets, and ivory disks with spokes (Fig. 5.3). The labor required to produce the beads alone has been estimated at a phenomenal 9,000 man hours, without counting the other objects or the fine buckskin clothing to which the beads were undoubtedly attached (White 1993). Such wealth and control over labor is inconceivable for any generalized hunter-gatherers. Sungir represents a major increase in political, economic, and social complexity in the world. In the Czech Republic the skeleton of the Brno "shaman" was accompanied by 600 fossil dentalia shells that probably took several generations to collect, according to Oliva (2000:150). Other, less extreme examples have been found in southwestern France and northern Italy.

Sixth, women and children, too, are more frequently buried than in previous periods—sometimes, as at Sungir, with great wealth. This is also a characteristic of more complex transegalitarian cultures in which women acquire more importance as a means of wealth transfer (via bride prices or dowries). Children can also become a means for the investment of surpluses as part of expensive maturation ceremonies meant to increase their value at marriage (Hayden 1995:44–45, 55). There are also indications of human sacrifice in the Upper Paleolithic (Fig. 5.7) that imply considerable social and economic inequalities and hierarchies (Beaune 1995:145, 179, 246; White 1993; Dickson 1990).

In addition, many of the distinctive stone tools of the Upper Paleolithic such as prismatic blades and endscrapers make sense primarily as tools for the mass processing of meat for storage and hides for clothing. All of the above six characteristics differ dramatically from generalized hunter-gatherer adaptations, but they are very typical of complex hunter-gatherers, such as those ethnographically recorded on the Northwest Coast. Thus, it is reasonable to seek answers to questions about Upper Paleolithic religion within the context of complex hunter-gatherers.

Although complex hunter-gatherer societies seem to appear first in Europe, they also appear on the Ukrainian steppes and in southern Siberia slightly later, around 25,000 B.P. (Soffer 1985:228–31). They subsequently spread to areas *with abundant resources* in the Near East, Africa, the Far East, the Americas, and Australia, as well as persisting in coastal Europe during the following Mesolithic period.

The Mesolithic was originally defined on the basis of chipped-stone technology. It was the period between the Old Stone Age (the Paleolithic), characterized by chipped-stone tools, and the New Stone Age (the Neolithic), characterized by ground-stone tools. The Mesolithic

Fig. 5.7. One of the most intriguing burials in Upper Palaeolithic Europe was excavated at Dolni Vestonice in Moravia, Czech Republic. An older and physically deformed woman (some suggest a shaman) is flanked by two men; the one on the left has his arms stretched out to touch her, while the man on the right was buried face down. Both men wore bone and ivory jewelry. Some archaeologists suggest that this may represent early evidence for human sacrifice. Whatever the cause of death, the situation certainly must have been unusual. Photo by Bohuslav Klíma, published in *National Geographic* 174(4):466 (1998).

often had both types of tools, and it also had very small ones (called microliths) that were often associated with bows and arrows. Later in the twentieth century, the Neolithic was redefined in terms of economic adaptations focused on domesticated foods. Like others (Cauvin 2000a:xii), I will follow the same economic approach here in defining the Mesolithic as the period of widespread subsistence strategies featuring the massive use of grass seeds, fish, and boiling and other extractive techniques that made complex hunting and gathering lifeways possible (see Hayden 1993a). In most areas, the Mesolithic amounted to no more than a hiccup in cultural evolution, lasting only a few thousand years in the 2.5 million-year trajectory of human technological development—a few centimeters near the end of our football field of cultural history. However, in some special areas, complex hunter-gatherer ways of life persisted well into the nineteenth and early twentieth centuries.

Complex Hunter-gatherers Expand Rituals

Under the more extreme conditions of generalized hunter-gatherers, it makes little sense for anyone to invest time or effort in the production of prestige goods, since most things are shared and individuals generally derive only a very fleeting, ephemeral enjoyment of attractive objects that they have made or acquired before someone else appropriates them. Among contemporary Australian Aborigines, I often heard reports of a person who would work diligently to get enough money to buy a pair of shoes or binoculars, or even a car, only to have these items "borrowed" by a "brother" and never returned. This situation has proved frustrating for administrators trying to integrate Aborigines into the national cash economy. Thus, in the past, as now, there would have been very little incentive to produce prestige objects, and very few of them occur in the archaeological or ethnographic record of generalized hunter-gatherers. Similarly, fine art objects related to rituals are generally rare and are always considered corporate community property. They are always cached in remote, hidden locations.

In contrast, when complex hunter-gatherers arrive on the scene, some rituals become part of public displays as prestige demonstrations of success. Moreover, ritual is often used by individuals such as shamans in order to gain personal power or other benefits. Since private ownership is recognized among complex hunter-gatherers, many individuals, families, or corporate groups invest considerable amounts of time and effort in the production and display of prestigious ritual paraphernalia that is meant to impress people. I suggest that this is the basic reason why there seems to be an explosion of art and elaborate ritual paraphernalia in the Upper Paleolithic. In the ecologically rich areas where complex hunter-gatherers developed, there is a dramatic increase in the representations of virtually every aspect of religion that could be inferred to have existed in the earlier phases in the Paleolithic. New aspects of religion also develop.

ANCESTOR CULTS

Burials are more elaborate and indisputably intentional, providing clear evidence for concepts of the afterlife and spirit world (Binant 1991). There are consistent patterns of bone manipulations after burials that are very similar to patterns of later Neolithic times when they are generally associated with ancestor cults (see Chap. 7 and Cauwe 1996, 1997, 2001a, b; van Berg and Cauwe 1996; Oliva 2001:210–12). These include skull cults, scalping or defleshing skulls, removal of bones from burials, burials in living areas, and secondary burials (Beaune 1995:251–52). The bones removed from burials were probably carried around much as "saints" bones (relics) were kept and carried as objects of supernatural power, or talismans, in medieval times. Moreover, moderate-sized or even large stones are used in a few Upper Paleolithic burials or for other offering deposits. Some people refer to these burials as "megalithic" tombs, although megaliths generally only occur in later Neolithic cultures (Cauwe 1996, 1998b, 2001a, b; van Berg and Cauwe 1996; Beaune 1995:245; Freeman and Echegaray 1981:9).

Thus, there seems to be good evidence for ancestor veneration in the Upper Paleolithic, and it continues into many Mesolithic areas of Europe (Schulting 1998b; Schulting and Richards 2001, 2002). The remarkable structural and sculptural remains of the late Mesolithic site of Lepenski Vir in Serbia probably also represent mortuary feasting houses and totemic sculptures, since the structures are quite small and little domestic refuse was found at the sites. Burials were also key elements inside the structures (see pages 159–62). In another Mesolithic site nearby, a communal tomb was cut into the bedrock (Radovanovic 1996:122, 220)—a feature usually found only in ancestor-oriented megalithic cultures during Neolithic times.

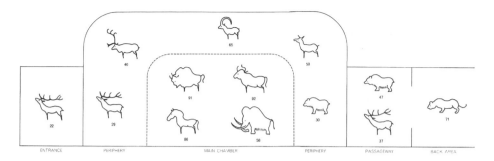

Fig. 5.8. After carefully mapping the locations of paintings within Upper Paleolithic caves, André Leroi-Gourhan discovered that they tended to form a pattern in the larger chambers with bison, cattle, horses, and mammoths portrayed on central panels while deer, reindeer, bouquetins, and bears were painted in more peripheral locations. Felines occurred almost exclusively in the more remote passageways. From A. Leroi-Gourhan, "The Evolution of Paleolithic Art," *Scientific American* 218(2):60–61.

ANIMAL CULTS

Thousands of depictions of animals in cave sanctuaries constitute a vast testimonial to the importance of animals in the religious life of Upper Paleolithic communities. André Leroi-Gourhan (1968) carefully recorded the positions of all animals within the major painted Upper Paleolithic caves and discovered, much to everyone's surprise, that the distribution of animal species was highly patterned. On the large chamber walls of the caves, wild cattle, bison, horses, and mammoths together with what Leroi-Gourhan identified as female symbols overwhelmingly dominated (Figs. 5.8, 5.9). Surrounding these central panels were depictions of stags and ibex as well as motifs that Leroi-Gourhan identified as masculine symbols. While some subsequent analysts have expressed reservations

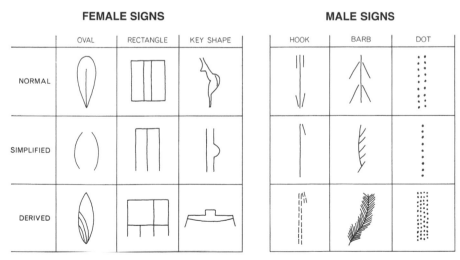

Fig. 5.9. There were also different sets of relatively abstract signs associated with the central panels in the caves and the peripheral areas. Some of these signs were interpreted as having female or male connotations, as suggested here. From A. Leroi-Gourhan, "The Evolution of Paleolithic Art," *Scientific American* 218(2):66.

Fig. 5.10. In Chauvet Cave, Upper Paleolithic people clearly moved and used the skulls of cave bears that they found in the cave, presumably for ritual purposes. Here a bear skull has been set up on a large rock near a hearth surrounded by numerous other bear skulls. From J.-M. Chauvet, E. Deschamps, and C. Hillaire, *La Grotte Chauvet,* Fig. 44. Paris: Seuil, 1995.

about interpreting this patterning in terms of sexual dualism, there is, nevertheless, a pattern that strongly indicates not only that animals were viewed in some sort of complementary dualism central to religious cults of the time but also that the large chambers in caves were used for rituals involving animal cults. It is also clear that human sexuality was a dominant symbolical theme in the caves, with stalagmites portrayed as phalluses and dissolution cavities portrayed as vaginas. This is particularly explicit at Pergouset Cave (Lorblanchet 2001:127, 164–66) and Font de Gaume, where vagina-shaped fissures were painted red.

Other evidence for animal cults was discovered in the form of a striking feline mural in one side sanctuary chamber in the French cave of Les Trois-Frères near the central Pyrenees. This chamber was called the "Lion Chapel" and contained the remains of a large fire and tools or bones placed vertically into crevices (Bégouën and Clottes 1986/87). At Kostienki in the Ukraine, lion skulls were also put on top of some dwellings where there was abundant ochre (Klein 1969:181–86). At the western end of the Pyrenees, Professor Arambourou (1981:3) excavated a remarkable collection of horse remains and horse sculptures at the rockshelter of Duruthy, which he felt certainly represented a cult sanctuary centered on horses. In southeastern France, at Chauvet Cave, one large chamber has a cave-bear skull carefully placed on a large, flat limestone block where a fire had also been lit (Fig. 5.10). This block was surrounded by more than 30 other bear skulls intentionally placed on the ground (Chauvet, Deschamps, and Hillaire 1995:42)—a situation remarkably similar to the early-twentieth-century description of bear skulls placed on ledges at Petershohle during Neanderthal times (see Chap. 4) and reminiscent of the special treatment of bear skulls at Régourdou.

At Dolni Vestonice and other nearby sites in Moravia (Czech Republic), excavators uncovered the earliest documented production in the world of purposefully baked clay (Adovasio et al. 1996; Vandiver et al. 1989), from over 23,000 years ago. There were some 2,000 fragments of small images of animals purposefully placed in a kiln while still damp so that they would break apart or explode when heated (Fig. 5.11). Experiments demonstrated that when properly dried, the fragmentation of these animals during firing was difficult to achieve, so the explosions were almost certainly intentional. Moreover, their production in a secluded part of the site indicated production for special purposes by a few unusual people, not by ordinary households. Thus, it appears that these clay animals were being used in divinatory rituals, and their use in this context again under-

scores the central role of animals in the supernatural concepts of the Upper Paleolithic.

In addition, many of the major Upper
Paleolithic depictions of men are as half animals and half men (therianthropes; Fig. 5.12),
indicating either totemic ancestors in animal
forms, masters of animals, shamanistic transformations, or perhaps all of these. There are
more than 55 such images in the Upper Paleolithic (Dickson 1990:131). It is curious that
there are no depictions of women as half
animals or in animal costumes. Similarly,
although there are many depictions of naked
women, there are very few images of naked
men other than in transformed animal states.
This is a pattern worth noting since it continues on into the Neolithic, as we shall see in
Chapter 6.

One striking sculpted face excavated by
Leslie Freeman and Jorge Echegaray (1981) at
El Juyo in northern Spain has been interpreted
by them to be half lion or leopard and half
man with a moustache (Fig. 5.13). This
sculpted stone is substantially larger than life
size (35 × 32 cm) and was carefully propped
up between two of the most remarkable offerings anywhere in the Upper Paleolithic. The
offerings consisted of clean sands, feet from
deer, layers of pink ochre, large animal bones,
decayed organic remains, seashells, numerous
bone spear points, and carefully created
rosettes of black and red 10-centimeter circles
of soil. These materials formed offering
mounds that were 75 centimeters high, sealed

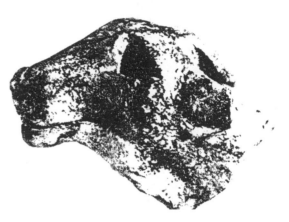

Fig. 5.11. Indications of belief in animal spirits during the
Upper Paleolithic also comes from thousands of clay fragments of simple modeled animals that were put into a special
kiln at Dolni Vestonice. Apparently, these clay animals were
meant to explode, perhaps as part of a divination ritual. These
are some of the earliest pieces of fired clay in the world, about
23,000 years old. From P. Vandiver, O. Soffer, B. Klíma, and
J. Svoboda, "The Origins of Ceramic Technology at Dolni
Vestonice, Czechoslovakia," *Science* 246:1004 (1989).
Reprinted with permission from *Science*. Copyright 1989
American Association for the Advancement of Science.

with clay, and connected by some sort of underground tube. One of the mounds was
capped by a "megalithic" one-ton slab of limestone that had been brought into the cave.
It was supported by smaller stone slabs. An even more dramatic representation of a half
man–half lion—or a man transformed into a lion—was found in Germany (Fig. 5.21).

Many of these animal cult elements, including the use of megalithic slabs, seem reminiscent of the bear cults of earlier times at Régourdou and perhaps the remains in Petershohle and Drachenloch. Bear cults are particularly interesting not only because of their
apparent great antiquity, but also because of their very widespread occurrence, especially
in circumpolar regions (Fig. 4.20; Campbell 1983:147ff; Hultkrantz 1967:142; Watanabe 1994). They also occur in other areas and time periods such as classical Greece.

Professor Jean Clottes (1996) has documented a change over time from early Upper

Fig. 5.12. There are more than 50 Upper Paleolithic representations of men that are part animal and part human, or at least of men wearing animal disguises. It is intriguing that there are no clear examples of women that are part animal. From S. de Beaune, "Chamanisme et préhistoire," *L'Homme* 147:204 (1998).

Paleolithic animal cults that featured carnivores and dangerous animals to later cults emphasizing more herbivorous ungulates such as horses and reindeer, although at least feline and bear cults seem to persist into later time periods as noted at Trois-Frères. The nature of these animal cults probably continued to revolve around concepts of totemic ancestors (Laming-Emperaire 1959, 1962), spirits of killed animals returning to the spirit realm, masters of animals, and creator animals, or some combination of these. Totemic ancestors are supernatural beings (often animals) that are thought to have passed part of their essence on to their human descendants who belong to the "totem" of that ancestor. Thus, individuals may have a wolf or frog or other animal totem and be able to invoke or channel the original totemic ancestor energy under appropriate ritual conditions. It is difficult to determine the exact nature of the concepts represented in the Upper Paleolithic at this point without undertaking much more detailed studies of specific prehistoric cultures, but sexual reproduction is often associated with the return of plant or animal spirits in newly regenerated bodies (Dickson 1990:207–14). And so, Leroi-Gourhan's view of an underlying sexual duality in Paleolithic religions may ultimately turn out to be fairly accurate.

As we shall see shortly, there is also much better evidence than in previous periods for other religious phenomena, such as cults featuring ecstatic rituals, initiations, and shamanism. But these topics are better discussed in the context of some of the new developments of this period.

Complexity Brings New Dimensions to Rituals: Feasting

As Polly Wiessner (1996) notes, simple hunter-gatherers constantly share all meat from large game or other large food harvests without any expectation of immediate or exact return. She makes a strong argument that such sharing is ecologically adaptive for everyone concerned, although it may benefit some individuals more than others (see also Hawkes et al. 2001; Winterhalder 1986). Food sharing even takes place among male chimpanzees, apparently in order to create more solidarity in the defense of home ranges (McGrew 1992:114). In this context, anything resembling "feasting" that takes place among simple hunter-gatherers has a rather ordinary character (Hayden 2001a). The closest equivalents to feasts seem to occur only when unusually large or prized animals are killed or when unusual abundances of other relished resources are obtained. However, there are rarely any host or organizing families, and there are few preparations since these events are largely unpredictable. There is no accumulation period prior to the giving of a feast. There is no account keeping or repayment record. There is little ritual involved other than that normally observed when animals are killed. No special status or honor is conferred upon the hunter who made the kill. While many people may contribute to these "feasts," and although feasts may serve to enhance group solidarity or alliance relationships between bands, there is nothing very much out of the ordinary about them compared with other daily meals.

With the appearance of complex hunter-gatherers, feasts take on new dimensions of meaning. Private ownership, sedentism, storage of food, and socioeconomic inequalities all combine to render feasting probably *the* major event in most communities. More than any other activity, feasts embody the customs, beliefs, arts, values, social relationships, politics, and rituals of transegalitarian communities. Above all, it is the new ability to produce owned food surpluses on a regular basis and to use those surpluses to compete for labor and power that

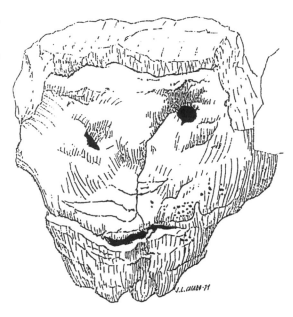

Fig. 5.13. At El Juyo in Spain, Upper Paleolithic individuals modified this block of stone and set it up in their ritual area. The excavators suggest that it was intended to represent a face that was half man (possibly with a mustache) and half lion. From L. Freeman and J. Gonzalez Echegaray, "El Juyo: A 14,000 year old Sanctuary from Northern Spain," *History of Religion* 21:12 (1981). Reprinted with permission of the University of Chicago Press.

transforms feasts into spectacular events involving large amounts of time and effort together with splashy displays of art and ritual. There are many types of feasts, but the potlatch of the Northwest Coast Indians of North America is probably the best-known ethnographic example of transegalitarian feasting, with its lavish consumption of food, startling ritual dances, exorbitant gift giving, and detailed record keeping of gift debts (Fig. 5.14). Less extreme variations of this kind of feast occur in most, if not all, transegalitarian societies, whether they are complex hunter-gatherers, simple horticulturalists, or pastoral nomads. We will expand our consideration of feasts in the next chapter, but it is important to note here that the first evidence for feasting comes from the complex hunter-gatherers of the Upper Paleolithic and Mesolithic.

When I visited the caves of Enlène and Les Trois-Frères near the central Pyrenees, Count Bégouën showed me his current excavations in a small, dark vestibule of the cave. I was astonished by the enormous quantity of bone and the charcoal-stained earth on this prehistoric surface dating back at least 14,000 years. I was also struck by the fact that it must have been very dark and that it was right at the entrance to a very long cave system containing several of the most remarkable sanctuaries known from the Upper Paleolithic. Living in such dark places was very unusual for hunter-gatherers as was the sheer density of material accumulated there. Thus, I think that the remains in the

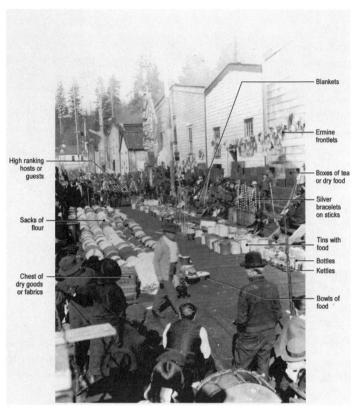

High ranking
hosts or
guests

Sacks of
flour

Chest of
dry goods
or fabrics

Blankets

Ermine
frontlets

Boxes of tea
or dry food

Silver
bracelets
on sticks

Tins with
food

Bottles

Kettles

Bowls of
food

Fig. 5.14. Lavish feasts and reciprocal gift giving of wealth on a grand scale seems to have originated with complex hunter-gatherers. The tradition of potlatching on the Northwest Coast became even more elaborate with wealth garnered from trading furs with Europeans, but its basic form and the presentation of surplus wealth undoubtedly go far back into the prehistoric past. Here, food and wealth to be given away are displayed at an Alert Bay potlatch sometime before 1914. Royal British Columbian Museum photo 2307-b.

vestibule at Enlène probably constitute some of the earliest good evidence for specialized ritual feasting in the Upper Paleolithic that we currently have, although Margaret Conkey (1980) has argued that several caves in northern Spain, such as El Juyo, served as aggregation sites where a number of different bands from the surrounding area would meet to conduct rituals and participate in feasts. These locations are unusually rich in animal bones and include art motifs that seem to originate from different subregions in the vicinity of the larger cave sites. Slightly later in time, in the Near East, there is much more dramatic evidence of feasting at the site of Hallan Çemi, in Turkey (c. 12,000 B.P.), where a central depression in a village of complex hunter-gatherers was used for cooking and consuming meat on a large scale (Rosenberg 1994; Rosenberg and Redding 2000). Smaller roasting deposits may have been used for feasting in sites of the Natufian culture in Jordan (Byrd 1989:78–80). Feasts were also prominent parts of funerals during the European Mesolithic (Schulting 1998a, 1998b).

As one might expect from the emergence of surplus-based feasting (especially competitive feasting), record keeping of gift debts and the display of prestige items to demonstrate economic success also appear at the same time. Alexander Marshack (1991a) has carefully documented record-keeping notations from the European Upper Paleolithic (Fig. 5.15). He views all of the series of lines and dots from this period in terms of calendrical notations, especially related to lunar cycles. His argument is convincing in some cases, but less so in others. What could the other cases of notation represent? Why would keeping track of lunar cycles be important?

I suggest that the most plausible other reason for keeping track of numbers of things would be for debts, specifically feasting debts. This is consistent with everything that we now know about complex hunter-gatherers and the feasts that the richest members of these communities hold. Frequently, dozens, scores, or hundreds of valuable items of food or gifts and debts must be monitored and remembered for each important feast, of which there are many. The magnitude of the task must have rapidly outrun human mental capacities, especially in areas with the richest resources and the largest feasts. In fact, Denise Schmandt-Besserat (1992) has traced our own writing system back to the use of simple clay geometrical shapes employed by Mesolithic-level complex hunter-gatherers in Iraq, some 12,000 years ago. She argues that these were used for keeping track of loaned animals and debts, just as clay tokens are still used today by some pastoral nomads in the region (Fig. 5.16). Tally devices were also discovered at Hallan Çemi (Rosenberg 1994; Rosenberg and Redding 2000).

In order to give as large a feast as possible and give as many gifts as possible, the coordination of the calling in of debts and the timing of feasts is of critical importance, as illustrated in the

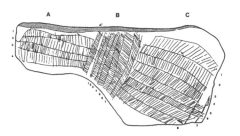

Fig. 5.15. There are a number of examples of Upper Paleolithic objects carefully engraved with series of lines. Alexander Marshack has suggested that they may be time-keeping devices. Another possibility, especially for the more complex items such as this one, is that they were for keeping records of gifts and reciprocal debts given or owed from important feasts. From A. Marshack, "Beyond Art: Pleistocene Image and Symbol," in M. Conkey, O. Soffer, D. Stratmann, and N. Jablonski, eds., *Beyond Art*, Fig. 15. California Academy of Sciences, Memoir 23, 1997. Used with permission of the California Academy of Sciences.

Fig. 5.16. These are clay "tokens" excavated from Middle Eastern sites spanning the end of the Paleolithic until the emergence of the first cities. Similar clay tokens are still used by some Middle Eastern herders for keeping records of animals given or loaned to others. Such token records eventually led to the development of the alphabet that we use today. Photo by D. Schmandt-Beserat.

documentary video, *Ongka's Big Moka*. I suggest that this is the real significance of the calendrical notations that Alexander Marshack has documented in the Upper Paleolithic and later times.

Finally, Sophie de Beaune (1995:125, 212) notes that prestige serving spoons of antler and ivory were also used in the Upper Paleolithic. At Hallan Çemi, prestige serving vessels of stone were unearthed (Rosenberg 1994; Rosenberg and Redding 2000). Prestige serving items would certainly be expected at feasts meant to impress guests. Some sculptures were also intentionally broken in the Upper Paleolithic, probably for the same reasons that Northwest Coast potlatch hosts intentionally burned or broke valuable items at the height of potlatches—in order to demonstrate their great wealth. Other sculptures (Fig. 5.1) were used to display the wealth and success of households, undoubtedly primarily at public ritual and feasting events (Beaune 1995:213).

Therefore, the key feature to note about these feasts is the role of rituals, for the first time, in sanctifying the use of surpluses in order to establish social, economic, and political advantages for households or lineages. People use feasts to create debts and forge political alliances. Therefore, many rituals probably become public spectacles for the first time. They are characterized by the lavish display of ritual objects, such as carvings, masks, costumes, paintings, and other symbolic paraphernalia. Very often special foods are obtained and prepared for these ritual feasts, as for the Ainu bear ceremony portrayed in the film *Iomande*. In this ceremony the bear is one of the special foods, and a bear cub is caught, fattened, and raised for a year. It is then ceremonially killed and eaten, and its spirit is fêted and sent back to its mountain home so that it will remember its happy experiences among the Ainu and return to them with a new body (Fig. 5.17). The ritual dispatch of animals to their spiritual homes so that they will return is an old and widespread theme among hunter-gatherers in North America and Asia (Watanabe 1994; Lajoux 2002), as are the singing, drumming, and masked dramas that form part of these ritual feasts. However, among complex hunter-gatherers like the Ainu, these rituals were transformed so that it was probably only the richest families that could afford to capture and feed animals such as bears on household surpluses during an entire year. It would only have been the richest families that could have afforded to fête the spirit of the bear properly, with impressive ritual items and abundant alcohol and food. Bear meat was highly valued because of its fat content, and hosts gave the best parts of the bear to other high-ranking members of the community and thus created debts that had to be returned. It would also have been the richest family that expected the gratitude of the community for providing the feast and for ensuring the continuing supply of bears and other animals from their mountain spirit homes. Rich sponsors of bear feasts might also use the gratitude of the bear spirit as a reason for being better off than other families. Such wealth-related feasts and rituals were likely used as a kind of advertising to draw other wealthy families into marriage and wealth exchanges, and they certainly conferred great prestige on the sponsors (Lajoux 2002).

The likelihood of similar rituals occurring among European complex hunter-gatherers has been highlighted by the identification of remains of a kept and harnessed bear in the French Mesolithic (Chaix, Bridault, and Picavet 1977) as well as captive boars in northern Mesolithic Europe (Gronenborn 1999:129). Similarly, in the Paleolithic, although the aurochs (wild bull) was a featured animal in many cave paintings, it was a

Fig. 5.17. Along the lower Amur River in Siberia, the Gilyaks, like the Ainu, had a ceremony in which a bear that had been raised from a cub was ritually killed and eaten, as shown in these early illustrations. Bear meat was greatly relished in cold climates for its high fat content, and raising such animals for feasts required considerable surpluses and wealth. Similar practices may well have led to the domestication of animals for feasting in other parts of the world. From J. Campbell, *Historical Atlas of World Mythology: The Way of the Animal Powers,* Figs. 260 and 261. New York: A. van der Marck Editions, 1983. Originals from the American Museum of Natural History.

rarely hunted or eaten prestige animal because it was so dangerous. It may have been procured only by those with great feasting ambitions (Dickson 1990:186; Beaune 1995:83).

Thus, the sudden appearance of ritual items and carvings in the context of Upper Paleolithic domestic refuse (versus their nearly complete absence in earlier periods) most likely reflects the transformation of egalitarian feasting and rituals into transegalitarian ritual feasting as a means of increasing prestige, power, and wealth in communities on the part of the most enterprising, ambitious, and gifted members.

Cave Rituals: Secret Societies
Open the Doors to New Dimensions

There have been many theories about why people began to paint and engrave magnificent images of animals deep inside European caves in the Upper Paleolithic. Early researchers thought the images were for hunting magic or were related to totemic cults or were used in tribal initiations (Bahn and Vertut 1988). Later scholars noted a repeated organization of the images that seemed to indicate that caves were used as sanctuaries (Leroi-Gourhan 1968) or suggested that it was primarily shamans who used the caves and painted impressive images in them (Clottes and Lewis-Williams 1998).

I would like to propose a somewhat different role for Upper Paleolithic caves, based on certain characteristics of complex hunter-gatherers. It should be kept in mind that, as in all archaeological problem solving, theories, models, or ideas about the past need to be tested. Thus, I encourage future testing of all ideas on cave art as well as the other theories proposed in this book.

If transegalitarian feasting transformed secretive egalitarian rituals into public displays of prestige and success, transegalitarian politics probably also maintained a secretive aspect of ritual that was much more exclusive. I propose that this aspect of Upper Paleolithic and Mesolithic religion is related to the development of secret societies. Secret societies are more or less like exclusive ritual clubs that feature severe initiatory trials, symbolic death, the revelation of a secret doctrine, and masked ancestral spirits (Eliade 1969:114–15). Understanding complex hunter-gatherer politics and secret societies is a relatively new area of research, but in my estimation it may hold the key to understanding much of the archaeological evidence from this early period. As Michael Dietler (2001:70) emphasizes, contemporary studies of religion have begun to emphasize the "instrumental role of ritual in creating, defining, and transforming structures of power."

In order to investigate this role for the Upper Paleolithic, D'Ann Owens and I (Owens and Hayden 1997) began to examine ethnographic accounts of complex hunter-gatherers around the world. We started with a simple observation and a simple question related to the use of the painted caves. On the basis of pioneering research by Leroi-Gourhan (1965, 1968), David Lewis-Williams (Lewis-Williams and Dowson 1988), and others, it was clear that the painted caves were used for some sort of ritual purposes, an issue that will be discussed in more detail later in the chapter. However, there was no agreement on the nature of those rituals. Owens and I began with the well-documented observation that a large portion of the footprints and handprints recorded from deep caves used in the Upper Paleolithic were consistently those of children (Clottes 1989:323). We then turned to the ethnographic record and asked the question: What rituals generally involve children among complex hunter-gatherers?

While there were a number of interesting results, the one that was most consistent and most pronounced and seemed to fit the Upper Paleolithic cave data the best was that children were characteristically initiated into secret societies. Although not all complex hunter-gatherers have secret societies, these ritual organizations become increasingly common as food surpluses and social complexity increase. The fact that secret societies appear to be absent among generalized hunter-gatherers supports this notion. It was also evident from the ethnographies that while these secret societies could theoretically be open to everyone, only the wealthier and more influential families became members or advanced to higher ranks. Using techniques that had been pioneered much earlier in human evolution, these elite members of society forged close emotional ties among themselves using ecstatic rituals in order to build and broker political and economic power. In these societies, leading members also acquired powerful spirit allies (generally, "power animals") through ecstatic experiences that were used to support, sanction, and solidify the basis of secular power.

Among the Chumash of California, only high-status individuals were allowed to be members. Their secret society was responsible for "maintaining, directing, and controlling man's interaction with his celestial, physical, and social environments" (Hudson and Underhay 1988:29). Meetings of such societies almost seem more like political strategy planning sessions than religious events. In general, secret societies appear to provide important material benefits in terms of establishing alliances and trade relationships or political support using supernatural reinforcement controlled by high-ranking members (La Fontaine 1985:95). On the Northwest Coast, some secret society members held hereditary rights to the religious experiences sponsored by the societies (Drucker 1965:167) or acquired their guardian spirits as marks of aristocratic rank (Jilek 1992:89). Among the complex hunter-gatherers of the Northwest Interior, the guardian spirit quest was open to everyone. But the quests of elite children were generally more severe and longer than those of other people, resulting in the acquisition of more numerous and more powerful guardian spirits (usually power animals) by the elite children (Schulting 1995:50–52).

These facts, together with other observations about the use of the Upper Paleolithic painted caves, support the idea that caves were being used for initiation and probably other rituals by members of secret societies during the Upper Paleolithic. And what place could be more secret than a deep cave? These observations can be summarized briefly.

1. The most ritually complex cultures of the Upper Paleolithic were clearly complex hunter-gatherers.
2. The most complex hunter-gatherers have a strong tendency to develop secret societies as one strategy to enable aspiring elites to consolidate economic, social, and political control within communities.
3. While initiations can be used for a number of purposes and in different ways in various types of societies, some of the most important initiation events for children in *complex hunter-gatherer societies* occur when they become junior members of secret societies and later attempt to advance in the society's hierarchy.
4. Secret society initiations often involve achieving ecstatic states and spiritual visions or acquiring animal guardians. Caves are ideally suited for inducing such states, especially through sensory deprivation and the amplification of drumming, whistles,

flickering torchlight, and other dramatic effects. At Tuc d'Audubert, which is also part of the Enlène–Trois-Frères cave system, there are indications that adolescents carried out energetic dances by using their heels, perhaps in imitation of animals (Campbell 1983:77–78).

5. The painted caves in Europe were *not* used on a regular basis, as might be expected of routine initiations for all tribal members. Dates for paintings within single caves are spread out episodically over hundreds or thousands of years rather than being clustered in shorter time periods of intensive use. Remains of torches, fires, tools, and food bones are also relatively rare. If the caves had seen regular use, one would expect much more abundant remains. Thus, visits to caves appear to have been rare events (Clottes 1989:322; Beaune 1995:192, 238, 274), as might be expected of exceptional initiations and ceremonies.

6. The spaces used were sometimes relatively small and more fitting for small segments of communities rather than entire communities. For instance, according to my estimates, the main chamber at Font de Gaume (one of the most masterfully painted caves in France) could hold only about 20 standing people, with no room for movement. Thus, those visiting the caves constituted a privileged minority of the community (Beaune 1995:238; Lewis-Williams 1994, 1995a).

7. It is clear that considerable preparatory work went into creating some of the cave paintings. They required training of art specialists as well as the underwriting of the actual forays into the caves, the construction of scaffolds to paint animals high on the walls or ceilings, and the elaborate preparation of pigments (Arlette Leroi-Gourhan 1982; Beaune 1995:191). Undertakings of such scope and quality imply artistic specialists who would have to be maintained by commissions or who might be members of elite families and supported by surpluses of others' work (Beaune 1995:274). Perhaps the most extreme of these creations were the masterful life-sized sculptures in the round of horses and bisons created in rock shelters such as the Abri Cap Blanc in the Dordogne (Fig. 5.18). Such works required great training, great skill, and extended periods of labor to create. They were not simply the result of impulsive fits of creativity boiling up inside the psyches of a new race of individuals seeking some outward expression, as implied by some writers. Upper Paleolithic art was not doodling. It was a "great art" tradition; and great art traditions require special training and substantial economic support to develop and maintain. The art in the major caves was clearly meant to impress and awe viewers by its sophistication and effort—and it still does, over 30,000 years later. While entire communities sometimes undertake complex projects such as irrigation, mining, or houses of worship, these generally have either a practical or public display purpose. Forays into the caves lasting hours or days in order to paint images or conduct rituals were expensive affairs for a select few. These forays might be better viewed as underwritten by wealthy families at infrequent intervals for special clandestine events such as elite initiations.

8. The animals depicted in the caves are generally not the most important animals used for food on a daily basis (Bahn and Vertut 1988:157). The animals portrayed in paintings were selected for symbolical reasons, such as strength and wildness (aurochs, bison), power (mammoth), ferocity (lion), or swiftness (horse), or perhaps

for totemic affiliations (Beaune 1995:83, 198–99, 209).

9. Painted caves are usually located in areas that would have been unusually rich in resources during the Upper Paleolithic, often near good hunting grounds, migration routes, or fishing locations in river valleys or near the confluence of rivers (Beaune 1995:204, 216). This indicates that groups using the caves were rich in resources. As we have seen, groups with abundant surpluses are most likely to have secret societies and associated rituals.

10. Secret societies often use masks and high drama as part of their rituals and initiations (Eliade 1958b:33). This certainly seems to have been part of cave rituals (see Figs. 5.12, 5.13, and 5.21; also Beaune 1995:248).

11. Feasts are usually held after secret society initiations (La Fontaine 1985:131, 181, 185), and there is evidence at El Juyo and Enlène that substantial feasting occurred in these caves. Other caves also contain evidence of meals having been consumed around fires, although no detailed analysis of these remains is available and feasting could also have taken place in the vicinity just outside the caves.

Fig. 5.18. The most time-consuming pieces of art created in the Upper Paleolithic were probably the life-sized animals sculpted in the round on the walls of Cap Blanc rockshelter in France. The magnificent horse (above) and wild bull (below) were heavily damaged by quarry men who did not realize that they were sculptures. Photo by B. Hayden.

In my estimation, all of these observations provide a compelling case for the use of many of the painted Upper Paleolithic caves as special sanctuaries and places of initiation for secret society members, as were caves on the Northwest Coast (Eliade 1958b:69). Certainly, caves may well have also been used for other purposes such as shamanistic trances, especially if the shamans were members of secret societies, which is likely (Eliade 1958b:39). As sanctuaries for elite initiations and rituals, the painted caves of Europe were designed to make powerful impressions on people. Such an interpretation also accords well with observations by David Lewis-Williams (1994, 1995a:150; 1995b:19), who argues that these deep caves were used in order to restrict access and exclude the general public so that a more select group would have control over rituals involving altered states of consciousness and over supernatural claims that could legitimize political power. The cosmos, like human society of the time, was probably viewed as being hierarchical. I fully concur. In order to test the theory that caves were used for secret society initiations and special rituals, I have developed a series of hypotheses and begun a research project to see if my hypotheses are supported by the evidence available. Specifically, if caves were used by secret societies, I expect that:

- sanctuary types of spatial organization, such as that proposed by André Leroi-Gourhan, should be confirmed with clear display areas as well as areas more suitable for individual perceptual initiation experiences (Baffier and Girard [1998:109–10] and Lorblanchet [2001:149, 160] have also proposed these two distinct types of use for Upper Paleolithic caves);
- some panels of display art would only be viewable by a small number of people (ca. 20–25) because of the postulated restricted nature of the secret societies and the events;
- evidence for use of caves will continue to indicate infrequent, episodic rather than regular visits;
- definite evidence for feasting may be confirmed for some of the caves (but not all since such feasts could also be held outside the caves);
- and an analysis of material items left in the caves (stone or bone tools) will reflect ritual or feasting activities.

If these expectations are all met in future research, the case for the secret society theory of cave use should be considerably bolstered.

It is interesting to note that as transegalitarian societies become more complex, women's status tends to increase, largely because of the investments that women represent in terms of bride wealth and dowries (Hayden 1995:55). Thus, unlike the ecstatic cults of some generalized hunter-gatherers, which rigidly segregated the sexes, many secret societies admitted women. However, in most cases, women had minor roles or they were not permitted to participate at all in the higher levels of the organization (Owens and Hayden 1997:143; Eliade 1958b:2). In other cases, the initiates were usually segregated by sex at secret society initiation rituals (La Fontaine 1985:90, 109, 117; Eliade 1958b:2). Thus, the predominance of animals and hunting motifs in the caves may indicate that the caves were used for initiating boys. While the value of marriageable women might have been increased by initiations into secret societies, this seems to have been more commonly achieved through special training and/or the hosting of maturation feasts for elite children (Owens and Hayden 1997). Precisely how the value of girls and boys might have been enhanced by elite families in the Upper Paleolithic is difficult to determine at this point.

Even if the specific interpretation of cave art that I have advanced should eventually prove to account for the data less well than other explanations, it seems likely that increasing socioeconomic complexity played a critical role in both the more intensive use of deep caves and the creation of great art within them. Wiessner and Tumu (1998, 1999; Wiessner 2001), for example, document how aggrandizive big men in New Guinea promote cult activities in order to mobilize community labor and surpluses for projects that primarily benefit big men. Such models are certainly worth investigating and testing (if we are ingenious enough!) in the context of understanding Upper Paleolithic cave paintings.

The Next Generation of Ecstatic Experiences

As with feasting, the most ambitious agents of social and religious transformation in complex hunter-gatherer societies used the age-old religious practice of inducing ecstatic states rooted in the ancestral, genetic, emotional, and psychological adaptations discussed in Chapters 2 and 3. But they cast these traditional practices into a new mold to suit their ambitions. Initiations and animal cults featuring ecstatic experiences were probably developed among some of the earliest generalized hunter-gatherers in order to ensure adherence to group survival values and to create strong emotional bonds between individuals and communities. However, much later, among well-off complex hunter-gatherers, sharing and intergroup alliances were no longer as critical for survival. I think that aspiring elites increasingly sought to restrict access to ecstatic contact with supernatural forces in order to claim privileged divine directives, in order to justify the new values that they wanted to propagate such as the ownership of resources, private property, bride wealth, ancestral powers, and many other self-serving concepts. Thus, in a curious twist of events, as life became more secure for most people, the ability to endure pain and to experience ecstatic states seems to have become transformed from a required ordeal for all adolescents living in stressed environments to a hallmark of elite superiority, demonstrating that elites had supernatural powers and strength beyond those of normal people. This became a device used by elites in many parts of the world, including the powerful aristocrats of the Mayan empires (Schele and Friedel 1990) and Northwest Coast nobles.

This entire new complex of feasting, secret ritual societies, and elite ecstatic initiations that I postulate here must have constituted a decisive turning point in the evolution of religions, because it was the beginning of a fundamental division between popular cults and elite cults. This represents a change in traditional religions brought about by those in power who used religion as a means to manipulate and control other community members. It is the harbinger of exclusivity and the decline of all-inclusive participatory sacred experiential cults. This is the vanguard of new religious practices in which the right of the individual to contact and participate in the sacred aspects of the universe is curtailed by self-aggrandizing individuals who see the desire to be one with the sacred forces of the universe as a political tool and a means to their own self-serving ends. For instance, among the complex hunter-gatherers of the Northwest Coast, supernatural encounters became a hereditary right (Drucker 1965:167). Perhaps this development was not too extreme during the Upper Paleolithic. Many of the same animal deities may have been revered in both the public and secret cults, although some animal deities seem to have been ritually revered exclusively in the caves. In particular, images of animal predators (with warrior or power connotations that become manifest in later epochs) and therianthrope forms seem to occur only in the caves. With the exclusion of the general public from cave rituals (no matter what their more precise nature), we can certainly see this trend toward elite-controlled cults beginning. It will continue to grow throughout the succeeding millennia. It also seems certain that both feasts and cave rituals were predicated on the production and strategic display of economic surpluses, whether this was in the context of secret societies or some other surplus-driven ritual organization.

SHAMANISM

Under these new conditions, what became of shamanism? In a ground-breaking study, David Lewis-Williams and Thomas Dowson (1988) drew world attention to the probable existence of shamanism in the Upper Paleolithic and to its role in creating much of the art of the period, especially the cave paintings. Somewhat earlier, Lommel (1967)

Fig. 5.19. The supernatural character of the animals painted and engraved deep inside Upper Paleolithic caves is clearly demonstrated by the occurrence of imaginary beasts, such as this two-horned horselike creature in Lascaux, France. Compare this form to the mythical animal ancestor portrayed in Fig. 1.3. From A. Leroi-Gourhan, *Préhistoire de l'Art Occidental,* Fig. 440. Paris: Mazenod, 1968.

had argued that shamanism was the origin of art, but he did not develop the argument in as much detail. What are the main arguments that can be adduced to show shamanism existed in the Upper Paleolithic?

First, it can be persuasively argued that the painted caves were used for ritual purposes (Clottes and Lewis-Williams 1998:38). Ethnographically, caves are widely associated with the underworld and spirit homes for animals, rainfall, or human spirits (Eliade 1958b:58; Clottes and Lewis-Williams 1998; Campbell 1983:79). Moreover, the painted animals on the cave walls are never portrayed in natural or narrative contexts; rather, they seem to float in the air as if disincarnate. They are also frequently drawn over by subsequent artists, as if the act of drawing them was the most important aspect of the art rather than the actual resulting depictions. There are also at least five examples of mythical animals portrayed on the cave walls (Dickson 1990:131–35), animals that never existed, such as the horselike creature with two long horns projecting from its forehead in Lascaux Cave (Fig. 5.19). As previously discussed, the paintings are also organized in a structured fashion indicating clear symbolism and ritually preferred locations for depicting certain animals and, possibly, reflecting a sexual division of the conceptual world. Dowson and Porr (1999) argue that the specific animals portrayed and their postures indicate shamanic types of concerns. All these characteristics indicate that caves were used for ritual purposes.

Second, the underworld was a place to which shamans often traveled in order to effect their cures and deal with the spirit world. Caves would have been ideal locations for conducting the most important of these journeys, physically as well as mentally, because of their isolation from outside disturbances and the total elimination of visual and auditory sensations that could be achieved in them.

Third, there are a number of convincingly shamanic motifs depicted at some sites. In Lascaux, at the bottom of a deep and narrow shaft, there is a painting of a wounded bison above a human figure who seems to be falling or lying on the ground in a rigid posture with a full erection. Next to him is a staff with a bird on it (Fig. 5.20). Many people consider this to be a portrayal of a shaman in ecstasy, since both staffs and birds are generally associated with shamans (Davenport and Jochim 1988). I might add that erections sometimes occur in states of ecstasy but not in death. Moreover, battles between shamans and animal spirits are common aspects of their journeys to the underworld. The Lascaux figure can certainly be interpreted in this fashion (Dickson 1990:131–35).

Mythic animals or spirit monsters also occur in many shamanic accounts of travels and battles in the underworld, and these, too, occur in Upper Paleolithic cave paintings. In the cave of Les Trois-Frères, which connects with the cave of Enlène, exists one of the most famous Paleolithic paintings of all: a half-man, half-stag creature with additional traits of other animals (Fig. 5.12 top center). Many authors have argued that this therianthropic image represents the well-known claims of shamans to be able to transform themselves into animals. Similar interpretations can be made of the lion-headed man carved in ivory (Fig. 5.21), the stone head at El Juyo (Fig. 5.13), and more than 50 other depictions of men with antlers or other animal elements (Fig. 5.12; Dickson 1990:131–35). At the very least, men appear to have worn animal costumes, also a typical shamanistic characteristic. This tradition continued into the following Mesolithic period, for at the site of Star Carr, in England, excavators found numerous shaped pieces of antlers still attached to the upper skulls of deer, but with eye holes carved out, exactly as shown in ethnographic illustrations (compare Fig. 5.22 with Fig. 3.3). The fact that shamans generally use animal spirit allies in their work is yet another reason for viewing the caves where animals are the dominant motif as shamanistic products. This close association of men with animals or animal transformations will be a recurring theme in other transegalitarian and even more complex cultures.

A fourth reason for thinking that shamanism was present is the depiction of altered and ecstatic states. For example, there is the very strange-looking prostrate man in Lascaux (Fig. 5.20). However, Lewis-Williams's main contribution was to demonstrate that many of the puzzling symbols depicted in the caves resembled entoptic phenomena as described in "Entoptics" (see page 152). These indications, as well as the eminently suited environment of the caves, provide strong reasons to believe that people in the caves were experiencing ecstatic states, just as hunter-gatherer shamans in South Africa entered trances and depicted their experiences in the rock art of the region. There are far too many parallels between the shamanistic rock art of South African Bushmen and the Paleolithic cave art of Europe to dismiss them as coincidences. Entoptic images occur frequently in both Paleolithic and ethnographic Bushmen art traditions. South African shamans considered rock walls to be boundaries or veils between their middle world and the realms of the animal spirits. They believed that animal spirits could be induced to

Fig. 5.20. A shamanic ecstatic state of travel to other worlds seems to be represented in this simple scene of a prone man with a notable erection, as often occurs in profound ecstatic states, but not death. The nearby association of a bird on a staff also probably indicates shamanic flight. Compare Fig. 3.20. From D. Davenport and M. Jochim, "The Scene in the Shaft at Lascaux," *Antiquity* 62:559 (1988).

Fig. 5.21. Shamans commonly experience inner visions of being transformed into animals. One of the most likely meanings of the half-man, half-animal representations, such as this lion-man from a German Upper Paleolithic cave at Hohlenstein, may be related to shamanic trance experiences (see also Fig. 5.12). From a photo by A. Marshack, *The Roots of Civilization*, Fig. 231. Mount Kisco, N.Y.: Moyer Bell, 1991.

come out of the rock walls with paintings. Red ochre and other paints constituted magical fluids that made this possible (Lewis-Williams 1995a:150; 1995b:17). Similar beliefs have been inferred for those who frequented Paleolithic caves such as Les Trois-Frères, where bones were stuck into the crevasses of chamber walls (Bégouën and Clottes 1986/87; Clottes 1989:310; Bégouën et al. 1993:304–13). And in Chauvet Cave, painted animals seem to be literally coming out of fissures in the walls (Clottes and Lewis-Williams 1998:85–86).

A fifth reason for thinking that shamanism was involved in the creation of cave art is the use of very deep passages and small, hidden diverticules. In these areas, as Leroi-Gourhan noted in his analysis, there are depictions of dangerous animals and ghostlike images. Lewis-Williams suggests that these were the places that shamans went in order to achieve the deepest ecstatic states or that they were perhaps places that shaman initiates were taken in order to increase the terror and effectiveness of their initiation.

Other reasons for thinking that shamans were present in the Upper Paleolithic include the positioning of some paintings at locations in caves where any sounds would be amplified (Scarre 1989; Reznikoff and Dauvois 1988). While vocal sounds could have been used to create powerful effects, drums, whistles, and rattles would have been even more dramatic, especially given the effects of sonic driving used to put shamans and initiates into altered states, as described in Chapter 3. The clay animals used in divination rituals at Dolni Vestonice provide yet another possible indicator of shamanic activity. The sheer quantity of these objects (thousands of fragments) indicates that animal spirits were being invoked or used on behalf of a community population rather than by a single individual for private purposes. A carved portrait of a person with one side of the face disfigured or distorted was also associated with these ceramic figurines. A nearby remarkable burial was discovered of an individual (perhaps a woman) between two men in unusual positions (Fig. 5.7). One side of the facial bones of the central individual were congenitally disfigured. This person also had spinal scoliosis and a poorly developed right leg, leading to the suggestion that she may well have been singled out for shamanic training, as were many individuals with physical or psychological disabilities (Eliade 1964:495; Putman 1988:466).

I feel that all of these arguments, plus the antiquity implied by the widespread distribution and apparent adaptedness of shamanism to hunting cultures (discussed in Chap. 3), are persuasive arguments for its existence in the Upper Paleolithic of Europe. Some prehistorians such as Sophie de Beaune (1998) have objected to the excessive invocations of shamanism to account for almost every aspect of Upper Paleolithic culture as well as rock art throughout the world. David Whitley (1992), for example, proposes that ecstatic shamanism is an explanation for all rock art in western

Fig. 5.22. At the Mesolithic site of Star Carr, numerous sets of antlers were found that had been modified almost exactly in the same fashion as the antlers shown on the Saami shaman's head in Fig. 3.3. Of special note are the two intriguing eyelike holes carved into the bone just below the antler bases. Photo by B. Hayden. Printed with permission of the University of Cambridge Museum of Archaeology and Anthropology.

North America. De Beaune agrees that altered states of consciousness are certainly very ancient and may well be implicated in the production of some art, but she argues that ecstatic trance states are hardly enough to demonstrate convincingly the presence of shamanism, since such states also occur in initiations of all kinds, possession cults, among monks and meditators, and in many other religious and secular contexts. While she is technically correct that it is difficult to demonstrate the presence of shamanic travel to the spirit world in order to cure or obtain other community benefits, I feel that the balance of probabilities weighs in favor of shamans having been present and active in Paleolithic cave rituals. Lewis-Williams has made an important contribution to our understanding of cave art and Upper Paleolithic religion, even if it is, as he readily admits, not the entire picture.

My own interpretation concerning the pivotal role of secret societies is in no way contradictory to Lewis-Williams's views on shamanism, although some small adjustments would make the two views even more compatible. In particular, I would point out that powerful families may well have had their own trained shamans who helped them control access to the supernatural and interpret it, just as priests later conducted secret society rituals elsewhere in the world (Eliade 1958b:39). Such elite-sponsored shamans could have supervised the initiations of elite children into secret societies and perhaps the initiation of elite adults into the higher ranks of those societies. Shamans may well have presided over secret society ritual activities and used the caves on occasion for their own deeper ecstatic visions. I suspect they would have been well remunerated for their services, just as they were in Northwest Coast communities and the transegalitarian tribes where I worked in Southeast Asia. What seems to occur as transegalitarian societies become more complex is that shamans begin to specialize and create hierarchies; only those at the top are authorized to conduct the most important initiations or other ceremonies and thus collect the most lucrative fees or favors. In all this, we can see the dilution or subordination of the original ecstatic spiritual nature of the shaman in order to accommodate political goals of the families or groups that sponsor their own shamans and underwrite their training. Eventually this trend will produce priests who

ENTOPTICS: THE BRAIN CREATES ITS OWN IMAGES

ENTOPTIC PHENOMENA		SAN ROCK ART		PALAEOLITHIC ART			
		ENGRAVINGS	PAINTINGS	MOBILE ART		PARIETAL ART	
A	B	C	D	F	G	H	I
I							
II							
III							
IV							
V							
VI							

From J. Lewis-Williams and T. Dowson, "The Signs of All Times: Entoptic Phenomena in Upper Paleolithic Art," *Current Anthropology* 29:Figs. 1, 2 (1988). Published by the University of Chicago Press, copyright© 1988 by the Wenner-Gren Foundation for Anthropological Research.

When the human mind is tired or under stress, especially if it is also plunged into darkness with little or no visual stimulation, patterns appear in the field of vision for many people. In the simplest form, these images are dots, zigzags, concentric arched lines, chevrons, and lattice patterns. These images derive from the way the human nervous and visual system is constructed. It is simply a function of the physical brain, just as we sometimes see afterimages if we stare at objects too long. If the periods of stress and sensory deprivation continue longer or become more intense, various familiar images start to appear associated with the earlier entoptic forms. Under these conditions, contemporary university students might start seeing beer cans with strange symbols or cryptic-looking books. For Paleolithic people, animals formed central themes of their lives and their deeper entoptic visions. At still deeper levels, imaginary animals, monsters, and therianthropes (half-man–half-animal creatures) similar to some of the images depicted in the caves begin to appear. Entoptic vortex images, in particular, were viewed as doorways to supernatural realms by ethnographic shamans. David Lewis-Williams has shown that many Upper Paleolithic cave paintings as well as rock paintings of other hunter-gatherer cultures fit such an explanation of the cave art. He thus suggests that artists were shamans who attempted to record their entoptic visions after trance experiences.

follow their books without any concern for ecstatic experiences or spiritual travel. However, we have not yet arrived at that point in our story.

FERTILITY BECOMES A MAJOR CONCERN OF ELITES

While elite members of secret societies may have confronted the mysteries of the spirit world deep in the bowels of the earth, a substantially different cult appears to have flourished in the bright light of day in the habitation areas of Upper Paleolithic communities. These more public cults probably incorporated many of the same animals that were painted in the caves, perhaps as totemic or general power animals, although the most powerful and secret rituals involving these animal spirits were undoubtedly reserved for secret societies. Power animals or totemic animals were most likely publicly displayed as sculptures, masks, and costumes at major ritual feasts where dramatic ritual performances undoubtedly took place, much as they did at the Northwest Coast potlatches.

However, there was another aspect to the public domestic cults that rarely made its appearance in the deep caves. These are the small statues of naked faceless females that became widespread during the Upper Paleolithic from Europe to Siberia. They are often referred to as "Venus" figurines, and they were carved in ivory, bone, and stone and even modeled in clay (Fig. 5.23). Approximately 200 of these figurines have now been recovered. Most female figurines in Western Europe have no

Fig. 5.23. Ritual concerns with fertility seem well attested by the occurrence of approximately 200 faceless female figurines, almost all of which exhibit ritual nudity and frequently have accentuated breasts and buttocks. One is even depicted back to back with a reptilian or carnivorous animal. The figurine shown here, from Dolni Vestonice, has a series of perforations on the top of her head presumably for inserting feathers, flowers, or a few strands of hair. Photo by Greg Ehlers.

recorded archaeological context, having been dug up by amateurs or art seekers. However, specimens with engraved vulvas from archaeological excavations from Eastern Europe have been dated between 12,000 and 23,000 years ago, and a recent figurine dated to almost 30,000 B.P. (Bahn 1989; Marshack 1991b).

Most examples are clearly associated with habitation areas, rather than deep cave recesses ("Distribution of Venus and Male Figurines by Type of Site," page 155; see also Dickson 1990:213–14). Some figurines in the Ukraine were found inside structures in shrinelike niches. The only figurines to be found in the completely dark parts of caves

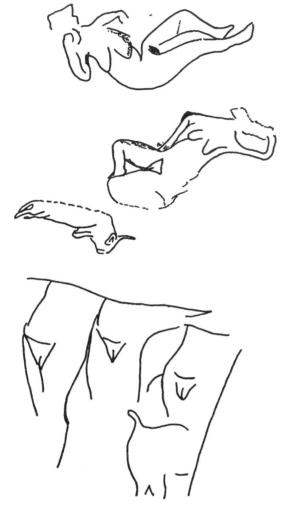

Fig. 5.24. Female sexuality was sometimes emphasized on the walls of rockshelters, such as La Madeleine, in France (top), the Roc aux Sorciers rockshelter (bottom), or sometimes inside caves such as Les Combarelles. Most full female figurines are found in habitation sites, rockshelters, or in the sunlit entrances of caves, but not deep inside caves where animals and animal-men are depicted. Ronald Hutton, *The Pagan Religions of the Ancient British Isles,* Fig. 1.3. Oxford: Blackwell, 1995. Reprinted with permission of Basil Blackwell Ltd.

were two male figurines. Female figurines found at cave sites were always located in the much more public and well-lit front entrance areas where people might live. For instance, two large bas relief sculptures of reclining nude females were engraved at the entrance to the La Madeleine rockshelter in southwestern France, providing a very public display of these types of women (Fig. 5.24). Large graphic depictions of female thighs and pubic areas also occur in some caves such as Les Combarelles. There are also a smaller, but still substantial, number of phallic carvings from Upper Paleolithic sites that underline symbolic fertility concerns (Fig. 5.25; Soffer 1985:83; Zervos 1959:79–80); to these can be added a large number of realistic to stylized incised or painted phalluses such as those near the vulvas at Les Combarelles (Fig. 5.25). As in the later Neolithic times, these phalluses are more numerous than depictions of males, but phalluses are still less numerous than portrayals of females. A great deal of debate has occurred concerning the meaning of the female Venus sculptures and whether they are Paleolithic pinups, goddesses, objects for fertility magic, or sculptures with other meanings.

In my estimation, the facts that they are naked, often have enlarged abdomens, buttocks, and breasts, and represent a considerable investment of time and effort to carve indicate that these are religious figurines, probably related to fertility. This has always been the most generally accepted interpretation. Eliade (1958a:333–34) observes that female nudity is generally a symbol of fertility, and Wymer (1982:246) argues that nudity would not have been normal tenure in the Ice Ages of Europe but must have been a ritual pose, as it was to be in later times. Soffer, Adovasio, and Hyland (2001:242) also argue that the hair pieces, cords, and bracelets sometimes depicted are all ritual items. It is difficult to imagine anyone going to such efforts at this technological stage merely to produce a "pinup," much less hundreds of people doing the same thing. Moreover, such an explanation does not really account for why such figurines occur in these Upper Paleolithic cultures but not others and not at other times. The high quality of some sculptures also indicates that these figurines were the products of special-

Distribution of Venus and Male Figurines by Type of Site

	Site Types		
Figurines	Open Air	Rockshelters	Caves
Female	17	3	6[a]
Male	1	0	4[b]
Indeterminate sex	8	1	11[c]

Data compiled from Pales and Tassin de Saint Péreuse 1976.

a. All female figurines were found in the penumbral front part of the caves, areas that would be most suitable for habitation

b. Two male figurines were found in the penumbral parts of the caves; two were found in the fully dark parts of the caves, areas most suitable for rituals.

c. All figurines of indeterminate sex were found in the penumbral areas.

ists, that they were prestige ritual items, and that they were probably commissioned.

Some popular writers have seized on these figurines in order to promote ideas of Paleolithic matriarchies and goddess worship based on the control that women have over life by virtue of giving birth. However, reality is probably more complex. Why should only Europeans and those living on the northern Asian plains have come to this realization? Why did they formulate such ideas only during the Upper Paleolithic, but not before or later? Why did such ideas lapse when the vast migratory herds of animals disappeared at the end of the Ice Age? Cognitively based interpretations have few testable answers to such questions. However, if we examine complex hunter-gatherers from a cultural ecological point of view, a number of characteristics make more sense. Several points about the ecology of Upper Paleolithic groups may help in understanding how this approach can provide more compelling explanations.

As was noted earlier, in many complex hunter-gatherer societies, the most influential and powerful families own or control some of the most productive resource procurement sites, like fords at rivers where animals cross or highly productive fishing locations. However, in situations where there are massive amounts of resources available for very short periods of time, as is the case with herd migrations, the ability to procure those resources depends on the labor available and how hard people are willing to work. Thus, labor availability determines the amount of surpluses that can be produced, which in turn determines the number and magnitude of feasts that can be given, which determines the amount of political and social support that one can create in a community, which determines the control that one can exert over resources, and so on in a circular chain of cause and effect. The amount of surplus and feasting also determines the number of wives and the quality of wives that ambitious men can obtain, which in turn determines how much meat or fish can be processed and stored and how many children can be raised to help in all aspects of subsistence and surplus production.

Fig. 5.25. The presence of a number of sculpted phalluses (above and below) and testes (below) in the Upper Paleolithic is probably also related to a concern with fertility. Photos by Philiippe Jugie, courtesy of the National Museum of Prehistory, Les Eyzies de Tayac, France.

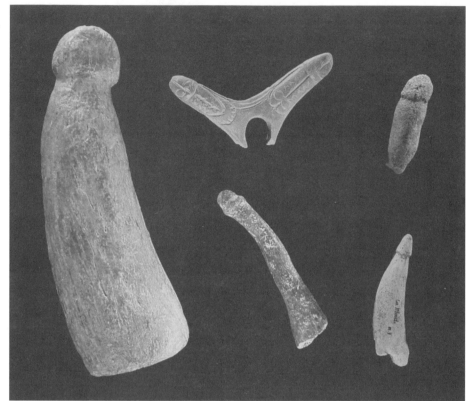

The most ambitious families, therefore, compete for the best wives, the largest families, the most surplus, the most feasting debts, the most political power, and the most spiritual power—all on the basis of the ability to pay—although such competition is not always overt. Women seem to have been unscrupulously manipulated and exchanged in many hunter-gather and horticultural societies (Tiechelmann 1841:7, 9; Meyer 1846:4–5; Smith 1880:3–4; Roth 1899:44, 88–89, 103, 107, 113–15; Withnell 1901:8; Reay 1959:22, 57, 111; Elkin 1964:134–38; Woodburn 1982; Speth 1990:161; Hampton 1997:612). Given the labor-intensive nature of buckskin preparation and the abundance of endscrapers among Upper Paleolithic tools, it seems very likely that some women were also valued for their ability to produce valuable buckskin clothes that constituted wealth and could be used in trade or to acquire more wives or as feasting debt-gifts. Among ethnographic hunter-gatherers, women generally seem to have used endscrapers and been responsible for making buckskin and the highly valued garments made from buckskin (Hayden 1990a).

Thus, I would argue that it was the need for labor among the wealthier Upper Paleolithic families that led to competition for wives and extra efforts to produce children, who would carry on the ownership and lucrative exploitation of resource procurement sites. Such enterprises could not have been left to the demographic vicissitudes of single couples. Moreover, the cost of procuring wives and their critical roles in producing wealth may have meant that the status of some women was relatively high, at least for first wives in elite families, although probably not as high as elite males (Hayden 1995:55). Besides acquiring several wives (as is typical of ambitious men in most transegalitarian societies), it would have made sense for the elite owners of the best resource procurement sites to try to enhance the fertility of their wives and other women within their group. This is why I think prestige-grade female fertility statues were produced and why fertility cults became popular primarily among wealthier families. Interestingly, among ethnographic transegalitarian societies with cults focused on *female* fertility and fertility goddesses, the status of women is not always very elevated. Men often try to make claims for powerful fertility magic or for being responsible for fertility, and in some ironic cases, such as those of New Guinea and Australia (Eliade 1958b:47; Lawrence and Meggitt 1965:15; Feil 1987:187–89, 221; Wiessner and Tumu 1999), membership in these female fertility cults is restricted to men! Complications such as these are why some archaeologists are reluctant to interpret many of the symbolic items that they find in the archaeological record in any specific social or gender terms. However, given appropriate cultural ecological models, I think much of this patterning can be deciphered. The inheritance of productive sources of wealth by successive generations probably also provided the impetus for developing ancestor veneration and the wealthy burials that occur in the Upper Paleolithic.

A similar emphasis on fertility seems to occur in some later Mesolithic-level cultures such as the Jomon in Japan, where female figurines occur in coastal areas and large stone phalluses were erected in ritual areas in the highlands (Fig. 5.26; see also Kidder 1993).

COMPLEXITY SPREADS

Many of the traits of European complex hunter-gatherers spread during the later Paleolithic across the Eurasian steppe to Siberia. I would argue that, as in southwestern

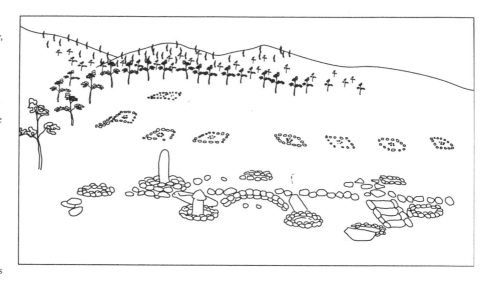

Fig. 5.26. Concern with fertility, or at least the ritual worship of the organs of procreation, continued during the Mesolithic in a number of places in the world, including the Jomon area in Japan, where stone phalluses were erected at ritual sites such as the Kinsei site, shown here, and ritually naked female figurines were made. Adapted from J. E. Kidder Jr., "Kinsei Site, Yamanashi Prefecture," *Ritual in the Late Jomon Period*. Mitaka, Tokyo: International Christian University, n.d.

France, complexity took hold and flourished in locations where resource and technological characteristics fostered it. For instance, the migration routes of mammoths and other animals along the rivers of the Ukraine appear to have been especially favorable. It was here that the fabulously wealthy burials of Sungir were found, as well as many other artistic or ritual indicators of complexity, including fantastically constructed and decorated structures of mammoth jawbones that may well have served ritual or secret society functions (Fig. 5.27). The most elaborate structures contained female figurines, amber beads and other prestige objects, a rabbit's foot talisman, lamps, notched tallylike bones, and even spits for roasting meat (Pidoplichko 1998:150–52, 198–200, 212–13, 247).

At the end of the Ice Age, climates, vegetation, and sea levels all changed dramatically in Europe and Asia. As the vast grasslands were replaced by forests, the great migratory herds dwindled in Europe, and many animals became extinct. However, once complexity had obtained a foothold in the human experience, it seems to have been difficult to eradicate. People began to look for other ways of producing food surpluses and maintaining their privileged positions through feasting and marriages. The result was a concerted effort to develop new technologies with the aim of extracting and storing massive amounts of previously untapped food resources. These new technologies characterize Mesolithic level adaptations. The most important of these included the large-scale harvesting of fish and cereal grains and innovations such as the bow and arrow. The environmental changes that occurred could not sustain complex cultural systems throughout much of the ensuing Mesolithic in Europe except in coastal areas where large amounts of fish could be captured to produce surpluses and sustain complex societies very similar to the ethnographic groups of the Northwest Coast. For instance, the Iron Gates region of the Danube River was rich in migrating fish and produced remarkable structures, prestige items, and ancestral or totemic sculptures. Similar developments occurred in the Near East, where the subsistence economies focused primarily on the harvesting of large amounts of cereal grains such as wheat and barley.

Fig. 5.27. Other possible indications of secret society ritual structures include this remarkable example of a structure made of mammoth bones by Upper Paleolithic inhabitants of the Ukrainian steppes near Mezhirich over 14,000 years ago. It is the most complex structure of the region and would have taken 10 men about six days to assemble, thus indicating an exceptional effort. A decorated mammoth skull to the right of the entrance also indicates its special status, while associated pieces of amber and seashells (from sources 600–800 km away) as well as ivory jewelry point to a transegalitarian social organization. Other structures using mammoth bones were not nearly so complex. From M. Gladkih, N. Kornietz, and O. Soffer, 1984, "Mammoth-bone dwellings on the Russian Plain," *Scientific American* 25(5):165.

The Case of Lepenski Vir

Lepenski Vir is situated on a high bank of the Danube River where it cuts through the Carpathian Mountains, a region known as the Iron Gates, about 200 kilometers above its mouth at the Black Sea. It was used during the later Mesolithic period, about 8800 to 7800 B.P. It is special in several respects, even in the context of the local Mesolithic culture. It is one of the few sites to have elaborate permanent structures, about 50 in all (Fig. 5.28). These structures feature distinctive slab-lined hearths, often with plastered floors and boulders carved into abstract forms or nebulous faces (Fig. 5.29). These boulders were situated at the far end of a long hearth in the center of the structure, around which were often placed real human jawbones or stylized carvings of human jaws (Fig. 5.30). The disposition of these objects around the hearths would seem to get in the way of ordinary domestic cooking tasks, and I know of no other instance like this in a purely

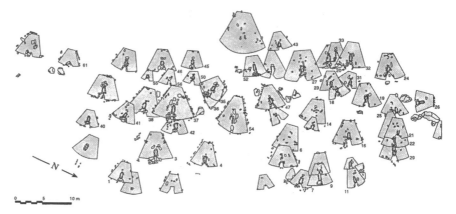

Fig. 5.28. The Mesolithic site of Lepenski Vir on the Danube River contained many small structures with unusual features and artifacts. This is the plan of the center of the site. Structures generally contained a central stone-lined hearth, a sculpted boulder at the end of the hearth, and frequently one or more burials under the floor. From Dragoslav Srejovic and Ljubinka Babovic, *Umetnost Lepenskog Vira,* p. 40. Belgrade: Izdavacki Zavod, 1983.

Fig. 5.29. Some of the stone sculptures clearly display a humanoid, perhaps totemic quality; others are made up almost entirely of abstract forms that probably indicate supernatural entities or forces. These boulders were placed at the head of the hearths. From Dragoslav Srejovic and Ljubinka Babovic, *Umetnost Lepenskog Vira,* pp. 107, 113, 116. Belgrade: Izdavacki Zavod, 1983.

domestic context. Thus, these objects and their placement (as well as the formal aspect of the hearths) seem to indicate a more ritual use of these hearths. The carved boulders were placed at the head of the hearths, near special graves, or incorporated into sacrificial platforms located at the center of the site. The carved boulders were probably the focal point of sacred activities, acting as axis mundi (Srejovic and Letica 1978:157). Although not all structures had burials, people may have had alternative burial rituals (such as on platforms or in distant parts of the territory), but still have been honored by the construction of a mortuary feasting structure. Such practices are not uncommon in more complex societies and may be indicated at Lepenski Vir by the many "scattered" and ochred bone remains at the site (Roksandic 1999:66, 77). Ancestor cults are indicated not only by burials in structures but also by the select number of people buried at the site, the retention and use of skulls, and the exceptional way that older men were buried. Two unusual burials occurred in circular stone structures with offering platforms at the center of the site. These may well have been burials of big men or chiefly elites set up

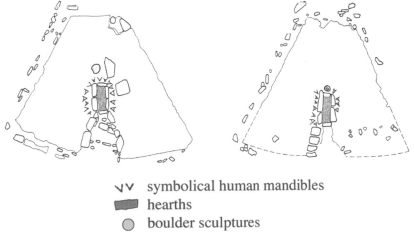

Fig. 5.30. Lepenski Vir hearths were much larger and much better made than hearths in any other contemporary hunter-gatherer cultures of the world. These hearths were also surrounded by ritual items such as sculpted boulders, real or symbolic human jaw bones (mandibles), and often burials such as the one displayed here. These seem to indicate a special function for Lepenski Vir structures beyond simple habitations. Top: from I. Radovanovic, *The Iron Gates Mesolithic,* Fig. 4.3. Ann Arbor, MI: International Monographs in Prehistory, 1996. Bottom: adapted by Greg Holoboff from Dragoslav Srejovic and Ljubinka Babovic, *Umetnost Lepenskog Vira,* pp. 153, 175. Belgrade: Izdavacki Zavod, 1983.

⋁⋁ symbolical human mandibles
▬ hearths
◉ boulder sculptures

by their descendants for homage from all members of their clan or kindred (Srejovic and Letica 1978:156–57).

Prestige items were also relatively common (Fig. 5.31), whereas little in the way of ordinary domestic refuse was recovered from the extensive excavations at the site. Even the animal bones are unusual in being composed of trophy animals and parts (bears, deer skulls with antlers). A complete bear was even butchered between two of the structures. This is definitely not a normal archaeological assemblage (Dimitrijević 2000). At

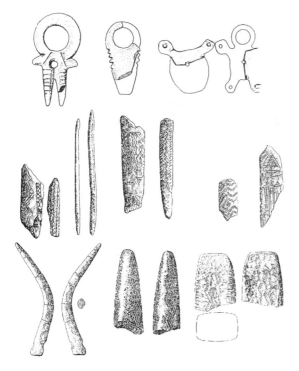

Fig. 5.31. Archaeological remains around the Lepenski Vir structures contained an unusual number of highly decorated stone and bone pieces that would ordinarily be associated with feasting and reciprocal gift giving as prestige objects. This is a small sample of such objects. From Dragoslav Srejovic and Ljubinka Babovic, *Umetnost Lepenskog Vira,* pp. 28, 29, 47, 58, 190. Belgrade: Izdavacki Zavod, 1983.

other nearby sites of the same culture exactly the opposite was the case, that is, daily domestic tools and bone refuse predominated in the other sites, although they contained few ritual or special items and much simpler structures. This has led Srejovic and Letica (1978:157) to argue that Lepenski Vir was a religious center or "priestly city" where the shrines held the most treasured and hallowed objects of the entire Iron Gates region. Large ritual sites are known from even earlier times in Anatolia (for example, Göbekli in Anatolia; see Chap. 6), but it seems more likely that Lepenski Vir is actually a cemetery site for the veneration of ancestors, similar to some sites on the Northwest Coast, like Scowlitz on the banks of the lower Fraser River, where numerous burial mounds up to 4 meters high were situated (Fig. 5.5) but with little evidence of contemporaneous occupation (Lepofsky et al. 2000). Burial houses that imitate normal houses are not uncommon among other transegalitarian societies such as the Maya Indians, Melanesian islanders (Fig. 5.32), and the Northwest Coast Indians. Such structures frequently serve as feasting locations in honor of ancestors and their living lineage members but are usually smaller than ordinary houses. The structures at Lipenski Vir are also notable for their unusually small size.

It is difficult to explain the presence of large carved boulders, the elaborate and unusually large hearths, the burials, the numerous elaborate prestige items, the unusual prestige animal bones, and the special representation of mandibles as domestic features. They do make sense in terms of a mortuary and feasting cult complex. The sparse domestic refuse is also consistent with an intermittent use for feasts rather than a daily residential use. Thus, Lepenski Vir is perhaps one of the most striking examples that we currently have of Mesolithic mortuary complexes in Europe. It is also interesting to note that a large number of individuals at Lepenski Vir died violent deaths (Roksandic 1999), as was the case in the complex hunter-gatherer societies of the Northwest Coast and elsewhere in the Mesolithic. This likely indicates high levels of competition over resources and wealth.

In Mesolithic Japan, at San'nai Maruyama, a remarkable Jomon site, intensive fishing, hunting, and plant use sustained a community with over 80 houses, a large public building, and two mounds with great amounts of large decorated pottery (probably used in feasting or rituals), elite burials, and the foundation posts of an astonishing monu-

Fig. 5.32. In other cultures, special structures that resemble homes are sometimes built for the dead and can even constitute small communities of the dead, as in the case of this cemetery (above) in the Tzeltal Maya community of Chanal (Chiapas, Mexico). Feasts to honor the dead take place at these structures. Photo by B. Hayden. The houses for the ancestors (below) that were built in Vanuatu (New Hebrides) bear a striking resemblance to the structures at Lepenski Vir. From F. Speiser, *Ethnographische Materialen aus den Neuen Hebriden*, Plate 88. Berlin: Springer-Verlag, 1923.

mental wooden structure (Iizuka 1995). The six posts of this structure were 85–100 centimeters in diameter, and the superstructure must have been proportionately massive—an estimated 20 meters tall. Each of the posts must have weighed anywhere from 12 to 20 tons. The control over labor necessary to undertake such a project is extraordinary for a hunter-gatherer society reliant only on stone tools, as is the size of the settlement itself. Ethnographically, one of the few types of structures that I have encountered that might require such large foundation posts the enormous triangular scaffold (up to 60 meters high) erected by Maori chiefs to display foods that they had amassed for their feasts (Fig. 5.33). Whether the Jomon structure at San'nai Maruyama was specifically used to display feasting food or not may never be known. However, we can conclude with some

Fig. 5.33. For chiefly feasts in New Zealand, the Maori would erect huge scaffolds, sometimes up to 60 meters high, as shown in this early drawing. When they were completed, gifts and food for the feast would be piled high on all the levels of the scaffold. Similar structures may have been erected by Mesolithic people at Stonehenge and in Jomon Japan. From W. Yates, *An Account of New Zealand.* London, 1835.

confidence that the structure was meant to display something related to status and economic success. Three similar massive foundation posts, virtually the same size, have been recovered from Mesolithic deposits at Stonehenge in England (Vatcher and Vatcher 1973), raising many interesting questions about just when the Stonehenge ceremonial tradition began and what its original nature was. The Stonehenge posts were not aligned, as they are in Japan, and so they could well have been similar to totem poles, mortuary posts holding burial boxes of elites, or display scaffolds for feasts.

In Northern Europe, Lars Larsson (1987/88) has excavated a small (4 × 4 m) structure associated with the Skateholm Mesolithic cemetery and a similar structure at Bredasten (M. Larsson 1985/86). These probably represent ancestral (or other) cult shrines, possibly where rituals and feasts took place similar to those described in the next chapter. On the other side of the world in Vietnam, Mesolithic Hoabinhian groups gathered 200 human skulls together, again possibly to honor ancestors and their descendants (Higham 1989:38–39).

The Mesolithic, and complex hunter-gatherers in general, are turning out to be one of the most fascinating periods of human prehistory for understanding the emergence of our present culture traditions and our past religious beliefs and practices. In resource-poor locations, such as the Australian Western Desert, hunter-gatherers probably continued the generalized forager type of religion. But at locations rich in resources, with the new Mesolithic technology, new, more complex types of religious developments occurred. The succeeding Neolithic period extends these developments to even further remarkable limits.

Summary

Complex hunter-gatherer cultures and complex religious expressions first appear during the Upper Paleolithic in Europe about 35,000 years ago. These cultures differed substantially from the generalized hunter-gatherers that had preceded them, although modest expressions of complexity can sometimes be detected in Neanderthal communities living in the richest resource areas of Europe—the same areas that produced the most abundant and sophisticated ritual art during the Upper Paleolithic. From what we can tell, many religious elements of the previous periods continued to be important in the Upper Paleolithic: concepts of the afterlife and spirit world, ecstatic rituals and initiations, animal cults, ancestor veneration, and possibly shamanism. However, new elements were also added, and some of the old elements were transformed into new complexes. These changes are primarily understandable in terms of more fundamental changes that were occurring in the economic and subsistence base.

The complex hunter-gatherers of the Upper Paleolithic probably owned or controlled resource procurement locations and produced surpluses with which they created wealth and political power through feasts and marriages. Marked differences in social and economic statuses emerged, together with competition based on the production of surpluses. Competition over resources, women, and political power also seems to have led to a much higher incidence of conflict and warfare among many complex hunter-gatherers (Hayden 1995; Schulting 1998a). While there are few clear religious expressions of these concerns in the archaeological record from these periods, other than the possible association of aurochs, felines, or other predator images in caves used by secret societies, they become much more important in subsequent Neolithic and following periods (Chap. 6).

The elites of the Upper Paleolithic may have established secret ritual societies in order to consolidate their secular positions of control, and they apparently tried to restrict access to ecstatic supernatural experiences in caves. While painted caves are usually seen as the result of the arrival of fully modern humans in Europe (or as the result of nebulously defined needs for symbolic expression stemming from larger populations), political ecological models suggest that cave sanctuaries were probably used for costly initiations and rituals of secret societies. Shamanism likely existed at this time, and it is possible that powerful elites may have tried to co-opt many shamans or even to sponsor their own shamans for their own political purposes. A division between elite cults (secret societies, shamanic rituals) and common or public cults probably also appears for the first time among the Upper Paleolithic complex hunter-gatherers. Fertility cults, too, were likely established in order to promote elite interests, particularly the birth of children to enable them to more effectively exploit the resources that they owned and to provide security in old age. This is also a pattern that becomes common with the production of foods based on domesticates, as in the Neolithic and other non-Industrial agrarian societies.

Perhaps the most important lesson to emerge from considering the religious developments of the Upper Paleolithic is the way in which resource characteristics and technology play a fundamental role in the nature of social and religious expression. This is most vividly demonstrated in the effect that surplus production and storage had on feasting, social and economic inequalities, burial rituals, ancestor veneration, the emergence of secret societies, the use of caves, the nature of initiations, the hierarchical transformations in the nature of shamans, and the emergence of fertility cults. Most of these features are recurring elements in what I refer to as the complex hunter-gatherer type of religion. With the development of food production, it became possible to create even more substantial surpluses, and as might be expected, these changes, too, had dramatic impacts on the nature of religions, as we will see in the next chapter.

A Cauldron of Change in the Fertile Crescent

Five bulls! Five bulls! The family was going to sacrifice five bulls for the funeral of the recently deceased elderly lineage head. Excitement was in everyone's eyes, I saw them leading the bulls in with their horns bedecked with streamers, flowers, and decorations. I saw them tied to the sacrificial poles. Hundreds of people stood around in their finest, most colorful clothes, handwoven and embroidered, decorated with multihued beads and shining, tinkling silver. A man with a long bush-clearing machete calmed one of the bulls, turned his back as though he was walking away, and then suddenly pivoted all the way around, holding his blade out, powerfully swinging it into the bull's throat. Blood gushed forth instantaneously and the great beast collapsed, struggling to regain its feet, flailing in the dust until it was too weak to move. Grain was heaped over the dead animal to mollify its spirit. Then the butchering began, with work crews of men dividing up the meat and sending some portions off for immediate cooking but reserving other portions as special gifts to be publicly presented to the most important guests. Many squealing pigs and chickens were also killed. There were half a dozen large cooking fires with huge cooking vats and squadrons of helpers for the preparation of the vast piles of meat and grain. Allied lineage elders remained together and were served the best portions by the many younger lineage members, who were constantly coming or going, refilling the grain bowls, the meat platters, the soup bowls, and the cups of alcohol (Fig. 6.1). This was a typical transegalitarian funeral feast sponsored by a successful lineage among the hill tribes of northwest Thailand. It could just as easily have been a funeral feast in a Neolithic European community or even in a rich Mesolithic community (except for the use of domesticated grain and animals).

On the one hand, the complex Mesolithic cultures of Europe *might* have stayed very much the same until historic times, just as the American Northwest Coast Indians remained hunter-gatherers until they encountered Europeans about 200 years ago. Like the Northwest Coast, northern Europe was not a particularly favorable area for domesticating plants or animals. The land was heavily forested and the most productive resources were

Fig. 6.1. The center of a traditional Akha tribal feast in Thailand consists of the most important elders of the village and the elders of the principal lineages. They consume meat, liquor, and other delicacies, and they occupy places of honor (shown here). Other participants of lower rank eat in adjacent areas after the elders have been served. Photo by Michael Clarke.

fish and sea mammals. On the other hand, the competitive forces in the more complex societies of Mesolithic Europe might eventually have stirred the inexorable process of domestication into movement, just as the Northwest Coast Indians cultivated small gardens of carefully tended clover and cinquefoil roots, which they used in their potlatches (Deur 2002; Turner and Kuhnlein 1982). We will never know what would have happened in Europe if the ancestors had been left to their own devices, for a major disruption occurred. It took about 3,000 years for repercussions to extend to Western Europe.

In Europe, this disruption began in the Balkans about 8,000 years ago. It was caused by the arrival of a new Mediterranean type of people, originating from the Near East, who brought a new Neolithic technology with them including ground-stone axes and domesticated animals and plants. In many respects, this event appears similar to events that transpired at the beginning of the Upper Paleolithic, when a new people brought new technology, social complexity, and new religious forms into Europe from the Near East. This time, however, the effects were far more pervasive and had many major repercussions. From the archaeological remains of the new Neolithic occupation of Europe, modern social visionaries have tried to infer the existence of utopias, and their visions need to be evaluated. But before delving into these aspects, it is essential to understand what transpired in the Near East and the nature of the economic and social changes that resulted in the cauldron of change that was to affect Europe.

The Neolithic Emerges from Complex Hunters and Gatherers

Early archaeologists initially defined the Neolithic (New Stone Age) on the basis of the appearance of a new type of stone technology: axes and other stone items shaped by grinding rather than by the chipping techniques used earlier. As research advanced over the decades, it was realized that this technology was almost always associated with domesticated animals or plants and that pottery was often present. Because these economic changes were considered to be more fundamental than the mere technique of shaping stone tools, the Neolithic was redefined as the period when food production and domestication began.

Generally, domestication implies controlled food production, in which humans protect species from natural selection forces and artificially select characteristics that are more beneficial to the food producers (such as size or lipid content) than the species' ability to survive in the wild. This results in changes in the species' genetic makeup. Sometimes, however, genetic changes can also be the accidental products of food production without intentional selection of seed or offspring to promote desirable characteristics. Domestication started around 9000 B.C.E. in the Near East and gradually spread to Europe and other areas. Similar events were unfolding in China about the same time and, only slightly later, in the Americas. In the Old World, the Neolithic came to an end when bronze tools began replacing stone tools about 4000–3000 B.C.E. This relatively short period (by Paleolithic standards) encompassed a great deal of cultural variation, from simple agricultural communities as described in the introduction to this chapter, to powerful chiefdoms that erected colossal monuments like Stonehenge. We will discuss the earlier, and generally simpler, expressions of the Neolithic in this chapter and the more complex expressions in the next chapter. We will also be switching from dates recorded as years B.P. (before present) to dates recorded as years B.C.E. (before the common era—I will use uncalibrated dates wherever possible), since this is the general practice of the scholars working with this and subsequent time periods.

The wild forms of the plants and animals brought into Europe by Neolithic colonizers are found in the Near East, where archaeologists have found the earliest dates of domestication. Therefore, it is to the Near East that we turn in order to learn more about this pivotal development. In the hilly northern and western parts of the Fertile Crescent (Fig. 6.2), a series of related Mesolithic-level cultures developed around 12,500 to 10,000 B.C.E. The best known of these is the Natufian. It was a complex hunting and gathering culture with an economy probably based on the collection, processing, and storage of wild wheat, as well as intensive hunting of gazelle and the exploitation of a wide range of other animals, plants, and fish. The Natufian is also known for its unusually large settlements and cemeteries, semipermanent or permanent architecture (complete with domestic house mice indicating a high degree of sedentism), elaborate burials with shell jewelry, and a range of symbolic and prestige sculptures in polished stone or bone. Of considerable interest is the occurrence of the earliest known domesticated dogs (and their occasional sacrifice as prestige grave offerings). As might be expected of complex hunter-gatherers, the dominant symbolic motifs continue to be animals (Fig. 6.3), although a few schematic representations of human heads have been found, as well as one sculpture of two people in a sexual embrace. The Natufian stone technological tradition continues on into the Neolithic with very little change. However, by 9000 B.C.E., there are changes in many settlement locations and sizes, and domesticated wheat, barley, and lentils begin to appear at famous sites like Jericho. Archaeologists refer to this as the Pre-Pottery Neolithic-A culture, or PPNA.

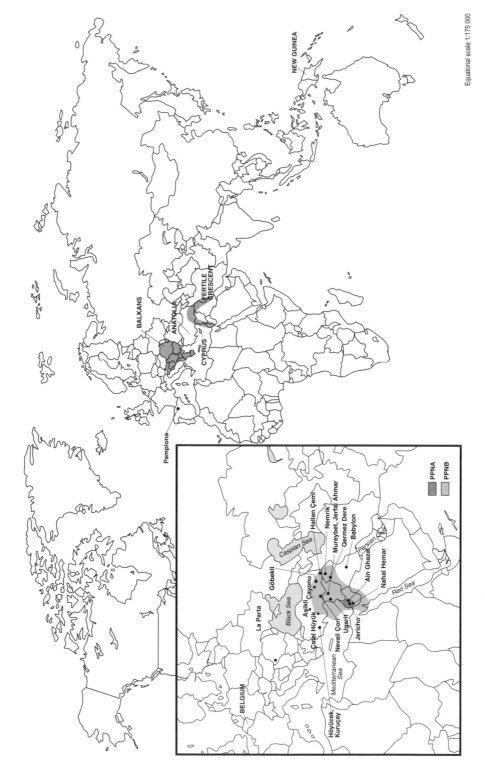

Fig. 6.2. Some of the most important regions, cultures, and sites of the early Neolithic are identified on this map. Drafted by Greg Holoboff.

Along the upper reaches of the Euphrates River in northern Syria, similar sedentary Natufian cultures were developing, especially at and around the site of Mureybet. Here, too, domesticated wheat began to appear about 9000 B.C.E., with barley domesticated shortly afterward. However, the most recent work in this area puts the domestication of rye back another 2,000 years, at 11,000 B.C.E. (Moore, Hillman, and Legge 2002; Pringle 1998a). The first domesticated animals (goats) do not appear until almost 8000 B.C.E. and they appear first in this region (Cauvin 1994:169).

Even farther north, at Hallan Çemi in Turkey, Rosenberg (1994, 1999; Rosenberg and Redding 2000) has located a slightly earlier (c. 9200 B.C.E.) Mesolithic-level settlement with considerable evidence for complexity. It is a relatively large and sedentary site, with permanent architecture. There is a central feasting area. There are prestige serving bowls made of ground stone and polished stones with some sort of tally marks similar to what one might expect for keeping track of major feasts. There was an aurochs skull attached to the interior north wall of one structure, foreshadowing later shrine developments. It is also possible that people were beginning to domesticate pigs and lentils at this site by 9000 B.C.E. (Pringle 1998b).

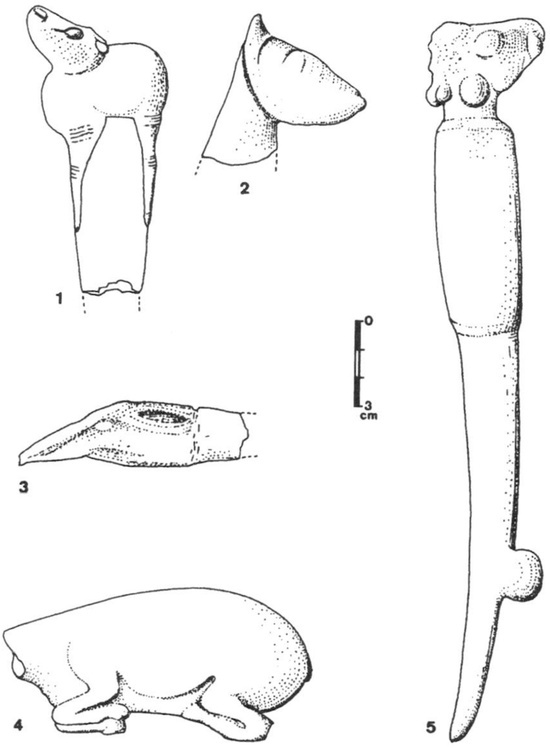

Somewhat similar developments were also occurring at Qermez Dere in northern Iraq (Watkins 1990, 1993). Thus, early domestication was occurring over a fairly broad area of the Fertile Crescent and neighboring Anatolia (Willcox 1998). As Cauvin (1994:83–84) has noted, by the time archaeologists can identify domesticated plants, they are already substantially different from their wild forms. Thus, the process of domestication must have been a long one and must have been going on for some time previous to the usually recognized beginning of the Neolithic. Cauvin argues that the initial experiments in domestication must have extended back into the Natufian or other complex Mesolithic types of cultures. The very early dates for rye domestication indicate that this was so. In fact, settlement-pattern changes foreshadowing those of the Neolithic begin occurring in the late Natufian (also known as the Khiamian) indicating that the basic economic shift was already under way.

The beginning of food production was not a momentous occasion. From an archaeological point of view, it seems to have slipped almost unnoticed into the cultural fabric of Mesolithic life. It sputtered along for thousands of years before the full potential of this new technology was explored. As Özdogan (1999:234–35) and others have emphasized, Pre-Pottery Neolithic subsistence was essentially a complex hunter-gatherer one

Fig. 6.3. As in the Paleolithic, animals continue to be the most represented art motifs in many Mesolithic-level complex hunter-gatherer cultures, such as the Natufian cultures, which produced these sculptures in the Levant. From J. Cauvin, *Naissance des Divinités, Naissance de l'Agriculture*, p. 36. Paris: CNRS, 1994.

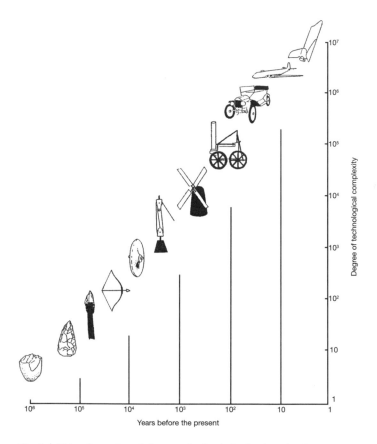

with domesticated foods playing very minor roles. The eventual ultimate effect of domestication, however, was the virtual transformation of the face of the globe and its natural environments. Domestication and food production made possible the thousand-fold increase of human populations from a few million hunter-gatherers into the billions of people who occupy the world today. It made possible the development of much more complex social and political systems such as chiefdoms, city states, and empires. It supported technological specializations that resulted in the dizzying rate of cultural change that began in the Neolithic and is still accelerating today (Fig. 6.4).

Fig. 6.4. Using domesticated plants and animals for food production enabled people to devote more surpluses to craft specialization and other endeavors resulting in a geometrically increasing rate of technological and cultural change since the beginning of the Neolithic. From B. Cotterell and J. Kamminga, *Mechanics of Pre-industrial Technology*, Fig. 1.3. Cambridge: Cambridge University Press, 1990. Reprinted with the permission of Cambridge University Press.

The critical difference between the wild resource base of hunter-gatherers and the resources of domesticated food producers is that the natural constraints on the abundance of wild foods are beyond the control of humans. In fact, for many resources, the more effort that is put into harvesting foods, the lower the return rate eventually becomes because of overexploitation and the degradation of the species—a lesson we are still learning in managing our fisheries and wild animals. For food producers, however, the major constraint on the abundance of their food resources is under human control. The more work one puts into producing food, the more food one generally gets. The more land that is cleared for planting, the more crops will be produced, barring calamity. Moreover, the more work that one invests, even in a given area of land, by weeding, manuring, spading, watering, and other techniques, the more food will be produced. This, in effect, becomes an open-ended, bottomless pit of production potential. When pressure is applied to food producers to increase production, they eventually find ways to do so. And it is this that has fueled the intensification of production and increasing complexity of political systems over the millennia. Social and political demands of ambitious individuals for using surpluses must have always risen to, or surpassed, the current potential for producing surpluses (Blackburn 1976; Modjeska

1982; Dickson 1990:169; Blanton and Taylor 1995). As Hampton (1997) and others have noted, in New Guinea, there are never enough pigs to meet social and political demands. These demands and the work that individuals are prepared to undertake to accumulate higher bride prices, foods for larger feasts, and more impressive prestige objects are probably responsible for the intensification of food production and the development of new technologies to achieve it. The process is still going on today with the mechanization of agriculture, genetic modification, pesticides, chemical fertilizers, hydroponic hothouses, water-diversion projects, and even weather control.

In ecological terms, it can be said that domestication and food production opened up a new ecological niche, a new way of obtaining food resources. Usually when such niches are opened up, populations increase rapidly to fill the niches and diversification takes place among those exploiting the new niche—in this case cultural diversity increased rather than genetic diversity. An accelerating rate of cultural change also takes place on the part of those who are attempting to maximize their adaptation to the new niches and thus dominate control over new resources and improve fitness for themselves and their descendants. This is perhaps the ultimate reason for the intense underlying competition in transegalitarian and subsequent societies. People fight to gain the maximum control over new resource niches—even today in the business world.

Thus, human labor and know-how become the key elements in producing surplus food. Surplus food, in turn, becomes the key to wealth, prosperity, political influence, and all of the comforts of civilization. Without domesticated food production, everyone would still be living, at best, in small villages of complex hunter-gatherers with no industrial products, no electricity, and no protection from the vicissitudes of Nature or other people. In fact, in a number of Mesolithic-type cultures, the incidence of violent deaths was around 20–30 percent, one out of every 3–5 people—on average at least one person in every family (Cybulski 1994; P. Walker 1989; Wendorf 1968; Vencl 1984; Gronenborn 1999:134–35). In this respect, too, complex hunter-gatherers are very similar to horticulturalists who frequently incur overall male mortality rates from warfare of 20–30 percent (Meggitt 1977:110, 201). It is intriguing that this does not seem to have been the case everywhere. For instance, there seem to be few violent deaths in the Natufian. If this is true, it will be interesting to determine how that culture dealt with the strong competitive pressures that must have existed. One of the most likely techniques must have been to use surpluses to hold competitive feasts.

The early food-producing societies of the Neolithic were not radically different from those of the preceding complex hunter-gatherers. Therefore, they are both referred to as "transegalitarian" societies and have many characteristics in common (see Hayden 1998). There were no chiefs or rigid social classes, but there were wealth differences and private ownership of resources and produce. Feasting and bride-wealth payments provided the main avenues for the ambitious to use surplus food in order to improve economic and political positions. Feasting and marriage thus became relatively competitive arenas and provided occasions for lavish displays of wealth and success such as described in the opening of this chapter. However, simple food producers, often called horticulturalists or "garden" growers, were able to expand many of the potentials that complex hunter-gatherers could only realize to a limited extent. The horticultural potential for producing food was higher and thus population densities had higher limits, as did village sizes, although there was still considerable overlap in these ranges with complex hunter-gatherers. Horticultural settlements tended to be more sedentary although many communities would move seasonally or every few years. Human labor became far more critical for success and well-being. More surplus food was used to create or procure valued prestige items, and rituals became more complex in ways that we shall explore shortly.

ARCHAEOLOGISTS SEARCH FOR THE KEY TO DOMESTICATION

Because of the profound repercussions that food production has had on the evolution of culture, archaeologists have viewed domestication as one of the most critical watersheds in human prehistory. Trying to understand why this development took place is still one of the greatest intellectual challenges of the discipline today, with no broad consensus as to why domestication occurred. I think that this has largely been because the question has been poorly formulated. Rather than seeing domestication as the critical turning point, I would argue that we should focus on *competition using economic surpluses as the key development.* Economically based competition was a fundamental characteristic of all complex hunter-gatherers. Once economically based competition becomes established— for it is not part of simple hunter-gatherer cultures—an entire array of *prestige* technologies develop to display the successful production and deployment of surpluses, in ways suggested by Barbara Bender (1975, 1978, 1985). These include pottery and ground-stone serving or ritual vessels, the first use of metals, nephrite or jade polished-stone axes, polished-stone bracelets, shell bead jewelry, sophisticated sculpture, great art traditions, complex ocean-going watercraft, megaliths, permanent and massive architecture, domesticated dogs, narcotics, and domesticated prestige foods.

I have explored these archaeological developments in detail in other publications (Hayden 1990b, 1998) so I will only give a brief outline here. Essentially, I argue, as Bender does, that competitive feasts, or perhaps even intercommunity feasts that used surpluses to befriend allies, provided the cauldron of conditions required to invest extra energy in the production of special foods that were meant to favorably impress guests and spectators. Feasts were opportunities to vaunt one's successes. They were predicated on *surpluses,* and they were held under only the most favorable surplus conditions. In addition to the fish oil, clover roots, and cinquefoil roots used at feasts by the complex hunter-gatherers of the Northwest Coast, wild meat—always difficult to obtain in the rainforest—was carefully dried and stored for feasts.

The same was probably true of Upper Paleolithic hunter-gatherers who may have especially relished the meat of the difficult-to-obtain wild cattle for its taste or spiritual powers. The Ainu adopted a slightly different approach. As discussed in the last chapter and depicted in the film *Iyomande,* it was the most successful families with the most surpluses that captured, fed, and raised bear cubs for a year before sacrificing and eating them as part of a major feast. Bear meat was highly valued in northern climates because of its high fat content (Le Jeune 1643:25). Similar practices involving bears and boars seem to have been followed in the European Mesolithic (Chaix, Bridault, and Picavet 1997; Gronenborn 1999:129). My contention is that it is not a very big step from these situations (in which wild animals are raised to eat) to a situation in which animals are being kept on a more permanent basis for sacrifice and consumption in alliance or competitive feasts or to situations where more plants are tended and actually selected for desirable feasting properties. This process is still going on in Sulawesi, where special albino breeds of cattle have been developed for their prestige value in feasts. The fact that early Neolithic people transported sheep, goats, boar, and cattle to the island of Cypress by 8200 B.C.E., *before* some of these animals were domesticated in their homeland of the adjacent Near East (Guilaine et al. 1998), also indicates that animals were being captured, kept, transported, and, one supposes, used for feasting since it would be impossible to import enough for daily meals. In fact, the disappearance of cattle from the island shortly afterwards only emphasizes their small numbers and the special contexts in which they must have been used. Initial food *production* must have involved much more effort than obtaining food from the wild. To produce food, fields had to be cleared and spaded. Seed needed to be sorted and stored for the following year. Just the storage of produce would have been a major undertaking. Fields had to be weeded and constantly monitored against intrusions of wild animals or birds. Animals would have to be fed during lean seasons and especially for fattening prior to their consumption at feasts. Animals would also have to be monitored so that they stayed under household control and were protected from predators or prevented from damaging others' fields or property.

The fact that traditional horticultural societies today *only* kill and eat domesticated animals for feasts, notably to impress guests, provides strong support for my interpretation. In these societies, whether in New Guinea, Africa, the Near East, Southeast Asia, or peasant villages of Europe, meat is not eaten as part of the daily meal (e.g., Lincoln 1981:43–46, 155–56). Animals are sacred wealth items and are only sacrificed and eaten for special occasions. Many groups view domestic animals as a way of storing surplus food, a kind of bank. Surplus food or wild fodder are fed these animals to increase their fat content so that they will be more appetizing for guests. As a means of storing surplus food, domesticated animals constitute the most important wealth items in many non-monetary societies. They are, thus, very much like bank accounts or stock investments. From the Neolithic onward, the daily consumption of meat occurs only among chiefly or state-level elites, followed much later by modern Industrial populaces. Even the poorest Industrial households today have become like the richest elites of the past in terms of their food consumption.

In New Guinea, pigs are raised only for feasting and gift exchanges at feasts. Among Southeast Asian hill tribes, there are more types of domestic animals, from chickens to water buffalo, but they are all used exclusively for feasting. The size of the feast and the wealth of the family determine the size and number of the animals to be sacrificed. The fact that the first domesticated animal at Hallan Çemi, the pig, was not a staple of the diet (Rosenberg 1999:31) is also consistent with a postulated role in feasting and the importance of feasting documented at the site. In Southeast Asia, rice plays a similar traditional role in feasting, and some of it is always converted into rice wine, drunk in extravagant amounts at feasts. It has been suggested by more than one author (e.g., Katz and Voigt 1986; Braidwood 1953) that the real reason why wheat, barley, and maize were originally domesticated was to produce beer, which again is traditionally used only in feasting contexts (Dietler 1990). If this is so, it may explain why rice, wheat, and maize were considered to have souls or even to be deities or some type of "spirits." I suspect that these grains may also have been used in feasts, especially to make such labor-intensive special foods as breads or cakes, which require laborious grinding of grain into fine flour—another of the past's delicacies that people today perhaps too easily take for granted.

Another compelling reason for viewing early domestication as the product of feasting is that morphologically domestic species actually formed only a small proportion of the entire diet of early communities for hundreds or thousands of years. In addition, as Cauvin observed, the process must have been going on for a long time even before the first appearance of fully domesticated wheat forms were archaeologically recognized. This is a consistent pattern of initial domestication almost everywhere and is difficult to explain if food production provided obvious subsistence advantages. In fact, it was probably exactly because early domesticated foods were so labor intensive that people did not use them on a daily basis, but reserved their use for special occasions when they wanted to impress guests, much as people today spend more time, effort, and money on preparing food for special guests than they ever would think of spending on a daily meal for themselves. Gordon Hillman told me that wild lentils are extremely time consuming to gather, and it is precisely this plant that was first domesticated in Anatolia (Cauvin et al. 1999:101). Thus, use of initial domesticates as parts of feasts nicely explains their small overall importance in subsistence for long periods during the beginning of the Neolithic and why there were not necessarily any major technological changes that occurred prior to discernible evidence for domestication (Cauvin 1994:38, 92).

Once surplus-based competitive feasting began, an inexorable juggernaut of cultural change was put in motion, leading to the inevitable domestication of animals and plants wherever the climate and indigenous species favored such developments. In some areas such as the dense forests of boreal Europe, northern Japan, the Northwest Coast of North America, and the Alaskan coasts, where land is difficult to clear and growing seasons are short, it was much more difficult to domesticate wild species, and the process was delayed or stalled. However, even in these locations, some steps had been taken toward domestication, as with the clover-root gardens of the Northwest Coast and the domesticated dogs of the more complex Eskimo cultures.

There are many other archaeological observations that fit the surplus and feasting model well, including the appearance of prestige serving vessels and the obvious delicacy of many initial domesticates, such as chilies and avocados in Mesoamerica. Many archaeologists (Cohen 1977; and authors in Price and Gebauer 1995) endorse alternative explanations, especially involving the development of food production as a response to increasing demographic pressures from climatic changes or other resource imbalances. I find these explanations unsatisfactory for a number of reasons (Hayden 2000), such as the recurring episodes of population compression and stress that occurred throughout the Ice Age as glaciers repeatedly advanced and retreated, causing sea levels to rise and fall dramatically and deserts to expand and contract in their wake. If stress on resources was the key factor in domestication, and if there were repeated episodes of major stress throughout the Ice Ages, why did domestication only happen so recently and in so many different places at once? Researchers such as Jacques Cauvin (1994:87–90; 2000a) dispute that there is any real evidence for population pressure or resource stresses before domestication occurred in the Near East. Moreover, the very recent documentation of domesticated rye almost two thousand years earlier than previously recorded for domestication in general and the most recent revisions in the dating of the climatic changes in the region no longer fit climate-driven scenarios for resource imbalances very well (Pringle 1998a). Nevertheless, research and dialog are far from finished in the fascinating quest to explain why domestication originally began. Thus, we continue to develop hypotheses to try to test the various theories. Cognitively based theories that were once popular almost a century ago still continue to appear in popular books, such as Kathryn Rabuzzi's *Motherself*. She suggests that Paleolithic people were unaware of the facts of biological reproduction—a highly dubious starting assumption. Then she suggests that domestication was the result of a sudden insight resulting from imitation rituals using digging sticks. There are very few archaeologists who would endorse such cognitively based, or "genius-insight," kinds of arguments today.

THE NEOLITHIC EXPLODES OUT OF EDEN

From the preceding discussions, it should be evident that the new Neolithic cultures were poised on the brink of a hitherto unknown state of disequilibrium, and all the forces were in their favor. In some areas, such as the Northwest Coast, the initial stage of food production for feasting did not fundamentally change the nature of society for complex hunter-gatherers. However, in other areas, the continued process of selecting plant seeds for their desirable characteristics in feasting, such as size and ease of processing, together with eventual refinements in gardening techniques, all must have gradually increased the efficiency and returns of the newly produced kinds of foods. Even today, I have watched traditional farmers carefully selecting the largest seeds of the year's crop for planting the following year. Eventually, a point must have been reached where formerly labor-intensive, specially produced foods for feasts became as easy to produce as ordinary gathered foods of wild species—perhaps easier. This process of striving to increase crop returns still goes on today with Industrial technology and genetic manipulation. With the development of new technologies and plant varieties, food items like white bread, once so labor intensive to produce that only the rich could afford them, have now become so economical that they have become staples of the poor.

A similar development can be seen for rice in many tribal areas of Southeast Asia, such as Tana Toraja. Here, rice was formerly used only for feasts or by elites but has now become everyday fare, although it is still a highly symbolic and prestigious food. One of the additional advantages of looking at the domestication process from a surplus and feasting perspective is that no fundamental technological changes were necessary to account for the dramatic expansions that occur. In fact, looking at stone technology, very little change occurred between the advent of complex hunter-gatherers and the full-blown expansion of agriculture. Only the use of domesticated prestige foods in feasting changed, followed by the progressive genetic manipulation of these wild forms. Thus, Cauvin's observation that technology remains remarkably stable is easily accommodated, while his observation that no shortage of resources preceded domestication is entirely consistent with what we expect among complex hunter-gatherers everywhere and especially those engaged in feasting using food surpluses to acquire social and political advantages.

With the transformation of some food production from a prestige economy to a practical economy that was productively competitive with the harvesting of wild foods, dramatic changes took place. The real potential for expanding the subsistence base through increased labor inputs was realized for the first time, and with this development population expansion began in earnest. By all accounts, these developments took place first along the upper Euphrates in the region of Mureybet in northern Syria, where a distinctive form of early Neolithic architecture, prestige items, and ideology evolved from the local Natufian cultures. This early Neolithic culture is called the Pre-Pottery Neolithic-B culture (PPNB), and it is characterized by the first square houses that are plastered, as well as domesticated animals, female anthropomorphic and bull figurines, a skull cult, specialized ritual buildings, and specially decorated, polished, grooved stones (see below; see also Cauvin 1994:106–23, 176–77; 2000a, 2000b).

As might be expected from ecological theory, once appropriate conditions were established, expansion proceeded apace. Hayden's self-evident law of expansion states that whenever food or other forms of energy can be converted to desired goods and services, and where resources are capable of expanding, there will be competition over the control of those resources. In accordance with this law, the PPNB culture expanded out of its Fertile Crescent paradise to control good farming land wherever it might be found. This diaspora began perhaps as early as 8700 B.C.E. By 8200 B.C.E., it overwhelmed the PPNA culture in the Levant and eastern Anatolia. By 7000 B.C.E., it or its derivatives had spread to central Anatolia, Cypress, the southern Levant, and the eastern reaches of the Fertile Crescent (Cauvin 1994, 2000a). By 3500 B.C.E. its offshoots and repercussions had extended all the way to the British Isles.

In many cases, it is abundantly clear that the PPNB culture displaced indigenous cultures. In other instances, however, such as at Aşikli in central Anatolia, it seems that local complex hunter-gatherers adopted selected aspects of PPNB culture through trade or other contacts and retained their own cultural integrity, sometimes not even bothering to adopt food production, presumably because in those specific environments domesticates were not as productive as the wild resources (Cauvin 1994:123–24; Balter 1998). Cauvin suggests that the special status of Aşikli may have been the result of its control over the obsidian trade that seems to have been eagerly sought by PPNB peoples. The community at Aşikli certainly ranks as one of the most complex hunter-gatherer societies anywhere in the world because of its public buildings and possibly temples.

This dual pattern of migration and cultural diffusion was to be repeated in Europe, where there was a clear intrusion of Neolithic cultures from the Near East (either descendants of the PPNB culture or of spin-off cultures that adopted food production from PPNB contact). There were also many Mesolithic groups that either remained independent or adopted selected aspects of culture from their new neighbors (Gronenborn 1999:180ff; Zvelebil and Zvelebil 1988; Zvelebil 1992). The first Neolithic groups in Europe undoubtedly arrived in the Balkans from Anatolia bringing cereal crops such as wheat and barley and domesticated animals like goats and sheep, as well as cultural elements like pottery that were totally foreign to eastern Europe. The displacement of the indigenous hunter-gatherers in the Balkans seems to have been complete, since little if any of their culture was carried over into the new Neolithic occupations (Cauvin 1994:186). The new Neolithic colonizers, or derivative groups, then spread throughout Europe in two directions, one taking advantage of, and following, the fertile and easily worked loamy soils of the Danube River and its tributaries. Other groups took advantage of easy coastal transport and fertile soils along the coasts, especially around riverine deltas. The latter route took Neolithic colonists along the northern Mediterranean Coast and then out along the Atlantic Coast until they reached the British Isles by 3500 B.C.E. The Danube River route eventually brought Neolithic colonizers or imitators to the Belgian lowlands around 4000 B.C.E. (Fig. 6.5). Thus, in a scant 5,000 years, the PPNB culture or its derivatives had expanded over 5,000 kilometers to the farthest reaches of Europe—an average rate of 1 kilometer a year. Along the way, pottery was developed and continued to form an integral part of Neolithic culture for the rest of the period and all subsequent periods. The first pottery in the Near East appears around 7000 B.C.E. Similar expansions of Neolithic groups were also taking place in China about the same time.

Jacques Cauvin (1994) has drawn attention to some of the implications that have usually been overlooked by earlier archaeologists con-

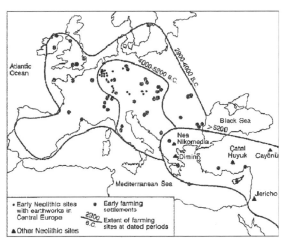

Fig. 6.5. The first domestication of plants and animals took place in the Near East between 9,000 and 11,000 B.C.E. These developments gradually spread across Europe, largely following the major river valleys such as the Danube River system and Mediterranean coastal plains. From B. Hayden, *Archaeology*, Fig. 7.5. New York: W. H. Freeman, 1993.

cerning this surprising cultural expansion. His main thesis is simply that where migrations and cultural replacements occurred, such an expansion into areas already occupied by hunter-gatherers or other agriculturalists could not have occurred without aggressive and brutal tactics backed up by an aggressive ideology. However, when boundaries stabilized, it was always possible to establish more mutually beneficial interactions that undoubtedly did result in the diffusion of ideas, materials, and practices to surrounding indigenous groups, as suggested by the Zvelebils' (1988; Zvelebil 2000), Whittle (1996: Chap. 6), and various other authors (in Price 2000).

The initial expansion of the PPNB in the Near East has all the hallmarks of cultural replacement by force (Cauvin 1994:163ff). This process seems to have continued throughout what must have been a very selective colonization of Europe. Lawrence Keeley and Daniel Cahen have documented early Neolithic fortified settlements in Belgium and many other areas in central Europe (Fig. 6.6; see also Chap. 7 and Keeley 1996; Keeley and Cahen 1989) that seem to represent hostile intrusions of frontier Neolithic groups into the territories of the resident complex hunter-gatherers (see also Milisauskas 1986:787; Evans and Rasson 1984:720). Using isotope analysis, Douglas Price (Price et al. 2001) has also demonstrated that the first Neolithic populations in Europe were intrusive, while Cavalli-Sforza (2000; Cavalli-Sforza and Cavalli-Sforza 2000; Ammerman and Cavalli-Sforza 1984) has shown that there was a massive intrusion of farmers from the Near East into Europe on the basis of the distribution of certain gene frequencies in both areas (also King and Underhill 2001; Benedetto et al. 2000). Yet in many regions of Europe there is substantial continuity from Mesolithic hunter-gatherer to Neolithic cultures in stone-tool characteristics, exchange patterns, burial traditions, decorative patterns, and other aspects (Zvelebil and Zvelebil 1988; Dennel 1992; Whittle 1996;

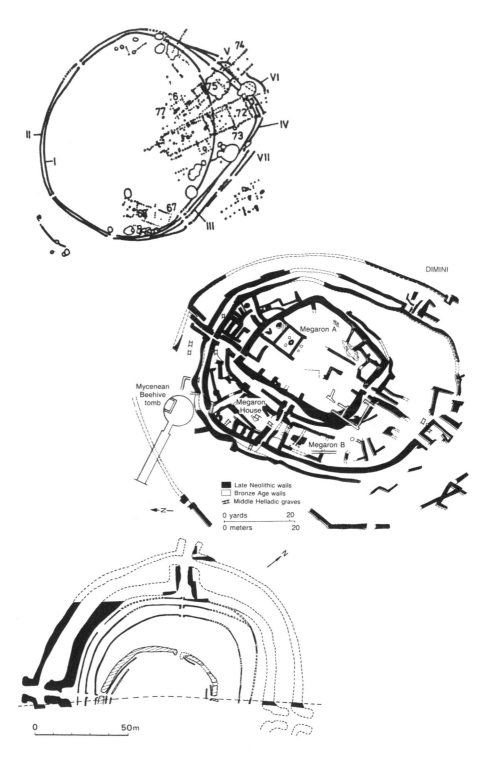

Fig. 6.6. Fortified sites were common during the early Neolithic spread into Europe. Here are three different styles of settlements commonly interpreted as fortified villages. Zlkovce (top) in Slovakia is surrounded by a double or triple wooden palisade; Dimini (center) in Greece is surrounded by two or three sets of stone walls with complex entrances; Svodin (bottom) in Slovakia is surrounded by deep ditches. Top and bottom: from J. Pavuk, "Lengyel-Culture Fortified Settlements in Slovakia," *Antiquity* 65(1991):349, 352. Center: from J. Hawkes, *Atlas of Early Man*, p. 49. New York: St. Martin's Press, 1976.

Cauwe 2001b). This indicates that local Mesolithic hunter-gatherers adopted and imitated foreign Neolithic food and pottery production techniques—perhaps for their feasts. Thus, the question of migration versus diffusion of the Neolithic in Europe is a highly complex one, but it is clear that both modes of spreading the Neolithic way of life took place (Gronenborn 1999:180ff; Bogucki 1999:176–80; Zvelebil 2000).

All these observations have changed our understanding of Neolithic society dramatically. In the middle of the twentieth century, when archaeological observations were still limited, it was thought that Neolithic settlements were self-sufficient, egalitarian, and very peaceful. It was also fashionable at that time to entertain similar idealized views about the Maya elites of such great centers as Tikal and Palenque in Mesoamerica. Maya nobles were thought to have been philosophers, mathematicians, and ritualists who ruled benevolently over a populace that supported them because of benefits derived from elite understanding of calendrics and their influence with the gods. Today, we marvel at how naïve such interpretations were, and we wonder how early archaeologists could have ignored the abundant evidence for slavery, warfare, and sacrifices of captives that has long been apparent in the well-known murals and stone carvings of the Maya.

A similar idealized view has long been held about the European Neolithic, perhaps a post–World War II reaction (Kristiansen 1999:175). However, the sheer mechanics of the PPNB expansion, together with more recent excavations of fortified settlements, genetic analyses, and isotopic analysis, makes it abundantly clear that the Neolithic expanded by force in some areas rather than through trade or friendly interactions that undoubtedly took place where land was not as good for farming (see Zvelebil and Zvelebil 1988; Gronenborn 1999: 180ff). Today, we, too, wonder why earlier evidence of fortified sites in the Neolithic was ignored by preceding generations of archaeologists. There are still a few who cling to the earlier views (e.g., Whittle 1996), but it is becoming increasing evident that from its inception Neolithic society was not particularly peaceful, nor particularly utopian, nor particularly egalitarian (a topic dealt with in more detail in Chap. 7; see also Fig. 6.7 and Gronenborn 1999; Bogucki 1999:206–14). It was a fairly typical transegalitarian group of cultures with economic and political inequalities, surplus-based competition, feasting, and probably frequent violence.

We can probably glean some notions of what the early Neolithic was like from looking at ethnographic societies with similar agricultural technologies, community characteristics, and subsistence practices. There are even some simple transegalitarian horticultural societies that used Neolithic stone technology and persisted into ethnographic times without being incorporated into larger state societies. These include the New Guinea Highlanders, the Amazonian Indians, the Iroquoian tribes, and the Southeast Asian hill tribes. They all conform to the basic pattern of moderate inequality, war, feasting, and surplus production described above. These observations will be important in the consideration of Neolithic rituals to which we now turn.

OLD RELIGIOUS THEMES TAKE ON NEW FORMS

With the increased levels of food surpluses made possible by the new Neolithic subsistence economy *in favorable places,* with aggressive population expansions, and with the enhanced importance of labor for producing surpluses, some of the religious changes

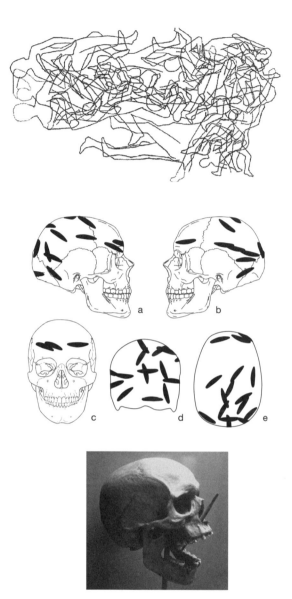

that occur in the Neolithic may be guessed at even at this point. Many of these developments are natural extensions of trends that began among Upper Paleolithic and other transegalitarian hunter-gatherers, but ultimately, Neolithic changes in the nature of the resource base and subsistence economy enabled these trends to develop further. I will discuss these religious developments in terms of feasting, ancestor cults, fertility cults, militaristic and secret cults with initiations, and public cults. While we will be concerned primarily with the various *forms* of ritual life, some of the symbolical content of Neolithic rituals also seems apprehendable from archaeological remains and surviving agricultural traditions. Where possible, we will examine these Neolithic symbolic and ritual details in order to better understand how the religions of this time were organized and what they probably meant in people's ideologies.

FEASTING FITS ALL OCCASIONS

The heights attained by complex hunter-gatherers in feasting would be difficult to surpass in most Neolithic transegalitarian societies. In historic times, Northwest Coast potlatches sometimes involved the consumption of huge quantities of salmon; tens of thousands of blankets were given away, valuable coppers and masks were destroyed, dentalium and other coveted beads were given away by the lineal meter, bottles of precious eulachen oil were

Fig. 6.7. Evidence of warfare and violence in the Neolithic includes clear indications of fighting, such as the mass grave at Talheim, Germany, where the bodies of 18 adults and 16 children were thrown into pits (top) after many of their skulls had been pierced by "shoe-last" adzes some 7,000 years ago. The center figure shows a composite tally of the blow locations. Other indications of violence include projectile points lodged in the bodies of victims, such as this man from Porsmose in Denmark (bottom), who died from two bone arrows around 5,000 years ago (the other arrow was in his chest). Top and center: from J. Wahl and H. Konig, "Anthropologisch-traumatologische Untersuchung der menschilichen Skelettreste aus dem banderamischen Massengrab bei Talheim, Kreis Heilbronn," *Fundberichte aus Baden-Württemberg* Band 12(1987):174. State Office for Historical Monuments of Baden Württemberg. Bottom: photo by B. Hayden with permission of the National Museum of Denmark.

burned, and thousands of dollars of cash were distributed. All of this consumption represented surplus that was, in effect, being invested much as we invest money in a bank. In transegalitarian feasts, food and gifts had to be repaid unless they were explicitly used to advertise the success of a group. However, many of the excesses of the Northwest Coast potlatch were the result of windfall profits from European trade and the reduced number of indigenous people caused by introduced diseases. Prehistoric feasts were almost certainly more modest, but they still must have been impressive. What is important is the use of feasts in many different contexts in order to use surpluses to create political or social debts or to achieve political or social ends (such as desirable and profitable marriages between rich and powerful families). Feasts could also be used to make investments that theoretically would either store wealth and place others under obligations, or even provide some interest on gift-loans.

In transegalitarian societies, a bewildering array of different types of feasts develop. As surpluses increase, it seems as though people use almost any pretext for feasting and investing surpluses in social or economic obligations. However, some feasting pretexts are more powerful than others, and these are the most commonly found ones ethnographically. Feasts for marriages, funerals, new houses, planting, harvests, and curing or health are particularly popular symbolic reasons used for hosting feasts. Except for funerary feasts, archaeologists cannot generally identify the symbolic purpose of holding prehistoric feasts. On the one hand, we can determine that feasts were being held, their general size, and the general amount of surpluses consumed. We can probably assume that such feasts included very strong ritual elements to justify the collection and use of surpluses and to enforce debt obligations with ritual pacts and sanctions, but we cannot tell if they were held for marriages or for new houses or purely for prestige. On the other hand, funeral feasts can usually be recognized since they were often held at burial sites.

Feasts generally were also accompanied by music and dance and the display of sacred items such as pipes, ancestral objects, and masks. Prestige ritual items are an ideal way of displaying a group's economic and social success without seeming too arrogant or offensive. They display the favor bestowed on certain groups by the spirits. The putative need for prestige ritual paraphernalia also provides a powerful means that ambitious individuals can use for justifying demands on others to increase and surrender surplus production (i.e., to ensure the spirits are pleased and continue to bestow good fortune on the group). In the context of the large public feasts hosted to achieve political and social goals, many aspects of ritual developed into public displays and public cults. It is important to appreciate the many types and purposes of ritual feasts in transegalitarian societies in order to understand the archaeological remains that are sometimes associated with ancestral and other cults in the Neolithic.

Ancestors Warrant the Wishes of the Living

While archaeological evidence for ancestor worship is somewhat limited in most complex hunter-gatherer societies, it becomes a common and sometimes dramatic theme in the Neolithic, stretching from the Fertile Crescent to the islands north of Scotland. It also emerges as a strong element in East Asia. In general, the importance of ancestor worship and its material expression in archaeological remains seems to vary with the relative wealth and the surpluses that a society could produce. Some of these remains testify to very different attitudes toward the dead than generally prevail in Industrial societies today. It is therefore worth pointing out that there is a wide range of attitudes and practices concerning the dead in different societies throughout the world. What is your attitude toward people you have known who have died? Do you like to look upon their bodies in their coffins? Are you hesitant to touch them? Are you relieved to have a funeral home take the body away for burial preparation or cremation? Do you ever pray to the dead person for help, or are you content simply to know that they have played out their role on earth and have gone to rest somewhere in the spirit realms? Do you hesitate to talk about them? Are you ever afraid of them? Are you afraid of ghosts?

Ancestor worship is a unique attitude and practice that is only found under certain cultural ecological conditions. We might well think of it as a distinctive "ancestor type" of religion. As mentioned earlier, even chimpanzees exhibit an innate fear of deathlike appearances of other chimpanzees. Generalized hunter-gatherers, like those in Australia, may revere mythical totemic ancestors who were half human and half animal, but their attitudes toward dead family or band members were generally those of extreme avoidance. Among the Australian tribes that I worked with, fear of the recently dead was so pronounced that there was a prohibition on anyone speaking the name of the dead person for years after they died. This often created problems for people who had the same name as the dead person. In general, I would suggest that there is probably an innate dislike or fear in most people toward dead bodies and their spirits. Most people feel rather uneasy at the prospect of ghosts hanging around their living quarters. Therefore, it comes as quite a surprise to find, in some societies, recently dead members being worshipped, even to the point of burying their bodies under the house floor! How would you feel if your grandfather was buried in the basement and your parents went down to talk with him from time to time?

What could motivate people to systematically engage in such activities over thousands of years? Ethnologists like Maurice Freedman (1965, 1970) have repeatedly observed that the worship of ancestors is intimately tied to the inheritance of valuable resources such as good farmland. From this perspective, the archaeological indications of ancestor worship in the Paleolithic and Mesolithic make a great deal of sense if key resource procurement locations, such as prime fishing sites and river fords along animal migration routes, were owned by families as they were among recent complex hunter-gatherers. Ownership of such resource locations would have been the key to prosperity and health, and ownership would have depended upon inheriting them from one's immediate ancestors. Moreover, obtaining the maximum benefit from these seasonal resources generally entailed considerable labor, and there were undoubtedly a number of other brothers and sisters who were also interested in benefiting from inherited rights to wealth-producing resources. As a result, ownership sometimes became the basis for the formation of corporate types of lineages or kindred, with everyone in the lineage having some rights to the inherited resources and the management of the corporate estate. With this mode of ownership, rules were required for determining rights and leadership roles: who had the right to make decisions; what rules would govern the roles of women and men and older and younger members of the lineages; or any number of details concerning the relationships between members or with other lineages. Under such conditions, appeal to some authority was required, and lineage ancestors provided a natural source for such authority. They could also be portrayed as providing spiritual guidance for important decisions, at least to those capable of contacting them—generally the living heads of the lineages. In order to retain as much claim to supernatural power as possible, leading lineage members often asserted that ancestors were reincarnated in their own children (Carlsen and Prechtel 1991).

Ambitious lineage members without the appropriate pedigree could claim to be channeling more remote ancestors (Lewis 1989:125). If they were wealthy enough and successful enough at feasting, they might well be able to convince others of the validity of their claims. Ancestors could also be portrayed as meting out spiritual and real-life retribution for transgressions of lineage rules (Lewis 1989:102–32). Ancestors, crops, and fertility all tended to be interrelated (Eliade 1958a:350). Since the lineage vital force, or lineage "soul," was often viewed as residing partially in the crops or in the fat of the lineage domestic animals, any poor harvests or herd diseases could readily be attributed to transgressions by some living lineage members of cultural or lineage rules. Poor crops and herd diseases were common occurrences and so could be easily used as supernatural leverage to promote behaviors that were in the interests of lineage leaders. Thus, ancestor worship helped lineage and household heads consolidate their control over their children (reinforced by actual control over inheritance) and other junior lineage members. Lineage heads would also have exerted control over surplus lineage resources and wealth held "in trust" for the entire lineage, in the form of corporate ritual wealth such as drums, masks, costumes, carvings, or other prestige paraphernalia or even domestic animals. This surplus wealth could be used for specific political and economic ends, for arranging desirable marriages that carried with them wealth exchanges or access to valuable resources, for waging wars or making peace, or for paying compensation for transgressions by lineage members. As Freedman (1970) notes, the high costs of lineage rituals was often a source of wealth for the lineage segment that owned the lineage shrines and halls. Elders, in particular, often gave large amounts of wealth to have their memorial tablets placed in the lineage shrines. *None of these aspects existed among egalitarian generalized hunter-gatherers.*

Resource conditions among horticulturalists *in suitable environments* were much more stable and richer than among generalized hunter-gatherers. As a result, subsistence alliances between communities were no longer as critical for survival. However, individual households were still subject to a number of risks, and being part of a lineage corporate group that would help in times of trouble was certainly a major adaptive feature of most transegalitarian societies (Clarke 1998, 2001). Ancestor cults were probably actively promoted by household heads as they became older (and closer to achieving ancestor status) in order to ensure that they were well taken care of in their old age. After all, who would want to anger or offend a person who was about to become your spiritual benefactor or who could mete out supernatural retribution for having been treated poorly? Thus, under cultural ecological conditions where inherited resource ownership could bring wealth or even subsistence security, ancestor cults and lineages tended to thrive (Collier 1975:76ff).

What is the archaeological evidence for ancestor cults in the Neolithic? As in the European Mesolithic, there is some evidence in the Near Eastern Mesolithic Natufian

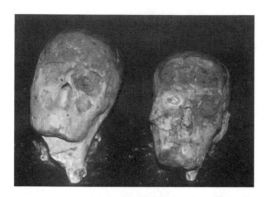

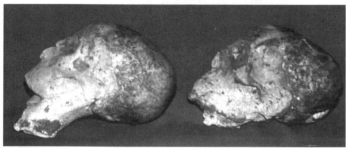

culture for ancestor worship. Here, substantial cemeteries occur for the first time in prehistory. It has been repeatedly argued that cemeteries in traditional communities indicate the existence of corporate groups such as lineages or clans (R. Chapman 1981a, 1981b, 1995). In the Natufian, there are other indications of ancestral cults (Cauvin 1978:127). Some burials occur within houses, and rare cases even occur where burials are covered with large flagging stones. Secondary burials (the removal of bones from decayed bodies and their reburial) also occur, and these seem to be almost exclusively associated with ancestral veneration. Skulls in particular appear to have been selected for secondary burial, and as previously noted, these are often considered to contain a person's soul. Watkins (1990:344; 1993:85–86) provides additional documentation for this skull cult. There are even stronger indications of ancestor worship in the Neolithic Natufian-derived PPNA culture where a number of skull deposits were discovered, all arranged in circles with the skulls facing inward (Cauvin 1978:127).

Skull and ancestor cults, however, are also one of the key features of the PPNB culture, both in its north Syrian homeland and in areas that it expanded into toward the east, north, and west. In its homeland area and in Jericho to the west, skulls were placed on pedestals or

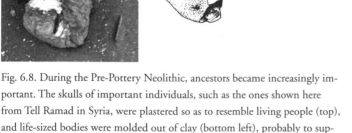

Fig. 6.8. During the Pre-Pottery Neolithic, ancestors became increasingly important. The skulls of important individuals, such as the ones shown here from Tell Ramad in Syria, were plastered so as to resemble living people (top), and life-sized bodies were molded out of clay (bottom left), probably to support the skulls in special ancestor shrines. Similar plastered skulls have been found at a number of sites from this culture, such as Jericho (bottom right). Photos from Francis Hours (unpublished originals). Drawings from J. Cauvin, *Les Premiers Villages de Syrie-Palestine*, p. 129. Paris: Maison de l'Orient, 1978.

clay statues along walls and their faces were modelled in clay with shells in the place of eyes (Fig. 6.8; see also Cauvin 1978:128). It is difficult not to see in this practice the attempt to depict the image of the deceased person and make their presence more tangible. Although the plastering of skulls may have only occurred archaeologically in the Levant during the Neolithic, similar practices are still carried out in some traditional ancestor-worshipping tribal societies.

In the expanding PPNB world, some skulls or portrayals of heads are found in public contexts (at Çayönü and 'Ain Ghazal), others occur in household shrines (at Çatal Hüyük), some are coated with bitumen (a natural tarry substance) and painted with radiating solarlike rays (Fig. 6.9), and in some sites, 'Ain Ghazal, for example, crude but carefully crafted human statues, some almost life-sized, appear to replace skulls as ancestral representations (Fig. 6.10; see also Rollefson 2000:185). Some of these latter statues also have solar-like rays engraved on their faces. In some sites, collections of skulls appear to be predominantly male, in others they appear to be predominantly female (Cauvin 1994:152–54). While household shrines undoubtedly represent the worship of family or lineage ancestors, the more public shrines probably represent the promotion of elite ancestors as overarching community authorities, such as lineage or clan heads or ancestral

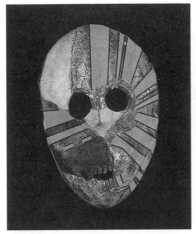

Fig. 6.9. Some of the representations of powerful people or supernatural entities such as ancestors or deities seem to have solar associations indicated by radiating lines on their faces. The two examples shown here include a full-sized mask from Nahal Hemar Cave in the Levant (perhaps used for secret society rituals during the PPNB) and a clay statue's head from the PPNB of Jericho. Left: Adapted from O. Bar-Yosef and D. Alon, "Nahal Hemar Cave," *Atiqot* 18 (1988). Right: from J. Cauvin, *Naissance des divinités, Naissance de l'agriculture,* p. 150. Paris: CNRS, 1994.

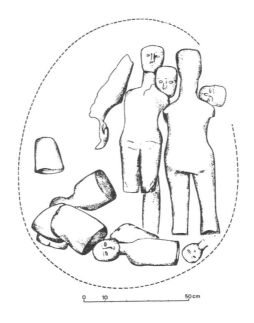

Fig. 6.10. An alternate way of depicting ancestors for worship in the Pre-Pottery Neolithic was probably to make statues that represented them. The half-life-sized clay statues here were discovered in a pit at 'Ain Ghazal in Jordan. They very likely were part of ancestor worship paraphernalia. From J. Cauvin, *Naissance des divinités, Naissance de l'agriculture,* Fig. 40. Paris: CNRS, 1994.

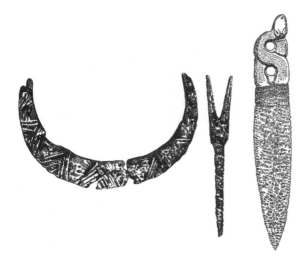

Fig. 6.11. During the early Neolithic at Çatal Hüyük, some important burials were accompanied by rich arrays of prestige objects such as this exquisitely made flint dagger (right), the fine bone neck ring (left), and the carefully carved symbolic item. These indicate that wealth and status differences existed within the community. From J. Mellaart, *Çatal Hüyük: A Neolithic Town in Anatolia,* p. 92. New York: Thames & Hudson, 1967.

chiefs (Rollefson 2000). These instances, and others that we shall review shortly, appear to constitute further attempts by elites to create cults in which they have privileged communication with supernatural forces and over which they could exercise control.

Probably the most fascinating of all the indicators of ancestral worship are the shrines uncovered by James Mellaart at Çatal Hüyük in central Anatolia (1967). Çatal Hüyük was an extremely prosperous and large Neolithic settlement, dating from about 7000 to 6000 B.C.E.—an offshoot of the PPNB expansion or one of its derivative cultures. At Çatal Hüyük, families and lineages seem to have become wealthy from the fertile land, abundant game, and lucrative obsidian trade in the area. Under these conditions, ancestor worship might well be expected to have flourished. In fact, about half of the domestic structures that James Mellaart excavated had elaborate shrines on their ground floors, apparently reached only by ladders from upper floors. In these shrines, there were bench platforms, mural paintings, human skulls, and sets of bull horns (bucrania) cemented into the walls or onto pedestals. Numerous burials occurred under the floors, almost certainly of lineage members, that is, ancestors. In fact, probably only the most important lineage members were buried in the shrine locations, indicating that burial in shrines may have been a costly affair (Wason 1994:159–60) as it was in the Chinese lineage halls described by Freedman. There seems to be little doubt that the shrines at Çatal Hüyük represent lineage ancestral shrines rendered more or less elaborate and member-inclusive according to the wealth of the family members or their benefactors.

Wealth differences there certainly were. Half the dwellings had no shrines and most graves contained no offerings or prestige goods. But some graves were richly provided with status items such as obsidian mirrors, stone bowls, maceheads, and finely made flint daggers (Fig. 6.11; Fiedel 1979; Wason 1994:161–64; Hodder, Stevanovic, and Lopez 1998:16–17, 20). Shrines were usually built over these exceptional graves (Wason 1994:161–62). In fact, a wide range of status materials were present, including copper, lead, carnelian, alabaster, apatite, serpentine, as well as dentalium and many other types of sea shells (Wason 1994:154). Shrine rooms also varied in terms of size, the extent of murals, and the number of bucrania incorporated into the architecture (Hodder, Stevanovic, and Lopez 1998:20). Thus, there seem to have been substantial differences in the relative wealth of each lineage, a situation characteristic of lineages in transegalitarian cultures today. The murals in some shrines are particularly instructive in terms of the actual ritual procedures, for they clearly show headless bodies with carion-eating birds hovering over them, perhaps for the purpose of stripping flesh from the bodies (Fig. 6.12).

Fig. 6.12. Carrion-eating birds, like buzzards or vultures, are depicted on some of the shrine walls at Çatal Hüyük. The bodies over which they hover are headless, and human skulls were found on some of the platforms beneath the murals. It has been suggested that the birds were depicted because they were part of the process of defleshing bodies before burial. However, it could be argued that they symbolized war, like the ravens the Celts thought were harbingers and followers of battles. If so, they would be preying on the bodies of decapitated enemies whose heads were displayed as trophies on shrines (see also Figs. 6.20 and 6.21). From J. Mellaart, *Çatal Hüyük: A Neolithic Town in Anatolia*, Figs. 14, 15, 47. New York: Thames & Hudson, 1967.

Fig. 6.13. One of the dominant patterns that James Mellaart observed among the shrines that he excavated at Çatal Hüyük was the tendency for bull representations to occur on north and east walls and for female images to occur on west walls. His observations are summarized here and seem to indicate a basic duality in Neolithic ideology between masculine forces (represented by the bull) and feminine forces, seemingly associated with different cardinal directions. From J. Mellaart, *Çatal Hüyük: A Neolithic Town in Anatolia,* pp. 102–3. New York: Thames & Hudson, 1967.

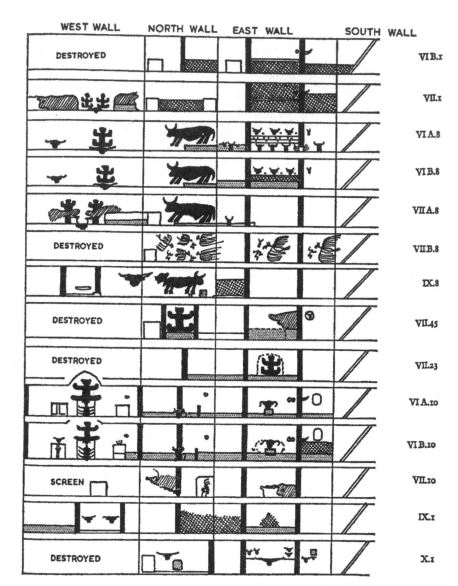

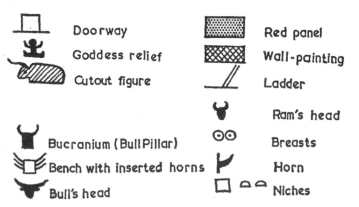

This may be the first clearly documented case of "excarnation," the exposure of dead bodies to birds or animals in order to remove the flesh prior to final burial. This practice was to become central to the rituals revolving around the great megalithic tombs of Western Europe (Chap. 7).

Since the promotion of procreation is generally a major reason for seeking the spiritual aid of ancestors, it is not surprising to find a basic, possibly sexually related dualism represented in the iconography of the ancestral shrines at Çatal Hüyük. James Mellaart (1967:125) has interpreted the human figures modeled in plaster, predominantly on the south and west walls (sometimes giving birth to animals) as goddesses, while the other walls feature images of bulls (Fig. 6.13). More recently, Hodder, Stevanovic, and Lopez (1998) have questioned the identification of the modeled plaster figures as being either female or human. On the basis of Mellaart's drawings and photographs showing these figures with human navels or breasts or giving birth, the interpretation of these figures as human or some anthropomorphic female form seems reasonable to me, although the incorporation of bird beaks inside some of their breasts and their giving birth to animals certainly indicates that they were viewed as having some unusual qualities

Fig. 6.14. There are many reasons for thinking that bulls represented cosmic or supernatural forces in the Neolithic. One reason shown here from Çatal Hüyük is the very elaborate painted motifs used to decorate the plastered bull's skulls and the shrine areas around them. Such elaborate decoration is typical of most sacred objects, such as Easter eggs and Christmas trees. From J. Mellaart, *Çatal Hüyük: A Neolithic Town in Anatolia*, Figs. 35, 36. New York: Thames & Hudson, 1967.

not entirely consistent with ideas of nurturing, comforting goddesses. As among the hunter-gatherers such as those in Australia and the Northwest Coast, these figures may represent totemic ancestresses that were both animal and human.

The other aspect of the ancestral shrines at Çatal Hüyük that is of immediate interest involves the bucrania. Why are these such central features of the ancestral shrines? What do they represent in terms of the rituals? The bucrania at Çatal Hüyük were clearly meant to represent sacred forces because they were intricately decorated, almost like Ukrainian Easter eggs (Fig. 6.14). Let us explore their possible feasting significance.

In transegalitarian and more complex traditional societies such as chiefdoms, funerals are one of the most common events for competitive displays of family and lineage wealth. There are a number of reasons why funerals might be especially suited for such displays. Michael Dietler (2001) has suggested that the most emotionally compelling and effective political symbols are those that are not overtly political but those that meld intense personal experiences involving one's existential identity with broader structures of power. Funerals provide a highly charged emotional environment that favors the

Fig. 6.15. Tribal groups throughout Southeast Asia use valuable domestic animals such as water buffalo as sacrifices at feasts to impress guests with the host's wealth and success. After feasts, horns from cattle are typically put on display to remind everyone of the economic and social successes of the hosts. Here, horns are displayed on a village leader's house among the Akha of Thailand. Bull horns in shrines at Çatal Hüyük and other Neolithic villages undoubtedly also were primarily derived from feasts and constituted displays of wealth and power. Shrines at Çatal Hüyük may well have been used primarily for important feasts for lineages similar to Fig. 6.1, where lineage heads sit on platforms similar to those at Çatal Hüyük. Photo by B. Hayden.

manipulation of economic realities and political symbolism. The addition of emotionally powerful music, dancing, rhymed verse, costumes, staging, and intoxicating substances enhances the power of these rituals for rendering people receptive to particular values that feast promoters wish to promulgate, such as the worship of ancestors, identification with lineage or clan, socioreligious organizations, mutually supporting relationships between those in powerful positions, and adherence to lineage rules. References to the ageless traditions established by mythical ancestors in the distant past can be used to create the impression of seamless continuity with the present and can limit the perception of alternatives. Thus, current or ideal practices are portrayed as "natural." Feasts provide an excellent context for expressing idealized concepts and the way people ought to act, at least from the often self-serving view of the organizing hosts. For these or similar reasons, funerals are well suited for hosting feasts by lineage leaders.

In fact, all transegalitarian funerals that I am aware of take the form of feasts such as the one described at the beginning of this chapter. Typically, a family and lineage use all their available surplus to host such feasts. They send special invitations to high-ranking members of allied lineages and make special meat or prestige gifts to those people. Such invitations must be reciprocated when members of the allied lineages die. Funeral feast costs are graded according to the importance of individuals within families and lineages. For transegalitarian groups with domestic animals, the most costly items are generally the largest domesticated animals. Among the hill tribes of Southeast Asia, where I worked, the most costly funerals in oral memory involved the killing of only nine cattle or water buffaloes. Most families owned no such animals or had perhaps only two or three. Only rich families had large numbers of cattle. The horns of the animals killed at these feasts were later attached to the house as a constant reminder to everyone of the prosperity and power of the family and lineage (Fig. 6.15).

I propose that the bucrania set up on display in the ancestral shrines of Çatal Hüyük represent exactly the same thing: a display and constant reminder to everyone in the lineage rituals, and to guests, of the power and wealth of the lineage as represented by the amount expended for funerals of important members. If there was any question about the role of feasting in these funeral rituals, the presence of kitchens and storerooms within the shrine areas and the use of prestige stone serving bowls and rare pottery vessels offers further support for a feasting interpretation (Wason 1994:164, 175). In addition, the presence of low platforms around the shrines of Çatal Hüyük are very similar to the low platforms on which the most important lineage elders feast in hill tribe communities today (in Fig. 6.1, these elders are seated on a platform although it cannot be clearly distinguished). Recent excavations have revealed much more evidence for feasting at Çatal Hüyük (Russell and Martin 1998, 2000). The incorporation of bucrania into house walls begins in the homeland of the PPNB culture in northern Syria at Mureybet and is also found in some PPNA structures at Jericho (Cauvin 1978:110; 1994:120), Jerf el Ahmar (Stordeur and Abbès 2002:590–91), at Hallan Çemi (Rosenberg 1994:125), and at other sites (Fig. 6.27). It seems very likely that these, too, were part of funeral feasts and rituals, but it is also possible that they were part of other major kinds of feasts, such as those for house dedications or making alliances.

Thus, the elaboration of ancestral cults in particularly rich, wealth-producing areas seems to be a hallmark of most transegalitarian societies everywhere, but it becomes especially prominent in the richest Neolithic communities of Eurasia (e.g., Lee and Zhu 2002). Such practices continue today in our popular celebrations. With a moment's reflection, one may come readily to mind.

FERTILITY PROMOTES PROSPERITY

Perhaps not all resources used by transegalitarian societies required intensive labor inputs or cooperating groups of families in order to achieve maximum or even adequate returns. However, grain farming is certainly a risky subsistence system, and labor is the key bottleneck to producing grain surpluses (Izikowitz 1951:293–94; Falvey 1977:55; Condominas 1977; Gregg 1988:156, 161). Under these conditions, it should come as little surprise that human fertility became a major concern of human interactions with the supernatural in most Neolithic societies. In my estimation, it is difficult to account in any other terms for the striking shift from dominant animal religious motifs in the Paleolithic and Natufian to the Neolithic, when female symbolic images play a major role in the overall artistic repertory of many regions. The fact that most of the figurines are fecund, female, naked, and obviously well-fed supports this notion, for as Eliade (1958a:333–34) has noted, nakedness and especially pregnant females are associated with fertility (Fig. 6.16). Marija Gimbutas claims that there are some 30,000 goddess figurines, but many of these are actually of indeterminate sex. Nevertheless, there are a considerable number, and the occurrence of numerous carved phalluses also seems to reflect a preoccupation with fertility. Similar Venus figurines and phalluses appeared for a while in the Upper Paleolithic (Figs. 5.23 and 5.25), and sexual symbols or female figurines occur in a few Mesolithic cultures such as the Jomon. However, this theme only becomes predominant over wide areas in the Neolithic, probably with the much more critical role of children and labor for family prosperity under food production conditions.

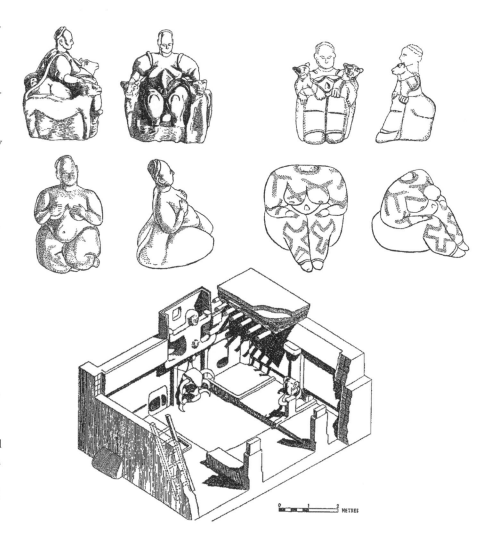

Fig. 6.16. Numerous figurines of obviously fecund women occur in the Neolithic, representing a major shift away from the predominantly animal icons of the Paleolithic. Neolithic female figurines seem most plausibly related to fertility concerns, as indicated also by the depictions of apparently pregnant women in some shrines at Çatal Hüyük (sometimes giving birth to animals). Occasionally the Neolithic female figurines are associated with animals, as in two of the examples from Çatal Hüyük, possibly indicating a relation between female goddesses and the general fertility of people, animals, and perhaps plant life. From J. Mellaart, *Çatal Hüyük: A Neolithic Town in Anatolia*, Figs. 40, 49, 50, 52, 53. New York: Thames & Hudson, 1967.

In spite of this shift, animal figurines are still the most common type, especially the bull and the goat. As in the Upper Paleolithic, the representation of these animals was not for their economic importance but for their symbolic attributes (Cauvin 1994:96). Thus, they should be viewed as aspects of religious or political life. It can be suggested that, as humans began to control the breeding and raising of animals, and with prosperity largely determined by the number of animals one owned (especially as investments to be used in feasts for economic and political benefits), Neolithic farmers began to take a much more active interest in promoting the reproduction of the domestic animals under their care. This change in vested interests may well account for the change in iconography from the Paleolithic to the Neolithic. As Waal Malefijt (1968:301) has argued, among hunter-gatherers, life depends to a large degree on hunting and in this realm man is considered subordinate to the will of supernatural powers.

In food-producing societies, people take a more active role in the production of crops and animals and thus also adopt a more proactive spiritual role in promoting fertility, growth, and health of both animals and plants. It is perhaps not surprising that fertile-looking goddesses dominate wildlife or are flanked by wild lions, as in the case of the famous statue from Çatal Hüyük (Fig. 6.16, top left). Such a theme fits in very well with earlier hunting and gathering concepts of a master or mistress of animals who controlled the fertility of animals and their appearance on the earth. Perhaps for the first time, the fertility of the earth became a central concern in human religions, too, and goddesses were addressed in order to make efforts at tilling the soil as productive as possible. Figurines of rams, bulls, and billy goats seem like natural symbols of virility and reproduction. These are, in fact, probably their most important common symbolical attributes in most traditional societies. Nor does it seem unusual that fertility statues might be found in grain bins or simple domestic contexts, as at Çatal Hüyük. Early farmers might well want to attract fertilizing forces to such places.

Representations of human males also occur in the Neolithic. However, as in the Upper Paleolithic, they are usually less frequent than portrayals of females, although at some sites they can be quite significant. At Nevali Çori, for instance, there were 179 male figurines, 159 naked and seated female figurines, and over 300 other indeterminate anthropomorphic figurines or fragments (Hauptmann 1999). In many cases, the expression of masculine supernatural forces largely seems to take the form of isolated carvings of phalluses (Cauvin 1994:68; Hutton 1991:42) or man-animal forms. Both occurrences follow the same patterns as in the Upper Paleolithic. Phalluses tend to be more numerous than depictions of males, but less numerous than depictions of females. Females are rarely, if ever, portrayed in animal masks or as therianthropes. Females are almost always naked, whereas males are often clothed or disguised. In fact, male supernatural forces may be symbolically represented most commonly by animal motifs rather than human ones. The masculine associations with animals will become more evident in our discussion of military cults. But the association between males and animals probably derives from the almost universal division of labor in traditional societies where men hunt but women do not. Men take animal lives and are responsible for properly conducting the rituals that will bring the animal spirits back in new bodies. Men are, in many respects, the brothers and allies of the animal spirits.

Another indication of fertility cults in the Neolithic is the emergence of a divine pair of deities whose sexual union was thought to guarantee the fertility of the land. Certainly, Leroi-Gourhan argued that the transegalitarian hunter-gatherers of the Upper Paleolithic conceived of their world in terms of a complementary sexual duality that might reflect a concern with fertility. However, there is no convincing evidence for the Paleolithic that this extended to sacred male-female pairs of divinities. At the other end of the prehistoric time scale, in the later religions of the Near East, such as Babylonian, this sacred marriage, or divine union, was celebrated by the divine king and a high priestess of the main temple (see Chap. 11). A similar concept may well be behind the Natufian statue of two people making love (Fig. 6.17), but such scenes are rare. The first suggested Neolithic representation of a divine pair seems to occur in the PPNB occupation of Nevali Çori, in Anatolia (Cauvin 1994:120). The concept seems to have spread rapidly (Cauvin 1994:98) and may underlie the division of shrine walls at Çatal Hüyük into animal and "goddess" oppositions.

At the Neolithic site of La Parta in the Balkans, there is a remarkable divine pair represented in life-sized forms in a public sanctuary (Fig. 6.18; see also Lazarovici 1998;

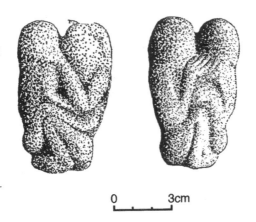

Fig. 6.17. Concerns of fertility in the ideological and ritual domains seem to occur initially among some complex hunter-gatherers such as those of Upper Paleolithic Europe and the Mesolithic-level Natufian culture of the Levant, where this sculpture of a sexual embrace was found. This is the earliest archaeological candidate for a depiction of the "sacred marriage" between supernatural beings responsible for community fertility. From J. Cauvin, *Les Premiers Villages de Syrie-Palestine*, Fig. 23. Lyons: Maison de l'Orient, 1978.

0 ___ 3cm

Monah 1997:211–12). Of particular note are the horns of the male deity, once again underlining the graphic representation of male divinities as animal or therianthropic forms, whereas images of females never seem to be represented in this way. In this case, and perhaps all cases of divine couples, the fertility cults may take on a public aspect, whereas the small Venus figurines and phalluses appear to be entirely related to domestic worship or prayers for fertility and thus are relatively numerous in Neolithic sites and occur overwhelmingly in household contexts (Hauptmann 1999:77; Rollefson 2000:184; Lesure 2002:599).

All in all, there are strong theoretical grounds for expecting fertility worship to be important in the Neolithic. It is interesting to note that phalluses continue to be religious domestic cult items in many agrarian cultures of the third world today, just as they were in the Neolithic and in classical Greece and Rome. These sculptures are often viewed simply as good luck charms to bring prosperity (Fig. 6.19). Their role and basic meaning has perhaps not changed significantly since the Upper Paleolithic. Other instances of divine couples or female and bull pairs occur on ceramic vessels or as sculptures in the Romanian Neolithic (Monah 1997:211–12).

MILITARISTIC CULTS MAKE MIGHT RIGHT

While it was fashionable in the 1950s to think of Neolithic societies as peaceful and egalitarian, this view has changed dramatically. At the outset, conflict seems to have been moderate in intensity and focused primarily at the active expansion fronts of Neolithic colonizations (Gronenborn 1999:185–89). As the Neolithic evolved, however, the incidence of conflict everywhere seems to have increased significantly (Milisauskas 1978:121, 177; Cauwe 2001a:100–102), until at the end of the Neolithic there were major fortifications and mass graves (see Chap. 7). For now, it is interesting to consider how military concerns were expressed in Neolithic religious terms. Jacques Cauvin (1994, 2000a) has provided the most comprehensive treatment of this topic. His main observations are that the PPNB culture could not have expanded without aggressive armed force and that a militaristic ideology was necessary to legitimize such actions. He thus describes the PPNB people as true conquerors and colonizers.

WEAPONS

Many of the grave goods accompanying PPNB men indicate a dominant concern with military weapons and prestige wealth. Cauvin (1994:168; 2000a) argues that their arrowheads and daggers were no longer simple, expediently made utilitarian items but had become technically elaborated to the point that they constituted impressive prestige items (Fig. 6.11). Moreover, they became most abundant when game was declining, a trend also noted by Keeley (1997:309) for the European Neolithic. Thus, it is unlikely that

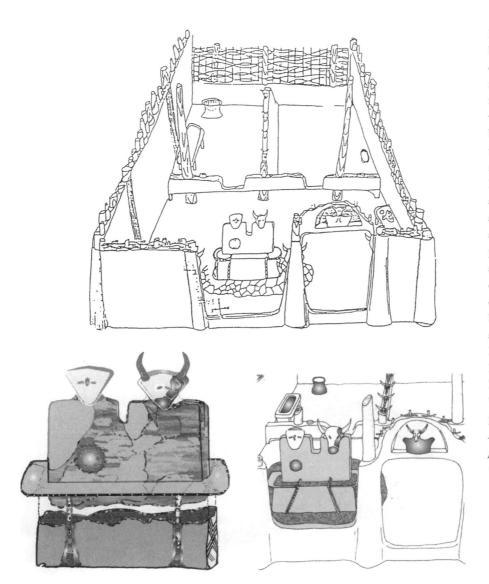

Fig. 6.18. The basic cosmological duality between male and female forces in the universe also seems to be represented in the Neolithic Romanian site of La Parta; a shrine altar appears to represent a horned god and a female deity, possibly pregnant, as the main objects of worship. Similar concepts seem to be displayed in the shrines of Çatal Hüyük (Fig. 6.13). From G. Lazarovici, "Monumentale plastik in Parta," *Acta Musei Napocensis* 35, no. 1 (1998): Figs. 1, 2.

these armaments were related to hunting. Rich males were also accompanied by knives, blades, and finely crafted maceheads—symbols and weapons of war and conquest that came to be used throughout much of Europe, North Africa, and Asia (Fiedel 1979). In fact, British royalty still carry ceremonial maces as emblems of power and authority for important state occasions. Maces also occurred at Qermez Dere (Watkins 1993). As we shall see in the next chapter, axes and adzes also served as weapons of war in fashions similar to maces. These, too, often became elaborated and costly and were used as ritual symbols of prestige in burials and other contexts (Milisauskas 1978:177; Patton 1991).

VIOLENCE AND SACRIFICES

There are additional, more grisly testimonies of aggressive dominating males in PPNB religious life. These consist of a headless body lying in the center of a ritual structure at

Fig. 6.19. Phalluses constitute important items during the Upper Paleolithic and the Neolithic in Europe and many other parts of the world. They were also important in Greek and Roman times and continue to be important in many traditional cultures of the world such as those in India and Southeast Asia. Historically and ethnographically, phalluses were associated with fertility and all the benefits that fertility brought: wealth, happiness, good fortune. The upper and lower left examples shown here are from Thailand and are inscribed with symbols and characters as well as being fitted with internal rattles to enhance their good luck powers. The lower right example is a Neolithic phallus of chalk from Maumbury Rings in the Dorset County Museum, England. Photos by Greg Holoboff and B. Hayden.

Jerf el Ahmar (Fig. 6.20), one of the earliest Neolithic settlements in the Near East (Stordeur et al. 2001:36–37; Arnaud 2000). The fingers of this individual were still dug into the earth, and there were two human skulls at the bottom of post holes in the same building. Depictions of similar headless people on the walls indicate that this was not an isolated incident, as do the three cooked human heads found in a hearth outside (Stordeur and Abbès 2002:553). Somewhat later at Çatal Hüyük, three human babies were put under the entrances to a shrine and the depictions of headless bodies continues (Hodder 1999:160). Houses at 'Ain Ghazal have at least one headless body (of varying ages) buried under their floors, perhaps as house foundation sacrifices. At Çayönü there is also a special cult building, dubbed the "House of the Dead," where 66 human skulls were found. Rather than being from older individuals who might be considered ancestors, these skulls were primarily of young adults, both men and women. When analyzing animal bones, archaeologists use high ratios of young individuals as a major indication of controlled killing. Under the floor were the partial remains of another 400 people. There were vertical stone stelae erected in the main room, and an analysis of the chemical residues on these stones indicated the presence of human blood as well as animal blood (Cauvin 1994:120, 122–23; 2000a). Two other buildings at this site also contained large slabs of stone with traces of human blood. One of these stelae was ornamented with a sculpted human head. Similar stelae, sculptures, and buildings have been found at other Anatolian PPNB sites and probably created the template for later Middle Eastern altars with their sacrificial stones. The famous "horns of consecration" of the Minoan cultures in the Aegean probably derive from the same tradition, for blood residues have also been found on them (Marinatos 1993:207; Cauvin 1994:159; 2000a). Pillars with anthropomorphic heads (often horned males) occur in later Neolithic shrines in Cyprus and Romania as well (see also Lazarovici 1989: Abb. 19(2); 1991: Fig. 3; 1998).

Additional evidence of competition between males is provided by the high incidence of major head wounds among males at Çatal Hüyük (27 percent) as well as the occurrence of frequent parry fractures in men's arm bones (7 percent; Wason 1994:157). At Nemrik, a number of skeletons had projectile points embedded in them (Watkins

1990:344). It is of further interest that Çatal Hüyük seems to have been established suddenly, without a long evolution, and that two racial groups seem to be represented among the skeletal remains. The higher incidence of female burials to male burials may indicate that males were dying more frequently in raids or while away on trading expeditions (Wason 1994:157).

In Jericho, during the PPNA occupation, a massive wall and tower were built requiring a great investment of labor, indicating considerable hierarchical control over labor. Early Neolithic fortifications are also present at Halula and possibly Jerf el Ahmar in Syria (Stordeur and Abbès 2002:567), at Aşikli and Kuruçay in Anatolia (Esin and Harmankaya 1999:125–26; Duru 1999:184), and at Tenta and Khirokitia on Cyprus (Ronen 1995:177). Both the wall and tower at Jericho have traditionally been considered military defenses, although some people have argued that the tower may have actually been built for ritual purposes. Even if this ritual explanation may eventually prove to be correct, the stuffing of its passageways with human skeletons during PPNB times seems to indicate a sacrificial cult similar to that documented at Çayönü (Cauvin 1994:157; 2000a). It is highly unlikely that these bodies represent a normal burial rite. Minimally, they may represent victims of an armed confrontation who were sacrificed.

As a result of these discoveries, one must wonder if all the skulls present in the ancestral shrines at Çatal Hüyük are in fact those of ancestors. Some if not all of them might be trophy heads or heads of sacrificed victims retained as victory and prestige items in the lineage sanctuaries. Such practices are typical of headhunters in most places in the world (Fig. 6.21). Fairservis (1975) observes that the disposition of prisoners of war through ritual execution, head removal, or sacrifice is common. He thinks that some of the human remains in the shrines may be those of captives. In many headhunting cultures, a death in the family must be avenged by killing an enemy and removing the head

Fig. 6.21. While the skulls associated with many Neolithic shrines may be those of revered ancestors, in some cases they may be skulls of detested enemies. Many warrior societies, such as the Celts, Amazonian tribes, Polynesians, and Southeast Asian tribes, kept the heads of those they had killed in battles and placed them on the altars or shrine areas of their houses. The examples shown here are the skulls of enemies killed by Torajans and placed next to high status (pedestalled) feasting vessels in a traditional household. Warfare may also be the origin of skulls in the Çatal Hüyük shrines (Fig. 6.12) and of skulls recovered from many Neolithic ceremonial centers in Europe. Photo by B. Hayden.

before proper burial of one's dead family member can take place. Enemy heads or skulls are typically kept and displayed on household shrines. The interval of time necessary to successfully complete such an undertaking may explain why many of the burials in shrines at Çatal Hüyük were secondary interments of bones after the flesh had decayed or been removed. Additional research is necessary to determine whether the skulls were, in fact, those of ancestors or enemies.

Assuming that at least some of these examples represent human sacrifices, this implies the existence of a warrior or enforcement cadre in early Neolithic communities. Some people would have to be responsible for obtaining and subduing the person to be sacrificed. One possibility is a militaristic secret society type of organization, even if the sacrifices may have been conducted as part of an elite-controlled fertility or ancestor cult rather than as part of a military cult's rituals. Many ethnographic secret societies were centered on elite ancestors (Eliade 1958b:39). However, military secret society cults also seem to be particularly prevalent among tribal and more complex societies where conflict was a recurring phenomenon. Because of their critical role in the survival of the community and the importance of unswerving mutual support between allies during combat, it is reasonable to expect warriors to create strong bonds between each other through the creation of secret societies with severe initiation rituals and occasional horrific rituals such as cannibalism or human sacrifices. They undoubtedly also used some of the ecstasy-inducing techniques forged millions of years earlier to create alliances. In Neolithic tribal societies, these alliances were probably being forged via rituals between warriors for defensive and offensive purposes rather than to secure access to sources of food and water (Shaw 1990:51, 85ff).

Human sacrifice appears to occur only in transegalitarian or more complex societies where there are pronounced differences in wealth and power. It is the ultimate form of hierarchical behavior. It is used to display control of one group over another. Typically, the subordinate groups are war captives, slaves, children, or, more rarely, the poorest members of one's own community. For instance, under the aegis of their chiefs, the Konds of India used to purchase a child to sacrifice to their earth goddess every year for the fertility of their fields (Padel 1995:110–13). At Jericho, 'Ain Ghazal, and Çatal Hüyük, infants were buried under the doors or incorporated into the walls of buildings (Rollefson 1986:50; Hodder 1999:160). These are exceedingly unusual locations for normal burials, leading the excavators to postulate that the children were probably house foundation offerings like the skulls placed under the posts at Jerf el Ahmar. Such sacrificial offerings are common in many traditional agricultural societies. In the Maya Highlands, I recorded many instances of offerings buried in pits beneath new house floors for the purpose of keeping the house spirit content and avoiding troubles, for houses were viewed as animate creatures whose souls were perhaps strengthened by offerings. However, all of the Maya offerings were of chickens in the poorest cases or larger animals for richer households. Human offerings obviously represent an entirely different order of magnitude of power and control.

WARRIOR SYMBOLS

Finally, Cauvin points to the blatantly aggressive symbols and iconography used everywhere in the PPNB culture. These consist primarily of bull images but also include wolves, lions holding human heads between their paws, snakes, vultures, scorpions, and males with erect penises as represented at Göbekli Tepe. To appreciate the importance of the wild bull, or aurochs, for both Paleolithic and Neolithic peoples, it is necessary to realize the stark terror that wild bulls evoked. Wild cattle were ferocious, probably worse than grizzly bears (Beaune 1995:83; Dickson 1990:186). In the Paleolithic, wild bulls were rarely hunted, although they were often portrayed in cave art and sculptures. In the Mesolithic-level cultures of the Near East, the situation was the same (Beaune 1995:83; Cauvin 1994:81). There were good reasons for this. Even today, confronting the much tamer domesticated descendants of the wild bulls can be one of life's most frightening experiences, whether on the farm or inside bullrings. How much more terrifying were confrontations of the wild ancestors, which were considerably larger (almost the size of a small elephant) and much nastier (Fig. 6.22).

From the Upper Paleolithic onward, wild bulls seem to have been symbols of power, virility, brute instinctual force, and violence (Cauvin 1994:166; Rice 1998). Bull symbolism pervaded every aspect of early Neolithic cultures to the extent that Cauvin has suggested that the PPNB culture should more accurately be referred to as the "Culture of the Bull." In contrast to earlier portrayals by archaeologists of the Neolithic as a peaceful and egalitarian culture, living in equilibrium with its environment, it is now evident that the early Neolithic was an expansive culture featuring periodic armed conflicts as well as very substantial power and wealth inequalities. The central iconographic role of the bull certainly fits this newer understanding of the Neolithic, for the bull is no symbol of peaceful sedentary communities living in harmonious equilibrium. It is the symbol of dynamic, aggressive, and violent communities (Cauvin 1994:176; 2000a). It is an ideal supernatural patron for warriors wielding maces, arrows, and daggers, just as bears were the supernatural patrons of Nordic berserker warriors, and jaguars and eagles were used as supernatural symbols by Aztec military orders in Mexico. Bruce Lincoln (1981:163) points out that warrior groups in pastoral societies always adopt an ideology that emulates powerful animals, such as lions or leopards (see also Eliade 1958b:81). Moreover, eating the meat of wild bulls must have been viewed as conveying many of

Fig. 6.22. Some sense of the awe with which Neolithic people looked upon wild cattle is revealed in this mural mural at Çatal Hüyük. The hunters or warriors are tiny beside the fierce, huge, terrifying bulls. It is not surprising that bulls were used as symbols of power during the Neolithic. Similar symbolic associations may have been responsible for the depiction of bulls on cave walls during the Paleolithic (see Fig. 5.18). From J. Mellaart, *Çatal Hüyük: A Neolithic Town in Anatolia,* Fig. 48. New York: Thames & Hudson, 1967.

those same spiritual qualities to its consumers. However, obtaining such meat must have been exceedingly dangerous, broached by only the strongest, hardiest, and best organized groups of hunters or warriors. Such a confrontation of warriors and a bull is graphically depicted at Çatal Hüyük (Mellaart 1967: pl. 64). Thus, eating beef was perhaps a very special ritual act from Upper Paleolithic times onward. You might keep this in mind the next time you have a steak. Relax with some wine and see if you can imagine consuming the powerful spiritual qualities of the bull, even diluted as they have been by domestication and Industrial stock raising.

In the PPNB culture, eating beef became much more common than in preceding periods, again probably underscoring the increasingly important role of feasting and warriors in Neolithic societies. The people of Mureybet were the first to hunt the bull systematically. Successful hunts were perhaps required for holding the most important feasts, because these people were the first to incorporate bull horns inside their walls, probably as house offerings. Later, bucrania were put on walls to display the power and prestige of the household (Cauvin 1994:166). At 'Ain Ghazal, cattle were not domesticated, but there is good evidence that they were captured, probably as calves, and kept (Rollefson 1986:50). The resemblance is striking to the Ainu practice of capturing young bears and raising them for sacrifices during feasts. Similar instances may have occurred of Upper Paleolithic groups raising reindeer, horses, (Bahn 1978, 1980), and even wolves (Beaune 1995:90). In the case of raising and fattening captured wild bulls at 'Ain Ghazal, probably for prestigious feasting purposes, I think we can perceive the beginnings and motivations for the initial domestication of cattle. In a similar fashion, goats, too, may have been domesticated for feasting purposes, although much earlier because they are easier to procure and handle. At least one faunal expert dealing with the Near East argues that animal domestication was not undertaken for subsistence reasons or to stabilize meat resources (Digard 1990:215). If this scenario is correct, then it may be that plants such as wheat were domesticated in order to rapidly raise, feed, and fatten captured animals for feasts, for Thomas Hakansson (1994, 1995) has documented that this was the cause of agricultural intensification in East Africa in more recent times.

Assuming a prestige feasting origin for domestic cattle, it is not surprising that in subsequent periods and in traditional ethnographic societies, cattle came to embody the greatest expressions of surplus investment, wealth, and power in a community. They became the major commodity for underwriting all important social and political transactions, whether marriages, funerals, compensation payments, or the creation of military alliances. Family and lineage success came to be viewed largely in terms of the number of cattle that they controlled, much as in the funeral depicted at the opening of this chapter. Ethnographers describe traditional cattle-raising people as being obsessed with cattle. Conversations can begin on any topic but within ten minutes they always turn to the discussion of cattle and the minutest details concerning them.

In later periods, the bull was clearly associated with masculine anthropomorphic deities such as Zeus, who abducted Europa in his bull form. Dionysus also appeared in bull form, as did the warrior-hero Baal of Ugarit (Cauvin 1994:166; 2000a). In the cuneiform writings of the Near East, the bull was An, the sky deity and the most important of all deities. The storm god, Adad, was also a bull (Schmandt-Besserat 1997:55). In these cases and others in written records, the bull is associated with masculine gods of the sky, the sun, and violent storms (for example, the Phoenician Baal and Hittite Hadad, and perhaps the god representations at Çatal Hüyük). He is often referred to as the "Bull of Heaven" (see Conrad 1957 and Rice 1998). Later, the Near Eastern and Roman Mithras cult members slaughtered a bull in order to keep the world in balance as part of a sun cult. Cauvin suggests that the bull-human-solar connections were already present in the PPNB when there are some male representations such as those at Nahal Hemar and 'Ain Ghazal that seem to have solar lines radiating from their faces. Thus, *the warrior sun and bull gods of later times very likely had their beginnings in the earliest Neolithic PPNB cultures of the Near East.* Similar aggressive themes may even have permeated some of the transegalitarian hunter-gatherer Upper Paleolithic cave cults, where special sanctuaries to bulls, bears, and lions were created.

PUBLIC CULTS AND SHRINES

While there are no cave sanctuaries in the Near East like those of the Upper Paleolithic, there are special buildings containing stelae and sacrifices at Çayönü. These have often been interpreted as public cult centers. However, their relatively small size, with a capacity of only six or seven people (Fig. 6.23), and the fact that several such buildings occur in the same settlement indicate that these early ritual buildings were more likely for select members of the community, such as militaristic secret societies in the case of buildings with sacrifices or perhaps lineage halls in other cases. Probably only the more high-ranking members of the societies or lineages would have actually used the sanctuaries, while junior members, wives, and children would have gathered outside to share in feasting and perhaps some public ritual displays. This is essentially how the lineage common houses operate that I observed during my visit to rural Vietnam (Fig. 6.24), and it is even the way large feasts were structured when held in family households. The Vietnamese lineage houses are very similar in size and architectural plan to the first "public" architecture or sanctuaries constructed in the Neolithic. In Vietnam, the actual buildings are small and primarily used to create a high-status feasting and ritual environment for the highest-ranking members of the lineage who can thus undertake some of their rituals and discussions in privacy. A similar arrangement seems to be reflected at Çatal Hüyük, where cooking facilities adjoin the lavish shrine rooms, and at Höyücek, where shrines

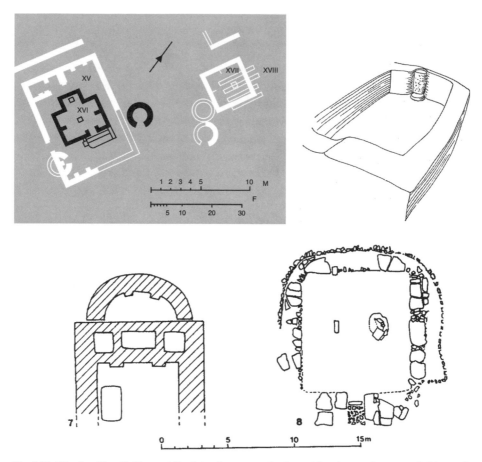

Fig. 6.23. The first identifiable specialized ritual structures in the prehistoric record are remarkably small buildings, usually not more than 3–5 meters on a side. Such small buildings could never accommodate the inhabitants of an entire community and must have been used by a relatively select number of privileged people in the community. Small ritual spaces are commonly used to restrict access to sources of supernatural power. These are some of the earliest ritual structures that have been found; see also Figs. 6.25–6.27. Top left: Eridu, levels xv–xviii; top right: Jericho PPNB levels; bottom left: Çayönü; bottom right: Nevali Çori. From A. Parrot, *Sumer: The Dawn of Art,* Fig. 70. New York: Golden, 1961; J. Cauvin, *Religions Néolithiques de Syrie-Palestine,* Fig. 10. Paris: CNRS, 1972; J. Cauvin, *Naissance des Divinités, Naissance de l'Agriculture,* Fig. 27. Paris: CNRS, 1994.

include storage bins, marble basins, and stacked ceramic bowls as well as antlers, goddess figurines, and ritual vessels (Duru 1999:177). Ritual structures at Jerf el Ahmar and Mureybet also had large food storage bins (Stordeur et al. 2001).

This is probably the real meaning of the appearance of the first "ritual," or "public," architecture in Neolithic communities rather than any upsurge in community spirit or spiritual enlightenment. Such structures reflect the importance of hierarchically organized secret societies or lineages and the attempt to manipulate surplus wealth on the part of elite members through feasting and ritual events. Other authors, too, have drawn attention to the fact that these early structures seem calculated to restrict access of the

Fig. 6.24. Some ritual structures in contemporary traditional societies are very similar to the earliest prehistoric ritual structures. Here a modern Vietnamese lineage house is used exclusively for feasting and the honoring of ancestors. Only the most important male lineage elders use the interior for feasting, rituals, and communicating with spirits and deities. Junior members and women eat and socialize outside the structure. This structure is similar in size and basic layout to those depicted in Fig. 6.23. Photo by B. Hayden.

supernatural to a very select group of people (Wason 1994:150–51). Ethnographically, it is relatively common to find that big men or aspiring aggrandizers try to claim exclusive access to, or control over, powerful ancestral spirits (e.g., Hampton 1997:435, 444). At Jerf el Ahmar the small cult structures were sunk deep (2 m) into the ground, much like kivas in the American Southwest (Fig. 6.25). This was certainly one good way to achieve privacy. Early versions had very limited open inner space (only 3 × 4 m) surrounded by platform benches and storage chambers probably used for society feasting food stores and ritual paraphernalia.

At 'Ain Ghazal, cult paraphernalia was often cached inside these structures and probably brought out only for use on ritual feasting occasions (Rollefson 1983, 1986). Cult paraphernalia was also sometimes stored in small isolated caves far away from settlements, such as the remarkable ritual remains found at Nahal Hemar (Bar-Yosef and Schick 1989). Here, Neolithic stone masks and other ritual materials were stored, but unfortunately many of them were looted before they could be properly excavated (Fig. 6.9). The rare occurrence of similar masks over a fairly wide area indicates their probable use in a regionally based secret society with a unified underlying iconography, as might be expected of militaristic or even cannibal societies such as those that existed among the complex hunter-gatherers on the Northwest Coast. In Nordic areas, the berserker warriors also formed some type of cannibal secret society (Eliade 1958b:81). Other European Neolithic caves bear evidence of having been used by small groups engaged in secret rituals that sometimes involved cannibalism (Skeates 1991, Villa 1992, Whitehouse 1992). These, too, seem to represent secret society ritual locations.

Some authors have referred to the Near Eastern groups as "male sodalities" (K. Wright 2001:116) that involved real or ritualistic hunting of unusual wild animals for display purposes. With their hierarchical organization (reflected in differing headdresses) and their ideologies emphasizing virility, domination, removing human heads,

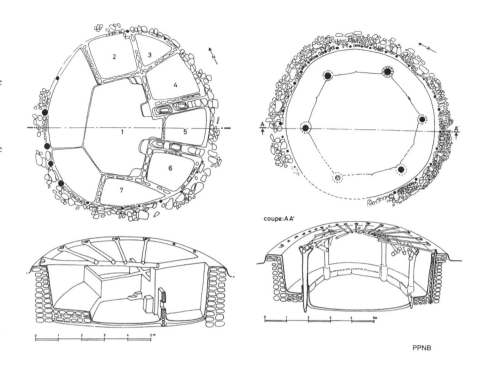

Fig. 6.25. Recently, remarkable ritual structures have been discovered in some of the earliest Neolithic sites of northern Syria, such as Jerf el Ahmar. Note the semisubterranean nature of these structures, emphasizing the privacy or secrecy of the space, and the open interior central areas. The structure from the lowest occupation level (to the left) is particularly notable for its copious storage bins (probably for storing grain for feasts and ritual paraphernalia) and its *very* limited seating area and central performance area. From D. Stordeur, M. Brenet, G. der Aprahamian, and J.-C. Roux, "Les batiments communautaires de Jerf el Ahmar et Mureybet horizon PPNA (Syrie)," *Paléorient* 26, no. 1(2001): Figs. 5, 9.

coupe: A A'

PPNB

and initiation of young men, these sodalities in essence constituted secret societies. Wright identifies another important aspect of these cults: ritual sites such as Nahal Hemar appear to have been used by groups composed of individuals from different villages. This site is not near any known Neolithic community and materials at the site were made in different places (Wright 2000:116). Thus, remote, secret society ritual sites appear to have been places where the highest-ranking members of different villages (but belonging to the same secret society) assembled to perform the most important rituals, to broker alliances, and to determine the political fate of regions.

Similar, but even more impressive, isolated early PPNB ritual sites have been excavated in southeastern Turkey at Göbekli Tepe. There, on a high point of the once-rich region, huge monolithic T-shaped columns carved with lions, cattle, snakes, birds, and other animals formed roof supports for the almost subterranean cult buildings (Fig. 6.26; see also Hauptmann 1999, Schmidt 2001). Ithyphallic men and sex scenes are also portrayed. Benches inside the structures recall cult structures at Hallan Çemi and Jerf el Ahmar. The site is an unexpected and extraordinary testimonial to the amount of political integration, complexity, and control over labor that some of the secret societies or other forms of sodalities of the early Neolithic created in productive environments. Its discovery shocked most archaeologists who thought of the Neolithic in terms of simple egalitarian societies. Now it appears as though Göbekli was probably a center for the regional elites to hold their rituals (Bar-Yosef 2001:22). It is worth considering whether other Neolithic sites with well-made structures might not have been similar regional ritual centers rather than normal residential villages.

Given the spectacular nature of Göbekli Tepe, were some of the other late Mesolithic or early Neolithic sites of the area used for intervillage rituals? Two of the earliest sites

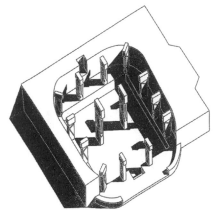

Fig. 6.26. Perhaps the most extraordinary early Neolithic ritual structures yet discovered occur at the site of Göbekli Tepe in southeast Anatolia (photos). The ritual structures are on a hilltop. Like the ritual structures at Nevali Çori (drawn reconstruction), the structures at Göbekli are semisubterranean, and the roof support columns are T-shaped megaliths engraved with animal images. Because of its monumentality, the site was long assumed to date from the Bronze Age. From H. Hauptmann, "The Urfa region," in M. Özdogan and N. Basgelen, eds., *Neolithic in Turkey*, Figs. 9.22–9.24. Istanbul: Arkeoloji ve Sanat Yayinlari, 1999.

with ritual architecture are Hallan Çemi and Qermez Dere. Hallan Çemi is a late Mesolithic site (10,500–10,000 B.P.) where the only substantial structures excavated to date have been identified as "public" buildings. There are two of them. They are associated with prestige items like copper ore and obsidian and food preparation. They are small (5 – 6 m diameter), round semisubterranean structures with plastered floors, stone benches or platforms, and walls lined with sandstone slabs. The complete skull of an aurochs once hung on the north wall of one structure. It seems clear that this is a prototype of ritual structures that are to be found in more elaborate forms several hundred years later at Jerf el Ahmar (Fig. 6.27) and Mureybet in village contexts (see below) and perhaps even Çatal Hüyük, where bucrania preferentially adorned the north walls. If this site is not an intervillage secret society cult site, then perhaps the structures served for lineage rituals within a community of less substantial domestic structures (Rosenberg and Redding 2000:56).

The structures at the contemporaneous site of Qermez Dere in northern Iraq have similar elements but a slightly different design. Like Hallan Çemi, there are only two structures that have been excavated and these may be the only substantial buildings at the site. Trevor Watkins (1990, 1992, 1993), the excavator of Qermez Dere, considered

Fig. 6.27. The use of bull skulls dates from the earliest Neolithic levels in the Near East. Here three sets of wild cattle horns adorned a small ritual structure at Jerf el Ahmar. From D. Stordeur and F. Abbès, "Du PPNA au PPNB," *Bulletin de la Société Préhistorique Française* 99(2002): Fig. 18.

the possibility of a ritual function for these structures but decided to view them as domestic buildings. However, I feel a strong argument can be made for their ritual use. The two structures were about the same size as those at Hallan Çemi, and they had plastered floors as well as walls. One or two substantial pillars were constructed in the center of the floor of each structure. At the top, they were modeled into shoulders and arms, not too dissimilar to the T-shape of the pillars at Göbekli Tepe and Nevali Çori. These pillars were entirely symbolical rather than functional. Later versions of these structures were built precisely on top of the earlier structures and even incorporated parts of the earlier pillars, as if to preserve sacred aspects of the original buildings. The initial building as well as the later demolition and rebuilding of these structures must have represented a considerable investment of time and resources and been quite labor intensive. Moreover, very little domestic refuse was recovered from these structures, whereas food preparation tools and remains were concentrated in another part of the site. Human skulls were also associated with these structures, indicating either ancestor worship or human sacrifices or headhunting.

All of these observations, together with the very small size of the buildings (4 × 5 m), are good grounds for considering the structures as ritual or feasting structures similar to the ones that we have been reviewing. It might also be noted that large rock slabs were used inside the pillars and that similar slabs were erected in shrines at Nevali Çori, Göbekli Tepe, and Çayönü, some of which were carved with human heads (Watkins 1993:85; Cauvin 1994:120–23; 2000a). Somewhat later, even better examples of pillars in shrines modeled into horned males, or horned males next to females, occur in Neolithic Romania (Fig. 6.18). This, too, seems to indicate that the structures at Qermez Dere were ritual buildings rather than domestic houses. The presence of large animal bones and special artifacts (bone pins, stone beads) in the fill of these structures (but the lack of other domestic refuse; Watkins 1990) seems to indicate that they were used as special ritual feasting structures, as does the placement of offerings in the construction fill. In Mesoamerica, the first ritual structures were also distinguished from ordinary houses by the use of plaster on floors and walls and the lack of domestic refuse (Drennan 1983)—the same pattern found at Qermez Dere. The Mesoamerican buildings were co-incidentally exactly the same size as the structures at Qermez Dere. Thus, I think there are many reasons to view these structures as serving specialized ritual functions. Even if it should eventually be demonstrated that the buildings at Qermez Dere were domestic, it seems that the pillars and the skulls constituted part of a shrine and ritual complex for a family or lineage that took up much of the floor area and was probably associated with feasting, comparable to the much later basement shrines at Çatal Hüyük.

I suspect that labor-intensive buildings with plastered floors and walls may have originally been built as specialized community or lineage shrines. Subsequently, with in-creasing surpluses and competition to display economic success, these features may have been copied inside domestic houses as family shrines. At neither Qermez Dere or Hallan Çemi were any clearly residential houses identified, although the size of the excavations was limited. Thus, the possibility that they were special intervillage elite ritual sites like Nahal Hemar, Göbekli, or perhaps Höyücek should be considered. Ofer Bar-Yosef (2001:23) has suggested that the Levantine site of Kefar Hattoresh may have functioned as another regional ritual center.

Other ritual structures clearly occur within the context of villages and may have been the village secret society cult locations, very similar to the way kivas functioned in the American Southwest. The best early examples of these occur at Mureybet and Jerf el Ahmar in northern Syria during the early PPN period (Fig. 6.25, see also Stordeur et al. 2001), although this tradition may begin in the Mesolithic Natufian deposits at Mal-laha, where a "public" structure 9 meters in diameter was discovered. In the PPN ex-amples in northern Syria, elaborately decorated bench platforms, carvings, and storage bins for food and ritual paraphernalia (including three enormous aurochs skulls at Jerf el Ahmar; Stordeur and Abbès 2002:590–91) characterize the remarkable almost subter-ranean buildings (Fig. 6.27). Aside from Göbekli and Nevali Çori, these are the most complex shrines in the Near East for this early phase of the Neolithic.

In sum, the earliest religious buildings in the Neolithic (in prehistory) seem to repre-sent meeting places of powerful elites in remote areas or meeting places for important people within communities (either elite secret societies, warrior secret societies, or shrines for lineage heads). Such structures were generally more elaborate than domestic structures but not larger.

RELIGION TAKES A DECISIVE TURN

As socioeconomic inequalities increased and some Neolithic communities gradually evolved toward chiefdom-level societies, aspiring elites undoubtedly attempted to extend the influence of their own lineage ancestral cults to veneration by the entire community. Some of the early ritual structures and statues of the Neolithic might represent these de-velopments (for example, the large statues from 'Ain Ghazal; see Fig. 6.10; Rollefson 1986, 2000:184). The substantial wealth of the largest communities also indicates a probable increase in political complexity and socioeconomic differentiation. If these public cults were promulgated by local elites and reflected elite aspirations or actual behaviors, it is significant that deities were sometimes depicted on regal thrones dominating ferocious beasts (Fig. 6.16; see also Cauvin 1994:98). Whether elites actually used thrones or not, it seems clear that they were aspiring to do so and would certainly succeed in the next millennia. At this time, it is difficult to distinguish elite ancestor cults from other secret society cults dominated by elite interests and, in fact, Eliade (1958b:39) notes that secret societies frequently focus on ancestors and are led by socially and politically dominant high-ranking initiates.

In any event, in a pattern that we shall see repeated from Egyptians to the Aztecs, the actual sanctuary of "public" cults always seems to have been reserved for the highest-ranking elites, whereas the public aspect of the cult took place adjacent to the shrines or temples. Thus, the largest temples in traditional communities were always reserved for the exclusive use of the rulers. The largest temples were not like contemporary churches or cathedrals meant to house large numbers of people, although even in modern churches, the most sacred areas can only be approached by the officiating priests.

In this way, religion took a decisive turn. On the one hand, elites seem to have developed, dominated, and promoted one set of public cults for nonecstatic worship by the public. They also probably developed a set of militaristic or other ecstatic secret cults. On the other hand, domestic cults appear to have continued many of the ritual concerns of earlier times, but they probably also developed some internal lineage ranking and cult control. Individual families used clay or other carved images of fertility and animal symbols to attract desired spiritual qualities either through prayer, magic, making vows, or as foundation deposits in houses (Schmandt-Besserat 1997:55; Rollefson 2000:184). The division of transegalitarian religion into elite-controlled public and secret society cults versus domestic cults constituted a profound change from the ecstatic community rituals of generalized hunter-gatherers.

If ecstatic ritual states played any role in these newly formed cults, secret societies, and lineage organizations, it seems likely that they were being reserved largely for the most important individuals. Ecstatic experiences were probably emphasized during initiations of new members (especially those from elite families) into secret societies or military cults. This seems to have been the case in other transegalitarian societies or complex hunter-gatherers, although considerable variability probably existed in this domain. In some societies, such as among the hill tribes of Southeast Asia, ritual ecstatic states are almost entirely missing from religious life, except for the curing trances of shamans. In other societies, such as those on the Northwest Coast and the former Maya elites in Mesoamerica, major efforts and wealth were expended to induce ecstatic ritual states among the more elite members of a community, while poorer members might be able to have similar experiences if they were sufficiently motivated and had innate penchants for entering these states. I suspect that this situation also characterized the Middle Eastern and European Neolithic. This certainly seems to have been the case in Western Europe as Neolithic society became more complex (Chap. 7).

What of shamans in all these developments? There are some indications of shamanic type activities, in the form of antlers used for wearing or for displays (Koch 1999). If Neolithic elites did not take on the roles of head shamans themselves, as was the case among the Maya elites, then shamanic roles were likely reduced to those of specialized and controlled curers. In this way, shamans could be isolated, marginalized, and more easily manipulated by elites bent on transforming community rituals to suit their own agendas. In the new cults, priests began to administer the public rituals in controlled fashions and to oversee public feasting. There was little trace of ritual ecstasy other than the altered states brought on by inebriation. Today, in Southeast Asia, shamans operate basically at the level of domestic cult curers. They are called in for cures and divinations only, a pale reflection of shamanic roles among earlier hunter-gatherers. A ranked priest-hood takes care of other religious functions, such as marriages, funerals, and household or community rituals. This Southeast Asian type of situation probably typified most complex societies from this point on, including many early states. On the other hand, in many transegalitarian societies family-sponsored shamans with expensive training and high rank may have played key roles in the ecstatic initiations of secret society members. Where shamans acquire high rank because of their elite connections, they could become wealthy and powerful, even to the point of claiming the right to deflower community virgins (Lewis 1989:131).

Symbols Persist from the Neolithic to Today

We have focused thus far on the major changes that took place with the emergence of transegalitarian Neolithic societies: the elaboration of feasting, fertility and ancestral cults, the upsurge in secret society and militaristic cults, the emergence of the first specialized ritual structures, and the advent of priests. The fundamental division between elite and popular cults is also much more in evidence at this time. We have touched upon the symbolic content of many of these rituals, for which the symbolism was relatively self-evident and pertinent to understanding specific aspects of Neolithic rituals, such as ancestor worship and bull symbolism. However, there is a much broader array of symbols that become popular in the Neolithic, the popularity of which continues for millennia, sometimes persisting into the present. Perhaps you have already been able to identify some Neolithic elements in your cultural surroundings or in some of the rituals that are common today. For instance, bullfights, the ritual running with bulls at Pamplona (Spain), and the general bull image are still potent symbols in many Mediterranean countries. In some countries wine is even referred to as "bull's blood." Examining the symbolic history of concepts can provide many insights about meaning that the examination of formal characteristics alone cannot provide. If we want to know why clocks have 12 hours, for instance, and not 10 or 5 or 20, we cannot derive this information from cultural ecology or formal analysis. We must turn to the history of cultural symbols. This is the best means of dealing with symbolic meaning, which frequently persists for centuries or even millennia after the behavioral form with which it was originally associated has completely disappeared. Why this should be so is still a bit of a mystery.

The honoring of ancestors was the original purpose of Halloween, and although ancestor worship is no longer practiced in Industrial societies, much of the symbolism related to the dead and the spirits of the underworld are still evoked in the popular masquerades of North America. Offering food and other gifts to the ancestral spirits was a main feature of traditional ancestral feasts going back to the Neolithic if not before. We still offer food and gifts to those spirits that appear on our doorsteps on this important feast day. Other countries, such as Spain and Mexico, have stayed closer to the original intent of the feast and specifically honor dead family members on All Souls Day, 1 November.

If we were to pick one main symbolical theme of traditional agrarian cultures, it would be the link between life, death, and rebirth. In the archaeological record of the Neolithic, we can detect these two themes separately (fertility and honoring the dead). However, there are few explicit examples of the two themes being linked in an overall conceptual scheme (see Chap. 7). It is on the basis of ethnographic analogy, later written texts, and the reasonableness of the relationship that we can assume that death leading to rebirth was a major leitmotif of Neolithic religion. Ethnographically, we have seen that most hunter-gatherers believe that after animals are killed their spirits return to a supernatural realm where they wait to return in new bodies. This belief seems to be very ancient, going back to the Upper Paleolithic, if not well before (Hultkrantz 1994).

Similar beliefs pervade crop producers who conceive of their plants as having souls. In tribal Southeast Asia, only rice has a soul as people do. In Mesoamerica, maize was a deity. In peasant Europe, wheat had a kind of soul. As the wheat was harvested, its soul retreated further and further until it was all concentrated in the last sheaf of wheat to be cut in the family fields. This sheaf was therefore very important. It held the spiritual essence for the next year's crop, and thus all the family's hopes for weal and wealth. The last sheaf of wheat was very carefully cared for. Ancestors and the dead were associated with the harvest and could personify the life force in the last sheaf (Eliade 1958a:341–43). Some people even say that before the last sheaf was cut human sacrifices were made to add to its vital forces, rather like the offerings made to house structures. Human sacrifices are not uncommon in many agricultural rituals (Padel 1995). But spirits of the dead were also attracted to fertility displays, so copulation in fields or orgies could occur as well (Eliade 1958a:341–55). After the grain harvest, stems from the last sheaf were woven into special shapes called "corn dollies." These were hung in the house and thought to bring blessings and prosperity. The next spring, they were scattered over the fields. At most craft fairs in North America and in many European or Latin American countries, corn dollies are still popular decorative items (Fig. 6.28), although few people are aware of their underlying symbolical significance, which may well date from Neolithic times. One traditional form is still called the "neck," perhaps referring to sacrificial rites.

The idea that the crops died but that their spirit lived on and was reborn in the following season must be extremely ancient, paralleling beliefs about animals. In both animal and plant realms, one of the great themes is that death is necessary for the regeneration of life (Bloch and Parry 1982:8, 28). Again, traditional religious insights come remarkably close to contemporary scientific biological concepts. The soul of the crops and herds is often considered part of the lineage soul, thereby bringing human beings into the same conceptual scheme. So, grandchildren were often thought to be reincarnations of their grandparents. In fact, the idea that genetic and personality characteristics often skip a generation is still a popular notion. Ancestors, crops, and fertility were typically all interrelated, and the fate of one was closely bound to the others (Eliade 1958a:350).

The concepts of crop and human death followed by regeneration also form part of traditional and contemporary popular folklore or songs. The Ballad of John Barleycorn, beloved of many Englishmen, has countless variations and verses. However, here is one of the more popular renditions (see "The Ballad of John Barleycorn," p. 214). See if you can identify the relevant Neolithic themes.

As we saw in Chapter 3, the descent into the underworld and return to this world is a very pervasive shamanistic theme. In this respect, the central mythic theme of Christianity—the death and resurrection of Jesus Christ—is hardly new. Like the story of John Barleycorn, it is a good example of one of the most eternal religious themes. It is simply a recycled Neolithic myth with much more ancient roots. There is little doubt that without incorporating the death and resurrection of its deity, early Christianity would not have had much of a chance competing in rural areas with the many other religions of the time that did accord central importance to death and resurrection themes. When the writers of the Bible had Christ say that wine was his blood and that wheat bread was his body (thereby creating the mystical transubstantiation of bread and wine into the literal body and blood of god), there can be little doubt that they were appealing to basically Neolithic attitudes of their listeners and followers. The parallels with John Barley-

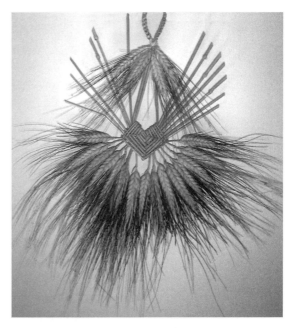

Fig. 6.28. "Corn dollies," or "wheat weavings," are traditional items used for recognizing and capturing some of the beneficent vegetative spirits (the soul of the wheat) in peasant European cultures. They represent concepts and traditions that may well go back to Neolithic times and have survived into our contemporary Industrial society in the form of a folk craft. They are thought to bring good luck today just as they did in the past. Photo by Greg Holoboff.

corn may be more apparent now. Sacrifice and rebirth, especially of males, has been a longstanding social, political, and religious motif. Males sacrifice themselves in war; males are more biologically expendable; male figures go to their deaths while female figures remain immortal (Adonis-Aphrodite, Isis-Osiris, Tammuz-Ishtar, Baal-Anath, Uranus-Gaea, Attis-Cybele); the royal king is sacrificed in order to renew the life of the tribe. This was the central theme of Sir James Frazer's *Golden Bough*. Although methodologically flawed, *The Golden Bough* attempted to show that Christianity was not very different from many other mythic systems in the world, and the book still stands as a research landmark in the history of religious studies.

There is another popular Neolithic ritual in Western Industrial societies with which you are certainly familiar. This is the recreation of the world every year. This event occurs in the spring and is still determined by the spring equinox, as well as the full moon and the day dedicated to the sun. It involves the mythic creation of the world in the form of a cosmic egg. The name of the ritual day is Easter, named after the Saxon goddess of the dawn, Eostre. And there is nothing Christian about the making of cosmic eggs to celebrate this day. It was Marijia Gimbutas (1982:101) who proposed that some of the symbols on Neolithic clay vessels actually represented painted cosmic (Easter) eggs

The Ballad of John Barleycorn

There were three men came from the west,
Their fortunes for to tell,
And the Life of John Barleycorn as well.

They have laid him in three furrows deep,
Laid pods upon his head.
Then these three men made a solemn vow,
John Barleycorn was dead, John Barleycorn was dead.

They let him live for a very long time,
Till the rain from heaven did fall,
Then little Sir John, he sprang up his head, and
He did amaze them all; He did amaze them all.

And they let him stand till mid-summer day,
Till he looked both pale and wan,
Then little Sir John he grew a beard and
He so became a man; He so became a man.

So they have hired men with scythes so sharp
To cut him off at the knee,
And they rolled and tied him around the waist,
And they served him barbarously; they served him barbarously.

And they have hired men with the crab-tree sticks
To cut him skin from bone,
And the miller has served him worse than that,
He ground him between two stones; He ground him between two stones.

And they have wheeled him here and they have wheeled him there,
They've wheeled him into a barn.
And they have served him worse than that,
They've bunged him in a vat; They've bunged him in a vat.

Well they have worked their will on John Barleycorn,
But he lived to tell the tale,
For they poured him out of an old brown jug,
And they call him home-brewed ale; And they call him home-brewed ale.

(Fig. 6.29). In examining the old traditions of agricultural communities in Europe and in early written texts, she found that the myth of the creation of the world from an original cosmic egg was extremely widespread. Even in Egypt, the world was conceived as created from a primordial egg in some regions (David 1982:49). Therefore, Gimbutas suggested that the Neolithic representations probably reflected the same myth. I, too, think that this is very likely.

It is obvious that the decorated eggs depicted on the pots and those made by people today are no ordinary eggs, for they are colored in ways unknown in the natural world. These are sacred eggs, cosmic eggs. According to one variant of the story, when they break open, the yellow yolk ascends up into the air and is transformed into the sun, while the shell behind it becomes the sky. The bottom half of the egg is transformed into the earth with all of its many hues and shapes. The very carefully made and elaborate *pysanky,* or Ukrainian Easter eggs, incorporate many intricate symbols, both supernatural and earthly (Fig. 6.30). The next time you paint an Easter egg or break one open, it may bring more satisfaction to you to think about the roots of this ancient tradition and its basic meaning.

Fig. 6.29. Some of the motifs painted on Neolithic ceramic vessels may represent decorated (cosmic) eggs. Eggs certainly are portrayed on some vessels and the above designs from the Balkans may be schematic representations of eggs. If so, the myth of creation from a cosmic egg probably also extends back to Neolithic times. From M. Gimbutas, *The Goddesses and Gods of Old Europe,* Fig. 6.26. Berkeley: University of California Press, 1967. Copyright, The University of California Press, Berkeley, and Thames and Hudson, Ltd.

Eliade (1959:78) has pointed out that traditional cultures believed that before the world could be reborn, it had to revert to the condition of chaos that existed before the world was created. He maintains that this is why chaotic celebrations typify the end of the year with reckless abandon of many social norms and the reversal of roles, aided, of course, by the consumption of copious intoxicating beverages (Miles 1912:302ff). These kinds of events were traditional during the Roman Saturnalia as well as English New Year's celebrations. Orgies were also part of many of these celebrations in some cultures because it was thought that these would increase fertility and prosperity in the next cycle of the world's creation. In fact, chaotic celebrations still characterize our own New Year's celebrations, although we are largely unaware of why we engage in these traditions. For cultures in which the earth was reborn in the spring rather than after the winter solstice, Carnival, leading up to Easter, served the same function of turning the world up-so-down and temporarily obliterating all the social and cultural conventions so that they could be recreated anew and in a better way—to wit, our New Year's resolutions. There were almost certainly other seasonal ritual celebrations for harvests (presaging our Octoberfests and Thanksgivings) that we have not been able to identify in the archaeological record.

Fig. 6.30. Today, Ukrainian eggs (and in a more degraded form, our Easter eggs) clearly derive from a tradition in which the earth's rebirth and renewed fertility is associated with magical eggs that can bring fertility and good fortune. From A. Kmit, L. Luciow, J. Luciow, and L. Perchyshyn, *Ukrainian Easter Eggs*. Minneapolis: Ukrainian Gift Shop, 1979.

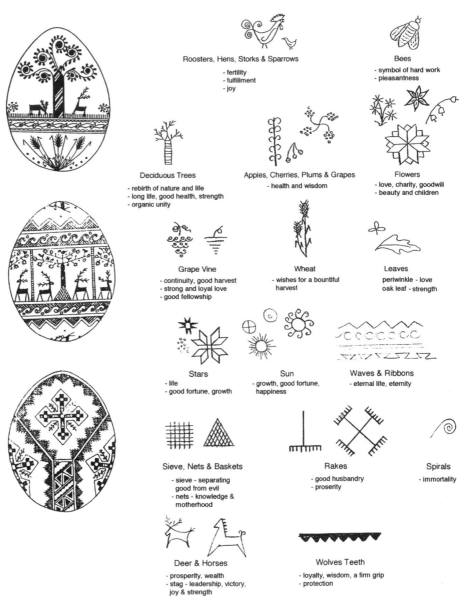

Symbols for Ukrainian Easter Eggs

Roosters, Hens, Storks & Sparrows
- fertility
- fulfillment
- joy

Bees
- symbol of hard work
- pleasantness

Deciduous Trees
- rebirth of nature and life
- long life, good health, strength
- organic unity

Apples, Cherries, Plums & Grapes
- health and wisdom

Flowers
- love, charity, goodwill
- beauty and children

Grape Vine
- continuity, good harvest
- strong and loyal love
- good fellowship

Wheat
- wishes for a bountiful harvest

Leaves
periwinkle - love
oak leaf - strength

Stars
- life
- good fortune, growth

Sun
- growth, good fortune, happiness

Waves & Ribbons
- eternal life, eternity

Sieve, Nets & Baskets
- sieve - separating good from evil
- nets - knowledge & motherhood

Rakes
- good husbandry
- proserity

Spirals
- immortality

Deer & Horses
- prosperity, wealth
- stag - leadership, victory, joy & strength

Wolves Teeth
- loyalty, wisdom, a firm grip
- protection

Gimbutas (1982) also pointed out the persistence and basic meaning of a number of other Neolithic symbols, including the equal armed cross (Figs. 6.29 and 6.30), which is a common designation for the four cardinal directions, signifying also the entire world or universe in either its supernatural and/or natural form. The cross is a natural symbol for these concepts, especially among people who follow the movements of the sun and other astral bodies. The rising and setting points provide the horizontal line of the world, and the midpoint of the sun in the sky provides a perpendicular bisecting line that, if extended, encompasses the highest point in the sky and the lowest point in the underworld. The same symbol was popular in pre-Christian Ireland and is sometimes called the Celtic cross. It is also found in prehistoric Mesoamerica and probably many other areas of the world. When this type of cross is rotated so as to bend the outer parts of the arms, it becomes a spinning solar emblem, often called a "swastika," although technically, this term only applies to crosses that are rotating in a counterclockwise direction. The earliest representation of a rotating cross is in the Upper Paleolithic, possibly indicating the importance of astronomical observations even then and possibly related to spiral motifs of the same and later time periods (Chap. 7; Campbell 1969:328). Gimbutas illustrates other examples of rotating crosses from the Neolithic.

Finally, it might be mentioned that the cup, bowl, and urn appear as important symbols during the Neolithic in ritual contexts, especially as "beakers," probably used to serve beer, wine, or mead and usually included as grave items with burials of important people. Beakers and urns were almost certainly used in feasting rituals and may have symbolized religious authority of social elites whose role was to share food and drink with guests (Littleton 1973). They may also have symbolized other, more supernatural traits, as in modern Tarot cards.

A number of virile animals noted for their fertilizing acts tend to be associated with the sun, as we have seen. These typically include the bull, the ram, and the goat. The snake appears to take on underworld, and therefore spirit-world, connotations, and there are many agricultural societies that feature the snake, perhaps as a phallic spirit-world figure, having various kinds of relations with maidens. According to Campbell (1969:385), such myths occur in Africa, the Near East (as in the biblical account of the Garden of Eden), India, Southeast Asia, and New Guinea. The snake features prominently in sculptures from early Neolithic sites like Göbekli Tepe and Nevali Çori. Eliade (1958a:164) sees the snake as a universal phallic symbol associated with rebirth (because it sheds its skin) and fertility because it lives in the realm of the underworld where the spirits of the unborn reside. As we shall see in the next chapter, the mace and the axe were almost certainly important emblems of authority in many Neolithic cultures, and the mace still plays the same role among royalty today.

Summary

The Neolithic was a time of dramatic changes that extended the trends already apparent in complex hunter-gatherers much farther than in the Paleolithic or Mesolithic. From a cultural ecological and political viewpoint, the domestication of plants and animals can be seen as the logical outcome of the new surplus resources opened up by Mesolithic technologies and the efforts to convert these surpluses into social and political advantages through feasting. There are several archaeological and ethnographic examples of wild animals being captured and raised specifically as prestige foods for feasts. Domestic animals in most traditional societies play exactly the same roles. Domestic animals are not used for daily meat consumption in these societies. This is a pattern that I think explains the origins of domestication.

When domestication and food production developed to the point that domesticated food was as efficient to produce as wild foods, or more, the production of food staples and surpluses became dependent on human labor and the great Neolithic expansion began. The effect on Neolithic religion was to increase the emphasis on human fertility as well as on animal and plant fertility.

Feasting transformed surpluses into social and political or economic advantages, and thus feasting undoubtedly developed in new and more dramatic ways. Lineage ancestral cults developed in response to inheriting valuable resources such as land and the desire to derive the maximum benefit from it. Militaristic or other secret societies also seem to have developed, replete with human sacrifice and numerous symbols of warrior elites such as maces and wild bulls. Aspiring members of Neolithic communities appear to have tried to monopolize the most important contacts with supernatural forces through the establishment of secret societies or public cults, in which the highest positions were held exclusively by elites.

The first ritual structures, like some of the Upper Paleolithic cave sanctuaries, were relatively small and seem suited for only a small number of people. Lineage rituals were probably led by the most important members of lineages and were used to control the activities of younger members of the lineages. In such contexts, ecstatic ritual experiences were probably restricted to the highest-ranking members of cults, or they may have faded almost entirely from religious life except for relict shamanistic healers. Elite priests or their designates undoubtedly became the main religious functionaries at most public events. However, individual household domestic religious activities appear to have ministered more directly to household concerns for fertility and prosperity. Many of the clay figurines and phalluses used in households during the Neolithic undoubtedly represent symbols for attracting fertility or fructifying supernatural powers to the household by means of prayers, magic, or offerings just as they do in some traditional societies today. Thus, the outlines become clear in the Neolithic of a division between elite and commoner religious activities and beliefs.

Many Neolithic symbols and rituals continue to play an important role in contemporary Industrial cultures, especially concerning reverence for the dead, world rebirth and renewal, and at least the subliminal acknowledgment of death as a precursor of resurrection and rebirth or eternal life. There have been many claims in popular publications about the utopian nature of Neolithic life. Given the research that has taken place in recent decades, it is worthwhile examining some of these claims in more detail. This and the more impressive achievements of later Neolithic societies are the topics for the next chapter.

CHAPTER 7

Megaliths and Mages

Of all prehistoric remains yet discovered, none seem to fascinate people more than the spectacular megalithic remains of Western Europe. These huge, rough-hewn stone monuments of the past loom like gray icebergs out of the ground and incite passionate discussions about why they were erected and what they could possibly mean. Above all, they are impressive in terms of their size and number. The most famous megalithic monument in Europe, if not the world, is Stonehenge (Figs. 1.9, 7.1), but it is not the largest by any means. Avebury, a scant 40 kilometers to the north, is far larger (Fig. 7.2), while the Grand Menhir Brisé in Brittany, France, is an astonishing 350 tons and 20 meters high, probably the largest megalith in the prehistoric world. What motivated prehistoric people to undertake such enormous projects?

Although prehistorians agree that these megaliths played an important role in the ritual life of the people who erected them, there is little agreement beyond this initial premise. Ardent advocates of ley lines and tapping into the earth's energy fields clash with hard-nosed archaeologists who view these stones as territory markers or funerary monuments. In trying to sort out the more meaningful responses to the conundrum of what these megaliths mean, it will be particularly useful to keep in mind the distinction between the formal characteristics of these stones (their presence or absence and the energy put into their construction) versus their symbolic significance.

The kinds of religions associated with the erection of megaliths can be referred to as a "megalithic type" of religion since it seems to occur predominantly under certain ecological and political conditions involving fairly advanced transegalitarian societies or socioeconomically stratified chiefdoms. However, in order to comprehend the role that megaliths played in such societies, it will first be useful to examine the dynamics of the transegalitarian societies in greater detail.

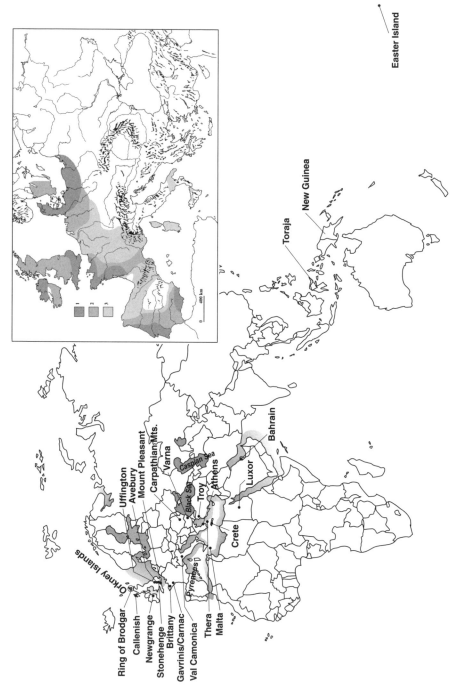

Fig. 7.1. Some of the most important megalithic and complex Neolithic sites mentioned in this chapter are located on this map. The inset map shows the spread of megalithic constructions: (1) fifth and early fourth millennia B.C.E.; (2) fourth millennium; (3) third millennium. From N. Cauwe, *L'heritage des chasseurs-cueilleurs*, p. 107. Paris, Editions Errance, 2001. Drafted by Greg Holoboff.

Aspiring Aggrandizers Transform Transegalitarian Societies

To understand the kinds of social-political developments that we have been discussing, as well as many related technological developments, archaeologists establish models of change. In some of these models, the primary reason that cultures change is attributed to new concepts, values, or other cognitive factors such as new insights. In other models, shifts in social relations or political life feature as the underlying causes for broader changes. In ecological models, the key factors that are thought to cause changes in culture and religion are related to energy resources and new technological developments that affect people's use of resources. This last approach has provided the most insights into the basic formal changes in religion that we have so far reviewed, and it also offers new insights into megalithic religious developments.

There are a few simple assumptions underlying the cultural ecology approach that illuminate the social-political features that emerge in transegalitarian and chiefdom-level societies. First, in accord with the most basic tenets of biological evolution, we can assume that at least some members of every population were striving to promote their own self-interests above the interests of others. Perhaps not all people in a community are self-centered, but every community has some such people, and their existence is probably important for preventing the human race from straying too far from the mainstream of evolutionary processes. I refer to individuals who promote their own self-interests whenever the opportunity presents itself as "aggrandizers."

The second assumption is that under certain resource conditions, such as scarce and fluctuating food resources and reliance on types of resources that are easy to overexploit, aggrandizing behaviors are destructive to resources and threaten the existence of all community members. As a result, the community limits aggrandizing behavior and does not permit the

Fig. 7.2. Avebury is perhaps the largest prehistoric stone ring and ditch site in the world. A small contemporary village is located within its earthworks. Many of the stones that once ringed its circumference have been destroyed by religious zealots or practical farmers, but some of those that are left are truly enormous (top). The embankment and ditch that encircle the site were originally remarkable in depth and size (below). Top photo by B. Hayden; bottom photo from D. Clarke, T. Cowie, and A. Foxon, *Symbols of Power at the Time of Stonehenge,* Fig. 3.39. Edinburgh: National Museum of Antiquities of Scotland (H.M.S.O.), 1985.

ownership of resources or the use of resources in competitive activities. This is typically the situation that is found in the generalized hunter-gatherer societies discussed in previous chapters (Wiessner 1998; Cashdan 1980), and it probably characterized most hunter-gatherers during the Paleolithic.

The third assumption is that when resource conditions improve to the point that aggrandizing behaviors no longer pose a major threat to other community members, then aggrandizers are permitted to indulge in activities that provide benefits to themselves as long as the community also feels that it is benefiting. But, just as in business, the most successful people always seem to benefit themselves the most in transactions with others. As Reay (1959:110–11, 129, 190, 192) observed of New Guinea aggrandizers, they give lip service to group solidarity, but greed and narrow self-interest dominate their behavior. They publicly appear generous and fair, but they find ways of getting advantages by hiding their wealth or by other means. They adhere to cultural values or rules publicly, but they see themselves as above such rules and use them to their own advantage through ruthless calculations. Their apparent self-restraint is a mask for shrewdness. Typically, the greater the food surpluses, the more such surpluses are used in aggrandizing activities.

A fourth ecological assumption is that aggrandizers actively seek as many ways as possible to promote their own self-interests. Aggrandizers use every technique that they can think of to cajole, entice, coerce, or lure other family or community members into their schemes. Aggrandizers organize events and are in good positions to manipulate the use of goods intended for events. Typically, aggrandizers try to get others to contribute, or pledge, specific amounts of their surplus production for community causes, such as feasts for creating alliances, community feasts, payments for making peace or settling disputes, ritual events for ancestors or good crops, wealth exchanges, desirable marriages, status, investments, curing, or dealing with emergencies of any kind. Aggrandizers use any pretext to push people into producing more and more surpluses as well as relinquishing some control over their goods to the aggrandizers who organize these purportedly beneficial events.

The outcome is that once aggrandizers are given an inch of leeway under favorable resource conditions, they quickly stretch that inch into a mile and keep on going. Aggrandizers are the internal motor of change when resource conditions are favorable. They gravitate toward the roles of big men, chiefs, elites, businessmen, and politicians. They aggressively promote changes in society that are in their own self-interest. In extreme cases, they are aggressive, ambitious, acquisitive, accumulative, adversarial, and adventurous. I call them "Triple-A" personality types.

Some people argue that this view of society is ethnocentric and colored by the values and norms of Western Industrial society. Many people who have never lived in traditional societies suggest that tribal and traditional non-Western societies are different. While there certainly are differences, in my experience, the suggestion that tribal societies are somehow immune to the basic realities of ecology and evolution is an unwarranted romantic notion. Having lived in a number of tribal societies, I have found them all to be basically as materialistic as Western citizens, with self-promoting aggrandizers present in every community. People in every traditional society that I am familiar with are all concerned with obtaining access to adequate food, medical treatment and Western medicines, the reduction of parasites and insect pests, and basic material comforts, as well as with adequate communication to the outer world. To be sure, material priorities and styles in traditional transegalitarian societies are sometimes different from Western priorities, and the techniques used by aggrandizers to promote their own self-interest are often much more subtle and devious than the techniques used in Western societies. But they are still very effective.

If we turn to the ethnographic descriptions of tribal and chiefdom societies, we find ample documentation for the aggressive self-aggrandizing behavior of many individuals in all tribal culture areas (e.g., Reay 1959). I have described these instances and strategies elsewhere (Hayden 1995, 2001b). A few examples from Oceania, one of the last pristine transegalitarian tribal areas in the world, are worth citing for further understanding. Polly Wiessner and Akii Tumu (1998, 1999) note that big men (aggrandizers) in New Guinea are viewed by other community members as providing benefits for the group and the supporters of the big man. Conversely, the success of individual big men was viewed as necessary for group success, and big men often took advantage of this unequal balance of power and interests. They also note that big men generally kept their real motives hidden. For example, Paul Sillitoe (1978) gives numerous examples of big men scheming to foment warfare or promote peace according to the benefits that either situation might provide for them. Wiessner (2001:36) similarly documents big men starting up new religious cults specifically in order to mollify feelings of inequality within the community and thus keep community members involved in the large-scale gift exchanges from which big men were handsomely profiting. People who did not participate in these gift exchanges could neither attract allies for defense nor suitable brides for marriage.

Similarly, Hampton (1997:435, 444–46) observed in New Guinea that big men tried to claim exclusive control of powerful ancestral spirits and to request favors from them. Big men typically also tried to claim control over women's fertility and played the dominant, if not exclusive, role in fertility cults (Wiessner and Tumu 1998:318; Lawrence and Meggitt 1965:15; Feil 1987:187–89, 207, 221). It was the big man's magic that was claimed to produce the biggest yams, and therefore big men competed with each other to grow the largest yams and claim the most powerful spiritual abilities or ancestral patrons (Young 1971 cited in Clark and Parry 1990:296, 333). Ancestral spirits were considered to reside in certain sacred stones resembling very long ground-stone axes, and big men often used their personal spiritual power to infuse these stones with power. Big men frequently claimed the role of shamans and acted as leaders of sun worship cults in the form of secret societies. These big men and their cults were very powerful in parts of New Guinea (Hampton 1997:374, 485). The myths and rituals of Oceania generally concern the economic well-being and the social-political organization of communities (Lawrence and Meggitt 1965:12, 18–19). In contrast to book religions, New Guinea religion is viewed as a technology for dealing with these socioeconomic aspects of life, not as a moral spiritual force for salvation.

Ethnographically, it is evident that many initiations, especially those that were painful, were being used by parents in order to increase the worth of children for marriage exchanges and to prepare their children's claims of special access to supernatural powers as revealed by their ability to withstand unusual pain and enter into trance states during initiation and subsequent ordeals. The scarification of girls in transegalitarian societies, their genital mutilation, or their neck or foot deformation make no sense in practical terms. They do make sense as attempts to increase marriageability or the value of children for marriage. Some procedures and training, such as the spirit quest, might last years for elite children (Owens and Hayden 1997). Cognitive explanations for intentional mutilations and body deformations generally must revert to the kinds of fanciful explanations given for the subincision of boy's penises in Australia (Chap. 5). Female mutilations, in particular, are often viewed as evidence that women have been "trained in moral and practical responsibilities" (Sanderson 1981:23) and are therefore suitable for high-status marriages. Excision and infibulation of girls' genitals is especially prevalent where virginity is highly prized, particularly for elite marriages (Dorkenoo 1994:21, 58). As more and more people aspire to arrange high-status marriages for their children, such practices become widespread. While ecological perspectives help us to understand why such mutilations exist, ecology cannot explain why specific forms of mutilation were adopted by specific cultures—why the Chinese chose foot binding rather than neck elongation, for instance. To deal with these kinds of questions, cognitive and historical frameworks are certainly best suited.

One other strategy used by aggrandizers to promote their own political control and wealth is the creation of prestige objects, both ritual and profane. This strategy is of particular interest to archaeologists, for we find the broken or buried offerings of such objects in our excavations. Prestige objects are objects that are invested with much more labor than would be necessary for any utilitarian function. In fact, in extreme cases, these objects have no practical use at all; they are simply considered beautiful or desirable for their own qualities as is the case with freestanding sculptures, jewelry, and paintings. These objects, like all prestige objects, are created in order to achieve social or political goals, not to solve practical problems such as crossing a river or making a spear.

Typically, aggrandizers develop prestige objects

- to display and symbolize their economic power;
- to convert some of their perishable surpluses into more durable material forms;
- to create inherently attractive and desirable objects that other people will want to acquire as both symbols of success and pleasurable objects; and
- to use in social or political transactions such as marriage payments or compensation or death payments.

To the extent that aggrandizers succeed in these goals, other people will also try to acquire prestige objects and will have to produce surpluses to acquire them (Taçon 1991; Hayden 1998). Frequently, aggrandizers try to monopolize the sources of prestige objects by choosing items that can only be obtained from other regions through trade connections that aggrandizers establish or that can only be obtained with large amounts of wealth. Aggrandizers use their control of these goods to indebt other people, as is often the case with expensive bridewealth payments that young men must borrow from their elders. I have provided further details of prestige technologies elsewhere (Hayden 1998). Given aggrandizers' attempts to occupy the most important ritual roles, many prestige objects that they produce are strongly ritual in character. Acquiring exotic or costly ritual prestige items was probably far easier to justify for community events than the direct acquisition of prestige goods by aggrandizers since ritual prestige items are used and displayed on behalf of the entire group. Thus, early aggrandizers often indulged in the most luxurious lifestyles in ritual contexts, and rituals became the events where the best foods were consumed, the most ostentatious clothes were worn, the most impressive prestige objects were manipulated, the most lavish furniture or buildings were used, and the finest arts enjoyed. The magnificent ritual palaces of Minoan Crete and the opulent priesthood of Ancient Egypt come readily to mind (see below). It is the link between prestige display and aggrandizer strategies that enables us to examine the underlying reasons for the use of megaliths in Neolithic Europe.

With aggrandizers underwriting the production of specialized crafts, the first "great art" traditions emerge during the European Upper Paleolithic. Several areas of Neolithic Europe also developed great art traditions, including the art engraved on megaliths and the megalithic forms themselves. The Western notion of creating art for art's sake, as a pure expression of the human spirit, is entirely antithetical to the ecological view that labor-intensive art is a symbolic economic expression produced for specific social and political objectives. In fact, in this respect, it is Western culture that is aberrant and bizarre. Ellen Dissanayake (1988) has cogently argued that art in traditional societies throughout the world is never made for its own sake. It always has a specific social or economic purpose. Traditional art is always for prestige or ritual purposes, and generally both (that is, for prestige purposes couched in terms of ritual embellishments pleasing to the spirits, as in the case of the elaborate gold crucifixes in the Vatican).

The idea that human internal creative urges by themselves would ever produce great art, much less a great art tradition that continued over hundreds or thousands of years in a large region, is simply not tenable. By "great art," I mean art that displays skill and care in execution as well as a coherent sense of style, proportion, balance, and color. Great art is time consuming to produce and so is developing the requisite skill to produce it. That great art was not produced by creative urges alone is amply demonstrated by its restricted and specialized occurrence in most hunting-gathering cultures except for complex hunter-gatherers. Among generalized hunter-gatherers such as the Australian Aborigines, art is almost exclusively reserved for secret ritual locations far away from general living areas. Art is used to enhance the effectiveness of rituals for creating ecstatic states.

The later appearance of great art in domestic living areas indicates that art is no longer being used strictly for ritual purposes, but that it has taken on social and economic significance in the everyday lives of transegalitarian or more complex communities. It is above all this latter use of art that requires underwriting from the wealthy, who seek finely crafted art as symbols of success. It is the economic stability of resource surpluses on a regular basis over centuries and millennia that creates and maintains great art traditions. Creative urges on their own would tend to be much less constrained by tradition, more variable, more sporadic, displaying much less continuity in tradition over time. In Western Industrial cultures, creative individuals are sought precisely because they are creative and develop new ideas and new approaches. Traditional artists are rarely sought for these qualities. Their role is to imitate the traditions of the past, not develop new ones. In order for symbols of success to be readily recognized, they must maintain traditional meanings, much as stags must maintain traditional symbols of biological health and strength (their antlers) in order to attract females. In fact, the great public art traditions are much like stag antlers, or peacock feathers, or ram horns. They are all unnecessary physical additions, the primary function of which is to advertise the biological or economic success of an individual in order to attract desirable mates or other followers (Beardsley 1993; Zahavi and Zahavi 1997). Today, sleek sports cars and other prestige items have largely replaced the genetic role of musculature, stature, beards, and silver-backed hair to show off success and lure mates. Prestige ritual items were used for this purpose in transegalitarian and more complex traditional societies (Reay 1959:98). If art is valued today in Industrial societies as a means for individuals to express themselves, this is largely because of an expanded middle class and a consequent demand for status-related goods. This has led to the creation of a significant subculture of artisan-specialists, especially in urban environments, and a generally high value placed on innovative artistic abilities typically with formal training in the arts.

The Neolithic Undergoes Dramatic Changes

There is relative consensus among prehistorians that the initial Neolithic colonization of Europe was characterized by relatively small transegalitarian communities that were not particularly complex or overly wealthy. However, within a few hundred years of their arrival in western Europe, substantial social and economic changes began taking place in favored locations, eventually culminating in the creation of powerful chiefdoms that controlled the exchange of prestige items and dominated megalithic centers (Gronenborn 1999:161; Cassen and Pétrequin 1999). Equally complex societies with rich prestige technologies emerged in favorable environments in eastern Europe. While the first Neolithic impacts occurred in southeastern Europe around 8000 B.C.E., it was not until 5300 B.C.E. that Neolithic colonists or influences arrived in France and only 3500 B.C.E. when they arrived in the British Isles. There, and along the west coast of France and Spain, some of the Neolithic colonizers found fertile ground for raising cattle and crops. By 4500 B.C.E., if not earlier, they had begun to erect megaliths in some locations. Above all, the great variability that existed over the span of the European Neolithic must be emphasized. This was due to regional traditions, Neolithic migrants versus indigenous Mesolithic groups, varying productivity of environments, megalithic versus non-megalithic traditions, and changes over time.

Indications exist that the incoming Neolithic colonists may have adopted the practice of erecting megaliths from some of the more complex Mesolithic hunter-gatherers that were native to Western Europe or that Mesolithic groups in this region adopted Neolithic technology and domesticates themselves. In Chapter 5, we saw that complex burial practices resembling megalithic burials were emerging in a number of Mesolithic (and perhaps Upper Paleolithic) cultures. Communal burials with rock slabs occur at a few Mesolithic sites, and the earliest megaliths occur in areas where the Mesolithic populations were already very dense. In fact, the earliest dated megaliths actually fall in the Mesolithic time period (Hutton 1991:18, 20–21; Sherratt 1990; Schulting 1998a, 1998b; Schulting and Richards 2001; Cauwe 1998a, 1998b, 2001a:135–36, 171–75, 2001b). It is clear, however, that in especially favorable locations, the greater productivity of the Neolithic food-producing economy permitted the elaboration of these mortuary structures to sizes far beyond anything known in the Mesolithic. Moreover, we have also seen in Chapter 6 that Neolithic groups at centers like Jericho and Çatal Hüyük also used communal graves, and thus some of the funeral practices of incoming

Neolithic groups may have been quite compatible with native Mesolithic traditions.

In the Western European megalithic religions, there is an overwhelming emphasis on ancestor worship—especially elite ancestor worship—as well as evidence for solar and lunar cults and an underlying domestic fertility cult. Feasting, shamanism, and the bull cult seem to have been incorporated into ancestral cults. We will examine each of these aspects of the megalithic type of religion in turn—but first, a look at megaliths.

The Megalithic Menagerie

Megaliths (literally, "very big stones") occur in a number of forms and were obviously important symbols in Neolithic times. Stone slabs or stelae were used in PPNB sanctuaries; the Semites used upright stones as representing their deities; Minoans incorporated bedrock outcrops in some of their altars; and the Europeans viewed large stones as housing extrahuman powers of ancestors and fertility that could be transmitted by physical contact. Stone is a symbol of permanency and power. It was called the "material of eternity" by the Egyptians.

Fig. 7.3. The simplest form of megalithic monument is the single standing stone, or *menhir*. In the Torajan highlands of Sulawesi, these menhirs are erected for the wealthiest elites of the community. The size of the stones reflects the family's wealth. Many pigs and water buffalo were sacrificed to hold feasts for people to quarry, carry, and erect them. Photo by B. Hayden.

Archaeologists have developed many complex classification schemes to describe the European megaliths, but most can be grouped into five categories: menhirs, dolmens, passage graves and long barrows, rock-cut tombs, and circles. The most basic form is a simple oblong standing stone called a *menhir* (Fig. 7.3). Burials are not always associated with menhirs, but they generally seem to have commemorative functions and ethnographically are usually associated with funeral rituals (Parker Pearson and Ramilisonina 1998; Sandarupa 1996).

Fig. 7.4. Constructions consisting of large vertical stones supporting one or a few horizontal stone slabs are referred to as *dolmens*. Dolmens may have originally been covered with earth while the space between the slabs was used for burials. This example (The Three Maidens) of such a tablelike construction is in Dorset, England. Photo by Peter Larkworthy.

Fig. 7.5. Elongated, tunnellike passages with large stones for walls and roofing slabs are known as passage graves. At Man Kerioned (Carnac, Brittany), the entrance to this imposing passage grave is in the foreground, while the covered tunnel extends to the background. Bodies were usually placed at the end of the passage inside the chambers. Only a small proportion of the community that constructed these tombs were usually buried in them—probably elites. Originally, all these stones would probably have been covered with earth. Photo by B. Hayden.

Fig. 7.6. *Long barrows* are generally passage graves with earth coverings that extend far beyond the actual stone passage. Shown here is the longest long barrow in Europe, located at West Kennet near Avebury. The stone-faced entrance to the passage can be seen at the far left with the barrow mound extending all the way across the photo and off the border to the right. The entrance is shown in more detail at bottom left, while the inside of the passage is shown at bottom right. Photos by B. Hayden.

Dolmens, or "stone tables," are large horizontal slabs of rock supported on two or three sides by large upright slabs of rock. It is generally thought that these were formerly covered with earth and that the earth has been subsequently removed by farmers (Fig. 7.4). Dolmens appear to be always associated with burials and funerals (Joussaume 1988:17).

Passage graves are mounds of earth that were entered through a stone-lined passage leading to a chamber where people were buried under a dolmenlike arrangement of large stones (Fig. 7.5). *Long barrows* are similar except that they are greatly elongated (Fig. 7.6). A number of people have suggested that the elongated shape of these burial monuments was meant to imitate the shape of the houses that people lived in.

Rock-cut tombs are chambers for burying the dead that are cut into cliff faces or enormous boulders (Fig. 7.7). They are generally used for communal burials consisting of the members of a family or lineage.

Circles are arrangements of large stones in circular or oval forms, like Stonehenge, although most are much smaller (Fig. 7.8). Stones can also be set up as more or less straight alignments or in such a fashion that they form avenues (Figs. 7.9, 7.10). Sometimes large poles or slabs of wood were used in place of stones for circles as well as tombs.

In addition to these megalithic structures, there are types of construction associated with them that are made without large stones. *Enclosures* are generally made only of earth and are associated with possible wooden structures. They usually have a ditch and bank around them (henges; Fig. 7.10). Enclosures usually have ritual remains in their ditches together with human skeletal remains, so they appear to have been used in mortuary rituals (Andersen 1997:309). *Cursuses* are elongated areas enclosed by low mounds of earth and shallow ditches (Fig. 7.10). They can be extremely long, ranging up to 10 kilometers in length. It is often suggested that these were used for funeral races, processions, or initiations (Stover and Kraig 1978:89), but little is known about them with certainty. Their ditches contain ritual and skeletal material, as do the enclosures.

Bone is not preserved in all the megaliths, but where it is preserved, megaliths are generally associated with human skeletal remains or funeral rituals (Joussaume 1988:17). This seems to be true throughout the world both archaeologically and ethnographically. In fact, there is a large body of beliefs about souls being

Fig. 7.7. Many megalithic societies also created rock-cut tombs such as this example in the Torajan highlands. In Europe, some such tombs were adorned with bull skulls or stylized sculptures. Here, the rock has been sculpted and painted in the form of a bull head beneath the entrance of the tomb. Tombs are closed with wooden panels. This one is decorated with a stylized bull head—a popular symbol of success and happiness in Torajan society. Sacrificing bulls was considered necessary for the dead to get to heaven. Similar concepts probably characterized Neolithic society as well. Photo by B. Hayden.

able to dwell in stones (Kaliff 1997:106ff). Thus, we are on fairly firm ground in assuming that megaliths were probably associated with funeral rituals. We might well suspect that ancestor veneration was involved. Additional observations will provide more detail to this basic level of interpretation.

MEGALITHS WERE MEGALOMANIAC MONUMENTS TO THE DEAD

There is good evidence for ancestor worship among the distant original Neolithic cultures in the Near East. It is present in PPNA and PPNB sites like Jericho with its plas-

Fig. 7.8. Megalithic stones were also set up in circular arrangements usually inside ditches, such as at Avebury in England and the Ring of Brogdar in the Orkney Islands of Scotland (shown here). Photo by B. Hayden.

Fig. 7.9. Processional "avenues" often led from stone circles or henges to other important ritual centers. These avenues were sometimes lined with megaliths, as was the case at Avebury, shown here. Photo by B. Hayden.

tered skulls and at Çatal Hüyük with its shrines and burials under the floors. Similar ancestor-oriented practices appear to have taken place in the megalithic cultures of Western Europe. In the megaliths and the enclosure ditches, there is often an emphasis on skulls, indicative of an ancestor cult; bones are often removed from funerary crypts apparently as talismans (Cauwe 1996, 1997, 1998a, 1998b; Berg and Cauwe 1996); and as at Çatal Hüyük, bodies were often defleshed on raised platforms outside the megalithic tombs or in special wooden funerary structures over which tombs were built (Hedges 1984:133ff;

Fig. 7.10. The area surrounding Stonehenge is one of the richest concentrations in Europe of different kinds of ritual structures and elite burial mounds (round and long barrows). Stonehenge is the most famous of the monuments; however, Durrington Walls is far larger, Woodhenge is almost as big, and the Cursus is almost 3 kilometers long, representing a major investment of time and labor. All of this construction and rich burial activity indicates that the Stonehenge chiefdom was exceedingly rich in Neolithic times. From D. Clarke, T. Cowie, and A. Foxon, *Symbols of Power at the Time of Stonehenge,* map. Edinburgh: National Museum of Antiquities of Scotland (H.M.S.O.), 1985.

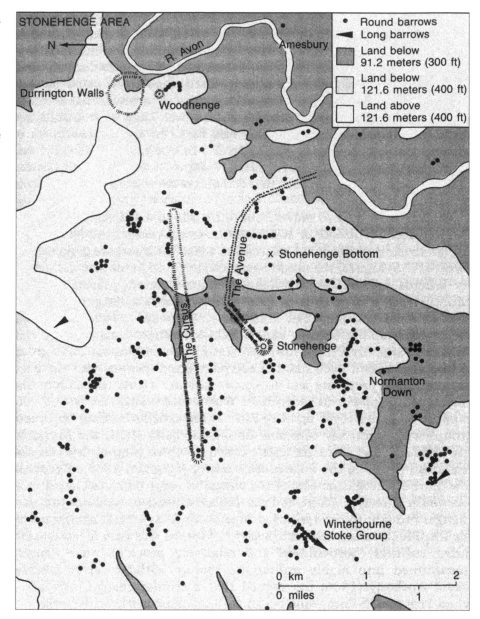

Hutton 1991:27; Joussaume 1988:31–32). The pattern of ditch enclosures being used as regional centers for funeral rituals also occurs in the European Iron Age. This may represent an unbroken tradition from the Neolithic (or even earlier periods) until the demise of the Celts (see Chap. 9 and Andersen 1997:280, 309).

Feasting was also a major characteristic of almost all megalithic structures, but particularly at the passage graves, long barrows, and enclosures. In fact, bodies or defleshed skeletons appear to have been placed in the tombs as part of annual ceremonial feasts (Hedges 1984:135; Cauwe 2001:156ff). Frequently, pots were left along the outside walls of the tombs or even in the passages, undoubtedly with food offerings in them.

Food refuse and broken pots are generally found in front of the tombs or in the ditches of enclosures. These occurrences and the rarity of pottery elsewhere have led to the suggestion that Neolithic pottery was used only in ritual feasting contexts (Sherratt 1991:56), an interpretation that is consistent with my general assessment of prestige technologies and feasting (Hayden 1998). Special offerings tend to be found inside the tombs consisting of unusual foods or animals with spiritual qualities such as eagles (Hedges 1984:145ff). Concentrations of different kinds of animals in different tombs may indicate a totemic aspect of Neolithic ancestor worship. One burial chamber even contained the remains of a kind of "witches' brew": fish, frogs, toads, snakes, shrews, mice, and hare (Joussaume 1988:73). Thus, people appear to have been conducting special rituals inside these tombs while more normal feasting was taking place outside. This is a pattern very similar to the Vietnamese lineage houses described in the last chapter. However, there was tremendous variability in all of the funerary practices, tomb styles, and treatment of human skeletons at the same time periods and even in the same localities. It is as if each lineage competed to develop a distinctive, more impressive, or more powerful funerary ritual than other lineages. Other variations of funerary rituals include what must have been impressive boat burials in rivers and lakes (Koch 1999:130).

One aspect that did not vary much was the relatively restricted access to the tombs, both for the dead and the living. With a few notable exceptions the majority of archaeological excavations have indicated that the people placed in megalithic tombs represented only a small portion of the population that must have helped to construct them. According to modern experiments and estimates, it would have taken 170 adults to move and raise a 32-ton block of stone, while 700–800 people would have been required to move a 100-ton block of stone (Joussaume 1988:21). In contrast, many of the early long barrows contained only a single burial while even those with a number of burials must have included only the most important or wealthiest families in a lineage (Hedges 1984:124, 138; Joussaume 1988:21, 30–32, 78, 126; Hutton 1991:68). This, too, is consistent with known ethnographic ancestor cults and lineage monuments, such as those described by Freedman (1961), where only the most important and wealthiest members of the lineage could have tablets or be honored in the lineage halls. It seems that megalithic tombs were probably a type of lineage hall where ancestors were worshipped.

There are also good indications that megalithic society began as a complex form of transegalitarian society but rapidly became dominated by powerful chiefs, who commanded vast human and natural resources that enabled them to erect very large monuments. Archaeologically, chiefdoms are usually recognized by monumental architecture (which the megaliths certainly are), the existence of a political hierarchy (which Stonehenge and other large centers certainly represent; Hedges 1984:114–26), and the development of refined specialized craft products (which are certainly found in the tombs and elsewhere; Fig. 7.11; Patton 1991). Chiefdoms also display an inordinate ritual emphasis on elite ancestors, especially the ancestors of the chief. Chiefly ancestors could become almost semidivine and serve to justify the chief's claims to supernatural and secular power. Archaeological evidence often emerges of these elite ancestor cults in many forms elsewhere in the world, too, from Mayan platform burial mounds surmounted by ancestor temples, to large statues of ancestors such as those on Easter Island, to the burial and

Fig. 7.11. Elaborate and costly prestige items such as these are sometimes found as isolated items, but more typically they furnished some of the most important Neolithic tombs in Western Europe. Their mere existence testifies to considerable wealth and power differences in Neolithic society. At top is a collection of jet and amber beads together with an unusually long and thin prestige axe. Below (left) is an elaborately carved flint macehead with a spiral motif on its side and (right) an enigmatically carved symbolic stone sculpture with no practical use. From D. Clarke, T. Cowie, and A. Foxon, *Symbols of Power at the Time of Stonehenge,* Figs. 3.16, 3.17, 3.38. Edinburgh: National Museum of Antiquities of Scotland (H.M.S.O.), 1985.

totem poles of chiefly elites on the Northwest Coast, to large lineage cemeteries and shrines in China (Lee and Zhu 2002).

While many people like to think of the Neolithic as being egalitarian, most of the evidence from the megalithic cultures indicates that there were very substantial social and economic inequalities throughout the society. Not only was burial in the megalithic tombs restricted to a small proportion of the population, but the sheer authority or wealth necessary to command the labor needed to construct the larger tombs and monuments is a major reason for believing that these societies were hierarchical if not stratified, as chiefdoms are with clearly separated classes and probably slaves. In some graves there were rich burial goods, such as prestige axes, sculptures, maces, beads, pendants, many pots, unusual animals like eagles, rare types of stone—all valuable items of successful aggrandizers (Fig. 7.11; see also Hedges 1984:155, 218; Joussaume 1988:35, 86; Clarke, Cowie, and Foxon 1985; Patton 1990, 1991).

It is my contention that the megaliths themselves must be viewed as one more manifestation of aggrandizer strategies for displaying success and their socioeconomic power, just as the cathedrals of Europe and the Olympic stadiums of today are essentially prestige symbols of successful and powerful people and polities (Icher 1998). This is the ecological (formal) meaning of the megaliths. If we want to know why the megaliths were built, it is the formal aspect that we must focus on. It is obvious that they were also built for the ancestors in symbolic terms, but this does not explain why so much energy was invested in their construction. Ancestors appear to have been venerated for thousands of years before megaliths were constructed. It is far easier to put up a wooden tablet for one's ancestors that involves few resources and little effort. Megalithic monuments were not built because one group was more religious or more zealous than another in the worship of their ancestors. Promoters of megalithic constructions were only using religion and their ancestors as a means to express their wealth and success while simultaneously pumping up their claim to ancestral sources of preternatural power. It was, perhaps, a natural path to pursue since success could in turn be attributed to powerful ancestors that successful people claimed helped them become economically successful. In New Guinea, Hampton (1997:404) observed that the strength of allies was judged by the power of their ancestors, and in Neolithic Europe the power of the ancestors was demonstrated by the impressiveness of their tombs or enclosures. The more one invested in honoring ancestors and making them happy, the more the ancestors made a lineage or group prosperous and successful—or so the story goes. Aggrandizers who claimed the closest connections to the ancestors could easily manipulate such a system for their own self-serving purposes and could justifiably demand ever more surpluses from their kin and supporters.

A number of authors have drawn attention to the very restricted access passages in the megalithic tombs leading to the unusually small burial chambers. As in the case of Paleolithic caves, these spaces seem to have been created small deliberately, so that only a few people could be present when offerings were made and rituals or communications with ancestors were taking place. Clearly, the hundreds or thousands of people who worked to construct the megalithic tombs would never be able to participate in the most intimate rituals with the ancestral spirits inside the tombs. Lower-ranking individuals undoubtedly celebrated rituals outside the tombs. Who, then, entered the tombs? The most logical persons would be the highest-ranking lineage family or family heads, perhaps together with a lineage priest or shaman, if that person was not also the lineage head. Thus, megaliths were undoubtedly used to control spiritual access to ancestors and enable aggrandizers to exert spiritual and political authority more easily and more convincingly (Patton 1990:555; Lewis-Williams and Dowson 1993). When the megalithic tombs were not being used for annual ancestor rituals, the entrances to the tombs may have been sealed by large stones in order to prevent any unauthorized entry (Hutton 1991:34; Joussaume 1988:62). When lineages died out or tombs were full of skeletons after hundreds of years of use, the tombs were often purposely filled with earth.

There is good evidence that the tombs were also constructed to induce or enhance the altered states of consciousness that were probably experienced by those entering the tombs for rituals. In some tombs, the upright slabs of stone were decorated with carved or painted images that resemble some of the entoptic forms found in Upper Paleolithic caves. David Lewis-Williams and Thomas Dowson (1993) have argued that these forms probably represent visions seen by those entering the chambers in altered states, or perhaps they were also meant to stimulate visual patterns and convey traditional symbolic images to those entering the chambers. Others have suggested that both the locations of paintings in Upper Paleolithic caves and the construction of the megalithic passages and chambers were meant to create striking sound effects, especially with the use of drums (Watson and Keating 1999). Furthermore, Andrew Sherratt (1991) has persuasively argued that psychotropic substances like Amanita mushrooms and opium were used to induce ecstatic states in Neolithic rituals.

Still other dramatic effects were incorporated into the building of these tombs. At Newgrange in eastern Ireland, a corbelled vault was constructed of stone slabs over the

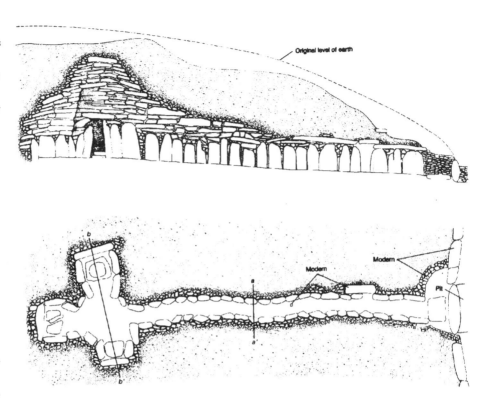

Fig. 7.12. Newgrange in Ireland is one of the most spectacular passage graves in Europe. The mound is very large, and it contained an unusually long passage tunnel ending in three small chambers. The chambers were roofed by a remarkable and unique megalithic corbelled vault, while the front of the mound was faced with gleaming white stones to impress viewers even at considerable distances. From G. Daniel, "Megalithic Monuments," *Scientific American* 243(1):80.

central chamber creating an amazing cone in stone (Fig. 7.12). This was a remarkable architectural achievement for the time, and it has earned Newgrange the title of a "Neolithic cathedral." The walls around Newgrange were faced with gleaming white quartz pebbles, while the base of the outside was lined with oblong stones intricately carved with spirals, lozenges, and solar symbols. There are even more spectacular alignments at a number of megalithic tombs and monuments to be discussed shortly. All of these features indicate extremely sophisticated architectural planning and engineering on the part of these Neolithic societies. While not all community projects may be outcomes of aggrandizers' strategies, the nonutilitarian nature and magnitude of megalithic structures testify to great wealth and surpluses that were being harnessed in order to display success and group "fitness." The aggrandizers who built the megalithic tombs were doing everything they could to enhance the impressiveness of these monuments, using sheer size, decoration, darkness, hallucinogens, and celestial alignments.

Authors like Colin Renfrew (1976) and Robert Chapman (1981a, 1981b) have tried to argue that the megaliths were constructed in order to establish firm boundaries of land ownership under conditions of increasing population pressure, land shortages, or other stresses. However, comparative studies indicate that strong lineages such as those capable of erecting megalithic tombs do not occur under conditions of resource scarcity (Collier 1975:76–77). Moreover, when the first megaliths were being constructed, there could not have been much population pressure, for the first monuments were built almost as soon as the first Neolithic colonists arrived in some locations (Hutton 1991:21). Rather, these megaliths testify to families, lineages, and aggrandizers that found new lands capable of producing great wealth. They are displays of success, just as an elephant's tusks show off the biological power and might of individuals. Just as an elephant's tusk is only one part of an entire organism, so the megaliths were really only a part of the entire economic system of the Neolithic communities that built them. The megaliths were like economic icebergs, with the vast bulk of the economy that produced them hidden in the mists of the past, hidden in the ground among countless animal remains.

MEGALITHS WERE ECONOMIC ICEBERGS

What was the source of the wealth that produced the megaliths of Europe? It may well have been cattle—the same factor that drove the surplus economic and social system of Neolithic communities in the Near East and that still drives the surplus economies and social systems in Southeast Asian tribal and chiefdom communities, as well as many of those in Africa and peasant Europe. In the dense forests of central Europe, it is difficult to clear forests and maintain good pasture for cattle. However, near the northern coasts of Scotland, rocky plains and severe climates could provide lush grasslands for cattle. Easily cleared chalk uplands were also very favorable for cattle because they did not quickly reforest but with some maintenance could retain grass pasture coverage for long periods. These were the advantages of the chalk downs surrounding such major centers as Stonehenge and Avebury in England. The same is true of the alpine areas in the Pyrenees Mountains, where megaliths are also found. In Brittany, too, the soil is so poor on this granitic rocky peninsula jutting into the Atlantic Ocean that agriculture normally yields poor returns. The area today is relatively impoverished. However, grass grows well in the wet climate, and dairy farming is one of the few viable livelihoods, as tends to be true today in many of the areas where megaliths are found such as the Orkney Islands and Ireland.

The overriding importance of cattle in the Neolithic may explain why so few Neolithic houses have been found in megalithic areas (Cauwe 2001a:137). People may have been constantly moving their herds to better pasture areas and moving with their herds. The fundamental importance of cattle to the Neolithic economy also explains the recurring symbolism of cattle at many megalithic tombs and their presence in feasting remains, just as they were used as sacred symbols in the ancestral shrines of Çatal Hüyük (Joussaume 1988:73, 96, 119, 217, 220, 222, 259, 261). As we shall see in Chapter 8, societies that depend heavily on the herding of domestic animals tend to develop hierarchical political organizations, like chiefdoms, especially if they are producing substantial surpluses. All these factors strongly indicate that most megalithic societies were hierarchically organized with substantial differences in wealth and power between families and lineages.

Because of the industrialization of meat production in today's global economy, cattle (like white bread) have become common, and beef is frequently eaten in all socioeconomic groups and in a wide range of fast-food outlets that serve burgers by the billions. Megalithic areas today may produce poor returns, being only suited for devalued cattle raising or dairying, but in the Neolithic, cattle were the gold of the economies. Even today, the first letter of our alphabet represents the inverted head of a bull, and our "stock" market is named after the trading of cattle. When we write a capital "A" or give term papers the grade of "A," it is as if we are still invoking the power of the bull. Cattle were probably the single most valuable material item in Neolithic society. If contemporary tribal societies are any indication, everything from marriage to warfare to peace must have hinged on one's ability to produce or procure cattle. It is likely that no large ritual, no claim to political office, and no social transaction could have taken place without exchanging or killing cattle. As in today's tribal communities in Africa and Southeast Asia, there must have been major exchanges between importing and exporting regions of cattle. I think this is the fundamental reason why there is a great deal of stylistic homogeneity between such distant megalithic centers as Brittany, Ireland, and the Orkneys, as well as a second style region all throughout northern Europe (Joussaume 1988:32, 36, 46, 62–63, 70; Hayden 1993a:320). In order to make sea journeys between such distant locations on a regular basis, cattle owners must have had to brave extremely adverse sea and weather conditions and to encounter many risks. It is a wonder that anyone made these voyages at all, much less on a regular basis. But the motivation to become wealthy through the trade of cattle can certainly account for these contacts as well as for the strong architectural and artistic similarities in these regions that reflect elite interactions, tastes, and priorities. Megaliths were constructed not only to impress local inhabitants but also to impress visiting elites from distant Neolithic lands, so as to encourage them to continue their trading relationships and mutually profitable exchanges. This is undoubtedly why the Carnac region, with the largest single concentration of megaliths in the world, became so important. It was an ideally protected Neolithic port adjacent to very productive pasture areas.

I became aware of just how small a proportion of the total Neolithic economy was probably represented by megaliths when I worked in the Torajan highlands in Sulawesi, Indonesia. Here, people still erect menhirs to the dead, but only for the wealthiest members of the upper class. Torajan society was traditionally a stratified chiefdom. It has made some accommodations to the modern world but retains many of its old funeral rituals and class distinctions. I was astonished to see the extent to which surplus wealth was invested in the decoration and exaltation of lineage house structures (requiring the killing of many water buffaloes and pigs) and feasts for many different occasions, especially funerals. Funerals are the most costly events in traditional Torajan communities. The deceased person is wrapped in special cloths like a cocoon and kept for months or years until a family has amassed enough wealth to provide a suitable funeral. Funerals for wealthy members of the elite class lasted many months, with elaborate rituals and constant small feasts occurring throughout that period. These minor events involved the sacrifice of hundreds of large pigs, chickens, and an occasional water buffalo or head of cattle. The major events, however, featured grand receptions of guests during which valuable heirloom items were displayed, guests were received by richly dressed and bejewelled junior lineage members, and a minimum of 24 buffaloes were slaughtered before the assembled guests, as well as dozens or hundreds of large pigs. The maximum number of cattle or buffalo sacrificed at a funeral such as this was about 200. Hundreds or thousands of people attended these funerals, including the most important elites from other lineages, villages, and political centers. To accommodate them all, elaborate temporary structures were erected, sometimes taking months to construct. These were then taken down immediately after the funeral.

If a family wished to have a menhir erected for someone who died, this constituted an additional cost that was incorporated into the funeral. A work crew to quarry the

Fig. 7.13. People often wonder how the large stones used in megalithic structures could have been transported. While some people resort to exotic explanations involving magical powers or extraterrestrial help, the ethnographic and archaeological records demonstrate fairly conclusively that these tasks simply required a great deal of muscle power, political power, economic underwriting, and organizational skill, as shown in this early photograph from Sumatra. Brian Cotterell and Johan Kamminga (1990:216–33) provide one of the most thorough discussions of the mechanics involved in moving megaliths. From F. Schnitger, *Forgotten Kingdoms of Sumatra,* Plate 24. Leiden: E. J. Brill, 1939.

menhir had to be hired months prior to the funeral, depending on the size of the monolith. The monolith had to be moved during the funeral, and for this hundreds or thousands of people were needed from many villages. They were paid for their labor by the sacrifice of a buffalo and many pigs for every day required to move the large stone. Most large stones took at least a week to move into place and stand upright. These stones were simply dragged on the ground with ropes if they were small enough or were placed on log rollers (Fig. 7.13). When the stone was erected, yet more buffalo or cattle were slaughtered, and feasting continued for days and weeks while the body of the deceased was eventually put to rest in its tomb a few hundred meters from the menhir (Figs. 7.3, 7.7).

Deceased family members who had such elaborate funerals and menhirs erected to them were considered to become ancestral deities that would send supernatural and material prosperity to the family that sponsored the funeral (Sandarupa 1996). Wealth, power, and the sacrifice of many water buffaloes were necessary to get to heaven. And having an ancestral sponsor in heaven was necessary to become prosperous and powerful in Torajan conceptual ideology. The more buffalo that were sacrificed, the more powerful the ancestor would become and the greater was the inducement for those receiving meat gifts to recognize claims of high supernatural status for the dead person.

The animal bones discarded from feasting, the proximity of the bones of the dead, the inclusion of burial goods and ritual paraphernalia at the Torajan funerary sites, and the bull and solar symbolism used are all extremely reminiscent of the European Neolithic enclosure ditches with feasting and ritual and human remains, as well as the megalithic tombs with feasting remains scattered in front of their entrances. In short, the megalithic cultures of Sulawesi seem to provide a reasonably close parallel to the rituals and societies of megalithic Europe. However, the amount of economic power represented by megalithic construction was only a small fraction of the total costs of funerals, and only a small fraction of the total economic power of the families or lineages that erected them. Moreover, even the largest megalithic structures of the Torajans tended to be dwarfed by the more spectacular megalithic centers of Western Europe such as Avebury, Carnac, Stonehenge, Mount Pleasant, and Newgrange. If these centers represented only the tip of the economic iceberg, the power and wealth of the elites at these centers must have been phenomenal.

MEGALITHIC RELIGION FOCUSES ON ELITE ANCESTORS

Archaeologists undoubtedly have a very biased view of megalithic religion. Virtually all the attention has been focused on the megaliths and monuments constructed by and for the elites, while very little attention has been paid to other members or other religious aspects of the society. This is natural in many respects because the elites are the ones that had the means to create enduring prestige materials and monuments. Others did not. The elites wanted to impress other people with their accomplishments and successes in order to forge trade and military alliances. They succeeded admirably, for we are still admiring their creations 6,000 years later, just as we are still admiring the exquisite prestige paintings and sculptures that aggrandizers commissioned in the Upper Paleolithic and the cathedrals that aggrandizers commissioned in medieval Europe. Dwellings of the people who actually built the megalithic monuments have been unusually elusive in archaeological excavations (Cauwe 2001a:137). As a result, little is known about the rituals and religions of common people. The presence of relatively common phallic sculptures (Fig. 6.19) betrays an underlying concern with fertility at the domestic level (Burl 1976:88) and probably a fertility cult similar to that inferred to have existed in the Near Eastern Neolithic cultures discussed in Chapter 6. Thousands of isolated finds or hoards of pots, axes, food, and even people were also ritually deposited over the landscape in streams or other wet places, probably as offerings by households to achieve fertility, wealth, respite from adverse conditions, or personal goals (Karsten 1994:186ff; Stafford 1999:133; Koch 1998, 1999). Three-quarters of the deposits were single items, probably indicating that offerings were made only episodically for special reasons. The common thread of these offerings was that the objects represented a great amount of labor investment. Offerings inside houses for their construction also occurred. Small cult houses such as that at Herrup (displayed in the Danish National Museum) were only about 6 × 6 meters, but they contained dozens of vessel offerings and probably had cult figures carved on the posts. These may well have been rural ancestral or deity shrines of common people during the Neolithic.

As in the Chinese lineage rituals described by Freedman (1961), it seems reasonable to assume that there was a poor version of a domestic fertility and ancestral cult as well as an elite version. Domestic cults may have also focused on the worship of various nature deities and spirits as documented for Greek peasants by Nilsson (1940). He points out that the Greek Olympian gods described by Homer and in most of the standard mythologies, such as Zeus and Athena, were really the gods of the elites and reflected elite social and political life. In contrast, Greek peasants primarily worshipped nature spirits such as pans, satyrs, water spirits, and gods of fertility and growth such as Diony-sus. As suggested in Chapter 5, this trend of establishing separate elite and nonelite religious cults probably started with the secret societies and ancestor veneration of transegalitarian hunter-gatherers or horticulturalists. With the emergence of chiefdoms, the process of establishing a separate cult for the worship of elite ancestors undoubtedly became even more distinct from the nature-fertility–oriented domestic cults of common people. The most powerful elite ancestors often became deified or semidivine.

It would have been in aggrandizers' interests to promote their ancestors as founders of entire clans or tribes, thus garnering the spiritual allegiance of everyone to the chief as the most direct descendant of the founding ancestor. Allegiance to elite ancestor cults could also be used as the basis for extracting surpluses from the populace in order to construct suitable temples, monuments, ritual areas, and tombs for the clan ancestors and their descendants. Surpluses would have to be obtained for the required ritual feasts to honor the ancestors properly and ensure prosperity for the entire clan. It is no coincidence, I would argue, that ethnographic chiefs and even rulers of early states collected tribute from the populace under the pretext of holding ritual feasts for the deities. In this respect, the abundant feasting debris associated with ancestral monuments implies ritual feasting on a much larger scale than has been detected in previous periods. This may be directly related to the use by chiefs of large-scale ritual feasting to extract surpluses from the populace, part of which would be used for a general feast and part of which would be retained for elite uses (see Kirch 2001; Schmandt-Besserat 2001; Junker 2001).

While this new elite ancestor cult could potentially embrace everyone in a chiefdom at the level of feasting and public rituals, running of the cult and the actual contact with ancestral spirits must have been restricted to a very small number of the most important elite members. Similar events were transpiring in several other complex societies elsewhere on the globe. For instance, on the Northwest Coast, complex hunter-gatherer elites claimed hereditary rights to supernatural encounters (Drucker 1965:167). And, among Mayan chiefs and kings, Schele and Freidel (1990) document the use of ecstatic rituals to contact ancestors (see Chap. 11).

STONE CIRCLES FEATURE THE SUN AND MOON

If most megalithic monuments seem closely associated with ancestral cults, megalithic stone circles are less clearly so, although the larger examples must certainly have been constructed by chiefly elites and were situated at the regional centers of political and economic power such as Avebury and Stonehenge. At least the larger examples, therefore, probably played a role in the elite ideology, and I suspect that smaller ones did as well. Stover and Kraig (1978:119) argue that all stone circles are essentially expressions of chiefly power. They occur almost exclusively in the British Isles and are late Neolithic and Bronze Age constructions. Aside from the great amounts of manpower that their construction implies, these circles frequently display significant alignments to the rising or setting points of the sun or moon at various points in their cycles (Hutton 1991:110–15; MacKie 1997; Milisauskas 1986:787). Some Portuguese megalithic tomb passages were even aligned to the first full moon after the spring equinox (Roslund et al. 2000). This is essentially how the celebration of Easter is determined in Europe even today. Aubrey

Burl suggests that lunar orientations probably also indicate that rituals were held monthly at night (Hutton 1991:116).

Solar alignments are present not only at Stonehenge but in a number of passage graves such as Newgrange in Ireland, Maes Howe in the Orkneys, and at Gavrinis in Brittany (Joussaume 1988:66, 118, 156). I suggest that the reason for this emphasis on solar symbolism in the largest of the megalithic monuments is related primarily to the development of chiefly ancestor cults. The sun is one of the most common deity concepts that occur throughout the world, even among some simple hunter-gatherers (Singh 1993). It is a deity form that is featured over others when it is advantageous to do so. For instance, the sun is empha-

Fig. 7.14. The sun is a popular symbol of power, rebirth, and dominance in many societies with developed political power and elites. In the Torajan culture, the sun is often used in funerary contexts for important individuals, as indicated on these wooden doors to rock-cut tombs. Here, the sun is also associated with bull imagery and with spirals very reminiscent of the spirals used in European Neolithic funerary monuments (see Fig. 7.17). Photos by B. Hayden.

sized among generalized hunter-gatherers who experience frequent adverse weather conditions (Hayden 1987). The advantage to elites with aspirations of extending their control over vast territories and many different communities is that the sun as a deity is a powerful symbol capable of transcending or assimilating local ancestors and deities. It is the highest, brightest, and most powerful symbol. It shines over all the land. In northern Europe, in particular, it is viewed as essential for life. Its dominant position among the forces that people had to contend with could not be disputed. The same symbolic logic led many other rulers to adopt this symbolism in later millennia, from the elites of the complex hunter-gatherers on the Northwest Coast, to the pharaohs of Egypt, to the Roman emperors, to the sun king of France, Louis XIV.

By associating their ancestors and themselves with the worship of the sun and its power, ambitious elites could create a universal cult that made good intuitive sense to many people. Elites hoped that others could become favorably disposed to contribute to, and participate in, the cult. Including the roles of the sun, ancestors, and fertility for crops and animals in the same cult must have been an especially powerful combination. Moreover, by claiming that the chiefly ancestors had entered the solar realms, or even become united with the solar spirit, chiefs in essence claimed control over the cult and fertility because of their special close relationships with their ancestors. Creating large temples, obtaining lavish ritual paraphernalia, and entering into privileged ritual states via training or use of psychotropic plants were all means of reinforcing or validating these claims.

Among the megalithic Torajans in Sulawesi, for example, the wealthy elite travel after death to heaven, where the sun is viewed as the source of life and features very prominently in elite mortuary motifs (Fig. 7.14). The sun is also a prominent symbol on decorated elite houses and rice granaries (Fig. 7.15). There are a number of other striking similarities between Torajan and prehistoric European societies. Cattle were the main form of wealth for both Torajans and the European megalithic builders, and both societies had chiefdom-level political organizations. The Torajan ancestors, in heaven with the sun, in turn send rice, buffaloes, children, and riches to the family that helped them get to heaven (Sandarupa 1996:52, 57). Traditionally, rice was only used by Torajan elites, and the same may

Fig. 7.15. The sun and the bull both feature prominently in many prestige displays of the wealthy and powerful in Torajan society. At left, an elaborately decorated rice granary features two suns depicted under the eaves, both surmounted by cocks (also symbols of the sun), while the walls of the rice granary are decorated with a number of stylized bull heads and spirals. The elite house at right displays an impressive number of horns from water buffaloes sacrificed during the major feasts that the household sponsored. Photos by B. Hayden.

have been true for wheat among European Neolithic elites, especially for feasts (Kaelas 1981:88; Jennbert 1984, 1985, 1987; Lidén 1995).

Interestingly, the spiral is one of the major art motifs used by Torajans in their mortuary structures and on their houses, and it was also one of the major motifs used in European megalithic tombs. There are many symbolic suggestions for the meanings of the European spirals, ranging from portals to other dimensions (Campbell 1969:120), to snake symbols (Helfman 1967:73), to lunar symbols (Stover and Kraig 1978:110), to symbols for the sun, women, life energy, cosmic energy, the flow of time, other flows, the womb, death, and rebirth (Walker 1988; Marshack 1991a:27). Perhaps the association of the sun with the spiral was derived from the spirallike path through the sky that the sun follows over the course of a year, as its rising and setting points along the horizon slowly expand from the winter to the summer solstice and then slowly contract until the winter solstice. The earliest clear representation of spirals occurs in Upper Paleolithic bone engravings from Malta (Siberia) and Mezin (Ukraine) (Marshack 1991a:27). At least one spiral also occurs in the European Mesolithic (Fig. 7.16; see also Larsson 1975/76, 2000c:Fig. 9). Whether this is the origin of Neolithic spirals and whether they had the same significance as Neolithic spirals are open questions, but even if the specific meaning was different, the use of this symbol in the Neolithic may be another indication that the megalithic tradition originated in the Mesolithic or earlier culture of Western Europe.

Fig. 7.16. One of the earliest depictions of a spiral comes from the Mesolithic site of Ageröd in southern Sweden. This occurrence may indicate symbolic continuity in this area from the Mesolithic to the Neolithic. Photo by B. Hayden, with permission from the Lund University Historical Museum.

Fig. 7.17. At Newgrange, a large megalithic stone carved with spirals and lozenges was placed in front of the entrance to the passageway. Above this entrance the builders had constructed a "window box," the function of which was at first very enigmatic. Photo by B. Hayden.

Some archaeologists enjoy speculating about such symbolical meanings, and most often there is no real way of telling if their speculations bear any relationship to past concepts. However, in at least one megalithic instance, there is very compelling evidence that both the spiral and the ancestors were conceptually tightly bound to the cycles of the sun. In one of the most remarkable architectural achievements of the Neolithic, the architects and builders of Newgrange not only constructed an enormous, impressive burial mound with a stone-lined passage leading to a vaulted chamber, but they also incorporated an ingenious eternal interactive architectural device in the design of the monument. Excavators in the twentieth century discovered a strange, windowlike feature immediately above the entrance into the passage (Fig. 7.17). They puzzled over its meaning for many months until they learned of a local legend that suggested the sun would shine through the window when it rose on the morning of the winter solstice. In good scientific fashion, the most hardy excavators—skeptics and converted alike—set

Fig. 7.18. Local traditions maintained that at the winter solstice, the sun shone through the window box and lit up the passageway at Newgrange. Archaeologists substantiated this tradition and were amazed to find that the burial chamber at the end of the passage was also lit up through this box on the winter solstice. This demonstrated the important symbolical role the sun played in elite ideology concerning their ancestors. Courtesy of the Office of Public Works, Ireland.

out to test the idea. They got up before dawn on 21 December and crawled into the narrow, damp, cold passage of Newgrange to see if there was any truth to the old legend. After long, anxious moments, the sunrise finally came, and the archaeologists were amazed to find not only that the sun shone directly through the stone window (Fig. 7.18), but also that it illuminated the entire passage and lit up the back wall of the burial chamber where the ancestral spirits resided. This was an event that would only occur on the winter solstice, and it would have occurred every year for what must have seemed like an eternity. We can only marvel at the sense of drama, the creativity, the imagination, and the engineering skills of the people who built Newgrange.

Significantly, close to the place where the sun's light fell on the burial chamber wall, there is an engraved triple spiral. In Neolithic times, it would have been illuminated when the rising sun shone down the entrance passage on the winter solstice. This is the kind of context and association that enables archaeologists to say with confidence that the ancestor cult, the solar cult, and the spiral were all conceptually associated in some of the megalithic monuments. The spiral may well represent death and rebirth, but it is certainly associated with the sun, and the sun was probably viewed as undergoing a death and rebirth at the winter solstice as well. Thus, powerful ancestors were associated with the sun and with megalithic stones. As we have noted, it is a common belief that such ancestors can also send fertility, riches, and children to those who honor them (Berglund 1976:110ff). In some Scandinavian communities, women still go to cemeteries for inspiration in naming their infants. Elsewhere in Europe, megaliths still play such roles in popular peasant folklore, for offerings are often left at megaliths in rural areas and women who want to become pregnant have been known to visit these old stone erections at night when the moon is full. They leave offerings, recite spells, and rub themselves against the huge ancient stones (Eliade 1958a:Chap. 6; Kaliff 1997:107ff).

This discussion of solar symbolism is a circuitous way of establishing the overarching importance of the solar cults for elites. While the Irish megalithic builders created exclusive megalithic tombs for the chief's ancestral solar cult, in England it appears that the chiefs erected huge and impressive stone circles that were monuments to the sun (and probably elite ancestors assimilated to the sun). The largest example is Stonehenge. In a recent article, Parker Pearson and Ramilisonina (1998) argued that Stonehenge was a monument to the dead and therefore not used much, while the nearby contemporaneous structure, Woodhenge, was a monument to the living and more intensively used. They also argued that the circle form is symbolical of life, death, and ancestors and that ancestors were related to the sun and moon.

While I think that some of these interpretations are correct, other aspects fall into the nonverifiable speculative tradition in archaeology. Certainly, there is widespread agreement that Stonehenge was part of a solar cult. On the basis of the solar ancestral cult at other megalithic centers such as found in Ireland, the Orkneys, and in Brittany, I, too, think that a convincing argument can be made that Stonehenge was the center of an ancestral sun-related cult. Stonehenge is located at the center of a very dense elite mortuary complex (Fig. 7.10), and it exhibits the same construction style as some other passage graves with its sun-orientation, circular form, and upright stones (Stover and Kraig 1978:103–4). It simply lacks the earth covering.

On the other hand, there is considerably less support for Parker Pearson's idea that nearby Woodhenge was a center for a cult of the living. This is one possible way of explaining the differences in construction material (stone versus wood) and the high density of feasting debris at Woodhenge compared with the much lower density of feasting debris at Stonehenge. Since these two structures were used at the same time and are so close to each other (only 3 km apart), they must have been built and used by the same community but in different ways or by different sectors of the community. In view of the likelihood that other clearly solar-symbolic megalithic monuments such as Newgrange were exclusive elite shrines, I would suggest that Stonehenge makes more sense as another example of a monument that was for elite use only. Like Newgrange, it must have been built by the general populace, was enormously expensive, and required complex engineering. And, like Newgrange, it was probably used for chiefly ancestral-solar cult activities including the prediction of solar events like the solstices and eclipses. Stonehenge was a monument meant to awe and impress rival as well as allied elites, in terms of its size, its complex engineering, and its fabulous functions. Impress and awe it still does. Stonehenge is simply the crowning jewel in one of the richest megalithic complexes anywhere in Europe, for there are scores of burial and other monuments all over the Salisbury Plain, where Stonehenge is located (Fig. 7.10). This includes a cursus that is almost 3 kilometers long. Stonehenge was at the center of an extraordinarily rich and powerful chiefdom based on cattle production and trade. If other megalithic monuments are any indication, access to it would have been restricted only to the elites and those serving them. Because these elites constituted only a small proportion of the entire population, it is normal that feasting refuse would be less abundant compared with other locations where the rest of the population gathered to celebrate such events as the summer or winter solstice.

Rather than viewing stone versus wood structures as representing death versus life cults, it seems more consistent to view stone versus wood as representing elite versus common structures, with the different amounts of feasting refuse reflecting the relative proportions of elites versus commoners in the general population. Wood was used to construct Woodhenge because it was cheaper than stone and easier to use in roofing over a large area to accommodate hundreds of people. If Woodhenge was the equivalent of later feasting halls used by commoners, it may well be that elite and common ancestors were all fêted on the same day, in broadly similar fashions, but simply in different locations. If this was the case, then Woodhenge would be equally involved in ancestral cults, just as Freedman (1961) described commoner ancestor cults of the Chinese as separate from the much more lavish ancestral shrines and feasting halls of the elites. On the other hand, there may have been other religious themes played out at Woodhenge. It may have simply been a general public building for any kind of open, public ritual event, feast, or gathering. It certainly seems to have been large enough to accommodate very large numbers of people (Fig. 7.19). A similar contemporaneous woodhenge also occurs near the great stone circle at Avebury, and the same feasting debris pattern obtains there as well. Other stone circles, such as the Ring of Brodgar in the Orkney Islands (Fig. 7.8) or the Callanish circle in the Hebrides Islands, may or may not have solar alignments, but it seems highly probable that they, too, would have been part of an elite ancestor cult on the basis of what we can infer about Stonehenge.

Is the view of Stonehenge as an elite cult center realistic? I think it is. This picture of Stonehenge fits in very well with the tradition that was established by Upper Paleolithic elites using caves for secret society rituals, the restrictive use of megalithic passage graves, and the later exclusive use of the largest temples by kings and elites. The largest temple in the Aztec empire was reserved exclusively for use by Montezuma, and the inner sanctum of the great temple at Luxor in Egypt was reserved for the exclusive use of the pharaoh. In all cases, we find that the largest and most lavish temples were commissioned by the elites, built with elite resources, and used exclusively by the elites.

Fig. 7.19. Wood-
henge is located
only 3 kilometers
from Stonehenge
and was used at
the same time (see
Fig. 7.10). It was
probably a large
covered wooden
structure used pri-
marily for feasting
and rituals, per-
haps by nonelite
members of the
chiefdom. It is
more likely that
the highest-
ranking members
of the elite would
have celebrated
rituals and feasted
at the more im-
pressive site of
Stonehenge. From
R. Atkinson,
*Stonehenge and
Neighbouring
Monuments*, p. 35.
London:
H.M.S.O., 1978.

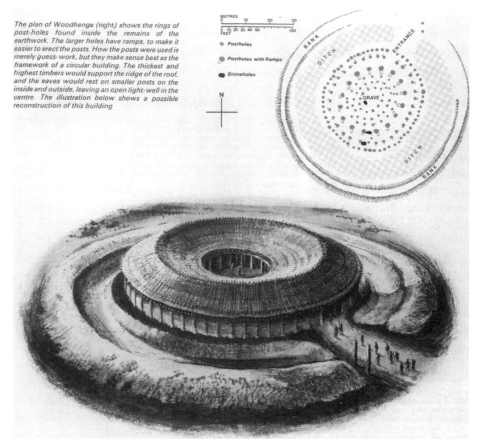

The plan of Woodhenge (right) shows the rings of post-holes found inside the remains of the earthwork. The larger holes have ramps, to make it easier to erect the posts. How the posts were used is merely guess-work, but they make sense best as the framework of a circular building. The thickest and highest timbers would support the ridge of the roof, and the eaves would rest on smaller posts on the inside and outside, leaving an open light-well in the centre. The illustration below shows a possible reconstruction of this building

OTHER ASPECTS OF MEGALITHIC CULTS AND CULTURE: SEX, POWER, AND VIOLENCE

As we have seen, ancestor cults dominated megalithic societies in Europe, but it seems reasonable to view the everyday domestic fertility cults as continuing to exist along with varying levels of shamanism. In chiefdom societies, the higher-level shamans probably ministered to the elite cults and perhaps elite secret societies. Lower-level shamans prob- ably helped to heal commoners. However, except for the entoptic images in the passage graves and occasional burials with ritual paraphernalia, there is little direct evidence of shamanism in the Neolithic. Priests who did not enter into ecstatic states but followed set liturgies may have taken over many of the shamans' former ritual functions.

In the realm of megalithic symbols among elites, axes were given phallic symbolic meanings and used as grave offerings sometimes in association with rings indicating fe- male genitals (Fig. 7.20; see also Patton 1991). Almost the same practice characterizes axe-using groups in New Guinea even today (Hampton 1999). In the European Neo- lithic, axes can be inferred to have had special ritual and prestige values on the basis of the special types of rock they were made from (including jadeite), the long distances they were traded, their inclusion in high-status burials, their use as offerings, often burned (Karsten 1994:189ff; Stafford 1999:127; Larsson 2000a, 2000b), their manufac- ture at large enclosed ritual sites like Dösjebro in Sweden (Svensson 2002:46–49), and their prominence as megalithic art motifs. The only clear evidence that we have of feasting is associated with funerary monuments or monuments like Woodhenge, for which no clear religious symbolism has been established.

The great animal cults of the Paleolithic and earlier Neolithic seem to have become subsidiary aspects of the ancestral cults although there are still some striking representations of these animals, especially in France, Malta, and Iberia (Joussaume 1988:73, 96, 116, 119, 176, 222). Cattle and other domestic animals must have continued to play an important symbolic role in ritual life, being required for the most important ritual sacrifices and used as forms of wealth to obtain wives, settle compensation payments, make peace, and obtain allies.

Some megalithic constructions like Gavrinis near Carnac also seem to have been built not as tombs but as specially decorated sanctuaries without burials (Joussaume 1988:90, 96, 118). These are probably the best indications that we have at present for the existence of elite-controlled secret societies other than elite ancestor cults. Only elites could have organized the construction of these lavish ritual edifices, and they were clearly intended for use by small numbers of people. Like some of the decorated cave sanctuaries of the Upper Paleolithic, these Neolithic sanctuaries seem best-suited for secret society rituals.

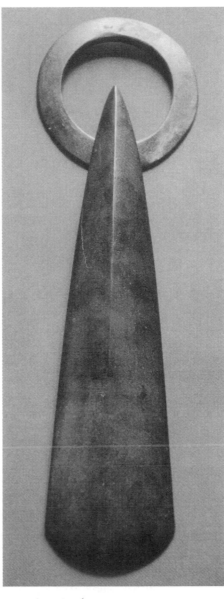

Fig. 7.20. One of the greatest finds of the nineteenth century in France was this jade bracelet and polished axe blade from Mané er Hroëk near Carnac. The jade must have come from the Alps, some 800 kilometers away. The forms may have had sexual connotations or symbolic meanings. Many of these prestige axes had never been used or were too thin to be functional but were closely associated with high-ranking males. From G. Bailloud, C. Boujot, S. Cassen, and C.-T. Le Roux, *Carnac, Les Premières Architectures de Pierre,* p. 116. Paris: CNRS, 1995. Courtesy of the Musée des Beaux-Arts de Vannes.

We have already discussed the major symbolic themes of megalithic societies as they have been represented in the archaeological record of the British Isles. On the Continent, megaliths can be grouped into broad regional art styles with many of the art motifs displaying evident connotations of power and authority. Joussaume (1988:116, 119) notes that war paraphernalia often accompanied the dead of western France. The major art motifs in this region consisted of axes, rayed circles (suns), arcs, crooks, boats, snakes, and "shields." Crooks are generally assumed to have been symbols of authority and are often associated with sunburst images (Joussaume 1988:119, 123, 203–5). At Locmariaquer, near Carnac, four rows of crooks pointing left and right surround a blazing sun in their midst (Joussaume 1988:119). The message seems clear: Those who carry crooks

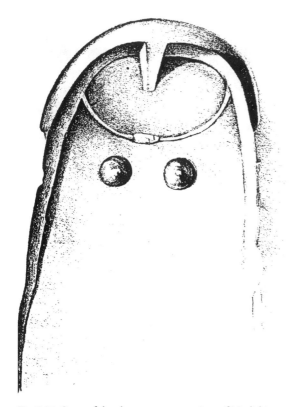

Fig. 7.21. Some of the clearest representations of Neolithic goddesses or ancestral spirits occur in megalithic tombs of the Paris basin and surrounding areas. This example is from Champagne and, like most of these figures, she clearly displays a neck ring, or torc, probably indicating her elite status. These figures occur only in the Late or Final Neolithic period. From J. de Baye, *L'Archéologie Préhistorique,* p. 164. Paris: Leroux, 1880. (See also Villes 1998).

also carry the power of the sun as well as the authority of the ancestors entombed in the graves with the sculptures. This is simply a variation on a theme well established at Newgrange, Maes Howe, Stonehenge, and other monuments. Crooks also appear as symbols of power and divinity in southeast Europe, where there

is even a crook made of copper dating from 5000 B.C.E. (Gimbutas 1973b:167–68). Crooks appear to be symbols associated with men or male deities or ancestors, as are axes, serpents, and horned figures (Bailloud et al. 2001:97). Perhaps they represent herding roles, not only herders of cattle, but perhaps of men or even all creatures.

Clearly female symbols occur less frequently. But sculptured, faceless female breasts, usually with necklaces, occur on three late Neolithic menhirs or carved stones in the Brittany area and are slightly more common in the Paris basin megalithic tombs (Fig. 7.21). Interestingly, these representations are always on the left of the antechamber entrance to the tomb (Joussaume 1988:74, 82, 120, 122, 132, 141), possibly reflecting a directional association similar to that displayed in the ancestral shrines at Çatal Hüyük in Anatolia. Axes and axe representations are always in the main tomb chamber (Patton 1991:69). In regions bordering the Paris basin, both male and female sculptures appear as tomb guardians or ancestors. They seem to represent complementary concepts as at Çatal Hüyük (Villes 1998:34, 37, 44). In France, the female representations are often called the Goddess of the Dead. There are no representations of any goddesses in Britain or Ireland, where the sun and axes are the dominant art motifs (Burl 1976:83). In both the British Isles and in France, there are abstract symbols and lines, frequently in the shape of diamonds. Interpreting the meanings of these symbols is much more subjective and problematical.

What does emerge from the above review of megalithic ritual is the central role of symbols of authority: the crooks, the axes, the suns, the bulls, the shields. Boats may have also been symbols of wealth or authority. Axes were not only the principal tools used by men for clearing forests, but they were also weapons of war. Axes were extremely valuable wealth items as well, sometimes made so long (up to 46 cm) and thin that they could be used only for prestige displays (Figs. 7.11, 7.20; see also Patton 1990, 1991). They were also sometimes made of valuable types of stone traded from long distances. In addition to being one of the most frequent art motifs, axes were frequent grave goods in the ancestral tombs. They thus seem to have been strongly associated with the ancestors both in art and in reality. Axes also appear associated with solar symbolism in some areas (Burl 1976:81). Similar uses and symbolism occur in New Guinea, where axes are closely associated with woodworking, warfare, wealth exchanges, rituals, men, and ancestors (Pétrequin and Pétrequin 1993; Hampton 1999).

As we have seen, representations of a goddess are certainly present, although they are infrequent and her role is not as clear as the fertility images of women in the Neolithic of the Near East. It is entirely possible that the goddess depicted in megalithic tombs was revered as a matrilineal ancestor or as the guardian of the dead and of rebirth or fertility. If so, descent or inheritance was probably traced through the female line, as it is among some tribal groups like the Rhadé in Vietnam, where breasts are carved on the entrance ladders to longhouses—presumably the breasts of the matrilineal ancestors. Anyone mounting Rhadé house ladders is encouraged to touch the carved breasts for good luck and prosperity (Fig. 7.22).

Fig. 7.22. In traditional Rhadé longhouses, like the one pictured here in Vietnam, the steps of the main entrance led up to a pair of female breasts carved in wood, which people were supposed to touch upon entering the house in order to obtain good luck. In most agricultural societies "good fortune" is strongly associated with fertility. The Rhadé are matrilineal and so the breasts probably depict ancestral founding mother's breasts. Photo by B. Hayden.

Whether most European Neolithic communities were organized along patrilineal or matrilineal lines is difficult to determine. On the one hand, there are many female figurines in eastern Europe and there are carvings of breasts in some areas of France and Switzerland (Clutton-Brock 1991). These certainly seem to reflect a concern and reverence for fertility or female ancestors. On the other hand, most agricultural societies are patrilineal, especially those in which herding is a dominant activity (Hutton 1991:18). However, societies in which men are away for prolonged times, either trading or raiding in distant lands, are far more likely to develop matrilineal forms of inheritance (Harris 1975:347–48). Even here, and in the case of strong fertility cults, males may dominate, as they dominate goddess-centered fertility cults in New Guinea (Lawrence and Meggitt 1965:15; Feil 1987:221; Wiessner and Tumu 1998:318). Brothers generally are the ultimate authorities in most matrilineal societies, such as the Rhadé of Vietnam or the Northwest Coast Tlingit (Blackman 1982:50; Hayden, field notes), even if women take on important roles in running everyday household affairs.

Certainly, there seems to be more equality between the sexes in some matrilineal societies than in the more staunchly patrilineal tribal or chiefly societies. In the Neolithic, there is little to tell what the relative status of the sexes was other than grave goods and sculptures. Grave goods vary considerably from region to region. In the British Isles and in Brittany, high-status, rich graves tend to be those of older adult males (Hutton 1991:81–83; Patton 1990). This is also the case in many areas of eastern Europe (Sherratt 1976), although there are some cases where females seem to have had richer graves than males, perhaps reflecting matrilineal social organization (Skomal 1986:181). Thus, the determination of sexual roles during the Neolithic is very complex, and it may be many years before any real pattern is evident or any consensus is reached.

However, it seems fairly evident that megalithic society was organized in a hierarchical fashion with major power vested in big men or chiefs and their supporting elites. The sheer size of the megalithic constructions and all that they imply concerning control over labor attest to this. The burial goods and symbols of power attest to this. The highly selective burial of individuals and the restricted space for ritual participants attest to this. The occurrence of major henge or enclosure centers such as Stonehenge and Avebury governing large expanses of territory attests to this (Fig. 7.23). The high degree of craftsmanship displayed in the creation of prestige and ritual items attests to this (Fig. 7.11). Finally, the human sacrifices at the henge monuments, in the burials, and elsewhere attest to great power (Hutton 1991:81–83; Schulting 1998a). In this regard, the seated corpses attached to megalithic tomb walls described by Joussaume (1988:100, 116, 176) may have been sacrificial victims meant to accompany their lords. Sacrifices, above all, indicate a high degree of hierarchical power within a society.

Given the prevalence of conflict and warfare among ethnographic chiefdoms in general and in view of the especially common occurrence of raiding among herding societies (see Chap. 8), one might well expect European megalithic society to have been involved in raids or warfare on a relatively frequent basis. In fact, the archaeological record seems to reflect just such a situation. The emphasis on war paraphernalia (axes, maces, and shields) in both megalithic art and grave goods belies a preoccupation with defense and offense. Violent deaths certainly occurred during this period and are represented in megalithic burials as well as in areas without megaliths (Joussaume 1988:29, 60, 64; Hutton 1991:18–19; Cauwe 2001a:100–102).

Rick Schulting (1998a:277–86) provides a useful summary of evidence for violence in the Neolithic. Schulting points out that for the *early and middle* Neolithic there is evidence of violent death for over 20 individuals in Denmark (see also Bennike 1999:29; Koch 1999:129) and 60 individuals in the British Isles, or about 5–10 percent of analyzed skeletons. A more recent analysis of 350 early Neolithic skulls in Britain revealed that 7.4 percent had head injuries (Schulting 2002). How many more of these same individuals may have died from injuries below the head? In Sweden, human sacrifices in the Neolithic are not uncommon and there is at least one good case of scalping (Karsten 1994:194; Larsson 1998:73; 2000b:183–84). These included possible bog sacrifices, house abandonment sacrifices, and burned sacrifices. In Germany and Austria, there were at least three mass graves representing probable massacres of entire villages (see also Hoffman 1971). In addition to the massacre at Talheim (Fig. 6.7), Cauwe (2001a:102) also notes an estimated one thousand massacre victims thrown into the defensive ditches of a Linearbandkeramik (early Neolithic) village near Herxhheim, Germany, and another 60 in the ditches at Schletz in Austria. As Cauwe notes, these events largely coincided with an increase in the importance of trade and the manufacture of prestige items.

Aside from such massacres, men overwhelmingly seem to have been the victims of violence. The indications include arrowheads embedded in bones, decapitations, cut marks indicating cannibalism and sacrifices, skull injuries, and parry fractures. The evidence has led authorities such as Stuart Piggott to suggest that cannibalism and head-hunting were part of life from the *early* Neolithic onward. The skeletal evidence indicates that at least 5–10 percent of these populations died violently. There are other indications of warfare as well. Clubhead maces are relatively common (96 in Denmark alone), and arrowheads seem to have been used primarily for war rather than hunting. There are at least 20 known palisaded or defended sites in the British Isles (many from the early Neolithic), plus numerous forts in Central Europe, Germany, and France, where sites were being chosen for their defensive locations during the middle Neolithic (Schulting 1998a; Howell 1987:120ff; Pavúk 1991; Wainwright 1979:241; Grygiel and Bogucki

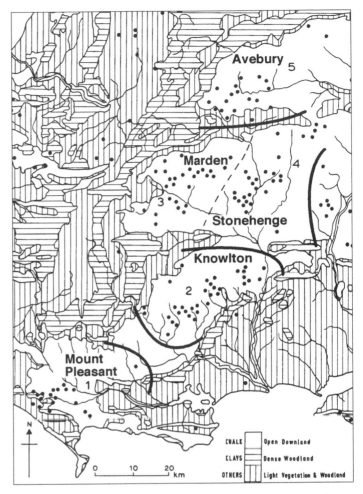

Fig. 7.23. In southern England, long barrows are distributed almost exclusively in chalk lands that would have been ideal for creating pasture for raising cattle. The long barrows additionally are grouped into clusters, each of which was dominated by a major ceremonial enclosure such as Stonehenge and Avebury. These centers and their surrounding barrow clusters are generally interpreted as separate chiefdoms or tribal alliances. Adapted from C. Renfrew, "Monuments, Mobilization and Social Organization in Neolithic Wessex." Adapted from C. Renfrew, ed., *The Explanation of Culture Change,* p. 546. London: Duckworth Publishers, 1973.

1997; Andersen 1997:277). To Schulting's list can be added other instances of violence in the Neolithic, such as two arrow-shot victims in Germany (Ortner 1991), another case from the Grotte Bibiche in Belgium, another case from Porsmose in Denmark (Fig. 6.7), and the cannibalization of 22 people at the megalithic site of Fosie in southern Sweden (Bradley 1993:95).

Schulting concludes that while the traditional view has been of gradually increasing levels of conflict from the beginning to the end of the earlier Neolithic, the growing evidence of conflict even in the earliest phases of the Neolithic period may simply indicate that the type of conflict, rather than its intensity, changed. Indeed, as the Neolithic progressed, fortifications became more and more common in England, while in France, many fortified sites have been identified, typically at the apex of local settlement hierarchies (Scarre 1984a:242; 1984b:335; Evans and Rasson 1984:720).

Overall, the picture that emerges of European megalithic society and religion is fairly typical of chiefdoms as we know them from the ethnographic literature. Chiefdom polities encompass several thousand to several tens of thousands of people; they are based on fairly abundant surplus resources and the generation of wealth through exchanges and feasting; they emphasize the importance of elite ancestors in rituals and monumental architecture; they are highly competitive and emphasize the display of success through wealth or monumental architecture; they are hierarchical and usually have slaves and human sacrifices; and they tend to be expansive and combative. Because of their competitiveness, political reigns tend to be relatively unstable, and chiefly families are not infrequently unseated by rivals. Such overthrows of elite rulers may account for the intentional breakage of carved megaliths and stelae noted in Brittany and their reincorporation into the funeral monuments of other elites (Joussaume 1988:119).

Southeastern Europe Serves as a Touchstone for Modern Ideals

From the time of Bachofen, who first popularized the idea of prehistoric matriarchies in 1861 in his book *Mother Right,* to Neumann (1963), who renewed the argument, and up to the present, there have been people who have postulated the existence of utopian matrifocal societies where women ruled in egalitarian harmony, settled their differences without recourse to warfare, and nourished the production of art, all under the aegis of a patron mother goddess. Subsequent archaeological, historical, and ethnographic research has not been kind to the concept that such matrifocal, matrilineal, or matriarchal societies existed in the ancient Mediterranean or Near East or anywhere else in the world (Hutton 1991:338). Even the concept of a great goddess was largely a nineteenth-century romantic invention of German scholars who felt that such a goddess should be part of pure prehistoric religions (Hutton 1997).

The most notable proponents of these utopian ideas in recent years have been Marija Gimbutas and a number of popular writers that she has inspired (Gimbutas 1989a, 1989b, 1991; Eisler 1987; Orenstein 1990; Spretnak 1992; Gadon 1989; Stone 1976). One recent variation on this theme is Shlain's (1998) claim that writing caused the collapse of utopian matriarchies and ushered in dominating patriarchal societies. Gimbutas originally argued her case on the basis of a Neolithic "Old Europe" culture tradition that she initially defined as comprising the Balkan peninsula and adjoining parts of central

Europe and the Aegean. She later extended this to encompass virtually all of Europe. Gimbutas's concepts of the European Neolithic were developed at a time when it was still fashionable to portray the Neolithic as a peaceful, egalitarian culture of small, self-sufficient communities living harmoniously in nature. We have already seen that the archaeological evidence for Western Europe and the Near East does not support the idea of an egalitarian or particularly peaceful Neolithic society. Whether Neolithic society was matrilineal or patrilineal, matrifocal or patrifocal, or somewhere in between is difficult to determine, but at present, there is scant archaeological support for either matrifocality or a pantheon dominated by a mother goddess. What we see is evidence of a typical chiefdom with a typical emphasis on ancestral cults strongly associated with solar deification. If Western Europe does not support the notion of a utopian Neolithic society, how does the heartland of Old Europe fare in an archaeological assessment of Gimbutas's ideas?

There certainly are many female figurines in this area and many very artistic creations. Some areas appear to be more peaceful than others. There undoubtedly was some form of commonly revered fertility goddess who may have exhibited varying other characteristics according to different local traditions, just as there was in the PPNB cultures of the Near East. However, this is only one component of what was almost certainly a much more complex religious and cultural ensemble. Maxim-Alaiba (1993), for instance, has pointed out that many of the "goddess" figurines in Old Europe sites were probably part of pairs of male-female figurines representing ancestral couples and ancestral cults. Similar observations have been made by Ian Hodder (2000:11) concerning rituals and beliefs at Çatal Hüyük and by Hood (1971:131–32) for Minoan Crete, while Özdogan (1999:234–35) noted that the first deity represented in southern Turkey was masculine.

Whereas the wealth of the Neolithic elites to the west was expressed in the construction of awesome stone, wood, and earth structures in conjunction with large-scale feasts, the wealth of Old Europe was largely expressed in the production of highly crafted prestige goods such as pottery, jewelry, sculptures, and the first metal ornaments of copper and gold (Fig. 7.24). Such high levels of specialization and craftsmanship are characteristic of chiefdom and more complex societies. In reading Gimbutas's and derivative popular accounts, the emphasis on beauty-loving, art-producing cultures of Old Europe often carries the flavor of the Western Industrial ideal of people creating art for art's sake. As we saw earlier, sophisticated, artistic craft products do not simply appear spontaneously as the results of creative human urges. Rather, specialized crafts must be supported by patrons who control surpluses. Great art requires great surpluses, and this is predicated on the existence of elites who can accumulate inordinate amounts of surpluses in their own hands. Elites obtain control over surpluses by establishing hierarchies or heterarchies with substantial control over resources and labor. There can be no question that Old European elites were producing fine art and loved beautiful things. But this should not be over-idealized. It should be viewed for what it was: an elite strategy for social control that involved the production of attractive prestige goods. Such prestige goods motivated people to participate in the elite credit and debt system, just as they do today. If these lavish items were used in ritual, this does not mean that Old European groups were any more religious or art-loving than other groups; it simply means that ritual items were being used as symbols of wealth and power and success in the same way that

medieval monarchs used gold crosses and church embellishments and that megalithic chiefs used menhirs, henges, and passage graves.

Large populations and large settlements for the residence of chiefs and their attendants also characterize chiefdoms. Settlement hierarchies are considered to be critical characteristics of chiefdoms by many archaeologists (Johnson 1973:2). In Old Europe, there are certainly some very large settlements at the top of settlement hierarchies, the largest reaching a staggering 300 hectares (Anthony 1995:94; Milisauskas and Kruk 1989; Demoule and Perlès 1993; Dinu 1993). However, instead of chiefs ruling from funerary and feasting centers like Newgrange and Stonehenge, the Old European elites ruled from centers for the production of prestige goods rather than centers of cattle production and exchange. Old southeastern Europe seems to have thrived on an almost marketlike exchange of elite prestige goods rather than on cattle production (Russell 1993:58–65, 470; Chapman 1991). Given our current archaeological and ecological understanding, it is inconceivable that Old Europe, with its large settlements and production of prestige goods, could have functioned on an egalitarian basis, and Dinu (1993) even argues that

Fig. 7.24. Toward the end of the Neolithic some communities in the Balkans began to produce extremely sophisticated luxury items including ones made of copper and gold. Powerful elites were buried in magnificent costumes decorated with gold disks, armlets, and beads. This burial at Varna is exceptional not only in terms of the quantity of gold items buried with this man, but also because of the gold collared mace that he holds in his right hand and a unique gold penis sheath found in his genital area. There is little doubt that some men were powerful figures in this society, a conclusion that is far removed from the egalitarian and nonhierarchical kind of society envisioned for this time period by some popular writers. From A. Sherratt, "The Transformation of Early Agrarian Europe," in B. Cunliffe, ed., *The Oxford Illustrated Prehistory of Europe,* p. 197. Oxford: Oxford University Press, 1994. Courtesy of the Varna Museum, Bulgaria.

patriarchal societies began in Old European cultures rather than being brought in by invaders. The lavish burials at Varna and Duronkulak in Bulgaria (Fig. 7.24) were filled with gold. They hardly represent an egalitarian society (Anthony 1995; Chapman 1991; see also Chokadzieu 1995). Moreover, as in Western Europe, there is considerable evidence for human sacrifice in Old Europe, most importantly in Minoan Crete and Italy, where children were apparently cut up for ritual sacrifices or perhaps even cannibalistic meals and young men seem to have been sacrificed on altars like young bulls (Warren 1984; Villa 1992; Villa et al. 1986; Skeates 1991:126–27; Schulting 1998a; but see Branigan 1982).

The most remarkable of these reports came from a mountaintop Minoan shrine, where excavators claim that an 18-year-old youth had been placed on the temple altar, trussed up like a young calf, and bled to death. However, at that point, the excavators claim that a catastrophic earthquake shook the temple and caused the roof, walls, and altar to collapse, killing four of the officiating attendants in the process. One woman was crushed as she was fleeing from the scene with a large ritual jar in her hands, perhaps containing blood from the victim (Sakellarakis and Sapouna-Sakellaraki 1981). Not all archaeologists are convinced of the accuracy of all of these details. But, needless to say, sacrificial rituals can hardly be viewed as consistent with egalitarian, peaceful societies. They are the supreme form of hierarchical domination.

In general, when profits and fortunes are to be made from exchange, warfare is viewed as disruptive and undesirable (Hayden 1995:53). Thus, warfare tends to be attenuated in societies that indulge extensively in wealth exchanges, although it is never really eliminated. This may well have been the case in the heart of Old Europe. There is recurrent evidence, however, of some conflict in the form of both fortifications and violent deaths from the beginning of the Neolithic onward (Schulting 1998a; Keeley 1996; Milisauskas 1986:787; Milisauskas and Kruk 1989; Webster 1990:343; Demoule and Perlès 1993). Even in Crete and Thera, frescoes show soldiers standing near palaces or going off to war in boats (Marinatos 1993:59, 244). As in Western Europe, weapons were used in Crete as symbols of high status, and some sanctuaries were dominated by offerings composed of weapons and male figurines (Marinatos 1993:125), perhaps an aspect of Minoan secret warrior societies. In any case, the relative peacefulness of Old European cultures, if established, would make more sense as the result of practical commercial decisions rather than cognitive factors such as goddess worship or rule by women. Women such as Queen Victoria, Elizabeth I, and Catherine the Great have presided over some of the most expansive militaristic empires in history, and ideology, no matter how nobly formulated, has never prevented groups from going to war or persecuting minorities, as Western history amply demonstrates.

Minoan Religion Reaches toward an Elite Utopia

Gimbutas and her followers have made much of the depictions of goddesses and priestesses in Minoan art in order to bolster their ideas of matrifocal and goddess-dominated cultures in Old Europe. It is, therefore, worth reviewing Minoan religion in some detail, for it is one of the most spectacular archaeological records of religion that has been unearthed. We are fortunate that Nano Marinatos (1993) has conducted a major synthesis of Minoan religion on the basis of archaeological discoveries. The periods most relevant for this discussion are the Prepalace period (2900–2000 b.c.e.) and the Palace period (2000–1450 b.c.e.). The Prepalace culture may have developed in place or come from elsewhere, but it displays strong influences from Anatolia, Egypt, and North Africa. A very lucrative trade seems to have developed with these areas, based on the surplus pro-

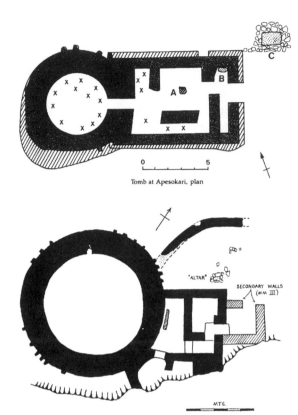

Tomb at Apesokari, plan

Fig. 7.25. In Crete, early burial chambers were built in a different style from the megalithic tombs of Western Europe; however, the basic idea of building a collective tomb for families wealthy enough to do so, and of holding ancestral rituals or feasts at regular intervals in front of the tombs in order to commemorate powerful ancestors, is the same pattern that is found at megalithic tombs. The top example is at Apesokari, the bottom example is at Kamilari. From N. Marinatos, *Minoan Religion,* Figs. 19, 20. Columbia: University of South Carolina Press, 1993.

duction of grapes (wine) and olives (oil). Minoans undoubtedly also reaped generous profits by acting as seafaring middlemen in the area's exchange network. As we have seen previously, the control of valuable agricultural lands that produce trade surpluses constitutes conducive ecological conditions for the development of strong and richly embellished ancestor cults. Not surprisingly, Marinatos concludes that the Prepalace religion of Crete largely revolved around funeral and tomb cults, as is consistent with everything else that we know of the richer Neolithic centers elsewhere in Europe and the Near East.

Tombs were built of carefully shaped stone blocks and were meant to be impressive monuments (Fig. 7.25). As in the megalithic cultures farther to the west, copious feasting accompanied ancestor rituals at the grave sites (Fig. 7.26). Other aspects of the funerary rituals at these rich tombs included bull vessels, showing men hanging onto bull horns, and female-shaped vessels, probably representing a fertility or regeneration goddess or ancestor, perhaps playing the same role as the goddess represented in the antechambers of Parisian megalithic tombs and the Neolithic goddesses of the Near East. As Marinatos (1993:28–29) notes, bullfighting and wrestling between men was a feature of Egyptian funeral art, and similar practices seem to have been adopted by the early Minoans. The bull was probably a sacrificial and sport victim in a fashion similar to its role in Torajan funerals, that is, to help the dead achieve immortality, or perhaps even to help the dead be reborn, since the bull is commonly associated with growth, the sun, the underworld, and rebirth (Campbell 1969:297; Rice 1998:7, 57). In this role, the bull would be a natural complement to the invocation of a goddess of rebirth. As we saw in Chapter 5, the badgering of captive bears or other animals before sending them to their animal masters in the underworld or mountains has probably been an important aspect of some sacrificial rites since the emergence of transegalitarian hunter-gatherers, and it is probably the origin of the bullfighting tradition that has persisted into modern times. In the Minoan and Egyptian cases, the *symbolic* concept was extended so that the spirits of sacrificed animals could accompany human spirits to the nether realms. However, the *formal* meaning of these sacrifices was still the display of wealth and surpluses in the

Fig. 7.26. We are fortunate that Minoans on Crete recorded some of their ancestral offerings and feasts in graphic form. This scene of liquid (probably wine) and animal offerings to the ancestral statue and tomb (at far right) was painted on the Hagia Triada sarcophagus. From N. Marinatos, *Minoan Religion,* Fig. 27. Columbia: University of South Carolina Press, 1993.

form of sacrificed animals and the ability to control them by sporting with them and sacrificing them—something only elite families could do.

In the first Palace period (2000–1700 B.C.E.), "palaces" or elaborate ritual centers, were established where elites resided in comfort. With increases in wealth, even more material items and structures were devoted to ritual life. There are no indications of individual kings or queens, but this is not uncommon among chiefdoms or early states organized as heterarchies based on a number of elite families cooperating to exert political control. It is clear from Marinatos's data that much of the ritual life of the Palace period was an extension of the elite funeral cults in the preceding period. She notes that small feasting shrines are especially numerous in the palaces and that rulers seem to have legitimized their authority by monopolizing access to supernatural contacts with powerful ancestors or other deities (Marinatos 1993:98, 110)—a common theme in transegalitarian and stratified societies. As in other early states and complex chiefdoms, the collection of surpluses from the populace may have taken place on the pretext of needing supplies to host general feasts or to propitiate the gods or divine ancestors (Schmandt-Besserat 2001; Junker 2001; Kirch 2001), for there are large storage rooms and jars associated with the Minoan temples. The feasting rooms were very small and could only accommodate a few, select people (Fig. 7.27). The abundance and distinctive display nature of the Kamares Wares at Knossos show that feasting was a major preoccupation of the Minoan elites and was undoubtedly used in structuring political power, although couched in a ritual format (Day and Wilson 1998; Dietler 2001). Marinatos also argues that the "throne room" was most likely for cult dramatizations in which impersonators would appear as the cult deities.

Many of the concepts for costumes, deity impersonations, processions, libations, offerings, sacrifices, and dances seem to have been inspired by contacts with Syria (Marinatos 1993:145). In particular, the bull and the stone-sculpted "horns of consecration" resembling bucrania of the Near East play extremely prominent roles in the Palace period cults (Fig. 7.28). Earlier occurrences of horns of consecration occur all the way to Bahrain in the Persian Gulf and as early as 8000 B.C.E. at Hallan Çemi (Rice 1998:173; Rosenberg 1999:30, Fig. 9). Just as blood was poured onto stone stelae or slabs in the

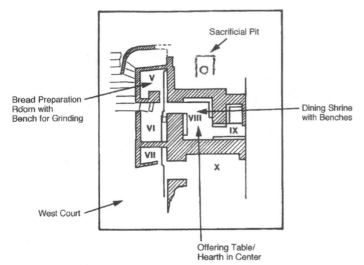

Sacrificial Pit

Bread Preparation
Room with
Bench for Grinding

Dining Shrine
with Benches

West Court

Offering Table/
Hearth in Center

Fig. 7.27. Inside Minoan palaces there were many shrine rooms, some of them quite small and only suitable for use by a small group of people, presumably for the most elite cults or the rituals of the most secret societies. Small shrines with pillars in their centers (such as the one pictured here from Knossos—bottom) recall some of the early Neolithic shrines with pillars in the Near East (e.g., Fig. 6.23; Qermez Dere also has a central pillar). Frequently, these shrine rooms were furnished with cooking and dining facilities undoubtedly for feasting, as in the example of the dining shrine from Phaistos (top). From N. Marinatos, *Minoan Religion,* Figs. 73, 74. Columbia: University of South Carolina Press, 1993. The central post of Austronesian houses (like those of Thai hill tribes) was also an axis mundi, where ancestors were venerated.

PPNB sanctuaries, blood was also poured onto the horns of consecration representing the most sacred objects for sacrifices (Marinatos 1993:207). Stone pillars also were central features in some Minoan shrines, just as stelae or slabs of stone were central features of PPNB sanctuaries. Horns of consecration are probably the most prolific symbol in Minoan ritual areas, and there is little doubt that they represent sacred bulls. Bulls are also strongly represented in sculptures and in paintings, including the famous ritual bull jumping scenes (Fig. 7.29). The bull seems strongly connected to elite ancestor cults, and Rice (1998:61, 68) argues that it became widely used as a universal and popular symbol of power, domination, and virility for elite purposes, just as the sun was being used by megalithic elites farther to the west. In fact, as we have noted earlier, the bull is often linked with the sun. Another common ritual symbol in Minoan culture is the double-headed axe, or labrys (visible in Figs. 7.26 and 7.30 bottom), which bears a striking resemblance to some battle axes of the Battle-axe culture farther north and contemporary with the Prepalace period (Fig. 7.31).

As is consistent with other elite cults, techniques for inducing ecstatic states seem to be attested in the images from this time, including ecstatic dancing (Warren 1984), drinking of wine, and possibly the use of psychotropic substances or more tra-

Fig. 7.28. "Horns of consecration" occur sporadically throughout the Middle East during the Neolithic in the form of bucrania or modeled stylized bull horns. However, in Minoan Crete, they become the principal icon indicating sacredness and connections with supernatural realms. They are clearly depicted adorning walls and roofs of temples at Zakros (above); forming the overall shape of shrines as well as being placed above and beside the entrance at Petsofas (bottom left); as the largest ritual objects on the altar of the Shrine of the Double Axes at Knossos (bottom center); and as the foci where deities appeared to mortals as in this seal from Kydonia (right). From these contexts, it appears that the horns of consecration probably functioned as axis mundi. Their use may be derived from early Neolithic practices as shown in Figs. 6.22 and 6.27. From N. Marinatos, *Minoan Religion,* Figs. 85, 86, 160, 228. Columbia: University of South Carolina Press, 1993.

ditional ecstasy-inducing techniques. Human sacrifice and possibly cannibalism were probably added to this ritual repertory as a further means of disrupting and disorienting normal mental states during initiations into secret societies or for special rituals (Warren 1984). Cannibalistic rituals certainly occurred in remote Neolithic caves during the French and Italian Neolithic (Villa et al. 1986; Skeates 1991), and these instances, too, probably formed part of elite or warrior secret society rituals much like the cannibal societies of Northwest Coast chiefdoms. In effect, the early Minoan "palaces" were primarily exclusive temples (and residences) for the elite, just as the Western European megalithic chamber tombs, the stone circles, and monumental temples elsewhere were probably constructed exclusively for elite use (Marinatos 1993; Day and Wilson 1998).

Fig. 7.29. The importance of bulls for Minoan rituals and ideology is nowhere more dramatically displayed than in the famous bull jumping fresco from the royal palace of Knossos depicted here. These specific practices seem to have originated from Egyptian funeral rituals involving bulls. From N. Marinatos, *Minoan Religion,* Fig. 57. Columbia: University of South Carolina Press, 1993.

Elites also established shrines and temples in remote locations. Some of the simpler examples of shrines may have been popular cult locations for honoring nature deities by the rural populace. The more elaborately built locations, however, were much more likely to have been constructed for the assembling of members of elite secret societies similar to remote early Neolithic ritual sites like Göbekli in the Near East. Some Minoan shrines are lavish and far from other habitations; often they are situated on mountaintops or in caves—ideal locations for secret society rituals. If we believe the excavators, there was good reason to keep some of these rituals secret, too, given the previously noted human sacrifices that occurred in some of these locations. The frequency of what appear to be initiation scenes for elite boys and girls in the Minoan centers (Marinatos 1993:203, 212) emphasizes the probable existence of elite secret societies.

On the basis of scenes of lavishly dressed or costumed women with bared breasts in frescoes, on carved seals, and on pottery, it is evident that women played important roles in many of the cult activities on Crete (Fig. 7.32). Bared breasts were possibly a part of ritual costumes rather than everyday dress, since nakedness and bare breasts are often associated with fertility and the dead ancestors who are associated with harvests and rebirth. Ancestors are often considered to be attracted to displays of fertility or sexual acts (Eliade 1958a:333–34, 349, 350, 355). That women would have played prominent roles in rituals and society is entirely in accord with what we know about the important role of trade and military campaigns in Minoan society. With men frequently being away for many months on sea voyages to Syria, Egypt, or North Africa, it is not at all surprising that they would have left family affairs in the hands of their sisters. Sisters, rather than wives, would have the best interests of their families and lineages at heart when any decisions had to be made. Wives would have married into families from other lineages and could have retained many more loyalties to their natal families rather than their husband's family. Thus, it seems entirely possible that Minoan society was matri-

Fig. 7.30. As depicted in these murals from Akrotiri (top) and Knossos (center and bottom), women often played major or leading roles in rituals and ideology. While both men and women participated in some rituals (center and bottom), other rituals seem to have been exclusively for women (top). Men may have been the exclusive or dominant participants in the more athletic rituals such as boxing and bull jumping (Fig. 7.29) and in the cave shrines where offerings of weapons are common. From N. Marinatos, *Minoan Religion*, Figs. 41, 213. Columbia: University of South Carolina Press, 1993.

lineally organized and became extremely affluent largely from middleman-trading enterprises that catered to the already established elites in Egypt and the Near East.

In evaluating claims for a matrifocal utopia in Old Europe, it is evident that the elite images from Minoan art create a picture of opulent beauty with elegant priestesses or goddesses. These images are wondrous to behold, veritable feasts for the eyes that bring to life a sumptuous society replete with beautiful women, magnificent landscapes, impressive temples and buildings, captivating rituals, and exotic scenes. There is much to

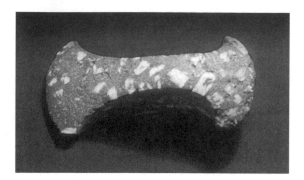

Fig. 7.31. The double axe, or labrys, symbol that is prominent in many Minoan ritual scenes may have originated from double axe forms in the Battle-axe cultures to the north of the Balkan region, where Minoans had trade contacts (see also Fig. 8.3). Photo by B. Hayden, courtesy of the Lund University Historical Museum.

be learned from studying these images alone. However, the images must be tempered with the more complete picture that is provided by examining all the archaeological evidence, together with the general trends in cultural development in neighboring regions. The Minoan frescoes portray the ideals of the elites and the important symbolical messages that the elites wanted to display. In the nonelite rural communities of the countryside, fertility goddesses were probably worshipped along with trees, snakes, and the moon (Willets 1965:42, 128–32).

The burial data cited previously indicates an overall heavier emphasis on rich authoritative males in the Old European area. In the fabulously wealthy graves at Varna and Duronkulak, the richest sexable graves are those of males (Anthony 1995; Chapman 1991). The highest-status burial was of a male and contained a remarkable amount of gold (Fig. 7.24). In his hand, he held a war adze or mace, and he wore a gold penis sheath (Chapman 1991; Renfrew and Bahn 1996:387). This is similar to the central European and Minoan practice of high-prestige weapons being buried with men, especially older men who were probably at the top of the socioeconomic hierarchy given their age (Keeley 1996). On the other hand, elite women were sometimes buried with substantial amounts of wealth as well, and in a few instances such as the Lengyel culture, women seem to have been slightly more richly buried than men, indicating possible matrilineal organization among these Old European societies (Skomal 1986:187).

All these observations provide a very different view of Neolithic Europe than the peaceful, artistic, egalitarian, matrifocal interpretations of Gimbutas. Additional critiques of Gimbutas's "paleopsychological" theories and interpretations have been presented by Meskell (1995), Eller (2000), Hutton (1991, 1997), Hayden (1986), Anthony (1995), and Chapman (1991). They criticize her deficient methodology, subjective interpretations, inability to explain why similar developments did not occur elsewhere (or why they occurred where they did), her ignoring of evidence that contradicts her theories, the lack of congruence between myth or god forms and sociopolitical realities in the real world, and the evidence for the in situ gradual transformation of Old European cultures into hierarchical warring polities during the Neolithic.

In addition to the previously mentioned problems involved in viewing Old Europe as a utopia, by focusing only on the idyllic human representations and opulent prestige items, the darker side of elite domination and power has been neglected, including the use of military force, the sacrificing of humans, the extraction of surpluses from the general populace, the transformation of extracted surpluses into prestige objects of domination, the dominating ideology of the bull and sacrifices, and evidence of conflict or warfare. Even the proto-writing system so often touted by Gimbutas and others as an example of enlightened civilization is simply another example of an accounting device

for recording elite wealth exchanges and transactions like those documented in the Near East
(Schmandt-Besserat 1986). Such record-keeping systems are not unexpected in trade-domi-
nated or large-scale feasting societies. If there
was a lower incidence of warfare in Minoan society, it was probably because of the central role
of trade profits in the economy and because of
the relatively protected location of Crete, being
isolated from enemy access by the open seas.

Minoan society may well have been matrilineal and it may have accorded relatively high
status to women, although ultimate authority
could have still resided with male members of
the families, as is the case elsewhere in the
world (Rosaldo 1974; Sanday 1981:165; Whyte
1978:167–68; Fluehr-Lobban 1979). However,
to claim that Old Europe was an idyllic, egalitarian, peaceful, goddess-dominated, matrifocal
society is a serious distortion of the archaeological and ethnographic evidence. Above all,
proponents of these views might be reproached
for displaying a naïve grasp of how traditional
societies actually function and the cultural me
chanics involved in producing prestige items or
monumental architecture. Such views are the
outgrowth of cognitive reverie rather than ecologically based reality. As John Chapman
(1991:154) observes, these utopian views do
not really help to explain why great concentrations of wealth accumulated at Varna but not
throughout all of Old Europe.

Fig. 7.32. Images of snake-wielding priestesses or goddesses,
although rare, are some of the most captivating depictions of
Minoan religious concepts that have been unearthed by
archaeologists. The women here may well be in ecstatic states.
The symbolism of the snakes has been the topic of a wide
variety of opinions. Ethnographically and historically, snakes
have been symbols for many things including evil, danger,
death, ancestors, the earth, the underworld, regeneration,
fertility, the phallus, guardians of the home, and rain. It is
therefore difficult to tell precisely what they represented for
Minoans. From N. Marinatos, *Minoan Religion*, Figs. 140,
141. Columbia: University of South Carolina Press, 1993.

Neolithic Europe Contributes to Contemporary Rituals and Classical Pantheons

We have already seen in Chapter 6 that a number of important, perhaps even archetypical, Neolithic symbols have persisted over the millennia and constitute the basis for
many of the most popular rituals of contemporary Western society, including Easter, the
resurrection of our gods, annual feasts for the dead, the making of corn dollies, bullfights, and the celebration of the spirit of the grain in the form of John Barleycorn. We
can now add our celebration of the New Year and Christmas, or more properly, Yule, to
the list.

Yule is a pagan solstice festival, and in popular symbolism today, it is still fundamentally a winter solstice celebration. The celebration of the birth of Christ was a relatively
recent addition. December 25 is almost certainly *not* the actual date of Christ's birth

(Miles 1912). Neolithic settlers, such as those who built Newgrange and Maes Howe, were the first people that we know of to have celebrated an astronomically based Yule. There is no doubt that the seasonal growth and enfeeblement of the sun played a central role in megalithic religious life. This solar cycle must have been intimately connected with the human birth and death cycle, the birth and death cycles of plants and animals, and the spiritual powers of the ancestors. The original winter solstice rites must have been a combination of the more modern Halloween and Yule themes. A large assortment of festivals, each with its own origin and calendar, are historically related to our own winter solstice celebration (Miles 1912). The essential theme of solar and life renewal undoubtedly began with the Neolithic or even earlier in hunter-gatherer transegalitarian cultures, though most of the detailed information that we have comes from historical times. Ethnographic complex hunter-gatherers such as the Thompson and Shuswap Indians of the interior of British Columbia used trees aligned with the rising position of the sun to determine the winter solstice date, which in turn determined their winter ceremonial feasts (Teit 1900:239, 1909:604, 610).

In the old days, calendars were not so precise as they are today, and so the celebration of astronomical events might vary slightly from century to century or place to place. The Roman New Year, the Kalends, was almost certainly supposed to celebrate the new solar year at some period of the past. Even in Roman times, it was a popular folk festival that extended over three days of feasting and general license. As Eliade (1963:51–52; 1959:78ff) notes, this return to chaos and the dissolving of social conventions is a common theme in many traditional rites of regeneration. It is necessary for a new birth of the world with new hopes of a better generation of life. We still carry out the dissolution of the old, usually with the help of alcohol and parties, and we still try to create a better new world with our New Year's resolutions. During the Roman Kalends festival, houses were decorated with evergreens and candles. Presents or good wishes were also exchanged between family and friends to encourage good fortune (Miles 1912:277). The Roman Saturnalia festival (December 17–23) was even more similar to the Neolithic winter solstice celebration, since it honored Saturn, the ancestor of the Roman gods, during whose reign everything was idyllic, probably very similar to the myths associated with founding ancestors of lineages and clans during the Neolithic. Saturn was portrayed as the jolly king of prosperity, joy, and justice. In his honor, the Romans engaged in much feasting, drinking, and singing. They also held processions as signs of good times under his reign, burned candles to welcome the new sun, and exchanged presents. While not all of these elements may have been part of the Neolithic celebrations, many of them may have been; and it is probable that the general flavor and meaning of the celebrations were very similar and that many of our own Yule traditions date back to the megalithic monument builders of 3000 B.C.E.

Late Neolithic society in southeastern Europe, however, has contributed even more to Western heritage than festivals. For the first time, it is possible to identify named deities that were worshipped and about which later writers recorded myths. Sometimes these stories have been obviously distorted by subsequent events that we shall deal with in the next chapter, but the underlying form of the myth is generally recognizable. The topic is a broad and complex one, but several examples will provide a basic idea of what these deities were like. By far, most of the recorded examples come down to us from early Greek writers and are derived from Greece and the adjoining regions. The Greeks invaded and took over the Old European centers around the Aegean Sea. They later recorded accounts about the earlier rulers and even adopted some of their deities.

The most famous and obviously pre-Greek myth is that of the Minotaur, a ferocious man-animal with the head of a bull. He was kept in a labyrinth of the palace of King Minos on Crete. Intriguingly, the Minotaur was the product of a union between Minos's queen and a sacred bull. Every year, the Greek cities subject to Minos had to deliver a tribute of seven young men and seven maidens who were to be given to the Minotaur as sacrifices to be eaten. A number of parallels have been drawn between this myth and archaeological facts. The association of the elites of Crete with bulls is well attested. The elite palaces on Crete resemble labyrinths. And it now appears that there were at least occasional human sacrifices and perhaps cannibalism in the Minoan palaces. In the Greek myth, the Minoan elites are ruthless and domineering. Such depictions may be accurate recollections of overbearing colonizing elites (which would be typical behavior in such situations), or these accounts may be tinged with political propaganda meant to justify the subsequent invasion of Crete by Athens. The overthrow of Crete's domination was led by Theseus—a mythological or historical figure who still features as a prominent constellation in our present-day maps of the stars.

Similarly, the Greek gorgon spirits like Medusa with their hair in the form of snakes appear to be derived from the often depicted snake goddess of Minoan religion (Warren 1984:49), while both Hera and Athena had typical Old European snake or bird associations (Robbins 1980) and the Minoan mistress of animals appears to have become the Greek goddess Artemis (Ginzburg 1991:127; Robbins 1980). Dionysus, Zeus, and Zagreus all seem to have originated in pre-Greek Old European pantheons and represented various fertility gods associated with bulls and ecstatic cults (Warren 1984:54; Sackett and MacGillivray 1989). It has been proposed that other fertility deities such as Demeter and Persephone are foreign to the dominant Greek pantheon as described in Homer and that they, too, have persisted from late Neolithic, Old European times (Nilsson 1940). In the case of Dionysian rituals, even during Greek times there was a strong underlying current of human sacrifice, as represented in Euripides' play *The Bacchae*.

Much less is known about the other Minoan or Old European deities. As Marinatos (1993:147) observes, there is a strong nature association in depictions of Minoan goddesses and priestesses. One of the most notable but rare representations is of a bare-breasted goddess or priestess entwined by snakes (Fig. 7.32), probably symbolizing fertility, rebirth, connections to the underworld and ancestors, or perhaps simply an ecstatic state (e.g., Whittlesey 1972). It may even be that snakes were part of ritual ecstatic images involving communication with ancestors similar to "vision serpents" that acted as communication conduits for elite Mayan men and women in ecstatic states (Fig. 11.5; see also Schele and Freidel 1990). However, there are many other various poses of goddesses or priestesses with bird features, or associated with dolphins, lilies, deer, goats, lions, monkeys, fish, or griffins, while some figures only had abstract forms for heads. With so much variation, it is impossible to tell if there was only a single goddess with many forms or whether there were many goddesses. Marinatos also suggests that many of the portraits of men or boys in the Minoan frescoes are actually depictions of gods, especially those with blue hair. Otherwise portrayals of masculine deities are fairly rare except in animal forms such as the bull. As we have seen, the portrayal of men or gods in animal guise and women or goddesses in nude or seminude human form is a ritual feature that dates back to the Upper Paleolithic and provides a continuous theme in early religions. On Crete there are a few representations of sacred couples, implying the persistence of the sacred union theme already noted for the Near Eastern Neolithic, where it is also relatively rare. In the next chapter, we will see how this entire pantheon of gods was transformed by the arrival of nomadic warrior groups with new interests and new types of resources that had predictable ecological effects on religious practices and concepts.

SUMMARY

In order to understand the religious developments that characterized the megalithic and rich trading centers of Europe during the Neolithic period, it is essential to understand how these societies operated and the kinds of strategies that were used by aggrandizers to concentrate power and wealth in their own hands enabling them to build megaliths and establish vast fortunes. These strategies are based on manipulating circumstances and people in order to gain control of surplus resources and labor. Transegalitarian, chiefdom, and early state organizations are all predicated on strategies such as bride prices, monopolization of the most productive resources, control of trade, compensation payments for deaths or injuries or transgressions, acquisition of allies, the use of force, peace payments, investment and wealth exchanges, exclusion of nonelites, and the creation of prestige items.

Creating special cults in which aggrandizer elites had exclusive access to supernatural powers was also an extremely common strategy for legitimizing inequalities in power or wealth, as well as for promoting changes in social values or practices that were beneficial to elites. Most commonly, these cults focused on elite ancestors promoted to positions of founders of entire communities, clans, or chiefdoms. Major building programs for temples and the acquisition of prestige ritual paraphernalia were justified to honor elite ancestors under the pretext of promoting prosperity for the community as a whole. While built by the populace at large, the interior of such temples, the rich ritual paraphernalia, and the best foods characteristically were only for the use of elites. This is a pattern found in Southeast Asian lineage houses as well as historically documented early state temples in Egypt and Mexico. This pattern explains why such early temples had small inner chambers only capable of accommodating a few people—a pattern that extends back to the earliest Neolithic sanctuaries, and even to the Upper Paleolithic cave sanctuaries.

Earlier in the twentieth century, it was popular to view megalithic and Neolithic society as being driven by idealistic social norms and enthusiastic religious beliefs. Stonehenge was conceived as being built out of religious zeal (Wernick 1973). The building of the great temples in Mexico was explained as "a chance to do something about poor crops" (Weaver 1972:75). The collapse of the great Olmec and Mississipian centers was thought to have occurred because people lost faith in the religious effectiveness of the elites (Heizer 1963). In this respect, archaeological explanations had not changed much in almost two hundred years, for in 1805, the Reverend George Barry had described the megalithic tombs of the Orkney Islands as having been built by members of a manic sect "inflamed almost to madness by the peculiar genius of their religion." These are all cognitively based explanations in which some belief inexplicably arises in a population and just as inexplicably spreads to everyone in a community to the extent that, for thousands of years, they devote enormous quantities of their time and labor and surpluses to building projects with no tangible advantages. Collapse of these centers is viewed as the inexplicable loss of belief in the religious system or its leaders. Such explanations confound and confuse the *symbolic* content with the *formal* material aspects of major building projects like those represented by the megaliths.

From the ecological perspective described in Chapter 1, we might expect that new religious ideas would be constantly generated by innovative and adventuresome individuals in most societies. While such individuals, and even their immediate families, might devote their own efforts to building a tomb or monument for their ancestors or for other purposes, how would they convince other people to help them, or even to copy them? Why would people continue to invest such large amounts of time and energy in projects over thousands of years if no demonstrably real benefits ever materialized from the supernatural realms? For such labor-demanding religious programs to develop, spread, and persist, ecologists argue that there should be real benefits associated with them. The benefits of becoming affiliated with a successful big man or a chief (and contributing to the worship of their ancestors) typically revolve around their ability to make loans, arrange marriages, provide privileges or training for one's children, permit access to resources, reduce penalties, protect followers from social predators, pay debts, acquire powerful military allies, and supply food in times of starvation. To be excluded from such powerful networks meant becoming marginalized within one's own society, if not eventual enslavement. Such systems were, however, entirely based on surplus production and creating wealth that was capable of motivating people to support aggrandizers through feasting and other uses of surpluses.

While the aggrandizers may have been initially supported because they were viewed as providing benefits for their constituents, aggrandizers increasingly pursued their own self-interest wherever possible and promoted the notion that their individual success was necessary for group success (Reay 1959:110–11, 129, 190, 192; Wiessner and Tumu 1999:xx, xxv; Earle 1998:158). In Western Europe, cattle and megaliths were the supreme expressions of surplus production and wealth. By that standard, megalithic monument builders were exceedingly rich and used much of their wealth to underwrite ancestral monuments and rituals that legitimized their authority, displayed their success, and attracted lucrative relationships. Erecting such a monument was very advantageous for ambitious aggrandizers. Similar tactics can still be observed today among the megalithic societies of Indonesia. Public religious life in these wealthy chiefly societies is heavily dominated by elite ancestor cults, almost to the exclusion of other types of rituals or cults. Stonehenge appears to reflect an innovative combination of an elite solar and ancestor cult. However, in Neolithic Europe, there is also some archaeological evidence of other elite secret society cults and common domestic fertility cults.

Developments in southeastern Europe follow a generally similar pattern to those in the megalithic areas of Western Europe, although the main form of wealth in these cultures is prestige goods rather than cattle, and formal architectural buildings take the place of megalithic constructions. An "Old European" cultural tradition was established in southeastern Europe toward the end of the Neolithic including the renowned Minoan culture of Crete. Many claims have been put forward that Old Europe was an egalitarian, peaceful, artistic, matrifocal, goddess-dominated culture. While these ideas may have seemed credible half a century or more ago, when they were formulated, it is evident from more recent advances in archaeological excavations and cultural reconstructions that such claims were highly idealized and distorted versions of what these cultures were actually like. Few archaeologists today would support Marija Gimbutas's notions about the nature of Old European society or culture. She did, however, provide a much firmer understanding for the dramatic events that appear to have brought the downfall of the great centers of civilization in this region, like Minoan Knossos on Crete as well as other centers of civilization such as the fabulously wealthy city of Troy on the other side of the Aegean Sea. The fall of Troy was described in vivid detail in Homer's *Iliad* and *Odyssey*—the oldest epic literature of Western civilization. To see how and why that war and many related battles unfolded, we turn the page to the next chapter in the development of prehistoric religions.

CHAPTER 8

Pastoral Nomads Turn
the World on Edge

He [Cuchulainn] trembled violently, from the soles of his feet to the highest strand of his hair. A red mist, like a fog of vaporised blood, rose off him and each strand of his hair became an electrified, impaling spike. As he stood upright, ready to climb into his chariot, a column of thick dark red blood spouted high into the air from the centre of his crown. . . . His eyes took off on journeys of their own, one inward, the other, outward. His mouth opened huge and red, gaping back to his throat's edge and his jaws gnashed together in bites that would kill a beast
Delaney 1989

This is a remarkable early description of the mythical hero of an Irish cattle raid. In this monstrous form, Cuchulainn was capable of prodigious feats (Fig. 8.1). The story reveals a great deal about pre-Christian culture and religion in Ireland during the first centuries before and after the beginning of the Common Era. Other examples of early writing, such as Homer's *Iliad* and the earliest Hindu sacred book, *The Rig Veda,* involve similar supernatural battles and feats of heroes, all rooted in historical events. These myths form an important core of what linguists and archaeologists refer to as Indo-European society and religion.

Indo-European is an enormous language family that is now spread over half of the globe. Some six thousand years ago, however, it was confined to a small group of speakers on the steppes north of the Black Sea, perhaps only a few thousand in total. The expansion of Indo-European languages and culture is one of the most remarkable stories of prehistory and is the focus of this chapter. This spread is largely synonymous with the spread of bronze technology in Europe. So with the Indo-Europeans, we leave the Neolithic behind and enter the Bronze Age—a transition that occurred between 4000 B.C.E. and 2500 B.C.E. in various parts of Europe.

The entire notion of language families, languages that are closely related to each other and presumably derived from the same ancestral language, is a relatively recent

Fig. 8.1. Heroic warrior figures capable of performing extraordinary feats through their supernatural and physical abilities characterize many early Indo-European myths and pantheons. The scene above from the Gunderstrup cauldron may not depict an exact event from the stories about Cuchulainn, but it is certainly consistent with the general flavor of these stories. From A. Duval. *L'Art Celtique de la Gaule au Musée de Antiquiquités Nationales,* Plate 47A. Paris: Editions de la Réuiobn des Musées Nationaux, 1989. See also Fig. 9.16.

concept. The idea that there was an Indo-European linguistic family began only about 1767 with James Parsons's musings on the similarities of certain words in various European languages. For instance, the word for "god" in Latin, *deus,* is similar to Italian and Spanish *dia* and *dios* and French *dieu.* The Greek name "Zeus" and the English word "day" come from the same root word *deiwos,* which carries connotations of gods dominating the skies and the days (Mallory 1989:9; Eliade 1959:120; 1978:189). Recognition that the ancient Indian language Sanskrit was closely related to European languages came a few decades later, and by the middle of the nineteenth century the existence and study of the Indo-European language family was firmly established.

The historical implications resulting from the study of Indo-European languages catapulted scholars into a protracted series of debates that are still among the most hotly contested issues in archaeology and linguistics today. Much of the heat generated in these arguments was engendered by nationalist concerns about where ethnic homelands were situated in the past and when ethnic groups arrived in their historical locations, for nations generally strive to justify their occupation of national territories (Dietler 1994). In order to identify these homelands, scholars attempted to reconstruct the ancient ancestral languages of Europe by identifying the words that they had in common, paying particularly close attention to words for various kinds of plants, animals, and geographical features. In doing so, they established a robust methodology that could also be used to reconstruct past social structure and religious life. The list of known Indo-European languages is long and comprehensive (see "Indo-European Languages").

A new political dimension has been added to the Indo-European foment in recent years by claims that Indo-European groups invaded Europe and brutally ended a European Neolithic utopia. Unfortunately, as J. P. Mallory (1989) has demonstrated, the archaeological data is generally not abundant or refined enough to be able to determine which of many competing interpretations best accounts for all aspects of the present distributions of Indo-European languages. There are a few widely accepted points of agreement, however, and I will summarize these briefly.

The ancestral, Proto–Indo-European (PIE) culture and language are generally thought to have developed sometime between 4500 and 2500 B.C.E. on the steppes north of the Black Sea in a region that later came to be known as Scythia (Fig. 8.2). Some authors would extend this homeland considerably farther to the northwest and to

INDO-EUROPEAN LANGUAGES

Major Branch	Member Languages
Anatolian	Hittite, Palaic, Luwian
Indo-Iranian	Avestan, Old Persian, Sanskrit, Pali, contemporary languages of Pakistan and northern India
Greek	
Italic	Oscan, Umbrian, Latin, contemporary Romance languages (French, Spanish, Romanian, Italian, Portuguese, Provençal, Catalan, Romansch)
Germanic	Scandinavian languages (Danish, Swedish, Norwegian, Icelandic, Faeroese), German, Netherlandic (Dutch, Flemish, Afrikaans), Frisian, English, extinct Gothic languages
Armenian	
Tocharian	(Spoken in Tarim Basin, Chinese Turkistan, in the later first millennium A.D.)
Celtic	Irish, Welsh, Manx, Breton, extinct Gaulish, Cornish
Balto-Slavic	Lithuanian, Latvian, Russian, Polish, Czech, Slovak, Serbo-Croatian, Bulgarian, Kashubian, Ukrainian, Belorussian, Lusatian, Serb, Slovene, Macedonian, Old Prussian
Albanian	

the east. Up until 5000–4000 B.C.E., the steppe grasslands of Eurasia were difficult to live in for agriculturalists, and even the few hunters and fishermen who originally inhabited the region were probably largely tethered to the riparian environments near rivers. The domestication of the horse and the invention of the wheeled wagon around this time changed the situation dramatically. Both the horse and the wagon made it possible to move much greater distances and to exploit much larger territories for good pasture and other resources. Moreover, by emphasizing cattle, sheep, and goats as economic staples, it was possible to move animals, people, and settlements over the landscape in order to avoid bad local conditions or to take advantage of distant pasture in its prime. These grasslands usually provided abundant fodder for many animals.

Proto–Indo-Europeans relied primarily on domesticated animals for their wool, hide, milk, and cheese as well as plowing the tough grasslands and transporting all their belongings. These were all parts of the "secondary products revolution" that occurred midway through the Neolithic (Sherratt 1981, 1983). Proto–Indo-Europeans took advantage of all the secondary products as well as the primary product, meat. With the horse and wagon, Indo-Europeans made living on the steppes an attractive and

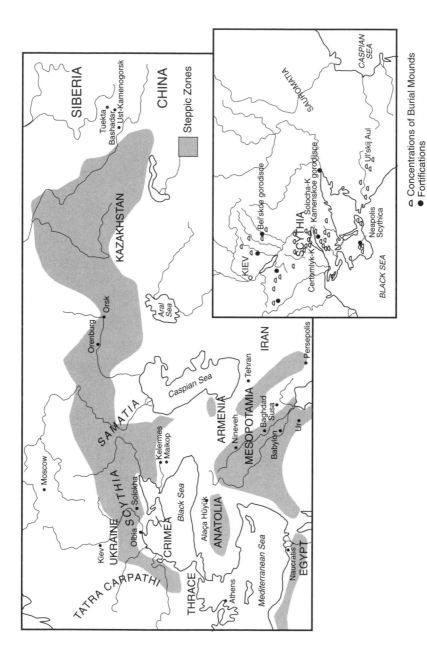

Fig. 8.2. This map shows the major areas of grassland steppe in the Near East and Asia as well as some of the ethnic groups referred to in the text. The area of densest kurgan burial mounds is shown in the inset and is thought to correspond to the Indo-European homeland by many authors. Adapted by Greg Holoboff from *From the Lands of the Scythians*, pp. 10–11. New York: Metropolitan Museum of Art, n.d.; and R. Rolle, *The World of the Scythians*, p. 12. London: Batsford, 1989.

worthwhile undertaking for the first time in human history (Anthony 1986). In effect, the secondary product technologies made pastoral nomadism possible. They opened up a new ecological niche, and the resources in this niche had their own distinctive characteristics, which shaped Indo-European society and religion as we shall see shortly. Indo-Europeans also had one other advantage, the use of metal weapons. At first, perhaps, they had only copper, but they soon acquired bronze, which was much more valuable and must have further enhanced the other effects of pastoral nomadism.

One of the most fundamental characteristics of this new pastoral steppe adaptation was the high mobility of groups. Given the vast open expanses of the Eurasian steppe (Fig. 8.2), it is not surprising that there was a rapid expansion of populations throughout the steppe extending even as far as western China, where remarkably preserved European types of bodies dating to the time of this diaspora have been preserved together with their clothing (Mallory and Mair 2000; Hadingham 1994). Throughout the steppes there was a high rate of interaction between groups, reflected by generally similar styles of artifacts and ritual practices. Some of these groups began coming into contact with the more settled agricultural communities of southeast Europe around 4000 B.C.E. Marija Gimbutas (1973a, 1973b) has been instrumental in developing some of the most widely accepted models for this interaction. She showed that there were intrusive groups from the steppes entering southeast Europe between 4000 and 3000 B.C.E. According to Gimbutas, their arrival precipitated the fortification of settlements and the collapse of many Old European centers. Similar events were transpiring in Anatolia, where early Indo-European Greeks were sacking the wealthy city of Troy. The story of a Greek queen, Helen, being abducted by a Trojan prince was likely only a trumped-up pretext for launching the war. Other Indo-European groups extended their movements to eastern, central, and northern Europe, where, Gimbutas argues, the effects were the same. In her view, incoming Indo-European warriors usurped the positions of local elites and imposed their language on the native populace, much the way European colonists spread English, French, and Spanish throughout the Americas from 1500 C.E. onwards. Like the spread of the Neolithic, there is considerable debate concerning the extent to which actual migration, population displacement, and warfare were responsible for the spread of the Bronze Age culture in Europe (versus cultural diffusion). Like the Neolithic, this was almost certainly a mix of migration and diffusion. There are strong indications of its spread via population movements in many areas (e.g., Price, Grupe, and Schröter 1998).

The earliest archaeological cultures in Europe that might be associated with Indo-European intrusions or influences comprise the Battle-axe, or Corded Ware culture (3000–2000 B.C.E.) and various kinds of Beaker cultures that spread over Europe about 2000 B.C.E. (Figs. 8.3, 8.4). The Battle-axe culture, which occupied large parts of central Europe, was characterized by its use of elongated stone battle axes (used like maces), the production of large corded-ware vases (probably used for brewing and/or serving alcoholic beverages at feasts) similar to those still used in Africa and Southeast Asia, and by burials of elites under kurgans (earth mounds).

On the steppes, population growth and competition to control the new grassland resource niche kept the entire area in a turmoil. Major ethnic movements and replacements occurred on a regular basis, pushing a continuous stream of displaced pastoral nomadic groups toward the forested European frontier. As a result, there seems to have

Fig. 8.3. The Battle-axe culture, also know as the Corded Ware culture, is named after the characteristic cord-impressed pots like these (probably used for brewing or consuming beer or other psychotropic drinks in ritual feasts) and ground stone axes probably used in warfare. This culture seems to correspond to the earliest appearance of Indo-Europeans in central Europe. Courtesy of the National Museum of Denmark.

been little long-term stability in Europe during the copper-using Beaker period or the succeeding Bronze and Iron Ages. Beaker cultures were characterized above all by the use of smaller and more refined drinking vases (beakers) than those at Corded Ware sites. Beakers appear to have been individually owned and were often buried with their elite owners. Prestige objects in copper or gold are often found in elite burials as well.

Not everyone agrees with the details of this scenario. Colin Renfrew (1987) argues that the original Indo-European expansion of language, cultural influences, and perhaps people was carried out by Neolithic groups originating in Anatolia, several thousand years earlier. Mallory (1989) is probably correct in rejecting this suggestion on linguistic and other grounds. However, even if Renfrew's ideas should eventually be supported by new archaeological discoveries, I suspect that Marek Zvelebil's (1995) suggestion will prove to be correct: that it was subgroups of Indo-Europeans who adapted to the steppes and later impacted parts of Europe. Certainly different physical types and diets of elite Beaker-culture males seem to indicate non-European origins for some of these groups (Harrison 1980:160; Price, Grupe, and Schröter 1998). Ultimately, whether the European Neolithic was Indo-European–speaking or not is of minor importance for the present discussion. What is important are the cultural mechanisms behind the very rapid spread of Indo-European languages and culture (or some branches of it) and how the adaptations of the expanding Indo-Europeans affected their religious life.

While Gimbutas's invasion hypothesis may be correct for southeastern and parts of central Europe (Price, Grupe, and Schröter 1998), the actual dynamics of contact and cultural change may have been much more complex in other areas of Europe, as indicated by Zvelebil (1995). In particular, there is now a general consensus that there was increasing population pressure in much of Europe throughout the Middle and Late

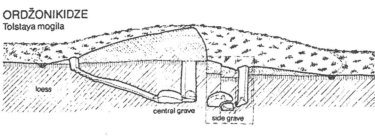

ORDŽONIKIDZE
Tolstaya mogila

loess

central grave   side grave

Reconstruction of the side grave

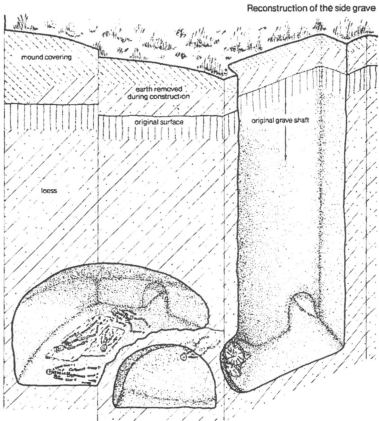

mound covering

earth removed
during construction

original surface

original grave shaft

loess

Fig. 8.4. Burial of elites under mounds (kurgans) was one of the distinguishing characteristics of early Indo-European cultures, according to many archaeologists. Pictured at top is an unusually complex group of kurgans at Perepyaticha in the Scythian area. Details of the shaft grave burial under the kurgan at Ordzonikidze are shown below. From R. Rolle, *The World of the Scythians,* Figs. 2, 6. London: Batsford, 1989.

Neolithic, accompanied by the "secondary products" revolution and increasing social stratification (Shennan 1986; Hutton 1991:92; Mallory 1989:260). Major changes in ritual monuments, warfare, and the construction of costly defensive works occurred with the advent of the *Middle* Neolithic rather than the arrival of the new Bronze Age technology at the close of the Neolithic. In fact, many of the most important Neolithic ritual monuments, such as Stonehenge and Avebury, were maintained and enhanced by the new bronze-using groups. There seems to be little change in ritual life with the transition to the Bronze Age in many parts of Europe. As noted in Chapter 6, there is no lack of evidence for violent conflict in the European Neolithic. Most archaeologists in Western Europe have been impressed with the dramatic changes in society, subsistence, settlements, warfare, and ritual that took place in the *middle* of the Neolithic, especially when compared with the generally smooth transition to the Bronze Age in western and northern Europe (Hutton 1991:92). The elites of the Beaker cultures that populate this transition period largely continue using the earlier types of megalithic monuments (which themselves evolved slowly over the centuries within western regions rather than being brought in by invaders; Hutton 1991:88–91). We have already noted that the presumed Indo-European Beaker culture elites seem to have fully adopted the Stonehenge and Avebury sanctuaries and carried their construction to new and greater heights. Alternatively, Richard Harrison (1980), Susan Skomal (1986:189), and Andrew Sherratt (1994) have argued that in many parts of Europe, there was no Indo-European invasion, but simply local Neolithic elites adopting the new international styles, prestige objects, and the trade language of the Indo-European elites, much as English and Western prestige objects have spread throughout the Industrial world. Thus, in Western Europe, the dominant archaeological view is that much of the symbolism and the general types of cults of the Late Neolithic persist without much change into the Bronze Age Indo-European cultures except for new styles or types of elite items. Although Gimbutas's reconstruction of events is partially supported (Price, Grupe, and Schröter 1998), her claims for the utopian nature of Old European Neolithic society and for the nature of Indo-European incursions in many parts of central and Western Europe are not well supported by archaeological data.

Pastoral Nomads Live in a Unique World

Before dealing with specific archaeological evidence for ritual behavior and beliefs among the Indo-Europeans, it will be worthwhile to establish a general cultural ecological framework for pastoral nomadic cultures and explore some of the underlying dynamics that constitute the foundations for most of these societies. Pastoral nomads have some very intriguing and rather unique characteristics related to the kinds of resources on which they rely for their living. Cultural ecologists have conducted some excellent studies on the reasons for certain adaptations of pastoral nomads (Barth 1961, 1964; Spooner 1973; Barfield 1993), and Bruce Lincoln (1981) has extended this line of research into pastoral nomadic religions. I will refer to the general type of religion that Lincoln describes as the "pastoral nomad type."

The basic ecological facts about pastoral nomadic societies are related to mobility and the dynamics of stock herding. Mobility favors the independence of individuals and groups. The animal resource base of pastoral nomads is, however, highly prone to fluctuations. It is unreliable and risky. Vast fortunes can sometimes be easily accumulated, but they can just as easily be lost. It is very much like investing in the stock market, and, in fact, the stock market was originally based on trading or investing in "stock," that is, cattle. How do people cope with such conditions?

Most animal herds have remarkable potential growth rates under favorable conditions, easily doubling or tripling in size within a year. If this growth continues for very long, herd sizes soon outstrip the ability of a single family to care for them, and the surplus must be sold, slaughtered, or loaned out. A successful herder can become very wealthy in a short time. Unfortunately, animal herds are also prone to dramatic depletions because of disease and raiding. Among the hill tribes of Southeast Asia, epidemic diseases devastate pig herds about once every 18 months, killing 75 percent of the pigs in a village, while cattle suffer an average 10 percent mortality from diseases (Falvey 1977:64). If nomadic livelihood depends on herd animals, and if disease or other adverse conditions suddenly wipe out one's herds, what options are left for survival? One can borrow more animals from others, resulting in an enormous debt that could result in enslavement if the loan cannot be paid back. One can sell oneself or family members into servitude. One can go off to raid cattle from other groups, as described at the beginning of this chapter. One can try to obtain a foothold in an agricultural community. Or one can perish. None of these options is particularly attractive. In reality, it is primarily the rich who are able to successfully take up a more settled agricultural way of life (Fratkin and Roth 1990; Starr 1987). Probably the most common solutions to loss of herds were raiding and indebted servitude.

These problems and their solutions created a distinctive, indelible stamp on the pastoral nomadic way of life and cultures (Fig. 8.5). First, they created major inequalities: some extremely rich individuals became chiefs, and others became indentured servants or slaves who could be sacrificed (Fig. 8.6; see also Glob 1974:60, 113). Fortunes might fluctuate among herders, but rights and privileges often were also strictly defined by class. The need to coordinate grazing rights to the best pasture lands in very large areas may have also favored the emergence of a hierarchical political power structure featuring chiefs. Barth (1961:127–30) has observed that chiefdoms develop primarily in the richer environments or where trade becomes important. The high mobility of nomads and their ability to transport materials in bulk on pack animals or in wagons makes them well adapted to acting as traders.

Because animals are so mobile, stealing and raiding are also attractive alternatives to disaster and poverty. For rugged individuals, raiding was undoubtedly a preferred means to achieve power and wealth in a very short time (Lincoln 1981:173). As Louise Sweet (1965) has argued, these factors made raiding and fighting an endemic part of life among many pastoral nomads. Moreover, those who had horses became especially effective warriors with whom foot soldiers from more sedentary communities could only poorly contend. Whether one was herding in Mongolia, Ireland, North Africa, or on the plains ranches of nineteenth-century America, these characteristics tended to recur (Spooner 1973; Barfield 1993).

In an excellent ecological study of the impact of pastoral nomadic resources on native cultures, Frank Secoy (1953) demonstrated how the introduction of the horse on the American High Plains totally transformed native societies from sedentary agricultural and

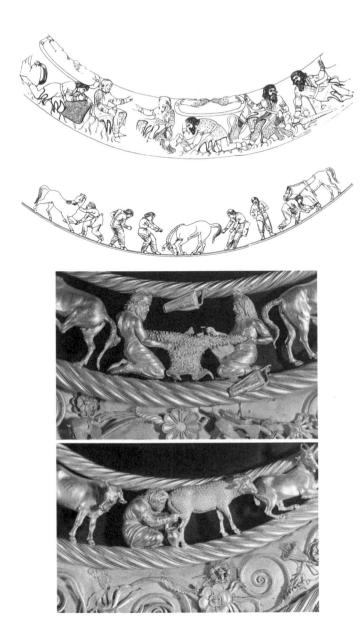

Fig. 8.5. Scenes from the pastoral nomadic way of life of the Scythians are portrayed on this embossed silver bowl (above) and on gold neck rings, or "torcs" (center and below). Men are never far from their quivers or swords or drinking vessels in the scenes on the bowl, while they are occupied with the care of their horses, sheep, and cattle in the scenes on the neck rings. The importance of herding animals reflects the basic adaptation to the steppe environment as well as the value of such animals. Note that men typically wear pants, probably an adaptation to horse riding. R. Rolle, *The World of the Scythians,* Figs. 32b, 77, Plates 15, 16. London: Batsford, 1980.

hunting communities, leading fairly routine daily lives, to the highly mobile warrior and raiding societies that we are more familiar with from historical records and popular films. David Anthony (1986) has argued that a similar change took place on the steppes north of the Black Sea when Proto–Indo-Europeans began to herd their domesticated animals with horses and move their settlements with wagons.

It is for these reasons, as well as the early historic documentation of events such as the Irish cattle raids, that Bruce Lincoln (1981:122ff) has argued that warrior bands were common in Proto–Indo-European cultures. The men who banded together to go out on raids were considered a special class of society and in many ways seem to have written their own rules (Fig. 8.1). Most early Indo-European histories refer to the existence of such bands or alternatively to bands that ventured out to attack cities for lucre and spoils, as in the Greek attack on Troy or the many accounts of battles in the *Rig Veda* (Fig. 8.7). Greek epics repeatedly refer to fighting for "the city and the women," and there was even a Greek title of honor called "the sacker of cities." If raiding herd animals could provide a good livelihood, the stealing of precious metals such as gold, silver, and bronze brought great wealth—wealth that was easily transportable because of its compactness, very high value, and ease of exchange for other commodities

(Fig. 8.8). The prospect of picking up precious metals in raids must have fired the ambition of many war band leaders to boiling points perhaps even higher than Cuchulainn's. Bronze could also be used to make elite weapons that conferred further advantages in fighting—the first real military-industrial complex of history.

With stakes and risks at unusually high levels, competition between individuals must have been extraordinarily intense. Rugged individualism seems to have been remarkably unrestrained, particularly among the warriors. As a result, public prestige was undoubtedly important for success in organizing raids and managing political affairs. Factions were almost certainly constantly vying with each other for the best spoils, the most power, the greatest reputation, and the most effective symbols of success. Those with aspirations probably took offense easily and egos were undoubtedly fragile. As might be expected, with their emphasis on herding and warfare, most pastoral nomad societies tended to be dominated by men. Many of them could legitimately be called patriarchal. Divale and Harris (1975) have shown that patriarchal societies tend to occur when militarism becomes a dominant factor in community life. Men probably not only brandish weapons of force and use them with less provocation than in

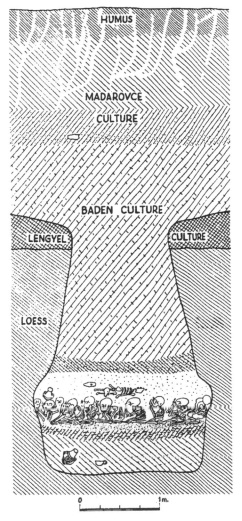

Fig. 8.6. The degree of absolute power wielded by some Bronze Age Indo-European elites can be gauged by incidents such as those that transpired at Nitriansky Hradok-Zamecek in Slovakia. In the "death pit" shown here, the archaeological remains revealed that people in power apparently ordered 10 individuals to be buried alive while kneeling in a large pit. Their arms were raised and hands were held in front of their faces. A dog and stone battle axe were placed in the pit after the people had been covered with earth. From A. Sherratt, in P. Garwood, D. Jennings, R. Skeates, and J. Toms, eds., *Sacred and Profane: Proceedings of a Conference on Archaeology, Ritual, and Religion*, p. 58. Oxford: Oxford University Committee for Archaeology, Monograph 32, 1991. Courtesy of Anton Tocik (the original excavator), Institute of Archaeology, Nitra.

other cultures, but women's safety becomes more dependent upon men, and poor protection could easily lead to rape, abduction, enslavement, forced marriage, and/or death.

The above characteristics do not seem to be entirely foreign to many Near Eastern and European Neolithic societies where cattle were of major importance, such as in the megalithic and PPNB and its derivative cultures (see Chaps. 6 and 7). Flint arrowheads and daggers were technically refined in the Neolithic, while warriors carried maces and axes and appear to have formed more modest war bands than in the Bronze Age. This may account for some of the seeming continuity from the Neolithic to the Bronze Age found in a number of regions.

Fig. 8.7. The eroded ruins shown here are all that remain of the fabled city of Troy, which controlled trade between the Mediterranean and the Black Seas. In true Indo-European tradition, the Mycenaean Greeks targeted Troy as a war prize ripe for plucking. Perhaps as a pretext, they claimed that the Prince of Troy had abducted one of the Greek queens, and the Greeks subsequently launched the Trojan war as recorded by Homer. From H. Schliemann, *Ilios, the City and Country of the Trojans,* title page. 1881.

Fig. 8.8. Heinrich Schliemann excavated parts of the ruins of Troy in the 1870s and recovered remarkable examples of gold jewelry and other items such as the gold bowl, head coverlet, earrings, beads, and ingot bars shown here; at right is also a bronze adze or battle-axe. This wealth undoubtedly was derived from the control over trade that Trojans exerted in the region. Such wealth also made Troy a prime target for Indo-European warrior elites. From H. Schliemann, *Ilios, the City and Country of the Trojans,* Figs. 688, 772, 822–28. 1881.

Given this background, it should not be too surprising that Indo-European religion incorporated gods of war or deities wearing weapons (Fig. 8.9). Sacred texts deal to a large degree with battles or raids, and weapons are imbued with supernatural forces—topics to which we shall now turn in greater detail.

Pastoral Nomadic Religions Reflect Their Societies

In a classic cultural ecological study of religion and herding societies, Bruce Lincoln (1981) drew attention to the surprising similarities exhibited by cattle-herding societies with clearly different historical and genetic origins, for example, the Nuer or the Masai in East Africa and the historical Indo-European cattle herders of the steppes. He observed that the warrior groups in these pastoral societies symbolically adopted powerful wild animals such as lions, leopards, wolves, bears (Lincoln 1981:125, 163), and probably wild bulls during the Neolithic (Chap. 6). Identification with such animals seems to have had strong influences on the rituals and ideologies of these groups. Moreover, warriors in herding cultures tend to form exclusive and independent social groups or classes, with their own deities, rituals, myths, and ritual leaders. Priestly elites also formed a separate class that endeavored to maintain dominant control over raids, spells, initiations, and, I suspect, basic cattle herding or production (Lincoln 1981:39ff, 126ff). Thus, in the pastoral nomad type of society,

Fig. 8.9. The Indo-European preoccupation with warfare heavily influenced their ideas of the nature of gods and the supernatural. Many of the early Indo-European depictions of deities, like this one from Arco, Trentino, in Italy incorporate weapons of war in their raiment. Clearly depicted are multiple daggers, halberds, and ritual belts and necklaces or torcs. From R. C. de Marinis, "Chalcolithic Stele-statues of the Alpine Region," in K. Demakopoulou, C. Eluere, J. Jensen, A. Jockenhovel, and J.-P. Mohen, eds., *Gods and Heroes of the Bronze Age: Europe at the Time of Ulysses*, p. 148. London: Thames & Hudson, 1999.

there is an evident conflict of interest between the major power-wielding sectors (warriors versus priestly elites) resulting in problems of integrating both social groups together, not to mention the people that do most of the herding and gardening. In this respect, religion can be adaptive in both defining special-interest groups within a society and in integrating groups together. This represents a further politicization of religion, a tendency that we saw beginning in the Upper Paleolithic.

Lincoln also noted that the creation myths of all pastoralists seem to involve the sacrifice of animals (Lincoln 1975). Animals are never killed simply for meat; they are always sacrificed for special events involving both social and religious purposes. Like the hunter-gatherer concepts of killing animals so that their spirits may return to the master of animals, who will send them back again in new bodies, pastoralists kill domestic animals so that the animal spirits will go to the gods and the gods in turn will send more cattle and other gifts and create the world anew. Pastoralists viewed the original creation of the world as resulting from just such a primordial sacrifice of a sacred animal (Lincoln 1981:90–92), perhaps giving the world its life force just as sacrifices in newly constructed houses give the structures life. This is the significance of the animal sacrifices that typified almost all Greek and Roman worship at temples and at their major undertakings like the sacking of Troy. It is also reflected in the biblical sacrifices offered by Cain and Abel when Jehovah found the animal sacrifice of Abel (a herder) much more favorable than the vegetable sacrifice of Cain (a farmer).

Some authors have also remarked on the strong tendency for pastoral nomads to emphasize a supreme deity usually associated with the sky, lightning, and the sun (Lincoln 1981:16; Eliade 1959:122). Such conceptions fit well with what we know already of the tendencies for chiefs to promote universal kinds of deities. Supreme deities can be seen as an attempt to create a divine model for the kinds of social and political relationships that elites wanted to foster in their spheres of influence. Certainly, the sun seems to have been the main deity represented in many Indo-European elite works of art and ritual (Glob 1974:99–106; Anati 1961:156). Whether invading Indo-European elites brought these concepts and practices into Europe or whether they were adopted by indigenous peoples as part of the status package of influence from the steppes is not critical for our discussion of the pastoral nomad type of religion. As we have seen (Chap. 7), supreme solar deities even began to develop among many megalithic groups in the European Neolithic.

INDO-EUROPEAN WARRIORS WENT BERSERK

Hand-to-hand combat is a terrifying experience in which all the hormones, endorphins, and adrenaline available within the brain mix together in potent, mind-altering chemical brews. By themselves, however, these are not enough for battle victories, for the ultimate effect may well be flight instead of fight, or even paralysis. In order to avoid such outcomes, warrior groups often "psych themselves up" using a number of psychological techniques. One such technique involves the creation of frenzied altered states of euphoria in warriors like Cuchulainn's state, described at the beginning of this chapter. Eliade (1958b:81ff) argues that induction into such states formed part of men's initiation into warrior secret societies. Similar tactics were used by nomadic Plains Indian warriors who sometimes entered into altered states of consciousness in which they felt that they were invulnerable to enemy weapons (as described in Neihardt 1961). This resulted in daring feats of bravado, in which some warriors would go up to the enemy and touch them without themselves being hurt (counting coup). Those who could do this successfully achieved great reputations for being spiritually powerful.

In Indo-European societies, many warriors felt themselves transformed into powerful animals that went out to fight with men (Lincoln 1981:126; Littleton 1982:80). Drugs were frequent aids in achieving such states (Lincoln 1981:30; Littleton 1982:44). The resulting blind fury induced by the creation of these altered states was undoubtedly a major factor in Indo-European military successes over other ethnic groups, and it probably accounts for much of the sacred symbolism of these Indo-Europeans. According to the Irish story, Cuchulainn became so dangerous that the king was afraid that the hero would kill all the warriors, friends and foes alike. Therefore, after the battle he placed a number of naked women in his path, and while the warrior was distracted, the king's men lifted him up and placed him in three successive vats of cold water. The first burst apart, the second boiled with bubbles as big as fists, and the third succeeded in quelling his inner fires. Above all, inner fire is an Indo-European symbol of divine possession and magical energy (Eliade 1958b:85). Thus, blacksmiths, warriors, and shamans are sacred, as are firewalkers.

The transformation of individuals into animal forms, in particular, is part of a long tradition seeming to originate far back in the Paleolithic, as expressed by artistic representations of lion- or antlered-headed men and the transformation of ritual participants into ancestral totemic animals under ecstatic conditions (Chaps. 4 and 5). It is therefore not surprising that Indo-Europeans seeking to induce wild ecstatic states preparatory to battle would also see themselves as becoming transformed into animal spirits or real animals. They became berserkers, the Norse warriors who took on characteristics of bears in battle. They became werewolves, the Baltic "dogs of God" who fought against the forces of evil. These werewolves fought for the good of the community and were considered beneficial up until the fifteenth century, when the church turned them into religious pariahs along with witches and others that did not conform to its ideology (Eliade 1958b:88ff; Ginzburg 1991:153–57).

While Indo-Europeans certainly had no monopoly on the use of psychotropic substances to achieve ecstatic states, they seem to have used drugs as the basis for many of their religious experiences, whether in military, shamanistic, or elite contexts (Sherratt 1991; Allegro 1970). Like warriors, shamans, too, waged battles, but instead of taking place on a physical battlefield, they took place in the realm of spirits. Thus, it is not surprising to find many of the same ritual elements of the Indo-European war bands also cropping up in nonmilitary contexts. These ritual elements include drinking a sacred drink or inhaling special fumes, entering into ecstatic states, being transformed into animal forms, and engaging in battles on spiritual planes, usually in the air.

The drink that keeps recurring in early Indo-European myths and sacred texts has many local names, but it is always the "Drink of Immortality." In India, it was called "Soma" (see "Soma, the Elixir of Life, the Drink of Immortality," pp. 286–87). In Greece, it was "ambrosia." In Ireland, it was "madhu." There has been a great deal written on this subject and the myths surrounding it. The drink itself was viewed as a god or an extension of a god, just as Dionysus was said to have been poured out in cups of wine and to have instilled sacred euphoria. Littleton (1982:44) has argued that it always contained alcohol, while other scholars think not. They have suggested that the key ingredient was the fly agaric mushroom (*Amanita muscaria*), opium poppies, cannabis, datura, or other herbs (Wasson 1968, 1972; Sherratt 1991; Furst 1976:96ff). The specific materials used by different groups may well have varied.

The important point is that Indo-Europeans had a strong tradition using some form of drink to enter into ecstatic states for sacred experiences and transformations. Whatever the psychoactive contents, by consuming it, individuals attained direct contact with a deity and were transported to his realm or became united with the godhead. This is perhaps why the cup in its many forms became an important sacred symbol for Indo-Europeans (Littleton 1982:9–10, 44, 205). The ceramic "beakers" and corded-ware vessels that typically constitute the grave goods of elite burials of the earliest Indo-Europeans in

SOMA, THE ELIXIR OF LIFE, THE DRINK OF IMMORTALITY

Many Indo-European groups had special drinks that helped them enter into ecstatic contact with the gods and sacred forces. Perhaps none of these sacred drinks was as revered and renowned as Soma, repeatedly referred to in the *Rig Veda,* the oldest Hindu sacred book. Unfortunately, no one today is sure exactly what plants were used to make Soma. It is a forgotten secret—one of the sacred mysteries of the Indo-Europeans. Here is one of the hymns to Soma (Book I, Hymn 91) from Griffith's (1992) translation.

Thou, Soma, art the Lord of heroes, King,
yea, Vrtra-slayer thou:
Thou art auspicious energy.
And, Soma, let it be thy wish that we may live and may not die:
Praise-loving Lord of plants art thou.
To him who keeps the law, both old and young, thou givest happiness
And energy that he may live.
Guard us, King Soma, on all sides from him who threatens us: never let
The friend of one like thee be harmed.
Well-skilled in speech we magnify thee
Soma, with our sacred songs:
Come thou to us, most gracious One.
Enricher, healer of disease, wealth-finder prospering our store,
Be, Soma, a good Friend to us.
Soma, be happy in our heart, as milch kine in the grassy meads,
Soma, wax great. From every side may vigorous powers unite in thee:
Be in the gathering-place of strength.
Wax, O most gladdening Soma, great through all thy rays of light, and be
A Friend of most illustrious fame to prosper us.
In thee be juicy nutriments united, and powers and mighty foe-subduing
    vigor,
Waxing to immortality, O Soma: win highest glories for thyself in heaven.
Wealth-giver, further with troops of heroes, sparing the brave, come,
    Soma, to our houses.
To him who worships Soma gives the milchcow, a fleet steed and a man
    of active knowledge,
Invincible in fight, saver in battles, guard of our camp, winner of light
    and water,
Born amid hymns, well-housed, exceeding famous, victor, in thee will we
    rejoice,
O Soma.

Europe were undoubtedly used for drinking some form of intoxicating sacred drink,
such as beer or mead, perhaps spiked with other psychoactive herbs (Harrison 1980:69).
The drink certainly seems to have been used to invigorate warriors (Lincoln 1981:97,
130). Some of these containers could be quite large, rivaling the high-status brewing and
drinking pots of Africa and Southeast Asia that probably functioned in fashions similar
to the larger beakers (Dietler 2001).

This may well be the basis for the Indo-European symbol of the cauldron: a vessel of transformation and a means of contacting the deities. The cauldron features prominently in Celtic legends such as the *Mabinogian* and appears prominently on carts or wagons in a number of archaeological representations going back to the Bronze Age. Magical cauldrons were borne on wheels and were often associated with supernatural beings (Fig. 8.10). In classical Greece they could be used to bring rain but seem to have been strongly associated with grape harvests and drinking. Many people suggest that the British myth cycle involving the Holy Grail is simply another variation of this mythical Indo-European cup of transformation and immortality—a cup that is typically stolen or lost, thereby consigning humanity to its unfortunate mortal and flawed existence. In any event, such cups and drinks were probably used by warriors and priestly elites alike. Michael Dietler (1990, 2001) has demonstrated that the making and drinking of beer tended to be confined to the affluent members of tribal and chiefly societies and that alcohol was exclusively used for important ritual and social occasions. Beakers also seem to have been only used by the rich and powerful (Harrison 1980:14–15, 68).

Fig. 8.10. Magical cauldrons and magical animals were important aspects of Indo-European mythology. Animals, people, a goddess, and cauldron were carried on this cult wagon. The wagon seems to symbolize sacred carriage. Gods, the sun, the cauldron of immortality, dead elites, and other sacred items were all borne on sacred wagons. This bronze cult wagon was found at Steiermärk, Austria. Courtesy of the Steiermärkisches Landesmuseum Joanneum, Graz, Austria.

Whether ecstatic states were achieved through drugs, sensory deprivation, or other means, it is relatively clear that Indo-Europeans seeking religious experiences generally sought to put themselves into states of ecstasy (Littleton 1982:80; Ginzburg 1991:102, 123, 150ff). In a masterful synthesis of historically recorded European folk traditions and religious disputes, Carlo Ginzburg (1991:183ff) has argued that medieval accusations of witchcraft, portraying the transformation of ritual practitioners into a variety of animal forms, reflected the persistence of a much older Indo-European religious tradition. He documented the remnant occurrences in Europe of various ecstatic cults. Members of these cults would gather together at specific times of the year, enter into ecstatic states, become transformed into wolves or other animals, and then fly into the air to do battle with malicious forces that wanted to keep harvests or fertility from their villages, or the cult members would contend with forces bent on doing harm to the villagers. These cults continued up until the nineteenth and twentieth centuries in some remote areas of Italy, Slovenia, Croatia, Hungary, and the Ukrainian steppes (Ginzburg 1991:153ff). All these elements are familiar aspects of shamanism that we noted in Chapters 3 and 5. However, in the Indo-European context they become group activities and cults.

These cults may well have originally been types of secret societies in Indo-European communities in which elites and their supporters undertook supernatural contacts in order to claim that they had protected the village and perhaps by implication had some rights over its produce. We find similar claims among aggrandizers in transegalitarian and chiefdom-level societies. The Indo-European concept of the king or, more probably, the chief, as the supernatural overseer of the welfare of the land and all its people probably derives from such claims. This was presumably one of the ideological justifications that Indo-European elites used to vindicate their claims to privileges. They undoubtedly used other claims, too. At the village level, the psychic battling of young members (7–12 years old) of the European ecstatic transformation cults may simply have been an elite initiation into the first rank of secret society membership, in a fashion similar to Upper Paleolithic cave initiations or to initiations into warrior societies (Eliade 1958b:182).

Moreover, as is typical of more complex societies based on relatively abundant surpluses, the Indo-European shamanistic and priestly class tended to fragment into a hierarchy of ritual specialists: magicians, poets, diviners, curers, pourers of libations, reciters, sacrificial priests, fire ritualists, and ritualists for cattle raids (Lincoln 1981:60–63). Like the priestly elite Brahmin class of India, the Indo-European priests were at the top of the socioeconomic hierarchy. The presence of such individuals is indicated archaeologically by burials with shamanic or priestly materials such as hawk claws, snake tails, amber, squirrel jaws, and stones in pigeon guts (Glob 1974:114, 116, 162). This class appears to have promoted their own deity concepts and rituals, just as chiefly elites did in Neolithic Europe and elsewhere. It is difficult to tell whether the Bronze Age portrayals of deities armed with weapons (Fig. 8.9) relate to the priestly elite cults (as they presumably did in megalithic monuments) or to more specialized warrior cult deities such as the cult of Indra (see "The *Rig Veda*").

THE *Rig Veda*

The *Rig Veda* is the oldest religious text from India. It is clearly Indo-European and illustrates many of the religious features of the early Indo-Europeans in India, such as the importance of warfare and war deities like Indra, the concern with the spoils of war, capturing cattle, and the drinking of Soma to induce altered states in rituals or before battles. Also of interest is the explicit imagery of the war god Indra as a bull—an association that began in the Neolithic, and perhaps in the Upper Paleolithic (Chaps. 5, 6).

The following excerpts addressed to Indra are from Book I, Hymns 7, 8, 32, 33, 53, 132, 176 and Book X, Hymns 102 and 103 (Griffith 1992).

Come, fain for booty let us speak to Indra:
yet more shall he increase his care that guides us.
Will not the Indestructible endow us with
perfect knowledge of this wealth, of cattle? (33:1)

Mid all his host, he bindeth on the quiver:
he driveth cattle from what foe he pleaseth:
Gathering up great stores of riches, Indra.
be thou no trafficker with us, most mighty. (33:3)

Help us, O Indra, in the frays, yea, frays,
where thousand spoils are granted,
with awful aids, O awful One. (7:4)

In mighty battle we invoke Indra, Indra
in lesser fight,
The friend who bends his bolt at fiends. (7:5)

Even as the bull drives on the herds, he
drives the people with his might,
The Ruler irresistible: (7:8)

Indra, bring wealth that gives delight, the
victor's ever-conquering wealth,
Most excellent, to be our aid; (8:1)

Aided by thee, the thunder-armed, Indra,
may we lift up the bolt,
And conquer all our foes in fight. (8:3)

His belly, drinking deepest draughts of
Soma, like an ocean swells,
Like wide streams from the cope of heaven. (8:7)

Impetuous as a bull, he chose the Soma,
and in three sacred beakers drank the
juices. (32:3)

Indra, the Bull, made his ally the thunder, and
with its light milked cows from out the darkness. (33:10)

Indra broke though Ilibisa's strong castles,
and Susna with his horn he cut to
pieces:
Thou Maghavan, for all his might and
swiftness, slewest thy fighting foemen
with thy thunder. (33:12)

Fierce on his enemies fell Indra's weapon:
with his sharp bull he rent their forts
in pieces.
He with his thunderbolt dealt blows on
Vrtra; and conquered, executing all
his purpose. (33:13)

Let us obtain, O Indra, plenteous wealth
and food, with strength exceeding glorious, shining to
the sky:
May we obtain the Goddess Providence,
the strength of heroes, special source
of cattle, rich in steeds. (53:5)

These our libations strength-inspiring,
Soma draughts, gladdened thee in the
fight with Vrtra, Hero Lord,
Thou goest on from fight to fight intrepidly, destroying
castle after castle here with strength.
Thou, Indra, with thy friend who
makes the foe bow down, slewest from
far away the guileful Namuci. (53:7)

This day that now is close at hand bless
him who pours the Soma juice.
In this our sacrifice may we divide the
spoil, showing our strength, the spoil of
war. (132:1)

Mark thou the man who injures us and
kill him like the heavenly bolt. (176:3)

Slay everyone who pours no gift, who,
hard to reach, delights thee not.
Bestow on us what wealth he hath: this
even the worshipper awaits. (176:4)

Here look upon this mace, this bull's
companion, now lying midway on the
field of battle.
Therewith hath Mudgala in ordered contest won cattle for
himself, a hundred thousand. (102:9)

Bristle thou up, O Maghavan, our
weapons: excite the spirits of my warring heroes.
Urge on the strong steeds' might, O
Vrtra-slayer, and let the din of conquering carts go
upward. (103:10)

May Indra aid us when our flags are
gathered: victorious be the arrows of
our army.
Advance, O heroes, win the day. May
Indra be your sure defence.
Exceeding mighty be your arms, that
none may wound or injure you. (103:13)

What does appear evident is that, in addition to powerful warrior dieties, there was a broad range of deities in the elite Indo-European pantheon and that they were portrayed as similar to elite society. That is, they were arranged in a social and political hierarchy. There was a dominant chief deity (the sun, the sky, deus, Zeus, the day, the thunder and lightning, the great bull). There were male and female deities with specialized characteristics such as blacksmiths, hunters, warriors, wives, or lovers. And interactions between the deities were quarrelsome and intensely political, with alliances and intrigues, feasting and conflicts. As Martin Nilsson (1940) has argued, the deities depicted by Homer in the Bronze Age epics *The Iliad* and *The Odyssey* exclusively represent the elite and warrior pantheons and probably reflect what Greek elite life was like in the Bronze Age on a daily basis. In contrast, the deities worshipped by common peasants were largely the nature deities of fertility and the woods: the pans, the sylphs, the satyrs, the grain goddess, the grape god, the fairies, the undines, and centaurs. The Olympian pantheon headed by Zeus represents one of the more notable examples of the development of elite deities and cult rituals so as to promote elite interests. While commoners may have given lip service to some of these deities and rituals, it appears that their hearts remained with the more traditional land-based rites and spirits. Unfortunately, the ritual remains left by poorer common people rarely survive archaeologically, whereas the more permanent and more costly monuments, burials, and paraphernalia of the elites do tend to be preserved. Thus we must contend with some major biases, not only in the archaeological record but also in the historical record for it was the elites such as Homer who were literate and the elites who wrote our historical documents.

The Third Estate

Although the common herders and farmers forming the third class of people in Indo-European communities may not have left as much indication of their ritual life as the other two classes (the priestly elites and warriors), there is one domain where we can perceive their ritual importance, albeit indirectly. This is in the the symbolic domain of myth and ritual. Georges Dumézil (1958) was one of the first scholars to apply the comparative techniques used to study Indo-European languages to the study of Indo-European religion and society. He pointed out that the number three was a recurring feature in many European myths and ritual practices. There are often three deities that rule tribal life. Deities like the Roman Matronae or Graces come in threes (Fig. 8.11); kings typically have three sons who vie to succeed their father by successfully obtaining a cup, an axe, and a plow. Fairy tales often have heroes that fail in a task twice but are successful the third time (Mallory 1989:132ff). Religions in other parts of the world have different sacred numbers, such as the sacred duality of Taoism or the sacred four directions of native American religions. The Indo-European sacred number was three.

Dumézil suggested that this was because early Indo-European society was divided into three basic classes, or estates: priestly elites, warriors, and herder-farmers. Because of the inherent conflicts that were especially divisive between the warriors and priestly elites, all rituals of importance had to refer to each of the three classes in turn and had to be done three times. Any major decisions that had to be made had to explicitly invoke blessings from the patron deities of the three major interest groups. Even the symbols of the chiefdom and battle banners had to symbolize the three major groups. Dumézil and others have argued that these traditions were so fundamental to Indo-European life that they have persisted in our culturally unconscious patterns of behavior down to the present day. Thus, we refer to the three estates in society. Our myths, fairy tales, and occult practitioners encapsulate the magical number of three. Most European flags prominently display three colors. In the Indo-European symbolical system, white is the color of purity and high priests, red is the color of warriors, and darker colors such as green or blue are more related to the earth or the sea. Perhaps from cultural habit, it is also sug-

Fig. 8.11. The sacredness of the number three for Indo-Europeans was expressed in many fashions, one of which was the representation of triple gods and goddesses, such as the three water nymphs of Celtic derivation at Coventina's Well by Hadrian's Wall. From B. Cunliffe, *The Celtic World,* p. 89. New York: McGraw-Hill, 1979.

gested that Europeans naturally tend to divide things up into threes, such as the Lower, Middle, and Upper Paleolithic (Littleton 1982:98, 231).

It is in the importance of the number three as a cultural symbol that we obtain a dim, distant notion of the ritual role of nonelites and nonwarriors in Indo-European religious life. It is even suggested that the Indo-European third estate emulated the other two social estates by pursuing religious experiences via ecstatic means. In particular, agricultural harvest festivals may have been occasions for ecstatic drinking and celebration (Littleton 1982:80), and even love may have been an ecstatic adventure. There are reports of folk magicians "bringing down the moon" in fifth-century B.C.E. Greece (Nilsson 1940:112); this may well have been in relation to agricultural and fertility folk rituals, since the moon is widely thought to influence crop growth in European cultures. Many of the Greek folk deities such as pans and satyrs are clearly fertility spirits, while phalluses and balls continue as popular fertility talismans in Bronze Age England (Hutton 1991:91), also indicating the persistence of domestic fertility cults.

There was likely a domestic cult for supernatural house protectors, too. Most early Greek houses are supposed to have had an image and house sanctuary for Zeus-the-Protector, who often took the form of a snake that guarded the household food stores and seems to have been associated with souls of the dead as well. While this may have been derived from contacts with Minoan societies, similar concepts are found in other European countries such as Italy and Sweden (Nilsson 1940:67–72).

Hearth cults, too, were very widespread throughout Indo-European areas. Hearth cults were certainly part of elite rituals, with offerings of food and drink being given to the hearth or placed on the floor near the hearth before and after meals (Nilsson 1940:73–75). In India, these cults focused on the fire god Agni—related to English terms like "ignite." The hearth was an extremely sacred place for the household, as was noted in Chapter 3 in connection with the axis mundi by which spirits visited the household. It is difficult to tell to what extent the early descriptions of hearth and household protector cults refer to elite versus common households, but it would not be surprising if this cult was a part of most common domestic ritual life.

While the number three is a symbolical feature of Indo-European religion and cannot be claimed to derive from cultural ecological laws or principles, the underlying logic of this development is certainly consistent with the cultural ecological framework. This theoretical framework leads us to expect warrior groups to form part of pastoral nomadic societies under appropriate resource conditions. We also expect elites to emerge under these same conditions and for there to be a less-privileged producing group. How the conflicts and tensions between these groups are resolved in a structured or ritual fashion depends on many other historical and situational factors. However, the Indo-European solution of ritually recognizing all three main interest groups was certainly an adaptive solution to the problem, one so successful that it persisted as the basis for invoking deities and supernatural help or for cementing social bonds for over 6,000 years.

Religious Dynamics and Symbols in Indo-European Cultures

We have seen that when the Indo-Europeans arrived in Europe, they adopted much of the symbolism already present in the Neolithic elite cultures, if indeed the Indo-European and Neolithic communities had not evolved along parallel paths all along, especially concerning elite solar, bull, ancestor, and warrior cults. They took over cults in Greece and in megalithic centers like Stonehenge farther to the west, to which they probably added some of their own deities and symbols, as well as their bronze technology. Ancestors were the foci for prominent elite cults, just as they were in the Neolithic. Shrines and sanctuaries continued to be small, restrictive enclosures (Anati 1961:198; Brooks 1989), probably used only by important social leaders. Caves continue to be used for rituals, probably by secret societies (Jelinek 1990). The inner chamber of Nakovana Cave in Croatia was recently excavated and yielded a large collection of finely made feasting cups, plates, and jugs distributed around a phallic shaped stalagmite placed in the center of the chamber (Kaiser 2001; Forenbaher and Kaiser 2001). Our earliest recorded myths portray life in the Indo-European Bronze Age together with the deities worshipped and the rituals practiced such as offering strips of skin and fat from sacrificed animals to the gods. There is a great deal of detail available for this time period that is simply lacking in previous periods. This is due not only to the survival of written records but also to the greater wealth produced in some regions during this period and consequently the greater ability of elites to construct enduring ritual monuments and to obtain greater quantities and higher qualities of ritual paraphernalia. It is impossible to explore all of the many issues of Bronze Age religion in such a brief overview, but some features are of particular note.

From an ecological perspective, it is interesting to observe that there is an increasing emphasis on individual burials and rich individual grave goods (similar to kurgan mound burials), rather than megalithic communal structures used for the burial of a number of select individuals. This is a trend that actually begins in the Late Neolithic but becomes very pronounced with the arrival of the more individualistic Indo-European cultures (Hutton 1991:87). Individual mound burials seem to reflect the growing power and wealth of the elite.

Another major theme of Indo-European religion and mythology is the stark dichotomy between the forces of good and evil, which are in eternal combat with one another (Eliade 1978:190; Littleton 1982:144). This extreme dualism is the theme behind the ecstatic transformation cults that were so well documented by Carlo Ginzburg, and it is a theme that pervades our own mythologies, including modern versions such as *Star Wars,* Tolkien's *Lord of the Rings,* and many other popular gothic stories. The Indo-Europeans probably adopted this religious theme from Middle Eastern religions that they came into contact with on their nomadic travels across the steppes. In particular, Zoroastrianism, which originated in Iran, features two antagonistic forces: light and darkness, good and evil, fighting battles for the world (Littleton 1982:103; Eliade 1978:320ff,188ff). Such ideologies were probably promulgated by elites trying to motivate their supporters and subjects to fight against competitors. By demonizing competitors, they could wage much more effective campaigns against their enemies. Typically, the priests fight against the forces of evil for fertility and good harvests; the god of spring growth fights against the god of winter dormancy to free the vitality in the plants and animals of the world (Littleton 1982:47).

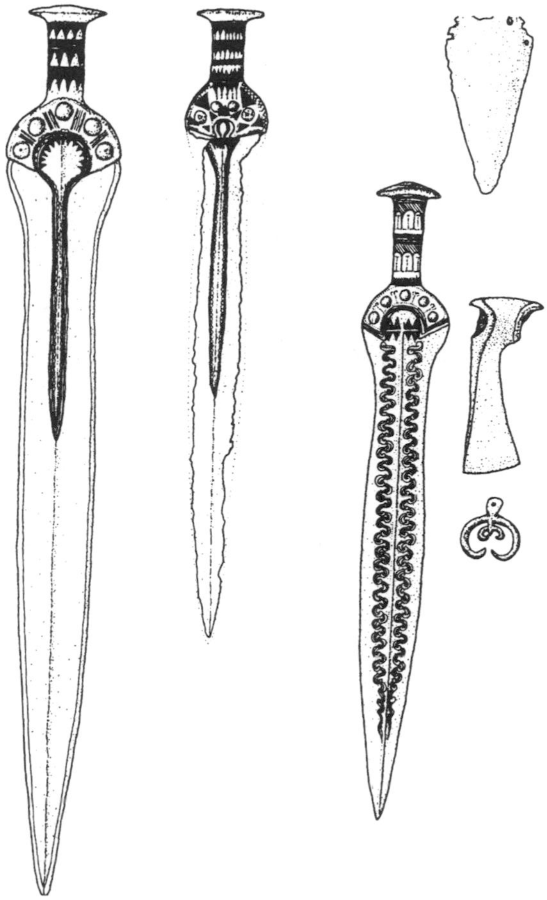

Another commonly occurring element throughout Indo-European myths, as well as many other pastoral nomadic cultures, is the concept of magically imbued weapons (Fig. 8.12), such as Thor's hammer (essentially a mace), which could even be viewed as part of a deity's persona (Stover and Kraig 1978:111). Other nomadic groups such as East African cattle herders also placed magical emblems on their weapons and used drugs for raids and sacrifices (Lincoln 1981:30). Magical weapons appear in many traditional Indo-European myths, such as King Arthur's magical sword, Excalibur. Magical weapons continue to occupy an important place in modern versions of traditional themes as well. Thus, the swords used by Tolkien's hobbits glow in the dark when enemies are near. In fact, many of the gothic tales of disincarnate spirits of evil warriors guarding tombs among the barrow tumulus graves are probably derived from illicit excavations of Bronze Age or Neolithic graves in which clandestine excavators entered into the funerary crypts of long-dead elites hoping to find treasures. Sometimes the well-preserved bodies of the Bronze Age elites, with their death grins staring out from oak coffins and their swords at their sides, must have been profoundly disturbing (Fig. 8.13).

Fig. 8.12. Bronze Age swords were not only extremely costly to make, but they were also elaborated with designs that enhanced their prestige value. Such swords undoubtedly were imbued with magic to enhance their effectiveness, as indicated by these examples from Scandinavia and the Carpathian Basin. From T. Kovacs, *L'Age du Bronze en Hongrie,* Fig. 7.6. Budapest: Corvina Publishers, 1977; J. Coles and A. Harding, *The Bronze Age in Europe,* Fig. 53. London: Methuen, 1979.

Fig. 8.13. In centuries past, when people dug into barrows, they sometimes found the log coffins of elite individuals still clutching their weapons, and in some cases still wearing their preserved clothes, hair, and jewelry, their death grins staring out at the excavators, as in these cases from Olby and Skrydstrup. From P. Glob, *The Mound People,* Figs. 15, 24. Ithaca: Cornell University Press, 1974.

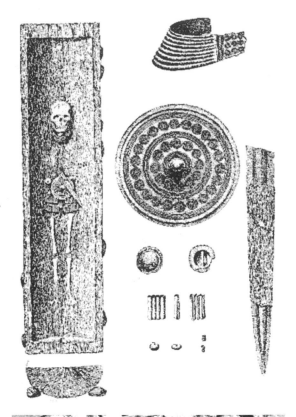

Indo-European chiefs, like their more settled Neolithic counterparts, seem to have displayed their power by means of human sacrifices (Jelinek 1990; Hutton 1991:81–95; Glob 1974:60, 113). There are human sacrifices associated with the Bronze Age megaliths, but beginning with the Neolithic, there is also a remarkable series of sacrifices that occur in bogs and surrounding elite burials. In one Bronze Age pit, about 10 individuals were buried alive while kneeling and probably drugged (Fig. 8.6; see also Sherratt 1991). Some of the bodies placed in bogs were probably simple executions of individuals for crimes or transgressions. However, others bear the signs of having been ritual sacrifices: There are many ways that death was delivered to some individuals: some bodies were staked to the bottom of bogs; other ritual offerings were staked into the bogs near the human bodies; many bog bodies appear to have been elite individuals; and bog sacrifices occurred at known cult centers (Figs. 8.14, 8.15; see also Sanden 1996:174–77). Human sacrifices are also known from early historical accounts of Indo-European tribes, but they usually entail burning or wounding. Some authors suggest that these different techniques of sacrifice or punishment may reflect appropriate forms of death in honor of each of the major deities presiding over each of the three major social divisions of Indo-European society (Mallory 1989:138). In any event, human sacrifices, whether justified in religious or other terms, must be viewed primarily as an ecological expression of power while the symbolical justification is largely incidental and arbitrary.

As in the Neolithic, Indo-European chiefs used feasts as a major means of gathering people together, extracting surpluses from them, and redistributing a nominal return of goods to the populace. The extent of these ritual feasts, almost certainly held in honor of titular deities, far surpasses anything that was known during Neolithic times. Enormous mounds of feasting and ritual debris occur in England during the Bronze Age, attaining proportions as large as 65,000 cubic meters (McOmish 1996).

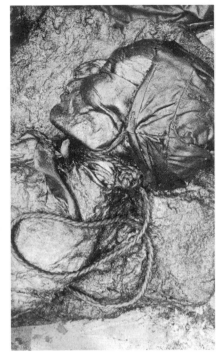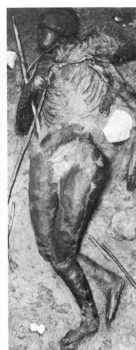

Fig. 8.14. Bogs were favorite places for leaving offerings, making sacrifices, and sometimes disposing of bodies. The tannic acids in the bogs frequently preserved organic materials so that the intact bodies of victims could be recovered. The Tollund man still has the cord used to strangle him around his neck while this young naked girl found in the Windeby bog was blindfolded and pinned down to the bottom of the bog by wooden rods. Both were probably ritual sacrifices. From P. Glob, *The Bog People*, Figs. 2, 38. London: Paladin, 1971.

Indo-Europeans also used animals as harbingers of supernatural powers and carriers of messages from spirits to humans. Gods or spirits could appear in the form of birds or animals and by observing their approach and behavior, one could divine the messages that they carried for humans. Sunwise (clockwise, or deosil) was considered beneficial, countersunwise (widdershins) was considered baleful. This symbolism may well extend back to the Neolithic sun cults, but it is difficult to be certain. Perhaps because of their high mobility, many Indo-Europeans also had few large-scale sanctuary structures (Fig. 8.16). Rather, they seem to have emphasized rituals that consecrated chosen spaces with chanting and animal sacrifices, perhaps delimited by carrying flaming brands of sweet-smelling herbs deosil (sunwise) around the perimeter of an enclosure, such as performed by the Kalash of the Hindu-Kush Mountains (Eliade 1978:190; Loude and Lievre 1984, 1985). The large megalithic centers were obvious exceptions.

While the bull continued to play an important role in social transactions and rituals, the horse became an even more important symbol of the elites and ritual honor. Horse goddesses, such as Rhiannon and Epona, are common in Indo-European pantheons. The great turf-cut chalk horse overlooking the Uffington hill fort in Britain (Fig. 8.17)

Fig. 8.15. Bogs seem to have been preferred places for contacting supernatural forces, and they are still viewed as "eerie" places at night, when mists form and marsh gas can create mysterious lights. Many Indo-European shrines were in or near bogs, and many offerings were left there such as this fertility goddess from the bog at Vikso. From P. Glob, *The Bog People*, Fig. 52. London: Paladin, 1971.

has also been recently dated to the Bronze Age (Miles and Palmer 1995). Horses are common sacrificial animals that accompany their masters to the grave, and they feature prominently in Indo-European rites pertaining to royalty and fertility. Even in the Southeast Asian cattle-centered rituals, horse sacrifices are far more prestigious than cattle sacrifices. In both early Ireland and early India, royal rituals included the sacred copulation of queens or kings with horses (Littleton 1982:208).

Being nomads originally, Indo-Europeans would have had a difficult time keeping track of the sun's movements across fixed points on the horizon. As a result, they used a lunar calendar even until relatively late times in Italy and some other regions. Nevertheless, the sun was an important supernatural being, and Indo-Europeans clearly adopted the solar symbolism and solstice celebrations of established solar cults when they came across them, as at Stonehenge. If the sun was not critical for determining the timing of the initial Indo-European calendrical rituals, it was certainly an important elite symbol of the highest deity. Solar symbolism is rampant in the European Bronze Age (Glob 1974:99–106; Green 1991; Hutton 1991:110;

Fig. 8.16. Aside from usurped megalithic monuments, there are few imposing early Indo-European temples or shrines. Many ritual areas seem to have been in remote areas, such as oak groves deep in forests or this simple shrine (reconstructed) located in a bog area at Bargeroosterveld, Drenthe, in Holland. The high mobility associated with the early Indo-European lifeway may have been an important factor in the modest nature of most of their ritual areas. J. H. F. Bloemers et al., *Verledan Land*. Amsterdam: Meulenoff en Co, 1981.

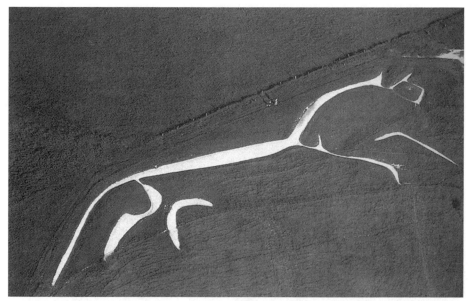

Fig. 8.17. The great importance of the horse in Indo-European economy and ritual is revealed not only by the horse sacrifices in Indo-European elite burials but also in horse goddesses, rituals involving horses, and the impressive images of horses that Indo-Europeans carved on the landscape, such as this monumental figure of a horse carved into the chalk subsoil at Uffington, England. From A. Ross, *The Pagan Celts,* Fig. 15. London: B. T. Batsford, 1986.

Stover and Kraig 1978:113). It is generally thought that the wheel is a solar symbol in Indo-European art (Figs. 8.18, 9.5). In this connection, a number of authors have claimed that the typical Bronze Age celebrations of the dead at Halloween and of new life on May Day may have been established in relation to solar calendars as far back as the Neolithic, but also celebrated using Bronze Age, Indo-European megalithic monuments to establish their proper timing (Stover and Kraig 1978:164; MacKie 1997:357–58; Burl 1976:127; see also Littleton 1982:171–74).

A great deal can be gleaned from the Bronze Age rock art that carpets particular areas of Europe, such as the Val Camonica region of Italy, where there are numerous representations of horned and phallic gods, marriages, fights, and circles with crosses in them (Fig. 8.19). Aside from the Neolithic crosses noted in Chapter 6, the earliest "Celtic" cross motif in a circle seems to occur in the Carpathian Mountains about 3000 B.C.E. (Hutton 1991:103). The occurrence of an equal-armed cross inside a circle in many Bronze Age rock carvings is often interpreted as representing the sun or a solar wheel. However, in some cases, it seems equally probable that the cross within a circle may represent a typical shamanic round drum with the crosspieces in the back. This could well have been a popular subject for representation in ritual art, given the presence of shamans in Indo-European society and rituals and perhaps the use of such drums at many important occasions.

INDO-EUROPEANS WERE CONNECTED TO THE WORLD

Although these elements seem to have been established by the Indo-Europeans between 4500 and 2500 B.C.E., Carlo Ginzburg has argued that many of the traits were not confined to the Indo-European ethnic groups. As a number of other scholars have noted even earlier, the vast steppes and the high degree of mobility of the Indo-Europeans across the steppes must have brought them into contact with many other people and facilitated the spread of cultural characteristics over large parts of the steppes. These

Fig. 8.18. The sun was undoubtedly one of the most important symbols in the religious life of the Indo-Europeans. Here it is represented by a disk (originally covered in gold) that is being drawn on a sacred wagon by a celestial horse, not very dissimilar to the (Indo-European) Greek idea that the sun was drawn across the sky in a chariot. The wheel may be symbolic of this chariot or of the sun itself (see also Fig. 9.5). This model is from Trundholm, Denmark. Courtesy of the National Museum of Denmark.

grasslands stretched from eastern Europe all the way across to Siberia and northern China (Fig. 8.2). Ginzburg (1991:214–20) argues that ethnic groups all along this enormous corridor were constantly intermixing and exchanging ideologies, myths, prestige goods, art styles, marriage partners, and rituals. Thus, the captivating "animal art style" of the Ukrainian Scythians is similar to the animal style of the Irish Celts, the Scandinavians, the Iranians, and the northern Chinese from 1000 B.C.E. to 1000 C.E. (Fig. 8.20). Even the archaeological remains of textiles are distinctive and similar throughout this area (Good 2000).

Myths also are uncannily similar from the far extremes of this region, such as versions of Cinderella that are found in China and Europe, but not in Africa, which is outside this zone of influence (Ginzburg 1991:249). Because of these interactions, exchanges, and similarities across the Eurasian steppes, it is often difficult to tell exactly where classic Indo-European pieces of art such as the Gunderstrup Cauldron were manufactured (Taylor 1992). Ginzburg even suggests that shamanism as we know it originated in this zone and diffused throughout it, never reaching Africa, where ecstatic spirit possession is common but the typical shamanic battles with the forces of evil are not.

SUMMARY

On linguistic evidence alone, the Indo-European language family can be shown to have spread rapidly over Europe, Asia Minor, the Iranian Plateau, and northern India between 4000 and 2000 B.C.E., the estimated time period for the breakup of Proto–Indo-Europeans. Linguistic evidence indicates that the best candidate for the homeland of the Proto–Indo-Europeans just prior to this diaspora was on the steppes north of the Black Sea. Archaeologically, this corresponds best with a group of cultures collectively known as "kurgan" cultures, so named after their burial of elites in pits under mounds of earth. While the initial kurgan groups had only copper, they soon acquired bronze technology and spread it throughout Europe. Thus, the history of Indo-Europeans in Europe is largely the history of the Bronze Age, and the study of Bronze Age religions is part of the study of pastoral nomad types of religion, even if these were introduced into forested, nonnomadic environments in Europe.

There are good archaeological indications that some groups from the steppes began invading or impacting the relatively wealthy territories of southeastern Europe and Italy between 4000 and 3000 B.C.E. Invasions may also have taken place in central, western, and northern Europe, although many archaeologists argue for a more complex scenario in which already existing elites in some of these areas were eager to acquire new prestige goods and therefore sought out the emblems of status that early Indo-Europeans made available, such as drinking beakers and copper or bronze weapons and ornaments. In this view, Indo-European

Fig. 8.19. Many ritual and daily scenes were recorded in rock art left by the Indo-Europeans. At top appears to be a marriage. At center and bottom are battle scenes. The two individual figures in the center represent supernatural entities, one with a solar symbol at the end of his penis, the other horned individual with a mace resembling Thor's hammer. These are only a few of the many scenes from Val Camonica in Italy. From E. Anati, *Camonica Valley*, p. 237. New York: Knopf, 1961.

languages associated with these new prestige items acquired a high status, just as the English language has a high status in most industrial nations today because of its trade and economic advantages. Elites, and then nonelites, would have adopted many aspects of Indo-European languages as a status symbol and thus spread the linguistic elements throughout their areas (Harrison 1980:164; Zvelebil 1995). This scenario would account for the marked cultural continuity observed archaeologically in many regions (Hutton 1991:88). A contending theory is that Indo-Europeans invaded all parts of Europe and usurped the position of local elites, imposing their language and culture on all matters of importance. As Mallory (1989) has documented, there is no simple expla-

Fig. 8.20. The "animal" art style spread across the steppes from northern Europe to China. Indo-Europeans adopted this style and helped spread it across the grasslands with their high mobility. At top is a a lion used to decorate a capital letter in the Book of Kells. At center is a Scythian lion using the exact same motif as a decorative element. At bottom are other examples of the Scythian variant of this animal art style from opposite ends of the steppes. Top: from G. Bain, *Celtic Art: The Methods of Construction,* p. 116. New York: Dover, 1973; second figure from R. Rolle, *The World of the Scythians,* Fig. 20. London: B. T. Batsford, 1989; third figure from *From the Land of the Scythians,* Fig. 20, Plate 3. New York: Metropolitan Museum of Art; Courtesy of The State Hermitage Museum, St. Petersburg. Bottom figure "Reindeer carved on coffin in the second Tuekta kurgan, Altai," after Rudenko, from *Arctic Anthropology* 11(1974):cover. University of Wisconsin Press.

nation that fits all the archaeological and linguistic data satisfactorily. Thus, a mix of situations and factors may be necessary to account for this extremely complex and dynamic period of prehistory and its religious changes.

It is possible to reconstruct Indo-European religion in some respects, thanks to the comparative cultural ecological studies that have been carried out concerning pastoral nomads, historical documents of early Indo-European life, and archaeological remains. It is clear that the original Indo-Europeans were primarily herders. Although they became farmers in many places or their customs were adopted by farmers, a number of aspects of their society and religion continued to reflect typical pastoral nomadic adaptations, including the increased importance of raiding and warfare and the existence of warrior groups within Indo-European society. Deities and rituals became distinctive for both these warrior groups and the elites, and both probably differed to some degree from the deities and rituals of common herders and farmers, which undoubtedly emphasized fertility, the home hearth, and the sacred protection of the home. There is good evidence that warriors and elites emphasized the importance of warrior deities and sacrifices, including human sacrifices that displayed the ritual and temporal power of those in charge. Their pantheons were hierarchically arranged, mirroring elite society of the time. The most powerful elites strove to establish similarly powerful gods, often associated with the sun and bulls.

The division of Indo-European society into three complementary classes (priestly elites, warriors, and food producers) is the foundation for understanding the symbolism of the number three in many Indo-European rituals. A strong dualistic view of good versus evil is another dominant Indo-European conceptual element. Sacred experiences appear to have been sought primarily using psychotropic drinks. Both warriors and priestly elites used such drinks in all important social or religious events and especially before going into battles for the community, whether in this world or in supernatural realms. Typically, they mystically transformed themselves into animals. The battles with the forces of evil may well have been organized by elite secret society cults. Members of these cults were probably demonized as sorcerers or witches in Medieval Europe by church authorities.

These insights provide a number of important keys to understanding the underlying meaning (both formal and symbolic) of some of the rituals and symbols that we still use in contemporary society, but that have slipped into our cultural unconsciousness in many cases, carried along by tradition, habit, and subconscious resonance. There are many more such symbols that become apparent if we examine some of the dominant Indo-European cultures of the past 2,000 years such as the Celts. It is to them that we now turn to gain further insights into the meaning of the rituals that we carry out today.

CHAPTER 9

Celts and Saxons Embellish
Western Rites

When the Roman legions under Julius Caesar expanded into Gaul (France), they confronted howling naked Celtic warriors wearing only their swords and shields and the blue dye they used on their skin (Bahn 1991). When the Romans advanced into Iberia (Spain), they confronted Celts. When Romans disembarked in Albion (Britain), they had to battle Celts. It was the Celts who twice sacked Rome and looted the treasures from its temples in the third century before the common era. It was the Celts who sacked the sacred temples of Greece in 278 B.C.E., carrying off precious metals and jewels. The Celts nearly drove the Romans out of Britain even after the Roman conquest. Julius Caesar is reported to have killed a million Celts and enslaved another million. It was the Celts who told fabulous wonder tales, such as the story of Cuchulainn, and who are among today's most gifted storytellers and lovers of creative, playful speech forms. The French comic book character Asterix still provokes laughter with his skillful play on words and antics referring to many Celtic myths. The Celts loved colorful, showy clothes, jewelry, and bravado. Mockingly, they told Alexander the Great that the only thing they feared was that the sky might fall on their heads. Some of them bleached their hair or formed it into spikes in imitation of Cuchulainn, not unlike recent punk fashions.

Above all, the Celts represent one of the most direct sources for many of the beliefs and rituals that the English-speaking world still adheres to. In order to provide a general understanding of those beliefs and rituals, we will take a brief look at the history and symbolic content of Celtic culture, as well as some of the other influences derived from the Angles and Saxons, which represent Germanic influences. The Celts maintained many general Indo-European traditions, such as cattle raiding and fractious fighting, even though many of them had become more agricultural and sedentary. Thus, this chapter will focus a bit more on the symbolic aspects of Celtic religion, for which there is considerable historical and ethnographic documentation.

Who Were the Celts?

Celtic speakers constitute one branch of the Indo-European language family. There are a number of separate Celtic languages and regional differences, but we will focus primarily on the British Isles, where traditional Celtic culture persisted the longest and where the influences on the English-speaking world were the most direct. English is not a Celtic language, but a Germanic one, the tongue of invaders who came into the British Isles during the fifth and sixth centuries of the common era. The Germanic languages are also Indo-European, as are the Roman-derived languages and the Viking languages. One of the major characteristics of Indo-Europeans is that they not only fought with non–Indo-Europeans, but they also fought bitterly among themselves, one tribe against another, even if they spoke the same language. The history of Indo-European cultures is one of very rapid and widespread expansions, often followed by just as rapid reductions in size when other groups began expanding. Roman historians recorded no fewer than three massive Celtic migrations impacting their territories around 600 B.C.E. and 400 B.C.E. and in 58 B.C.E. The latter two involved 300,000 and 368,000 people, respectively, and seem to have been motivated by the prospect of acquiring richer, wine-producing lands (Cunliffe 1997:69–74, 89). There is no reason to believe that such expansions as well as declines and migrations did not occur throughout Indo-European history. Thus, some groups like the Thracians and Illyrians expanded to the point that they became known as the most populous people north of the Greeks. Now they are linguistically extinct. The Celts, after expanding over almost all of Europe in a mere 200 years, are now reduced to a relict population of only a few thousand speakers, mainly in the British Isles, with some pockets in Brittany (France) and Nova Scotia (Canada).

The origins of the Celts must be traced back to the initial Indo-European arrival in central Europe (or at least to diffusion of their languages and status items, sometime around 3000 B.C.E.). From 1200 to 800 B.C.E., a regional culture called the Urnfield Culture developed in what is now southern Germany, Austria, and Bohemia in the Czech Republic. This culture was noted for its burial of the dead in urns. The urn funeral rite appears to be linked to the origin of the Celtic culture, which spread rapidly throughout much of Europe after 800 B.C.E. (Fig. 9.1). While a Celtic expansion definitely did occur during this period, there are some scholars who argue for a much wider initial distribution of Celts outside this generally accepted homeland. Specifically, some authors suggest that Celtic speakers moved into the British Isles with the first Beaker influences or during the early Bronze Age (Harbison 1975; Burton 1979). If this is true, according to Irish mythology, there seems to have been no shortage of subsequent Celtic invaders.

The Celts, like most other Indo-Europeans, were predominantly fair skinned and fair haired. Society was divided into the normal three Indo-European classes (Ross 1967:54; Richards 1980). The monumental hill forts they constructed, together with smaller farmsteads, specialized prestige goods, and the historical-linguistic accounts of elite rulers leave little doubt that most Celts were organized into chiefdom types of societies accompanied by fairly intense competition over animals, land, labor, and trade, although in poorer environments one might find some transegalitarian communities. They did not form any coherent ethnic group or have an ethnic identity beyond local confederations. Rather, they were fractious and treated other Celtic or linguistic groups as enemies

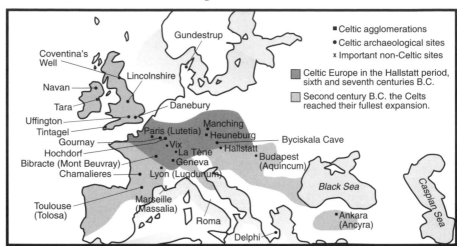

The Emergence of the Celts

Fig. 9.1. This map shows the initial distribution of Celtic tribes prior to the sixth century and their subsequent expansion throughout much of Europe. Adapted by Greg Holoboff from B. Cunliffe, *The Celtic World*, pp. 18–19. New York: McGraw-Hill, 1979.

as often as allies. Warfare was a major aspect of Celtic life, and the Celts erected victory shrines to their patron deities. These shrines consisted of monumental wooden structures where the bodies and weapons of hundreds of decapitated warriors could be hung (Brunaux 2000:101ff). Human heads were some of the most prized spoils of raids and battles (Fig. 9.2). In fact, an entire head cult grew up among many Celtic groups (Dietler 1997:321; Brunaux 2000:153). The human head seems to have been considered the seat of the soul or an aspect of divinity, and it was associated with supernatural powers, as suggested in the story of Bran, whose head is supposed to be buried at the Tower of London, still guarding it from attack. Heads were certainly part of elite cult sanctuaries in the south of France, perhaps as part of warrior secret society cults.

THE CELTS EXPAND

When one group or culture expands at the expense of other groups or cultures, it is usually because some key feature of technology or sociopolitical organization provides critical advantages. In the case of the pervasive Celtic expansion, one of the key features appears to have been the adoption of iron smelting and technology, probably acquired from contacts to the east, where this technology had been developed. Iron smelting is far more difficult than making bronze because much higher temperatures are required to turn iron ore into metal than is the case with copper and tin (the constituents of bronze). Some idea of the time, effort, and risk involved can be gleaned from traditional iron smelters and workers in Africa (Fig 9.3; also David 1988). Given the high temperatures that must be attained and maintained as well as the considerable risk of failure, it is not surprising that iron smelting was accompanied by elaborate magical spells, incantations, and the sacrifice of animals. In Africa, smelting was portrayed as a type of battle to extract the precious metal from its earthy prison. Master iron smelters purposefully created imagery and rituals around their furnaces emphasizing the importance of fertility (David 1988; Larick 1991:353). They also used their iron-producing position, their

Fig. 9.2. The Celts were warriors of renown, and they used many tactics to terrify their enemies including thunderous drums, blaring instruments, ecstatic Druids working magic on the battlefields, and brazen appearances. They also used head-hunting to intimidate enemies and worshiped the human head as the seat of the soul, as indicated by this figure of a warrior god from Entremont, Provence, In France (above), and these columns with niches for human heads in a temple at Roquepertuse in Provence. Above: from M. Green, *The Gods of the Celts,* Fig. 11. Phoenix Mill: Alan Sutton Publishing, 1986. Below: from Julius Caesar, *The Battle for Gaul,* ed. A. Wiseman and P. Wiseman, eds., p. 125. London: Chatto & Windus, 1980.

lineage, and their rituals to legitimize their considerable economic control and political power within their societies. All this, too, was undoubtedly true of Celtic if not all Indo-European smiths, given the magic associated with all metal weapons, as noted in the last chapter.

In the Arthurian legends and other Celtic myths, swords have names and special magical properties (Fig. 8.12). They are key components of the Celtic wonder tales. Another prominent feature of the African smelting process is the incessant beating of the hand bellows, which must go on nonstop for ten or more hours. I suspect that in order to render this extremely monotonous and tiring task more bearable, many iron smelters using hand bellows began to develop and elaborate rhythms that went well beyond the

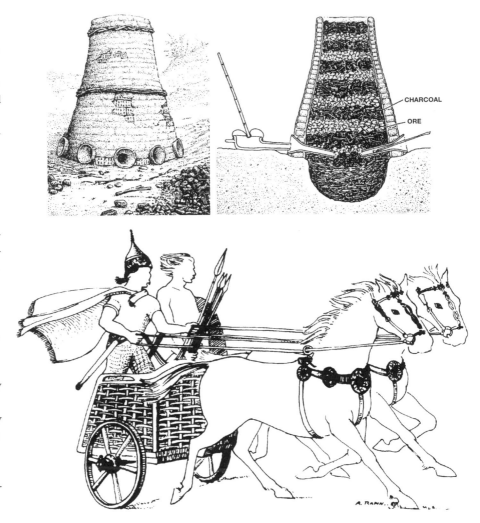

Fig. 9.3. Behind the Celts' military successes were several major technological innovations that they borrowed from cultures farther to the east, including the smelting of iron, which enabled them to produce relatively inexpensive weapons and lightweight wheeled vehicles like chariots (below). These technologies gave them critical advantages in battles. Above is one type of traditional iron furnace historically used by African tribes but probably similar to the ones used by the Celts. Top: from F. van Notten and J. Raymaekers, "Early Iron Smelting in Central Africa," *Scientific American* 258(6):110. Bottom: from A. Duval, *L'Art Celtique de la Gaule au Musée des Antiquités Nationales,* p. 34. Paris: Editions de la Réunion des Musées Nationaux, 1989.

basic beats that tend to characterize hunter-gatherer or simple horticultural music. Thus, the smelting process may have been the impetus behind the development of the more complex jig rhythms of the British Isle Celts and the polyrhythms that characterize the music of iron-making societies in Africa.

Although iron smelting was much more difficult than making bronze, it had one critical advantage: it was cheaper. The reduction in cost had nothing to do with the manufacturing process; rather it was due simply to the fact that the key ingredient for making bronze was tin, and tin was extremely rare and costly to procure. By itself, copper is relatively soft and not well suited for making tools or weapons. It requires the addition of tin to stiffen the copper and make serviceable edges. Even though bronze swords were highly effective in hand-to-hand combat, bronze weapons were so expensive that only the very wealthy could afford them.

In contrast, iron ore could be procured in almost any environment where there were volcanic rocks or bogs. By adopting iron smelting, the Celts could effectively reduce the cost of making swords and arm many more warriors. Iron was every bit as effective as bronze for making weapons. Iron weapons therefore gave the Celts a major military advantage over other groups, just as it provided major military advantages to initial iron-using groups elsewhere in the world. The Scythians of the Asian steppes and the Bantu speakers who occupy most of sub-Saharan Africa are only two of many well-known examples of groups that expanded rapidly after the adoption of iron technology.

In addition to weapons, iron technology enabled the Celts to make a wide array of other tools, some of which also provided military advantages, such as the iron-rimmed wheel that made lightweight war chariots so effective in combat. In fact, after the Celts perfected their wheel technology, few changes were made until the twentieth century, when rubber wheels were developed. Above all, the expansion of the Celts or their culture heralded the arrival of the Iron Age in Europe. Other groups later adopted iron-smelting technology, but the initial adoption by the Celts and their imitators gave them decisive advantages in the early Iron Age, beginning about 800 B.C.E. in Europe. Celtic blacksmith wizards went on to create other wonders with the new technology, including most of the basic metal hand tools still in use today (saws, pliers, gouges), barrels with iron bands, iron horseshoes, and metal locks (Severy 1977). Their silver- and gold-smiths produced phenomenally sophisticated and artistic cups, mirrors, shields, brooches, pitchers, wheeled couches, horse fittings, ritual wagons, cauldrons, swords, helmets, and countless other metal items. Most of these metal items were reserved exclusively for the wealthy elites or warriors. The metal chokers, or torcs, in particular were a sign of elite lineage. The elite Celts loved artistic embellishments, and they decorated almost everything they could.

With increasing contacts between Roman merchants and Celtic elites, some Celtic chiefdoms developed into major trade centers with very large fortified hilltops called "oppida." Some of these centers verged on becoming small states or at least large confederations of powerful chiefdoms. The Manching oppida in Bavaria, for instance, had timber walls enclosing an area about 6.5 kilometers in circumference. The iron nails used in making these walls alone are estimated to weigh about 300 tons. The Celtic elites had always sought the exotic prestige goods that Etruscan, Greek, and Roman traders had to offer. The French town of Marseilles began as one of many Greek trading posts. Thus, Greek and Roman metalwork, glass, beads, and amphora containing wine were traded far into the European hinterland in exchange for Celtic furs, cattle, specially bred hunting dogs, slaves, salt, and many other Celtic products.

DRUIDS: CELTIC PRIESTLY ELITES

Of all the aspects of Celtic society described by the Romans, the Druids held a particular fascination (Fig. 9.4). Druids still hold a great fascination for many people interested in the occult. They evoke images of arcane knowledge, natural wisdom, and great spiritual power handed down across generations upon generations of mystical adepts. Some archaeologists have gone to great effort to demonstrate that the Druids could not have built Stonehenge or other megalithic monuments. While this may be technically true, it is almost certain that other priestly Indo-European groups similar to the Druids did officiate at Stonehenge and other large Bronze Age megalithic monuments. The Druids, if you like, represent only one order of Indo-European priestly elites, perhaps comparable

Fig. 9.4. Since the time when they were first encountered and described by the Romans, Druids have held a special fascination for many people interested in Celtic culture. Druids were powerful priests, mystics, poets, politicians, and judges. This somewhat fanciful, but perhaps not entirely unrealistic, view of what Druids looked like was published in the late nineteenth century and was based on recent finds of Bronze Age gold ornaments.

in distinctiveness to the way that Dominicans or Jesuits represent different orders of priests within the Catholic Church but are still all priests.

The Druids were the priests of the Belgic-influenced Celts, and they were undoubtedly internally ranked with many specializations. They formed one of the Celtic social classes. They administered rituals, sacrifices, and justice, cast magical spells, and performed divinations. As in many shamanic cultures, certain individuals were likely marked from birth as destined to become Druids or to play special roles within the Druid class, especially those born with a caul (amniotic sac) or with deformities or who were otherwise impaired (Ginzburg 1991:155, 165, 247). In many Indo-European cultures, those who were blind or partially blind seem to have been considered to have special gifts of supernatural sight or "second sight." Such concepts are embodied in the Norse god of runic magic, Woden, who had one eye missing, and in Homer, the master bard of the Greeks, who was blind.

According to Caesar, Druids seem to have been a particularly British order of priests that developed relatively late in prehistory, eventually spreading to parts of Gaul. However, Brunaux (2000:29, 40, 53) argues that they more likely developed among Belgic Celts in the fourth century B.C.E., in conjunction with large sanctuaries. This complex spread throughout northern France and England via Belgic invasions and influence. Druids, like other Indo-European priests, were recruited from elite and warrior families. They undoubtedly concerned themselves primarily with elite matters and helped induce ecstatic states as part of elite initiations into warrior or other secret societies. There are even suggestions that Celtic Druid elites may have been promoting the worship among all Celtic groups of certain Celtic deities like Cernunnos and Lugh (a sun god) in an attempt to create one or more unified Celtic states (Ross 1967:54). We can only assume that lower-ranking Druids or more common shamans, or perhaps village wisewomen, administered to the needs of common folk. Such women may have become the witches condemned by the church in later centuries. Druids were rooted out and exterminated much earlier by the Romans because they fomented, or represented, opposition to Roman rule.

There is considerable debate as to whether the Druids were shamanistic in nature or more priestly. As you may remember from preceding chapters, it appears that with increasing sociopolitical complexity, shamans become more ranked and more specialized. The highest-ranking individuals eventually became politically powerful priests divorced from ecstatic experiences, while lower-ranking shamans became marginalized curers. Where did Druids fit along this continuum of development? Different levels of the Druid hierarchy probably would be placed at different points, with those at higher levels becoming priestlike. However, many Druids appear to have shared a number of characteristics with shamans, including the use of sensory deprivation induced by being enveloped in bull hides for divinations. The discovery of cannabis in a Celtic tomb at Hochdorf, Germany (Green 1997:33), also indicates the use of psychotropic substances to achieve altered states of consciousness. Druids also used typical shamanistic costume elements such as bird's wing headdresseses, antler headdresses, and bull's hides (Piggott 1975:110; Ross 1967:57; Green 1997:33). Moreover, transformation into animal forms, a common shamanic belief, is rampant in Celtic art, myths, and beliefs. All these elements are consistent with the idea that some kind of ecstatic shamanism was likely practiced by some Celtic Druids. Given what we know about the ecstatic states used by Indo-European warriors, it would be surprising if the Druid elites did *not* induce similar ecstatic states for their rituals. It is not clear whether some Druids specialized in ministering to the ritual needs of warriors or whether the warriors may have had their own ritual specialists, but the former seems likely.

Some Druids may have been women (Green 1997:97), although Markale (1975:38, 43) finds no proof that women were Druids, even though they clearly did serve as seers and sorcerers. Some elite women certainly held important positions of leadership and authority in Celtic society, perhaps when no suitable male heirs were available, as in Boudicca's case, but usually politics and public life were dominated by men (Markale 1975:47; Green 1997:94ff; Hutton 1991:171). Some women also became warriors. Elite women outranked common men, and the dominant spouse in a marriage appears to have been determined by the relative wealth of the partners (Markale 1975:35).

In addition to fulfilling ritual and healing roles, Druids played key roles in settling disputes and administering justice. According to the Romans, the major penalty that the Druids could mete out was to ban offenders from the Celtic feasts. Unfortunately, the Roman commentators do not specify whether individuals were banned from all forms of feasting or only major feasts. This may seem to be a trivial punishment by Industrial culture standards, but in traditional societies, the world revolved around feasting, a point made in Chapters 5, 6, and 7. Feasting is generally a means of exchanging wealth, investing surpluses, acquiring political and social support, organizing war bands, earning recognition and status for economic success or success in other domains (war, politics, alliance making), and getting married. The Celts based their social and political organization on patron-client relationships. Attracting clients was largely based on competitive feasting and drinking to show who could provide the most benefits and defend themselves best. This is sometimes referred to as "Celtic potlatching." Given this situation, the ability to hold significant feasts became synonymous with socioeconomic advancement and the right to rule (Murray 1995). Thus, exclusion from feasts would have been devastating for anyone with the slightest ambition. Michael Dietler (1989, 1990, 1996) has been particularly important in documenting the critical role that feasting played in all domains of elite Celtic life and how a person's political, social, and economic fortunes absolutely depended upon feasting activities. Persons banned from all these activities would soon find themselves in a precarious position in the intensely competitive Celtic world, and probably in other Indo-European societies as well.

Although the Roman reports seem to have distorted the Celtic judicial system, banishment from feasts as an "extreme" form of punishment may have applied only to the elite and warrior classes, for we know archaeologically and from written sources that a considerable number of people were executed or sacrificed (Brunaux 2000). Evidently, elites, and presumably Druids, had life or death powers at least over their slaves' lives. Perhaps transgressors from other classes could incur lethal retribution as well. A number of scholars have argued that the many hundreds of bog bodies from the Iron Age represent, in part, executed criminals (Sanden 1996:166ff). Indo-Europeanists have suggested that there were probably three different ways criminals could be executed, corresponding to the nature of their transgressions or the class of the wrongdoer in the Indo-European tripartite division of society (Mallory 1989:138). Most executions took place by hanging, drowning, or burning.

Moreover, there is abundant linguistic evidence that blood feuds were common but constrained by rules and that fines were imposed for the breach of rules. A standard case of inexcusable murder resulted in a fine of seven female slaves or 21 cows. If the victim was of noble class, the fine increased accordingly (Richards 1980:83). Each person had an established "honor price" calculated on the basis of a person's class, rank, and wealth. If the person was injured, killed, or wronged, the guilty person would have to pay compensation determined by both the nature of the wrong and the victim's honor price. As is typical of many transegalitarian and chiefdom societies, there was probably an entire battery of lawyer-Druids to argue clients' best interests, as well as a judicial body that likely included community Druids. So, it would seem that Druids did have much more than just the power to ban people from feasts.

ELITE CELTIC CULTS

There is a remarkable diversity of gods populating the mythological geography of Celtic Europe. Seventy-five percent of the god names occur only once. It seems that each community or region had their own patron god and a goddess of the land (Cunliffe 1997:185–86). Later deities with more specialized functions may have been adopted for war, fertility, and other important concerns. There were also a few deities whose cults seemed unusually widespread such as Lugh, the sun-related fertility god, and Cernunnos, the antlered god of the hunt and fertility. As in the Neolithic and Bronze Age, solar symbols and deities are particularly prevalent. In the case of the Celts, the solar wheel is one of the most common indicators of deities found archaeologically, and sanctuaries are usually aligned to solstice or equinox positions of the sun (Fig. 9.5; Green 1986, 1991; Brunaux 2000:94). The cults of the more widespread gods were probably promoted by elites, especially high-ranking Druids who considered themselves to be important "international" (intertribal) figures and who needed a common religious context in order to interact effectively with allied or other elites (Piggott 1975:34).

Many of the Celtic deities seem like little more than deified ancestors, which they may well be. The general character of these clan or tribal gods (Cunliffe 1997:186) certainly is consistent with idealized, deified, ancestral figures. It seems plausible that the Celtic aristocracy promoted cults for ancestors from whom they claimed to have derived their powers, both corporal and spiritual. These ancestor cults would have provided the ideological foundation for establishing and governing Celtic clans. Many surnames in the English-speaking world are derived from this Celtic clan structure. Names like MacDougal and O'Sullivan mean "the son of Dougal" and "the son of Sullivan." In the past, everyone with these names would have been considered a member of the Dougal or Sullivan clans, and all members would have been considered descendants of the original founding Dougal or Sullivan

Fig. 9.5. The solar symbolism shown here is widespread in Celtic art. Solar symbols usually revolve around the wheel metaphor, which is still used today in phrases like "the wheel of the year" or the "solar cycle." The rotated three-armed triskelis and the rotated four-armed cross are variants of the solar symbols, as are the more usual rayed figures. From M. Green, *The Sun-Gods of Ancient Europe,* Fig. 17, 23, 25. London: B. T. Batsford, 1991.

ancestor whom the living chief represented. Despite such obvious ancestor features in Celtic society, the great emphasis on individual achievement and wealth may have attenuated the overall importance of ancestor cults in favor of war or tribal deities (unless these were ancestors) as well as limiting the number of generations involved in ancestor worship.

ARISTOCRATIC ANCESTORS WERE WORSHIPPED AT HOCHDORF

Following contacts with the Scythians to the east, who followed the old kurgan tradition of burying elites under mounds, the Celts, too, often buried their elites under mounds, although regional burial practices varied considerably, including cremations, water burials, and excarnations. In groups that used mounds for burial, a timber chamber was generally constructed in the ground and then buried with the elite person and his or her grave offerings inside. Everything needed for a happy afterlife in "Summerland" (the Celtic paradise) might be included.

At Hochdorf, Germany, a series of unusually large burial mounds was constructed, dating to the early phases of Celtic culture, around 600 B.C.E. Jorg Biel (1987) was fortunate enough to excavate one of the tombs that had remained undisturbed by looters. The mound was originally 7 meters high and covered half a hectare of land. The inner

Fig. 9.6. The Celtic prince shown here, from Hochdorf, Germany, was buried in fine Indo-European tradition under a large earth mound, in a log chamber accompanied by a sacred wagon, drinking horns, a large cauldron, feasting paraphernalia, gold-decorated clothes, and a remarkable wheeled iron couch or throne (below), the supports of which were in the form of maidens. From J. Biel, "A Celtic Grave in Hochdorf, Germany," *Archaeology* 40(6):23 (1987).

core was composed almost entirely of large rocks. Digging through such material was difficult; however, the discovery of a collapsed but otherwise intact burial chamber was a reward far surpassing Biel's hopes: the Celtic find of the century. Inside the timber funeral chamber, Biel found the remains of a 40-year-old man reposing on a bronze funerary couch mounted on a series of small wheels, each surmounted by a bronze female figurine holding up the couch (Fig. 9.6). Such a technically advanced piece of furniture is remarkable at this time period, and it is quite rare in the Celtic world. The chief was buried in embroidered silk, and he clearly had contacts with Greek and Etruscan merchants, for their pottery and prestige items were also found in the tomb. He had a gold-handled dagger, a belt with gold ornaments, ornate gold brooches, an arm band, a necklace, and gold-trimmed shoes. Many of these items appear to have been made expressly for the funeral. There had undoubtedly been a funeral feast, and the feasting was intended to continue into the afterlife, for there inside the funeral chamber was a huge Greek cauldron rimmed with lions, filled with 500 liters of mead at the time of burial,

together with a Celtic gold
serving bowl. Nine drinking
horns were hung on the
walls. There was also a din-
ner service for nine piled on
a ceremonial wagon plated
with iron. The afterlife, it
appears, was viewed as a literal heaven, where one might
wait to be reborn. Perhaps
discoveries such as these in
earlier centuries provided the
basis for stories of "fairy
folk" or elves living inside
mounds where great ban-
quets took place and where
mortals who were lured to
eat or drink by fairy queens
found themselves ensorcelled
for many years, if not the
rest of their lives.

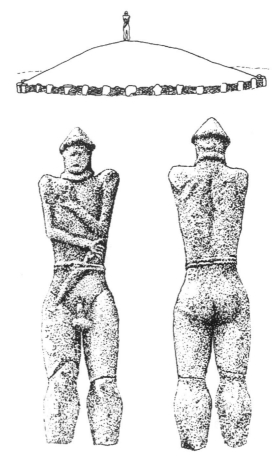

Fig. 9.7. The use
of elite burial
mounds for
ancestral worship
is indicated by the
erection of statues
at some of the
mounds, like this
one of a warrior
chieftain at
Hirschlanden,
Baden-
Wurttemberg, in
Germany. Statues
and burial
mounds were
probably vener-
ated by surviving
members of
lineages and their
allies. From
J. Collis, *The
European Iron
Age*, Fig. 25b, c.
London: B. I.
Batsford, 1984.

Although some archaeol-
ogists using linguistic evidence argue that there is
scant evidence for ancestor
worship in Celtic society
(Richards 1980:82), it is difficult to imagine that the tremendous effort expended in displaying the greatness of dead Celtic aristocrats such as the ones buried at Hochdorf was
unrelated to ancestor veneration or the use of ancestors in order to legitimize the reign of
current rulers. Indeed, the nearby discovery of a lifelike statue of a warrior-chief at the
perimeter of another tomb (Fig. 9.7) indicates that these tombs and their occupants were
meant to be venerated well after their funerals. Samhain, the popular Celtic feast of the
dead and probably the most important Celtic celebration, also indicates that ancestors
played a significant role in Celtic life.

Celtic Sanctuaries and Secret Societies

There are a number of cases of small, square sanctuaries placed in the midst of communities with round houses (May 1991:264; Piggott 1975:54ff; Cunliffe 1988:43; Dietler
1997:320). As in earlier periods, these sanctuaries are relatively small, often only suitable
for 1–13 people. These shrines were probably primarily for the use of the chief and/or
the highest-ranking elite Druids for honoring elite ancestors or community patron
deities and communicating with them spiritually. As with Vietnamese lineage shrines, if
there were public events and feasts associated with this worship, these activities seem to
have been carried on outside the shrines.

Fig. 9.8. One of the strongest indications that secret societies featuring elite or warrior cults existed from the Neolithic period onward is the recurring discovery of evidence for cannibalism, usually in secluded places like caves far away from normal living areas. Particularly macabre remains were found at Byci skala Cave in Bohemia, where animals and women were sacrificed and mutilated in the sixth century B.C.E. An artist's rather romanticized idea shows what the scene may have looked like. The man is holding a cup at the site (fashioned from a human skull), and another skull was found inside the cauldron. Drawing by Paul Jenkins. From Miranda Green, *The World of the Druids,* p. 84. London and New York: Thames & Hudson, 1997.

Elites appear to have continued the use of secret societies also. Warriors could certainly be expected to have formed secret ritual and feasting societies, and there may have been other types of secret societies. Armed warrior gods feature prominently in the archaeological record of the Iron Age (Cunliffe 1979:75: Green 1986:103). Especially noteworthy are the many variants of deities that continue the Neolithic tradition associated with bull horns. There is enough evidence of cannibalism in Celtic societies to indicate that this probably formed part of some secret society rituals, plausibly related to warrior cults (Cunliffe 1988:41; Hutton 1991:194). Probably the most dramatic archaeological example of such a secret cult was found in Byci skala Cave, in the Bohemian area of the Czech Republic. Here, abundant offerings of pots, grain, and animals were left in a cave, along with the grisly remains of 40 people, mostly women, whose heads, hands, or feet had been cut off (Fig. 9.8). One human skull was still inside a cauldron, and another skull had been shaped into a drinking cup (Jelinek 1990; Green 1997:84). Other caves and remote groves were undoubtedly used for other secret society rituals by elite groups.

As Celtic chiefdoms prospered from trade with the classical world, they also became bigger, more powerful, and more complex. After the fourth century B.C.E., large, rich burials occur as well as substantial sanctuaries such as the carefully excavated site of Gournay-sur-Aronde in northern France. These are rectangular areas, usually 15–50 meters on a side, surrounded by a ditch and a palisade to ensure that all activities were hidden from the noninitiated. They generally had an impressive entryway oriented to equinox or solstice positions of the sun. Festooning the entryway were statues of the sanctuary deity or ancestor as well as displays of his favor in the form of human trophy

Fig. 9.9. Celtic sanctuaries appear to have begun as small shelters with a simple offering pit dug into the ground to convey sacrifices to the underground, or chthonic, spirits, as shown below in a reconstruction of the sanctuary at Montmartin (Oise), France. A human skull was found in the offering pit. As chiefdoms developed, larger, more complex regional sanctuaries evolved such as the enclosed sanctuary of Gournay-sur-Aronde (Oise), depicted above with its surrounding ditch and displays of captured weapons and severed heads—offerings to the gods or ancestors for their support in warfare. These sanctuaries were oriented to solar positions. From J.-L. Brunaux, *Les Religions Gauloises,* pp. 100, 117. Paris: Editions Errance, 2000.

heads and sacrificed bull skulls (Fig 9.9; see also Brunaux 2000:84ff). A simple, small roof over an offering pit for chthonic sacrifices and poles for displaying captured weapons were the only other important elements in these sanctuaries. Considering the large amounts of animal bones and weapons thrown in the ditches, it is obvious that these sanctuaries were used by elite warriors, nobles, and priests for feasting, celebrating victories, seasonal changes, or ancestors, as well as for forming alliances (Brunaux 2000:130).

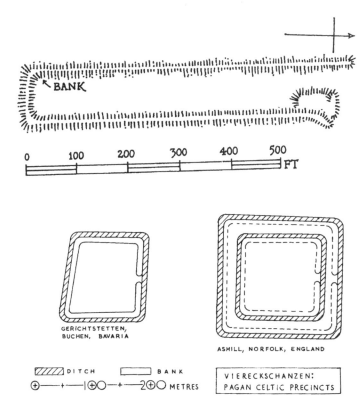

Fig. 9.10. As Celtic chiefdoms became larger and more powerful, enclosures for ritual meetings also became larger, sometimes reaching impressive dimensions. Examples of some of the largest enclosures include the one at Tara, Ireland, over 200 meters long and 30 meters wide; Ashill in England, over 200 meters on a side; and Gerichtstetten in Bavaria, a more modest 150 meters square. Whether these enclosures were used for assembling elite warriors with their retenues or were for a much broader segment of the population as might occur for tribute feasts organized by chiefs in honor of tribal deities is unclear. Similar types of events probably occurred in the complex societies of earlier times, including the Neolithic. Above: from S. Piggott, *The Druids,* Fig. 85. London and New York: Thames & Hudson, 1985. Below: from A. Ross, *The Pagan Celts,* Fig. 42. London: B. T. Batsford, 1986.

Smaller versions of these sanctuaries occur in habitation areas (especially elite living areas), but the great majority are located far away from any settlements. These isolated locations and the palisaded walls not only indicate that these were elite secret society sanctuaries devoted to particular (ancestral?) gods, but that they probably also served to politically unite a number of settlements in a region—thus their considerable size. Brunaux (2000:85) thinks these sanctuaries and their rites probably developed from earlier funeral rituals involving banquets, open spaces, processions, and sacrificial offerings. They are often associated with or located near barrow burials. He is undoubtedly right, for we have seen similar indications of the promotion of chiefs' ancestor cults to regional deity status in the Neolithic and Bronze Age as well. This appears to be a common tendency in religious evolution at this level of social complexity.

Dietler (1997:321) clearly links the development of these sanctuaries to the political ambitions of elites. He thinks they transformed a traditional funeral rite into a religious form that would promote the glory of the chiefs and make their claims to political power seem more natural. In some regions, sanctuaries grew to enormous size, up to 20 or more hectares (Fig. 9.10). These seem to have functioned in a similar fashion to the smaller versions, but on still larger political scales. They served entire chiefdoms or perhaps even segments of emerging Celtic states for the purpose of elite reunions, feasting, and politicking in the heyday years just before the Roman Conquest (Murray 1995; Brunaux 2000:89).

As with the construction of monumental burial mounds and hill forts, elites also demonstrated the great importance and power of their cults or ancestors by engaging in monumental rituals. Sometimes these projects defy rational analysis and must simply be

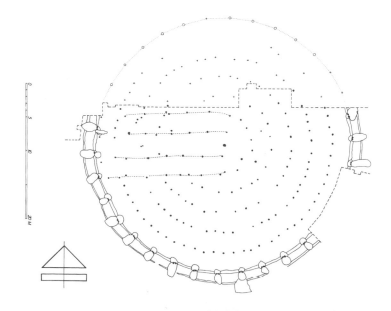

Fig. 9.11. The Celts sometimes built enormous structures for symbolic and perhaps ritual reasons, such as this one at Naven in Ireland—the largest known prehistoric Celtic building. They then sometimes just as quickly destroyed them. This building was filled with stones before it was completely burned down, almost as in a fairy tale. From Chris Lynn, "Navan Fort," *Current Archaeology* 134(2):45, 46.

viewed as displays of cult power meant to advertise the greatness of certain social and economic groups or certain patron ancestor deities (see the later discussion of offerings). Some of these ritual remains consist of enormous earthen-banked enclosures suitable for large gatherings of people. Other examples consist of very large structures, somewhat like the Neolithic woodhenges. However, in the case of Naven, one of the Celtic regional capitals in Ireland, the most remarkable wooden structure built anywhere in the Celtic world was constructed and then immediately filled with rock. After this, the entire complex was burned (Fig. 9.11). This building was an enormous 40 meters in diameter (Lynn 1986, 1993).

Fig. 9.12. Fertility was a constant religious and practical concern for the Celts, as with most food-producing cultures. While the elites may have worshipped the sun and produced impressive prestige objects symbolizing the sun, the more crudely represented concerns of the agriculturalists and herders clearly focused on fertility, as demonstrated by these simple carvings. The one at left is from Ireland, the one at right, referred to as the Broddenbjerg god, was found in Denmark. Left: from E. Kelly, "The Archaeology of Ireland 3: The Pagan Celts," *Ireland Today* 1 (March 1984): 7. Reprinted with permission from the National Museum of Ireland. Right: from P. Glob, *The Bog People,* Fig. 75. London: Paladin, 1971.

COMMON CULTS

On a more popular, as well as elite, level, fertility cults continued to be quite important. According to Cunliffe (1997:186, 189), the local or tribal goddesses embodied the land and its fertility. The mating of the tribal god and goddess at Halloween was meant to ensure fertility for the next year. The many offerings in springs and rivers or pools of water were most likely meant to bring fertilizing energy of water to worshippers, their land, and their herds. Phallic carvings, sometimes crudely made of wood (Fig. 9.12), are clearly part of popular fertility cults, while the horned or antlered depictions of Celtic gods frequently emphasize the phallic associations of these deities as well as their ability to provide abundant harvests, such as the Cernunnos sculpture holding a cornucopia from Reims, France (Fig. 9.13). As was true from the Neolithic onward, fertility was essentially synonymous with prosperity, wealth, and the good life. Barry Cunliffe (1979:72) and Miranda Green (1986:72) suggest that most, if not all, of the Celtic goddesses were agents of procreation, the earth, and fertility, especially the triple goddesses.

However, there is additional evidence for common, third-estate special rituals. Commoners undoubtedly celebrated some household ancestral rituals as well as the major religious festivals of the Celts. They were most likely excluded from secret society cult membership or the inner sanctuary rituals of more public cults, but they may well have participated on the periphery of these cults, and they undoubtedly paid special homage to sacred wells, springs, and other sacred places associated with fertility or healing, just as they do today. While some beautiful prestige objects were left at these locations by elite Celtic worshippers, there are also very crude sculptures of wood that seem to have been made with minimal skill or time investment. These were deposited in such large numbers as to indicate popular cults—over 5,000 were deposited in the springs at Chamalières in France (Fig. 9.14, Deyts 1971; Piggott 1975:80). These crude, simple offerings are probably the offerings of common people—a good example of the kind of art that is generally produced in contexts where there is no training or support for artisans.

The only other evidence that we have of common rituals occurs in the burial record. In contrast to the elite burials, which could be under large mounds, there were no cemetery areas or special burial rites for commoners. At Danebury in Britain, commoners seem to have been defleshed by excarnation—exposure to the elements—the bones then simply scattering

Fig. 9.13. The horned deities of the Celts such as the opulent Cernunnos from Reims, France, often represented abundance and wealth, and by implication, fertility. Sometimes these figures were phallic, but in this case, Cernunnos simply holds a cornucopia overflowing with agricultural produce. Horned deities also represented virility and strength and were therefore frequently called upon for their warrior attributes as indicated in the carving (above) from Maryport, Cumbria, in England. Above: from M. Green, *The Gods of the Celts*. Phoenix Mill: Alan Sutton Publishing, 1986; courtesy of the Senhouse Museum Trust. Below: Altar of Cernunnos. Reims, rue Vauthier-le-Noir, first century C.E., Inventory No. 978.20189, collection Musée Saint-Remi, Reims, photo courtesy of Musée Saint-Remi.

(Cunliffe 1988:40). In general, it appears that only about 5 percent of the population was buried, but these were not always elites (Hutton 1991:196). There is much variability in burial practices throughout the Celtic world. Cremation seems to be the normal funerary practice in many areas and times, but in some areas aristocrats seem to have been consigned to watery graves along with their most cherished prestige items, perhaps being set adrift in boats (Bradley and Gordon 1988). In other areas, ritual wagons were central elements in elite burials (Paré 1989). Thus each time period and each region should be analyzed separately—a vast topic that we cannot attempt to cover here.

Fig. 9.14. Thousands of crudely carved wooden objects and figurines were deposited in the sacred waters at Chamalières in France. The number of these offerings and their crude craftsmanship indicate that they were part of a popular rather than an elite cult. Left: from S. Piggott, *The Druids,* Fig. 63. London: Thames & Hudson, 1985. Right: from A. Ross, *The Pagan Celts,* Fig. 46. London: B. T. Batsford, 1986.

Offerings and Sacrifices

Ritual pits were dug deep into the ground, some of them reaching surprising depths of over 120 feet (Fig. 9.15). These pits were filled with special sacrificial animals, pottery, statues, coins, and many other types of ritual offerings. They first begin to appear in the Bronze Age but are most common during the Iron Age (Piggott 1975:72–75; Cunliffe 1979:92). Sometimes they end in wells and are associated with sacred enclosures. Stover and Kraig (1978:165, 175) suggest that these ritual pits were dug in order to provide the spirits of the dead with water and to pour libations and offerings to the dead, for the dead have great thirsts (more indications of elite ancestor worship). Presumably, the more important ancestors were for a chief, the deeper their offering pits were dug and the more esoteric were the offerings given to them. In fact, pits of less dramatic sizes with special ritual offerings in them are central features of many formal sanctuaries; they are also common occurrences at many Celtic settlements such as Danebury (Cunliffe 1988:41). This seems to be about as much sense as we are able to extract from these ritual deposits at this time.

The ritual logic of these offering pits and wells stems from a broader Indo-European concept concerning natural sources of water as portals to spiritual domains, a topic that we will turn to shortly. Offerings of priceless gold and bronze objects were placed in pools of water or rivers, undoubtedly with the expectation that the greater the offering, the more difficult it would be for deities to refuse requests, especially for battle victories (Cunliffe 1979:90). However, there must also have been a very great element of prestige display in making these labor-costly offerings, especially when performed in front of allied elites. Following a similar logic and display strategy, the aristocrats of the Northwest Coast tribes of

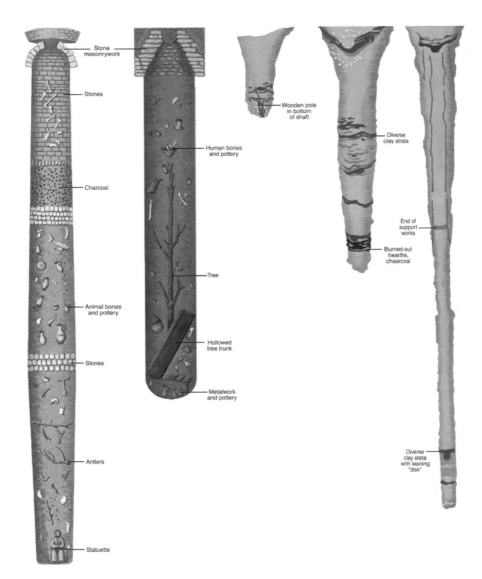

Fig. 9.15. During the Bronze Age, but especially in the Iron Age, impressive deep pits were dug in ritual areas only to be filled in with ritual offerings, fires, and dirt. These deep shafts were undoubtedly considered portals of communication with the underworld and ancestors, but whatever their symbolic meaning, they were certainly meant to be impressive displays of elite power. From B. Cunliffe, *The Celtic World*, p. 93. New York: McGraw-Hill, 1986.

North America made great displays of dropping their most valuable copper objects into the sea. Such displays created renown that was talked about for generations. The presence of human skulls or skeletons in all of the Celtic contexts (pits, pools, and rivers) may reflect burial rituals for special people, war trophies, or human sacrifices as special offerings or displays of power (Bradley and Gordon 1988; Hutton 1991:188, 190).

Human sacrifices are part of the offering pits in some instances and probably served as religiously justified displays of the power of the Celtic elites. Roman histories are replete with accounts of human sacrifices by Druids as part of rituals. Head-hunting by warrior elites for the supernatural power contained in skulls also features prominently in early historical accounts of the Celts. Archaeological remains amply support these early accounts (Piggott 1975; Green 1997; Sanden 1996; Dietler 1997:321).

The Bog Bodies

Over the last few centuries, almost 600 bodies, or parts thereof, have been recovered from the peat bogs of northern Europe. Peat generally forms in marshy areas where shallow pools of water collect. Marshes may be reasonable places for getting rid of the unwanted and defiling bodies of those who, like Germanic transgressors, committed shameful crimes. Thus, many "cowards, shirkers, and sodomites" were probably "pressed down under a wicker hurdle into the slimy mud of a bog," as recorded by the Roman historian Tacitus. Many of the bog bodies seem to fit such a scenario fairly well. They are older men who have been strangled or stabbed or had their throats cut. Some such bodies may also have simply been murder victims. Other bodies, however, have a much more ritual-sacrifice character to them. For instance, a substantial number of the bodies are young adolescents, especially girls who were pinned to the bottom of bogs naked and blindfolded without any clear indications of how they were killed (Fig. 8.14). As noted in the previous chapter, some are associated with other ritual offerings or occur near known sanctuaries. Moreover, there are certain periods when bog bodies are particularly numerous although major deposits of the spoils of war ("booty" offerings) are rare. In succeeding periods, these booty offerings increase dramatically but bog sacrifices almost disappear (Fabech 1991:97). This change indicates that bog bodies were predominantly sacrifices and that at some level they played the same ritual role as offerings of expensive weapons and precious metals, although the symbolic content and even the conceptual justification for each type of act may have been different.

Thus, bog bodies provide yet another glimpse into Celtic ritual life. The documentation of human sacrifices in bogs makes it all the more probable that the Roman accounts were relatively accurate when they described Druids disemboweling human victims for divinatory purposes or burning human and animal victims alive in wicker frames shaped like giant people. It also seems relatively likely that these victims were generally criminals, slaves, or war captives (Hutton 1991:193). In any event, tribal Celtic life was anything but peaceful. Between enemies, blood feuds, slave raids, one's own rampaging warriors, and priests looking for potential sacrifices, individuals must have had to be constantly on their guard. They must have had to cultivate strong mutual-help alliances with kith and kin alike to ensure a secure future.

The Celtic Seasonal Festivals

Like other Indo-Europeans, the Celts originally came from a nomadic background. They may have settled down into a more agricultural way of life after arriving in productive farming areas at some point after leaving their Indo-European homeland, but they carried many of their nomadic traditions with them, including raiding, fractious competition, and their seasonal festivals. Because of the difficulty of marking the rising and setting position of the sun when moving around the countryside, nomads tend to use seasonal markers for seasonal festivals. Markers such as the time when the maple leaves turn red, when harvests are ready, or when the herds are taken to spring pastures are common signals for seasonal ceremonies. Nomads also tend to use lunar calendars to keep track of time and to schedule festival events. In fact, the Romans and Celts used a lunar calendar long after they had settled down into civilized ways although they also adopted solar reckoning systems for some events, as indicated by their sanctuary orientations. It was not until the first centuries of the common era that European civilizations adopted the current, solar-based calendar. It seems likely that full moons would have been the optimal times for holding the most traditional Celtic festivals.

For large polities, the archaeological evidence indicates that some of these festivals must have been very large gatherings of people from a wide area. Huge enclosures, over 200 meters in diameter, were evidently used for seasonal gatherings (Piggott 1975:62), perhaps primarily for elites and warriors in federations, but there must have been major celebrations for more common classes as well, perhaps taking the form of tribute feasts held by chiefs or priestly elites (Fig. 9.10). Evidence for feasting is abundant at these large enclosure sites (Hutton 1991:167; Murray 1995; Brunaux 2000:130–38), and it seems most likely that such events would have been held at the time of the major Celtic sacred festivals: Samhain (Halloween, 31 October), Beltane (May Day, 1 May), Imbolc (Brigit's Feast, or Ground Hog Day, 2 February), and Lughnassa (1 August). None of these occur on any significant solar dates such as the solstices or equinoxes. They all appear to be seasonally determined.

The Indo-Europeans and the Celts may have adopted some of the more important indigenous Neolithic solar festivals when they arrived in new areas, especially for elite cults or secret society worship. However, it is evident that they also carefully preserved their own ritual traditions as any recourse to the folklore of Ireland or Scotland amply attests (McNeill 1959). In fact, these are still the major festivals in these areas. Lughnassa is by far the most important celebration in Ireland today (MacNeill 1982). In Western English-speaking cultures, Halloween and May Day are probably the most popular, nonofficial ritual holidays still celebrated, with fairly obvious symbolism and meanings. In Shakespeare's day, people were so excited by these festivals that no one slept on the eve before May Day (Squire 1975:408). The significance of Imbolc has faded with its renaming as Ground Hog Day, but it is still a popular day for casual divination, as is Halloween. All of these ritual festivals originally derived their meaning from a largely pastoral nomadic way of life, whether celebrating the new growth and fertility of the land (Beltane, or May Day), the coming into milk of the ewes (Imbolc), the first grain harvest (Lughnassa), or the slaughtering of surplus animals prior to winter, and the honoring of the dead (Samhain, or Halloween). These would have been events that everyone in a community probably participated in either at household celebrations or at larger gatherings within communities or between communities. There were undoubtedly rituals, sacrificed animals, drinking, games, sports, races, marriage arrangements, trading, and the formation of alliances. In many respects, they appear to have been similar to the country fairs that are still popular in rural Celtic areas (Stover and Kraig 1978:162; MacNeill 1982). Many of these festivals involved bonfires on the highest hills and new fires rekindled in home hearths. In modern and perhaps earlier times, jumping over bonfires was a prominent feature in these festivals, as was rolling flaming hoops representing the sun down hillsides into bodies of water. Fairies or other supernatural beings were unusually active during these festival times, and care had to be taken to placate them with small offerings of food or drink left in the house or at some sacred place like a spring. Dancing, music, and perhaps orgiastic behavior in the woods or fields at night all seem to have been common. Animal and even human sacrifices were carried out up until the nineteenth century in remote areas in order to promote the well-being of the community and to appease angry spirits (Squire 1975:412). Similar types of fairs and large-scale festivals probably extend back into the Bronze Age or perhaps into Neolithic times when the woodhenges (discussed in Chap. 7) were built and great enclosures similar to those of the Celts were also created at sites like Durrington Walls and Mount Pleasant.

Themes and Symbols Reemerge in an Age of Nostalgia

Mircea Eliade and Joseph Campbell, among others, have lamented the lack of viable living myths and meaning in our own contemporary society. People who do find meaning in symbols and myths generally focus on past cultures in which myth and symbols were alive and vibrant. Celtic cultures provide an unusually rich source for such symbols and traditions. The Celts were masters of visual arts and visual impacts; they were masters of myth, magic, and marvelous tales.

One of the most famous and ever renewing mythic traditions is King Arthur and his knights of the Table Round. The major theme of King Arthur's story is that of living in a noble utopian kingdom that was spoiled by individual moral weaknesses and by the existence of unscrupulous individuals in the world—a theme not unfamiliar to contemporary society. The story of Arthur is a story of paradise lost. It accounts for tragedy in the world in terms of evil and selfish men, but it is also a story of paradise to be regained, since the hope is always held out that Arthur, or another noble and capable ruler, will return, reunite the kingdom, restore moral order, and establish a new golden age. The Holy Grail is also used in this myth cycle as a symbol for the same theme: The sacred cup or cauldron of regeneration, rebirth, and prosperity is stolen or lost, plunging the kingdom into barrenness and discord, and so the quest to regain it is an ongoing one (Figs. 9.16 and 8.10).

There is some historical truth to the general Arthurian myth. After the initial Roman invasion, a "pax Romana" (an era of peace imposed by the Romans within their conquered domains) reigned over England for a few hundred years, putting an end to tribal warfare. The country prospered. However, by the fifth century, Rome was collapsing as a political power and could no longer afford to keep an army in England. The citizens of Romanized Britain were left to fend for themselves.

Bands of unconquered Picts from Scotland began raiding the wealthier regions to the south, and the unconquered Irish also took advantage of the situation to invade England. The central political authority in Britain collapsed, plunging the British Isles, once again, into a period of war between regional tribal groups and petty chiefdoms vying with each other for dominance. Groups of Germanic speakers called Saxons also took advantage of this state of turmoil to establish some settlements on the eastern shores of Britain. Some of the Celtic chieftains employed these Saxon newcomers as mercenaries to help stave off the raids by the Picts and Irish. By 450 c.e., the Saxon colonists had opened the gates to their Germanic kin and allies to mount a veritable invasion of England. Other tribes joined them, especially the Angles and the Jutes, forming an Anglo-Saxon coalition. They successfully overran much of what is known today as England (Angle-land) including London, Lincoln, and York.

However, according to Geoffrey Ashe's (1982, 1985, 1988) historical analysis, in 490 c.e. the native Celtic Britons managed to stage a successful counteroffensive. At this time in particular, the Britons seem to have become united into an effective military force,

Fig. 9.16. The Holy Grail, the miraculous chalice of many medieval stories including the Arthurian cycles (portrayed below), is very likely the continuation of a much more ancient Indo-European and Celtic tradition of magical sacred cauldrons that contain wisdom, rebirth, fertility, and prosperity. The Gunderstrup cauldron (above) was almost certainly one such magical cauldron used by the pagan Celts or Germanic tribes. See also Fig. 8.10. Above: courtesy of the National Museum of Denmark. Below: courtesy of the Bibliothèque Nationale de France.

and there was enough centralized power to construct an enormous fortified wall in Lincolnshire and East Anglia, apparently marking the Celtic-Germanic frontier. The *Historia Brittonum,* written in 830 c.e. by Nennius, refers to Arthur by name as leading the battles against Germanic chieftains whom other chronicles described as ruling around 500 c.e. Thus, it seems that there was a warrior-chieftain who managed to unite the Celtic Briton chiefs around 490 c.e. and reestablish a semblance of peace over part of Britain for a time. His exact name is unknown, but one of his many titles may have been Arthur, which, in fact, means "bear" and may have been more of a warrior title than an actual name, just as the Norse berserkers were referred to as bears.

Some scholars suggest that Arthur is actually a name from the continental Celts near Switzerland and that the entire story is a generic myth of the Celts, representing events that must have reoccurred many times during the centuries of tribal conflicts that were endemic to Celtic and Indo-European society in general (Ginzburg 1991:167). Nevertheless, there were chieftains in Britain at the appropriate time and places, who were referred to as "the Bear," such as Cuneglasus the Bear and his father, also referred to as "the Bear." There are even good candidates for other characters in the story, such as Maglocunos (Mordred?), who killed his uncle in an attempt to seize the throne and ended by dividing the kingdom. Recent excavations have also uncovered a piece of slate with the Romanized name "Artognov" from Tintagel, the birthplace of King Arthur according to legend (*Vancouver Sun,* 7 August 1998:A20).

The next wave of invaders on English soil, the French Normans, seem to have popularized the old stories of Arthur in order to vilify the Germanic tribes they conquered in 1066 c.e. The Normans could therefore justify taking political rule away from Germanic rulers since the Angles and Saxons had unjustly seized it from the British Celts. The Normans could present themselves as coming to fulfill Arthur's prophecy of a return to more noble and utopian times. How much of the other details about Arthur and his entourage is true is impossible to say, although it is very likely that Celtic chieftains did have counsellors like Merlin who were tutored in divination and magic, much as the Druids were, and it is entirely likely that the Celtic elites maintained close contacts with other Celtic elites across the English Channel in Brittany, France, as recounted in the early history of Arthur's family. Both archaeological and historical documents support this. Even the Round Table may reflect a Celtic tradition of sitting in a circle at feasts so as to minimize conflicts about rank and status (Cunliffe 1979:43).

The Arthurian stories incorporate many elements of pre-Christian religion and myth besides figures like Merlin and the search for the Holy Grail. When Arthur is mortally wounded, he is placed in a boat that carries him away, much like the earlier pagan Celtic and Bronze Age boat burials. The story of the Green Knight is basically an allegory of vegetative and human sacrifice/death and rebirth. There are magical springs and castles as well as the Lady of the Lake, who gives Arthur his magical sword, Excalibur. This story may harken back to some of the Celtic sacrifices of women in bogs or the deposition of valuable swords in lakes and springs. It certainly reflects Celtic myths about water. In Celtic beliefs, transition zones are always potential portals to the otherworld and must be approached carefully. Thus, the edge of a wood, the threshold of a house, hearths, twilight, dawn, times of pronounced seasonal change, and especially places where the earth meets water are all points at which supernatural forces can be contacted with comparative ease.

Springs, wells, and pools of water that seem to come from deep in the earth held a particular fascination for the Celts although they were also popular for making offerings during the Neolithic and Bronze Ages. These bodies of water were thought to communicate rather directly with a miraculous well in the center of the otherworld—the Well of Segais. In fact, there is an entire cult of springs that is still active in rural parts of Ireland and France today (Brenneman and Brenneman 1995). Many traditional rural folk go to certain springs or wells in order to drink their waters for cures of specific illnesses. The commercial success of Vichy and Perrier bottled water was perhaps originally built upon similar beliefs. In Ireland, springs and wells are frequently decorated with ribbons or other objects left as offerings to the spirits of the water, the fructifying forces from the underworld (Fig. 9.17). This is the origin of the contemporary tradition of wishing wells or the throwing of money or objects into any body of water while making a request of supernatural powers—a wish. The same logic and beliefs undoubtedly underlay the sacrifices in bogs, the offerings in springs, and the digging of ritual wells or pits that were filled with offerings during the Iron and Bronze Ages of Europe. In Roman Britain, Coventina's Well alone contained over 14,000 coins as well as small bronze statues, brooches, bells, pottery, glass, and a human skull (Ross 1967:29–30).

If sources of water represented fertility with a feminine cast, the masculine aspect came to be expressed in the form of Robin Goodfellow, a.k.a. Robin of the Wood, a.k.a. Robin Hood, a.k.a. Puck, a figure dressed in green and thought to cavort with the fairies, exhibiting many characteristics of the Greek pans and satyrs. He was immortalized in Shakespeare's *Midsummer Night's Dream* and countless plays and folk stories. In a more extreme form, the Green Man, with vegetation sprouting from all of his orifices (Fig. 9.18), also seems to be derived from a Celtic or perhaps Germanic folk concern for fertility of the land beginning at least in the time of the Romans (Hutton 1991:314).

As described in the opening chapter of this book, the Celts seem to have been one of the most consummate traditional religious people of the Old World. Everything surrounding them was imbued with magic and sacred forces. Each type of tree had special supernatural characteristics, and even the letters of the magical Ogham alphabet that the Celts developed after contact with the Romans were named after trees. All manner of supernatural qualities were attributed in particular to animals. However, as in the Bronze Age, of special significance was the horse as a sun and fertility symbol as well as a critical element for battle successes; the bull acted as a symbol of prosperity and divinity; and the dog was often sacrificed like a slave or considered to be a supernatural messenger. Birds, too, were especially noted for their portents or involvement in special events, such as the ravens that accompanied battles (Green 1986:171ff; 1992).

As in other traditional cultures, shamans, gods, animals, and people could all adopt each others' shapes, or "shape-shift." This is an extremely common theme in Celtic tales, often taking the form of magical punishments. Boars, in particular, were thought to be former swineherds, and lovers were often depicted as transformed into birds. However, the power to transform oneself at will into an animal and back again appears to be possible only for gods and specially trained ritualists or cult members, such as Druids and

Fig. 9.17. As in the pagan Celtic past, wells and springs are still revered in some Celtic regions today as magical places. At Doon Well in Kilmacrennan, Donegal, Ireland, those with pain have left bits of cloth on a small tree at the well hoping that their pain or illness would be left behind. Numerous offerings are also scattered over the rocks by the well. From W. Brenneman and M. Brenneman, *Crossing the Circle at the Holy Wells of Ireland,* p. 51. Charlottesville: University Press of Virginia, 1995.

warriors. As we noted in the preceding chapter, such transformation abilities undoubtedly derive from a more general Indo-European belief system involving secret societies in which individuals transformed themselves into animals and engaged in ecstatic battles for the good of the community (Ginzburg 1991:183ff). Many of these individuals were judged to be malevolent witches by medieval church authorities seeking to eradicate heresies. Some of the people the Church killed during the medieval period who claimed transformation powers were probably simple village wisewomen who were maintaining age-old Indo-European conceptual systems for healing on the spiritual planes.

So, with the Celts, we can detect the immediate predecessors for most of the contemporary rituals and many of the beliefs in the contemporary English-speaking world, even though we do not speak a Celtic language today. Contemporary English is a creolized Germanic-French language. There are not as many clearly Germanic traditions that have entered into the popular rituals of the Western world; however, there are several worth noting, beginning with the days (*deus*) of the week. As is common among many traditional people in the world, each day of a weekly cycle was thought to be ruled by a different god, and each day was thought to be propitious for different kinds

Fig. 9.18. It is difficult to know how far back in popular myth the Green Man goes. Sculptured depictions first appear during Roman times and clearly represent the wild, vital, and fructifying forces of nature. The image became extremely popular during the late medieval and Renaissance times and is still a popular figure in Mummer's plays and Morris dancers' celebrations, as shown by this lively Green Man in a Vancouver Morris dancers' May Day celebration. Above: from W. Anderson, *The Green Man: The Archetype of Our Oneness with the Earth,* Fig. 106. London: HarperCollins, 1990. Below: photo by Margaret Whale.

of things. It is probably not a coincidence that our most important day of the week is ruled by the Sun, followed by a day ruled by the Moon. The next four days are all ruled by different Germanic deities. Tiwaz, a Germanic god of war, rules Tuesday (Tiwaz's Day). Woden, the god of supernatural knowledge, rules Wednesday (Woden's Day). Thor, the sky god of thunder and lightning, rules Thursday (Thor's Day). And Frigga, goddess of love and fertility, rules Friday (Frigga's Day). The Romans also have a nominal representative in our weekly pantheon. Saturn, the ancestor of the gods as well as of utopias past, rules over Saturday (Saturn's Day)—a good day for parties and enjoyable activities.

As we noted in Chapter 3, many of the characteristics of Santa Claus are strikingly similar to the Germanic figure of Woden riding his magical eight-legged horse through the skies from the northlands to visit each household at midwinter and bring his blessings. The only other distinctive Germanic contribution to our ritual lives is the Saxon spring festival honoring Eostre, the goddess of the dawn who probably was also associated with rabbits. Spring rites in her honor may go back to very early Indo-European times (Rappaport 1999:337). She still presides over our spring ceremonies of world rebirth at Easter. The Anglo-Saxons also gave us the word, "witch," derived from *wicce,* meaning "knowledge" (Hutton 1991:335fn).

Because of their commonly shared Indo-European heritage, many of the other traditions of the Anglo-Saxons were so similar to Celtic traditions that it is impossible to tell whether some practices and beliefs came from Celtic or Germanic sources. The maypole is one example that is extremely widespread in Germanic and Celtic cultures. Although some authors like Hutton (1991:177) quip that there is no written evidence for maypoles before the 1300s, this is probably due to the nature of written records and elite interests prior to this time. The widespread distribution of maypoles and decorated ritual trees from Scandinavia to eastern Europe argues for a much longer history, at least in rural communities, versus their more recent adoption in urban centers. The same may be true of the Christmas tree and Yule log. While the earliest historically recorded Yule tree was noted in an aristocratic house in 1605 in Germany, this is probably only the beginning of the Industrial elite tradition. The widespread occurrence of sacred decorated trees again seems to argue for much deeper rural roots, although the tradition may have been mainly Germanic (Miles 1912:263–71). Certainly other Indo-Europeans like the Romans and the Kalash used evergreens in abundance during winter solstice ceremonies, and the custom of bringing in potted trees or bushes before Yule so that they would bloom at the winter solstice also appears to be of great antiquity. The Vietnamese have a similar tradition for miniature orange trees that are central to their lunar New Year festival, Tet. In the European cases, the sacredness of the trees is always indicated by the colorful decorations and lights that adorn them and transform them into fantastic and memorable apparitions that seem full of vitality, life, and abundant symbols of prosperity.

Summary

The Celts exemplify many of the strongest religious characteristics of the Indo-Europeans that were identified in the last chapter. They had three classes composed of warriors, priestly elites, and common herder-farmers. They had warrior bands and a chiefdom type of political organization. They excelled at warfare, and thanks to the advantages they gained from smelting iron, they were able to expand over most of the European continent as well as large parts of Anatolia. Under favorable trading and agricultural conditions, some Celtic regions developed into large confederacies with large, imposing fortified centers verging on primitive states. The Celtic Druids, too, seem to conform to the general pattern of priestly elites in other Indo-European groups. Celtic burials reflect the differential status of class membership and also reveal concepts of the afterlife that are surprising in their literal reproduction of earthly lifestyles. Ancestors undoubtedly continued to play an important role in elite Celtic religion, as did secret societies. However, (ancestral?) war deities and tribal deities appear to have dominated ritual life. Elites and Druids interacted intensely across political boundaries, participating in some pan-Celtic cults such as those associated with the sun god Lugh and the horned god Cernunnos. Themes of fertility and prosperity, too, are detected both in elite and common cults.

Large fairlike gatherings at seasonally important times of the year probably characterized the other major aspect of Celtic ritual life and provided the contemporary English-speaking world with some of their most beloved popular ritual events. Offerings and sacrifices were an integral part of the Celtic world. The richer and more powerful individuals were, the greater the sacrifice they could make to the gods and presumably the greater the rewards they received or could justify taking. These sacrifices were simple items for common people. For elites, they ranged up to the most expensive gold treasures produced by Celtic craftsmen and frequently included valuable animals, slaves, or captives. Elites sometimes dug impressive ritual pits for conveying these offerings to ancestors or other chthonian deities.

Many of our literary traditions, including the battles between good and evil in magical landscapes, owe their immediate origins to Celtic wonder stories such as the legend of King Arthur. Many other aspects of our daily lives that we perform as a course of habit also owe their origins to the Celts or the pagan Germanic tribes who invaded England in the fifth century of the common era. Tossing coins into pools for good luck and invoking the names of Germanic deities when we say the days of the week are only two examples of this. The study of traditions and folklore reveals many more such contributions to our cultural habits and gives them considerably more meaning than their usual unconscious iteration. They are capable of providing a magical and poetical element to our lives. Of particular interest in this regard are the fairy tales that almost all Europeans have grown up with. Aside from being entertaining stories for children, what meaning do these tales contain, if any? That is a topic of engaging interest to scholars and educators alike, and it is the topic of the next chapter.

CHAPTER 10

Once upon a Time

The Mystery of Stories

Traditional religions are above all else oral and participatory. Rituals and myths were not to be written or read, because writing robs ritual and myth of its spur-of-the-moment inspiration and dynamic interplay between performers, observers, surroundings, and inner spiritual forces. Writing saps the life out of organic sacred experiences and turns them into dull, dry, profane experiences stuck in fixed formats forever. Myths, like rituals, are meant to be sacred experiences for both listeners and tellers. You enter into a different dimension of time with the intonation of a magical formula—"Once upon a time . . ." You are gradually drawn into a different world and become the transformed characters in that world. That world becomes a part of your life. The myths, tales, and symbols are doorways—portals or points of entry into sacred realms where you can make connections with the deeper structure of the universe, a structure that has always existed and always will exist. Myths and tales are timeless. Their characters never age.

Today, some of our traditional culture is still passed on largely in a participatory context, such as traditional music and many crafts like woodworking. However, the traditional oral aspects of passing on myths, cultural forms, and information has almost completely disappeared, except in a few small cultural refugia such as our children's bedrooms or scout campfires, where stories are sometimes still told (or often read). There are also a few small circles of adults who attempt to keep alive the old storytellers' art.

There are some areas far removed from the Industrial bustle, from televisions or videos, where the art of telling myths and stories still thrives. These include the remote villages of the Scottish Highlands, the Aran Islands off the west coast of Ireland, the Amazonian jungles, and the parched lands of Nubia. An art it is. Just like playing music or painting, it takes training and practice to become proficient, to be able to captivate people's attention for long stretches and enrapture them with the mysteries of stories. Few people in Industrial societies today have much exposure to vibrant storytellers. They have been upstaged by Hollywood producers who have millions of dollars at their fingertips, all earmarked to capture the attention of children, adolescents, and adults. Traditional storytellers have no stage sets, no money to spend on their presentations, no scriptwriters, and no computerized special effects. They use only their wits, the vivid imaginations of their listeners, and the props that they find around them when telling a tale. They rely on the inner visions of their listeners to create all of the spectacular effects that the cinema has reduced to a mere spectator sham and an easy fillip. It is not surprising that the storytellers have been displaced. Yet, there are few experiences more memorable than listening to a master storyteller around a fire at night creating a totally imaginary and captivating world.

Traditional myth telling had all of these same entrancing characteristics. What has come down to us in the form of written records is but a dim reflection of what those myths were like in the living cultures. They are like the dry bones of a once-living creature. Trying to appreciate what the original myths and stories were like is usually like trying to get a feel for traditional music by looking at the printed versions. I have met traditional musicians who scorn attempts to write their music down. They claim that, at best, perhaps 10 percent of a tune is conveyed by the written versions, for traditional musicians are constantly changing nuances and making slight variations according to their inspiration of the minute. The tunes they play are rarely exactly the same twice, although the melody is clearly recognizable. Moreover, no two traditional musicians ever play the same tune exactly the same way. Traditional musicians also interact a great deal with other players and with their audiences, changing tunes to suit the flow of the energy at the time, the nature of the dance, and the reactions of the dancers or other players.

This is a good way of looking at traditional storytelling, for traditional storytellers never tell the same story exactly the same way twice, and no two tellers have exactly the same version although everyone would recognize a particular myth or tale (Guenther 1999:428). Committing myths and tales to writing eliminates this dynamic and their innovative characteristics or at least ignores them. Writing gives the false impression that there was only one, static, and unchanging version of myths, whereas in reality there were as many variants as there were tellers and communities and regions (Reay 1959:131). Greek scholars can attest to this fact, because they are aware of the bewildering array of versions of some of the Greek myths (Kraemer 1992:36).

The most devastating effect of writing, however, has been to remove the spontaneity of the telling and the interaction between the tellers and their listeners. Traditional tale tellers often use comparisons between the events in the tales and the personal experiences of individual listeners or events that everyone in a community knows about to enhance the interest and the spice in their tales. This is only one technique that traditional storytellers employ to make their tales come alive and to engage listeners' attention.

Very few film documents exist that capture the techniques of traditional tale tellers. However, one superb example, *The Myth of Naro,* was filmed by Napoleon Chagnon among the Yanomamo Indians of the Upper Amazon River in South America. In this film, the leading shaman of a village recounts one of the most important myths of his community. The myth is much like a Rudyard Kipling just-so story because it explains how many of the animals obtained their characteristics, such as the brown nose and slow behavior of the sloth and the bright feathers of the toucan. It is also like a transformation myth of the geographical landmarks of the area, since in it the distinctive mountains take on their shapes as a result of the events in the tale. There are also culture heroes, references to spirits, and moral lessons for those who break basic taboos such as wife-stealing and murder. The shaman uses many techniques to draw listeners into the story and maintain their attention. He states that the events are absolutely true events. He uses humor and coarse language, referring to one of the characters as "that stinky bastard." He spices up the interest with references to sex, wife-stealing, chases, and battles. He says that the events took place right in the village where the tale is being told, "in that house over there," or in the surrounding mountains. The shaman teller talks directly to the listeners and asks them rhetorical questions: "Did you know that?" or "Isn't what I say true?" He uses gestures to indicate dramatic events, such as the sloth being flung through the air and crashing into a mountainside. He uses props that happen to be at hand, such as a piece of string held between foot and hand to represent a bow. He also changes his voice to mimic the characters, and he uses many expressive facial gestures. The overall result is a thoroughly captivating and entertaining account that a standard written version simply could never convey.

Written accounts provide only a skeleton framework of a story or myth, usually in dry, matter-of-fact academic fashion. For this and other reasons, the invention of the printing press was strongly opposed by the guardians of traditional culture. They prophesied that printing would result in the sterilization and depauperization of culture as well as the transformation of children into introverted misfits incapable of normal social interactions. In extreme cases, these predictions have undoubtedly come true; however, home-made music and tellers of tales have not been eradicated completely, and most children seem sufficiently adept in social situations even after many years of intensive book learning. Perhaps our culture has become depauperized in many respects due to printed books, but it has also become much more enriched in other ways, extending to everyone a plethora of concepts, information, and experiences that were formerly only available to elites.

Today, of course, many of the same objections that were raised to printing are being raised concerning television and computers. Again, there is clearly the potential for further impoverishing real living culture through the substitution of facile, flaccid spectator observation for interaction and participation. There is also an increased potential for asocial, introverted personal development. However, as with printing, there are important benefits to television and computers, one of which is the potential for developing interactive stories as well as interactive musical experiences. The age-old creative sacred forces within human beings are difficult to eliminate completely, and they keep on resurfacing in new contexts and under new situations in new variations. It is up to us to be aware of these processes and to provide the encouragement and nourishment required to keep those aspects of our human heritage in good health. It is up to us to use new technologies for our own personal growth and benefit rather than for our impoverishment or the benefit of media moguls.

Fairy Tales Connect People with Sacred Forces

For many readers, fairy tales are perhaps the most familiar part of the oral tradition of storytelling. We do not know when fairy tales began or what their origin was, but they are especially prevalent among Indo-European speakers and in the cultures with which Indo-Europeans came in contact on the steppes. In the nineteenth century, the Grimm brothers, Jakob and Wilhelm, compiled one of the earliest and most extensive collections of European fairy tales (Fig. 10.1). It is probably no coincidence that they were linguists studying Indo-European languages and began to perceive many commonalities among the tales told in different Indo-European cultures. Because there are so many fairy tales and because they tend to shade into other kinds of tales, it is difficult to come up with a precise definition of fairy tales, although we can list a number of key characteristics. We can also describe fairy tales on the basis of what they are not. Fairy tales are not local legends that feature ghosts and scary events. Fairy tales are not myths focusing on gods, nor are they saints' tales with moralistic messages or reaffirmations of church faiths. Fairy tales are not just-so stories that attempt to account for animal characteristics on the basis of events that transpired in the distant mythical past. There is little overt philosophizing, moralizing, deep thinking, intellectualizing, political action, or social protest in fairy tales. Class inequalities are simply part of the world as it exists. Nor are there overt references to sex or any erotic images.

The characteristics of the fairy tale are that *people* are the central figures, not gods or saints or animals. Fairy tales do not purport to represent historical events in a region. Moreover, the heroes in fairy tales always experience a crisis. They are abandoned in the woods, they are trapped in drudgery, they have been put to sleep for an eternity, they are prisoners, they are to be killed, or they must perform impossible tasks or suffer horrible fates. These life crises are resolved by obtaining help from supernatural beings or realms. Finally, the ending of the fairy tale is always happy

Fig. 10.1. The Brothers Grimm published many traditional European fairy tales in the nineteenth century and made them available to wide audiences throughout the world. Many became classic favorites well before Walt Disney popularized them. Several collections were published in the early twentieth century, including this version of Sleeping Beauty. From A. Quiller-Couch (illustrated by Edmund Dulac), *The Sleeping Beauty and Other Fairy Tales from the Old French,* p. 41. New York: Garden City, n.d.

and represents the recovery of a state of bliss. Each of these characteristics warrants detailed examination, and there have been many books written about fairy tales and their meanings. Here we will briefly examine some of the more interesting aspects that relate to religious concepts, for there is a very strong underlying traditional cosmology imbedded in all fairy tales. This basic philosophical message of fairy tales has been eloquently presented by Max Luthi (1970, 1982, 1984) and I will summarize some of his key points.

At the core of the fairy-tale philosophy is a magical and poetic vision of the universe expressed in terms of certain fundamental truths. Most important is the truth that the world is supernaturally alive and will interact with people and can help them. Even if a person is physically or socially isolated, he or she is not alone but part of a much vaster network of life and spirituality. There are magical beings or forces around every person that can help when needed. These magical beings most often take the form of animals that can talk, animals that need help from humans, animals that have magical powers, or animals that can transform themselves. Even the wind or the stars or the moon can talk and help the central figures by supernatural means. Ancestral spirits or fairy godmothers are also frequent helpers. These are the kinds of spirits that one generally associates with nonelite worship, indicating that fairy tales probably originated as an oral form among common classes, who would also be those most likely to experience adversity and yearn to become benevolent princes or princesses.

The heroes of fairy tales are always vulnerable and cannot achieve their goals without help. They are also always open to contacts with nature and the supernatural. They accept spells and miracles as a matter of course. By nature, the heroes exhibit a deep-seated humanity that is extended to all people and to all living things in nature, even the poorest and ugliest beings. The heroes are always innocent and willing to help those in need. They empathize with people in trouble and rarely think of themselves first. The heroes are pure of spirit, and even when they become princes, kings, or queens at the happy endings of the tales, they are not adversely affected by the material riches around them; their personalities do not change. The good hero never expects or counts on help from others. Only when he or she is totally at a loss and despairs of ever overcoming their dreadful situation does the miraculous happen. Crying and despair are often presented as a metaphor for requesting help. The message of the fairy tale is that, if a person is pure of heart, then help will come from somewhere and will be guided by supernatural forces.

The fairy tale typically also presents the converse of this philosophy: If a person is self-centered, greedy, or selfish or performs good acts only as a ploy to obtain benefits for themselves (as typifies many elites), the supernatural powers will know this immediately and the gold of the greedy will turn to dung, or similar unflattering events will befall them. Those who perform certain acts expecting beneficial results are always disappointed and made the brunt of supernatural practical jokes. The fact that heroes are usually from poor or disadvantaged backgrounds and the fact that so much emphasis is placed on the value of helping others strongly indicates again that the fairy tale is predominantly a nonelite form of sacred oral tradition. Typically, in peasant communities, a great deal of mutual help is required for working the fields as well as in times of emergencies, such as sickness or accident. In small peasant communities, mutual help and sharing of food are the most important cultural values. It is probably no coincidence, either, that eating is so prominent a feature in fairy tales and is also a major preoccupation of peasant families (Luthi 1984:146).

Another important facet of fairy-tale philosophy is that evil and cruelty exist in the world as a given. Heroes always encounter cruel stepmothers, evil women in the woods, tyrant kings, or stepsisters who denigrate them. Those in power frequently abuse their might in cruel ways, as the evil queen does in Snow White. Many people today object to fairy tales because they portray cruelty rather vividly—victims being eaten by a wolf, pushed into ovens, forced into marriages, or abandoned by parents. However, adversity and danger are real aspects of the world and were especially important to deal with among common folk in pre-Industrial Indo-European societies. How does a person cope with vicious cruelty when it confronts them, especially from those in authority? How do we educate children to deal with such situations when they occur? Pretending that injustice and cruelty do not exist is a poor option. The philosophy of the fairy tale provides listeners with two important reference points in this regard. The first is that evil will eventually consume itself and be destroyed. The second is that adversity can be transcended if one is pure and innocent. The ultimate goal of the fairy tale is to instill trust in the listener that things will work out if one perseveres and if one is just. Such optimism undoubtedly provided major survival benefits for many people whose futures looked bleak. Rather than succumbing to despair, depression, anxiety, inaction, or even suicide, the fairy-tale hero instills hope and encourages persistent action that must have substantially aided many people to overcome seemingly hopeless situations.

One of the most common motifs of the fairy tale is the self-centered greedy individuals who succumb because of their own greed or their own evil intentions for others. In "Hansel and Gretel," the woman who wants to roast children is herself roasted in the oven that she built to cook the children. In one Balkan tale, the king requires a hero to bathe in boiling mare's milk. With the help of a magical horse, the hero comes to no harm, but when the king becomes envious and attempts the same thing he dies (Luthi 1984:97–102). Evil must be combated, but typically the heroes are far weaker physically and politically than their tormentors. They need help to overcome such adversity. Most frequently, this help comes in the form of supernatural aid; however, cunning also plays a central role, as exemplified when Hansel holds out a stick instead of his finger for the old woman to judge how fat he is. He also tricks her into looking into the oven. Heroes use their minds rather than their physical strength to overcome their problems. Self-reliance, perseverance, cunning, and opening oneself up to connections with supernatural forces are the major means of transcending adverse conditions. The hero is isolated or wanders and finds help by befriending nature and trusting his instincts ("Elements of Fairy Tales: The Golden Goose," pp. 340–43).

HOUSEHOLD STORIES, FROM THE COLLECTION OF THE BROTHERS GRIMM

Despite its title, "The Golden Goose," like most fairy tales, features people not animals or gods as the central figures of the story. Several typical fairy-tale themes can also be identified. The hero, the Simpleton, is disadvantaged and often belittled and insulted. When his brothers receive a fine pancake and wine for their lunch, the Simpleton is given a cake baked in ashes and sour beer. When they meet a little gray man in the forest, the

There was a man who had three sons, the youngest of whom was called the Simpleton and was despised, laughed at, and neglected, on every occasion. It happened one day that the eldest son wished to go into the forest to cut wood, and before he went his mother gave him a delicious pancake and a flask of wine, that he might not suffer from hunger and thirst. When he came into the forest a little old gray man met him, who wished him good day, and said,

"Give me a bit of cake out of your pocket, and let me have a drink of your wine; I am so hungry and thirsty."

But the prudent youth answered,

"Give you my cake and my wine? I haven't got any; be off with you."

And leaving the little man standing there, he went off. Then he began to fell a tree, but he had not been at it long before he made a wrong stroke, and the hatchet hit him in the arm, so that he was obliged to go home and get it bound up. That was what came of the little gray man.

Afterwards the second son went into the wood, and the mother gave to him, as to the eldest, a pancake and a flask of wine. The little old gray man met him also, and begged for a little bit of cake and a drink of wine. But the second son spoke out plainly, saying,

"What I give you I lose myself, so be off with you."

And leaving the little man standing there, he went off. The punishment followed; as he was chopping away at the tree, he hit himself in the leg so severely that he had to be carried home.

Then said the Simpleton,

"Father, let me go for once to the forest to cut wood"; and the father answered, "Your brothers have hurt themselves, by doing so; give it up, you understand nothing about it."

But the Simpleton went on begging so long, that the father said at last,

"Well, be off with you; you will only learn by experience."

The mother gave him a cake (it was only made with water, and baked in the ashes), and with it a flask of sour beer. When he came into the forest the little old gray man met him, and greeted him, saying,

"Give me a bit of your cake, and a drink from your flask; I am so hungry and thirsty."

And the Simpleton answered, "I have only a flour and water cake and sour beer; but if that is good enough for you, let us sit down together and eat." Then they sat down, and as the Simpleton took out his flour and water cake, it became a rich pancake, and his sour beer became good wine; then they ate and drank, and afterwards the little man said:

"As you have a kind heart, and share what you have so willingly, I will bestow good luck upon you. Yonder stands an old tree; cut it down, and at its roots you will find something," and thereupon the little man took his departure.

The Simpleton went there, and hewed away at the tree, and when it fell he saw, sitting among the roots, a goose with feathers of pure gold. He lifted it out and took it with him to an inn where he intended to stay the night. The landlord had three daughters who, when they saw the goose, were curious to know what wonderful kind of bird it was, and ended by longing for one of its golden feathers. The eldest thought, "I will wait for a good opportunity, and then I will pull out one of its feathers for myself"; and so, when the Simpleton was gone out, she seized the goose by its wing—but there her finger and hand had to stay, held fast. Soon after came the second sister with the same idea of plucking out one of the feathers for herself; but scarcely had she touched her sister, than she also was obliged to stay, held fast. Lastly, came the third with the same intentions; but the others screamed out, "Stay away, for heaven's sake stay away!"

But she did not see why she should stay away. "If they do so, why should not I?" and went towards them. But when she reached her sisters there she stopped, hanging on with them. And so they had to stay, all night. The next morning the Simpleton took the goose under his arm and went away, unmindful of the three girls that hung on to it. The three had always to run after him, left and right, wherever his legs carried him. In the midst of the fields they met the parson, who when he saw the procession, said,

"Shame on you, girls, running after a young fellow through the fields like this," and forthwith he seized hold of the youngest by the hand to drag her away, but hardly had he touched her when he too was obliged to run after them himself. Not long after the sexton came that way . . . but no sooner had he touched him than he was obliged to follow on too. As the five tramped on, one after another, two peasants with their hoes came up from the fields, and the parson cried out to them, and begged them to come and set him and the sexton free, but no sooner had they touched the sexton than they had to follow on too; and now there were seven following the Simpleton and the goose.

By and by they came to a town where a king reigned, who had an only daughter who was so serious that no one could make her laugh; therefore the king had given out that whoever should make her laugh should have her in marriage. The Simpleton, when he heard this, went with his goose and his hangers-on into the presence of the king's daughter, and as soon as she saw the seven people following always one after the other, she burst out laughing, and seemed as if she could never stop. And so the Simpleton earned a right to her as his bride; but the king did not like him for a son-in-law and made all kinds of objections, and said he must first bring a man who could drink up a whole cellar of wine. The Simpleton thought that the little gray man would be able to help him, and went out into the forest, and there, on the very spot where he felled the tree, he saw a man sitting with a very sad countenance. The Simpleton asked him what was the matter, and he answered,

"I have a great thirst, which I cannnot quench: cold water does not agree with me; I have indeed drunk up a whole cask of wine, but what good is a drop like that?"

Then said the Simpleton,

"I can help you; only come with me, and you shall have enough."

He took him straight to the king's cellar, and the man sat himself down before the big vats, and drank, and drank, and before a day was over he had drunk up the whole cellar-full. The Simpleton again asked for his bride, but the king was annoyed that a wretched fellow, called the Simpleton by everybody, should carry off his daughter, and so he made new conditions. He was to produce a man who could eat a mountain of bread. The Simpleton did not hesitate long, but ran off quickly to the forest, and there in the same place sat a man who had fastened a strap round his body, making a very piteous face, saying,

"I have eaten a whole bakehouse full of rolls, but what is the use of that when one is so hungry as I am? My stomach feels quite empty, and I am obliged to strap myself together, that I may not die of hunger."

The Simpleton was quite glad of this.

"Get up quickly, and come along with me, and you shall have enough to eat."

He led him straight to the king's courtyard, where all the meal in the kingdom had been collected and baked into a mountain of bread. The man out of the forest settled himself down before it and hastened to eat, and in one day the whole mountain had disappeared.

Then the Simpleton asked for his bride the third time. The king, however, found one more excuse, and said he must have a ship that should be able to sail on land or on water.

"So soon," said he, "as you come sailing along with it, you shall have my daughter for your wife."

The Simpleton went straight to the forest, and there sat the little old gray man with whom he had shared his cake, and he said,

"I have eaten for you, and I have drunk for you, I will also give you the ship; and all because you were kind to me at the first."

Then he gave him the ship that sailed on land and on water, and when the king saw it, he knew he could no longer withhold his daughter. The marriage took place immediately, and at the death of the king the Simpleton possessed the kingdom and lived long and happily with his wife.—Crane 1899

two brothers are selfish and refuse to share their food and wine. They are punished for their actions, hurting themselves in woodcutting accidents. The Simpleton, however, is humane and willing to help; he shares his meager rations with the little man and is rewarded with the golden goose. This event shows that although cruelty and greed exist in the world, humanity and empathy are rewarded.

Thus, during his travels with the golden goose, the Simpleton, who is pure and innocent, is the only one unaffected by its magic. All the others are punished for their greed or meddling by becoming stuck to the goose or its train of followers. When faced with the prospect of winning a wife simply by making her laugh, the Simpleton is up to the challenge and indeed makes the solemn girl howl with laughter. Before he can claim his wife, her father imposes several impossible tasks in an attempt to be rid of the Simpleton. The solution to each is found by trusting and enlisting the aid of supernatural forces in the form of the little gray (ancestral?) man of the forest. Again, several typical fairy-tale themes are illustrated. Appearances can be deceiving, as can be seen with the surprising abilities of the little gray man, as well as the golden goose. Those in power typically abuse it, as can be seen in the king's actions to be rid of the Simpleton despite the fact that he had already met the initial challenge of making the princess laugh and had rightfully won her hand. Adversity can be transcended if one is pure of heart and trusts in the supernatural, as demonstrated through all of the Simpleton's actions throughout the tale. And finally, the hero, good and pure, enters the elite class and lives out his life in happiness and bliss.

In many respects, the fairy tale is like an initiation. The hero-initiate generally begins in a state of childlike comfort or security. This state is disrupted by events in which the hero-initiate must transcend his or her former self and develop new skills or abilities, which are accompanied by important new revelations about the nature of the cosmos. Finally, the hero-initiate reestablishes himself or herself in a better condition than that in which the hero started out. Rather than a real initiation, this is a vicarious initiation, a formulaic blueprint for the trials and tribulations that constitute life's initiatory experiences—events that would be certain to occur later in life even if they were not accompanied by any formal rituals.

Although Max Luthi does not view the fairy tale as originating from shamanic tales, the resemblances are so striking that it is difficult to believe that there are no connections. Both the shamanic tales and the fairy tales feature a main protagonist (the shaman or the hero) who must venture out to battle evil. In shamanic tales, the evildoer is generally supernatural, whereas in the fairy tale the evildoer is usually human. In both cases, good and evil are presented in simplistic and extreme fashions. In both cases, animals (or other beings) with supernatural powers generally assist the hero or shaman; and in both cases, the hero or shaman achieves a successful and happy outcome. In both cases, the story is action-driven and involves little if any character development or psychological detail. Many of the details tend to be similar as well, including flying through the air and the use of cunning to turn evil against itself.

The ultimate aim of the fairy tale is to instill trust and optimism in the listeners, as opposed to local legends that are used to create fear. The underlying goal of shamans' tales may have been the same. The cosmos of the fairy tale is typical of all traditional religions and thus undoubtedly has prehistoric roots. Fairy tales are perhaps the strongest surviving element of traditional European religious stories. Most likely, the tales were developed as teaching and education techniques for children of common families in nonliterate Indo-European societies. I suspect they were modeled after shamanic stories that listeners in many traditional communities found entertaining and philosophically comforting. Shamanic tales undoubtedly were also meant to reinforce listeners' belief in the effectiveness of shamans' powers, thereby influencing the immune systems of shamans' clients (see Chap. 3). Many of the characteristics of fairy tales indicate that their primary audience was children: the lack of erotic scenes or sexual references (as opposed to myths like that of Naro), the negligible character development, the emphasis on action, the extreme forms of good and evil, and the simplicity of the plots. These same characteristics typify children's comic books today.

In particular, the fact that children feel extremely powerless and vulnerable in an adult world probably accounts for the inherent appeal of vicariously confronting evil and learning that it can be overcome (Luthi 1970:140). Such lessons undoubtedly helped prepare children for the adult world and reduced their anxiety about events over which they had no control. If one can endure suffering and sacrifices, adverse events will lead to transcendence, purity, and greater strength. In some of these stories, such as "Sleeping Beauty," even death can be overcome. This factor continues to provide the enormous appeal of fairy tales for children everywhere, even in contemporary societies. These are truths also reflected in shamanic initiations or stories of supernatural battles and in modern psychology. In shamanic contexts, it would have been especially important to instill deep belief in shamanic powers at early, formative stages of mental development in order to exert the greatest psychosomatic effect on the immune system of patients during shamanic curing ceremonies.

A number of other characteristics should also be mentioned in order to flesh out the character of fairy tales. In particular, people are generally evaluated and judged on the basis of their actions rather than on the basis of what they say. Appearances are deceiving, and many things are clearly not what they appear to be, including frogs or beasts that turn into princes. Becoming a prince, king, or queen or acquiring vast fortunes of gold are all symbolic images meant to convey mastery of one's destiny. They represent the developed, mature human spirit. The journey, or adversity, is typically the beginning of the process of mastering one's destiny.

Inner emotions are generally expressed by concrete visual symbols, such as the wearing out of iron shoes as an expression of extreme perseverance, determination, or motivation. Physical beauty is equated with goodness and innocence, and it, too, is expressed not by detailed physical descriptions, but generally by the effects that it has on other people or the surroundings. A princess may be so beautiful that her face shines like the sun and people are unable to look at her for long, or she may be so beautiful that flowers spring up in her footsteps as she walks across a field. Such beautiful heroes are often associated with solar imagery, while the absence of goodness/beauty is indicated by darkness. Thus, beauty is to be understood as humane, good inner qualities. Physical beauty is only a simile for inner realities. In fact, similes are typical features in fairy tales rather than metaphors, which tend to confuse listeners.

In general there is very little detailed description of physical characteristics of people or houses or the landscape. Listeners are required to imagine all of these aspects in their own minds, and doing so personalizes the stories and paradoxically makes their inner viewing more vivid and also more universal. Glass and metals are generally symbols of magical or supernatural situations. Music and poetry are rarely used or may indicate supernatural situations. Dragons represent evil or serious problems. Above all, the number three is central to almost all action for reasons discussed in Chapter 8. There are always three brothers, three sisters, three tasks to be performed, three trolls, three repeated attempts, or three fairy godmothers. The formula of three marks stories as typically originating from Indo-European sources. Like all good oral traditions, fairy tales incorporate a goodly amount of humor, especially using ironic turns of events in which evil, greedy people serve as the instruments of their own misfortune. We can assume that traditional tellers also used many of the other techniques mentioned earlier to entrance and enchant their audiences: action-driving, mimicking, audience interactions, props, reference to known locations, affirmations of the truth of the story, gestures, facial expressions, humor, and so on.

Not every aspect of religious oral traditions was meant to engage listeners in this way. Some ritual chants and phrases were meant to be recited exactly the same way, each and every time, as part of specific rituals. However, as far as we know, these kinds of liturgies were never very elaborate in traditional religions, except perhaps in elite ancestor or secret society cults. None of these texts has come down to us from prehistory, although some representative fragments may be preserved in the ethnographies of groups like the Polynesian chiefdoms.

The realm of fairy tales, myths, and religious oral traditions is vast and has been extensively explored by a number of authors. These oral traditions deal above all with symbolic contents and thus are not usually very amenable to archaeological or ecological study. However, in some cases, such as fairy tales and shamanic tales, it is possible to determine how the basic elements of these oral traditions can be viewed as helpful and adaptive for promoting healing, personal maturation, or coping with adverse conditions. There are many other alternative ways of achieving the same ends, including real initiations, children's group participation in the challenges of maturation via the formation of age grades, or other psychological approaches. But the fairy tale appears to be a common and relatively successful solution used by many Indo-European societies or at least by the nonelite portion of these communities.

Summary

In this discussion of the oral aspects of traditional religion and ritual, I have not dwelt upon the functions of myths or other kinds of oral rituals because this area is so contentious and so far removed from what can be determined archaeologically. Certainly, myths must have been told to accompany the rituals and ritual paraphernalia that we recover archaeologically. We can even make relatively educated guesses about the general nature of these myths. In the Paleolithic, they must have involved totemic animal ancestors, masters of animals, and even recognizable ancestors. In the Neolithic, they must have focused on lineage or clan ancestors or totems, great bulls, fertility goddesses, the sun, and the moon. In Indo-European times, we know that the elites told stories featuring Olympian types of pantheons of gods and goddesses that acted very much like people in elite society. Warrior gods were especially prevalent. Nonelites focused more on nature spirits and magical animal helpers or ancestors, more reminiscent of ancient shamanic worldviews and stories. In modern Industrial societies, the European fairy tale appears to be the sole surviving living representative from this long oral tradition— particularly the nonelite segment of this tradition. All of the above inferences about myths make sense primarily as ideological extensions of what we can infer were fairly straightforward ecological types of ritual adaptations to social and economic conditions based either on hunting, control over surplus-producing resources, herding, or other similar factors.

The main goal of this chapter has been to acknowledge the role that oral religious traditions play in the general scheme of rituals and religion and to provide a better understanding of their importance and enormous appeal. It is very difficult to appreciate what the telling of myths was like from written accounts. Like other aspects of traditional religion, the telling of myths and related stories must be experienced to be appreciated. If you would like to try your hand at telling stories (for instance bedtime stories), it is worthwhile trying to adopt some of the traditional techniques used by tellers of sacred tales, such as using props, asking rhetorical questions of listeners, mimicking characters' voices, using facial expressions or gestures, and adding humor. Fairy tales are an important part of our Western ritual heritage that deserves to be kept alive. The importance of fairy tales and the philosophy of the cosmos that they represent may provide renewed interest in this traditional ritual expression and help you appreciate the fundamental messages they convey. Fairy tales are not simply entertainment for children at bedtime. They teach children about the supernatural nature of the universe, about how to cope with adversity, about the value of helping without expectation of return favors, about the sacredness of all life, and about dealing with the world in general. If you want to see how the written "book" part of our religious tradition became established, we must go back to events surrounding the emergence of the first states and empires in the West. This is the focus of the next chapter.

CHAPTER 11

Religious Needs of
Early States and Empires

Mention archaeology in any gathering of people and immediately the room fills with visions of pyramids, Egyptian temples, and the jungle-shrouded monuments of the Maya. These are the consummate expressions of human spirituality and civilization for most people. There are few archaeological manifestations that can rival these magnificent constructions. They present mysteries. What could have inspired prehistoric people to create such beautiful art and to devote so much energy to building these enormous structures? What religious forces led to their construction? Climbing nearly 200 feet to the summit of the Temple of the Sun in Mexico and feeling the incredible mass of the structure supporting you as you gaze over far-reaching horizons and ant-sized people far below in distant fields is a breathtaking experience (Fig. 1.2).

Today, it seems inconceivable that such structures could have been built solely with human labor without mechanized equipment. However, there are no other viable explanations, and ancient carvings in stone show how laborers dragged huge blocks of stone to the construction sites (Heizer 1966; Cotterell and Kamminga 1990). How shall we make sense of these developments in our quest to understand the evolution of religion? To begin with, it will be useful to distinguish between early city-states and later empires, for the problems that they faced were somewhat different. It will also be helpful to pick up the thread of social and political changes where we left off, at the development of powerful chiefdoms that raised megalithic monuments and established sophisticated trading centers. Many of the characteristics of early states grow directly out of powerful chiefdoms, so this is where we shall begin.

ELITES IN EARLY STATES CLAIM DIVINITY

In archaeology, the term *civilization* has a fairly precise meaning. It represents the next major increase in political complexity and size after the development of chiefdoms. Thus, civilizations are synonymous with "states" for most purposes. Typically, chiefdoms are composed of several thousand people and, in exceptional situations, tens of thousands

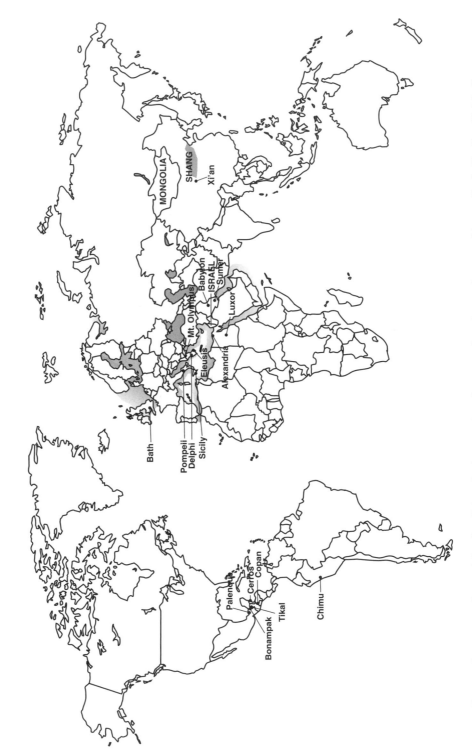

Fig. 11.1. Important regions and sites for religious developments in early states and empires are shown on this map. Drafted by Greg Holoboff.

(Sanders and Price 1968:82ff). In contrast, even small city-states have 10,000 or more people while the upper range of states extends into the millions. Craft specialization is usually more developed in civilizations, as is political centralization. While chiefdoms generally have two or three administrative levels and sizes of settlements, states typically have three or more levels (Johnson 1973). States also have standing armies or police forces to ensure compliance with elite decrees and to defend or advance the interests of the elites.

In Chapter 8, we saw that chiefly elites use religion to reinforce their political position of power in three ways. First, they create cults with which everyone in the chiefdom and its numerous communities can establish some affiliation: solar cults, fertility cults, and/or clan ancestral cults are particularly common. Second, chiefly elites also arrange to have themselves or their close elite affiliates established as the highest authorities in the cult with exclusive access to direct communication with the cult deities. While the general populace might celebrate the major events of the clan cult outside on plazas or in large halls filled with feasting, music, and dance, the elite cult directors worshiped in an inner sanctum, likely in altered states of varying degrees, conversing with the deities or the dead. Some of the Greek elites of the sixth century before the common era used shamanic types of techniques of sensory deprivation ("incubation") in their healing cults (Kingsley 1999). Third, elites created exclusive secret societies for brokering power among the leading members of communities.

Large feasts were used by chiefly elites not only to consolidate their ideological claims to legitimacy in wielding power but also to unify the populace and to collect surpluses from the populace for use during the feasts and for later use in the material support of the elites (Junker 2001; Kirch 2001). We find exactly the same tactics being used in the early Sumerian states of Mesopotamia (Fig. 11.1; see also Schmandt-Besserat 2001), South America (C. Morris 1979), and probably Mesoamerica (Fox 1996). Interestingly, consumption of enormous amounts of beer seems to typify most of these feasts, perhaps to facilitate feelings of euphoria in ritual, worship, and celebration. It may have more favorably disposed participants to surrendering their surpluses and accepting socioeconomic proposals by the elites. The aspect that changes in moving from chiefdoms to states is the scale and intensity of these developments. In order to establish an administration capable of governing tens or hundreds of thousands of people and to maintain a police force or standing army, a great deal more surplus food is required than is the case with simple chiefdoms, which only require a few administrators for a few thousand people. According to Rambo (1991:304–5), energy requirements for running institutions escalate exponentially with increases in social complexity. Thus, the degree of political complexity of a society bears an important relationship to basic ecological factors, especially to a society's ability to produce surpluses or obtain surplus benefits from trade. The religious developments that we will note, in turn, depend on the degree of political power exercised by various segments of a society and by the nature of their interests.

In the case of early states, which were usually city-states, or at least states with centralized administrations, we find the same drive to establish universal elite-dominated cults as in chiefdoms. These cults frequently featured deified kingly ancestors associated with the sun or other generative forces, as in the case of the Egyptian pharaohs. Other elite cults of early states featured pantheons of gods with elite characteristics similar to

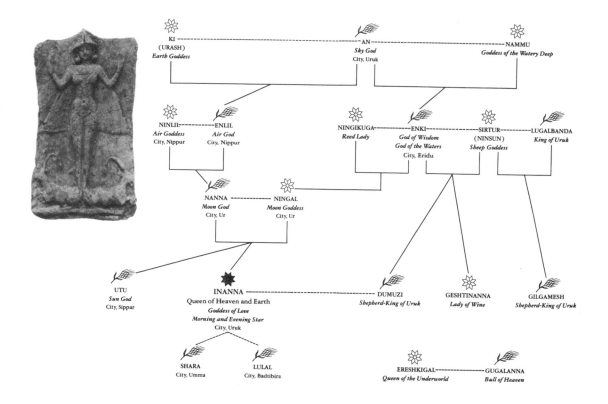

Fig. 11.2. In early city-states like those of Sumer, gods ruled over each city as their earthly counterparts did. And, like earthly kings and queens, the gods had family trees and family members who were often rulers in other cities. This diagram shows the goddess Inanna's family tree and the cities over which they ruled. From Diane Wolkstein and Samuel Noah Kramer, *Innana: Queen of Heaven and Earth*, pp. x–xi, 6. New York: Harper & Row, 1983.

the Olympian pantheon adopted by the Greek city-states or the Sumerian pantheon adopted by Sumerian city-states (Fig. 11.2 and "Inanna and the Mesopotamian Pantheon," pp. 352–55; see also Wolkstein and Kramer 1983). How might such pantheons develop? The Minoan city-states described in Chapter 7 began with predominantly ancestor worship but developed a basic pantheon as well, featuring Zeus, Dionysus, Artemis, and other gods. It is likely that the merging of several polities into city-states or larger confederations entailed merging several different local elite ancestor cults into more polytheistic pantheons. Alternatively, deified elite ancestors may have also had difficulty displacing more traditional, more established, and more popular local deities, resulting in several distinctive cults within early states: elite ancestor cults plus more popular deity cults.

Typically, one deity of the pantheon was chosen as a tutelary deity who served as the main supernatural patron of each early state. Large main temples were built for these patron deities by local elites. The temples and deities served as rallying points that helped to establish political solidarity in the early states, much the way home sports teams and their stadiums serve as a focus for community solidarity in the modern Western world.

Fig. 11.3. To build chiefdoms and states, early elites were constantly battling with internal competitors and other interest groups, as well as with external enemies and the adverse forces of nature. It is therefore not surprising that combat with the supernatural forces of chaos (represented by fabulous mythical animals) should be a recurring feature in the ideologies of early state religions, as shown in this early mythological depiction from the Izapan culture in Mexico. Similar scenes are common on early cylinder seals from Mesopotamia. In Europe, dragons filled the same role during medieval times. By demonizing such adversaries, elites always had someone to blame when things went wrong. From V. G. Norman, *Izapa Sculpture,* Part I, Plate 6. New World Archaeological Foundation, Brigham Young University, Paper 30, 1973.

In fact, a favorite theme in the myths of chiefdoms and early states are battles involving a main deity (like Gilgamesh) and supernatural monsters of chaos and disorder. I suspect that these themes are common because of the constant threats and dangers to the state leaders and the polities they organized. Droughts, floods, disruptions in trade, discontent among commoners, competition and intrigue within the elite ranks, tenuous alliances with other states, epidemics and other calamities, all could be blamed on rulers who claimed special influence with the gods. If discontent was widespread, these events could jeopardize elite life and livelihood. One ploy for dealing with such situations would be to blame misfortunes on supernatural forces of destruction and evil with which elites could claim they were in constant battle, much as the shamans of the past did, who battled with the supernatural forces that stole souls and caused illness (Fig. 11.3). In Mesoamerica, these battles were played out in the flesh upon ritual ball courts, with the defeated combatants sometimes losing their heads during the most important ritual events (Fox 1996; Scarborough and Wilcox 1991). In more recent times, these forces were demonized and fought on mock battlefields or in dramatic ritual dances like those of Bali.

Inanna and the Mesopotamian Pantheon of Elite Gods

Some of the earliest written accounts of deities come from the Sumerian city-states along the lower Tigris and Euphrates Rivers in southern Iraq. Inanna was the patron deity of Uruk. She was part of an entire family of elite gods and goddesses who ruled over various cities, just as their human counterparts did (Fig. 11.2). Her parents ruled over the city-state of Ur; her grandfather, Enki, ruled over Eridu, and it was to him that she traveled by boat to obtain the *me,* or sacred gifts, that would establish Uruk as an independent, fully empowered city-state. Inanna was greeted by Enki's servant, who poured water for her and offered her butter cakes and beer on a sacred table. Enki and Inanna drank beer together and Enki became besotted. He drunkenly gave away all his most precious *me,* including the crown of kingship, the crown of godship, priests and priestesses of various types, the throne of kingship, the dagger and the sword, the ability to descend to and ascend from the underworld, the art of lovemaking and phallus kissing, the art of prostitution, song, fire, various crafts, the art of treachery, the art of straightforwardness, and the plundering of cities. When he awoke from his stupor and realized what he had done, he sent his servant and minions to bring the sacred treasures back, but it was too late. With these treasures, Inanna set up her city and engaged in a sacred marriage with Dumuzi, king of the pastoralists of Uruk. As we can see from the following passages, reproduced from Wolkstein and Kramer (1983:37–48), their sacred marriage involves clear references to human-divine sexuality and agricultural fertility:

My vulva, the horn,
The Boat of Heaven,
Is full of eagerness like the young moon.
My untilled land lies fallow.

As for me, Inanna,
Who will plow my vulva?
Who will plow my high field?
Who will plow my wet ground?

As for me, the young woman,
Who will plow my vulva?
Who will station the ox there?
Who will plow my vulva?

Dumuzi replied:
    Great Lady, the king will plow your vulva.
    I, Dumuzi the King, will plow your vulva.

Inanna sang:

   Then plow my vulva, man of my heart!
   Plow my vulva! . . .

He has sprouted; he has burgeoned;
He is lettuce planted by the water.
He is the one my womb loves best . . .

My lord, the honey-man of the gods,
He is the one my womb loves best.
His hand is honey, his foot is honey,
He sweetens me always.

My eager impetuous caresser of the navel,
My caresser of the soft thighs,
He is the one my womb loves best,
He is the lettuce planted by the water.

Dumuzi sang:

   O Lady, your breast is your field.
   Inanna, your breast is your field.
   Your broad field pours out plants.
   Your broad field pours out grain.
   Water flows from on high for your servant.
   Bread flows from on high for your servant.
   Pour it out for me, Inanna.
   I will drink all you offer. . . .

Inanna sang:

   Before my lord Dumuzi,
   I poured out plants from my womb . . .
   I poured out grain before him.
   I poured out grain from my womb . . .

My lord Dumuzi met me.
He put his hand into my hand.
He pressed his neck close against mine . . .
My lord Dumuzi is ready for the holy loins.
The plants and herbs in his field are ripe.
O Dumuzi! Your fullness is my delight! . . .

Let the bed that rejoices the heart be prepared!
Let the bed that sweetens the loins be prepared!
Let the bed of kingship be prepared!
Let the bed of queenship be prepared!
Let the royal bed be prepared! . . .

I bathed for the wild bull,
I bathed for the shepherd Dumuzi,
I perfumed my sides with ointment,
I coated my mouth with sweet-smelling amber,
I painted my eyes with kohl.

He shaped my loins with his fair hands,
The shepherd Dumuzi filled my lap with cream and milk,
He stroked my pubic hair,
He watered my womb.
He laid his hands on my holy vulva,
He smoothed my black boat with cream,
He quickened my narrow boat with milk,
He caressed me on the bed. . . .

The Queen of Heaven . . . decreed the fate of Dumuzi:
    In battle I am your leader,
    In combat I am your armor-bearer,
    In the assembly I am your advocate,
    On the campaign I am your inspiration.
    You, the chosen shepherd of the holy shrine,
    You, the king, the faithful provider of Uruk. . .
    In all ways you are fit:
    To sit on the lapis lazuli throne,
    To carry the mace and sword,
    To guide straight the long bow and arrow,
    To prance on the holy breast like a lapis lazuli calf. . . .

Ninshubur, the faithful servant of the holy shrine of Uruk,
Led Dumuzi to the sweet thighs of Inanna and spoke:
    My queen, here is the choice of your heart,
    The king, your beloved bridegroom. . . .
    Let his shepherd's staff protect all of Sumer and Akkad.
    As the farmer, let him make the fields fertile,
    As the shepherd, let him make the sheepfolds multiply,

Under his reign let there be vegetation,
Under his reign let there be rich grain. . . .
In the forests may the deer and wild goats multiply,
In the orchards may there be honey and wine. . . .
May he enjoy long days in the sweetness of your holy loins.

Inanna spoke:
My beloved, the delight of my eyes, met me. . . .
He took his pleasure of me. . . .
My sweet love, lying by my heart,
Tongue-playing, one by one,
My fair Dumuzi did so fifty times.

Unfortunately, Dumuzi became satiated and after awhile no longer came to Inanna. For him, the results were disastrous. He was carried away to the underworld—a lesson for all kings who would court divinity!

There are many aspects of this elite sacred story that illustrate the special relation that kings were supposed to enjoy with the gods. Especially notable is the role that the king plays in ensuring the fertility of the land, the close connection between sacred human sexuality and the fertility of the land, the close correspondence between elite life and the life of the gods, and the sacred marriage between the king and the main goddess of the state, or at least one of her representatives (Eliade 1954:26; 1958a:353ff). Many of the statements in this myth are also transparently self-serving of elite interests, such as the divine sponsorship in battles and probably the right to lie with priestesses in sacred marriages. But then, it was the elites who dictated the contents of these myths and had them written down. It was the elites who promoted these early state cults and had all the rich paraphernalia and luscious ritual foods and settings established for their use, all on the pretext of trying to ensure the prosperity of the kingdom. A good ploy for getting people to contribute surpluses if you can get others to accept it! It is also relevant to note the continuing symbolism and association of the bull with the spiritual-political-military leaders, together with weapons of war, such as the mace and other fighting implements. As we have seen in Chapter 6, this is a pattern that began with the earliest Neolithic communities of the Near East.

Certainly, one of the most common themes from the religious records of these early states is the claim that local elites are descendents of deified ancestors or simply of deities. In Egypt, the pharaoh was considered to be the offspring of the royal mother and the main elite deity, Amun Re (David 1982:124). In order to retain as much divinity in the lineage as possible, pharaohs were generally supposed to marry their sisters in incestuous unions—another example of how elites frequently create their own moralities and ideologies in order to suit their own purposes. Similarly, genealogies were carefully kept, documenting the descendants from the original coupling of Zeus with Europa and other offspring arising from the sexual relationships between supernatural beings and humans.

> Ye coasts, pray tell my loving father that Europa has left her native land, seated upon a bull, my ravisher, my sailor, and, as I think, my bed-fellow.
> Europa in *Dionysiaca* 1:130

King Minos and King Rudamanthys claimed descent from this union. Helen of Troy claimed descent from the coupling of Zeus and Leda. Alexander the Great was said to have had a virgin birth with Dionysus as his father. Even in medieval Europe, lesser elite families often claimed descent from intercourse of one of their members with mermaids or other supernatural spirits, as in the French account of the Lusignan family being descended from a mermaid or even Richard the Lionheart being the offspring of a spirit (Thiebaut 1992:80–81; Seznec 1981:19–26). Olmec and Maya elites also promoted the idea that elite lineages were descended from the mating of jaguars or gods and humans (Coe 1972; Furst 1968; Grove 1972).

In the case of deified ancestors, such as the pharaohs of Egypt, the Mayan kings, Chinese emperors, Roman Caesars, and Tibetan Dalai Lamas, promoting one's predecessors to divinity conferred more authority on any communications that putatively were imparted to the reigning rulers, and it was only a small step from considering one's father to be a god to portraying one's self as a god. Such attitudes are epitomized by the Roman emperor Vespasian's wry comment on his deathbed: "Dear me! I must be turning into a god" (Suetonius 1957:241). At Cerros, in Belize, David Freidel (PBS 1981) has been able to document this change in ideology archaeologically from the worship of gods at temples to the worship of divine kings. Desmond Morris (1994) once quipped that the human species is unique in that the highest position in its hierarchy is not occupied by an individual but only by a spirit, a god. However, with the arrival of early states, we have come full circle, and the highest position in the hierarchy is occupied by an individual who also claims to be god. Thus, divine rulers are commonplace in complex chiefdoms, early states, and even in many historical kingdoms.

As divine or semidivine beings, these kings sometimes claimed to engage in the divine union, or "sacred marriage," with goddesses of fertility, thus ensuring the kingdom's prosperity. This was especially common in the Near East where, at key seasons of the year, rulers would copulate with a priestess of the temple as the representative of a goddess ("Inanna and the Mesopotamian Pantheon of Elite Gods"). It is sometimes suggested that the strong emphasis on royal or state religions in early states, in contrast to Industrial societies, was due to the relatively tenuous hold on power that characterized early political leaders. They could not entirely rely upon economic clout or their militias to fend off insurgency from discontented commoners or competing aristocrats within their own polities. Therefore, they used all the means possible to reinforce their claims to power, including economic controls, military might, popular feasts, and promoting impressive ideological claims. There is undoubtedly a strong relationship between the elite need for religious sanctification, or at least the need to demonstrate power, and the size of the temples or other state religious monuments like the pyramids in early states (Rappaport 1971:37; 1999:324–25).

In order to provide tangible proof of the power and importance of royal cult ancestors or deities, elites invested heavily in the construction of imposing temples or burial structures for their deified ancestors. The tallest pre-Columbian building in the Western Hemisphere is Temple IV at Tikal, Guatemala, the burial monument and ancestral shrine of a Mayan king. The largest pyramid at Giza in Egypt, one of the seven wonders of the world, was a burial structure and ancestral shrine for a deceased pharaoh, built by a royal family and maintained by their successors. The Mausoleum of Halicarnassus, one of the other wonders of the world, was also built for a deified ruler. Maintaining as large a display as possible for divine father pharaohs was entirely in the self-interest of the reigning rulers since it demonstrated the might and power of the royal sacred source of power. In ecological terms, these fantastic structures were promotional displays, pure and simple, meant to validate, render tangible, and make believable the power claimed by royal rulers (Aranyosi 1999). The pyramids were visible from great distances, with their gold-sheathed apexes flashing in the desert sun. They were built to instill awe in everyone who looked upon them. They generated myths and stories about Egyptian rulers that spread the state's fame over the entire Mediterranean world and guaranteed the respect and attraction of elites everywhere. The pyramids still effectively serve the same status function for the general populace and elites of Egypt, 5,000 years after they were built and long after Egypt had been eclipsed as the major power of the Mediterranean. At a symbolic level, for the Egyptians, the pyramid represented the sun, perhaps because of the shapes that are formed by the rays of sunbursts emanating from behind clouds (David 1982:50–52). Some people suggest that the sun's rays were supposed to shine down the sides of the pyramid over the pharaoh and link him with Ra the sun god (Macaulay 1975).

The pyramids of Egypt were not simply cenotaphs or monuments erected for a single funeral event. The pyramids were divine ancestral shrines that were meant to maintain the worship of dead pharaohs for all eternity. The pyramids were only the most prominent part of a large complex of temples, residences, and productive fields that were dedicated to the sole purpose of continuing the ancestral rituals of the pharaohs. Presumably, ruling pharaohs would travel to these temples to consult with their deified fathers or grandfathers about any issue of importance. Priests undoubtedly played important roles in this kind of process and thus wielded great influence over rulers. Large tracts of land were given to these ancestral corporations. Temples and residences were built for priests and workers along the banks of the Nile and a ramp connected these structures with a dock and with the funerary pyramid. The priests administered the growing of crops on these lands. The proceeds were used to feed the priests and workers and to obtain all the ritual paraphernalia or offerings required to perpetuate the ancestral rituals forever, or at least for as long as Egyptian economic health would permit.

There is no shortage of theories about why the pyramids were built, including the need to unite recently formed empires via work contributions from all regions, the maintenance of economic flows and productivity, and the validation of the supreme authority of royalty. However, the pyramids are simply the extreme expression of a much more general phenomenon of large mortuary temples built for early rulers of stratified societies, as exemplified by the megaliths, the Chinese tombs of emperors, and the burial temples of Maya kings. In all cases, these structures were primarily used to display the power of the immediate ancestor of the reigning monarch *and* as a prestige display of the greatness of the elite polities that built them.

Massive human sacrifices also formed part of the display of power at funerals of many early state rulers. A particularly graphic account of a traditional funeral with human sacrifices for a Balinese king is provided by Geertz (1980). Other royal funerals were notable for the sheer scale of human sacrifices. Five hundred people were immolated in some early Egyptian tombs (David 1982:32, 34); up to 3,000 slaves were killed for the funerals of certain sub-Saharan African potentates (Budge 1973:225–29); scores of soldiers, servants, women, and oxen at Ur in Sumer; hundreds of retainers for the first kings of Chimu in Peru; and scores of sacrifices for the first emperors of China. Oracle bone inscriptions of Shang China that have been recovered mention at least 14,197 human sacrifices and indicate that such sacrifices were a means to communicate with ancestors and restore harmony in the world (Shelach 1996:13–15). Such sacrifices cannot be reconciled with the standard economic theories for pyramid building. But they do make sense as prestige power displays. The practice of large-scale sacrifices for dead rulers was short-lived everywhere, perhaps because of the strong opposition that such brutality and waste evoked. In a number of cases, such as China and Egypt, live human sacrifices were replaced by expensive ceramic or carved statues of retainers. At Xi'an in China, the founder of the Qin (Chin) dynasty was buried with 7,000 life-sized ceramic warriors, 600 clay horses, and 100 war chariots, plus immense quantities of real weapons (Fig. 11.4). Religion in early states—or at least those aspects underwritten by the elites—was primarily for the benefit of the ruler and the state hierarchy. Egyptian temples were not for community worship but were owned estates that received taxes. Being a priest was generally very lucrative, and only professionals or elites were admitted to the ranks of the temple. There they had access to higher education, yet another aspect of elite culture (David 1982:52, 134–35).

The Maya kings used the ancestral shrines that they built not only to display the power of their ancestors but also to communicate with the ancestors buried beneath the shrines. Linda Schele and David Freidel (1990; Freidel, Schele, and Parker 1993) have carefully documented the elaborate rituals used by Maya elites who drew their own blood, suffered painful piercings, and consumed noxious psychoactive brews at their temples in order to contact ancestors or other deities. As columns of incense and burning blood rose into the air, they turned into supernatural "vision serpents." From the mouth of these serpents, the head of an ancestor's or a deity's spirit emerged and communicated with the supplicating descendant (Fig. 11.5). These events are displayed in elite stone sculptures and on pottery vases. As one might expect, funerals were especially important affairs for the elites. Allied royalty traveled many miles to participate in each others' funerals. From the scenes and inscriptions on vessels, it is clear that these ceremonies involved dancing in richly costumed clothes, often mimicking animals such as jaguars (McAnany 1995).

The Minoan rituals reconstructed by Marinatos (1993) seem very similar. In both cases, major participants probably entered into ecstatic states as a result of stress, blood-

Fig. 11.4. Most rulers of early states claimed divine descent and almost absolute authority. In order to demonstrate the power and importance of themselves and their family members, rulers began to sacrifice large numbers of people to accompany the most important dead elites into the afterlife—logical developments if one accepts the basic premises of elite religion and power of those times. However, such excesses were short-lived and were often replaced by symbolic or "spirit" offerings consisting mostly of sculpted imitations of people or spirits. To date, the Chinese emperor Ch'in, who lived in the seventh century before the common era, holds the record for such offerings. He had an entire spirit city of 500 acres built for his final resting place, and he constructed a fully life-sized spirit army of 7,000 ceramic figurines to guard the city, as shown here. The emperor was also a despot who had 460 Confucian scholars buried alive and the Great Wall built at a high cost of human life. From Cultural Relics Publishing House, Beijing; appearing in J. Campbell, *The Way of the Seeded Earth,* Part 1, Fig. 193. New York: Harper & Row, 1988.

letting, dancing, drumming, and/or the use of psychoactive substances. There is now abundant evidence that the Maya elite used drugs to induce ecstatic states during their rituals, including the use of toads, tobacco, mushrooms, and many other psychotropic plants (Furst 1974, 1976). These substances may well have been ingested prior to some of the painful piercings that the Maya elites endured, such as the use of stingray spines to pierce their penises or the passing of cords laced with spines through holes pierced in their tongues (Fig. 11.6). All of these techniques strongly recall the shamanistic initiations and ecstatic visions of a much earlier time. As we have seen, such ecstatic experiences were progressively expropriated by the elites and eventually claimed as their exclusive domain. Elites entered these states as rightful descendants of powerful ancestors, as leaders of state cults, and as members of secret society cults.

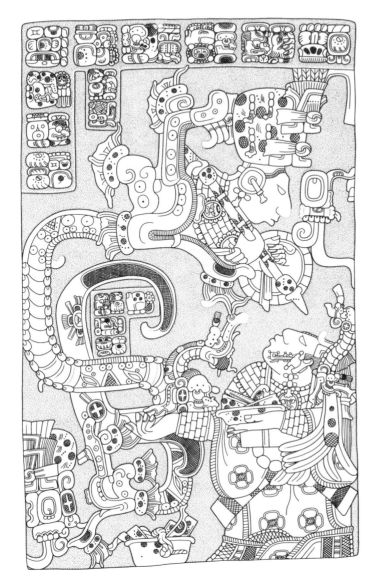

Fig. 11.5. Elites in early states often claimed privileged communication with the world of gods and spirits, especially the most powerful ones. Some elites undoubtedly claimed that their most important decisions were actually commands that they received from the gods, just as Moses claimed to have obtained the Ten Commandments directly from God. Here, a noble Maya woman of Yaxchilan is shown receiving the words of an ancestor or deity who appears out of the head of a serpent rising from a bowl. This "vision serpent"—a central concept in Maya elite ideology—was evoked by drawing blood from a noble's body (Fig. 11.6) and by burning the blood on slips of paper in a bowl, the column of smoke creating the impression of a serpent. From Ian Graham and Eric von Euw, *Corpus of Maya Hieroglyphic Inscriptions,* Vol. 3, Pt. 1, Fig. 3:55. Cambridge: Peabody Museum, Harvard, 1977.

We have seen evidence for these secret society cults continuing into Minoan state-level organizations accompanied by human sacrifices. Similar events undoubtedly transpired in Maya kingdoms, where caves and inner "basement" chambers of the elite palaces provided ideal locations for secret society cult activities. The evidence for the ritual use of caves by small groups of people is abundant and frequently involves ritual offerings, cave paintings, burials, and evidence for sacrifices (Gibbs 1998; Brady and Stone 1986; Pendergast 1971). Some of these aspects recall the Upper Paleolithic and Neolithic use of caves in Europe. One remarkable figure incised on a plastered wall in a basement room at Tikal is depicted as dancing with an axe in his hand. The dancer is using the axe to cut off his own head. The figure is done so realistically that it appears to represent an actual event rather than a mythological story (PBS 1981). If so, the person must surely have been in a profound ecstatic state. Other incised figures are shown being sacrificed with arrows. Thus, there are good indications for the continuation of secret society cults in early Mesoamerican states. These secret cults continued the age-old functions of the earliest religions, that is, to create strong alliance bonds between individuals. However, whereas in the Paleolithic, everyone (or at least all adult males) was involved in forming these ritual alliances through mutual participation in ecstatic ritual states, by the time of powerful chiefs and kings, this function of religion had become an elite prerogative and was used almost exclusively by them.

Common people indulged in the less intense forms of religious experiences such as feasting, drinking, and watching perform-ances that were meant to awe and inspire. We are fortunate that the Maya have left a visual record of some of these performances car-ried out on the steps of the major temples and palaces. The extraor-dinarily elaborate costumes and headdresses reach to over twice the height of the dancers, and each dancer shimmers with hun-dreds of long, iridescent-green quetzal plumes. Their arms are extended by long fans. We can al-most hear the orchestra playing from the detailed mural represen-tation in these scenes (Fig. 11.7). The only full representation of these celebrations comes from a relatively small Maya center named Bonampak in Mexico. It is difficult to imagine how much more spectacular the correspon-ding rituals were at some of the truly great centers of the Maya world such as Tikal, Palenque, or Copan. The overall effect easily must have rivaled the most spec-tacular costumes and shows that Florenz Ziegfield developed for his Follies or that Las Vegas pro-duces today.

Fig. 11.6. In order to demonstrate that royalty is both superhuman and super-natural, elites sometimes underwent painful physical ordeals that ordinary people would be unwilling to accept voluntarily. Such ordeals were often linked with the induction of altered states of consciousness and privileged communications with deities. Here, a Maya queen at Yaxchilan has pierced her tongue and is pulling a cord spiked with thorns through her tongue in order to draw blood and communicate with the spirit world (Fig. 11.5). The event was so extraordinary that it was commemorated in a series of stone sculptures. Note the bowl with paper at her knees. From Ian Graham and Eric von Euw, *Corpus of Maya Hieroglyphic Inscriptions,* Vol. 3, Pt. 1, Fig. 3:53. Cambridge: Peabody Museum, Harvard, 1977.

The Egyptians and other royalty who built ancestral shrines also constructed impos-ing temples to national gods, such as the Temple of Luxor (Fig. 11.8) or the Temple of Huitzilopotchli in Mexico. The Maya temples surmounting the great tall pyramids at Tikal only contained a few square meters of floor space and could never hold more than a dozen people standing (Fig. 11.9). In all these cases, rulers or their confederates were

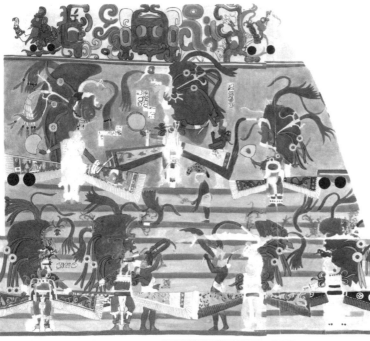

Fig. 11.7. After major battles, and probably for important calendrical festivals, Maya elites sponsored large and lavish ritual celebrations at which a great deal of feasting undoubtedly also took place. These events may have been occasions for collecting feasting "contributions" to help support the elites. At the relatively minor center of Bonampak, murals record the amazing costuming of dancers on temple steps as well as the large orchestra (below) and many elaborately costumed dignitaries (not shown) who were the main participants in these events. At the very top, deities and spirits watch over the display. From *Ancient Maya Paintings of Bonampak Mexico*. Washington, D.C.: Carnegie Institution, 1955.

the privileged communicators with the deities and these temples were built with the same aims as the imposing shrines to ancestral deities. Many of the principal festivals were undoubtedly held in the precincts of these major temples and were attended by representatives of the entire community, who provided feasting contributions as well as participating in the revels outside the temples, as seems to be indicated in Sumerian depictions (Fig. 11.10; see also Schmandt-Besserat 2001). It is difficult to determine the extent to which popular fertility or other cults may have persisted on a domestic level and to what extent these religious expressions had been replaced or assumed by the populist festival-and-feasting oriented cults promoted by early state elites. At least in Egypt, David (1982:143) indicates that popular religious worship took place primarily at the household and shrine level. Preferred deities were the masculine god, Bes, patron of love, dance, and fun, as well as the goddess Tauret, patroness of fertility.

The development of large-scale elite-sponsored spectator and feasting cults headed by educated, literate priests probably constitutes the beginning of the "book" religions that we began our discussion of religion with in Chapter 1. We can perhaps even detect the beginnings of these developments in some of the more complex chiefdom societies. In many, but perhaps not all, early states, it seems that elites attempted to isolate the general population from the more intense ecstatic ritual experiences. They appropriated these experiences for themselves in order to bolster their claims to privileged communication with divine entities (Rappaport 1999:447). As the size and complexity of early states grew, temples honoring a considerable diversity of deities were

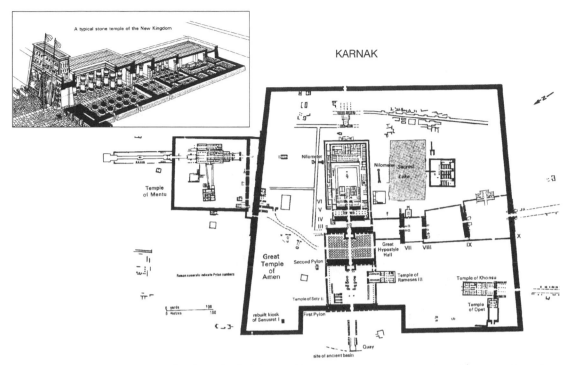

Fig. 11.8. In contrast to contemporary churches and cathedrals, one of the most consistent patterns in traditional societies indicates that the largest religious structures were for the exclusive use of the most important political and religious figures (often the same person) of a community or state. Although the outside grounds of large temples such as Karnak (bottom) might be used to host large numbers of common celebrants, the inside of a temple (top) was restricted to the most important figures. Access to the most sacred inner sanctum, where deities could be most easily contacted, that is, at the farthest reach the temple (top), was generally reserved almost exclusively for the use of the ruler or highest authority. Although congregations have been brought inside churches and cathedrals in the Occident, the altar areas are still restricted to the highest-ranking officials. From J. Hawkes, *Atlas of Archaeology*, p. 152. New York: McGraw-Hill, 1974.

built in the great metropolises of Mexico, Rome, and the Near East. How funds were acquired to build these temples and what inducements were offered worshippers to provide for the maintenance of temples and priests is not clear in all cases. At least in Rome, Greece, and Southeast Asia the ruling elite provided funds to establish temples. Many of the great temples and sculptures were erected by elites as parts of the fulfillment of vows to deities who were considered to have provided elite petitioners with military successes or answered other important requests (Burkert 1987:13). Other gifts to temples seem to have been intended to enhance the benefactor's reputation—another early form of promotional advertizing. From an ecological point of view, we would expect that some benefit would be provided to worshippers who systematically contributed food, effort, or other goods to the maintenance of the temples, but we do not have a clear idea as to what those benefits were.

ORACLES GUIDE THE SHIPS OF STATE—SOMETIMES

People have probably always sought some form of supernatural help in making critical decisions through divinations, prayers, or other means. However, it is only with complex

Fig. 11.9. The temples atop the imposing pyramids at the Maya site of Tikal in Guatemala (left) had extremely thick walls and inner chambers of only a few square meters in size. The interior view below was taken in Maler's Palace but is similar to the temple rooms on top of the larger pyramids. It is doubtful that any more than a handful of people could ever have occupied these temples at one time. Bottom photo courtesy of the University of Pennsylvania Museum Archives; photo at left by B. Hayden.

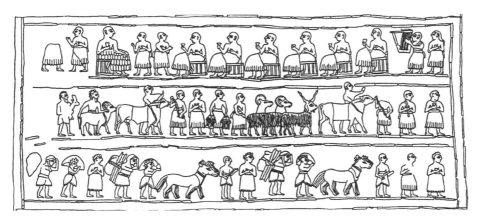

Fig. 11.10. Periodic feasts in honor of the principal deities seem to have been regular features of many chiefdoms and states. Citizens were expected to bring considerable amounts of surplus to these feasts, as shown in this depiction of a Sumerian feast. Much of the food and prestige paraphernalia offered to the gods was used to host a feast for everyone; however, a certain proportion of everything seems to have been retained by elites for the temple and for their own use as "tribute." From Denise Schmandt-Besserat, *Before Writing,* Vol. 1: *From Counting to Cuneiform,* p. 173. Copyright © 1992. Courtesy of the author and the University of Texas Press.

societies that these practices develop into veritable cults or systematic studies of astrology, calendars, or other techniques of prediction. Oracular cults such as that of Delphi in Greece developed large temple complexes and became a distinctive aspect of imperial or early state religious complexes. These developments may be understood in terms of the greater scale of consequences that are associated with important decisions made by rulers and other elites compared with normal individuals or households. Decisions by ordinary individuals normally only affect themselves or their families, whereas decisions by rulers or elites can entail important, sometimes life-and-death consequences for many thousands or even millions of people. Rulers and administrators in states or empires therefore invest heavily in predictive techniques. The movement of stars and planets provided one of the most structured manifestations of the state of the cosmos. Early Chinese rulers used oracle bones (often with sacrifices) and the *I Ching.* Direct ecstatic channeling of the will of the gods through oracular priests was also popular, and elites paid handsomely for useful guidance. However, many people used other considerations and would keep consulting various oracles until they got the predictions that they wanted. Then there is the story of Claudius Pulcher, a Roman naval commander who used chickens to perform a divination concerning an upcoming battle. He did not like the result, which indicated defeat, and threw the chickens overboard. He lost the battle, and the survivors never forgot his reckless disregard of the message from the gods (Suetonius 1957:114).

EMPIRES CONFRONT SOCIAL AND RELIGIOUS TENSIONS

By their very nature, large cities are amalgams of people from different racial groups, different cultures, different languages, and different religions. In very large cities, small ethnic subcommunities develop, but otherwise cities are usually populated with people from varied backgrounds with varied interests. This, too, is what large cities in empires were like. The cities of the Roman, Chinese, and Mongol empires were all mixtures of different ethnic groups. This characteristic created problems of social integration, anomie, and dangerous dissatisfaction. People who were uprooted, who had no family, and who had no social contacts sought common bonds with others in order to provide some security, help in times of need, and a means of decent burial. Desires for friendship and the warmth of company may have played a role in all this too, although more practical considerations must have impelled many people to invest significant amounts of time, effort, and resources in activities that created bonds of mutual aid and socio-economic safety nets. Ritual, of course, was a prime arena for forging such bonds and networks.

Thus, it should not come as a surprise to find that a new type of religion sprang up in urban centers of empires. In Rome, the elite-supported worship of Olympian deities was moderated as a result. These new cults owed little to the rituals and myths propagated by the elites to help consolidate their control and increase the solidarity of their kingdoms. Instead, these new cults tended to grow from the residues of previous fertility or other popular cults. As might be guessed, these tended to be ecstatic cults with strong influences on members. As was said of Eleusinian initiates, those who knew the mysteries were thrice happy. This cult and other similar ones were the "mystery cults" of the classical Mediterranean world. Certainly, there were other ways in which individuals who were uprooted by slavery, warfare, economic opportunities, or postings to distant locations might establish personal connections and safety networks. There were guilds, professional associations, business partnerships, clubs, and secret societies. Although mystery cults may not have been the only solution to urban social and economic isolation, they spread very rapidly from 500 B.C.E., when Rome was becoming an overgrown state but not yet an empire, until the ascension of Christianity about 400 C.E. This rapid spread indicates that these cults were providing some tangible benefits although many of the details of their operations are obscure. Mystery cults together with officially sanctioned imperial worship (often of the emperor or his ancestors and other state deities), ethnic cults, household ancestral cults, elite secret societies, and rural cults might well be called an imperial religious complex. Let us take a closer look at mystery cults to see how they differed from other religious practices.

First and foremost, it is important to point out that the basic socioeconomic conditions that made mystery cults adaptive were the same cultural ecological conditions that led to the rise of empires: notably, very high levels of surplus production that could sustain an extensive administrative structure as well as a large army; many non–food-producing crafts people; ritualists; and an effective long-distance transport system both for people and for massive amounts of food surpluses. The technology that made it possible for the Mediterranean world to produce large surpluses and to transport them, usually by ship, to major urban centers throughout the Roman Empire are what made the empire possible. It was these same conditions that created the gawdy mixes of people in the urban centers who had no ethnic cult to turn to, no ancestral cult, no large-scale fertility cult, and no real rapport with the imperial or dominant cults of the emperor or the Roman pantheon. The mystery cults flourished by filling this gap in the religious and social fabric of the classical world. Mystery cults were a direct outgrowth of the ecological conditions of the time.

Mystery cults of the classical period can be defined as cults that emphasized the transformation of individual experiences and spiritual fulfillment by means of establishing a personal closeness to a cult deity and a personal contact with the sacred. It was generally this contact that conferred salvation and instilled convictions of blissful eternal life after death (Burkert 1987:8–12). The more traditional Greco-Roman civic cults featured rituals that were predicated on, and displayed, individual public status within the state organization. Outside the cult there was little impact on personal lives. In contrast, mystery cults emphasized personal rather than public relations with deities, and this resulted in a new religion-based morality that would pervade all aspects of followers' lives all the time (Beard, North, and Price 1998a:289). Mystery cults, therefore, represent the advent of the first morality-based religions in the world, in sharp contrast to the pragmatic emphasis of traditional religions up to this point. Perhaps it was partly this feeling of intimate union with important deities and an inner link to moral codes that pervaded all places and times (in conjunction with socioeconomic stresses) that favored the manifestation of sacred ecstatic experiences within these cults.

Typically, these experiences were induced at the initiation rituals of new members by a variety of means ranging from the traditional 26 techniques used by shamans (Chap. 3) to overwhelming dramatic or emotional experiences such as being stripped and whipped, or being bathed in a bull's blood as the bull was being sacrificed on a grate above the initiate (this occurred in the rituals of Mithras and Cybele). Walking in circles, going down frightening paths in the dark, harassment, humiliation, pain, panic, shivering, sweating, sudden exposure to light, amazement, dances, sacred sounds, sacred words or sights, dramatic performances, fasting, baths, and jesting were other documented elements of the mystery cult initiations (Burkert 1987:91, 102). Generally, exhausting and terrifying events preceded sudden light and rejoicing. Polar-opposite concepts and experiences were strongly developed in the initiation procedures. The initiation was clearly meant to represent the psychological death and resurrection of the initiate, although not quite as literally as in Christianity (Burkert 1987:99). These experiences could be repeated at later events if one wished to do so and could afford the costs. A few authors have compared some of the mystery cults to modern secret societies such as the Masons (Cooper 1996:29, 34). Some of the general flavor may be similar, although it is not clear that groups like the Masons provided initiates with ecstatic experiences of sacred forces.

Special, secret versions of the cult myths were conveyed to the initiates at various levels of their advancement. The experience of direct contact with the sacred forces of the cult constituted the "mystery." Through these experiences, blessedness was achieved, and one's life here on earth became a more joyous experience. A dramatic description of one such encounter is provided in Apuleius' *Golden Ass* when the hero (Lucius) is delivered from his life as an ass and becomes a normal human being again through the intervention of the supreme goddess (Isis):

> Behold, Lucius, I have come in answer to your prayers. I am the mother of Nature, the mistress of all the elements, and the original child of time. I am the mightiest of deities, queen of the dead, and queen of Heaven. I am the single manifestation of every aspect of all the gods and goddesses. With a nod of my head I rule the starry firmament, the wholesome breezes of the sea, and the sorrowful silences of the underworld. I am worshipped everywhere in the world in many aspects, with different rites, and under many names, but my divinity is one. The first-born Phrygians know me as Pessinuntia, Mother of the gods. The Atticans, who sprang from their own soil, call me the Cecropian Min-

erva. On sea-washed Cyprus I am known as the Paphian Venus. To the archers of Crete I am Dictynna Diana. The trilingual Sicilians know me as Orygian Prosperina, and the ancient Eleusinians call me Ceres, their Mother of Corn.

Some call me Juno, some Bellona, others Hecate, and still others Rhamnubia. Both races of Ethiopia, who are the first to greet the morning rays of the sun, as well as the Egyptians, who excel in ancient lore, worship me with the proper rites and know me by my true name, which is Queen Isis. I have come in pity for your plight. I bring you sympathy and goodwill. Stop your tears now, and weep no more. Banish your grief; by my divine light your day of deliverance is dawning.—Translation by Fritz Muntean

The mysteries (sacred contacts and celebrations) were thought to continue in the same format after death. Immortality might be achieved within some mystery cults, but it was often an immortality similar to that of hunter-gatherer totemic ancestors, that is, of life flowing through generations one after another (Nilsson 1940:54–60; Mylonas 1961:283–84), or perhaps of reincarnation or an afterworld immortality as with the resurrection of Osirian adepts (David 1982:93, 108).

MYSTERY CULTS RESHAPE THE OTHERWORLD

The congregation of most mystery cults was predictably motley, but some of the mystery cults catered to specific segments of society, such as the Mithraic cult so popular among soldiers, the Dionysian cult that was almost exclusively for women, or the Orphic or Pythagorean cults popular among intellectual and philosopher elites. Ginzburg (1991:252) even argues that the Orphic cult never actually existed in terms of ritual gatherings, but that it was all in the minds and in the writings of a coterie of philosophers who tried to account for the discrepancy between an ideology in which the bad should be punished by divine retributions and a reality in which the wicked and cruel often seemed to get away with immoral or criminal behavior without ever seeming to suffer the consequences. To explain this discrepancy the Orphics invented the idea of divine retribution after death; that is, they came up with the idea of hell as a place where the wicked were punished. Before this time, the afterlife had always been a fairly nebulous concept. Among hunter-gatherers, there seems to be little philosophy on the matter. Their concepts are vague other than "happy hunting ground" notions (e.g., Teit 1900:342–43), although even these ideas may reflect the early influence of Christian missionaries. Perhaps more prevalent were notions of returning to a master of spirits, similar to the hunter-gatherer master of animals in the mountains or in underground caves. But the nature of these spiritual sanctuaries of repose was ill-defined, seeming at best to be almost like hibernation zones under the ground. Similar concepts were probably common among early horticulturalists, who likely took their models for human death and return to life from the grain or other plants that they grew. Just as the stalk of grain died but left the grain spirit and kernels either in the ground or in storage to be sprouted in a coming season, so humans might be thought to die and leave their bones and spirits dormant in some storage place from which they would return in new forms. Hesiod speaks of death as a sleep, and Psalm 88:13 in the Jewish Bible refers to the afterlife as "the land where all is forgotten," where the dead lose their individuality and are assimilated into an impersonal archetype of the forefather. A modern rendering of the

Irish story of Tuan by Jim Fitzpatrick (1978) gives much of the flavor of this kind of an outlook on the afterlife:

I am Tuan
I am legend
I am memory turned myth.

I have lived through life in many forms.
I have been man and beast, sea and sky.
I have died and been reborn more often
Than I can truly remember.

I, Tuan, was once a man of wisdom and renown. I was the White Ancient, chieftain of the tribe of Cessair, first men to dwell in green and fertile Eireann.

I lived in peace until the Great Flood drowned my race leaving me the solitary companion of bird and beast, alone in a land grown strange and desolate. . .

Then a great sadness came upon me and the horror of that night weighed on me pressing me down into a black slumber.

I slept for many days, floating loose in dream-time. I saw my mortal form change from aged man to powerful beast: in my dreams I became a stag. Through the heaviness of sleep I felt the beat of a new heart, the strength of young sinews and limbs.

I awoke from my sleep
I became my dream
I, Tuan, was a stag. . .

I, Tuan, grew old as a stag, but with old age another transformation awaited me and I slept.

I, Tuan, awoke from golden dreams in an empty land, hard with winter, white with snow.

Once I, a royal stag, raced the ocean's breezes, powerful as a storm, untiring as the sea-swell . . . Now . . . I woke as a black boar with sharp tusks and yellow teeth to tear my prey; on my back a mane of bristles so sharp and high a plump apple might stick there and rot.

But I was young again and I was glad. I was king of the boar-herds of Eireann; strong and powerful, afraid of nothing. . . . Then a great weariness came upon me and I felt the ache of change.

While this may represent commoner and perhaps even some elite views of the after-life, we have also seen that beginning at least with chiefdom levels of society, some elites began developing the notion of traveling to a privileged abode in the afterlife that was furnished with all of the luxuries of their actual life on earth. Only those that had luxuries (sometimes including attendants) buried with them could enjoy this privileged after-life. At least some Celts took it all quite literally with them to their Summerland, as did many Indo-European, Egyptian, and Chinese elites and others. For some groups such as the Torajans, it was the sacrifice of buffaloes that enabled the wealthy dead to get into heaven, where they would be happy and powerful (Sandarupa 1996). Similar notions must have characterized many early chiefdoms and state elites.

What happened to those who could not afford the fare to this heaven or the goods needed to set up a comfortable lifestyle in paradise? Few people talk of such things. Presumably, nonelites were simply relegated to the darker and dingier corners of the afterworld, excluded from the showy, sumptuous rituals or feasting that the wealthy loved so much on earth and which they tried to continue in their afterlife. The Romans thought that dead souls ascended into the sky and became one of the infinite number of stars, but otherwise they had very vague ideas about the afterlife. Some Romans released an eagle atop funeral pyres to carry the soul up into the skies. The Hebrews thought of the afterlife for the wicked as merely going to a place that was cut off from god's presence.

While heaven may have been an idea developed by the elites and for the elites, it provided good conceptual fodder for other religious developments, including some of the mystery cults such as the Orphic, Dionysian, and Eleusinian. Other mystery cults tended to focus on the help that deities could provide in the present world and left the next world traditionally vague (Burkert 1987:25). Like white bread, metals, indoor plumbing, and tombstones, the notion of heaven perhaps gives us yet another example of elite innovations being appropriated by nonelites (in mystery cults) as desirable status indicators, an issue discussed in Chapter 6.

Mystery Cults Originate from Telluric Cults

The major concerns of the general subsistence-oriented populace have always been the cosmic forces that directly affected their lives: fertility, the source of animals, and sacred alliances for help in times of need. We have seen that these concerns continued to be represented in popular, nonelite domestic cults during the Neolithic, the megalithic, and early state societies. We have also seen that elites in these societies progressively appropriated for themselves the ritual ecstasies that gave them credible claims for communication with the most powerful deities or spirits. However, various kinds of mystics, shamans, and trance healers must have continued to exist in nonelite parts of society, even if the majority of people were being shunted into more spectator types of religious activities. The household or local ancestral or fertility cults, shrines, and traditional healers constituted the populist religious movements. In Greece, phalluses were set up as grave markers, the place of life and death, where Hermes and Priapus stood erect and on guard (Kerenyi 1976:1224). Aside from the shamanic trances and the general euphoric dancing and feasting at harvests, weddings, or funerals, ecstatic states may have been largely eliminated from the ritual life of the populace.

The emergence of the mystery cults represents a revolution in the nature of religious life for the general populace because of their focus on morality and because they restored the participatory ritual ecstatic aspects to the religious life of everyone who wished to be initiated into the cults. Mystery cults again made it possible for everyone to obtain direct ecstatic contact with, and direct personal knowledge of, the gods, or at least the sacred forces that they represented. The very large populations in urban centers of the empire and the diverse origins of citizens made it difficult for rulers to control religious developments as they had more successfully done at the chiefdom and city-state levels. However, elites certainly did their best to keep a grip on all group rituals. In Rome, religion and politics were tightly intertwined by priest-politicians. Religious cults were regulated by the Senate, which portrayed itself as the central mediator between the gods and humans.

It had ultimate control over human approaches to the divine, while the local priests were simply technicians licensed by the Senate (Finn 1997:52; Beard, North, and Price 1998a:228). The Senate spent a great deal of time evaluating religious organizations to determine what were proper and improper cult activities. It repressed or regulated any cult or rite that was threatening to the moral or spiritual interests of the empire (Beard, North, and Price 1998a:91, 228, 230; 1998b:197, 204, 292). Priests had to be approved by politicians, and imperial rulers tried to create cults with deities that they claimed were more powerful than the various ethnic or mystery cult deities. Emperors were members of all priestly colleges. Some emperors even tried to identify themselves with mystery cult deities like Mithras and Dionysus to advance political integration in the empire (Burkert 1993:262–69). However, confronted with the massive socioeconomic forces at work in empires, none of these strategies were very successful for creating a unified religion.

The vast majority of the deities featured in the mystery cults seem to have derived from the old fertility cults of the countryside: the gods of plant growth and the vine such as Dionysus, Demeter, Bacchus. These deities are sometimes referred to as "tellurian" deities because they are so closely associated with the earth, as opposed to deities in elite pantheons like those of Mount Olympus, the "Olympian deities." While some authors may see the origins of specific mystery cults, such as those of Eleusis at Athens, as going all the way back to the Mycenaean period (1500–1000 B.C.E.), it seems most probable that the early forms of these cults were simply local fertility shrines at which celebrations for the sowing of crops were held (Nilsson 1940:23ff, 40; MacKenzie 1967:83). In this earlier period, statues of Demeter were erected on the family or village threshing floors, and the thrusting of the winnowing shovel into the pile of grain was performed with overt sexual symbolism, as in northern European harvest festivals. Phalluses were purposely placed in baskets full of fruit carried by women, and fruit was used to shower bridegrooms at weddings in order to confer fertility (Nilsson 1940:25ff). Similar activities with singing and dancing took place at wine-pressing gatherings. These kinds of rituals and cults were undoubtedly extremely widespread and common among almost all agrarian and horticultural communities from the Neolithic onward. While specific local fertility cults, such as that of Demeter, may have been transformed into mystery cults like the cult at Eleusis near Athens, they probably did not begin as mystery religions. Originally, they were simply ordinary rural fertility cults. What transformed them was the fact that large, interethnic, socially complex metropolises like Athens grew up around them and appropriated them. It was the needs of people in the metropolises of empires and trading emporia that transformed the local village fertility cults into something completely different—the mystery religions. While the original folk fertility cults were largely corporate family or community rituals, in which everyone participated for the good of the group, the new mystery cults emphasized individual benefits, individual experiences, and individual relationships with deities. The original agricultural myths of death and rebirth lost their earlier function and became allegories with personal significance for urban dwellers (MacKenzie 1967:83). What counted was the experience of the initiate rather than the revitalization of forces of growth in the natural world.

The earliest sign of this transformation took the form of urban "votive" religions, in which vows were made to specific deities. An initial gift and request was made at the shrine. If the deity would grant a favor—recovery from sickness, success in war, safe

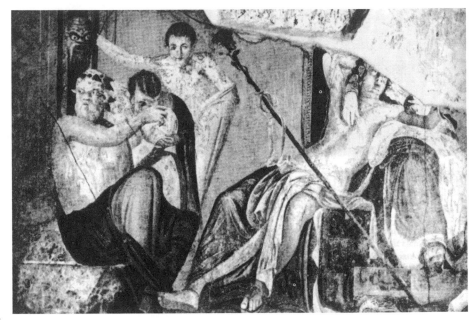

Fig. 11.11. The Villa of Mysteries in Pompeii was covered with ash by the volcanic explosion of Mt. Vesuvius in 79 of the common era, thus preserving many of the depictions of ritual and myth inside some of the most secret parts of the temples of mystery religions. The full mural in the Villa of Mysteries covers an entire room and shows the stages that an initiate goes through. Here, an old Silenus shows visions or cult revelations to a youth in a magical mirror, a mask used in sacred dramas of Dionysus hangs above their heads on the wall, and Dionysus reclines in the lap of Ariadne with a long thyrsus on his lap. From M. Grant, *Cities of Vesuvius,* p. 100. Harmondsworth: Penguin Books, 1971.

return from trips, a safe childbirth, recovery of stolen property—then the supplicant would carry out the terms of their vow, usually by making offerings, building shrines, or in some cases mortifying the flesh (Fig. 9.12). We have seen that votive offerings were popular among the Celts and that archaeologists frequently find votive offerings (Chap. 9), but they are also fairly common in many relatively complex cultures. Burkert (1987:12ff) suggests that votive offerings, like fairy tales, provided hope to people who felt oppressed by their material or social situation—they were a means of maintaining motivation in the face of bleak prospects or high-risk situations with uncertain outcomes. Votives were used by all classes of society, from generals to the poorest slave. Making the offering was a public act of faith in the deity, and fulfilling the terms of the vow frequently involved public announcements and feasts. However, votive cults were highly personal relations between individuals and deities who could provide salvation in this world. Obviously, success bred success. And if appeal to one deity did not work, there were always others that could be approached. Indeed, polytheism encouraged worship in more than one cult at a time and many members of votive or mystery cults undoubtedly divided their allegiances between several gods. Votive cults became particularly popular in the urbanized centers of the classical world, where they developed many of the characteristics of later mystery cults, especially personal dedication to a deity in the hope of salvation. Initially, many of the cults from the Near East came to Rome as votive cults with mysteries forming an auxiliary level of involvement within the cult (Burkert 1987:15). As urban centers grew and the need for more comprehensive religious frameworks developed, mystery cults acquired their characteristic forms.

As might be expected, votive and mystery cults blossomed all over the classical Mediterranean as well as in Roman Europe. For some, the more exotic and mysterious a cult was, the more effective it was thought to be. Thus, there were a number of cults imported from the Near East, like those of Isis, Cybele, Mithras, and Meter. At first, congregations consisted primarily of citizens or soldiers from the eastern realms where empires had long existed, but other urban Roman citizens, especially women, soon began to take an interest in the new cults. After the first flourishes, a few cults dominated the classical world in popularity and their priests became opulent in the elaborate ritual structures that they had built. The most popular mystery cults were those of Isis, Osiris, Dionysus (Bacchus), Cybele (Magna Mater), Mithras, and the Eleusinian cult of Athens. Egypt, too, had its mystery cults. From the Middle Kingdom onwards, the cult of

Fig. 11.12. In this scene from the Villa of Mysteries, a young female initiate is being scourged and having her hair cut in preparation for her spiritual death, transformation, and rebirth. From M. Grant, *Cities of Vesuvius,* p. 104. Harmondsworth: Penguin Books, 1971.

Osiris staged mystery plays and promised immortality for all initiates following successful trials of their souls after death (David 1982:93, 106, 110). The Greeks combined the cult of Osiris with that of Apis, creating another popular cult, that of Serapis.

Archaeologists have had the extraordinary good fortune to discover the well-preserved remains of one of the Roman mystery cult centers at Pompeii, replete with the original mural paintings on its walls—some of the greatest surviving archaeological murals in the Old World (Figs. 11.11, 11.12). This center, like the rest of Pompeii, was buried in 79 C.E. by a sudden volcanic eruption of hot pumice particles (volcanic "ash") similar to that of Mt. Saint Helen's. The buried cult center is called the Villa of Mysteries. It was the temple for a Dionysian mystery cult. The initiation chamber is relatively modest, only about 5 × 7 meters, but much of the public ceremonial life must have taken place outside, including processions through the streets. Many of the myths concerning deities of the mystery cults are different from the standard classical myths that are most familiar to us. Each cult seemed to try to develop more and more esoteric details about deities' lives that would be unknown to anyone outside the cult, and they were very eclectic in acquiring these details. At the Villa of Mysteries, we can see one such obscure myth portrayed, that of Dionysus reclining on Ariadne's lap apparently after he has been redeemed from Hades. The two have probably been united in a form of sacred marriage.

There are nine other groups of figures painted on the mural walls, indicating important details of the cult rituals and beliefs. There are people with sacrifices, ecstatic dancing, musicians, figures holding masks that were certainly used in rituals, preparations for a sacred marriage of an initiate with Dionysus, and a scene of the initiate being prepared for the ritual (Fig. 11.12). The ritual sequence begins with a maiden who appears successively in the other mural poses. She starts with preparations for the mystical matrimonial union with Dionysus. A priestess prepares her toilet including a special bridal veil. A young boy is holding a mirror up for her. Next, she approaches a naked young priest who is reading a charge relating to the mysteries and the oaths that she must follow. She then proceeds with a dish of food to a priestess seated by a table with food offerings. Here, an attendant is pouring a libation in preparation for the *agape,* or love feast, which also became part of early Christian celebrations. After the feast, there is a pastoral scene of a satyr and satyra with a fawn that represents Dionysus, who adopted this form to hide from other wrathful gods. The satyra offers Dionysus her breast. In another, older form, Dionysus (Silenus) acts as an instructor and shows a youth something fascinating in a magical mirror or sphere that was made for Dionysus by one of the gods. Dionysus also says something to the initiate that fills her with fear, perhaps relating to his own death by being torn apart, or perhaps relating to her own similar fate. The new bride of Dionysus displays her new status by revealing a huge phallus, which she has brought in a sacred basket. The phallus is placed on the ground and is observed approvingly by a winged seminude woman who may be the daughter of Dionysus. This figure then administers the ritual flagellation of the initiate, which represents in a symbolic form the initiate's death. Following this trial, the initiate is reborn as the bride of Dionysus and a semidivine being, a *bacchante.* We then see her naked and involved in a frenzied dance, watched by a priestess with a *thyrsus,* a pine cone on a rod symbolizing Dionysian spirit and life.

From another nearby town that was buried by the same eruption, archaeologists have recovered a mural depicting the afternoon banquet or service at another mystery cult center (Fig. 11.13). Further details of these cults can be gleaned from written documents of the times, such as philosophers' comments, references in plays such as *The Bacchae* by Euripides, remarks by early Christian detractors of paganism, and works of fiction such as the thoroughly enjoyable adventures of Lucius, who was turned into an ass but, as we have seen, was finally redeemed by Isis.

Archaeologists have been fortunate in identifying a number of other mystery cult sites, such as the remarkable, virtually intact underground meeting chamber of a Mithraic cult in Roman Britain (Ulansey 1989). However, the remains of most mystery cult buildings are usually in very poor states of preservation, generally with little more than foundations left. They were often intentionally destroyed. For instance, after functioning for over a thousand years, the center at Eleusis was destroyed by the Christianized followers of the barbarian leader, Alaric, in 396 C.E. However, a considerable amount of information about the cult was recorded by many early sources (Mylonas 1961; Nilsson 1940:42 ff; Burkert 1987). While there is some debate as to what exactly the mystery consisted of as revealed to initiates, the basic format of the ritual is quite well documented. Initiation was open to all citizens of Athens and presumably its allies. The full ritual lasted seven days. But, at the core, initiates began by fasting and making a 14-mile pilgrimage on foot from Athens to Eleusis, bringing a pig to sacrifice at the sanctuary. Upon arriving at the sanctuary, the physically stressed, fatigued, and verbally abused initiates were subjected to further disorientations and terrifying images, harassment, mockings, following frightening paths in the dark, walking in circles, and hearing

Fig. 11.13. The eruption of Vesuvius also buried the town of Herculaneum, where this mural was preserved. It shows the white-robed priests of the Isis mystery cult performing their relatively formal and highly organized afternoon ritual. From M. Grant, *Cities of Vesuvius,* p. 99. Harmondsworth: Penguin Books, 1971.

ominous sounds in the dark. Dancing, singing, offerings of cakes to the gods, and the drinking of potions were also key features of the ritual. At the critical point, the initiates were totally engulfed in a dark chamber and then suddenly exposed to a blinding bright light. It was at this point that the sacred mystery was probably revealed involving a drama, spoken words, and the display of a sacred object. Many people believe this to have been a simple stalk of wheat representing life and rebirth.

Certainly, life and death and the sprouting of a new crop (eternal life) were the main theme of the Eleusinian mysteries as well as the earlier fertility cults of Demeter. The central figures in the myth associated with Eleusis personify grain and vegetation (Demeter and Persephone). And, just as grain went into underground storage during the winter, so Persephone was taken down into the underworld by the ruler of the under-world, Hades. According to the mystery cult myth, the distress of her mother, Demeter, eventually succeeded in having Persephone returned to middle earth for the growing season of the year. Initiates who came to understand this mystery in an experiential and ritual ecstatic context must have felt as though they would live on into the afterlife and that their lives had acquired new meaning and new joy. After this revelation, the initiates and those formerly initiated joined together in feasting. In Aristophanes' play *The Frogs*, the Eleusinian initiates are found, after they die, in the land of the dead, still celebrating their torch-lit processions.

THE MYSTERIES APPEAL TO THOSE IN DISTRESS

There is a strong tradition in anthropology that views people's involvement in religion as the result of social distress or economic destitution as well as of the tendency for people under stress to lapse into ecstatic states (Chap. 2). While I think this is an inadequate explanation for all forms of religion in general, it clearly has some strong empirical support for specific kinds of religious phenomena. Accusations of malevolent sorcery, for instance, tend to vary in direct relation with economic hard times. Participation in ecstatic possession cults such as voodun is also strongly correlated with economic hard times and with those who are economically destitute (Lewis 1989). In general, new religions appeal primarily to those who feel deprived or excluded from prestige and rewards in society (Kraemer 1992:13). As we noted at the beginning of this discussion, the popularity of mystery cults, too, displays a very pronounced relationship with socially displaced, disempowered, and often poor individuals. Mystery cults were essentially an urban phenomenon oriented to helping people cope with urban anomie. Possession cults such as voodun may have had similar roots in the slaveholding societies of West Africa, the Caribbean, and the southern United States. Ross Kraemer (1979, 1992) has made a very compelling argument along these lines for the Dionysian mystery cult of Greece.

Dionysus was worshipped in early agricultural festivals of the countryside as god of the vine and fertility. However, by the fourth century B.C.E., he was featured in more exclusive mystery cult rituals as well. In these mystery cults, married women were the primary participants. Their secret rituals were renowned for the ecstatic madness that Dionysus induced in his followers. Those women who felt his calling but refused to follow Dionysus were often said to be stricken with madness that drove them to perform horrible acts, such as murdering and cannibalizing their own children, while followers were reputed to be capable of engaging in mad acts of a slightly more benign character. Dionysian rituals (*orgia,* from which our term "orgy" is derived) were also thought to be characterized by sexual promiscuity. All these portrayals may simply be vicarious and salacious fantasies of Euripides and a gossip-hungry Greek public. Depictions on archaeological Greek vases show much tamer rituals: libations to Dionysus, masks set up for his sacred appearance, satyrs and followers playing music and dancing, and processions with women carrying *thyrsuses* (Fig. 11.14). There is little doubt that drinking wine, sacrificing an animal, and feasting formed an important part of the nocturnal rituals as well as the appearance of the god in the person of a masked performer, probably a male. Historical accounts indicate that snake handling and ecstatic wanderings or dancing at night in the mountains by women were also major elements (Kraemer 1992:40–42). Priestesses were paid fees by the initiates.

Kraemer asserts that the cult of Dionysus had a powerful appeal to Greek women because they were one of the most repressed and suppressed segments of Greek society. Classical Greek society was extremely puritanical in its values toward women, rivalling fundamentalist Islam in its sequestering of women within the confines of patriarchal homes. Kraemer (1979:74) suggests that women's status in classical Greece was among the worst in Western society at any time. Even in Republican Rome, the male *paterfamilias* were often domineering and the traditional public Roman cults were controlled by men. Roman women may have even been banned from making sacrifices— the central ritual of these cults (Beard, North, and Price 1998a:295–96). Thus, women were weakly connected to the central social structures. It is probably conditions such as these that were responsible for the popularity of Bacchic and Isis cults as well as the authorities' fear of the cults as described by Livy. In Webber's terms (Webber, Stephens, and Laughlin 1983), this repression could lead to stress and psychological problems for many women. One way of venting pent-up frustration and repressed emotions would certainly have been to participate in an ecstatic cult in which all repressed emotions could be released in a more or less controlled environment. This, too, is the

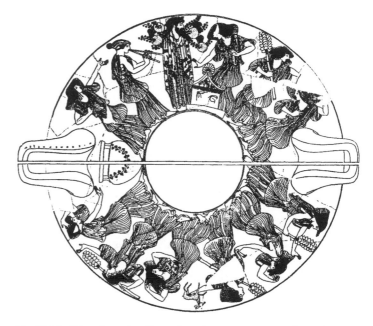

Fig. 11.14. Although stories of ecstatic madness, savageness, and sexual excesses were rampant concerning the secret meetings of the followers of Dionysus (mainly women), most actual depictions seem much more prosaic. In this scene from a Greek cup, women are probably engaged in ecstatic dancing with their sacred thyrsus wands around a pillar with a mask of Dionysus (or an actual man representing him), but there is no sex and no savagery. From W. Otto, *Dionysus, Myth and Cult,* p. 55. Bloomington: Indiana University Press, 1973.

logic behind the appeal of possession cults in Africa and the New World, especially among the poor and slaves. In this respect, possession cults are the equivalent of many classical mystery cults. In fact, Winkelman (2000:156ff) has shown that possession cults and mediums are strongly associated with politically complex cultures, presumably because these cultures create conditions of stress and anomie for so many people.

Under these conditions, it would be normal that people who repressed their emotions under stress but refused to participate in ecstatic cults that gave vent to their feelings might well experience emotional crises, breakdowns, and psychotic episodes in which they could perform exceedingly destructive acts—the madness sent by Dionysus to those who spurned his call. It is fascinating to note that similar cults probably originating with the worship of Cybele and Rhea as "women from outside," or "Mothers" (just as Dionysus was portrayed as being foreign), occurred in Italy, Sicily, and Crete sometimes right up to the nineteenth century. The women followers had to acknowledge these divinities and obtained direct ecstatic experiences or visions from them. Those who denied the reality of the cult goddesses became afflicted with mental tortures like the madness of Dionysus (Ginzburg 1991:122–26).

Amidst all the social, economic, and religious turmoil of the Roman Empire, there was one other mysterylike cult that we have yet to mention, a relatively late development among the mystery religions, but one that was destined to have a far greater impact on the classical and subsequent worlds than all of the other mystery religions combined. That was Christianity. Because of its distinctive features and its great impact in the world, we will take a closer look at its origins in the next chapter.

SUMMARY

The trends documented in previous chapters of elites trying to develop their own cults (in which they were the leaders and communicators with the gods while everyone else in the community was urged to follow along as spectators) achieved its greatest expression with the advent of early states and empires. Early states witnessed the formal assumption of divinity on the part of rulers in many cases. The king became god. The largest temples were built for royal use only and as expressions of the greatness and grandeur of the state's power and the king's rulership. Frequently, monumental ancestral temples or burial monuments such as the pyramids of Egypt were erected to dead rulers by their successors to legitimize the living ruler's claims of divine descent or at least very powerful supernatural connections. Frequently, elites attempted to curtail or eliminate direct ecstatic ritual experiences with sacred forces from popular religion by making rituals spectator events and closeting away those with natural ecstatic penchants in monasteries, relegating them to common shaman-curer roles, or by involving them in the priesthood. People who claimed to receive communications from deities could become politically troublesome for elites who wanted to make such claims exclusively for themselves. Divine kings also tried to assume credit for all the surpluses and wealth that their lands produced in order to back up their attempts to expropriate substantial amounts of citizens' produce. Additional justifications for collecting produce from citizens were made on the basis of requiring goods for feasts in order to honor the patron deity of the state. In later times, these contributions may have been demanded using military force backed up by the claims of divine rights. Famines and catastrophes were undoubtedly blamed on the forces of evil that were portrayed as the enemies of the divine polity patrons. At the popular level, ancestral and fertility cults seem to have remained ever present in many households and at rural community shrines; however, little archaeological evidence remains of these other than simple statues or phalluses.

Ecological and economic factors are critical in understanding religious developments in early states and empires, for they directly account for the emergence and relative power of elites. It is largely the elites pursuing their own self-interests who created the new religious forms. It was the elites who organized and underwrote the massive building programs for the impressive temples and monuments that form such a prominent and impressive part of the archaeological record of early states.

With the expansion of surplus-producing potential and the technological means of transporting food surpluses in bulk over long distances, powerful multiethnic empires emerged. Under these conditions, the simple religious forms of the early city-states were no longer adequate for the ritual or social needs of large urban populations. A new imperial type of religious complex developed. Emperors continued to try to unify the worship and rituals of the entire populace by imposing required worship of themselves as divine rulers. However, such edicts and laws were difficult to enforce and were not very convincing for the large numbers of ethnic tribal or foreign citizens who had little reason to embrace imperial values, customs, or religious concepts. One attempt to deal with such ethnic and racial diversity was to incorporate deities from all the constituent cultures into the imperial pantheon and to establish temples for all of them. Another strategy was to declare equivalences between local ethnic gods and the standard imperial gods so that, for example, people could worship both the Roman god Minerva and the local Celtic god Sulis at the Roman temple of Bath.

However, another development occurred that was probably unforeseen by the elites and had a more populist origin. This was the development of mystery cults that catered to socially displaced citizens and created individually meaningful experiences between initiates and the cult deities. These cults promoted ecstatic experiences and inner moral codes for all participants. This was the most dramatic religious development since the time when elites first began to create special cults that they could control, back in the Upper Paleolithic. As we shall see in the next chapter, Christianity was one of the most important mysterylike cults to emerge in this context.

CHAPTER 12

The New Synthesis
Judeo-Christianity

In the late Roman Empire, there was a veritable foment of religious activity. Conquered ethnic groups were bringing their foreign gods into urban centers. There was a particular fascination with cults that came from the Near East. The mystery cults created a new and vibrant ritual life throughout the realm. No cult wanted to be left out of the new developments. As a result, ritual elements and concepts were borrowed or adapted freely between cults. The old religions were threatened and new religions seemed to be springing up like weeds. In many ways, the first century before the common era to the first century of the common era was very much like the last half of the twentieth century and probably what a good part of the twenty-first century will be like. At the beginning of the common era, major empires were being established, incorporating diverse cultures into large interacting networks, accompanied by dramatic religious changes.

Born of this religious foment, Christianity has been viewed as similar to other mystery cults of the times (Metzger 1955; Wedderburn 1982; Burkert 1987). It arose from a local, more traditional cult, a sect of Judaism. It borrowed heavily from other mystery cults and offered salvation, spiritual rebirth, an idyllic afterlife, and a personal relationship or experience with the cult deity. There were initiations and mysteries that could only be understood by attaining certain levels within the cult (Eliade 1982:368ff). However, the local cults in Israel from which Christianity emerged were not fertility cults, but a relatively unique type of cult that the elites had managed to make the Hebrew populace accept completely to the exclusion of all other cults. Since this was the origin of Christianity, it is worth examining Judaism in more detail to note its distinctive characteristics.

JUDAISM SUCCEEDED WHERE OTHER ELITE CULTS FAILED

Beginning with the ancestor cults of chiefs, we have seen repeatedly how elites created new cults with themselves in key positions in order to further their political ambitions. We have also seen that elites tried to induce the entire population that they governed to accept these cults, usually with something less than the desired result. This trend certainly continued into Roman times, when a number of new cults were created by Roman or other emperors explicitly to strengthen their political rule. The cult of Serapis, the cult of Sol Invictus, and the cult of the divine emperors are some of the most notable examples. In some cults the service of the deity was exclusively in the hands of the Roman senators (Eliade 1982:290, 411). In others, cult priests and officials had to be sanctioned by the Roman government. Cults that were deemed unacceptable were banned or regulated (see Chap. 11). The elite political motivation for adopting or promoting certain religions played an important role in the history of Christianity, as we will see later, but the main point now is that elites had always tried to use religions in this fashion but had generally not been completely successful. Many people apparently preferred the older traditional deities that responded to their own needs rather than new deities that served the needs of the rulers, often rather transparently. However, because of historical circumstances and some astute religious-political leaders such as Moses, the elites of the early Israelite state did manage to achieve the age-old goal of elite religious domination, perhaps for the first time in history.

Although the early history of the Israelites is fraught with controversy (see Dever 1997), many scholars think that at least some of the more influential early Hebrews adopted a pastoral nomadic way of life and were divided into clans and chiefdoms with patriarchal political leaders. As among other pastoralists, animal sacrifices were the primary focus of clan rituals (Nakhai 2001). The House (clan) of Joseph appears to have been particularly important. Early Hebrew religion was probably similar to other chiefdom religions in that the main deities of the elites consisted of deified ancestors such as the "god of Abraham," the "god of Irene," or simply god the clan "Father" (Vriezen 1899:119; Albright 1957). Each chiefdom or clan probably had its own distinct ancestral deities. Whether all the Hebrews were pastoralists or not, it seems likely that their main deities were associated with the sky, much like megalithic chiefly ancestral deities, the Greek Zeus, and even the Islamic Allah (Eliade 1959:122). However, ancestral deities and supreme deities must have ruled within the context of a larger pantheon and not been the exclusive gods. There are several deity names in the earliest texts, such as Yahweh, Adonai, El, Elohim (used to denote the plural of god), Ashara, and a host of local fertility spirits or deities to which the Israelite commoners made offerings, sacrificed animals for feasts, and made crescent cakes. As part of a wider Middle Eastern interaction and economic sphere, the early Hebrews borrowed many elements of myth and ritual from their Canaanite neighbors and from the Egyptians and the Babylonians, who were the major powers of the time. This is typical of many nomadic or highly interactive societies. The story of Noah and the great flood is clearly borrowed from the Gilgamesh epic of the Sumerians; a number of verses in Ecclesiastes (e.g., 9:7–9) are also taken from the Gilgamesh texts; the Tree of Life in the Garden of Eden is an expression of the sacred world tree found in the myths of the region; the Song of Songs is similar to Inanna's song to Dumuzi (in Chap. 11); the monotheism of Moses was likely inspired, directly or indirectly, by the monotheism of Akhenaten in Egypt; the good-versus-evil dualism is derived from Zoroastrianism; the Book of Proverbs is taken from the Instruction of Amenemope; Psalm 104 is a revised version of the Hymn to Aten, as is the world's creation through the "word" (David 1982:175; Eliade 1978:172–86; Jastrow 1915:463).

During this period, Hebrew rural and common cults appear to have been very similar to the popular fertility cults of the Canaanites—the Philistine neighbors and sometimes enemies of the Israelites. Hebrews worshipped standing stones and set up shrines to their gods at the sacred places of the Canaanites. In fact, there is no clearly discernible break in the continuity of the Canaanite tradition from the Late Bronze Age to the Early Iron Age, when the Hebrews began to develop a distinctive culture.

Until about 1200 B.C.E., it seems that the Hebrews led a relatively peripheral existence as pastoral nomads or small-scale farmers in the poorer lands surrounding Bronze Age Canaanite towns and cities (Dever 1997). At least some early Israelites may have led nomadic pastoral lives and probably had typical pastoral religious practices. Typically, more powerful neighbors often raided these peripheral ethnic groups for slaves or to put an end to nomadic depredations against settled agricultural communities. Thus, the Israelites were overpowered and some were probably captured by the Egyptians, who appear to have enslaved them and taken them to Egypt. The Conquest Stela of Merneptah, dated at 1207 B.C.E., clearly states that the pharaoh "laid waste" to Israel, probably to avert any threat to Egyptian interests in the region. There may have been earlier campaigns as well by the Egyptians (Dever 1997:43ff). This was the first of two critical turning points in the development of Hebrew religion.

If biblical accounts are any indication, Moses appears to have been a key figure not only in negotiating the release of a small group of the Hebrews from the Egyptians around 1200 B.C.E. but also in maintaining political authority and unity over this group during the subsequent period of wanderings that culminated in the return to Canaan. During these wanderings, Moses seems to have become inspired by the beliefs of a bedouin tribe that worshipped Yahweh, a fairly typical pastoral nomadic deity that was the supreme and war-oriented deity of their hierarchical society. Moses probably realized that this concept of god could help unify defeated Israelite groups into effective military and political forces. It was a religious concept that he was able to induce many in his group of Israelites to adopt, perhaps because of the unusual political leverage that he could exert as the one responsible for freeing the Hebrew contingent from Egyptian bondage. Basically, Moses was able to use the historical defeat of the Israelites together with his inordinate political skills and power to promote what other elites had often dreamed of achieving but had always lacked the means of implementing: namely, the establishment of a single elite deity that everyone was obligated to worship to the exclusion of all others. Moreover, Moses was the leader of this cult, and it was to him alone that this supreme deity, Yahweh, spoke. It was Moses who went up on the mount to talk to Yahweh and brought down the Ten Commandments that would be instrumental in forging a new political force. Although this was a major turning point in religious evolution, the transformation was not immediately effective among the Israelite settlements that Moses returned to, as is demonstrated by his wrath upon returning from the mount and finding his Hebrews worshipping a golden calf like the early Israelites who had remained in the Transjordan. One of these Israelite bull cult sanctuaries complete with a small bronze bull has been discovered by archaeologists (Fig. 12.1; see also Dever 1997:37–39). Evidently, large proportions of the Israelite population still loved their fertility gods—the popular traditional deities of feasting, dance, and song.

By attempting to make Yahweh an exclusive deity with no other gods permitted to be worshipped—and with considerable leverage to enforce this dictum—Moses tried to create a powerful religious force that could help to resist the further breakup of the Israelite populace and its assimilation by more powerful polities in the region. Of course, such a religion was also an ideal tool for the political control by elites over their constituents. Thus, everything was done to promote the power and importance of Yahweh. He was portrayed as providing miraculous mana (food) in the desert; he enabled his followers to destroy heathen cities (although no de-

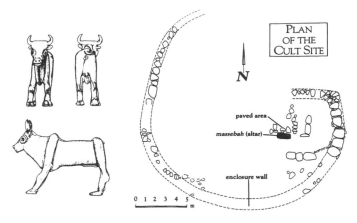

Fig. 12.1. Among the early Israelites, bull cults were popular and worship took place in open-air shrines such as this one, where a small, bronze bull statue was actually found, similar to "Bull El," the chief male deity of the Canaanite pantheon. Such cult practices undoubtedly were the basis for the biblical story of the golden calf. From W. Dever, "Archaeology and the Emergence of Early Israel," in J. Bartlett, ed., *Archaeology and Biblical Interpretation*, Fig. 2.12. London: Routledge, 1997.

struction of cities in this area occurs archaeologically at this time; Dever 1997:22–23); Yahweh took on the form of a pillar of smoke and flame guiding the Hebrews through the desert; he parted the seas; no ordinary mortal could see him and live; he was portrayed as infinitely powerful and eternal, totally beyond ordinary nature. Moreover, Yahweh was jealous and wrathful. He would not tolerate the worship of other gods, and he demanded absolute blind faith in his commands on the part of his followers. What more could an aspiring elite ask of a deity? Eliade (1978:176, 181) has called this last aspect of the new religion "Abrahamic faith," and it featured as one of the most distinctive aspects of Moses' religious innovations. It was probably this unique feature that subsequently enabled the Hebrews to keep their religion and culture intact even in the face of the destruction of their state and temples and the dispersal of the populace.

The return of the Egyptianized Israelites to Transjordan may have occurred at an opportune time, for the late–Bronze Age Canaanite cities and towns were undergoing a dramatic systemic collapse and abandonment. This undoubtedly created a relative power vacuum that the leaders of the Yahweh cult were well positioned to fill, using the cult to politically unify and organize their followers. As a result, within two centuries, a Hebrew state emerged with kings who assumed complete control over the cult of Yahweh. As typically occurred in similar situations, the general populace began to feel alienated from the overbearing elite cult with its list of "thou shall not" commandments. Many people chose to pay homage to the more popular agricultural deities of the Canaanites. The north part of the country reverted to the cult of the golden calf. Archaeologists commonly find female fertility figurines and private offering altars at sites throughout the area of the kingdoms of Judah and Israel (Silberman 1998a). Female figurines representing the goddess Asherah were popular in households, and kings even introduced her statue into the Hebrew temple in Jerusalem (Kletter 1996:78, 81). A number of elite priests, having adopted the use of ecstatic supernatural inspirations from the Canaanite cults, began prophesying dire consequences if the Israelites did not renounce the worship of all other gods except Yahweh and return to the keeping of the Ten Commandments. The prophets fulminated especially against the sacred prostitution and fertility cults of the Canaanites, their sacrifices, and their concepts of sacred forces as present in nature (Eliade 1978:180–86, 343, 354ff). They threatened divine retribution from Yahweh for these "sins." The prophets also began the tradition of claiming to work miracles, such as raising the dead and feeding multitudes.

The second major turning point in the development of Hebrew religion came in 586 B.C.E., when Jerusalem was destroyed by the Babylonian army. This time, large numbers of Israelites were taken into captivity and led away to Babylon. The elite priests used this political disaster as proof of Yahweh's anger and his power to punish those who had abandoned his worship and commandments. This event had a lasting impact on Hebrew consciousness and culture. Perhaps for the first time, a historical event was valorized in terms of religion. History became part of god's manifestation, in particular of his wrath against unfaithful followers, one of many themes that were to be adopted by later Christian sects (Eliade 1978:355–56). Traditional sacred time (which took place in a different dimension and was nonhistorical) was replaced with concrete events in history that constituted the major connections with the deity. From that point on, the religious life of the Hebrews was firmly rooted in the monotheistic worship of Yahweh.

Mircea Eliade (1959:72, 110; 1954:103–11; 1978:166, 338–55; 1975:64) has emphasized the unique features of this new Yahwism.

1. *A god that demanded absolute faith from followers and compliance with his will,* no matter how unreasonable it might seem, as in his command to Abraham to sacrifice his son or the attempt to shake Job's faith by taking everything from him including his wife and children. Evil and adversity simply became tests of one's faith that Yahweh sent or permitted to occur from time to time, as in the case of Job. This was a very new philosophical explanation for the existence of evil. This concept plus Abrahamic faith replaced the traditional logic of human relationships with deities whereby humans offered deities worship and sacrifices in return for fertility or other favors. With Yahwism, a chosen people became the servants and slaves of God, and people lived in constant fear of his wrath.

2. *The elimination of traditional sacred time* and its replacement by historical events considered as sacred events. Seasonal celebrations were transformed into celebrations of god's historical interventions, as in the example of Passover.

3. *An unusual monotheistic deity with purely anthropomorphic form that was wrathful and insisted on moral behavior and thought,* in contrast to traditional religions that emphasized correct rituals toward the deities but placed little importance on morality. Yahweh demanded constant moral behavior and thoughts from *all worshipers* in *all* aspects of their lives, *all* the time. Thus, a close personal relationship became established between worshippers and their god. This was one of the major turning points in the development of book versus traditional religions. It seems that only the very

powerful threat of another defeat and enslavement was strong enough to overcome popular opposition to this concept.

4. *The realm of God and the sacred forces was removed from the traditional realm of the natural world* and placed in a separate, inaccessible heaven, somewhere far above the world. The goal was to place God above nature and emphasize his all-powerfulness so as to ensure that only elites and their priests could access divine powers. The prophets were particularly incensed at the idea that God's essence could be in a tree or stone or natural object. They violently and totally rejected the traditional notion of cosmic religiosity. Similarly, they rejected the traditional link between life and death as the central element in the mystery of fertility.

5. *The celebration and joy of life as being part of a sacred world that was inherent in traditional cosmic religions was rejected* and repressed by the new philosophy of the prophets. Following Zoroastrian influences, salvation was to be found in the next world by adhering to the commandments of Yahweh during life, not in ecstatic fertility rituals in this world. Rappaport (1999:325) has suggested that this theme of waiting for a better life in the next world is actually common in many state societies for rather obvious reasons.

6. *The Hebrews were portrayed as the only chosen people of the only real god.* The reasons why God chose the Hebrews simply had to be accepted without reasoning as one of the mysterious decisions of Yahweh, as well as his decision to "give" them the promised land. If they did not accept his decision, they would be annihilated from the face of the earth—a concept that was ideal for the self-serving interests of the elites.

7. *A complete intolerance of other religious practices or beliefs* together with a condescending attitude toward followers of other faiths. This attitude often acted as a social irritant profoundly disturbing for the Romans. Hebrews became self-righteous in proclaiming that they were the only ones who knew the truth about God. In Roman eyes (and in some contemporary pagan eyes—Adler 1986:29) Hebrew zealots became religious totalitarians.

8. *A strong emphasis on good-versus-evil duality* and notions of conspiracies against God. This seems to have been adopted from the Zoroastrian religion while the Hebrews were captives in Babylon, but it served to further consolidate the cult of Yahweh and enhance the fanaticism of its followers. Strong good-versus-evil dualism tends to be a particularly well-suited ideology for promoting monotheistic religions.

9. *Religious-based wars appear for the first time* in known human history. While it was certainly true that other tribal groups had patron deities that members prayed to or sacrificed to for success in warfare, wars were always fought for more mundane purposes such as taking land, booty, or slaves, revenge, controlling trade, or other practical causes. The gods simply were implored to help and guide. With Yahwism, people were told to fight simply because Yahweh commanded it and because Yaweh had chosen a land for his chosen people. The justification for eliminating enemies was based on their beliefs, not their economic assets.

Thus, a new social and religious model was created beginning with Moses, who established a visionary blueprint to maximize the chances of survival for the Hebrews as a people but that also provided great control and benefits for the elites. This involved building a strongly disciplined society where obedience was total and unquestioning, where people were willing to make major sacrifices, and where self-discipline was a daily affair. The circumcision ritual of Hebrew males was undoubtedly originally an initiatory demonstration of individual boys' commitment to Hebrew solidarity. Ecstatic pleasure-indulgent fertility rituals became threats to ethnic political solidarity. Sybaritic behavior was castigated and rooted out by dour leaders, priests, and prophets. Many successful ethnic struggles for survival seem to incorporate these features, whether in the form of religious or political ideologies, as the example of the Vietnamese struggle against the Americans demonstrates. Individualism and unwillingness to make sacrifices for greater community goals weakens any polity. This is perhaps the real lesson behind the lapse of the Hebrews back into traditional pagan ways—and their subsequent conquest by the Babylonians.

CHRISTIANITY ESTABLISHES A NEW DIRECTION

If the Hebrews had been lucky, they could have used and transformed their unique monotheistic religious, social, and political system to forge a powerful, expansive empire. In time, they might have dominated the Near East, much the way that the nomadic Mongols, Aztecs, and Inca created vast empires in short periods using many of the same tactics of self-sacrifice, gods that demanded conquests, absolute obedience, and mobile military tactics. However, other great powers of the region never permitted the fledgling Hebrew state to become a major threat, and Jewish elites experienced continuous problems in implementing their program among the general populace until the Babylonian captivity. The ultimate effectiveness of the elite Hebrew strategy has been demonstrated repeatedly by the strong Hebrew ethnic and religious fabric that survived the Roman conquest and dispersal of Jews throughout the Roman world, as well as by the persistence of Judaism and Jewish culture in communities throughout the world over the last 2,000 years despite pogroms and holocausts.

However, some of the very features that made Yahwism so effective in this regard also limited its potential for becoming a major force in the world at large. The worship of Yahweh was closely tied to membership in a single ethnic group, the Hebrews, although exceptionally members of other ethnic groups might be admitted. The strong ethnic focus of Yahwism undoubtedly greatly limited the involvement of other groups and therefore the political potential of the religion. The rigor of the Hebrew religion made back-sliding and assimilation the greatest threats to the loss of local political power and ethnic identity, especially given the highly interactive world of commerce and conquest in which they lived. This effectively meant that Judaism could never be an expansionist or proselytizing religion.

It was as part of the religious foment of the last century B.C.E. and the first century C.E. that one sect sprang from the roots of Yahwism with a much greater potential for expanding beyond the confines of the Hebrew state—the Christian cult. The early Christian cult was an innovative blend of traditional, very conservative Hebrew beliefs and practices together with some new ideas and fairly heavy borrowings from other sources, especially other mystery cults introduced by the Romans. Early Christianity was initiatory and membership was a matter of choice rather than ethnic affiliation. Full submersion baptism was commonly understood as a symbolic death experience and the beginning of a new life—a spiritual resurrection similar to the death-rebirth-and-salvation experienced by initiates into other mystery cults. Christianity, like many other mystery cults, featured salvation through direct ecstatic experiences with the cult savior divinity who died and rose again. Initiation was also preceded by fasting, purifications, and trials, as well as circumcision. Once admitted, membership conferred equality within a given rank, and the individual experience with the Christ divinity was stressed. Involvement with the deity included moral precepts that pervaded one's thoughts and behavior. The Eucharist or agape ritual meals were meant only for the initiated. There were several ranks involving levels of mystery, and membership entailed new social relationships and commitments (Meyer 1987; Eliade 1982:368ff; Rappaport 1999:154).

As documented in Chapter 11, many of these characteristics were common in the mystery cults of the time. However, there were other more specific borrowings as well. Virgin birth of semidivine or divine individuals in human form is a common theme in many pagan traditions in Eurasia and the New World, but some of the Hebrews may have been familiar with this concept from dealings with the Egyptian pharaohs, who claimed to be born from the union of their royal mothers with Amun Re. There are also many similarities between Isis and the Virgin Mary (Fig. 12.2; see also Eliade 1982:294; Witt 1971; Warner 1976). Ideas about a triune godhead were also current in the Egyptian New Kingdom (David 1982:124, 175). The similarities between Osiris' death and resurrection and Christ's are probably not accidental, although myths with the same features characterized Dionysian cults, the cult of Zarathustra in Babylon (Eliade 1978:338), and a number of other mystery cults. In fact, Christ was often equated with Dionysus and vice versa (as gods of rebirth and as a savior or deliverer from punishment after death; see Burkert 1993:268; Henrichs 1993:28fn; Graf 1993:243, 252). The rites of Attis and Cybele were particularly similar to the Christian resurrection, for the priests of this cult fashioned an effigy of Attis and paraded it though the streets for four days before the spring equinox, letting their blood flow as part of the procession. The effigy was then buried and the tomb was opened on the vernal equinox with the proclamation that the god had risen from the dead. Today, the celebration of Christ's resurrection, too, is keyed to the vernal equinox. The equinox was also of great importance in the cult of Mithras, which featured sacrifices of bulls (representing the heavens). The basic theme of death and rebirth was probably extremely widespread among agricultural communities from the beginning of the Neolithic (if not Paleolithic) onward. In this respect, Christianity simply recycled the most fundamental Neolithic myth. In fact, it is doubtful that Christianity would have been able to compete successfully with other religions if it had not adopted this central myth.

Moreover, it is particularly telling that there was no mention of Christ's resurrection or passion in the earliest gospels that were written, nor was there any account of the miracle of the loaves and fishes. These all seem to be features added on to the cult myth at a later time (Funk and Hoover 1993). The followers of Osiris had long conceived of a trial of human souls after death like the Christian judgment (Fig. 12.3; David 1982:111). In a number of other mystery cults the eating of the ritual meal was considered to involve a sacred communion with the cult deity, usually involving bread, meat, and/or wine (Burkert 1987:111). The consumption of bread and wine was especially important in the Mithraic cults, conferring immortality in the afterlife but also provid-

ing strength and wisdom in this life (Eliade 1982:280). The birth, or rebirth, of many mystery cult divinities was also commonly celebrated at the winter solstice, or 25 December, especially the birth of Mithras—one of the major competitor deities of Christ (Eliade 1982:328, 348).

A number of mystery cults were also noted for their puritanical morality, particularly the Orphic, Pythagorean, and Isic cults (Burkert 1987:107). One Pythagorean catechism explicitly proclaimed that "pleasure is in all circumstances bad; for we come here to be punished and we ought to be punished"—a doctrine similar to the Christian concept of original sin (Dodds 1959:152). Gnostic views similarly held that the material world and pleasures were polluting and the antithesis of spiritual fulfillment or salvation. A number of cults were also permeated by the dualistic notion of a cosmic struggle between

Fig. 12.2. In Egypt, there are many portrayals of a seated Isis with a crescent moon crowning her head or cradling her feet while she holds her divine infant, Horus (left). It is fairly clear that this image and many of the spiritual qualities of Isis were adopted in Christian portrayals of the Virgin Mary, as shown here in a woodcut by Dürer from the sixteenth century (right). Many modern views and depictions of Mary still keep this tradition alive. Left: Photo by B. Hayden. Right: from R. Guiley, *The Encyclopedia of Witches and Witchcraft*, p. 140. New York: Facts on File, 1989.

good and evil, with the good going to paradise and the evil going to hell.

While the ultimate source of this extreme good-evil duality and ideas about the corrupt nature of the world may be found in religions farther east, such as the Babylonian cult of Zoroaster, Yahwism adopted these concepts as well. Thus, local Hebrew influences may more parsimoniously account for Christian attitudes concerning the battle between good and evil and the defiling nature of sex, pleasure, and material goods. An extensive literature exists on this issue and the influence of the mystery cults on Christianity. It is conveniently listed in the *Ancient Mysteries Sourcebook* (Meyer 1987:226–27; but see in particular Metzger 1955 and Wedderburn 1982).

The Christian borrowings and inspirations from the ultra-orthodox Hebrew Essenian sect have been of special interest to archaeologists since the discovery of the Essenes' sacred books near Qumrun in the Palestinian desert over half a century ago—the famous Dead Sea Scrolls (Fig. 12.4). The Essenes were a highly disciplined moral order that viewed pleasure and the material world as evil. Even marriage and procreation were forbidden, indicating the extremeness of many of their views since this dogma must have adversely affected the group's ability to perpetuate itself. They called their spiritual leaders "Sons of Light," similar to Christ's title as a "Son of God." Like Zoroastrians,

Fig. 12.3. Near Eastern religions provided many sources for the concepts and themes that occur in the Judeo-Christian religious tradition. The concept of a judgment of one's soul after death is one example. Here, the Egyptian dog-headed deity Anubis leads the dead person to the scale where his soul (in the form of a feather) will be weighed and the result recorded by the ibis-headed scribe. The dead person is then led to Osiris, god of death and rebirth enthroned in white at right, who will decide his fate.

they foretold the coming of an antideity and a final battle at the end of the world when a redeemer would come from God and proclaim the final salvation together with the end of the world and ordinary history, although last judgments at the end of the world were relatively common features in mystery cults as well (Eliade 1982:328, 353–58).

The Essenes established extremely close-knit communities isolated from the rest of society. Religion was used to create a very supportive communal environment in which mutual help, sharing, and confrontation of crises were all important aspects. To some degree this must have been essential for survival in their remote desert communities, just as mutual help had been essential for simple hunter-gatherers living in poor environments thousands of years previously. But in the context of early states and empires, with citizens dislocated and separated from their traditional families or tribes, such intense social support from strangers who were brought together in cults was an innovation. By the time of the Romans, the Essenes may have represented the strongest existing combination of religion with socioeconomic programs. They probably provided a blueprint for later Christian communities. While some mystery cults offered members new social identities and a new sense of community, Christians and Jews were the only groups that provided charity to their own members (Beard, North, and Price 1998a:278–88). Many Essene features of early Christianity have persisted in episodic forms down to the present; some sects still proclaim the imminent end of the world. Mormonism and many other less well-known cults provide a contemporary model for the establishment of religious socioeconomic communities, and Christian monasteries represent the most extreme form. However, Jesus, John the Baptist, and Paul used the Essenes and other traditional Hebrew cults as only one source for their new religious vision. The other main source was the mystery cults.

The early history of the Christ cult was not particularly notable. Like many other mystery cults, its first members were foreigners from the Near East. Its egalitarian practices and philosophy appealed primarily to women, slaves, the poor, and the displaced, most of whom appreciated the emphasis on mutual help, sharing, and the establishment of a real socioeconomic-religious community. Christianity promised followers a better life and, with their social programs, could frequently make good on their promises.

The original Christian philosophy was strongly antimaterialist and antiauthoritarian, which is what got Jesus into trouble. Saint Luke explicitly stated that the rich would go to hell while the poor would go to heaven. This, too, appealed to the urban proletariat

while the antiauthority tenor appealed to disenfranchised women, slaves, and the poor as well as to Hebrew nationalists who wanted to see Roman authorities overthrown and the Hebrew state reestablished (Robertson 1962:93). Early Christians vigorously spread their philosophy in missionizing drives among the poor, to whom they gave material help. Like the main source from which it sprang, followers of Jesus were fiercely intolerant of other belief systems to the point of being obnoxious in the conviction of their own deity's superiority. This and several other factors led to direct clashes with the dominant Roman culture and its administrators.

CHRISTIANITY COLLIDES WITH PAGAN ROME

Rome is often portrayed as cruelly persecuting the early Christians because of its intolerance of the new religion. However, the actual situation was rather different. The Christians were persecuted as much because they threatened the basic fabric of Roman civilization as because of the Christian self-righteous intolerance of other views. Roman policies on religion were as democratic as might be achieved in classical times and a model of tol-

Fig. 12.4. The Dead Sea Scrolls shown here were discovered in a cave in Palestine. When the radical religious community at Qumrun was abandoned in the first century before the common era, they carefully hid their scriptures and records in a cave. These records reveal important details about the radical religious movements of the period such as the Essenes, which seem to have heavily influenced Jesus' philosophy and doctrines. From C. Pfeiffer, *The Dead Seas Scrolls and the Bible*, pp. 48, 92. New York: Weathervane Books, 1969.

erance that many post-Roman governments could have emulated with considerable benefit. Technically, the worship of all deities was permitted and the most important ones were sanctioned by the Roman Senate, authorizing major temples to be built. Nevertheless, Roman leaders liked their older traditions and tended to be somewhat hostile to all new cults, which they regarded as potentially undermining the established sociopolitical order. Thus, Jews and Chaldeans were expelled from Rome in the second century

B.C.E., and the Bacchanals and the Egyptian mystery cults were banned or persecuted at various times, as were the Christians (Tentori 1982). Usually, after a century or two of increasing familiarity with new cults, Roman administrators reached a mutual accommodation with cult leaders and accorded them an official status.

Christianity was initially one of the most threatening of the new cults. Traditional Roman religions emphasized worship in the context of the family, the lineage, and the public for the well-being of these groups rather than self-interests of individuals. Christianity, in contrast, focused squarely on an *individual's* relation to God and individual salvation or benefits. Roman temples were the focal point of Roman civilized life. They were repositories for myths, history, poetry, works of art, and culture in general. They were centers for celebrations. When an individual and his or her family wanted to fête an important event, they went to the temple, offered a sacrifice on the altar, and settled in for a feast, often accompanied by music, poetry, dance, and song, all in the presence of the gods. Temples served as butcher shops, where those who wanted meat could purchase the excess from sacrifices. The poor might find some scraps, too. The deities were part of the world and participated in its daily events but particularly its celebrations.

According to Paul Veyne (1983), deities were not any more virtuous than their human counterparts, and they were often likened to aristocrats. They were powerful and worthy of veneration, and they generally favored virtue, but they had their weaknesses and unjust whims. The gods expected to be honored in the same way that powerful men were honored. Unlike Yaweh, the pagan gods were independent and self-sufficient; they had not created human beings, did not need human servants, and could destroy people if offended. For pagans, the human race did not occupy the central position of the universe, but was simply one rung on the ladder from inanimate, to plant, to animal life, to humans, to spirits, and then to the gods. The gods were simply "superhuman." Aristocratic rulers were more powerful than ordinary people, but less powerful than the gods, so they occupied an intermediate step between human beings and the gods. Rulers could make things happen that ordinary mortals could not. Nature was divine because people had no real power over it. In fact, *divinus* simply meant "superior." Worshippers were constantly petitioning their gods for favors in the same manner that they would petition powerful elites. Worshippers would also criticize the gods just as they might criticize political decisions of rulers. In some cases, irate worshippers even hurled insults and stoned temples, as after the death of Germanicus. Such attitudes also explain the penchant for making fun of the gods and telling jokes about them that were popular among the Greco-Romans, jokes not very dissimilar to those circulated about President Clinton. But the gods were not indifferent to morality. They generally supported virtuous men and good causes, even though they could sometimes swerve away from the most noble course of action as the result of gifts, jealousies, or revenge. These pagan Roman attitudes were clearly far different from the attitudes of the followers of Yahweh or Christ.

Christianity intruded into Hellenistic pagan cultures, proclaiming that all gods but Christ were false. Moreover, the other gods were proclaimed to be demons and part of the conspiracy of evil against good. Christians obstinately refused military service, refused to worship the emperor, refused to participate in basic Roman festivals, and seemed to be undermining authorities by giving assistance to the poor and sometimes refusing to pay taxes. Early Christians were viewed in terms similar to Communist atheists in the United States during the 1950s. In addition to the newness of the Christian cult, which must have rankled Roman traditionalists, Christians seemed to be bent on destroying Roman society. Not only were the Christians threatening the very fabric of Roman culture and political life, but they also were aggressive and provocative with their haughty attitudes of superiority and self-righteousness. They openly relegated the wealthy leaders of Rome to hell in the afterlife—hardly an endearing strategy for gaining official acceptance.

Moreover, the Roman political system was largely founded upon the incorporation of tribal groups through the assimilation of their gods into the Roman pantheon. It was a relatively open and democratic system. The insistence by the Christians that only Christians worshipped the true god jeopardized the entire foundation of Roman political integration as well as the Roman elite's attempts to establish a universal religion in which all Roman subjects would feel comfortable, such as the Sol Invictus cult.

Moreover, the Christian god was the antithesis of all the interactive negotiating characteristics that Romans usually attributed to gods. In essence, Christianity was perceived as a kind of religious totalitarianism that threatened the religious democracy that the Romans had worked hard to establish as well as the pleasure-loving habits of Roman civilization. The specter of the poor becoming united under a new, intolerant, and potentially violent god also must have given Roman elites cause for alarm. Some Romans spread rumors of scandalous orgies, cannibalism, and the killing of babies in the secretive Christian cult. These are typical rumors about many new or adversarial cults that recur throughout the ages, and ironically they are the same rumors that Christians later spread about pagans in medieval Europe. In Rome these rumors were fueled by the secrecy of Christians and allusions to the eating of the body of Christ (the Eucharist), drinking his blood, and the kiss of peace (leading to speculations of orgies).

Just as Fascism is viewed as a threat to democratic political systems today and is outlawed in most Western democracies, so the Romans outlawed early Christianity and in some periods decided to persecute those trying to spread its doctrine. In fact, it is worth considering the proposition that the spread of Christianity may have been a major contributing factor to the collapse of the Roman Empire (Gibbon 1960:525ff), although not all scholars would agree with this view (MacMullen 1988).

CHRISTIANITY OFFERS ADVANTAGES AT OPPORTUNE TIMES

Despite official attempts to limit or eradicate Christianity, it persisted in the Roman Empire, eventually becoming the official religion (Fox 1986). How can this spread be explained, especially if we reject contentions of moral superiority or the religious truth of Christianity in comparison with other religions? If we adopt a cultural ecological position, we are led to search for practical advantages that Christianity might have conferred on its followers. There were several stages in the development of Christianity.

Certainly, following the changes instigated by Paul, the spread of Christianity was a complex phenomenon with a number of contributing factors. However, several features stand out as critical from a cultural ecological perspective. First and foremost was the deteriorating state of the Roman Empire during the first centuries of the common era. We have already mentioned the rampant urban anomie created by the displacement of peoples and their congregation in the urban centers. Rodney Stark (1996:144) describes

Roman cities as "incredibly disorganized" cultural chaos. This fueled the popularity of the mystery cults in general. However, in addition to this general state of empire life, the Roman Empire soon found itself confronted by serious economic, social, and political collapse. Archaeologists have discovered that the earlier scattered farming villages were being consolidated into huge plantations, perhaps due to technological advances in plowing and farming. Large segments of the rural populations were either being turned into serflike tenant farmers or they were forced to migrate to expanding towns in search of work. Such a vast restructuring of the Roman economy impoverished great multitudes (Silberman 1998b:47). Under these ecological conditions, it became increasingly difficult to feed all the poor and indigent in the urban areas. Popular unrest turned to violence and crime, and occasionally broke out in popular, slave, or even military revolts. By the third century of the common era, there were no temple inscriptions and little financial support for temples from the Roman government. In fact, all public works and inscriptions dropped off dramatically (MacMullen 1981:128–29). There was little political stability in the rapid succession of emperors. Rome could no longer afford to finance its full army, and barbarian chiefs took advantage of Rome's weakness to attack the Roman borders. Hebrew nationalists saw their opportunity to stage revolts from Roman rule. As mentioned in Chapter 9, the army was also withdrawn from Britain at this time.

Under these circumstances, it would be expected that any religious cult that provided effective social and economic support for its members would become popular, especially among the lower classes and those displaced by military, commercial, administrative, or other duties. Christianity did this with its Essene type of heritage and emphasis on a mutually helping religious community. Many of the disadvantaged must have felt deeply that the world was made for suffering and that the best solution was to reject the material pleasures of life. In comparison with Christianity, the other mystery cults offered very limited social or economic support for members (Burkert 1987:51–53; Kraemer 1992:78). On this basis alone, one could anticipate a more successful spread of Christianity, especially in urban centers, which is where Christianity and the mystery cults did, in fact, first take hold. They were fundamentally urban developments that only made sense under the urban ecological conditions of the times. Rural areas remained heathen much longer. However, the mainstream mystery cults had other disadvantages according to Burkert (1987) and Gibbon (1960:143ff). The mainstream mystery cults grew out of a polytheistic tradition, where people could belong to several different cults and where there were few rigid boundaries between cults, little competition, no heresy, and no excommunication. The mainstream mystery cults did not form socially and ideologically coherent units with unshakable resolve. There was little total commitment among followers either to the cult or to each other. If a person was not satisfied with one cult, he or she could try out others, much as one might choose a favorite neighborhood pub to frequent.

Many Christian groups (for there was enormous variation within the early Christian movement), on the other hand, demanded total commitment and a large degree of control over one's economic resources. The Christian cult, in effect, set up an alternative, totally self-sufficient, independent, self-reproducing society within Roman jurisdictions. It was a parallel administrative system that collected taxes, redistributed resources to those most in need, took care of people in difficulty, arranged for marriages, burials, and induction into the community. The lack of extreme dedication in mainstream mystery cults put them at a serious disadvantage compared with the organization, drive, collective efforts, resources, and missionizing of the Christians. When Roman control over crime began to break down together with the judicial and economic system, the other mystery cults began to disintegrate along with the bulk of Roman society.

Christian communities, on the other hand, were well equipped to weather the social and economic storms that ravaged Roman towns and cities in the first centuries of the common era and the ensuing Middle Ages. Roman cities were frequently attacked and taken by unfriendly armies; they were disrupted by natural disasters; they were crowded and unsanitary population sinks; most people "lived in filth beyond our imagining" (Stark 1996:153). As a result, epidemic diseases ravaged urban populations on a regular basis, destroying the pagan Roman social fabric and overwhelming pagan philosophical explanatory concepts (Stark 1996:74–76). The largest of these epidemics (in 165 and 250 c.e.) may have killed 25–33 percent of the urban populations. Christian communities took better care of those caught up in the epidemics, conflagrations, and other disasters that plagued Greco-Roman cities, thus creating a survival rate for Christians that was far higher than that of pagans (Stark 1996:74). Christian communities provided a safe refuge of mutual aid for all who would make the commitment required. Christianity had an explanation for the epidemics (retribution for crimes and the refusal to accept Christ as the only true god); Christianity provided an alternative to the brutalities of Roman culture and the socioeconomic chaos. Moreover, unlike many of the mystery cults that catered to specific professional groups or social classes, Christianity was open to all. Like other new mystery cults, especially that of Isis, early Christianity had a strong appeal to women. Women's status in Greco-Roman culture and ritual was not very high and many felt marginalized. Males dominated most of the cults. Early Christian cults often accorded women more status and gave them some leadership roles. As a result, Christian congregations were largely composed of women, including women from the upper classes (Beard, North, and Price 1998a:295–96; Kraemer 1992:17–18, 73, 78, 128; Stark 1996:95). The cult of Isis, with its emphasis on the family and marital fidelity for both husband and wife, was an important rival for the support of women. However, the Isis cult was costly and did not have the same emphasis on community life.

Many of the poor must also have relished the idea that they did not have to be rich in order to reap spiritual rewards or participate fully in the Christian cult—quite the opposite; poverty was viewed as desirable and spiritually advantageous. For many people in the poorer or displaced social groups, life may have seemed divested of meaning. Christianity not only provided an acceptable meaning for life and suffering, based on the blind faith in God's great plan, but also promised redemption in the afterlife and provided some tangible relief in the present world.

The ability of the Christian cults to provide for the worldly needs of their members ultimately was dependent upon their ability to collect finances, resources, and labor from their members. Good Christians never needed to worry about where the next meal could be found or where they might sleep because the hospitality of the congregation took care of all brethren, even those from other towns (Benko 1984:32; Stark 1996:188). However, with a congregation composed almost exclusively of the poor, the ability of early Christians to help each other, not to mention to dole out food and material goods for new recruiting, must have been severely constrained. Stark (1996:34–35, 46) has argued that successful cult movements are never proletarian-based but are those that successfully recruit the rich and influential. Thus, in a strategic turnaround, the early cult directors decided to dilute the vitriol against the rich and to court their favor so as to swell church coffers and make greater expansion possible. At this point, Christianity entered a new stage in its evolution. It became the poor in spirit who would enter heaven, not simply the financially destitute. By the late second and early third century of the common era, the new policy was in place, and gradually a number of wealthy converts entered the church (Kautsky 1953:278). Modest increases in finances made great increases in missionizing possible. Thus, armed with their conviction together with the greater material benefits that they could provide, the Christian cult began making substantial numbers of converts by the beginning of the fourth century.

Roman Elites Appropriate Christianity

We have seen that state elites everywhere tried to institute a single religion in their domains that would unify the populace and enable the elites to exert better control over their subjects. This elusive quest was of special concern to the Roman emperors, who deified themselves; but they had no better success than imperial elites elsewhere. The cults like Sol Invictus that emperors created and headed, and the attempts by the Senate to regulate mystery or other cults, were all ineffectual. Whereas Roman emperors had repeatedly tried to create a unifying religion and failed, Christianity was in the process of successfully establishing just such a religion, but from a populist base rather than an elite one. One of the more astute emperors, Constantine, monitored the extremely rapid rise and popularity of Christianity, and he decided to publicly endorse the new religion. Since it had already become a major political force, Constantine may have hoped that it would be possible not only to establish Christianity as the principal ideological unifying force in the empire (tolerating no other deities), but also to co-opt its administration and direction to suit Roman political needs (Fowden 1993:82; Stark 1996:2). After many years of internal strife in Rome, Constantine probably perceived the church as a way to unify the Roman Empire—a force for reunification ready for his use (Westcott 1909:200, 233–34; Gibbon 1972:418).

Constantine claimed to have seen a vision of a flaming cross that indicated he would have an important military victory if he adopted Christianity. Whether this was a fabrication after the fact, a premeditated and calculated gamble beforehand, or a genuine dream, Constantine won the battle in 312 C.E. and, consequently, vigorously promoted the position of the Christian Church as a recognized religion. By 324, Christianity was the dominant religion in Roman society. With Constantine's support, it became popular among the middle and upper classes. After Constantine's conversion, in order to achieve important political positions or conduct large-scale business, it was necessary to be Christian (Markus 1974; Barnes 1981, 1993). Thus, many wealthy and well-educated people converted to Christianity, at least nominally.

The more militant Christians began to use the Roman legions to intimidate remaining pagan worshippers into converting and to destroy pagan temples or centers of learning, such as the temple at Eleusis (Fig. 12.5) and the library at Alexandria, the greatest collection of books in the Roman world. In 391 C.E., Emperor Theodosius made Chris-

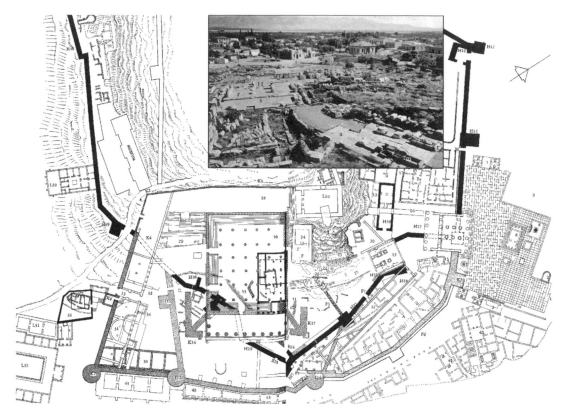

Fig. 12.5. The great pagan temples and centers of traditional healing, divination, and learning became targets for the ambitious leaders of the new, more universal Christian cult. In order to successfully wield this new religion for political purposes, other religions had to be suppressed. Many centers such as the temples at Eleusis (shown above), which had functioned continuously for over a thousand years, were torn down and destroyed by fanatical mobs. The inset photograph is a view from the right looking toward the remains of the main temple at Eleusis. From George Mylonas, *Eleusis and the Eleusinian Mysteries,* Figs. 4, 54. Copyright 1961 by Princeton University Press: Princeton, NJ.

tianity the only official religion and tolerated no other cults. Polytheism was pronounced a treasonable offense. Pagan temples were stripped of their art and closed or destroyed. Unauthorized cults that deviated from the official Church dogma were persecuted. Under the patronage of the Roman administration, the Church became increasingly concerned with rank and title, with a separation between elite and common people. The office of pope and the College of Cardinals were established in order to ensure hierarchical control of Church dogma. To further consolidate control of the Church administration, mass education was discouraged at the end of the Roman Empire, thus cutting the great majority of people off from directly knowing for themselves exactly what the Judeo-Christian Bible said. The elite dream of many millennia (to unify populations under a religion promoting elite interests either directly or indirectly) had finally become reality in the Western world with the "triumph" of Christianity.

Christianity continued to spread beyond the Roman borders either at the end of a sword or because of political considerations similar to those of Constantine and Theodosius. Any chief or monarch who wanted to establish powerful military or economic alliances with Rome eventually found himself confronting Roman-affiliated Christian elites who insisted on doing business exclusively with "true believers." Although many things have changed in 1,500 years, there has been some continuity in basic Church philosophy and strategies. For instance, in the contemporary world, I have seen Christianity continuing to spread among tribal societies by using many of the same tactics that the early Christians used: the demonization of other religions, the establishment of material help and a social network in exchange for total commitment to a Christian religious organization to the exclusion of other religious practices; restriction of access to political or business authorities so as to favor Christians; portrayal of Christianity as fighting the forces of evil in the world (including other religions); spiritual intimidation, using threats of damnation if individuals did not convert; and the establishment of an alternative Christian culture, generally resulting in the destruction of the original tribal culture (see also Lewis 1990; Tinker 1993). Whether in the Australian Desert among the Aborigines, in the villages of the Maya Indians of Guatemala, or among the hill tribes of Southeast Asia, the scenario is almost always the same, especially where evangelical missionaries are involved.

In many of these tribal societies, traditional religions and feasting created the mutual support network necessary to cope with uncertain ecological subsistence and political conditions (Clarke 1998, 2001). However, creating these feasting and support networks is always costly in terms of time, resources, and energy. With the advent of cash economies and national or regional aid programs, the costliness of traditional support systems becomes onerous for many people, especially the poor. Under these new economic conditions, Christian missionaries find it easy to move in and try to provide less costly alternatives, largely with the use of church funds built up in other, richer countries or collected from an unwary public under the guise of "relief work" or "third-world aid."

To return to late classical times, under the direction of the Roman administration, not only were the wealthy and powerful welcomed into the church, but subsequent attitudes toward a number of pagan practices also softened somewhat, and many pagan deities became incorporated as saints of the Church, such as Saint Brigit, Saint Christopher, and others. In essence, they came to play the same role as the minor pagan deities or nature spirits of former times (Brown 1981).

These developments bring us close to the present state of religions in terms of the major changes in the prehistory and history of religious developments for Western culture. Since the major focus of this book is on traditional, rather than book religions, we will not detail the subsequent history of the Church during the medieval and Renaissance periods. But it might be worth examining our own situation in the twenty-first century to see whether our overview of religion through the millennia can shed any light on current practices and beliefs. That is the goal of the last chapter.

Summary
Judaism is the basic root stock of Christianity, and to understand the latter we must understand the former. Cultural ecology can help us understand some of the characteristics of early Judaism, especially those features that it had in common with other pastoral

nomad societies: the presence of a high god, the emphasis on wrath and war, the cult of deified ancestors. However, historical circumstances are also important in understanding the unique features that some Hebrew elites such as Moses introduced and tried with varying success to have adopted by one segment of the Hebrew population. While the Hebrew elites were following an age-old political ecological pattern of trying to consolidate rule through the promotion of a universal religious cult under their control, they succeeded where other elites failed because of their prophets' predictions of the coming wrath of Yahweh and the actual subsequent destruction of Jerusalem, accompanied by the enslavement of many Hebrews by the Babylonians. The resulting cult of Yahweh had many unique characteristics, but it was especially noted for its intolerance of other religious beliefs, Abrahamic faith in the will of God, the removal of the sacred from the natural world, and the transformation of historical events into sacred events. This was the Hebrew elite's solution to combating the disintegration of the Hebrew ethnic group and to creating a solid sociopolitical force resistant to assimilation and attack.

Christianity adopted many of these features and combined them with notions derived from the other mystery cults of the period. Christianity succeeded to a far greater extent than other mystery cults primarily because of the important social and material benefits that it could provide. These benefits were especially important during the first centuries of the common era, when Roman social, economic, and political institutions were collapsing. Christianity also had major advantages in demanding total commitments from its followers, thus creating a coherent sociopolitical fabric that was largely absent in other religious cults of the time. While Christianity initially grew very slowly because it appealed to the poor and displaced, a change in strategy by Church leaders made it more palatable to the wealthy and powerful, especially women elites. With this change, converts and coffers increased, and Christianity became a political force to be reckoned with. By the fourth century, Roman emperors realized that they might be able to use Christianity to unite a fragmented and crumbling empire. They therefore endorsed it, probably in the hope of achieving an age-long elite dream of establishing and controlling a single universal cult in their domain. While this tactic did not prevent the Roman Empire from crumbling, it did establish the first world monotheistic religion. Whether this actually facilitated the governing of polities or nation states is a topic of debate for other specialists. Thus, let us turn to our present-day situation in order to see what role religion has to play today.

CHAPTER 13

Religious Foment in
the Industrial World

We shall not cease from exploration and the end of all our exploring will be to arrive where we started and know the place for the first time.
—John Fowles, *The Magus*

We began our journey into the past at a familiar starting point: our own religion. After exploring what may have seemed like endless permutations and transformations of religious expressions across the millennia and the globe, we have finally come full circle and are in a position to look again at our own beliefs, our own practices, and our own lives. Some of the religions that we have examined may have seemed totally alien to our own experiences, some may have seemed exotic, some cruel, others self-indulgent, but we have sought to understand them and make them comprehensible within the logic of ecological concepts. All of them have provided insights. Has this journey provided any new insights or understanding for our present situation? Yes. There are at least several basic perspectives emphasized in this book that can yield useful new ways of looking at our own religions.

OUR RELIGIOUS HERITAGE

First, we can look at our ancient human biological heritage in a new way—the aspects of our human emotional makeup that instinctively resonate within us. As discussed in Chapters 2 and 3, these include our natural reactions to rhythm, dance, song, drama, ritual, and all the myriad factors that tend to produce altered states of consciousness in us. These are not simply behaviors that we have learned because cultural traditions have taught us to enact them, with our minds serving as a blank canvas. I contend that these are all evolutionarily structured basic behavioral penchants, similar to the proclivity that human infants exhibit for learning and structuring language (Chomsky 1972). All these factors—language, play, family closeness, kinship, ritual, rhythm, dance—probably played important adaptive roles in the early evolution of the human race. Cultural traditions may model the styles and the details, but the basic penchants undoubtedly stem from ecological adaptations. Not everyone may feel the pull of each factor equally strongly. Some people seem more sensitive to music, others to ritual, others to masks and drama. However, there are probably very few people who do not naturally feel some reaction to at least one of these factors. Recognizing these aspects of our human nature and our human heritage and valorizing them as the essence of what it means to be human is an important step in coming to terms with our contemporary religious experiences.

Politicians, philosophers, scholars, scientists, and others have often expressed dismay that in this age of science and enlightenment, such large proportions of even the most modern populations continue to hold irrational, unverified superstitions or beliefs about the existence of a supernatural world, gods, ghosts, or spirits. In fact, an entire publisher, Prometheus Books, is devoted largely to promoting the point of view that these are all unfounded beliefs. For such people, science and modern social or political life should have eliminated the need for supernatural beliefs and ritual practices. But they have missed the point. Religion satisfies an inner craving for meaning, a feeling of wholeness or union with greater forces, and an inner satisfaction that comes only from ritual life, just as music and rhythm satisfy an inner emotional craving deep within our souls and minds for the trances, the ecstasies, and the profound experiences that only they can produce. These are fundamental adaptations of our biological heritage. To argue that advances in science or politics have eliminated the need for religion is tantamount to arguing that science and politics have eliminated the need for music or emotional attachments to family members. Such claims are clearly absurd. As Rappaport (1999:401) has phrased it, reason alone cannot provide a secure or sound basis for social life. Rational thought on its own becomes pathologically self-serving and destructive of life. Albert Einstein purportedly expressed a similar sentiment when he said that the intuitive mind is a sacred gift and the rational mind is a faithful servant; we have created a society that honors the servant and has forgotten the gift.

In fact, in many ways, Industrial science and politics have themselves developed into religions that, in a monotheistic world, view themselves as competing with the more traditional belief systems. For their ardent practitioners, the laws of science or the ideals of a political movement have become like gods. The principles of these movements dictate morality and behavior just as much as the Ten Commandments of Moses. The age-old internal drive to see fulfillment, meaning, and wholeness through the ecstatic merging of our individual identities with overarching entities, whether ancestors, gods, scientific principles, or political ideals, still motivates people, whether they embrace religions or reject them. The ecstasy of the scientist who has discovered the double helix structure of DNA or the grand unified theory of matter is probably fully comparable to the ecstatic state of the reborn Christian who has become part of the mystical body of Jesus Christ.

But not everyone in contemporary society is immersed in the monotheistic mold. As we noted in Chapter 2, many of the most brilliant scientists readily acknowledge the limited perceptions of science and the greater mysteries or sacredness that the universe holds. At the extremes, science and traditional religions that view the world as full of sacred forces seem to have many points in common.

A second source of insight into the dynamics of religion stems from a more detailed consideration of the role of resources in guiding people's beliefs and ritual behavior. We have seen that scarce, fluctuating, and vulnerable resources of simple hunter-gatherers created conditions favoring the emergence of ritual-based alliances between bands. Mythic totemic ancestors were the usual focus of this ritual life. Members of a given kin group or local group or ancestral track all shared an ability to become transformed into the totemic ancestors who created the world in the distant past—or at least to contact them and channel some of their energy. Those ancestors continued to exist in a parallel separate dimension that individuals could access through rituals. By reestablishing the rituals of creation, members ensured that the sacred, social, and human world as they knew it would continue to exist. We have also seen that once sacred ecstatic experiences became an established part of our human makeup, our religious emotions could be targeted for manipulation by ambitious individuals. So long as scarce resources maintained sharing and group survival as the ultimate sacred propositions, ambitious individuals were held in check; their schemes to advance their own self-interest over others' interests were thwarted and curtailed.

However, we have also seen that improved technology led to changes in procurable resource characteristics. Through innovation, ecological dynamics began to change in some areas. Where new technology and favorable environments made it possible to produce and store surpluses, complex hunter-gatherer societies developed. The foothill river valleys of Upper Paleolithic France with their painted cave sanctuaries supported very early forms of transegalitarian hunter-gatherers. Local abundances removed the constraints imposed on ambitious aggrandizers, leading to the privatization not only of the most productive resources but also of ritual life. Elites began to establish relatively exclusive new cults with hierarchies, such as ancestor cults and probably secret society cults. Their rituals were primarily for those who were most important in society; they took place in secret locations such as cave sanctuaries deep in the earth. Thus, the first discernible division between elite and popular religion probably occurred in the Upper Paleolithic caves. This is only one facet of a range of strategies that aggrandizers began to use to promote their interests when favorable resource conditions allowed them to. Other strategies (especially the use of ritual feasts to transform surpluses into desirable social relationships or items) created a new ecological paradigm in the world. In this new paradigm, surpluses were sought after because they could be transformed through fasting.

The strategies developed by complex hunter-gatherers toward the end of the Ice Ages continued to be used and elaborated by the transegalitarian farming societies of the Neolithic. Rituals that involved altered states of consciousness became especially effective arenas for the manipulation of public emotions, values, and political sympathies, as noted by both Dietler (2001) and Wiessner (2001). Rival cults often become political contestants representing conflicts of interest, as in the case of Ain's cult mentioned below.

Food production and domestication had further repercussions on the political ecological dynamics of culture. For the first time, it became possible to increase surpluses with additional labor rather than depleting resources through overexploitation. Combined with the use of surpluses to acquire allies, mates, wealth, or other benefits, societies became open-ended, positive feedback systems with ever increasing demands for energy resources—an ecological condition that we must still contend with. In many cases, as resource surpluses increased in magnitude, it became possible for aggrandizers to concentrate greater and greater amounts of political and economic power in their hands. We have seen that in addition to their exclusive cults, chiefly aggrandizers began to promote their ancestors as the spiritual and genealogical ancestors for everyone in their chiefdoms. The elites portrayed themselves as the most closely connected individuals to those ancestors. In elite ideologies, their ancestors became the source of well-being and success for everyone. Due to competition between lineages and chiefs for the most desirable marital, economic, and military partnerships, funerals became major events at which families, lineages, and chiefdoms displayed their strength and success for all to see. They honored their ancestors, who were portrayed as responsible for the successes of their descendants. In some parts of Western Europe, huge megalithic monuments were erected to display the power of those ancestors and their descendants. In Eastern Europe, ancestors were just as important, but funerals often concentrated more on highly crafted grave goods. Funeral rituals and ancestors seem to have formed the basis for many of the even more elaborate religious expressions in the early states and empires of Minoan Crete, Greece, and Egypt. In attempts to create universal deities that exerted their sphere of influence over the entire polities, chiefs and kings often associated their semidivine ancestors with the sun or promoted worship of the sun as a deity. The use of the sun as an elite religious focal point first emerges as a trend among some complex hunter-gatherers, but it achieves notable expression in the megalithic tombs in Neolithic Europe, as well as among the Indo-Europeans, the Polynesians, the Celts, and of course in places like Egypt where the pharaohs were incarnations of the sun.

In a like manner, we have seen that the increased resource and surplus base of early states made claims to divinity on the part of rulers quite common as a part of strategies to extend their control over the corporeal and spiritual aspects of their domains. And finally, we have seen how technological advances made it possible to funnel vast amounts of surpluses into the creation and running of empires. These same forces placed millions of people under a single political umbrella and created densely populated polyglot cities. These were the conditions under which mystery cults thrived.

Yet another ecological example of how resources affected religious beliefs and ritual behavior was provided by considering pastoral nomads and the vicissitudes of their resource base, resulting in endemic raiding, a warrior class, and warrior deities.

Perhaps one of the most telling examples of the effect that resource characteristics have had on behavior related to religion is the documentation that Polly Wiessner provides concerning the effects of the introduction of the sweet potato into New Guinea. She and Akii Tumu show how the increased surpluses made possible by sweet potato cultivation transformed relatively simple hunting-gathering or horticultural societies into highly competitive big man societies that revolved around large-scale ceremonial exchanges and a series of ritualized wars. They demonstrate how big men sought out and introduced new "egalitarian" cults like the Kepele cult to procure the cooperation of fellow tribesmen for more competitive and exploitative enterprises, such as ceremonial exchanges. Wiessner and Tumu also demonstrate how cults periodically emerged that appealed to people's frustration with the crushing demands and debts that the ceremonial exchanges and wars produced. When taken to extremes, competitive exchanges resulted in backlash cults, such as Ain's cult, that promised to abolish the debts and excesses of the institutions run by aggrandizers and ambitious individuals. In transegalitarian and stratified societies, similar backlash cults probably always appeared episodically, only to be ultimately absorbed, transformed, or co-opted by aggrandizers. Early Christianity can be viewed as one example of these backlash cults.

In addition to the basic types of religious adaptations to underlying resource conditions (which I refer to as the hunter-gatherer, the transegalitarian, the pastoral nomad, the early state, and the empire types of religious adaptations), there are other types of ecological effects that appear to crosscut these distinctions. In particular, a number of authors have suggested that where political succession is unstable, much greater effort is usually enlisted in order to display superior economic, social, and political abilities. Laura Junker (2001) has emphasized that when political power is based on personal relations rather than resource ownership, succession is likely to be very unstable. Under unstable conditions, therefore, one expects to find excessive material manifestations of success, such as the megaliths, the pyramids, and burials laced with gold (Douglas and Isherwood 1979:62; Brumfiel 1987:676; Randsborg 1982:135). These authors argue that stable or rigid rules of succession do not necessitate such expenditures, because everyone knows their relative rank and it is not necessary to advertise or vie for support among a number of potential backers. The relative stability or instability of political positions may be related to specific resource characteristics, although this would be a lengthy tangent to pursue at this juncture. We might add that whenever it is viewed as beneficial to attract support (whether for political, economic, social, marital, or other purposes), there may be considerable emphasis on the display of success. This is consistent with Aubrey Cannon's (1989:446–47) broader conclusion that any ambiguity in the perception of social distinction is enough to precipitate greater efforts to display status using material items.

Aside from ecologically based insights into religion, historical and cultural approaches provide additional valuable explanations for the symbolic reasons why we celebrate specific ritual days like Halloween, why Santa Claus comes down the chimney, and a host of other beliefs or practices. Many of these have been documented in the preceding chapters.

ECOLOGY STILL AFFECTS RELIGIONS IN THE INDUSTRIAL WORLD

The cultural ecological perspective has helped make past religions intelligible to us in a number of ways. What does such a perspective offer for our understanding of contemporary religions? Initially, it is worth examining the origins and some of the basic ecological characteristics of our own society, including the environment, resources, technology, and demographics.

Toward the end of the Middle Ages in Europe, agrarian-based lords began to obtain sufficient surplus production from their estates to support significant numbers of luxury item traders and prestige craftspeople. These more numerous merchants and artisans began to congregate in towns that governed themselves independently of feudal estates (Tuchman 1978). As polities became consolidated and potentates grew wealthier, so the

arts and urban centers flourished, culminating in the Renaissance. The mercantile interests of these new centers were often in conflict with the more traditional land-based
interests of the lords, who were generally supported by religious organizations tailored to
elite interests. In the ensuing struggles for political control within kingdoms, the free-
spirited new mercantile class promoted rational thought above dogma partially in order
to undermine the authority of the clergy and lords. This skeptical, probing, secular rationalism created the Age of Reason and is still a vibrant part of our intellectual heritage.
It also formed the conceptual basis for the emergence of the Industrial Revolution.

The Industrial Revolution has had profound implications for literally every aspect of
life and culture that we experience. At the most basic levels, industrial technology has
enabled far greater amounts of resources to be obtained, processed, and transported than
ever before with far less subsistence and other human labor costs. This has created a consumer society in which a large proportion of the population plays an active role, not just
the elites. It has also meant that slave labor is no longer necessary. Slavery was abolished
as the result of industrial technology. The fluctuating needs of industries have created
highly mobile labor pools that are no longer tied to extended families of more traditional
times (Hobsbawm 1962, 1968). Families have become independent economic units,
and with increasing affluence, even the nuclear family is breaking down, as individual
women and men become economically self-sufficient. Expanding resources have resulted
in a highly competitive, aggressive ethos (Hayden 1995). Thus, industrial technology
has created a much more competitive, individual-oriented society, which large multicul-
tural urban industrial environments have strongly reinforced.

Given these underlying characteristics, people in industrial cultures tend to seek
religious experiences that are individually fulfilling, much as in the mystery cults and
Christian cult of Rome. The broader emphasis on the welfare of society or the corporate
family has disappeared from the Industrial religious core. Fertility is no longer viewed as
the key to prosperity (rather the opposite is true). Nature's role in production has largely
been replaced by technology, and state legal systems or corporations have largely replaced the role of the ancestors. Also, like the Roman Empire, vast nation-states such as
Russia, the United States, and Canada have emerged, welded together by industrial
communications, transport, and the exploitation of resources. Rappaport (1971:37ff)
argues that unifying religious ideologies are simply impractical for most industrial
nation-states, given the huge numbers of people involved, the great diversity of origins
represented, and the need for flexible and rapid responses to threats or problems. Thus,
there is no concerted effort today on the part of industrial elites to establish any state religions. To a large extent, the elite desire for a religious ideology that could be used to
unify their domains has been achieved by the values of nationalism and national ideologies, both of which are largely products of industrialization. Before industrialization,
national ideologies and languages were affairs of only the elites, not the common people,
and even then the elites either held strong regional loyalties or tended to be "international" in outlook, neglecting national boundaries and interests in order to pursue their
own self-interests. The intended role of widespread national ideologies to replace religion as a political unifying force was most clearly evident in the attempts by many Communist regimes in the twentieth century to supplant traditional religions. The attempt
ultimately failed. Today's Industrial society is much more reminiscent of Imperial Rome,

in which all cults were tolerated provided that they abided by the laws of the land and respected the rights of others.

Industrialization has also required mass education so that people not only can consume industrial goods but also manufacture them and use them intelligently. Mass education together with the scientific underpinnings of industry have led to universal access to the actual Judeo-Christian Bible as well as to a wide range of other sacred and secular sources that call into question literal biblical interpretations and the authority of the clergy as interpreters of God's will. This, too, has led to a further exploration of alternative religious views, beliefs, and rituals. Thus, Industrial societies seem engulfed in an unprecedented diversity of cults, originating from all corners of the globe and encompassing dogmas ranging from ultrarational, to the utterly irrational, and even the self-destructive. Jonestown, the Davidians, and the Solar Temple are only some of the more extreme examples.

Mass entertainment, too, has become a prominent feature of Industrial societies, as we noted in Chapter 10. Oral traditions and the telling of myths are no longer a part of the standard experiences of adults or our children. The vast majority of our experiences are mediated through a screen or a book, or at best placed on a stage and viewed from afar. Industrialization has rendered live interactive music, myths, or sacred dramas rare experiences. We have largely become spectators rather than involved participants of our religions and our arts. On the other hand, large urban centers and modern Industrial transport, communication, and technology have made it possible and profitable to cater to a far larger diversity of tastes, lifestyles, and values than at any previous time in history. Thus, while the vast majority of the Industrialized citizenry may be happy with mainstream secular entertainment and religions, there are also innumerable small enclaves of ethnic groups, special interest groups, or alternative lifestyles that keep alive a plethora of artistic, performance, and religious traditions, ranging from folk dancing to belly dancing to storytelling to string finger games.

Industrialization not only eliminated slavery but also dramatically changed the role of women in society. The ability to control their own fertility, to use weapons to defend themselves, to command powerful machines, and to manipulate finances and communications technology has removed many of the previous constraints on the social roles of women. Even those women who have decided to retain more traditional lifestyles have found their world transformed by industrial aids that enable them to run households, take care of children, and engage in other activities on their own. Transportation aids, medical advances, and modern communications all make women's lives much easier and more secure than in traditional societies. Industrialization has made women more independent in all aspects of life and made it possible for many to establish their own spiritual goals and lifestyles. This change has resulted in a significant upsurge in women's spirituality movements in the Industrial world compared with their roles in most book religions (Adler 1986).

Industrialization has created large urban agglomerations that produce urban anomie and large numbers of disenfranchised poor or highly stressed individuals, just as in earlier imperial examples such as Rome. Industrialization and large megalopolises create other major problems, too, that have damaged the natural and urban environments. Industrialization has resulted in toxic pollution on an unprecedented scale: the water people drink, the air they breathe, the seas, the earth, the food they consume, as well as their audio and visual environments. Because of industrial activities and wastes, we are eliminating species of plants and animals at a rate completely unknown in the world's several billion years of life history. We are changing the atmosphere and climate of the earth, and we are beginning to tinker with the genes that nature has taken billions of years to evolve. The threat of nuclear war or accidents is yet another major concern produced by industrialization. These are all extremely serious issues that national governments and religions have not managed to successfully deal with. They are ecological factors that directly impact the lives of large numbers of people, animals, and plants, not only in Industrial states, but everywhere in the world.

The emphasis on mass education, mechanization, nationalism, science, modernity, and consumerism have clashed with the absolutist book religions in our societies. Judeo-Christianity removed the sacred from the natural world and forged a religious force based on exclusive monotheism and intolerance of other views. The Romans co-opted early Christian religion to serve their own interests. Industrialization has largely eradicated the remaining vestiges of prebook symbolism and direct participation in meaningful religious activities. Science and technology have sought to eliminate the irrational from human lives. It is surprising that anything of the original human passion for religion has survived these processes at all. However, we still have our cult gatherings, our weddings, our funerals, our wishes made under the moon or by special bodies of water, our Easter Eggs and chocolate rabbits, our nights with spirits on Halloween, and our celebrations of the northern spirits that descend our chimneys at the winter solstice—enduring testimonies to the deep-rooted and resilient nature of human yearnings for things spiritual.

Eliade (1959:203ff) has been among the most vocal of those lamenting the almost complete elimination of traditional sacredness from the mainstream Industrial world. He points out that in contemporary Industrial society, with its emphasis on individualism, the sacred nature of the world is often viewed as an obstacle to personal freedom as well as to business interests. For some people, their own freedom can only be achieved when the last god has been annihilated. The world has become a product of historical events where transcendent experiences with nature's sacred forces are rejected and individuals are responsible only to themselves for their successes. Fortunately, the extreme nonreligious person is not the norm, but for large numbers of people, these are the accepted ideals fostered by mainstream Industrial society. Many Industrial citizens no longer know what ecstatic experiences are or are only exposed to them in popular concerts or through drugs. Even then, the contexts are often profane, as are many of the resulting experiences. Industrialism and Judeo-Christianity have transformed almost every aspect of our interactions with this world from sacred ecstasies to gray mundane and profane expressions of existence. Mainstream society no longer is aware of the meaning of the remnant rituals that it enacts or the reasons why it indulges in them. The significance of the symbols that connect us to the sacred realms has lapsed into our cultural unconscious. They often can only be resurrected from scholarly treatises on folklore. But symbols are the raw material of internal religious meaning, and there are small groups of devotees who try to keep our folklore alive with old celebrations, customs, crafts, music, and stories. There are still a few people who promote the underlying philosophy of all traditional religions and fairy tales: *the world is, and should be, a magical place.*

The Cults of a New Age

Thus, industrialization and the resources that it has opened up have shaped our economic, social, political, and spiritual lives far more than we usually stop to think about. Industrialization, computers, and nuclear energy have virtually created a new age, a new cultural era that archaeologists of the future will certainly recognize as one of the most dramatic cultural upheavals in the entire history of the world, accomplished to a very large degree in a very short 300 years (to date). This has been a truly revolutionary development, accompanied by many corresponding political revolutions (Hayden 1993a:423ff). There are many parallels between Imperial Rome and contemporary urban centers, although there are certainly differences as well, in particular the ability of Industrial societies to support much higher standards of living for a much larger proportion of the population and the forging of nation-state ethics and identities that have replaced elite religions among the general population. Despite the desacralization of much of our cultural and natural world, there are still some people who feel their instincts pulling strongly at their thoughts, feelings, and dreams. Whether because of socioeconomic or fortuitous factors, or because some people feel strong emotions related to ritual life, there are significant numbers of Industrial citizens that have escaped the enculturation and the repression of our basic emotions that tends to characterize our educational and religious institutions. These people, together with disenfranchised or uprooted citizens, are often those that begin a quest to find more meaningful religious organizations in today's society. They are the ones that explore new cults and form new religious relationships or concepts. They are the ones that avidly read books on different forms of religions such as this one. Many seek traditional forms of religion such as Native American or African cults in order to put poetry, music, magic, and meaning back into their lives. Other groups have sought to recreate tribal types of communities within urban settings by establishing community rituals such as the popular "First Nights" of many communities or the dramatic participatory night parades of the Vancouver Public Dreams Society. Still others have tried to find deeper or original meanings of Christianity in specialized church groups or visionary sects.

Predatory Cults Seek the Vulnerable

Given this situation, it is perhaps not surprising that within contemporary urban populations there are some individuals who seek to establish religious cults in order to further their own ambitions of power and wealth. Many disillusioned, disempowered, or distraught people often become easy targets for the unscrupulous. There are certainly intelligent, socially astute, charismatic, but totally unscrupulous leaders of such predatory cults. Charles Manson and Jim Jones are among the most infamous. Using their natural instincts or picking up ideas from more traditional religions, they have learned to manipulate people by using the same innate characteristics that made ritual life adaptive millions of years ago. In the hands of the unscrupulous, ritual techniques are used for indoctrination rather than inspiration (Wiessner 1998). Leaders of these cults typically establish a set of cult ideals that are seemingly above reproach: humanitarian aid to the poor, helping orphaned children, feeding the starving in drought-stricken countries, community service, peace projects. Leaders often claim that god has chosen them to do his work. Alternatively, their goals are justified by claiming that they are scientifically valid, and therefore beyond question. Rather than being ultimate goals, these ideals are used as tools to engage people in the cult, to make them commit themselves to the cult, and to contribute most of their material possessions to the cult. Once committed to the ideals, conscious efforts are often made to get members to work long hours, followed by long prayer or chanting sessions in order to render members more susceptible to having ecstatic experiences in the context of the cult's value and symbolic system. The aim is to get members to feel a ritual ecstatic bond to the cult figurehead and the values being promoted. Jilek (1982:24, 28) has noted that ecstatic states provide excellent conditions for implanting beliefs in people, and Eliade (1964:12) observes that no other religious experiences are more subject to distortion and aberration than ecstatic ones.

In predatory cults, other techniques are generally used to achieve a total, unquestioning commitment of members, such as limiting contact with nonmembers or even forbidding communication with the outside world, poor diets that result in weakened physical conditions and reduced critical thinking, and repeated indoctrination in the guise of sermons, prayers, or chanting. The exhausted and poor physical and mental states of members make it easier to manipulate them and induce controlled ecstatic states, all of which is generally justified on the basis of achieving the humanitarian goals of the cult. Such tactics would hardly be tolerated in business or educational contexts, but unscrupulous leaders of these cults hide behind a façade of religious freedom in order to dominate people and extort their earnings—activities which ordinarily would be criminal offenses.

Thus, those who are seeking alternative religious experiences today must beware of the many pitfalls that lurk in the morass of contemporary cults and claims. There are certainly wonderful experiences and great spiritual and emotional rewards to be had by exploring and joining many of the alternative cults that now exist (see Enroth 1983; Adler 1986), but there are also some dangerous manipulative cults, just as there are good businessmen and there are con artists in the business world, honest doctors and quacks. Religion is no different. Rituals and ecstatic techniques are tools; they are parts of ritual technology, and like any technology, they can be used to benefit mankind or for its detriment. For those who would like some guidelines, I provide a convenient checklist with which you can analyze and rate cults or religious movements that seem potentially interesting (see "Evaluating Modern Cults").

I must emphasize that just because some individuals or groups manipulate our innate religious characteristics in unscrupulous ways, this does not mean that we should avoid or even try to abolish rituals or religion from our lives. Quite the contrary. Ecstatic states may be particularly prone to abuse, but, like sex, they are some of the most powerful of all human experiences. It would be a travesty to excise such basic experiences from our lives simply because we fear that they might make us vulnerable. Love, too, makes us vulnerable. It seems that the most powerful human emotions often make us vulnerable. Our religious characteristics are adaptations, just as our sexual drive, response to music, and our technology are adaptations. Just because these aspects of our lives can be used in abusive or destructive fashions does not mean that we should try to eliminate them. Nor should we try to eliminate technology or other aspects of humanity from our lives if they are sometimes misused. We should learn how to use all human abilities properly

Evaluating Modern Cults

In order to determine whether a particular cult or religious organization (or any organization for that matter) is truly interested in your spiritual development or spiritual ideals, rather than the benefit of its leaders, try to find out the following information.

1. Are you being *pressured* to make a decision one way or another about making a commitment to contribute time or to join the group? If you decide not to make a commitment, is that decision accepted simply by cult representatives or argued about?

2. What is the *magnitude of commitment* for work and worship or other activities expected of members? How many hours per day or week are required? Does this increase with advancement? Ask members how much sleep they get per night and how many hours per week they spend in cult-related activities.

3. Is there an established community or residence that members are urged to live in? How isolated or secretive are these locations or meeting locations?

4. Are members discouraged from communicating with other people or reading unapproved materials?

5. Are ordinary members visibly fatigued or undernourished?

6. How frequently are sermons, prayers, or singing sessions held?

7. Is music, chanting, dancing, or rhythm used excessively to induce ecstatic states? Is happiness primarily the result of these activities and performance of cult work?

8. How hierarchical is the decision structure of the cult? How charismatic are its leaders?

9. Do cult members appear to be troubled psychologically or to come from stressful backgrounds? Do those targeted for recruitment seem to have low self-esteem?

10. To what extent do cult practices assault and degrade the self-esteem or self-identity of members? Are members asked to perform painful or degrading acts? Asked to make public confessions of guilt? Are they ever asked to view themselves as sinful or to perform penances? To what degree is purity a requirement for membership? Is sex considered impure or used to manipulate people? Do members often break down and cry during confession sessions? Is strict obedience required of members? How difficult is it to adhere to cult rules? Are there punishments for transgressing rules?

11. To what extent is coercion used to obtain the compliance of those who hesitate? What guarantees exist that you will be able to leave the group easily if you wish to do so in the future?

12. Does the group use unusual words that have special meanings or definitions. Has it developed a code language of its own?
13. Can the basic premises or values of the cult be discussed or questioned?
14. How important are members' lives in comparison with the group's goals? How important are a person's own feelings in comparison with the group's doctrine?
15. To what extent are nonmembers demonized or depicted as forces of evil and damnation?
16. To what degree do unintelligible mysteries form part of the cult dogma or its ranking system?

If the group that you are considering joining exhibits several of the above characteristics, alarm bells should begin to sound. There is a very large literature on the topic of predatory cults. If you are concerned by this topic, the following references will provide a more in-depth discussion of the topic: Evans 1973; Hassan 1988; Appel 1983; Beckford 1985; Hexham and Poewe 1986; Ross and Langone 1988; Rudin and Rudin 1980; Galanter 1989; Hill 1980; Stoner and Parke 1977; Conway and Siegelman 1978.

and wisely. One of the main goals of this book is to help readers understand what religion is and how to use it for their own personal benefit and growth.

We have explored the nature of religion, its origins and its various forms. And we have seen how it can be misused. I have also endeavored to engage readers in some basic religious experiential exercises in order to familiarize them with some fundamental concepts and feelings, of traditional religious experiences. If we become familiar with these basic phenomena and know them for what they are, then we are less likely to be taken in by people who use them in manipulative ways. Nor are we likely to be frightened or intimidated when these experiences occur to us in other contexts. The experiential approach in both archaeology and the study of religion can be used to appreciate and value our basic human experiences as we interact with the world around us, while at the same time using our unique analytical abilities to understand how the world works and how we ourselves function. It has perhaps been assumed for too long that objective study or analysis precludes any emotional involvement or deep appreciation of the objects of our study. The writings of the great physicists referred to in Chapter 2 should have dispelled this notion. The experiential approach in archaeology explicitly rejects the exclusively objective approach. The experiential approach claims that it is possible to study something objectively and understand how it works while also maintaining deep feelings for the impact that various phenomena have on our emotions as well as our feelings for the mystery and poetry that is inherent in the world. Just because a vintner knows all the chemical reactions involved in making wine does not mean that he is any less appreciative of the delectable bouquet and flavor that a fine bottle of wine will produce in his nose and mouth. In fact, he may savor it even more than other people.

Where religion is concerned, we are fortunate that we have background training in applying skeptical secular rationalism as a defense against bogus cults. As long as we realize that the specific symbolic content—the specific deity, leader, goal, or ideal—that is associated with sacred ecstatic experiences is *not* being validated by the experience, then we may retain our mastery over the situation. The content of the experience is not the important part of the message. *The medium, the experience itself, is the message.* We can approach sacred ecstatic experiences at three levels of usefulness.

First, sacred ecstatic experiences can be self-directed, for example, when individuals decide on their own to undertake spirit quests. Under these circumstances, it might be possible to obtain real insights into the fundamental nature of the spiritual world without outside values or manipulations interfering. On the other hand, there is great scope for self-deception and wish fulfillment. Basic cultural experiences and values must also affect these outcomes.

Second, sacred ecstatic experiences can occur within an established cultural framework such as the initiation of Australian Aboriginal boys. In this case, the symbolic content of the experience is the product of long traditions that are shared by almost everyone in the community. These situations are not blatantly manipulative for self-serving personal goals but are considered part of the experiences that every member of society should have for proper personal and spiritual growth and to function properly in society. A number of psychiatrists (Jilek 1982; Wittkower 1970; Webber, Stephens, and Laughlin 1983) argue that ecstatic states used in these contexts contribute to individual mental health by providing drive release, ego support, aid in problem solving, relief from superego pressures, and atonement. The meaning and experiential content is determined by the culture but has moral backing. Whether the symbolic content of these experiences provides any useful insights into the fundamental nature of spiritual dimensions is entirely speculative.

Third, sacred ecstatic experiences can be crassly manipulated by predatory individuals as described above. It seems rather dubious that these experiences convey any valid symbolic information about actual spiritual realms.

Obviously, the first two ways of using ritual ecstatic experiences are to be preferred. Whether ecstatic states can ever serve as true doorways to other realities or not and how one can distinguish reality from illusion in such contexts is a fascinating topic, but one that is speculative at this stage of inquiry (recall the discussion in Chap. 2). Black Elk's visions were sometimes uncannily accurate and saved lives; other times they were fairly clearly pipe dreams and self-deception.

TRADITIONAL RELIGIONS RETURN

With the abandonment of elite attempts to use religion to forge their political spheres of influence in the Industrial world, religion has been set somewhat adrift. It has once again become almost entirely a matter of personal choice and a popular force to be used by individuals for their own personal fulfillment and growth. Secret societies like the Masons and Shriners have proliferated, however, not for aims of political control or warfare but largely for the innate love of ritual and the creation of a close-knit social fraternity similar to those that existed during our evolution in tribal or band societies. Women's spirituality has also witnessed an understandable increase in popularity. The older themes of book religions that emphasize suffering in this world in order to reap rewards after death all seem out of synch in an affluent Industrial world that emphasizes enjoying life now through spending, recreation, and accumulations. It is therefore hardly surprising that increasing numbers of people have begun to explore alternative spiritual paths that seem more relevant to modern Industrial conditions and problems.

The formidable environmental and social problems of Industrial society have given rise to many socially or environmentally oriented cults including New Age cults with simplistic solutions to complex situations. It is perhaps not surprising, too, that given the current ecological concerns, nature-oriented religions have become fashionable once again, particularly the many varieties of neopaganism (Adler 1986). Given the fundamental premise of traditional tribal religions about the sacredness of the natural world, if there is to be an ecologically oriented religion in the future, it will almost certainly emerge from a traditional religious substrate rather than from one of the book religions. While many aspects of the neopagan movement have been reconstituted from historical texts and surviving bits of folklore, it is the only cult movement in today's Industrial society that has any claim to represent a traditional religious system of the Western world. Some authors like Ronald Hutton (1991) generally dismiss any continuity between the pre-Christian pagan religions of Europe and contemporary neopaganism.

On the other hand, historians such as Carlo Ginzburg (1991) make strong arguments that typical pagan ecstatic groups continued to exist up into the nineteenth century if not later in certain parts of Europe and western Asia. In northern Europe, the Church branded members of such groups as witches. Their etheric battles with spirits to safeguard the well-being of their communities were denounced as demonic witch's sabbats. Ginzburg (1991:138, 148, 150) notes that in the twelfth century of the common era, Church members complained that up to one third of the European population were followers of Herodias and her nocturnal flights. As late as 1613, such practitioners were still using psychotropic salves to induce ecstatic states. The brothers Grimm also saw the Church's claims of witchcraft as largely stemming from popular pagan beliefs. Today, neopagan cults have incorporated many of the elements of these earlier cults in their own rituals. Some pagan cults probably constitute the closest analog that exists today to the Roman mystery cults. Individual experiences with Nature are at the core of the mystical experiences and, ideally an ecstatic union with Nature provides the feeling and context of salvation. There are initiations and mysteries to be unveiled as well as trials and sufferings. The basic pagan philosophy is very similar to other traditional religions such as those of the North American Indians or the Mayan Indians:

- The world is sacred and it is possible to contact sacred forces through the proper rituals at the proper places with the proper actions and intentions.
- Ritual ecstasy is the archetypical means of contacting the gods or sacred forces, and it is a highly desired experience open to all.
- Life is the central mystery of existence.
- The cosmos is a living organism.
- The cosmos communicates with individuals, and individuals are never alone.
- The main avenue of touching the sacred forces is by stimulating the creative capacities within ourselves through ritual, music, poetry, drama, and magic.
- Entering into contact with sacred forces takes place in sacred time, not historical time.

- The world is viewed in terms of sacred poetry and magic.
- Evil and misfortune are dealt with by assimilating them into universal themes and values, not evil forces conspiring against people and god.

With the meddling of early elites removed from religion as a result of the effects of industrialization, many individuals have begun to search introspectively inside themselves and listen to what their deepest emotions urge them to do. It is probably these people who have rediscovered the ancient roots of traditional religion and who have set about reconstituting a contemporary version of the long-suppressed Western traditions. The incorporation of practices or beliefs maintained by rural traditionalists and folklorists has added a legitimate dimension of meaning to many of these practices and has revitalized the meaning of many of the more popular rituals that Westerners still celebrate today: the seasonal festivals, the marriages, New Year's celebrations, gatherings at full moons, and house warmings. All these developments seem to be pointing in a more healthy direction toward balance with the environment and toward a more satisfying existence for those keen to experience life in a multihued sacred fashion rather than endure a gray profane existence. Whether these concerns will become widespread enough to overcome the personal psychological deleteriousness of today's mainstream consumer society may depend on the magnitude of environmental crises in the future and the impact that they may have on general priorities.

Summary

By casting a wide net over the diverse manifestations of religious beliefs and practices through time and space, we have been able to view our own religious backgrounds and practices from a new perspective and with a new appreciation. Using information from historical traditions has enabled us to understand the meaning of many symbols and symbolic acts that we engage in such as the decoration of trees or eggs. To complement this historical approach, the cultural ecological approach has enabled us to understand why we have basic feelings for religious experiences and how these have been molded by subsequent changes in technology, resources, and our societies. It has also enabled us to examine the ecological conditions of our present Industrial society to determine what kinds of forces are affecting our own religious institutions and practices.

Industrialization is by far the single most important factor in understanding the cultural ecological forces at play today. Industrialization has led to high standards of living for large numbers of people, high levels of education and information availability, a highly competitive business and social ethic, urban anomie, a deemphasis on elite-controlled religions for political purposes, a corresponding emphasis on science and nationalism as unifying ideologies, a strong emphasis on individualism and individual religious experiences, and a great number of extremely serious ecological problems. If religion was really nothing more than a body of superstition based on ignorance of how the world works (as some anthropologists have theorized), then it should certainly have faded from the Industrial scene and especially from Eastern Europe during the twentieth century. Similarly, if religion was only something that we learned during our early socialization to sanctify our cultural practices (as other anthropologists suggest), then modern schooling, political ideals, nationalism, and similar institutions should have long ago rendered religion obsolete. Yet, despite determined efforts to eradicate religion in some

Communist countries, it has proved surprisingly resilient, indicating that much more deep-seated factors are involved.

Because of Industrial ecological conditions today, many standard book religions have changed their focus so as to become more socially relevant and provide greater social integration for their members. Many urban dwellers, however, find the strict and relatively austere backgrounds of these formerly elite-controlled, spectator religions out of synch with the higher living standards of Industrial cultures and their emphasis on enjoying the pleasures of life today rather than enduring suffering for vague hopes of a better experience after death. Consumerism is only the extreme expression of this Industrial ethos. Those people who have felt overly constrained by book religion morality, by its austerity, by its spectator emphasis, by its tendency to devalue women, and by a basic spiritual philosophy that ignores the natural world, have sought to fulfill their spiritual yearnings in many other alternative cults.

As a result of Industrial ecological conditions such as increased literacy and information for very large and ethnically mixed populations, the variety of alternative cults today is truly amazing. As in any situation that creates a potential for exploitation of others, there is a certain proportion of these alternative cults that are predatory. I hope that this book has helped you to be able to identify these unscrupulous cults and to understand how they operate. On the other hand, there are many healthy and rewarding new cults ranging from relatively open native American sweat lodge groups or medicine wheel groups, to East Asian philosophies, to women's spirituality groups, to Druid groups, and a great variety of neopagan groups.

Given the critical role of the environmental problems that now face us and that will continue to confront us in the foreseeable future, together with the yearning of many urban dwellers for reestablishing some contact with Nature and the individual fulfillment that many neopagan groups offer through individual contacts and epiphanies with Nature, it seems that such cults have a particularly good potential for becoming more popular over the next centuries. Pagan attitudes toward pleasure are more congruent with the Industrial ethos, although not to the extent of embracing wanton consumerism that is environmentally destructive. Paganism exhibits considerable variability with many different types of cults, some of which may ultimately have an adaptive value in evolutionary and natural selection terms because of their core environmental values. Perhaps after a long detour of some 30,000 years during which aspiring elites sought to monopolize control of the supernatural, religion is finally returning to its popular and more universal roots. Just as industrialization freed the slaves, eliminated crushing work loads for many workers, and made politics more democratic, so it seems to be reconstituting religious life. I would predict that religious control, too, is returning to the hands of people in general, but only time will tell how far this trend will go and what forms it will take.

> All these events occurred in the long-past dreamtime, an epoch (which is also a category of existence) that not only preceded the historical past and present but also continues in parallel with them. Although the totemic beings either departed from (our) territory or vanished into the earth during the dreamtime, they still exist and their powers and actions directly affect contemporary society.
> (Meggitt 1965:60)

References

Abbie, Andrew
  1969   *The Original Australians.* American Elsevier, New York.
Achterberg, S. J.
  1987   The Shaman: Master Healer in the Imaginary Realm. In *Shamanism,* edited by
  S. Nicholsan. Theosophical Publishing House, Wheaton, IL.
Adler, Margot
  1986   *Drawing down the Moon.* Beacon Press, Boston.
Adovasio, James, Olga Soffer, and Bohuslav Klíma
  1996   Upper Palaeolithic Fiber Technology: Interlaced Woven Finds from Pavlov I, Czech
  Republic, c. 26,000 Years Ago. *Antiquity* 70:526–34.
Albright, W. F.
  1957   *From Stone Age to Christianity: Monotheism and the Historical Process.* John Hopkins
  University Press, Baltimore.
Allegro, John
  1970   *The Sacred Mushroom and the Cross.* Sphere Books, London.
Alpert, Richard
  1995   The Random Spinning of the Mind Must Be Centered by Prayer. In *High Priest,* edited by T. Leary, pp. 157–71. Ronin Publishing, Berkeley.
Alting von Geusau, Leo
  1983   Dialects of Akhazan. In *Highlanders of Thailand,* edited by J. McKinnon and
  W. Bhruksari, pp. 243–77. Oxford University Press, Kuala Lumpur.
Ambrose, S. H.
  1998   Late Pleistocene Human Population Bottlenecks, Volcanic Winter, and Differentiation of Modern Humans. *Journal of Human Evolution* 34:623–51.
Ammerman, A. J., and L. Cavalli-Sforza
  1984   *The Neolithic Transition and the Genetics of Populations in Europe.* Princeton Univer-
  sity Press, Princeton, NJ.
Anati, Emmanuel
  1961   *Camonica Valley.* Jonathan Cape, London.
Andersen, Niels, H.
  1997   *The Sarup Enclosures: The Funnel Beaker Culture of the Sarup Site Including Two
  Causewayed Camps Compared to the Contemporary Settlement in the Area and Other
  European Enclosures,* vol. 1. Jutland Archaeological Society Publications XXXIII.

Anthony, David

    1986   The "Kurgan Culture," Indo-European Origins, and Domestication of the Horse: A Reconsideration. *Current Anthropology* 27(4):291–304.

    1995   Nazi and Eco-feminist Prehistories. In *The Nationalism, Politics, and Practice of Archaeology,* edited by P. Kohl and C. Fawcell, pp. 82–96. Cambridge University Press, Cambridge.

Antoni, M., et al.

    1991   Cognitive Behavioral Stress Management Intervention Buffers Distress Responses and Immunologic Changes Following Notification of HIV-1 Seropositivity. *Journal of Consulting and Clinical Psychology* 59:906–15.

Appel, Willa

    1983   *Cults in America: Programmed for Paradise.* Holt, Rinehart, & Winston, New York.

Arambourou, R.

    1981   Les recherches de préhistoire dans les landes en 1980. *Extrait du Bulletin de la Société de Borda.*

Aranyosi, E. F.

    1999   Wasteful Advertising and Variance Reduction: Darwinian Models for the Significance for Non-Utilitarian Architecture. *Journal of Anthropological Archaeology* 18:356.

Arens, William

    1979   *The Man Eating Myths.* Oxford University Press, New York.

Arkani-Hamed, Nima, Savas Dimopoulos, and Georgi Dvali.

    2000   The Universe's Unseen Dimensions. *Scientific American* 283(2):62–69.

Arnaud, Bernadette

    2000   First Farmers. *Archaeology* 53(6):56–59.

Ashe, Geoffrey

    1982   *Kings and Queens of Early Britain.* Methuen, London.

    1985   *The Discovery of King Arthur.* Debrett's Peerage, London.

    1988   *The Arthurian Handbook.* Garland, New York.

Aurell, Carl

    1989   Man's Triune Conscious Mind. *Perceptual and Motor Skills* 68:747–54.

    1994   Man's Triune Conscious Mind: Part II. *Perceptual and Motor Skills* 78:31–39.

Bachler, E.

    1921   Das Drachenloch bei Vättis im Taminatal. *Jahrbuch der St.-Gallischen Naturwissenschaftlichen Gesellschaft* 57(1).

Baffier, Dominique, and Michel Girard

    1998   *Les Cavernes D'Arcy-sur-Cure.* La Maison des Roches, Paris.

Bahn, P. G.

    1978   The "Unacceptable Face" of the West European Upper Paleolithic. *Antiquity* 52:185–92.

    1980   Crib-Biting: Tethered Horses in the Paleolithic? *World Archaeology* 12(2):212–17.

    1989   Age and the Female Form. *Nature* 342:345–46.

    1990   Eating People Is Wrong. *Nature* 348:395.

    1991   Ancient Britons in Blue. *Nature* 350:382–83.

Bahn, Paul, and Jean Vertut

    1988   *Images of the Ice Age.* Windward, Leicester.

Bailey, Lee, and Jenny Yates, eds.

    1996   *The Near Death Experience: A Reader.* Routledge, New York.

Bailloud, Gérard, Christine Boujot, Serge Cassen, Charles-Tanguy Le Roux

    2001   *Carnac: Les Premiéres Architectures de Pierre.* CNRS, Paris.

Bak, P.

    1996   *How Nature Works: The Science of Self-Organized Criticality.* Copernicus, New York.

Bak, P., and K. Chen

    1991   Self-Organized Criticality. *Scientific American* 264(1):46–53.

Balter, Michael

    1998   Why Settle Down? The Mystery of Communities. *Science* 282:1442–45.

Bardens, Dennis

    1987   *Psychic Animals.* Holt, New York.

Barfield, Thomas

    1993   *The Nomadic Alternative.* Prentice-Hall, Englewood Cliffs, NJ.

Barnes, Timothy

    1981   *Constantine and Eusebius.* Harvard University Press, Cambridge, MA.

    1993   *Athanasius and Constantine.* Harvard University Press, Cambridge, MA.

Barrett, Marvin

    1998   Seeking the Transcendent. *Parabola* 23(2):46–55.

Barrow, John, and Frank Tipler

    1986   *The Anthropic Cosmological Principle.* Oxford University Press, Oxford.

Barry, George

    1805   *History of the Orkney Islands.* Edinburgh.

Barth, Fredrik

    1961   *Nomads of South Persia.* Allen & Unwin, London.

    1964   Capital, Investment, and the Social Structure of a Pastoral Nomad Group in South Persia. In *Capital, Saving, and Credit in Peasant Societies,* edited by R. Firth and B. Yamey, p. 69. Aldine, Chicago.

Bartop, R. W.

    1977   Depressed Lymphocyte Function after Bereavement. *Lancet* 1:834–36.

Bar-Yosef, O., and T. Schick

    1989   Early Neolithic Organic Remains from Nahal Hemar Cave. *National Geographic Research* 5(2).176–90.

Bar-Yosef, O., et al.

    1986   New Data on the Origin of Man in the Levant. *Current Anthropology* 27:63–64.

Bataille, Georges

    1980   *La Peinture Préhistorique Lascaux ou La Naissance de L'Art,* vol. 1. Skira Flammarion, Genève. Originally published 1955.

Beard, Mary, John North, and Simon Price

    1998   *Religions of Rome.* Cambridge University Press, Cambridge.

Beardsley, Tim

    1993   Honest Advertising. *Scientific American* 268(5):2–27.

Beaune, Sophie de

    1995   *Les Hommes au temps de Lascaux.* Hachette, Paris.

    1998   Chamanisme et Préhistoire. *L'Homme* 147:203–19.

Beckford, James

    1985   *Cult Controversies: The Societal Response to the New Religious Movements.* Tavistock, London.

Bednarik, Robert

    1994   Art Origins. *Anthropos* 89:169–80.

    1995   Concept-Mediated Marking in the Lower Paleolithic. *Current Anthropology* 36(4):605–34.

Bégouën, R., and Jean Clottes

    1986/87   Le Grand Félin des Trois-Frères. *Antiquités Nationales* 18/19:109–13.

Bégouën, R., et al.

    1993   Os, plantes et peintures rupestres dans la Caverne D'Enlène. In *Pyrenées Préhistoriques. Arts et Sociétés,* pp. 283–306. Congres National des Sociétés Historiques et Scientifiques, 118e, PAU.

Belfer-Cohen, Anna, and Erella Hovers

    1992   In the Eye of the Beholder: Mousterian and Natufian Burials in the Levant. *Current Anthropology* 33(4):463–71.

Bender, Barbara

    1975   *Farming in Prehistory.* John Baker, London.

    1978   Gatherer-hunter to Farmer: A Social Perspective. *World Archaeology* 10:204–22.

    1985   Emergent Tribal Formations in the American Midcontinent. *American Antiquity* 50:52–62.

Benedetto, Giulietta Di, et al.

    2000   Mitochondrial DNA Sequences in Prehistoric Human Remains from the Alps. *European Journal of Human Genetics* 8:669–77.

Benko, Stephen

    1984   *Pagan Rome and Early Christians.* Indiana University Press,1 Bloomington.

Bennike, Pia

    1999   The Early Neolithic Danish Bog Finds. In *Bog Bodies, Sacred Sites, and Wetland Archaeology,* edited by B. Coles, J. Coles, and M. Schou Jorgensen, pp. 27–32. Proceedings of a conference held by WARP and the National Museum of Denmark, in conjunction with Silkborg Museum, September 1996, Jutland.

Benson, Herbert

    1996   *Timeless Healing: The Power and Biology of Belief.* Simon & Schuster, New York.

Berg, Paul-Louis van, and Nicolas Cauwe

    1996   Magdalithiques et Mégaléniens: Essai sur les sources des structures spatiales du néolithique européen. *Bulletin de la Société Préhistorique Française* 93(3):366–87.

Berglund, Axel-Ivar

    1976   *Zulu Thought: Patterns and Symbols.* Swedish Institute of Missionary Research, Uppsala.

Berndt, R. M., and C. N. Berndt

    1964   *The World of the First Australians.* University of Chicago Press, Chicago.

Beyries, S., and P. Walter

    1996   Racloirs et colorants à Combe-Grenal: Le Probleme de la retouche Quina. *Quaernaria Nova* 6:167–84.

Biel, Jorg

    1987   A Celtic Grave in Hochdorf, Germany. *Archaeology* 40(6):22–29.

Binant, Pascale

    1991   *La Préhistoire de la mort.* Editions Errance, Paris.

Binford, Lewis, and Chuan Kun Ho

    1985   Taphonomy at a Distance: Zhoukoudian, "The Cave Home of Beijing Man"? *Current Anthropology* 26(4):413–42.

Black, S.

    1963   Inhibition of Immediate-Type Hypersensitivity Response by Direct Suggestion under Hypnosis. *British Medical Journal* 1:925–29.

Blackburn, T.

    1976   Ceremonial Integration and Social Interaction in Aboriginal California. In *Native Californians: A Theoretical Retrospective,* edited by L. Bean and T. Blackburn, pp. 225–43. Bellena Press, Socorro, NM.

Blackman, Margaret

    1982   *During My Time: Florence Edenshaw Davidson, A Haida Woman.* Douglas & McIntyre, Vancouver.

Blanton, Richard, and Jody Taylor

    1995   Patterns of Exchange and the Social Production of Pigs in Highland New Guinea. *Journal of Archaeological Research* 3:113–45.

Bloch, Maurice, and J. Perry

    1982   Introduction. In *Death and the Regeneration of Life,* edited by M. Bloch and J. Perry, pp. 1–50. Cambridge University Press, Cambridge.

Bloch, Maurice, and Dan Sperber

    2002   Kinship and Evolved Psychological Dispositions. *Current Anthropology* 43: 723–48.

Bodhi, Bhikku

    1984   *The Noble 8-Fold Path.* Buddhist Publication Society, Kandy, Sri Lanka.

Boff, Leonardo

    1987   *The Maternal Face of God,* translated by R. R. Barr, J. W. Diercksmeier. Harper & Row, San Francisco.

Bogucki, Peter

    1999   *The Origins of Human Society.* Blackwell Publishers, Oxford.

Bonifay, Eugène

    1964   La grotte du Régourdou. *L'Anthropologie* 68:49–64.

    1965   Un ensemble rituel moustérien à la grotte du Régourdou. *VI Congrès International de l'Union Internationale des Sciences Préhistoriques et Protohistoriques* (Rome), pp. 136–40.

    2002   L'Homme de Néandertal et L'Ours (Ursus Arctos) dans la Grotte du Régourdou (Montignac-Sur-Vézère, Dorgogne, France). In *L'Ours et l'Homme,* edited by T. Tillet and L. Binford, pp. 247–54. ERAUL, Liège.

Bonifay, E., and B. Vandermeersch

    1962   Dépôt rituel d'ossements dans le gisement Moustérien du Régourdou. *Académie des Sciences* (Paris) 225:1035–36.

Bonifay, M. F.

    1989   Analyse taphonomique des Ursidés de la grotte sépulcrale néandertalienne du Regourdou. In *L'Homme de Néandertal,* vol. 6, *La subsistence,* edited by M. Otte, pp. 45–49. ERAUL, Liège.

Boxall, Michael

    1990   Little Drummer Girl: Music Therapy Brings Healing, Learning, Calm. *Vancouver Sun* 23 June.

Boyer, Pascal

    1994   *The Naturalness of Religious Ideas: A Cognitive Theory of Religion.* University of California Press, Berkeley.

    2001   *Religion Explained: The Human Instincts That Fashion Gods, Spirits, and Ancestors.* Heinemann, London.

Bradley, Richard

    1993   Causeway Enclosures. In *People of the Stone Age,* edited by G. Burenhult, pp. 90–95. Harper Collins, New York.

Bradley, R., and K. Gordon

    1988   Human Skulls from the River Thames, Their Dating, and Significance. *Antiquity* 62:503–9.

Bradshaw, J., and L. Rogers

    1993   *The Evolution of Lateral Asymmetries, Language, Tool Use, and Intellect.* Academic Press, San Diego.

Brady, J., and A. Stone

    1986   Naj Tunich: Entrance to the Maya Underworld. *Archaeology* 39(6):18–25.

Braidwood, Robert

    1953   Did Man Once Live by Beer Alone? *American Anthropologist* 55:515–26.

Branigan, K.

    1982   The Unacceptable Face of Minoan Crete? *Nature* 299:201–202.

Brauchli, P., C. M. Mitchell, and H. Zeier

    1994   Electrocortical, Autonomic, and Subjective Responses to Rhythmic Audio-Visual Stimulation. *International Journal of Psychophysiology* 19:53–66.

Brenneman, W. L., and M. G. Brenneman

    1995   *Crossing the Circle at the Holy Wells of Ireland.* University Press of Virginia, Charlottesville.

Brooks, Howard

    1989   The Stansted Temple. *Current Archaeology* 10(10):322–25.

Brown, Peter

    1981   *The Cult of the Saints.* University of Chicago Press, Chicago.

Brumfiel, E. M.

    1987   Consumption and Politics at Huexotla. *American Anthropologist* 89:676–86.

Brunaux, Jean-Louis

    2000   *Les Religions Gauloises (V–I siècles av. J.-C.): Nouvelle Approaches sur les Rituels Celtiques de la Gaule Independante.* Editions Errance, Paris.

Budge, E. A. Wallis

    1973   *Osiris and the Egyptian Resurrection,* vol. 1. Dover Publications, New York.

Burgers, J. M.

    1975   Causality and Anticipation. *Science* 189:194–98.

Burkert, Walter

    1987   *Ancient Mystery Cults.* Harvard University Press, Cambridge, MA.

    1993   Bacchic Teletai in the Hellenistis Age. In *Masks of Dionysus,* edited by T. Carpenter and C. Faraone, pp. 259–75. Cornell University Press, Ithaca, NY.

Burl, Aubrey

    1976   *The Stone Circles of the British Isles.* Yale University Press, New Haven, CT.

Burton, Holly

    1979   The Arrival of the Celts in Ireland. *Expedition* 21(3):16–21.

Byrd, Brian

    1989   The Natufian Encampment at Beidha. *Jutland Archaeological Society Publication* XXIII:1. Aarhus University Press, Aarhus, Denmark.

Calvin, William, and Derek Bickerton

    2000   *Lingua ex Machina: Reconciling Darwin and Chomsky with the Human Brain.* MIT Press, Cambridge, MA.

Cameron, Julia

    1992   *The Artist's Way: A Spiritual Path to Higher Creativity.* G. P. Putnam's Sons, New York.

Campbell, Joseph

    1968   *The Hero with a Thousand Faces.* Princeton University Press, Princeton, NJ. Originally published 1949.

    1969   *The Masks of God: Primitive Mythology.* Penguin Books, New York.

    1983   *The Way of the Animal Powers,* vol. 1: *Historical Atlas of World Mythology.* Harper & Row, San Francisco.

    1985   Mythic Reflections. *Context* 52–56.

Cancian, Frank

    1965   *Economics and Prestige in a Maya Community.* Stanford University Press, Stanford.

Cannon, Aubrey

    1989   The Historical Dimension in Mortuary Expressions of Status and Sentiment. *Current Anthropology* 30(4):437–47.

Capitanio, J. P.

    1986   Behavioral Pathology. In *Comparative Primate Biology,* vol. 2A: *Behavior, Conservation, and Ecology,* edited by G. Mitchell and J. Erwin, pp. 411–54. A. R. Liss, New York.

Carlsen, Robert, and Martin Prechtel

1991 The Flowering of the Dead: An Interpretation of Highland Maya Culture. *Man* (n.s.) 26:23–42.

Carrasco, Pedro

1961 The Civil-Religious Hierarchy in Mesoamerican Communities. *American Anthropologist* 63:483–97.

Cashdan, Elizabeth

1980 Egalitarianism among Hunters and Gatherers. *American Anthropologist* 82:116–20.

Cassen, Serge, and Pierre Pétrequin

1999 La Chronologie des Haches Polies Dites de Prestige dans la Moitié Ouest de la France. *European Journal of Archaeology* 2(1):7–33.

Cauvin, Jacques

1978 *Les Premiers Villages de Syrie-Palestine*. Maison de l'Orient, Lyon.

1994 *Naissance des divinités, Naissance de l'agriculture*. CNRS Editions, Paris.

2000a *The Birth of the Gods and the Origins of Agriculture*. Cambridge University Press, Cambridge.

2000b The Symbolic Foundations of the Neolithic Revolution in the Near East. In *Life in Neolithic Farming Communities: Social Organization, Identity, and Differentiation,* edited by I. Kuijt, pp. 235–51. Academic/Plenum Publishers, New York.

Cauvin, J., et al.

1999 The Pre-Pottery Site of Cafer Hoyuk. In *Neolithic in Turkey: The Cradle of Civilization,* edited by M. Özdogan, pp. 87–104. Arkeoloji Ve Sanat Yayinlari, Istanbul.

Cauwe, Nicolas

1996 Les Sepultures collectives dans le temps et l'espace. *Bulletin, Société Préhistorique Françaises* 93:342–52.

1997 Les Morts en Mouvement. In *Actes, International Symposium o Neolitico Atlantico e as Orixes do Megalitismo,* edited by A. R. Casal, pp. 719–37. Consello da Cultura Galega/Universidade de Santiago de Compostela, Santiago de Compostela.

1998a Confrontation des espaces funéraires Mésolithiques et Néolithiques. *Anthropologie et Préhistoire* 109:141–53.

1998b Sepultures Collectives du Mésolithique au Néolithique. In *Sepultures D'Occident et Genese des Megalithismes,* edited by J. Guilaine, pp. 9–24. Editions Errance, Paris.

2001a *L'Heritage des Chasseurs-Cueilleurs dans le Nord-Ouest de l'Europe*. Edition Errance, Paris.

2001b Skeletons on the Move, Ancestors in Action. *Cambridge Archaeological Journal* 11:147–63.

Cavalli-Sforza, Luigi Luca

2000 *Genes, Peoples, and Language*. North Point Press, New York.

Cavalli-Sforza, Luigi Luca, and Francesco Cavalli-Sforza

2000 *The Great Human Diasporas: The History of Diversity and Evolution*. Addison-Wesley, Reading, MA.

Cawte, J. E.

1968 Further Comments on the Australian Subincision Ceremony. *American Anthropologist* 70:961–64.

Chaix, Louis, Anne Bridault, and Regis Picavet

1997 A Tamed Brown Bear (Ursus arctos L.) of the Late Mesolithic from La Grande-Rivoire (Isère, France). *Journal of Archaeological Science* 24:1067–74.

Chagnon, Napleon

2000 Manipulating Kingship Rules. In *Adaptation and Human Behavior,* edited by L. Cronk, N. Chagnon, and W. Irons, pp. 115–32. Aldine, New York.

Chapman, Anne
 1982   *Drama and Power in a Hunting Society: The Selk'nam of Tierra del Fuego.* Cambridge
          University Press, Cambridge.
Chapman, J.
 1991   The Creation of Social Arenas in Varna. In *Sacred and Profane,* edited by P. Gar-
          wood, pp. 152–71. Oxford University Committee for Archaeology, Monograph No.
          32.
Chapman, Robert
 1981a   The Emergence of Formal Disposal Areas and the "Problem" of Megalithic Tombs in
          Prehistoric Europe. In *The Archaeology of Death,* edited by R. Chapman,
          I. Kinnes, and K. Randsbortg, pp. 71–81. Cambridge University Press, Cambridge.
 1981b   Archaeological Theory and Communal Burial in Prehistoric Europe. In *Pattern of
          the Past,* edited by I. Hodder, G. Isaac, and N. Hammond, pp. 387–412. Cambridge
          University Press, Cambridge.
 1995   Ten Years After: Megaliths, Mortuary Practices, and the Territorial Model. In *Re-
          gional Approaches to Mortuary Analysis,* edited by Lane Anderson Beck, pp. 29–51.
          Plenum Press, New York.
Chauvet, J., E. B. Deschamps, and C. Hillaire
 1995   *La Grotte Chauvet.* Seuil, Paris.
Chokadzieu, Stefan
 1995   On Early Social Differentiation in the Struma River Basin. In *Prehistoric Bulgaria,*
          edited by D. Bailey and I. Panayotov, pp. 141–47. Prehistory Press, Madison, WI.
Chomsky, Noam
 1972   *Language and Mind.* Harcourt Brace Jovanovich, New York.
 1986   *Knowledge of Language: Its Nature, Origin and Use.* Praeger, New York.
Clark, Grahame
 1986   *Symbols of Excellence.* Cambridge University Press, Cambridge.
Clark, John, and William Parry
 1990   Craft Specialization and Cultural Complexity. *Research in Economic Anthropology*
          12:289–346.
Clarke, D. V., T. Cowie, and A. Foxon
 1985   *Symbols of Power.* National Museum of Antiquities of Scotland, Edinburgh.
Clarke, Michael
 1998   *Feasting among the Akha of Northern Thailand.* M.A. thesis, Archaeology Depart-
          ment, Simon Fraser University, Burnaby, British Columbia.
 2001   Akha Feasting: An Ethnoarchaeological Perspective. In *Feasts,* edited by M. Dietler
          and B. Hayden, pp. 144–67. Smithsonian Institution Press, Washington, DC.
Clottes, Jean
 1989   Le Magdalenien des Pyrénées. In *Le Magdalenien en Europe,* pp. 281–360.
          ERAUL 38.
 1996   Thematic Changes in Upper Paleolithic Art. *Antiquity* 70:276–88.
Clottes, Jean, and David Lewis-Williams
 1998   *The Shamans of Prehistory: Trance and Magic in the Painted Caves.* Abrams, New
          York.
Clutton-Brock, Juliet
 1991   Representation of the Female Breast in Bronze Carvings from a Neolithic Lake Vil-
          lage in Switzerland. *Antiquity* 65:908–10.
Coe, Michael
 1972   Olmec Jaguars and Olmec Kings. In *The Cult of the Feline,* edited by E. P. Benson,
          pp. 1–18. Dumbarton Oaks Research Library and Collection, Harvard University,
          Washington, DC.

Cohen, Erik

2001   *The Chinese Vegetarian Festival in Phuket: Religion, Ethnicity and Tourism on a Southern Thai Island.* Studies in Contemporary Thailand No. 9. White Lotus Press, Bangkok.

Cohen, Mark

1977   *The Food Crisis in Prehistory.* Yale University Press, New Haven, CT.

Cohen, S., and T. Herbert

1996   Psychological Factors and Physical Disease from the Perspective of Human Psychoneuroimmunology. *Annual Review of Psychology* 47:113–42.

Collier, George

1975   *Fields of the Tzotzil.* University of Texas Press, Austin.

Condominas, Georges

1977   *We Have Eaten the Forest: The Study of a Montagnard Village.* Hill & Wang, New York.

Conkey, Margaret

1980   The Identification of Prehistoric Hunter/Gatherer Aggregation Sites: The Case of Altamira. *Current Anthropology* 21:609–30.

Conrad, Jack

1957   *The Horn and the Sword.* Dutton, New York.

Conway, Flo, and Jim Siegelman

1978   *Snapping: America's Epidemic of Sudden Personality Change.* Lippincott, Philadelphia.

Cooper, D. J.

1996   *Mithras.* Weiser, York Beach, ME.

Cotterell, Brian, and Johan Kamminga

1990   *Mechanics of Pre-industrial Technology.* Cambridge University Press, Cambridge.

Cousins, Norman

1989   *Head First: The Biology of Hope and the Healing Power of the Human Spirit.* Penguin Books, New York.

Crane, Lucy

1899   *Household Stories, from the Collection of the Bros. Grimm,* translated by Lucy Crane. Macmillan, London.

Crellin, David, and Ty Heffner

2000   The Dogs of Keatley Creek. In *The Ancient Past of Keatley Creek,* edited by B. Hayden, pp. 151–65. Archaeology Press, Simon Fraser University, Burnaby, B.C.

Cunliffe, Barry

1979   *The Celtic World.* Greenwich House, New York.

1988   Celtic Death Rituals. *Archaeology* 41(2):39–43.

1997   *The Ancient Celts.* Oxford University Press, Oxford.

Cybulski, Jerome

1994   Culture Change, Demographic History, and Health and Disease on the Northwest Coast. In *In the Wake of Contact: Biological Responses to Conquest,* edited by G. Milner and C. Larsen. Wiley-Liss, New York.

Dart, R. A.

1974   The Waterworn Australopithecene Pebble of Many Faces from Makapansgat. *South African Journal of Science* 70:167–69.

Davenport, D., and M. A. Jochim

1988   The Scene in the Shaft at Lascaux. *Antiquity* 62:558–62.

David, A. R.

1982   *The Ancient Egyptians: Religious Beliefs and Practices.* Routledge & Kegan Paul, London.

David, Nicolas

1988   *Dokwaza: Last of the African Iron Masters.* Video Documentary, University of Calgary, Calgary.

David-Neel, Alexandra

    1932   *Magic and Mystery in Tibet.* Dover, New York.

Davies, Paul

    1980   *Other Worlds.* Simon & Schuster, New York.

Davis, Wade

    2001   Ideas. CBC Radio Interview, January 2001.

Day, Peter, and David Wilson

    1998   Consuming Power: Kamares Ware in Protopalatial Knossos. *Antiquity* 72:350–58.

Deetz, James

    1977   *In Small Things Forgotten: The Archaeology of Early American Life.* Anchor Press, Garden City, NY.

Defleur, A., et al.

    1993   Cannibals among the Neanderthals? *Nature* 362:214.

Defleur, A., et al.

    1999   Neanderthal Cannibalism at Moula-Guery, Ardèche, France. *Science* 286:128–31.

Delaney, Frank

    1989   *Legends of the Celts.* Hodder & Stoughton, London.

Demoule, J., and C. Perlès

    1993   The Greek Neolithic: A New Review. *Journal of World Prehistory* 7:355–416.

Dennel, Robin

    1992   The Origin of Crop Agriculture in Europe. In *The Origins of Agriculture,* edited by C. Cowan and P. Watson, pp. 71–100. Smithsonian Institution Press, Washington, DC.

Deur, Douglas

    2002   Rethinking Precolonial Plant Cultivation on the Northwest Coast of North America. *Professional Geographer* 54(2):140–57.

Dever, William

    1997   Archaeology and the Emergence of Early Israel. In *Archaeology and Biblical Interpretation,* edited by J. R. Bartlett, pp. 20–50. Routledge, London.

Deyts, S. A.

    1971   The Sacred Source of the Seine. *Scientific American* 225(1):65–73.

Diamond, A. S.

    1959   *The History and Origin of Language.* Citadel Press, New York.

Dickson, Bruce

    1990   *The Dawn of Belief.* University of Arizona Press, Tucson.

Dietler, Michael

    1989   Greeks, Etruscans, and Thirsty Barbarians: Early Iron Age Interaction in the Rhone Basin of France. In *Centre and Periphery: Comparative Studies in Archaeology,* edited by T. C. Champion, pp. 127–41. Unwin Hyman, London.

    1990   Driven by Drink: The Role of Drinking in the Political Economy and the Case of Early Iron Age France. *Journal of Anthropological Archaeology* 9:352–406.

    1994   Our Ancestors the Gauls: Archaeology, Ethnic Nationalism, and the Manipulation of Celtic Identity in Modern Europe. *American Anthropologist* 96:584–605.

    1996   Feasts and Commensal Politics in the Political Economy. In *Food and the Status Quest,* edited by P. Wiessner and W. Schiefenhovel, pp. 87–125. Berghahn Books, Providence, RI.

    1997   The Iron Age in Mediterranean France: Colonial Encounters, Entanglements, and Transformations. *Journal of World Prehistory* 11(3):269–80.

    2001   Theorizing the Feast: Rituals of Consumption, Commensural Politics, and Power in African Contexts. In *Feasts,* edited by M. Dietler and B. Hayden, pp. 65–114. Smithsonian Institution Press, Washington, DC.

Digard, J. P.

    1990   *L'Homme et les Animaux Domestiques.* Fayard, Paris.

Dimitrijević, Vesna

2000   The Lipinski Vir Fauna. *Documenta Praehistorica* 27:101–17.

Dinu, M.

1993   Sur le Début du Système Patriarcal dans le Centre et le Sud-Est de L'Europe. In *Actes du XIIe Congrès International des Sciences Préhistoriques et Protohistoriques,* vol. 2, edited by J. Pavúk, pp. 532–35. XIIe Congrés International des Sciences Préhistoriques et Protohistoriques, Bratislava.

Dissanayake, Ellen

1988   *What Is Art For?* University of Washington Press, Seattle.

Divale, W., and M. Harris

1975   Population, Warfare, and the Male Supremacist Complex. *American Anthropology* 78:521–38.

Dodds, E. R.

1959   *The Greeks and the Irrational.* University of California Press, Berkeley.

Dorkenoo, Efua

1994   *Cutting the Rose.* Minority Rights Publications, London.

Dossey, Larry, M.D.

1993   *Healing Words: The Power of Prayer and the Practice of Medicine.* Harper Collins, New York.

Douglas, M., and B. Isherwood

1979   *The World of Goods.* Basic Books, New York.

Dow, James

1986   Universal Aspects of Symbolic Healing: A Theoretical Synthesis. *American Anthropologist* 88:56–69.

Dowson, Thomas, and M. Porr

1999   Special Objects—Special Creatures: Shamanic Imagery and Aurignacian Art. In *The Archaeology of Shamanism,* edited by N. Price, pp. 165–77. Routledge, London.

Drennan, Robert

1983   Ritual and Ceremonial Development at the Early Village Level. In *The Cloud People,* edited by K. Flannery and J. Marcus, pp. 46–50. Academic Press, New York.

Drucker, P.

1965   *Cultures of the North Pacific Coast.* Harper & Row, New York.

Dumézil, Georges

1958   *L'Ideologie Tripartie des Indo-Européens.* Collection Latomus (vol. 31), Brussels.

Dunbar, R.

1992   Neocortex Size as a Constraint on Group Size in Primates. *Journal of Human Evolution* 20:469–93.

Durkheim, E.

1961   *The Elementary Forms of Religious Life,* translated by J. W. Swain. Collier, New York.

Duru, Refik

1999   The Neolithic of the Lake District. In *Neolithic in Turkey: The Cradle of Civilization,* edited by M. Özdogan, pp. 165–92. Arkeoloji Ve Sanat Yayinlari, Istanbul.

Earle, Timothy

1998   Comment. *Current Anthropology* 39:158.

Eibl-Eibesfeldt, Irenäus

1989   *Human Ethology.* Aldine de Gruyter, New York.

Eisler, R.

1987   *The Chalice and the Blade: Our History, Our Future.* Harper & Row, San Francisco.

Eliade, Mircea

1954   *Cosmos and History (Myth of the Eternal Return).* Princeton University Press, Princeton, NJ.

1958a   *Patterns in Comparative Religion,* translated by R. Sheed. Sheed & Ward, London.

1958b   *Rites and Symbols of Initiation.* Spring, Dallas

1959   *The Sacred and the Profane.* Harcourt Brace Jovanovich, New York.

1964   *Shamanism: Archaic Techniques of Ecstasy.* Bollingen Foundation, New York.

1969   *The Quest: History and Meaning in Religion.* University of Chicago Press, Chicago.

1973   *Australian Religion.* Cornell University, Ithaca.

1975   *Myth and Reality.* Harper & Row, New York. Originally published 1963.

1978   *A History of Religious Ideas,* vol. 1. University of Chicago Press, Chicago.

1982   *A History of Religious Ideas,* vol. 2. University of Chicago Press, Chicago.

Elkin, A. P.

1964   *The Australian Aborigines.* Doubleday, New York.

1977   *Aboriginal Men of High Degree: Initiation and Sorcery in the World's Oldest Tradition.* Inner Traditions, Rochester.

Eller, Cynthia

2000   *The Myth of Matriarchal Prehistory.* Beacon Press, Boston.

Enroth, Ronald

1983   *A Guide to Cults and New Religions.* Intervarsity Press, Downers Grove, IL.

Enserink, Martin

1999   Can the Placebo Be the Cure? *Science* 284:238–84.

Esin, U., and S. Harmankaya

1999   Aşikli. In *Neolithic in Turkey: The Cradle of Civilization,* edited by M. Özdogan, pp. 115–32. Arkeoloji Ve Sanat Yayinlari, Istanbul.

Evans, Christopher

1973   *Cults of Unreason.* Farrar, Straus, & Giroux, New York.

Evans, Robert, and Judith Rasson

1984   Ex Balcanis Lux? Recent Developments in Neolithic and Chalcolithic Research in Southeast Europe. *American Antiquity* 49:713–41.

Fabech, Charlotte

1991   Booty Sacrifices in Southern Scandinavia: A Reassessment. In *Sacred and Profane,* edited by P. Garwood, D. Jennings, R. Skeates, and J. Toms, pp. 88–99. Oxford University Committee for Archaeology, Monograph No. 32, Oxford.

Fairservis, Walter

1975   *The Threshold of Civilization: An Experiment in Prehistory.* Scribner's, New York.

Falk, Dean

1980   Language, Handedness, and Primate Brains. *American Anthropology* 82:72–78.

Falvey, Lindsay

1977   *Ruminants in the Highlands of Northern Thailand.* Australian Development Assistance Bureau/Tribal Research Centre, Canberra.

Farizy, C.

1990   Du Mousterien au Châtelperronien à Arcy-sur-Cure. *Memoires du Musée de Préhistoire, Ile-de-France* 3:281–89.

1991   Middle Paleolithic Specialized Sites. Paper presented at the 54th annual meeting of the Society for American Archaeology, New Orleans.

Fawzy, F., et al.

1993   Effects of Early Structured Psychiatric Intervention, Coping, and Affective State on Recurrence and Survival Six Years Later. *Archives of General Psychiatry* 50:681–89.

Feil, D. K.

1987   *The Evolution of Highland Papua New Guinea Societies.* Cambridge University Press, Cambridge.

Fiedel, Stuart Jay

1979   *Intra- and Inter-Cultural Variability in Mesolithic and Neolithic Mortuary Practices in the Near East.* Ph.D. diss., University of Pennsylvania. Printed in 1984 by University Microfilms International.

Fifer, F. C.

1987 The Adoption of Bipedalism by the Hominids: A New Hypothesis. *Human Evolution* 2:135–47.

Finn, Thomas M.

1997 *From Death to Rebirth: Ritual and Conversion in Antiquity.* Paulist Press, New York.

Fitzgerald, Sergeant

1999 Interview with Sergeant Fitzgerald. Canadian Broadcast Corporation, *Vancouver News* 11 August.

Fitzpatrick, Jim

1978 *The Book of Conquests.* Phin, Cheltenham.

Flannery, Kent

1968 Archaeological Systems Theory and Early Mesoamerica. In *Anthropological Archaeology in the Americas,* edited by B. J. Meggars, pp. 67–87. Anthropological Society of Washington, Washington, DC.

1986 *Guila Naquitz: Archaic Foraging and Early Agriculture in Oaxaca, Mexico.* Academic Press, Orlando.

Fluehr-Lobban, C.

1979 A Marxist Reappraisal of the Matriarchate. *Current Anthropology* 20:341–59.

Foley, R. A.

1994 Speciation, Extinction, and Climatic Change in Hominid Evolution. *Journal of Human Evolution* 26:275–89.

Ford, Richard

1977 Evolutionary Ecology and the Evolution of Human Ecosystems: A Case Study from the Midwestern U.S.A. In *Explanation of Prehistoric Change,* edited by J. Hill, pp. 153–84. University of New Mexico Press, Albuquerque.

Forenbaher, S., and T. Kaiser

2001 Nakovana Cave: An Illyrian Site. *Antiquity* 75:677–70.

Foulks, Edward

1972 *The Arctic Hysterias.* American Anthropological Association, Washington, DC.

Fowden, Garth

1993 *Empire to Commonwealth: Consequences of Monotheism in Late Antiquity.* Princeton University Press, Princeton, NJ.

Fox, John

1996 Playing with Power: Ballcourts and Political Ritual in Southern Mesoamerica. *Current Anthropology* 37:483–509

Fox, Robin Lane

1986 *Pagans and Christians in the Mediterranean World from the Second Century A.D. to the Conversion of Constantine.* Penguin, London.

Fratkin, Elliot, and Eric Roth

1990 Drought and Economic Differentiation among Ariaal Pastoralists of Kenya. *Human Ecology* 18:385–402.

Frazer, Sir James George

1959 *The New Golden Bough.* Criterion Books, New York.

Freedman, Daniel, and Peter van Nieuwenhuizen

1985 The Hidden Dimensions of Spacetime. *Scientific American* 252(3):74–81.

Freedman, Maurice

1965 *Lineage Organization in Southeastern China.* Athlone Press, New York.

1970 Ritual Aspects of Chinese Kinship and Marriage. In *Family and Kinship in Chinese Society,* edited by M. Freedman, pp. 164–79. Stanford University Press, Stanford.

Freeman, L. G., and J. G. Echegaray

1981 El Juno: A 14,000 Year-Old Sanctuary from Northern Spain. *History of Religions* 21:1–19.

Freidel, D. A., L. Schele, and J. Parker

    1993   *Maya Cosmos: Three Thousand Years on the Shaman's Path.* William Morrow, New York.

Freud, Sigmund

    1913   *Totem and Taboo.* In *The Basic Writings of Sigmund Freud,* edited by A. A. Brill, pp. 807–930. Random House, New York.

    1939   *Moses and Monotheism.* Random House, New York.

Funk, Robert W., Roy W. Hoover, and the Jesus Seminar

    1993   *The Five Gospels: The Search for the Authentic Words of Jesus.* Macmillan, New York.

Furst, Peter

    1968   The Olmec Were-Jaguar Motif in the Light of Ethnographic Reality. In *Dumbarton Oaks Conference on the Olmec,* edited by E. P. Benson, pp. 143–74. Dumbarton Oaks Research Library and Collection, Harvard University, Washington, DC.

    1972   *Flesh of the Gods.* Waveland Press, Prospect Heights, IL.

    1974   Hallucinogens in Precolumbian Art. In *Art and Environment in Native America,* edited by M. E. King and I. R. Traylor, Jr., pp. 55–102. Special Publications of the Museum of Texas Technological University, Lubbock.

    1976   *Hallucinogens and Culture.* Chandler & Sharp, San Francisco.

Futterman, A. D., et al.

    1992   Immunological Variability Associated with Experimentally Induced Positive and Negative Affect States. *Psychological Medicine* 22:231–38.

Gadon, E.

    1989   *The Once and Future Goddess.* Harper & Row, New York.

Gagnière, S.

    1963   Quinson: La Baume Bonne. *Gallia Préhistoire* 6:339–41.

Galanter, M.

    1989   *Cults and New Religious Movements: A Report of the American Psychiatric Association.* Washington, DC.

Gargett, R. H.

    1989   Grave Shortcomings: The Evidence for Neandertal Burial. *Current Anthropology* 30:157–90.

    1999   Middle Paleolithic Burial Is Not a Dead Issue. *Journal of Human Evolution* 37:27–90.

Gazzaniga, Michael

    1998   Ground-Breaking Work That Began More Than a Quarter of a Century Ago Has Led to Ongoing Insights about Brain Organization and Consciousness. *Scientific American* 279(1):51–55.

Geertz, C.

    1975   *The Interpretation of Cultures.* Hutchinson, London.

    1980   *Negara: The Theatre State in Nineteenth-Century Bali.* Princeton University Press, Princeton, NJ.

Gibbon, Edward

    1960   *The Decline and Fall of the Roman Empire. An abridgement,* by D. M. Low. Harcourt, Brace, New York.

    1972   *History of Christianity.* Arno Press, New York.

Gibbons, Ann

    1997   Archaeologists Rediscover Cannibals. *Science* 277:635–37.

Gibbs, Sherry

    1998   The Significance of Human Remains in Ancient Maya Caves. Paper presented at the annual meeting of the Society for American Archaeology, Seattle.

Gill, Sam

    1987   *Mother Earth.* University of Chicago Press, Chicago.

Gimbutas, Marija

    1973a   Old Europe c. 7000–3000 B.C.: The Earliest European Civilization before the Infiltration of the Indo-European Peoples. *Journal of Indo-European Studies* 1:1–20.

    1973b   The Beginning of the Bronze Age in Europe and the Indo-Europeans: 3500–2500 B.C. *Journal of Indo-European Studies* 1:163–214.

    1982   *The Goddesses and Gods of Old Europe.* University of California Press, Berkeley.

    1989a   *The Language of the Goddess.* Thames & Hudson, London.

    1989b   Women and Culture in Goddess-Oriented Old Europe. In *Weaving the Visions,* edited by J. Plaskow and C. Christ, pp. 63–71. Harper & Row, San Francisco.

    1991   *The Civilization of the Goddess.* Harper & Row, San Francisco.

Ginzburg, Carlo

    1991   *Ecstasies: Deciphering the Witches' Sabbath.* Penguin, New York.

Girard, C.

    1976   L'Habitat et la Mode de Vie au Paléolithique Moyen. In *Les Structures d'Habitats Paléolithique Moyen,* edited by L. Freeman, pp. 49–63. Papers of Colloque XI, IX Congres UISPP, Nice.

Glob, P. V.

    1974   *The Mound People: The Danish Bronze-Age Man Preserved.* Cornell University Press, Ithaca, NY.

Good, Irene

    2000   From Hallstat to Paxyryk? Theme and Variation in "Saka" Burial Modes. Paper presented at the annual meeting of the Society for American Anthropology, Philadelphia, March 9 2000.

Goodall, Jane

    1971   *In the Shadow of Man.* Collins, London.

    1990   *Through a Window.* Houghton Mifflin, Boston.

Gould, Stephen J.

    1989   *Wonderful Life: The Burgess Shale and the Nature of History.* Norton, New York.

Graf, Fritz

    1993   Dionysian and Orphic Eschatology. In *Marks of Dionysus,* edited by T. Carpenter and C. Faraone, pp. 239–58. Cornell University Press, Ithaca.

Graves, Robert

    1961   *The White Goddess.* Amended and enlarged edition. Vintage Books, New York. Originally published 1948.

Green, Miranda

    1986   *The Gods of the Celts.* Sutton, Gloucester.

    1991   *The Sun-Gods of Ancient Europe.* Batsford, London.

    1992   *Animals in Celtic Life and Myth.* Routledge, London.

    1997   *The World of the Druids.* Thames & Hudson, London.

Greer, S.

    1991   Psychological Responses to Cancer and Survival. *Psychological Medicine* 21:39–43.

Gregg, Allison

    1988   *Foragers and Farmers.* University of Chicago Press, Chicago.

Griffith, Ralph, trans.

    1992   *Sacred Writings: Hinduism: The Rig Veda.* Motilal Banarsidass, Delhi.

Gron, Ole, and Oleg Kuznetsov

    2003   Ethnoarchaeology among Evenkian Forest Hunters: Preliminary Results and a Different Approach to Reality. In *Mesolithic on the Move,* edited by L. Larsson, H. Kindgren. K. Kuntsson, A. Akerlund, and D. Loeffler, pp. 216–21. Oxbow Books, Oxford.

Gron, O., O. Kuznetsov, and M. G. Turov

    2001   Cultural Micro-Mosaics—A Problem for the Archaeological Culture Concept? *Proceedings of the Nordic TAG,* edited by J. Bergetol, pp. 342–50. Oslo Archaeological Series, vol. 1.

Gronenborn, Detlef

    1999   A Variation on a Basic Theme: The Transition to Farming in Southern Central Europe. *Journal of World Prehistory* 13(2):123–210.

Grove, David

    1972   Olmec Felines in Highland Central Mexico. In *The Cult of the Feline,* edited by E. P. Benson, pp. 153–64. Dumbarton Oaks Research Library and Collection, Harvard University, Washington, DC.

Gruet, M.

    1955   Amoncellement pyramidal de sphères calcaires dans une source fossile moustérienne à El Guettar. *Actes du IIe Congrès Panafricain de Préhistoire et de Photohistoire,* pp. 449–56. Paris.

Grygiel, Ryszard, and Peter Bogucki

    1997   Early Farmers in North-Central Europe: 1989–1994 Excavations at Oslonki, Poland. *Journal of Field Archaeology* 24:161–78.

Guenther, Mathias

    1999   From Totemism to Shamanism. In *The Cambridge Encyclopedia of Hunters and Gatherers,* edited by R. Lee and R. Daly, pp. 426–33. Cambridge University Press, Cambridge.

Guilaine, J., et al.

    1998   Les Débuts du Néolithique à Chypre. *L'Archéologue* 33:35–40.

Gurdjieff, Georges

    1963   *Meetings with Remarkable Men.* Routledge & Kegan Paul, London.

Gusinde, Martin

    1931   *Die Selk'nam: Von Leben und Denken eines Jagervolkes auf der grossen Feuerlandinsel.* Verlag der Internationalen Zeitschrift "Anthropos," Modling bei Wien, Austria.

    1932   *Die Yamana: Vom Leben und Denken der Wassernomaden am Kap Horn.* Verlag der Internationalen Zeitschrift "Anthropos," Modling bei Wien, Austria.

Hadingham, Evan

    1994   The Mummies of Xinjiang. *Discover* 15(4):68–77.

Hakansson, N. T.

    1994   Grain, Cattle, and Power: Social Processes of Intensive Cultivation and Exchange in Precolonial Western Kenya. *Journal of Anthropological Research* 50:249–76.

    1995   Irrigation, Population Pressure, and Exchange in Precolonial Pare, Tanzania. *Research in Economic Anthropology* 16:297–323.

Halifax, Joan

    1979   *Shamanic Voices.* Dutton, New York.

    1982   *Shaman: The Wounded Healer.* Thames & Hudson, London.

Hall, H. R.

    1983   Hypnosis and the Immune System. *American Journal of Clinical Hypnosis* 25:92–103.

Hamel, George

    1983   Trading in Metaphors: The Magic of Beads. In *Proceedings of the 1982 Glass Trade Bead Conference,* edited by C. Hayes III, pp. 5–28. Rochester Museum and Science Center, Research Records No. 16, Rochester, NY.

Hampton, Winston, O.

    1997   "Contemporary Stone Age: Ethnoarchaeological Perspectives and Systems Analyses." Ph.D. diss., Anthropology Department, University of Texas, Austin.

    1999   *Culture of Stone: Sacred and Profane Uses of Stone among the Dani.* Texas A & M University Press, College Station.

Harbison, Peter

    1975   The Coming of the Indo-Europeans to Ireland. *Journal of Indo-European Studies* 3:101.

Harner, Michael

    1980   *The Way of the Shaman: A Guide to Power and Healing.* Harper & Row, San Francisco.

Harris, Marvin

    1971   *Culture, Man, and Nature.* Crowell, New York.

    1975   *Culture, People, and Nature.* Crowell, New York.

    1979   *Cultural Materialism.* Random House, New York.

    1992   Anthropology and Postmodern Antiscientism. Paper presented at the Annual Meeting of the American Anthropological Association, San Francisco.

    1993   The Objectivity Crisis: Rethinking the Role of Science in Society. Paper presented at the Annual Meeting of the American Association for the Advancement of Science.

Harrison, Richard

    1980   *The Beaker Folk.* Thames & Hudson, London.

Hart, Mickey

    1990   *Drumming at the Edge of Magic: A Journey into the Spirit of Percussion.* Harper Collins, New York.

Hassan, Steven

    1988   *Combating Cult Mind Control.* Park Street Press, Rochester, VT.

Hatley, Tom, and John Kappelman

    1980   Bears, Pigs, and Plio-Pleistocene Hominids. *Human Ecology* 8:371–84.

Hauptmann, Harald

    1999   The Urfa Region. In *Neolithic in Turkey: The Cradle of Civilization,* edited by M. Özdogan, pp. 65–86. Arkeoloji Ve Sanat Yayinlari, Istanbul.

Hawkes, J., J. O'Connell, and N. Blurton Jones

    2001   Hunting and Nuclear Families: Some Lessons from the Hadza about Men's Work. *Current Anthropology* 42(5):681–709.

Hayden, Brian

    1981   Subsistence and Ecological Adaptations of Modern Hunter/gatherers. In *Omnivorous Primates: Gathering and Hunting in Human Evolution,* edited by G. Teleki and R. Harding, pp. 344–422. Columbia University Press, New York.

    1986   Old Europe: Sacred Matriarchy or Complementary Opposition? In *Archaeology and Fertility Cults in the Ancient Mediterranean,* edited by A. Bonanno, pp. 17–30. Gruner, Amsterdam.

    1987   Alliances and Ritual Ecstasy: Human Responses to Resource Stress. *Journal for the Scientific Study of Religion* 26:81–91.

    1990a   The Right Rub: Hide Working in High Ranking Households. In *The Interpretive Possibilities of Microwear Studies,* edited by B. Graslund, H. Knutsson, K. Knutsson, and J. Taffinder, pp. 89–102. Societas Archaeologica Upsaliensis, Uppsala.

    1990b   Nimrods, Piscators, Pluckers, and Planters: The Emergence of Food Production. *Journal of Anthropological Archaeology* 9:31–69.

    1993a   *Archaeology: The Science of Once and Future Things.* W. H. Freeman, New York.

    1993b   The Cultural Capacities of Neandertals: A Review and Re-evaluation. *Journal of Human Evolution* 24:113–46.

    1995   Pathways to Power: Principles for Creating Socioeconomic Inequalities. In *Foundations of Social Inequality,* edited by T. D. Price and G. Feinman, pp. 15–85. Plenum Press, New York.

    1997   *The Pithouses of Keatley Creek.* Harcourt Brace, Fort Worth.

    1998   Practical and Prestige Technologies: The Evolution of Material Systems. *Journal of Archaeological Method and Theory* 5(1):1–55.

2000   On Territoriality and Sedentism. *Current Anthropology* 41:109–12.

2001a   Fabulous Feasts. In *Feasts,* edited by M. Dietler and B. Hayden, pp. 23–64. Smithsonian Institution Press, Washington, DC.

2001b   Richman, Poorman, Beggarman, Chief: The Dynamics of Social Inequality. In *Archaeology at the Millennium,* edited by T. D. Price and G. Feinman, pp. 231–72. Plenum Press, New York.

Hayden, Brian, and A. Cannon

1984   *The Structure of Material Systems.* Society for American Archaeology, Paper No. 3, Washington, DC.

Hayden, Brian, and Rob Gargett

1990   Big Man, Big Heart? A Mesoamerican View of the Emergence of Complex Society. *Ancient Mesoamerica* 1:3–20.

Hedges, John

1984   *Tomb of the Eagles.* Murray, London.

Heizer, Robert

1963   *Excavations at La Venta.* (Film). EMC, University of California, Berkeley.

1966   Ancient Heavy Transport, Method and Achievement. *Science* 153:821–30.

Helfman, E. S.

1967   *Signs and Symbols around the World.* Lothrop, Lee & Shepard, New York.

Henrichs, Albert

1993   "He Has a God in Him": Human and Divine in the Modern Perceptions of Dionysus. In *Masks of Dionysus,* edited by T. Carpenter and C. Faraone, pp. 13–43. Cornell University Press, Ithaca.

Henry, James

1982   Shamans and Endorphins: Hypotheses for a Synthesis. *Ethnos* 10(4):394–408.

Hexham, Irving, and Karla Poewe

1986   *Understanding Cults and New Religions.* Eerdman's, Grand Rapids.

Higham, Charles

1989   *The Archaeology of Mainland Southeast Asia from 10,000 B.C. to the Fall of Angkor.* Cambridge University Press, Cambridge.

Hill, D.

1980   *Study of Mind Development Groups, Sects, and Cults in Ontario.* Government of Ontario, Toronto.

Hiraiwa-Hasegawa, Mariko

1992   Cannibalism among Non-Human Primates. In *Cannibalism and Evolution among Diverse Taxa,* edited by M. Elgar and B. Crespi, pp. 323–38. University of Oxford Press, Oxford.

Hobsbawm, Eric J.

1962   *The Age of Revolution, 1789–1848.* World, New York.

1968   *Industry and Empire.* Weidenfeld & Nicolson, London.

Hodder, Ian

1976   Material Culture Texts and Social Change. *Proceedings of the Prehistoric Society* 54:67–75.

1986   *Reading the Past.* Cambridge University Press, Cambridge.

1999   Renewed Work at Çatalhoyuk. In *Neolithic in Turkey: The Cradle of Civilization,* edited by M. Özdogan, pp. 157–64. Arkeoloji Ve Sanat Yayinlari, Istanbul.

2000   Developing a Reflexive Method in Archaeology. In *Towards Reflexive Methods in Archaeology: The Example at Çatalhoyuk,* edited by I. Hodder, pp. 3–15. McDonald Institute Monographs, British Institute of Archaeology at Ankara.

Hodder, I., M. Stevanovic, and M. Lopez

1998   *Çatalhoyuk. Site Guide Book.* Turkish Friends of Çatalhoyuk, Cambridge.

Hodges, Richard
    1992   *Drum Is the Ear of God: Africa's Inner World of Music.* Material for Thought No. 13.
           Far West Press, San Francisco.

Hoffmann, E.
    1971   Spuren Anthropofager Riten und von Schadelkult in Freilandsiedlungen der Sachsisch-
           Th, reingischen Bandkeramik. Ein Beitrag zur Geschichte der Anthropophagie und
           ihre Motivation. *Ethnographische-Archaeologische Zeitung* 12:1–27.

Hogg, G.
    1966   *Cannibalism and Human Sacrifice.* Citadel Press, New York.

Hood, Sinclair
    1971   *The Minoans: The Story of Bronze Age Crete.* Praeger, New York.

Hoppal, Mihaly
    1992   *Northern Religions and Shamanism.* Akadémiai Kiadó, Helsinki.

Horgan, John
    1992   Quantum Philosophy. *Scientific American* 267(1):94–104.

Hormann, K.
    1923   Die Petershohle bei Velden in Mittelfranken. *Abh. Naturhist. Ges. Nurnberg* 21:121–54.

Hovers, E., et al.
    1995   Hominid Remains from Amud Cave in the Context of the Levantine Middle Paleo-
           lithic. *Paleorient* 21(2):47–61.

Howell, John
    1987   Early Farming in Northwestern Europe. *Scientific American* 257(5):118–26.

Howells, William
    1948   *The Heathens: Primitive Man and His Religion.* Doubleday, New York.

Hudson, Travis, and Ernest Underhay
    1988   *Crystals in the Sky: An Intellectual Odyssey Involving Chumash Astronomy, Cosmology,
           and Rock Art.* Bellena Press, Menlo Park, CA.

Hultkrantz, Ake
    1966   An Ecological Approach to Religion. *Ethnos* 1(4):131–50.
    1967   *The Religions of the American Indians.* University of California Press, Berkeley.
    1973   A Definition of Shamanism. *Temenos* 9:25–37.
    1994   Religion and Environment among the Saami. In *Circumpolar Religion and Ecology,*
           edited by T. Irimoto and T. Yamada, pp. 347–74. University of Tokyo Press, Tokyo.

Hutson, Scott
    1999   Technoshamanism: Spiritual Healing in the Rave Subculture. *Popular Music and So-
           ciety* 23(3):53–78.
    2000   The Rave: Spiritual Healing in Modern Western Subcultures. *Anthropological Quar-
           terly* 73(1):35–50.

Hutton, Ronald
    1991   *The Pagan Religions of the Ancient British Isles.* Blackwell, Oxford.
    1997   The Neolithic Great Goddess: A Study in Modern Tradition. *Antiquity* 71:91–99.

Ianzelo, Tony, and Boyce Richardson, directors
    1974   *Cree Hunters of Mistassini.* National Film Board of Canada, Montreal.

Icher, François
    1998   *Building the Great Cathedrals.* Abrams, New York.

Iizuka, Toshio
    1995   *The Kingdom of Earth and Wood: The San'nai Maruyama Site.* Jomon Film Produc-
           tion Company, Japan.

Ikemi, Y., and S. Nakagawa
    1962   A Psychosomatic Study of Contagious Dermatitis. *Kyushu Journal of Medical Science*
           13:335–50.

Isaac, Glynn
    1978   Food-Sharing and Human Evolution. *Journal of Anthropological Research* 34:311–25.

Izikowitz, Karl
    1951   *Lamet: Hill Peasants in French Indochina.* Etnografiska Museet, Gothenborg.

Jacob, T.
    1972   The Problem of Head-Hunting and Brain Eating among Pleistocene Men in Indonesia. *Archaeology and Physical Anthropology in Oceania* 7:81–91.
    1981   Solo Man and Peking Man. In *Homo Erectus: Papers in Honour of Davidson Black,* edited by B. Sigmon and J. Cybulski, pp. 87–104. University of Toronto Press, Toronto.

James, William
    1961   The Final Impressions of a Psychical Researcher [1901]. In *William James on Psychical Research,* edited by G. Murphy and R. Ballou. Chatto & Windus, London.

Jastrow, Morris
    1915   *The Civilization of Babylonia and Assyria.* Benjamin Blom, New York.

Jaynes, Julian
    1976   *The Origin of Consciousness in the Breakdown of the Bicameral Mind.* Houghton Mifflin, Boston.

Jelinek, Jan
    1990   Human Sacrifice and Rituals in Bronze and Iron Ages: The State of Art. *Anthropologie* 28(2–3):121–28.

Jennbert, Kristina
    1984   Den Produktiva Gdvan. Tradition och Innovation I Sydskandinavien för Omkring 5300 ar sedan. *Acta Archaeologica Lundensia* 4(16). Lund.
    1985   Neolithisation—A Scanian Perspective. *Journal of Danish Archaeology* 4.
    1987   Neolithisation Process in the Nordic Area. *Swedish Archaeology Uddevalla,* pp. 21–35.

Jilek, Wolfgang
    1971   From Crazy Witch Doctor to Auxiliary Psychotherapist: The Changing Image of the Medicine Man. *Psychiatria Clinica* 4:200–220.
    1982   *Indian Healing.* Hancock House, Surrey, British Columbia.
    1989   Therapeutic Use of Altered States of Consciousness in Contemporary North American Indian Dance Ceremonials. In *Altered States of Consciousness and Mental Health: A Cross-Cultural Perspective,* edited by C. A. Ward, pp. 167–85. Sage, London.
    1992   The Renaissance of Shamanic Dance in Indian Populations of North America. *Diogenes* 158:87–100.
    1993   Traditional Medicine Relevant to Psychiatry. In *Treatment of Mental Disorders: A Review of Effectiveness,* edited by N. Sartorius, G. Girolamo, G. Andrews, G. A. German, and L. Eisenberg, pp. 341–90. American Psychiatric Press, Washington, DC.
    1994   Traditional Healing in the Prevention and Treatment of Alcohol and Drug Abuse. *Transcultural Psychiatric Research Review* 31:219–58.

Jilek, Wolfgang, and Louise Jilek-Aall
    1978   The Psychiatrist and His Shaman Colleague: Cross-Cultural Collaboration with Traditional Amerindian Therapists. *Journal of Operational Psychiatry* 11(2):32–39.
    1990   The Mental Health Relevance of Traditional Medicine and Shamanism in Refugee Camps of Northern Thailand. *Curare* (Heidelberg) 13:217–24.

Johnson, Gregory
    1973   *Local Exchange and Early State Development in Southwestern Iran.* University of Michigan Museum of Anthropology Papers No. 51, Ann Arbor.

Jones, Rhys
    1977   The Tasmanian Paradox. In *Stone Tools as Cultural Markers,* edited by R. V. Wright, pp. 189–204. Australian Institute of Aboriginal Studies, Canberra.

Joussaume, Roger
  1988   *Dolmens for the Dead.* Cornell University Press, Ithaca.
Jung, Carl
  1969a   *The Archetypes and the Collective Unconscious.* Bollingen Series, vol. 20. Princeton
             University Press, Princeton, NJ.
  1969b   *Synchronicity,* translated by R. F. Hull. Princeton University Press, Princeton, NJ.
Junker, Laura
  2001   The Evolution of Ritual Feasting Systems in Prehispanic Philippine Chiefdoms. In
             Feasts: Archaeological and Ethnographic Perspectives on Food, Politics, and Power, edited
             by M. Dietler and B. Hayden, pp. 267–310. Smithsonian Institution Press, Wash-
             ington, DC.
Kaelas, Lili
  1981   Megaliths of the Funnel Beaker Culture in Germany and Scandinavia. In *The Mega-
             lithic Monuments of Western Europe,* edited by C. Renfrew, pp. 77–90. Thames &
             Hudson, London.
Kaiser, Timothy
  2001   *The Secret Chamber.* Rotunda, Spring Edition, Toronto.
Kaliff, A.
  1997   *Grav och Kultplats. Eskatologiska Forestallningar Under Yngre Bronsalder och Aldre Jar-
             nalder I Ostergotland.* Aun 24. Department of Archaeology, Uppsala.
Kammerer, Cornelia
  1986   *Gateway to the Akha World.* Ph.D. diss., Anthropology Department, University of
             Chicago.
Kane, Steven
  1982   Acupuncture and the Endorphins. *Ethnos* 10(4):369–84.
Kaplan, H., A. Freedman, and B. Sadock, eds.
  1980   *Comprehensive Textbook of Psychiatry.* Williams & Wilkins, Baltimore.
Karsten, Per
  1994   Att Kasta Yxan I Sjön. *Acta Archaeologica Lundensia* 8(23).
Katz, Richard
  1982a   Holiness Ritual Fire Handling: Ethnographic and Psychophysiological Considera-
             tions. *Ethnos* 10(4):344–68.
  1982b   *Boiling Energy: Community Healing among the Kalahari Kung.* Harvard University
             Press, Cambridge.
Katz, Solomon, and Voigt Mary
  1986   Bread and Beer: The Early Use of Cereals in the Human Diet. *Expedition*
             28(2):23–34.
Kautsky, Karl
  1953   *Foundations of Christianity.* Russell & Russell, New York.
Keeley, Lawrence
  1996   *War before Civilization.* Oxford University Press, New York.
  1997   Frontier Warfare in the Early Neolithic. In *Troubled Times: Violence and Warfare in the
             Past,* edited by D. Martin and D. Frayer, pp. 303–20. Gordon & Breach, Amsterdam.
Keeley, Lawrence, and Daniel Cahen
  1989   Early Neolithic Forts and Villages in NE Belgium. *Journal of Field Archaeology*
             16:157–76.
Kelly, Robert
  1995   *The Foraging Spectrum: Diversity in Hunter-Gatherer Life-Ways.* Smithsonian Institu-
             tion Press, Washington, DC.
Kerényi, Karl
  1976   *Hermes: Guide of Souls,* translated by Murray Stein. Spring Publications, Woodstock.

Kidder, J. E.

    1993   Ritual in the Late Jomon Period. In *Actes du XIIe Congres International des Sciences Préhistoriques et Protohistoriques,* edited by J. Pavúk, pp. 297–304. Institut Archeologique de l'Académie Slovaque des Sciences, Bratislava.

King, Roy, and Peter Underhill

    2001   Congruent Distribution of Neolithic Painted Pottery and Ceramic Figurines with Y-chromosome Lineage. *Antiquity* 76:707–14.

Kingsley, Peter

    1999   *In the Dark Places of Wisdom.* Golden Sufi Center, New York.

Kirch, Patrick

    1984   *The Evolution of Polynesian Chiefdoms.* Cambridge University Press, Cambridge.

    2001   Polynesian Feasting in Ethnohistoric, Ethnographic, and Archaeological Contexts. In *Feasts,* edited by M. Dietler and B. Hayden, pp. 168–84. Smithsonian Institution Press, Washington, DC.

Klein, Richard

    1969   *Man and Culture in the Late Pleistocene.* Chandler, San Francisco.

Kletter, Raz

    1996   *The Judean Pillar Figurines and the Archaeology of Asherah.* Bar International Series 636, Tempus Reparatum, Oxford.

Koch, Eva

    1998   *Neolithic Bog Pots.* Det Kongelige Nordiske Oldskriftselskab, Copenhagen.

    1999   Neolithic Offerings from the Wetlands of Eastern Denmark. In *Bog Bodies, Sacred Sites, and Wetland Archaeology,* edited by B. Coles, J. Coles, and M. Schou Jorgensen, pp. 125–32. Proceedings of a conference held by WARP and the National Museum of Denmark, in conjunction with Silkborg Museum, September 1996, Jutland.

Kohler, Wolfgang

    1927   *The Mentality of Apes.* Kegan Paul, Trench, Trübner, London.

Kraemer, R. S.

    1979   Ecstasy and Possession: The Attraction of Women to the Cult of Dionysus. *Harvard Theological Review* 72(1–2):55–80.

    1992   *Her Share of the Blessings: Women's Religions among Pagan, Jews, and Christians in the Greco-Roman World.* Oxford University Press, Oxford.

Kristiansen, K.

    1999   The Emergence of Warrior Aristocracies in Later European Prehistory and Their Long-Term History. In *Ancient Warfare,* edited by J. Carman and A. Harding, pp. 175–89. Sutton Publishing, San Francisco.

Krueger, D.

    1975   Therapeutic Touch. *American Journal of Nursing* 75(5):784–87.

Kurten, Bjorn

    1976   *The Cave Bear Story.* Columbia University Press, New York.

La Fontaine, Jean

    1985   *Initiation.* Penguin Books, New York.

Lajoux, J. D.

    1996   *L'Homme et l'Ours.* Glénat, Paris.

    2002   Les Donnees Ethnologiques du Culte de L'Ours. In *L'Ours et l'Homme,* edited by T. Tillet and L. Binford, pp. 229–34. ERAUL, Liège.

Laming-Emperaire, A.

    1959   *Lascaux, Paintings and Engravings.* Pelican, London.

    1962   *La Signification de L'Art rupestre Paléolithique.* Picard, Paris.

Larick, Roy

    1991   Warriors and Blacksmiths: Mediating Ethnicity in East African Spears. *Journal of Anthropological Archaeology* 10:299–331.

Larsson, Lars

    1975/76   A Mattock-Head of Reindeer Antler from Ageröd, Scania. *Meddelanden från Lunds Universitets Historiska Museum,* pp. 5–19.

    1987/88   *A Construction for Ceremonial Activities from the Late Mesolithic.* Archaeological Institute, Papers, n.s., vol. 7, University of Lund. Lund, Sweden.

    1998   *Prehistoric Wetland Sites in Sweden. The Cultural Significance of Wetland Archaeology.* UBC Press, Vancouver.

    2000a   The Passage of Axes: Fire Transformation of Flint Objects in the Neolithic of Southern Sweden. *Antiquity* 74(285):602–10.

    2000b   The Role of Fire in Neolithic Ritual Activities. *Archeologija* 19:175–87.

    2000c   Expressions of Art in the Mesolithic Society of Scandinavia. In *Prehistoric Art in the Baltic Region,* edited by A. Butrimas, pp. 31–61. Vilnius, Lithuania.

Larsson, Mats

    1985/86   *Bredasten: An Early Ertebølle Site with a Dwelling Structure in South Scania.* Archaeological Institute, Papers, n.s., vol. 6, University of Lund. Lund, Sweden.

Laughlin, W.

    1980   *Aleuts.* Holt, Rinehart & Winston, New York.

Lawrence, P., and M. J. Meggitt, eds.

    1965   *Gods, Ghosts, and Men in Melanesia.* Oxford University Press, London.

Lazarovici, G.

    1989   Neolithic of Southeastern Europe and Its Near Eastern Connections. *Varia Archaeologica Hungarica* 2:149–74.

    1991   Venus de Zauan. *Acta Musei Porolissensis* 14–15:11–36.

Leach, Edmund

    1954   *Political Systems of Highland Burma: A Study of Kachin Social Structure.* London School of Economics and Political Science, London.

    1961   *Rethinking Anthropology.* Athlone Press, London.

Lee, Richard

    1979   *The !Kung San.* Cambridge University Press, Cambridge.

Lee, Yun Kuen, and Naicheng Zhu

    2002   Social Integration of Religion and Ritual in Prehistoric China. *Antiquity* 76:715–23.

Lefcourt, H., K. Davidson-Katz, and K. Kueneman

    1990   Humor and Immune System Functioning. *Humor* 3:305–21.

Le Jeune

    1634   *Relations des Jésuites.* 6 volumes. Editions du Jour, Montreal.

Lepofsky, D., et al.

    2000   The Archaeology of the Scowlitz Site, Southwestern British Columbia. *Journal of Field Archaeology* 27:391–416.

Leroi-Gourhan, André

    1965   *Préhistoire de L'Art Occidental.* Mazenod, Paris.

    1968   The Evolution of Paleolithic Art. *Scientific American* 218(2):58–70.

Leroi-Gourhan, Arlette

    1975   The Flowers Found with Shanidar IV, A Neanderthal Burial in Iraq. *Science* 190:562–64.

    1982   The Archaeology of Lascaux Cave. *Scientific American* 246(6):104–13.

    1999   Shanidar et ses Fleurs. *Paleorient* 24(2):79–88.

    2000   Rites et Langage a Shanidar? *Bulletin de la Societe Préhistorique Française* 97(2):291–93.

Lesure, Richard

    2002   The Goddess Diffracted. *Current Anthropology* 43(4):587–610.

Lévi-Strauss, Claude

    1963   *Structural Anthropology,* translated by C. Jacobson and B. G. Schoepf. Basic Books, New York.

Lewis, I. M.

    1989   *Ecstatic Religion.* Routledge, London.

Lewis, Norman

    1990   *The Missionaries: God against the Indians.* Penguin, New York.

Lewis-Williams, J. D.

    1994   Rock Art and Ritual: Southern Africa and Beyond. *Complutum* 5:277–89.

    1995a   Modelling the Production and Consumption of Rock Art. *South African Archaeological Bulletin* 50:143–54.

    1995b   Seeing and Construing: The Making and "Meaning" of a Southern African Rock Art Motif. *Cambridge Archaeological Journal* 5(1):3–23.

Lewis-Williams, J. D., and T. Dowson

    1988   The Signs of All Times: Entoptic Phenomena in Upper Paleolithic Art. *Current Anthropology* 29:201–45.

    1989   *Images of Power.* Southern Book Publishers, Johannesburg.

    1993   On Vision and Power in the Neolithic: Evidence from the Decorated Monuments. *Current Anthropology* 34(1):55–65.

Lidén, K.

    1995   A Dietary Study of Two Swedish Megalithic Populations. *Journal of Anthropological Archaeology* 14(40):404–17.

Lincoln, Bruce

    1975   The Indo-European Myth of Creation. *History of Religions* 15:121–45.

    1981   *Priests, Warriors, and Cattle.* University of California Press, Berkeley.

Littleton, C. S.

    1982   *The New Comparative Mythology.* University of California Press, Berkeley. Originally published 1973.

Lloyd, Seton

    1978   *The Archaeology of Mesopotamia: From the Old Stone Age to the Persian Conquest.* Thames & Hudson, London.

Lommel, Andreas

    1967   *Shamanism: The Beginnings of Art.* McGraw-Hill, New York.

Lopez, Mendel Thomas

    1941   Relacion (1612). In *Landa's Relacion de las Cosas de Yucatan,* edited by A. M. Tozzer, pp. 222–27. Peabody Museum of American Archaeology and Ethnography No. 18. Harvard University, Cambridge.

Lorblanchet, Michel

    1999   *La Naissance de L'Art.* Editions Errance, Paris.

    2001   *La Grotte Ornee de Pergouset.* Editions de la Maison des Sciences de l'Homme, Paris.

Loude, J. Y., and Lievre, V.

    1984   *Solstice paien, fêtes d'hiver chez les Kalash du Nord Pakistan.* Presses de la Renaissance, Paris.

    1985   *Kalash Solstice.* Lok Virsa Publishing House, Islamabad.

Lovejoy, C. O.

    1981   The Origin of Man. *Science* 211:341–50.

Ludwig, Arnold

    1969   Altered States of Consciousness. In *Altered States of Consciousness,* edited by C. Tart, pp. 9–22. Wiley, New York.

Lumley, Henri de

    1969   Une Cabane Acheuléenne dans la Grotte du Lazaret. *Memoires de la Sociéte Préhistorique Française,* vol. 7. Paris.

Lumley, H. de, and B. Bottet

    1962   Sol empierré dans le prémoustérien de la Baume Bonne. *Cahiers Ligurgique de Préhistoire et Archéologie* 11:3–8.

Luthi, Max

> 1970   *Once upon a Time.* Indiana University Press, Bloomington.

> 1982   *The European Folktale.* Indiana University Press, Bloomington.

> 1984   *The Fairytale as an Art Form and Portrait of Man.* Indiana University Press, Bloomington.

Lynn, Chris J.

> 1986   *Navan Fort: A Draft Summary of D. M. Waterman's Excavations.* Emania, Bulletin of the Navan Research Group, Belfast.

> 1993   Navan Fort. *Current Anthropology* 134(2):44–55.

Macaulay, David

> 1975   *Pyramid.* Houghton Mifflin, Boston.

MacKenzie, Norman, ed.

> 1967   *Secret Societies.* Holt, Rinehart, & Winston, New York.

MacKie, E. W.

> 1997   Maeshowe and the Winter Solstice: Ceremonial Aspects of the Orkney Grooved Ware Culture. *Antiquity* 71:338–59.

MacLean, Paul

> 1973   *A Triune Concept of Brain and Behaviour.* University of Toronto Press, Toronto.

MacMullen, Ramsay

> 1981   *Paganism in the Roman Empire.* Yale University Press, New Haven, CT.

> 1988   *Corruption and the Decline of the Roman Empire.* Yale University Press, New Haven, CT.

MacNeill, Maire

> 1982   *The Festival of Lughnasa.* Comhairle Bhealoideas Eireann, Dublin.

Malinowski, Bronislaw

> 1954   *Magic, Science, and Religion and Other Essays.* Doubleday, Garden City, NY.

Mallory, J. P.

> 1989   *In Search of the Indo-Europeans.* Thames & Hudson, London.

Mallory, J. P., and V. H. Mair

> 2000   *The Tarim Mummies: Ancient China and the Mysteries of the Earliest Peoples from the West.* Thames & Hudson, London.

Marinatos, Nanno

> 1993   *Minoan Religion.* University of South Carolina Press, Columbia.

Maringer, Johannes

> 1960   *The Gods of Prehistoric Man.* Alfred A. Knopf, New York.

Markale, Jean

> 1975   *Women of the Celts,* translated by A. Mygind, C. Hauch, and P. Henry. Gordon Cremonesi, London.

Markus, R. A.

> 1974   *Christianity in the Roman World.* Thames & Hudson, London.

Marshack, Alexander

> 1981   On Paleolithic Ochre and the Early Uses of Color and Symbol. *Current Anthropology* 22(2):188–91.

> 1991a   *The Roots of Civilization.* 2nd ed. Moyer Bell, Mt. Kisco, NY.

> 1991b   The Female Image: A "Time-Factored" Symbol. A Study in Style and Aspects of Image Use in the Upper Palaeolithic. *Proceedings of the Prehistoric Society* 57(1):17–31.

> 1997a   The Berekhat Ram Figurine: A Late Acheulian Carving from the Middle East. *Antiquity* 71:327–37.

> 1997b   Paleolithic Image Making and Symboling in Europe and the Middle East: A Comparative Review. In *Beyond Art: Pleistocene Image and Symbol,* edited by M. W. Con-

key, O. Soffer, D. Stratmann, and N. Jablonski, pp. 53–91. California Academy of Sciences, San Francisco.

Masataka, Nobuo

    1993   Effects of Experience with Live Insects on the Development of Fear of Snakes in Squirrel Monkeys, Siamiri sciureus. *Animal Behaviour* 46:741–46.

Mason, A., and S. Black

    1958   Allergic Skin Response Abolished under Treatment of Asthma and Hayfever by Hypnosis. *Lancet* 1958(1):877–80.

Maxim-Alaiba, Ruxandra

    1993   Considerations Concernant la Vie Spirituelle des Communautes de Cucuteni-Tripolje dans le Moldavie Meridionale-Roumaine. In *Actes du XIIe Congrès International des Sciences Préhistoriques et Protohistoriques,* edited by J. Pavúk, pp. 540–47. XIIe Congrés International des Sciences Préhistoriques et Protohistoriques, Bratislava.

May, Jeffrey

    1991   Tony Gregory: Reflections on Life. *Current Anthropology* 126:263–67.

McAnany, P. A.

    1995   *Living with Ancestors: Kinship and Kingship in Ancient Maya Society.* University of Texas Press.

Mcbrearty, Sally, and Allison Brooks

    2000   The Revolution That Wasn't: A New Interpretation of the Origin of Human Behavior. *Journal of Human Evolution* 39:453–563.

McGrew, William

    1992   *Chimpanzee Material Culture: Implications for Human Evolution.* Cambridge University Press, Cambridge.

McKee, J.

    1994   Hominid Evolution in the Context of Gradual Change among the Mammals of Southern Africa. *American Journal of Physical Anthropology* Supplement 18:145.

McOmish, David

    1996   East Chisenbury: Ritual and Rubbish at the British Bronze Age-Iron Age Transition. *Antiquity* 70:68–76.

McNeill, F. Marian

    1959   *A Calendar of Scottish National Festivals.* William Maclellan, Glasgow.

Meares, A.

    1978   Regression of Osteogenic Sarcoma Metastases Associated with Intensive Meditation. *Medical Journal of Australia* 2:433.

    1979   Meditation: A Psychological Approach to Cancer Treatment. *Practitioner* 222:119–22.

Meggitt, Marvyn

    1965   *Desert People.* University of Chicago Press, Chicago.

    1977   *Blood Is Their Argument.* Mayfield, Palo Alto, CA.

Mellaart, James

    1967   *Çatal Hüyük: A Neolithic Town in Anatolia.* Thames & Hudson, London.

Mermin, N. D.

    1990   What's Wrong with Those Epochs? *Physics Today* 43(11):9–11.

Meskell, Lynn

    1995   Goddess, Gimbutas, and "New Age" Archaeology. *Antiquity* 69:74–86.

Metzger, Bruce

    1955   Considerations of Methodology in the Study of the Mystery Religions of Early Christianity. *Harvard Theological Review* 72:223–35.

Meyer, H. E.

    1846   *Manners and Customs of the Aborigines of the Encounters Bay Tribe, South Australia.* Adelaide.

Meyer, Marvin W., ed.

    1987   *The Ancient Mysteries: A Sourcebook: Sacred Texts of the Mystery Religions of the Ancient Mediterranean World.* Harper & Row, San Francisco.

Miles, Clement

    1912   *Christmas in Ritual and Tradition.* Gale Research, Detroit.

Miles, David, and Simon Palmer

    1995   White Horse Hill. *Current Archaeology* 12(10):372–78.

Milisauskas, S.

    1978   *European Prehistory.* Academic Press, New York.

    1986   Selective Survey of Archaeological Results in Eastern Europe. *American Antiquity* 51:779–98.

Milisauskas, S., and J. Kruk

    1989   Neolithic Economy in Central Europe. *Journal of World Prehistory* 3:403–46.

Mishlove, Jeffrey

    1975   *The Roots of Consciousness: Psychic Liberation through History, Science, and Experience.* Random House, New York.

Modjeska, N.

    1982   Production and Inequality: Perspectives from Central New Guinea. In *Inequality in New Guinea Highland Societies,* edited by A. Strathern, pp. 50–108. Cambridge University Press, Cambridge.

Monah, Dan

    1997   *Plastica Antropomorfa a Culturii Cucuteni-Tripolie.* Bibliotheca Memoriae Antiquitatis III. Piatra, Neamt.

Moore, A. M., G. C. Hillman, and A. J. Legge

    2002   *Village on the Euphrates: From Foraging to Farming at Abu Hureyra.* Oxford University Press, Oxford.

Morphy, H.

    1991   *Ancestral Connections: Art and an Aboriginal System of Knowledge.* University of Chicago Press, Chicago.

Morris, C.

    1979   Maize Beer in the Economics, Politics, and Religion of the Inca Empire. In *Fermented Food Beverages in Nutrition,* edited by C. Gastineau, pp. 21–34. Academic Press, New York.

Morris, Desmond

    1994   *The Human Zoo.* (Video). The Learning Channel, Bethesda, Maryland.

Mulvaney, John, and Johan Kamminga

    1999   *Prehistory of Australia.* Allen & Unwin, St. Leonards, Australia.

Mukerjee, M.

    1998   Alan Sokal: Undressing the Emperor. *Scientific American* 280(3):30–31.

Murray, Mathew

    1995   Viereckschanzen and Feasting: Socio-Political Ritual in Iron-Age Central Europe. *Journal of European Archaeology* 3(2):125–51.

Mylonas, G. E.

    1961   *Eleusis and the Eleusinian Mysteries.* Princeton University Press, Princeton, NJ.

Nakhai, Beth Alpert

    2001   *Archaeology and the Religions of Canaan and Israel.* American Schools of Oriental Research, Boston.

Needham, R.

    1967   Percussion and Transition. *Man* 2:606–14.

Neher, A.

    1962   A Psychological Explanation of Unusual Behavior in Ceremonies Involving Drums. *Human Biology* 34:151–60.

Neihardt, John

    1961   *Black Elk Speaks.* University of Nebraska Press, Lincoln.

Neumann, Erich

    1963   *The Great Mother.* Princeton University Press, Princeton, NJ.

Nilsson, Martin

    1940   *Greek Folk Religion.* University of Pennsylvania Press, Philadelphia.

Oakley, K. P.

    1981   Emergence of Higher Thought. *Philisophical Transactions of the Royal Society of London* 292:205–11.

Oliva, Martin

    2000   The Brno II Upper Paleolithic Burial. In *Hunters of the Golden Age,* edited by W. Roebroeks, M. Mussi, J. Svoboda, and K. Fennema, pp. 143–52. University of Leiden, Leiden.

    2001   Les Pratiques Funeraires dans le Pavlovian Morave: Revision Critique. *Préhistoire Européenne* 16–17:191–214.

Olson, Ronald

    1936   *The Quinault Indians.* University of Washington Publications in Anthropology 6/1. University of Washington Press, Seattle.

Orenstein, G.

    1990   *The Reflowering of the Goddess.* Pergamon Press, New York.

Ortner, Donald

    1991   Case Report No. 16: Two Neolithic Arrow-Shot Victims. *Paleopathology Newsletter* 75:13–25.

Otte, Marcel

    1996   Aspects Spirituels. In *Neandertal,* edited by D. Bonjean, pp. 269–83. Andenne, Belgium.

Oubré, Alondra

    1997   *Instinct and Revelation: Reflections on the Origins of Numinous Perception.* Gordon & Breach, Fulda, Germany.

Ouspensky, P.

    1979   *Conscience: The Search for Truth.* Routledge & Kegan Paul, London.

Owens, D'Ann, and Brian Hayden

    1997   Prehistoric Rites of Passage: A Comparative Study of Transegalitarian Hunter/Gatherers. *Journal of Anthropological Archaeology* 16:121–61.

Özdogan, M.

    1999   *Neolithic in Turkey: The Cradle of Civilization.* Arkeoloji Ve Sanat Yayinlari, Istanbul.

Pacher, Martina

    2002   Polémique Autour d'un Culte de L'Ours des Cavernes. In *L'Ours et l'Homme,* edited by T. Tillet and L. Binford, pp. 235–46. ERAUL, Liège.

Padel, Felix

    1995   *The Sacrifice of Human Beings: British Rule and the Konds of Orissa.* Oxford University Press, Delhi.

Pales, Léon, and M. Tassin de Saint Péreuse

    1976   *Les Gravures de la Marche: Les Humains.* CNRS, Ophrys, Paris.

Paproth, H. J

    1976   *Studien uber das Bärenzeremoniell,* vol. 1. Bärenjagdriten und Bärenfeste bei den tungusischen Volkern. Uppsala.

Paré, Christopher

    1989   From Dupljaja to Delphi: The Ceremonial Use of the Wagon in Later Prehistory. *Antiquity* 63:80–100.

Parker, S. T., R. W. Mitchell, and M. L. Boccia

    1994   *Self Awareness in Animals and Humans: Developmental Perspectives.* Cambridge University Press, Cambridge.

Parker Pearson, M., and Ramilisonina

    1998   Stonehenge for the Ancestors: The Stones Pass on a Message. *Antiquity* 72:308–26.

Parsons, Talcott

    1952   Sociology and Social Psychology. In *Religious Perspectives in College Teaching,* edited by H. N. Fairchild, pp. 286–305. Ronald Press, New York.

Patton, Mark

    1990   On Entoptic Images in Context. *Current Anthropology* 31:554–58.

    1991   Axes, Men, and Women: Symbolic Dimensions of Neolithic Exchange in Armorica (North-west France). In *Sacred and Profane,* edited by P. Garwood, D. Jennings, R. Skeates, and J. Toms, pp. 65–79. Institute of Archaeology, Oxford.

Pauli, Wolfgang

    1984   Embracing the Rational and the Mystical. In *Quantum Questions,* edited by K. Wilber, pp. 157–63. Shambhala, Boston.

Pavúk, Juraj

    1991   Lengyel-Culture Fortified Settlements in Slovakia. *Antiquity* 65:348–57.

PBS

    1981   *Maya Lords of the Jungle* (video). Public Broadcasting Associates, Washington, DC.

Pei, Wen Chung

    1932   Preliminary Note on Some Incised, Cut, and Broken Bones Found in Association with Sinanthropus Remains and Lithic Artifacts from Choukoutien. *Bulletin of the Geological Society of China* 11:110–41.

Pendergast, D.

    1971   *Excavations at Eduardo Quiroz Cave, British Honduras (Belize).* Royal Ontario Museum Art and Archaeology Occasional Paper 21, Toronto.

Pétrequin, P., and A. Pétrequin

    1993   *Ecologie d'un outil: La Hache de pierre en Irian Jaya (Indonesie).* CNRS Editions, Paris.

Pidoplichko, I. G.

    1998   *Upper Paleolithic Dwellings of Mammoth Bones in the Ukraine,* translated by P. Allsworth-Jones. BAR International Series, Harvard University Press, Cambridge.

Piggott, Stuart

    1975   *The Druids.* Thames & Hudson, London. Originally published 1968.

Price, T. D.

    2000   *Europe's First Farmers.* Cambridge University Press, Cambridge.

Price, T. D., et al.

    2001   Prehistoric Human Migration in the Linearbandkeramik of Central Europe. *Antiquity* 75:593–603.

Price, T. D., and A. B. Gebauer, eds.

    1995   *Last Hunters—First Farmers: New Perspectives on the Prehistoric Transition to Agriculture.* School of American Research Press, Santa Fe.

Price, T. D., G. Grupe, and P. Schröter

    1998   Migration in the Bell Beaker Period of Central Europe. *Antiquity* 72:405–11.

Prince, Raymond

    1982   The Amino Acid Alphabet in the Brain. *Ethnos* 10(4):303–16.

Pringle, Heather

    1998a   The Slow Birth of Agriculture. *Science* 282:1446–47.

    1998b   Reading the Signs of Ancient Animal Domestication. *Science* 282:1448–50.

Putman, John

    1988   The Search for Modern Humans. *National Geographic* 174(4):439–77.

Quin, J. F.

    1984   Therapeutic Touch as Energy Exchange: Testing the Theory. Advances in Nursing. *Science* 6:42–49.

Rabuzzi, K. A.
	1988	*Motherself: A Mythic Analysis of Motherhood.* Indiana University Press, Bloomington.
Radin, Paul
	1920	The Autobiography of a Winnebago Indian. *University of California Publications in American Archaeology and Ethnology* 16:381–437.
	1937	*Primitive Religion.* Viking, New York.
Radojevic, V., P. Nicassio, and M. Weisman
	1992	Behavioral Intervention with and without Family Support for Rheumatoid Arthritis. *Behavior Therapy* 23:13–30.
Radovanovic, I.
	1996	*The Iron Gates Mesolithic.* International Monographs in Prehistory, Ann Arbor.
Rak, Y., W. H. Kimbel, and E. Hovers
	1994	A Neandertal Infant from Amund Cave, Israel. *Journal of Human Evolution* 26:313–24.
Rambo, A. T.
	1991	Energy and the Evolution of Culture: A Reassessment of White's Law. In *Profiles in Cultural Evolution: Papers from a Conference in Honor of Elman R. Service,* edited by A. T. Rambo and K. Gillogby, pp. 291–310. University of Michigan, Ann Arbor.
Randsborg, Klaus
	1982	Ranks, Rights, and Resources: An Archaeological Perspective from Denmark. In *Ranking, Resource, and Exchange,* edited by C. Renfrew and S. Shennan, pp. 132–40. Cambridge University Press, Cambridge.
Rappaport, Roy
	1971	The Sacred in Human Evolution. *Annual Review of Ecology and Systematics* 2:23–44.
	1999	*Ritual and Religion in the Making of Religion.* Cambridge University Press, Cambridge.
Reay, Marie
	1959	*The Kuma.* Melbourne University Press, Melbourne.
Renfrew, Colin
	1976	Megaliths, Territories, and Populations. In *Acculturation and Continuity in Atlantic Europe,* edited by S. de Laet, pp. 298–320. Dissertationses Archaeologicae Gandenses 16.
	1987	*Archaeology and Language: The Puzzle of Indo-Eurpoean Origins.* Cape, London.
Renfrew, Colin, and Paul Bahn
	1996	*Archaeology: Theories, Methods, and Practice.* Thames & Hudson, London.
Reynaert, C., et al.
	1995	From Health Locus of Control to Immune Control. *Acta Psychiatry Scandinavia* 92:294–300.
Reznikoff, I., and M. Dauvois
	1988	La dimension sonore des grottes ornées. *Bulletin, Société Préhistorique Française* 85:238–46.
Rice, Michael
	1998	*The Power of the Bull.* Routledge, London.
Richards, J. W.
	1980	The Celtic Social System. *Mankind Quarterly* 21(1):71–95.
Riel-Salvatore, J., and G. A. Clark
	2001	Grave Markers: Middle and Early Upper Paleolithic Burials and the Use of Chronotypology in Contemporary Paleolithic Research. *Current Anthropology* 42(4):449–60.
Robbins, Miriam
	1980	The Assimilation of Pre–Indo-European Goddesses into Indo-European Society. *Journal of Indo-European Studies* 8:19–29.
Robertson, A.
	1962	*The Origins of Christianity.* International Publishers, New York.

Robinson, Sarah

  1963   *Spirit Dancing among the Salish Indians, Vancouver Island, British Columbia.* Ph.D.
              thesis, Dept. of Anthropology, University of Chicago, Chicago.

Roebroeks, W., et al., eds.

  2000   *Hunters of the Golden Age: The Mid Upper Palaeolithic of Eurasia 30,000–20,000 BP.*
              University of Leiden, Leiden.

Rodriquez, E., and R. Wrangham

  1993   Zoopharmacognosy: The Use of Medicinal Plants by Animals. *Recent Advances in
              Phytochemistry* 27:89–105.

Roheim, Geza

  1972   *The Panic of the Gods.* Harper & Row, New York.

Roksandic, Mirjana

  1999   *Transition from Mesolithic to Neolithic in the Iron Gates Gorge.* Ph.D. thesis, Depart-
              ment of Archaeology, Simon Fraser University, Burnaby, British Columbia.

Rollefson, G. O.

  1983   Ritual and Ceremony at Neolithic 'Ain Ghazal (Jordan). *Paleorient* 9(2):29–38.

  1986   Neolithic 'Ain Ghazal (Jordan): Ritual and Ceremony, II. *Paleorient* 12(1):45–52.

  2000   Ritual and Social Structure at Neolithic 'Ain Ghazal. In *Life in Neolithic Farming
              Communities: Social Organization, Identity, and Differentiation,* edited by I. Kuijt,
              pp. 165–190. Academic/Plenum Publishers, New York.

Ronen, Avraham

  1995   *Core, Periphery, and Ideology in Aceramic Cyprus.* Sonderdruck aus Quartar, Band
              45/46.

Rosaldo, Michelle Zimbalist

  1974   Women, Culture, and Society. In *Women, Culture, and Society,* edited by M. Z. Ros-
              aldo, pp. 17–42. Stanford University Press, Stanford.

Rosenberg, Michael

  1994   Hallan Çemi Tepesi: Some Further Observations Concerning Stratigraphy and Ma-
              terial Culture. *Anatolica* 20:121–40.

  1999   Hallan Çemi. In *Neolithic in Turkey: The Cradle of Civilization,* edited by M. Özdo-
              gan, pp. 25–34. Arkeoloji Ve Sanat Yayinlari, Istanbul.

Rosenberg, Michael, and Richard Redding

  2000   Hallan Çemi and Early Village Organization in Eastern Anatolia. In *Life in Neolithic
              Farming Communities: Social Organization, Identity, and Differentiation,* edited by
              I. Kuijt, pp. 39–61. Academic/Plenum Publishers, New York.

Rosenblum, L. A., and G. S. Paully

  1984   The Effects of Varying Environmental Demands on Maternal and Infant Behavior.
              Child Development 55:305–14.

Roslund, Curt, Yasmine Kristiansen, and Birgitta Hårdh

  2000   Portuguese Passage Graves in the Light of the Easter Moon. *Fornvännen*
              95:1–12.

Rosman, Abraham, and Paula Rubel

  1971   *Feasting with Mine Enemy.* Columbia University Press, New York.

Ross, Anne

  1967   *Pagan Celtic Britain.* Routledge & Kegan Paul, London.

Ross, J. C., and M. Langone

  1988   *Cults: What Parents Should Know.* American Family Foundation, Massachusetts.

Roth, H. L.

  1899   *The Aborigines of Tasmania.* F. King & Sons, London.

Rouget, Gilbert

  1985   *Music and Trance.* University of Chicago Press, Chicago.

Roush, Wade

    1997   Herbert Benson: Mind-Body Maverick Pushes the Envelope. *Science* 276:357–59.

Rouzaud, François, M. Soulier, and Y. Lignereux

    1996   La Grotte de Bruniquel. *Spelunca* 60:28–34.

Rudin, James, and Marcia Rudin

    1980   *Prison or Paradise: The New Religious Cults?* Fortress Press, Philadelphia.

Russell, Narissa

    1993   *Hunting, Herding, and Feasting: Human Use of Animals in Neolithic Southeastern Europe.* Ph.D. diss., University of California Berkeley.

Russell, N., and L. Martin

    1998   *Catalhoyuk Animal Bone Report.* Catalhoyuk Archaeological Project, Archive Report.

    2000   Neolithic Catalhoyuk: Preliminary Zooarchaeological Results from the Renewed Excavations. In *Archaeozoology of the Near East IV A,* edited by M. Mashkour, A. M. Choyke, H. Buitenhuis, and F. Poplin, pp. 164–70. ARC Publicatie 32, Groningen.

Sackett, Hugh, and Sandy MacGillivray

    1989   Boyhood of a God. *Archaeology* 42:26–31.

Sahlins, Marshall

    1981   *Historical Metaphors and Mythical Realities.* University of Michigan Press, Ann Arbor.

Sakellaraki, Y., and E. Sapouna-Sakellaraki

    1981   Drama of Death in a Minoan Temple. *National Geographic* 159(2):205–22.

Sandarupa, Stanislaus

    1996   *Life and Death in Toraja.* Computer Ujung Pandang, Indonesia.

Sanday, Peggy Reeves

    1981   *Female Power and Male Dominance: On the Origins of Sexual Inequality.* Cambridge University Press, Cambridge.

    1986   *Divine Hunger.* Cambridge University Press, Cambridge.

Sanden, Wijnand van der

    1996   *Through Nature to Eternity.* Batavian Lion International, Amsterdam.

Sanders, W. T., and B. J. Price

    1968   *Mesoamerica: The Evolution of a Civilization.* Random House, New York.

Sanderson, L. P.

    1981   *Against the Mutilation of Women.* Ithaca Press, London.

Saver, J. L., and J. Rabin

    1997   The Neural Substrates of Religious Experience. *Journal of Neuropsychiatry and Clinical Neurosciences* 9(3):498–510.

Scarborough, Vernon, and David Wilcox, eds.

    1991   *The Mesoamerican Ballgame.* University of Arizona Press, Tucson.

Scarre, Christopher

    1984a   The Neolithic of West-Central France. In *Ancient France,* edited by C. Scarre, pp. 223–70. University of Edinburgh Press, Edinburgh.

    1984b   A Survey of the French Neolithic. In *Ancient France,* edited by C. Scarre, pp. 324–43. University of Edinburgh Press, Edinburgh.

    1989   Painting by Resonance. *Nature* 338:382.

Schele, Linda, and David Freidel

    1990   *A Forest of Kings.* William Morrow, New York.

Schleifer, S. J.

    1983   Suppression of Lymphocyte Stimulation Following Bereavement. *Journal of the American Medical Association* 250:374–77.

Schmandt-Besserat, Denise

    1980   Ocher in Prehistory: 300,000 Years of the Use of Iron Ores as Pigments. In *The*

Coming of the Age of Iron, edited by T. A. Wertime and J. Muhly, pp. 127–50. Yale University Press, New Haven, CT.

1986   An Ancient Token System: The Precursor to Numerals and Writing. *Archaeology* 39(6):32–39.

1992   *Before Writing,* vol. 1: *From Counting to Cuneiform.* University of Texas Press, Austin.

1997   Animal Symbols at 'Ain Ghazal. *Expedition* 39(1):48–58.

2001   Feasting in the Ancient Near East. In *Feasts,* edited by M. Dietler and B. Hayden, pp. 391–403. Smithsonian Institution Press, Washington, DC.

Schmidt, K.

2001   Gobekli Tepe, Southeastern Turkey: A Preliminary Report on the 1995–1999 Excavations. *Paleorient* 26(1):45–54.

Schmidt, Wilhelm

1912–55 *Der Ursprung der Gottes-Idee.* 12 volumes. Aschendorff, Munster, Germany.

Schnitger, F. M.

1989   *Forgotten Kingdoms in Sumatra.* Oxford University Press, Oxford.

Schulting, Rick

1995   *Mortuary Variability and Status Differentiation on the Columbia-Fraser Plateau.* Archaeology Press, Simon Fraser University, Burnaby, British Columbia.

1998a   *Slighting the Sea: The Mesolithic-Neolithic Transition in Northwest Europe.* Ph.D. thesis, Department of Archaeology, University of Reading.

1998b   Creativity's Coffin: Innovation in the Burial Record of Mesolithic Europe. In *Creativity in Human Evolution and Prehistory,* edited by S. Mithen, pp. 203–26. Routledge, London.

2002   Cranial Trauma in the British Earlier Neolithic. *PAST* 41:4–6.

Schulting, Rick, and Michael Richards

2001   Dating Women and Becoming Farmers: New Paleodietary and AMS Data from the Breton Mesolithic Cemeteries of Teviec and Hoedic. *Journal of Anthropological Archaeology* 20:314–44.

2002   Finding the Coastal Mesolithic in Southwest Britain: AMS Dates and Stable Isotope Results on Human Remains from Caldey Island, South Wales. *Antiquity* 76:1011–25.

Sears, William

1961   The Study of Social and Religious Systems in North American Archaeology. *Current Anthropology* 2(3):223–46.

Secoy, Frank

1953   *Changing Military Patterns on the Great Plains.* American Ethnological Society Monograph 21. University of Washington Press, Seattle.

Serban, G., and A. Kling

1976   *Animal Models in Human Psychobiology.* Plenum Press, New York.

Severy, Merle

1977   The Celts. *National Geographic* 151(5):582–33.

Seznec, Jean

1981   *The Survival of the Pagan Gods: The Mythological Tradition and Its Place in Renaissance Humanism and Art.* Princeton University Press, Princeton, NJ.

Shackley, Myra

1980   *Neanderthal Man.* Duckworth, London.

Shanks, M., and C. Tilley

1987   *Re-Constructing Archaeology.* Cambridge University Press, Cambridge.

Shaw, R.

1990   *Kandila: Samo Ceremonialism and Interpersonal Relationships.* University of Michigan Press, Ann Arbor.

Shelach, Gideon
    1996   The Qiang and the Question of Human Sacrifice in the Late Shang Period. *Asian Perspectives* 35(1):1–26.

Shennan, Stephen
    1986   Central Europe in the Third Millennium B.C.: An Evolutionary Trajectory for the Beginning of the European Bronze Age. *Journal of Anthropological Archaeology* 5:115–46.

Sherratt, Andrew
    1976   Resources, Technology, and Trade: An Essay in Early European Metallurgy. In *Problems in Economic and Social Archaeology,* edited by G. de G. Sieveking, I. H. Longworth, and K. E. Wilson, pp. 557–82. Duckworth, London.

    1981   Plough and Pastoralism: Aspects of the Secondary Products Revolution. In *Patterns of the Past,* edited by I. Hodder, G. Isaac, and N. Hammond, pp. 261–305. Cambridge University Press, Cambridge.

    1983   The Secondary Exploitation of Animals in the Old World. *World Archaeology* 15:20–104.

    1990   The Genius of Megaliths. *World Archaeology* 22:147–67.

    1991   Sacred and Profane Substances: The Ritual Use of Narcotics in Later Neolithic Europe. In *Sacred and Profane,* edited by P Garwood, D. Jennings, R. Skeates, J. Toms, pp. 50–64. Institute of Archaeology, Oxford.

    1994   The Emergence of Elites. In *The Oxford Illustrated Prehistory of Europe,* edited by B. Cunliffe, pp. 244–76. Oxford University Press, Oxford.

Shlain, Leonard
    1998   *The Alphabet versus the Goddess.* Viking Penguin, New York.

Shnirelman, Victor
    1990   Class and Social Differentiation in Oceania. In *Culture and History in the Pacific,* edited by J. Siikala, pp. 125–38. Finnish Anthropological Society Transactions no. 27, Helsinki.

Siegel, R. K., and M. Jarvik
    1975   Drug-Induced Hallucinations in Animals and Man. In *Hallucinations: Behavior, Experience, and Theory,* edited by R. K. Siegel and L. J. West, pp. 88–162. Wiley, New York.

Silberman, Neil
    1998a   Digging in the Land of the Bible. *Archaeology* 51(5):37–45.
    1998b   The Roots of Christianity. *Archaeology* 51(5):46–47.

Sillitoe, Paul
    1978   Big Men and War in New Guinea. *Man* 13:252–71.

Singh, Mandanjeet
    1993   *The Sun: Symbol of Power and Life.* Abrams, New York.

Skeates, Robin
    1991   Caves, Cult, and Children in Neolithic Abruzzo, Central Italy. In *Sacred and Profane,* edited by P. Garwood, D. Jennings, R. Skeates, and J. Toms, pp. 122–34. Institute of Archaeology, Oxford.

Skomal, Susan Nacev
    1986   In Search of the Proto-Indo-European Archaeological Assemblage. *Mankind Quarterly* 26:175–92.

Small, Meredith, F.
    2000   More Than the Best Medicine. *Scientific American* 283(2):24.

Smith, James
    1880   *Booandik Tribe of South Australian Aborigines: A Sketch of Their Habits, Customs, Legends, and Language.* Adelaide, Government Printer, North-Terrace.

Soffer, Olga

    1985   *The Upper Paleolithic of the Central Russian Plain.* Academic Press, Orlando.

    1989   Storage, Sedentism, and the Eurasian Paleolithic Record. *Antiquity* 63:719–32.

Soffer, O., J. Adovasio, and D. Hyland

    2001   Perishable Technologies and Invisible People. In *Enduring Records,* edited by B. Purdy, pp. 233–45. Oxbow Books, Oxford.

Solheim, Wilhelm G.

    1985   Korwar of the Biak. In *The Eloquent Dead: Ancestral Sculpture of Indonesia and Southeast Asia,* edited by J. Feldman, pp. 147–204. UCLA Museum of Cultural History, Los Angeles.

Speth, John

    1990   Seasonality, Resource Stress, and Food Sharing in So-Called 'Egalitarian' Foraging Societies. *Journal of Anthropological Archaeology* 9:148–88.

Spevakovsky, Alexander

    1994   Animal Cults and Ecology: Ainu and East Siberian Examples. In *Circumpolar Religion and Ecology: An Anthropology of the North,* edited by T. Irimoto and T. Yamada, pp. 103–108. University of Tokyo Press, Tokyo.

Spiro, Milford

    1955   Review of Symbolic Wounds. *American Journal of Sociology* 61:163–64.

Spooner, Brian

    1973   *The Cultural Ecology of Pastoral Nomads.* Addison-Wesley, Reading, MA.

Spretnak, C.

    1992   *The Lost Goddess of Early Greece.* Beacon Press, Boston.

Squire, Charles

    1975   *Celtic Myth and Legend.* Newcastle Publishing, Van Nuys, CA.

Srejovic, D., and Z. Letica

    1978   *Vlasac: A Mesolithic Settlement in the Iron Gates.* Serbian Academy of Sciences and Arts Monographies, vol. 62, Department of Historical Sciences, vol. 5. Belgrade.

Stafford, Michael

    1999   *From Forager to Farmer in Flint: A Lithic Analysis of the Prehistoric Transition to Agriculture in Southern Scandinavia.* Aarhus University Press, Aarhus.

Stark, Rodney

    1996   *The Rise of Christianity: A Sociologist Reconsiders History.* Princeton University Press, Princeton, NJ.

Starr, M.

    1987   Risk, Environmental Variability, and Drought-Induced Impoverishment: The Pastoral Economy of Central Niger. *Africa* 57(1):29–50.

Sternberg, Esther

    2000   *The Balance Within: The Science Connecting Health and Emotions.* W. H. Freeman & Company, New York.

Steward, Julian

    1955   *Theory of Cultural Change.* University of Illinois Press, Urbana.

Stocker, Brian

    1997   Sacred Stories We Live By: An Interview with Jonathan Young, Ph.D. *Kindred Spirits Magazine* (UK) 39(Summer):14–18; www.folkstory.com/articles.

Stone, A. A.

    1994   Daily Events Are Associated with a Secretory Immune Response to an Oral Antigen in Men. *Health Psychology* 13:440–46.

Stone, Merlin

    1976   *When God Was a Woman.* Harvest Books, San Diego, CA.

Stoner, C., and J. Parke

    1977   *All God's Children: The Cult Experience-Salvation or Slavery.* Chilton, Radnor, PA.

Stordeur, D., and F. Abbès

    2002   Du PPNA au PPNB: Mise en Lumiere d'une Phase de Transition a Jerf el Ahmar (Syrie). *Bulletin de la Societe Prehistorique Francaise* 99(3):563–95.

Stordeur, D., et al.

    2001   Les Batiments Communautaires de Jerf el Ahmar et Mureybet Horizon PPNA (Syrie). *Paleorient* 26(1):29–44.

Stover, Leon, and Bruce Kraig

    1978   *Stonehenge, the Indo-European Heritage.* Nelson-Hall, Chicago.

Strassman, B. I.

    1981   Sexual Selection, Parental Care, and Concealed Ovulation in Humans. *Ethology and Sociobiology* 2:31–40.

Strehlow, T. G.

    1965   Culture, Social Structure, and Environment in Aboriginal Central Australia. In *Aboriginal Man in Australia,* edited by R. M. Berndt and C. H. Berndt, pp. 121–45. Angus & Robertson, Sydney.

Suedfeld, Peter

    1980   *Restricted Environmental Stimulation.* Wiley, New York.

Suetonius, Gaius Tranquillus

    1979   *The Twelve Caesars.* Trans. Robert Graves. Penguin, New York.

Svensson, Mac

    2002   Palisade Enclosures. In *Behind Wooden Walls: Neolithic Palisaded Enclosures in Europe,* edited by A. Gibson, pp. 28–58. BAR International Series 1013, Oxford.

Sweet, Louise

    1965   Camel Raiding of North Arabian Bedouin. *American Anthropologist* 67:1132–50.

Symons, D.

    1979   *The Evolution of Human Sexuality.* Oxford University Press, Oxford.

Taçon, Paul

    1991   The Power of Stone: Symbolic Aspects of Stone Use and Tool Development in Western Arnhem Land, Australia. *Antiquity* 65:192–207.

Tart, Charles, ed.

    1969   *Altered States of Consciousness.* Wiley, New York.

Taylor, Timothy

    1992   The Gundestrup Cauldron. *Scientific American* 266(3):84–89.

Teit, James

    1900   The Thompson Indians of British Columbia. *American Museum of Natural History Memoirs* 2(4):163–392.

    1909   The Shuswap. *American Museum of Natural History Memoirs* 2(7):447–789.

Tentori, T.

    1982   An Italian Religious Feast. In *Mother Worship: Themes and Variations,* edited by J. J. Preston, pp. 95–122. University of North Carolina Press, Chapel Hill.

Testart, Alain

    1982   The Significance of Food Storage among Hunter-Gatherers. *Current Anthropology* 23:523–37.

Thiebaut, Michel

    1992   *Dans le sillage des Sirenes.* Casterman, Brussels.

Tiechelmann, G. C.

    1841   *Aborigines of South Australia: Illustrative and Explanatory Notes of the Manners, Customs, Habits, and Superstitions of the Natives of South Australia.* Adelaide.

Tillet, Thierry
        2002   Les Grottes a ours et Occupatios Neandertaliennes dans les Alpes. In *L'Ours et l'Homme,* edited by T. Tillet and L. Binford, pp. 167–84. ERAUL, Liège.

Tinker, George E.
        1993   *Missionary Conquest: The Gospel and Native American Cultural Genocide.* Fortress Press, Minneapolis.

Tkalich, A., S. Tkalich, and K. Van Deusen
        1993   *Music and Tales of Chukotka.* Word of Mouth Audio Productions, Hornby Island, British Columbia.

Toth, N.
        1985   Archaeological Evidence for Preferential Right-Handedness in the Lower and Middle Pleistocene, and Its Possible Implications. *Journal of Human Evolution* 14:607–14.

Trinkaus, E.
        1985   Cannibalism and Burial at Krapina. *Journal of Human Evolution* 14:203–16.

Trinkaus, E., and P. Shipman
        1992   *Neandertals: Of Skeletons, Scientists, and Scandal.* Vintage, New York.

Tuchman, B.
        1978   *A Distant Mirror: The Calamitous Fourteenth Century.* Ballantine, New York.

Turke, P. E.
        1984   Effects of Ovulatory Concealment and Synchrony on Protohominid Mating Systems and Parental Roles. *Ethnology and Sociobiology* 5:33–44.
        1988   Concealed Ovulation, Menstrual Synchrony, and Parental Investment. In *Biosocial Perspectives on the Family,* edited by E. Filsinger, pp. 103–23. Sage, Newbury Park, CA.

Turner, Nancy, and Harriet Kuhnlein
        1982   Two Important "Root" Foods of the Northwest Coast Indians. *Economic Botany* 36:411–32.

Turner, Victor
        1986   *The Anthropology of Performance.* PAJ Publications, New York.

Tuzin, Donald
        1984   Miraculous Voices: The Auditory Experience of Numinous Objects. *Current Anthropology* 25(5):579–89.

Tylor, E. B.
        1958   *Primitive Culture,* vol. 2: *Religion in Primitive Culture.* Harper Torchbooks, New York.

Ulansey, David
        1989   The Mithraic Mysteries. *Scientific American* 261(6):130–35.

Utts, Jessica
        1995   An Assessment of the Evidence for Psychic Functioning. *Journal of Parapsychology* 59:289–320.

Vale, V., and A. Juno, eds.
        1989   *Modern Primitives: An Investigation of Contemporary Adornment and Ritual.* Re/Search, San Francisco.

Valiente, Doreen
        1973   *An ABC of Witchcraft: Past and Present.* Phoenix Publishing, Custer, WA.

Van Deusen, Kira
        1996   The Flying Tiger: Aboriginal Women Shamans, Storytellers, and Embroidery Artists in the Russian Far East. *Shaman* 4:45–78.

Vandiver, P., et al.
        1989   The Origins of Ceramic Technology at Dolni Vestonice, Czechoslovakia. *Science* 246:1002–1008.

Vastokas, J. M.

    1977   The Shamanic Tree of Life. In *Stones, Bones, and Skin: Ritual and Shamanic Art,* edited by A. T. Brodsky, R. Danesewich, and N. Johnson, pp. 93–117. Society for Art Publications, Toronto.

Vatcher, Lance, and Faith Vatcher

    1973   Excavation of Three Post-Holes in Stonehenge Car Park. *Wiltshire Archaeological and Natural History Magazine* 68:57–63.

Vencl, S.

    1984   War and Warfare in Archaeology. *Journal of Anthropological Archaeology* 3:116–32.

Veyne, Paul

    1983   Les Paiens et leurs dieux. *L'Histoire* 55:18–25.

Villa, Paola

    1992   Cannibalism in Prehistoric Europe. *Evolutionary Archaeology* 1(3):93–104.

Villa, Paola, et al.

    1986   Cannibalism in the Neolithic. *Science* 233:431–34.

Villeneuve, L. de, ed.

    1906   *Les Grottes de Grimaldi,* vol. 2. Imprimerie de Monaco, Monaco.

Villes, Alain

    1998   Les Figurations Neolithiques de la Marne, dans le Contexte du Bassin Parisien. *Bulletin de la Société Archéologique Champenoise* 91(2):7–46.

Von Gernet, Alexander

    1993   The Construction of Prehistoric Ideation. *Cambridge Archaeological Journal* 3(1):67–81.

Vriezen, T. C.

    1899   *The Religion of Ancient Israel.* Butterworth, London.

Waal Malefijt, Annemarie de

    1968   *Religion and Culture.* Waveland Press, Prospect Heights, IL.

Wainwright, G. J.

    1979   *Mount Pleasant, Dorset: Excavations 1970–1971.* Society of Antiquaries, London.

Waldrop, M. M.

    1992   *Complexity: The Emerging Science at the Edge of Order and Chaos.* Simon & Schuster, New York.

Walker, Barbara

    1988   *The Women's Dictionary of Symbols and Sacred Objects.* Harper & Row, San Francisco.

Walker, Phillip

    1989   Cranial Injuries as Evidence of Violence in Prehistoric Southern California. *American Journal of Physical Anthropology* 80:313–23.

Walker, William

    1998   Where are the Witches of Prehistory? *Journal of Archaeological Method and Theory* 5(3):245–308.

Wallis, Robert

    2003   *Shamans/Neo-Shamans.* Routledge, London.

Warner, Maria

    1976   *Alone of All Her Sex: The Myth and Cult of the Virgin Mary.* Weidenfeld & Nicolson, London.

Warren, P.

    1984   Knossos: New Excavations and Discoveries. *Archaeology* 37:48–55.

Wason, Paul

    1994   *The Archaeology of Rank.* Cambridge University Press, Cambridge.

Wasson, Gordon

    1968   *SOMA, Divine Mushroom of Immortality.* Ethno-Mycological Studies no. 1. Harcourt Brace, New York.

1972   What Was the Soma of the Aryans? In *Flesh of the Gods,* edited by P. Furst, pp. 210–13. Waveland Press, Prospect Heights, IL.

Watanabe, Hitoshi

1994   The Animal Cult of Northern Hunter-Gatherers: Patterns and Their Ecological Implications. In *Circumpolar Religion and Ecology,* edited by T. Irimoto and T. Yamada, pp. 47–68. University of Tokyo Press, Tokyo.

Watkins, Trevor

1990   The Origins of House and Home? *World Archaeology* 21(3):336–47.

1992   The Beginning of the Neolithic: Searching for Meaning in Material Culture Change. *Paleorient* 18(1):63–75.

1993   The Origins of the Household in North Mesopotamia. In *Houses and Households in Ancient Mesopotamia,* edited by K. R. Veenhof, pp. 79–88. Institut Historique-Archaeologique Neerlandais de Stamboul, Leiden.

Watson, Aaron, and David Keating

1999   Architecture and Sound: An Acoustic Analysis of Megalithic Monuments in Prehistoric Britain. *Antiquity* 73:325–36.

Watson, Andrew

1997   Quantum Spookiness Wins, Einstein Loses in Photon Tests. *Science* 277:481.

Weaver, Muriel

1972   *The Aztecs, Maya, and Their Predecessors.* Seminar Press, New York.

Webber, M., C. Stephens, and C. D. Laughlin, Jr.

1983   Masks: A Re-Evaluation, or "Masks? You Mean They Affect the Brain?" In *The Power of Symbols: Masks and Masquerade in the Americas,* edited by N. R. Crumrine and M. Halpin, pp. 204–18. University of British Columbia Press, Vancouver.

Webster, Gary

1990   Labor Control and Emergent Stratification in Prehistoric Europe. *Current Anthropology* 31:337–66.

Wedderburn, A. J. M.

1982   Paul and the Hellenistic Mystery-Cults: On Posing the Right Questions. In *La Soteriologia Dei Culti Orientali nell' Impero Romano,* edited by U. Bianchi and M. J. Vermaseren, pp. 817–33. Brill, Leiden.

Weidenreich, F.

1943   *The Skull of Sinanthropus Pekinensis.* Geological Survey of China, Pehpei, Chungking.

Wendorf, Fred

1968   Site I77: A Nubian Final Paleolithic Graveyard near Jebel Sahaba, Sudan. In *The Prehistory of Nubia,* vol. 2, edited by F. Wendorf, pp. 945–95. Fort Burgwin Research Center, Taos, and SMU Press, Dallas.

Wernick, Robert

1973   *Monument Builders.* Time-Life Books, Alexandria, VA.

Westcott, Brooke

1909   *The Two Empires: The Church and the World.* Macmillan, London.

Whitley, D. S.

1992   Shamanism and Rock Art in Far Western North America. *Cambridge Archaeological Journal* 2(1):89–113.

White, Randall

1985   *Upper Paleolithic Land Use in the Perigord.* BAR, Oxford.

1993   Technological and Social Dimensions of "Aurignacian Age" Body Ornaments across Europe. In *Before Lascaux,* edited by H. Knecht, A. Pike-Tay, and R. White, pp. 277–99. CRC Press, Boca Raton.

White, Tim D.

1980   Evolutionary Implications of Pliocene Hominid Footprints. *Science* 208:175–76.

1986 Cut Marks on the Bodo Cranium: A Case of Prehistoric Defleshing. *American Journal of Physical Anthropology* 69:503–509.

Whitehouse, Ruth

1992 *Underground Religion.* Accordia Research Center, University of London, London.

Whittle, Alasdair

1996 *Europe in the Neolithic.* Cambridge University Press, Cambridge.

Whittlesey, E. S.

1972 *Symbols and Legends in Western Art: A Museum Guide.* Scribner's, New York.

Whyte, Martin

1978 *The Status of Women in Preindustrial Societies.* Princeton University Press, Princeton, NJ.

Wiedenfeld, S. A.

1990 Impact of Perceived Self-Efficacy in Coping with Stressors on Components of the Immune System. *Journal of Personality and Social Psychology* 59:1082–94.

Wiessner, Polly

1977 *Hxaro: A Regional System of Reciprocity for Reducing Risk among the !Kung San.* Unpublished Ph.D. diss., Dept. of Anthropology, University of Michigan, Ann Arbor.

1981 Measuring the Impact of Social Ties on Nutritional Status among the !Kung San. *Social Science Information* 20:641–78.

1982 Risk, Reciprocity, and Social Influences on !Kung San Economics. In *Politics and History in Band Societies,* edited by E. Leacock and R. B. Lee, pp. 61–84. Cambridge University Press, Cambridge.

1986 !Kung San Networks in a Generational Perspective. In *The Past and Future of !Kung Ethnography: Critical Reflections and Symbolic Perspectives,* edited by M. Biesele, R. Gordon, and R. Lee, pp. 103–36. Helmut Buske Verlag, Hamburg.

1996 Leveling the Hunter: Constraints on the Status Quest in Foraging Societies. In *Food and the Status Quest,* edited by P. Wiessner and W. Schiefenhovel, pp. 171–92. Berghahn Books, New York.

1998 Indoctrinability and the Evolution of Socially Defined Kinship. In *Indoctrinability, Ideology, and Warfare,* edited by I. Eibl-Eibesfeldt and F. Salter, pp. 133–50. Berghahn Books, New York.

2001 Of Feasting and Value: Enga Feasts in a Historical Perspective. In *Feasts: Archaeological and Ethnographic Perspectives on Food, Politics, and Power,* edited by M. Dietler and B. Hayden, pp. 115–43. Smithsonian Institution Press, Washington, DC.

Wiessner, Polly, and Akii Tumu

1998 *Historical Vines: Enga Networks of Exchange, Ritual, and Warfare in Papua New Guinea.* Smithsonian Institution Press, Washington, DC.

1999 A Collage of Cults. *Canberra Anthropology* 22(1):34–65.

Wilber, Ken

1996 *A Brief History of Everything.* Shambhala, Boston.

Wilber, Ken, ed.

1984 *Quantum Questions.* Shambala, Boston.

Willard, R.

1977 Breast Enlargement through Visual Imagery and Hypnosis. *American Journal of Clinical Hypnosis* 19:195–200.

Willcox, G.

1998 Archaeobotanical Evidence for the Beginnings of Agriculture in Southwest Asia. In *The Origins of Agriculture and Crop Domestication: The Harlan Symposium,* edited by A. Damania, J. Valkoun, G. Willcox, and C. Qualset, pp. 25–39. International Center for Agricultural Research in the Dry Areas (ICARDA), Aleppo, Syria.

Willets, R. A.

1965 *Ancient Crete: A Social History.* University of Toronto Press, Toronto.

Williams, Nigel

    1997   Biologists Cut Reductionist Approach down to Size. *Science* 227:476–77.

Williamson, Craig

    1982   *A Feast of Creatures: Anglo-Saxon Riddle Songs.* University of Pennsylvania Press, Philadelphia.

Wink, C. A.

    1961   Congenital Ichthyosiform Erythrodermia Treated by Hypnosis. *British Medical Journal* 2:741–43.

Winkelman, Michael

    1982   Magic: A Theoretical Reassessment. *Current Anthropology* 23:37–66.

    1986   Trance States. *Ethos* 14:174–203.

    1990   Shamans and Other "Magico-Religious" Healers: A Cross-Cultural Study of Their Origins, Nature, and Social Transformations. *Ethos* 18:308–52.

    1991   Physiological and Therapeutic Aspects of Shamanistic Healing. *Subtle Energies* 1(2):1–18.

    1992   *Shamans, Priests, and Witches: A Cross-Cultural Study of Magico-Religious Practitioners.* Anthropology Department, Arizona State University, Tempe.

    2000   *Shamanism: The Neural Ecology of Consciousness Healing.* Bergin & Garvey, London.

Winterhalder, B.

    1986   Diet Choice, Risk, and Food Sharing in a Stochastic Environment. *Journal of Anthropological Archaeology* 5:369–92.

Withnell, John, G.

    1901   *The Customs and Traditions of the Aboriginal Natives of North Western Australia.* Roebourne.

Witt, R. E.

    1971   *Isis in the Graeco-Roman World.* Cornell University Press, Ithaca, NY.

Wittkower, E. D.

    1970   *The Interface between Psychiatry and Anthropology.* Brunner/Mazels, New York.

Wolkstein, Diane, and Samuel Noah Kramer

    1983   *Inanna: Queen of Heaven and Earth.* Harper & Row, New York.

Wolpoff, M.

    1986   More on Zhoukoudian. *Current Anthropology* 27:45–46.

Woodburn, James

    1982   Egalitarian Societies. *Mankind* 17:431–51.

Wreschner, Ernst

    1980   Red Ochre and Human Evolution: A Case for Discussion. *Current Anthropology* 21(5):631–44.

Wright, Katherine

    2000   The Social Origins of Cooking and Dining in Early Villages of Western Asia. *Proceedings of the Prehistoric Society* 66:89–121.

    2001   Interpreting the Neolithic of Western Asia. *Antiquity* 75:619–21.

Wright, Robert

    1988   *Three Scientists and Their Gods.* Times Books, New York.

Wymer, John

    1982   *The Paleolithic Age.* Croom Helm, London.

Yengoyan, Aram

    1976   Structure, Event, and Ecology in Aboriginal Australia. In *Tribes and Boundaries in Australia,* edited by N. Peterson, pp. 121–32. Australian Institute of Aboriginal Studies, Canberra.

    1985   Digging for Symbols: The Archaeology of Everyday Material Life. *Proceedings of the Prehistoric Society* 51:329–34.

Young, Frank

    1965   *Initiation Ceremonies.* Bobbs-Merrill, New York.

Zahavi, Amotz, and Avishag Zahavi

    1997   *The Handicap Principle: A Missing Piece of Darwin's Puzzle.* Oxford University Press, New York.

Zervos, Christian

    1959   *L'Art de l'époque du Renne en France.* Cahiers d'Art, Paris.

Zvelebil, Marek

    1995   At the Interface of Archaeology, Linguistics, and Genetics. *Journal of European Archaeology* 3(1):33–70.

    1992   Farmers: Our Ancestors and the Identity of Europe. In *Cultural Identity and Archaeology,* edited by P. Graves-Brown, S. Jones, and C. Gamble, pp. 145–66. Routledge, London.

    2000   The Social Context of the Agricultural Transition in Europe. In *Archaeogenetics,* edited by C Renfrew and K. Boyle, pp. 57–80. MacDonald Institute, Cambridge.

Zvelebil, Marek, and Kamil Zvelebil

    1988   Agricultural Transition and Indo-European Dispersals. *Antiquity* 62:574–83

Glossary

adaptation Modification of an organism, people, or culture that makes them more fit for existence under the conditions of their environments.

anthropology The science of human beings, especially the study of human beings in relation to distribution, origin, classification, and relationship of races, physical character, environmental and social relations, and culture.

anthropomorphic Trait of attributing human forms or characteristics to something which is not human.

archetypes An inherited idea or mode of thought in the psychology of C. G. Jung that is derived from the experience of a race and is present in the unconscious of the individual.

aurochs An extinct wild European form of cattle.

barrow A mound of earth or rocks, usually marking a grave or tomb.

booty Valuables seized by force, usually spoils of a raid or war.

bride-wealth or bride-price Goods or wealth given by a groom (or his family) to the parents of a bride as payment for the privilege of marrying their daughter (often viewed as a compensation for the loss of a family member).

bucrania Bull horns attached to a bull's skull (or part thereof) and incorporated into architecture (as at Çatal Hüyük).

clans An early form of social group composed of several families claiming descent from a common ancestor; a tribal division, usually exogamous, of matrilineal or patrilineal descent from a common ancestor.

cult A system of religious beliefs and or practices usually not considered to be a mainstream religion in contemporary terms, but also referring to any small-scale religious organization as is typical of traditional societies.

culture A set of behavior and information passed from one individual to another by behavioral versus genetic means.

cultural ecology A branch of anthropology concerned with the interrelationship of people and cultures with their environments.

cuneiform A form of writing composed of wedge-shaped characters used in ancient Sumerian, Akkadian, Assyrian, Babylonian, and Persian inscriptions.

cursus Very elongated Neolithic earthen constructions forming two long, low mounds with external ditches on either side of a central alley, ranging in length up to 10 kilometers.

diffusionism A theory popular in the late nineteenth and early twentieth century, according to which technological sophistication and advanced civilization spread gradually from a very few (sometimes only one) central place (usually Egypt).

divination The act of attempting to foretell future or unknown events.

domestication Change in the genetic characteristics of wild species as a result of human manipulation of natural selection.

ecology A branch of science concerned with the interrelationship of organisms and their environments. Adaptation and energy use constitute major organizing concepts. The totality or pattern of relations between organisms and their environment.

ecstatic state An ineffable and altered state of consciousness characterized by a feeling of unity with suprahuman powers, entities or principles, often with sacred characteristics.

entoptics Images produced by the human neural and optical system under conditions of sensory deprivation and stress, ranging from simple spots to complex stylized representations of objects.

epiphany An appearance or manifestation of a god or other supernatural being.

estrus A regularly recurrent state of sexual excitability during which the female of most mammals will accept the male and is capable of conceiving; heat. In most primates estrus is indicated by swelling and color change around the sexual organs.

ethnoarchaeology An approach to archaeology that attempts to interpret the implications of remains by investigating the use of similar materials or objects in contemporary contexts.

ethnography The systematic recording of human traditional cultures.

ethnology (cultural anthropology) The branch of anthropology dealing chiefly with the comparative and analytical study of cultures.

excarnation The exposure of dead bodies to birds or animals in order to remove the flesh prior to final burial.

familiar In some belief systems, a spirit in animal form used for the purpose of interacting with humans.

genes An element of the germ plasm having a specific function in inheritance that is determined by a specific sequence of bases in DNA or sometimes in RNA and that serves to control the transmission of a hereditary character by specifying the structure of a particular protein or by controlling the function of other genetic material.

henge A circlular ditch and embankment, sometimes containing megaliths, as at Stonehenge (in Wiltshire, England).

heterarchies A relatively diffuse sharing of power by a number of groups within a community, or by groups that have specialized functions.

hierophany A sudden manifestation of sacred forces.

iconography The art of representing or illustrating concepts by pictures, figures or images.

industrial culture A culture whose social and economic organization is characterized by large industries.

Kurgan An early Indo-European culture known for their rapid expansion across Europe with the use of the domesticated horse. Kurgans refer to the burial mounds erected over elite burials.

ley lines Meridians of natural energy and/or sacred forces that flow through the earth according to advocates of the concept.

lineage All the direct descendants from an ancestor usually extending 2–5 generations and forming a recognized social unit with a recognized membership.

mace A clublike weapon.

mage A seer or wise person skilled in magic.

magic The use of means (charms or spells) believed to have supernatural power over natural forces. An extraordinary power or influence seemingly from a supernatural source.

magician One who uses supernatural magic in order to achieve desired ends.

matriarchal A social organization in which the mother is designated the head of the family, tribe or clan; government, rule, or domination by women.

matrilineal Lineage or descent traced through the females of the family.

megalith A very large stone used by Neolithic or other people to construct tombs or create other monuments.

mesolithic The cultural period between the Paleolithic and the Neolithic Ages usually dated from 12,000 to 8,000 B.P. or later in some regions. The Mesolithic is characterized by new technologies for resource extraction, such as fishing, boiling and seed processing technologies.

mousterian A late Paleolithic stone tool tradition believed to be used primarily by Neanderthals.

mystic A believer in mysticism, which is the belief that it is possible to achieve communion with spiritual forces, truths, or deities, through contemplation and intuition.

myth Usually a traditional story of ostensibly historical events that serves to unfold part of the world view of a people or explain a practice, belief, or natural phenomenon. A popular belief or tradition that has grown up around something or someone, especially one embodying the ideals and institutions of a society or segment of society.

natural selection The natural process that results in the survival of individuals or groups best adjusted to the conditions under which they live and that is equally important for the perpetuation of desirable genetic qualities and for the elimination of undesirable ones as these are produced by genetic recombination or mutation.

Neanderthal An extinct race of people living in the Middle Paleolithic period in Eurasia about 200,000–35,000 years ago.

Neolithic The cultural period following the Mesolithic in which ground-edge stone implements were made and domestication became widespread beginning about 8,000 B.C.E. in the Near East and lasting until about 3,000 B.C.E.

numinous Supernatural, mysterious; filled with a sense of the presence of divinity; holy; the nonrational part of the holy (versus moral or rational aspects).

ochre Naturally occurring iron oxide that was used prehistorically as pigments.

Paleolithic The cultural period preceding the Mesolithic in which chipped-stone tools were used. The lower Paleolithic (which lasted from about two million years ago to 250,000 years ago) was a long period of cultural stability. The Upper Paleolithic (about 35,000 to 12,000 years ago) saw significant development of art.

patriarchal A social organization in which the father is designated the head of the family, tribe or clan; government, rule, or domination by men.

patrilineal Lineage or descent traced through the males of the family.

physical anthropology Anthropology concerned with the comparative study of human physical evolution, variation, and classification.

political ecology Ecological studies that focus on the interaction between resources and the brokering of political power.

postmodernism A movement in reaction against the theory and practice of "modernism" in art and literature. Postmodernism emphasizes the relativity of interpretations and the equal validity of all interpretations.

postprocessual An archaeological theoretical school that adopts many postmodern views and assumptions, such as the difficulty or inability to establish real facts or generalizations, the relativity of all interpretations, and the validity of nonscientific points of view.

power grip A way of holding objects characterized by clenching the hand, as in holding a club.

precision grip A way of holding objects characterized by the use of the forefingers and thumb, as in holding a pencil or dart.

priest A person whose official function is to be an intermediary between the worshippers and the deity or supernatural forces by following a set liturgy.

profane Nonsacred; not in accord with sacred knowledge.

religion A personal set or institutionalized system of attitudes, beliefs, and practices about gods or supernatural forces.

rituals Any formal and customarily repeated act or series of acts performed according to religious law or social custom.

sacred Objects, places, or forces that are part of or closely associated with the fundamental supernatural energies of the cosmos.

secondary burials The removal of bones from decayed bodies and their reburial.

secret society Ritual organizations that typically have exclusive but voluntary memberships and secret rituals and dogmas.

secular Nonsacred; not in accord with sacred knowledge.

sedentism The act of remaining in one locality, as opposed to a nomadic way of life.

shaman A social functionary who, with the help of guardian spirits, attains ecstasy in order to create a rapport with the supernatural world on behalf of his group members.

shamanism A religious technique that involves going into altered states to achieve ecstasy.

social technology Social practices and relationships that are meant to provide or increase access to food or other important resources.

stele An upright stone slab or pillar engraved with an inscription or design and used as a monument or grave marker.

taphonomy The study of how objects become deposited in the earth and the processes leading to their occurrence over the landscape.

therianthropes Depictions of half-man/half-animal forms, sometimes interpreted as "master of the animals" or a shaman in costume.

thyrsus Staff adorned with a pine cone and ivy, which Dionysus, the satyrs, and their followers were represented as carrying. Probably symbolizing fertility or sacred power.

totem In many religious systems, a bird, animal, or aspect of nature believed to be related by blood to a specific group or clan and taken as their symbol.

transegalitarian Intermediate societies between egalitarian social organizations and strictly class-structured societies; characterized by private ownership of some resources and produce, significant social and economic inequalities, but unstable and weakly developed political centralization and authority.

tumulus A manmade earthen mound, often used for tombs.

Index

Page numbers for text boxes are in italics; page numbers for figures are followed by *f*.

A, letter, as bull's head, 237
Aboriginal. *See* Australia
Abrahamic faith, 383–84, 398
Abri Moula, 97
Academy, of Athens, ix, 12
access, restricted: to supernatural, to sanctuaries, to ecstatic experiences, 147, 188, 205, 210, 223, 233, 241, 247, 259, 268, 349, 362, 378, 402
adaptive benefits. *See under* benefits
afterworld, 39, 115, 117, 132, 165, 368–70, 375, 412; Celtic, 314–15; Christian, 390, 392, 394; Hebrew, 385; Torajan, 239, 243, 369, 388
agape, 374, 387
aggrandizers, 221–25, 234–35, 268–69, 288, 401–2. *See also* elites
agnostics, 15
'Ain Ghazal, 187, 198, 201–3, 205, 209
Ainu, 115, 174
Akha. *See* hill tribes
Akhenaten, 381
alcohol, 7, 275, 285–87, 376
alliances, 29, 44, 105, 143, 174, 200, 317, 397; ritual, 32, 360, 366, 401
Allah, 381
altered states of consciousness, 33, 49, 60–73, 84, 145, 149, 235, 284–85, 311, 399; criteria of, 62; in mammals, 33; types of, 61
amanita mushrooms, 235
ancestors, 183–93, 211, 235, 239, 266–67, 404; as authorities and punishers, 183–99; and crops, 185, 212, 246; cults, 115–18, 132, 157, 182, 227, 230–33, 241, 245, 255, 258, 294, 313, 315, 317, 321–22, 346, 349, 370, 380, 381, 398, 401; elite,

233, 241–43, 247, 254, 259–60, 268–69, 349, 355–59, 378, 381, 402; lineage, 208, 218; totemic (*see* totems)
Anglo-Saxons, 326–27
animals: art style, 300, 302; contact with Nature, 106, 297; cults, 105, 133–36, 208, 249; master of (*see* master of animals); mythical, 148–49; pastoral nomadic, 279, sacrifice (*see under* sacrifice); spirit allies (*see* spirit helpers); spirits, 135*f*; symbolic aspects, 194–95; transformation into, 284–85, 288, 295, 311, 330; as wealth, 175, 185, 192; as warrior icons, 147. *See also* shamanism, therianthropes
anthropomorphism, 38
Apuleius, 367–68
archetypes, 37–39, 58–59, 65, 98
Arctic hysteria, 84
Arcy-sur-Cure, 102
art, 54, 100–1; for art's sake, 225, 255; commissioned, 143, 155; great, 143, 146, 225, 255; specialists in, 143, 154–55. *See also under* animals
Arthur, King, 295, 307, 326–28, 333
Asherah, 381, 384
Asikli, 178, 199
astronomical alignments, 241–47
Atapuerca, 95
atheists, 15
aurochs. *See under* bulls, wild
Australia, Aboriginal, 3*f*, 184, 397
Australopithecus, 90–91
Avebury, 219, 220*f*, 221*f*, 237, 240–41, 252–53, 278
axes, 197, 217, 223, 234*f*, 248–251, 281
axis mundi, 77, 261*f*, 293
Aztecs, 201, 247

Baal, 203, 213
Bacchus, 371, 377, 391

crescent cakes, 381
crosses, Celtic, equal-armed, rotated, 216–17, 299
Cuchulainn, 281, 284, 304
cultural ecology. *See* ecology
cults. *See under specific entry:* ancestors, bears, elite, popular
cups, 217, 285, 326
curers, 48
cursus, 230, 247
Cyprus, 175, 178, 198–99

dance, 7, 33, 53–54, 373, 377*f*, 399
Danebury, 321–22
days, ruled by gods, 330, 332
death: as archetype, 58; attitudes toward, 184; and resurrection, 58, 212–13, 246, 266, 367, 374, 387–88 (*see also* rebirth); violent, 173
decoration, as indicator of sacred, 81, 191*f*, 215, 235
defleshing. *See* excarnation
demographic pressure. *See* population pressure
dimensions, physical, 43
Dionysus, 59, 203, 241, 267, 285, 350, 356, 371, 377; mystery cult of, 368, 370–73, 377*f*, 387
displays, 191–93, 254, 322–23, 357
divination, 365
divine couple, 195–96, 268, *352, 355*, 356, 373
divine human descendants and rulers, 356, 378–79, 381, 402
division of labor, sexual, 195
dogs, 169, 176, 329; of God, 285
dolmens, 228*f*, 229
Dolni Vestonice, 131*f*, 134–35, 150, 153*f*
domesticated animals and plants, 171, 176, 178, 202, 273
domestication, 169, 217, 401
domestic cults, 153, 196, 210, 240, 248, 293
Drachenloch, 108
Drochenhohle cave, 102
drama, 33, 399
drink, of immortality, 285–87. *See also* alcohol; beer
drugs, 75, 84–85, 235, 285–87, 303, 311, 358–59, 412
druids, 309–12, 324, 328, 329, 333, 414
drums, 59, 85, 299
dualism: good vs. evil, 294–95, 303, 381, 388; sexual, 134, 190–91, 195
Dumézil, Georges, 292

Easter, 213, 215, 241, 265, 332
Easter eggs, 213, 215
Ecclesiastes, 381
ecology, 12–13, 87, 120, 173, 178, 185, 349, 399–403, 405; cultural ecology 12–13,16, 44, 104–5, 123, 155, 211, 217, 221, 224–25, 234, 265, 269, 278–79, 283, 295, 297, 345, 357, 363, 366, 378, 392, 397, 399–403, 405, 412–14; political ecology, 13,16, 165, 217, 349, 398, 401
ecstatic states, 7, 32–33, 37, 39, 45, 60–77, 84, 87, 105, 149, 223, 285, 376–78, 400, 406, 412; intensity of, 63; in mammals, 32; in rituals, 31, 99, 103, 143, 165, 210, 218, 260, 267, 288, 293, 295, 310, 358–62, 365–66, 370, 377–78, 378–78, 384, 387,

408, 412; sacred 63, 367, 401, 411; shamanic, 50, 63, 65, 118, 210, 311; techniques, 65–73, 367; motivations, 73; intentions, 73; sex as, 71
eggs, cosmic, sacred, 191, 213–216, 406.
Egypt, 225, 227, 247, 258, 262*f*, 355, 381, 391, 402
Eleusinian mysteries, 366, 370, 371, 373–75, 395, 396*f*
elite, 147, 222, 292, 395, 414; ancestors (*see* ancestors); cults, 147, 218 240, 247, 264, 293, 346, 401, 407, 413; initiations, 147. *See also* aggrandizers
El Juyo, cave, 135, 137–38, 145
emotions: bonding, 30, 33; evolution of, 29–32; human characteristics, 22, 33–34, 44, 399–400, 408
emperor cults, 371, 381
empires, 365–66, 378
enclosures, ritual, 318, 325–26
Enlène cave, 137, 145
entoptics, 37, 149, *152*, 235
Epona, 297
equinoxes, 213, 312, 317, 387
erections, 149
Essenes, 388–89, 390*f*, 393
estrus, 30
ethnocentrism, 4, 222
Europa, 203
evangelical missionizing, 394, 397
evil, vs. good, 326, 339, 351, 378, 381, 384, 388, 392, 397, 413. *See also* dualism
evolution, human, 24–34. See also *Homo*
excarnation, 191, 321
excision, 224
exclusivity of Hebrew worship, 382–85
executions, 312
exhaustion, 69–70
experiential approach, 4, 410

fairy: folk, 315, 325, 329; tales, 292, 333–46, 406
familiars. *See* spirit helpers
families, 28
fatigue, 70
feasts, 7, 11*f*, 114, 117, 124, 136–42, 145, 155, 158, 162, 165, 171, 192, 202, 204, 217–18, 232–33, 238–39, 241, 254, 258, 260, 269, 275, 295, 297, 311, 314*f*; 315, 318, 362, 370, 376, 378, 381, 391 397, 401; competitive, 173–76, 181, 311; maturation, 146; structures for, 160, 260; surplus based, 138, 165, 172–77, 181; tribute, 325, 349, 365*f*, 378; types of, 183
feathers, as archetypes, 59
feet, evolution of, 26–27
Fertile Crescent, 169, 178
fertility cults, 153–57, 165–66, 182, 193, 195–96, 201, 215, 217–18, 223, 227, 240, 248, 258, 264, 267, 292–93, 298, 303, 306, 312, 320–22, 329, 333, 346, 370, 378, 381–84, 404; dominated by males, 252
festivals, seasonal, 317, 324–25
figurines: animal, 134–35, 194–95; bull, 178; female, 153–58, 178, 193, 194*f*; 255, 384; male, 154–58, 187, 195; Venus, 153–58, 196
flight, 77

food, 7, delicacies, 176, 217; production 173, 176, 177, 193, 401

footprints, 142

formal aspects of religion. *See under* religion

fortifications, Neolithic, 179–80, 199

foundation offerings. *See* offerings

Frazer, James, 213

friendship, 30

funerals, 8*f*, 192, 238, 402, 406; cults, 162–63; rituals, 117, 230, 258, 318, 358

Gavrinis, 242, 249

gender, 85, 157; ritual roles, 121. *See also* women, status

gifts, 30–31, 33

Gilgamesh, 351, 381

Gimbutas, Marija, 254, 264, 270, 275–78

Gnostics, 388

Göbekli Tepe, 206, 208–9, 217

gobbledegook, 73, *74*

goddesses, 250*f*, 251, 254, 258, 267; worship, 155, 257, 264, 267–68

gods, 118, 242, 291, 303; Celtic, 312–13, 320–21; limited existence of, 120; Old European, 267; Sumerian, 350. *See also* Olympian pantheon, supreme deity

gold, 255–56, 264, 276, 280, 314

Golden Ass, 367–68

Golden Bough, 213

golden calf, 382, 383*f*

Gournay-sur-Aronde, 316, 317*f*

graves. *See* burials

Graves, Robert, 54

great art. *See* art

Green Man, 329, 331*f*

Groundhog Day, 80

guardian spirit. *See* spirit helpers

Gunderstrup Cauldron, 300, 327*f*

Gurkhas, 64

Hallan Çemi, 138–40, 171, 175, 193, 206–9, 259

Halloween, 211, 266, 315, 320, 325, 403, 406

hand, evolution of, 26–27

handprints, 142

harvest festivals, 371

head: cults, 306, 307*f,* 317; wounds, 182*f*

head-hunting, 199–200, 208, 253, 306, 307*f,* 323

hearths, 79; cults, 293, 303

Hebrews. *See* Israelites

hell, 368, 375, 388, 390, 392

Hermes, 370

heterarchies, 259

hierarchies, 151, 199, 204, 233–34, 237, 252-257, 279, 288, 291, 310, 401

hill tribes, 298, 397; Akha, 10*f,* 11, 168*f,* 181, 192, 210–12, 279; Rhadé, 251–52

historical explanations. *See* cognitive

Hoabinhian, 164

Hochdorf, 314–15

Holy Grail, 287, 326–28

home bases, 28

Homer, 240, 270–71, 292, 310

Homo, erectus, habilis, sapiens, archaic sapiens, 90–92; modern, 91*f, 96, 96*f, 97,122

honor price, 312

horns of consecration, 198, 259–61

horses, 279, 297, 298, 299*f,* 329; domestication of, 273

house offerings. *See* offerings

Höyücek, 204, 209

human evolution. *See* evolution

hunter-gatherers 22, 46, 83, 87, 92-93, 104–5, 118; complex/transegalitarian, 122–32, 142, 147, 155, 158, 164–65, 168–69, 171, 173, 177–79, 182–83, 267, 401; generalized/simple, 124–25, 184, 401

hypnosis, 82

I Ching, 365

ideals, 75, 268

ideology: elite, 239, 402; militaristic, 196; national, 404

immortality, 368

imperial: religious complex, 366–67, 379; worship, 366

Inanna, 86, 350, 350*f, 352–55*

incubation, 349

individual relationships with deities. *See* personal relationships

Indo-Europeans, 271–302, 305, 332, 336–37

Indra, *289–91*

Industrial Revolution, 404–7, 413–14

inequality, socioeconomic, 124, 130, 157, 166, 173, 181, 188, 201, 210, 234, 237, 279

information theory, 43

inheritance, 157, 184

initiations, 57, 103–5, 143, 145, 166, 200, 210; in fairy tales, 343; into mystery cults, 367; shamanic (*see* shamans); into secret societies, 210, 262, 284, 310

intentions, in ecstatic states, 73

intolerance, 385, 392, 398

Ireland, 237–38, 271, 298, 300

Iron Age, 232; technology, 306–9, 333

Isis, 213, 367–68, 372, 375*f,* 377, 388*f,* 394

Israelites, 381–86

Japan. *See* Jomon

Jerf el Ahmar, 193, 199, 201, 204–7, 209

Jericho, 169, 186, 193, 199, 201, 226, 230

Jesus Christ, 86, 115, 213, 387–88

jewelry, shell, 130, 169

Jomon, 158*f,* 162–63, 193

Judaisim, 380–386, 397

Judgment: of souls, 387, 388–89, 389*f;* last, 389

Kalends, 266

Karnak, 363*f*

Kebara cave, 117

kinship, 30, 400

Konds tribes, 201

Kostienki, 134

kurgans, 277*f,* 295, 301, 313

sacred ecstatic experiences. *See* ecstatic states
sacrifice, 203; of animals, 7, 8*f*, 140–41, 174–75, 258,
    259*f*, 283–84, 306, 325, 329, 333, 373, 374, 376,
    381, 391; human, 130, 196–201, 212–13, 218,
    252–53, 257, 261, 264, 267, 269, 281*f*, 296–297,
    297*f*, 303, 323–25, 328–29, 358, 360
saints, 397
Samhain. *See* Halloween
sanctuaries, 312, 315–18. *See also* shrines
Santa Claus, 80, 332, 403
Saturnalia, 215, 266
satyrs, 241, 292–93, 329, 376
Saxons, 326
scarification, 223
Scythians, 271, 280*f*, 300, 313
secondary products revolution, 273–74, 278
secondary sexual characteristics, 30–31
secret societies, 142–47, 151, 158, 165–66, 182, 200,
    203–6, 210–11, 223, 241, 249, 257, 261–62, 284,
    288, 294, 295, 303, 306, 310, 315–18, 318, 325,
    330, 333, 349, 359–60, 401
self-awareness, 95
self-deception, 42
self-interest, 13–14, 147, 221, 269
self-organization, 43
Serapis, 373, 381
sex, as ecstatic state, 71
shamanism, 47–60, 87, 118, 145, 147–53, 165–66,
    248, 300, 349; effectiveness in healing, 82
shamans, 151, 210, 285, 288, 310, 329, 351, 367, 370;
    costume 49*f*, 59; definition, 46; initiation, 58; tales,
    344
Shanidar, 117
sharing, food, 136
shiny objects, 59
shrines, 145, 188, 191, 193, 203–4, 209, 210, 218, 240,
    260*f*, 298, 306. *See also* sanctuaries
Skateholm, 164
skulls, 188, 208, 231, 323; cults of, 186, 198; removal
    of, 118
slaves, 234, 254, 269, 324, 404, 414
Sleipnir, 80, 332
smoke hole, 80
snakes, 201, 206, 264, 265*f*, 267, 293, 376. *See also* vi-
    sion serpent
social component of religion, 393–95, 398
sociopolitical pressures, 173, 203, 217
sodalities, 205
solar symbolism. *See* sun
solstices, 245–47, 265–66, 312, 317
Soma, 285–87
Song of Songs, 381
souls, 95, 97, 106, 117
specialist artists. *See* art
spirals, 217, 243–246
spirit helpers, 60, 143, 149
spirit quest, 143, 224
sports, 350–51
springs, sacred. *See* wells

staffs, 149
Star Carr, 149
Star Wars, 50, 52, 295
states. *See* civilization
stele (stelae), 198, 203, 227, 260, 382
stock market, 279
stone: bowls, 140, 193; masks, 205; piles of, 108; sacred,
    223, 382; with holes, 109–10, 112
Stonehenge, 18*f*, 164, 219, 232*f*, 237, 240–41, 246,
    247, 250, 252, 256, 278, 294, 298, 309
storage: food 130, 166, 193, 205, 209, 259, 375; ritual
    paraphernalia, 205, 206*f*, 209
storytelling, 334–36, 345–46, 405
stratification, social, 278
stress, 376–77, 405
stylistic homogeneity, 238; regions, 238, 249
subincision, 224
success, advertising of, 226, 235, 237
Sumerian: elites, 358; feasts, 362, 365*f*; states, 349
Summerland, 314, 369
sun: cults, 223, 227, 241, 284, 325, 346, 349; symbol-
    ism, 187, 203, 217, 242–47, 250–51, 258, 294, 298,
    299–300*f*, 303, 313, 345, 402
Sun Dance, 69
Sungir, 130
supernatural, power, 147, 223
supreme deity, 119, 284
surpluses, 138, 147, 155, 165, 172–77, 181, 183, 193,
    204, 217, 222, 241, 253, 259, 264, 269, 349, 366,
    401–2
swastikas, 217
sweat lodges, 69, 414
swords, magical, 295, 307, 328
symbolic, contexts, interpretations, 13–19, 234,
    245–46, 269, 292, 295, 303, 304, 357, 406
symbols, 76, 182, 191–95, 201–3, 211–17, 237,
    242–43, 248, 249–51, 254, 257–58, 260, 265–67,
    283, 287, 294, 298, 298–99, 300*f*, 312–13, 313*f*,
    329, 345, 355, 371, 406
synchronicity, 39, 40–41, 43

tallies. *See* record keeping
Tata, 99
Talheim, 182*f*, 253
technology: early, 27–29; in empires, 366; Neolithic,
    168–69; Upper Paleolithic, 127
temples, 261, 268, 350, 357–64
Ten Commandments, 382, 400
Teotihuacan, 2*f*
therianthropes, 135, 136*f*, 147, 149, 150*f*, 152, 196
three, 292, 293*f*, 303, 332-333, 345
thrones, 210
Tikal, 357, 361, 364*f*
tokens, 139
Tolkien, 50
tombs. *See* burials, megaliths
Torajan culture, 8*f*, 177, 200, 227*f*, 230*f*, 238–40,
    242–43, 242*f*, 243*f*, 258
torcs, 309